APPROACHING THE POSSIBLE

APPROACHING THE POSSIBLE

THE WORLD OF STARGATE SG-1

JO STORM

ECW Press

Published by ECW PRESS
2120 Queen Street East, Suite 200, Toronto, Ontario, Canada M4E 1E2

Library and Archives Canada Cataloguing in Publication

Storm, Jo, 1972–
Approaching the possible : the world of Stargate
SG-1 / Jo Storm.

ISBN 1-55022-705-X

1. Stargate SG-1 (Television program). I. Title.
PN1992.77.S76S76 2005   791.45'72   C2005-904251-6

Developing editor: Jennifer Hale
Typesetting: Gail Nina
Cover and text design: Tania Craan
Cover photo: Courtesy Shooting Star
Color section credits, in order: Jonathan Cruz; Albert L. Ortega;
Peter Fallon; Charles Bush/Shooting Star; Tricia Byrne; Michelle;
Albert L. Ortega; Jonathan Cruz; Albert L. Ortega; Charles
Bush/Shooting Star; Courtesy Teryl Rothery; Jonathan Cruz; Ron
Davis/Shooting Star; Sue Schneider/Shooting Star; Ron Davis/Shooting
Star; Charles Bush/Shooting Star
Printing: Transcontinental

DISTRIBUTION

CANADA: Jaguar Book Group, 100 Armstrong Avenue, Georgetown, ON, L7G 5S4
UNITED STATES: Independent Publishers Group, 814 North Franklin Street,
Chicago, Illinois 60610

PRINTED AND BOUND IN CANADA

ECW PRESS
ecwpress.com

TABLE OF CONTENTS

Out of the Blue:
The Franchise of *SG-1*

No Red Shirts:
The "Fanchise" of *SG-1*

ACKNOWLEDGMENTS

Thank you to Jen Hale, Jack David, and ECW Press for the chance to put in text the abiding fandom that is "sgwun." Thanks also to my good friend and sometime agent Noelle Allen, who made my shyness seem like an okay thing to a very busy Jen Hale, who took on the project even though she was about to go on maternity leave. A very big and warm thank you to Eliza Bennett, who was an invaluable assistant and whom I cannot praise enough.

The shaping of this book was helped by fans all over the globe who sent me photos, offered suggestions, hounded cast and crew at conventions for info, and supported me through the entire endeavor. I'd like to thank Anthea Murphy, Tricia Byrne, Robin, Craig and Zoë Bennett, Jenifer Renieri, Julie Winningham. A warm thank you to the people who agreed to be interviewed — Meesh, without whom none of the interviews would have happened, AJ, Suz Voy, Tricia Byrne, splash_the_cat, Denise, and lab_brat. Thanks to all the cast (and their agents!) and crew who participated — James Tichenor, Joseph Mallozzi, Alex Zahara (who agreed to an interview even though he had food poisoning), and Teryl Rothery. Not only is she enthusiastic and friendly, but she is a genuinely brilliant woman. James Tichenor mentioned that everyone is welcome at his blog, "The Joint" (http://www.lehopictures.com/the_joint/), and as he's working on *Stargate Atlantis* these days, it's chock full of *Stargate* stuff. Thanks to Morjana Coffman and Denise for their excellent proofreading skills and general *Stargate* knowledge. Also to Morjana (SG-1-Spoilergate) and Darren Sumner (GateWorld), two *seriously* dedicated fans whose vast warehouse of knowledge I used.

Thanks to Aline Reinhard, Maureen Thayer, my "Convention Gals" (Robin, Zoë, Jenifer, Eliza, and Tricia), Douglas Thar of the US Air Force, Danielle MacNeil, Michelle, Jonathan Cruz of Cruz Photography and Peter Fallon of Best of Both Worlds (http://www.bobw.com.au/), for their great photographs.

This book is dedicated to all the *SG-1* fans around the world (and there are a lot of them!). After nine years, a split, a death (or two), and a spin-off, you still keep *SG-1* honest.

Approaching the Possible
The World of *Stargate SG-1*

Speculative fiction has roots that reach way back, but until recently it was loosely designated under the heading "fanciful." That phrase taps the shoulder of none other than the poet Samuel Taylor Coleridge. To Coleridge, the difference between what he termed "fancy" and "imagination" was the difference between "stuff" and "art." He maintained that fancy was merely a resetting of familiar things, whereas imagination took old things and made them new, a phrase reiterated by the Modernist movement. For a long time, speculative fiction in either the science or fantasy realm was derided as mere "fancy," not compressing or dissolving old themes and making new ones, but just putting them in space with a ray gun, or in the forest with a sword. Contemporary scholars however, have delved more deeply into the underlying structures of speculative fiction and realized that this genre is more than old tales retold with new costumes. Fantasy often offered spiritual or moral insights because it spoke to timeless truths, and science fiction presented insight into physical reality, because it was based on the laws of physics.

Traditionally, science fiction and fantasy are seen as two sides of the same coin (or universe); one employing the hard-and-fast rules of science to explain phenomena, and the other using magic, myth, or other more sublime rule sets to explain the ways in which a world and its inhabitants exist. In both cases, it is insight into our world and how we live in it that readers are looking for.

Speculative fiction television seemed to have landed heavily on the "science" side of things. Starting as far back as *Captain Video* in 1949, TV offered shows like the British *Dr. Who*, which ran from 1963 to 1993 — the longest running science fiction show to date. Across the pond in America, *The Outer Limits,* originally aired in 1963, went back into production in the 1990s. And, of course, there is the ubiquitous *Star Trek*, starting with the original series in 1966 and continuing to this day in its various spin-offs.

More fantastical series like *Battlestar Galactica*, which aired for one season in 1978 (though it's been renewed recently to greater audience acclaim) and Jim Henson's *Farscape* (1999–2003) didn't seem to have the same staying power. These kinds of shows were trying to ride the coattails of popular imagination — *Battlestar Galactica* aired directly after the movie *Star Wars* — or, like *Farscape*, they became mired in intricate, slow-moving plots that demanded close (and often repeated) viewings, something large television audiences weren't interested in. A few fantastical shows developed small followings but ultimately did not appeal to wider audiences. *Beauty and the Beast,* a cult romantic series that aired between 1987 and 1990, tailored its mythic characters to a grown-up audience, recasting the fable with a modern day premise. Occasionally, a show might seem to have a scientific premise, but it was really more about fantastical worlds — *Quantum Leap* is a good example, running from 1989 to 1994.

What was missing was a hybrid — a show that catered to viewers' taste for mythology and good storytelling while being "believable" due to its scientific, "realistic" premise. That brings us to the year 1997. *Stargate SG-1* started out as a movie in 1994 (like another hit series, *Buffy the Vampire Slayer*), and was a long anticipated brain-child of director Roland Emmerich. The concept of the movie was simple. It tied together all the hard-edged glare of physics with the tumbling, twisting stories of Egyptian mythology into one big package: a package completed by glowing eyes and a need to dominate.

Why mythology? We look to myths to give us an inner sense of why things appear and happen; they accentuate and broaden outer, rational explanations of how light works, what makes things fall to the ground, or where the sun is on the longest day of the year. Long before humans started writing, stories were oral, spoken from one person to another, told to groups. The tales bound groups together with a common sense of identity and purpose. Mythology gives us a common well from which to drink, a larger sense of self that lets us see both heroes and villains, sometimes in the same person. Egyptian mythology is a great example of this; many of its gods and goddesses harbor both good aspects *and* evil or unflattering aspects. For instance, Anubis — a character in later seasons of *Stargate SG-1* — was the god associated with death and embalming, offering his judgment on mortal lives, but his odd, jackal-headed features also brought peace to the deceased and were a symbol of intelligence. Another god associated with death —known as the god of the dead — was Osiris. But his rebirth myth (he was cut up into many pieces and thrown into the river, but he was revived and made whole again) also links him to creativity and the cycle of nature, of renewal.

In this age of shifting moral values, where many aspects of our lives are called into question, we turn again to mythology as a form of "source code" for our own moral compasses. The crises that we face — racism, marginalization, privacy, and threats to security — are reflected and recast in the framework of *SG-1*, whose original mandate is to "perform reconnaissance, determine threats, and make peaceful contact with the people of alien worlds." Bold enough in its plotlines and characterizations to bring in viewers who want fantastical stories, and with enough physics, rationality, and exploration to satisfy the science viewer, *SG-1* is like a dream meld of science and fantasy.

Besides closing the rift between genres, *SG-1* also seems at home catering to both American and British audiences. This could have a lot to do with where the show is shot (although, oddly enough, where new episodes are not aired) — Canada. Almost all filming of *SG-1* is done in and around the Vancouver, British Columbia area. The U.S.'s northern neighbor has always been seen as a hybrid between brash individualism and more conservative ideologies, legacies of both the American and British impacts, and the series reflects this. The combination of British humor, American idealism, and Canadian "grit" or character makes this series appeal to an increasingly globalized community of viewers.

Perhaps the most intriguing part of the Stargate itself is its instant gratification; when characters step through it, they are transported immediately to another world — there's no hundred-year space voyage, no fancy explanations for cryogenic sleep, or other, life-stretching scenarios so that characters arrive a billion miles away with nothing more harmful or aging than a five o'clock shadow. The Stargate is backed to an extent by scientific principles, fantastical in nature but not unbelievable, a feature premise that is then interwoven into fiction. Neither good nor evil, the Stargate is just that — a gateway to anywhere, affecting thousands of cultures and millions of lives. Each culture that is encountered has its own civilization — its own government, technology, and cultural characteristics. But each culture also embraces a universal desire to avoid trouble and seek happiness.

The operation of the Stargate relies on an ancient map — the stars. Star charting and navigating have been practiced since 3500 BC. They brought Columbus to America, and Marco Polo to China. And those explorers met some of the same struggles and hindrances the SG-1 team does, each voyage of exploration a chapter in the history of humanity, a different story for the storybooks.

The Stargate encircles all this; the stories, conflicts, triumphs, and setbacks. The alluring, silent grey ring is a gateway to innumerable worlds, with the reflective, soothing blue glow of the event horizon in its center — the Stargate excites and tempts us each week, as we wonder what the flagship team of Stargate Command, the SG-1 team, will find.

Anything is possible.

Making Myth
The Story of *Stargate SG-1*

A Colonel, a scientist, an archaeologist, and an alien step through a huge grey ring and end up on a distant planet: it sounds like the start of a bad joke, but it's not. That's actually the premise of *Stargate SG-1*, an award-winning series that's now tied with *The X-Files* for longest-running original U.S. science fiction show on the air. Now in its ninth season, *SG-1* tells of the adventures of a team of explorers who travel to alien planets to rid the galaxy of the evil Goa'uld. Far from being a typical space exploration story, *SG-1* uses mythology and popular science to recast old stories in a contemporary vein; and though it might sound like a hokey premise for a show, the steady mix of humor, adventure, and multifaceted characters have made it a cult hit. Today *SG-1* boasts one of television's largest fan bases, and it continues to gain popularity among fans and critics alike.

Like most good stories, the series has a long history. It's based on the 1994 movie *Stargate*, although it's very different in tone and setup. The movie, which starred Kurt Russell and James Spader in the lead roles of Air Force Colonel Jack O'Neil and Egyptologist Daniel Jackson respectively, was written and produced by Dean Devlin and Roland Emmerich, who went on to write such movies as *Independence Day* and *Godzilla*. *Stargate* opens in Egypt in 1928, with the discovery by a team of archaeologists of a set of "coverstones" and a mysterious grey disc. In the present, Professor Daniel Jackson, an archaeologist shunned by his peers for his unwavering belief that the Egyptian pyramids were in fact built by aliens, is invited to a top-secret military facility to decipher the cryptic hieroglyphs on the coverstones. He eventually realizes that the markings are not hieroglyphs but constellations, and that, combined, they plot a course through space. The function of the Stargate is thus uncovered, and a military team, led by Colonel Jack O'Neil, and accompanied by Jackson, goes through the Gate to the planet Abydos. There they discover an enslaved population who worship an alien creature posturing as the Egyptian Sun God, Ra. While Jackson tries to get the team home, O'Neil becomes involved in an uprising against Ra, who has discovered Earth's existence and is threatening to destroy it. At the last minute, Ra is defeated. Although Daniel has managed to get the Stargate to work, he decides to remain on Abydos with his love, Sha'uri, while the rest of the team goes back to Earth. The series would eventually pick up with that exact situation.

Although *Stargate* had little popular impact at first, its melding of myth and science fiction gradually drew attention, more through word of mouth than through advertising. Distributed by MGM, *Stargate*'s budget came in at about US $55 million; it was largely panned by critics for its plot but praised for its special effects. Still, it grossed approximately US $200 million at the box office, and a cult following of the film sprang up.

The origins of the movie *Stargate* are surrounded in mystery. The story goes that director Roland Emmerich conceived of the idea for the movie in film school in 1979. Other sources suggest that the premise was written by an Egyptologist (who later sued) and sent to Emmerich, who rejected the manuscript at that time. Whatever the origination of the material, the movie was made independent from MGM. "It was very simple," said Dean Devlin, in an interview with *IGN FilmForce*. "There was no studio involved when we made *Stargate*. It was financed through Le Studio Canal+ in France and, after the film was finished, it was sold to MGM."

In 1995, Jonathan Glassner was working as writer, executive producer, and director on *The Outer Limits* when Brad Wright was hired, mostly for Canadian content reasons (see "Everybody CanCon" for more on Canadian content). He quickly recognized Wright's potential, and made sure he was put to work writing. As Glassner put it, "Brad was originally brought in to work on the show for Canadian content reasons and some of my bosses didn't have a whole lot of faith in him because of this. They had it in their minds that this was the only reason he was hired and they couldn't see beyond that. When I read his first script I said, 'This guy is really talented.

Let's put him on staff.' So that's what we did and he became what I used to call our lean, mean writing machine." Both Glassner and Wright had seen the *Stargate* movie and firmly believed in its potential as a franchise. The movie was sitting prettily on the shelves of MGM, but so far had not developed into anything further, such as a series or second feature film. By coincidence, both men independently approached MGM to pitch the idea of a series.

It was the two men's effective and friendly working relationship that led MGM to assign the *Stargate* series to them, and so began the long creation process. John Synes, the then-presi-

Jonathan Glassner, seen here in a rare convention appearance, is the co-creator of the *SG-1* series, with creative partner Brad Wright (COURTESY MICHELLE)

dent of MGM, suggested that Glassner and Wright call Michael Greenburg, co-owner of Gekko Film Corp. to produce the series. Greenburg consulted his partner Richard Dean Anderson, of *MacGyver* fame, and the project was approved. As a bonus, Richard agreed to play the series' male lead, with some provisos (see Richard's biography for more details). *Stargate SG-1* was born.

When news broke of the series' creation, however, not everyone was happy. Despite Glassner and Wright's best intentions and intensive research (they even tried to communicate, to no avail, with Emmerich and Devlin to make sure the series would not undermine the original mythology and characters) the movie's creators were against *SG-1* from the start, and made no attempt to hide it. In an online chat, Glassner explained, "They were very bitter about it. They planned it as a series of movies, but the studio never had any intention of doing it as a series of movies. So that made them more angry. The studio decided it would be more profitable and lend itself better to a television franchise, and offered it to them. They wouldn't make the deal the studio wanted to make so the studio moved on, and that infuriated them. They've been bad-mouthing the series which I think is very unfair of them. I think we're doing the movie justice. We've been very careful to do it justice and stick to the mythology that was created by Emmerich and Devlin."

Glassner and Wright spent a whole summer working through the basics to make sure that the series would be faithful to the intent of the movie. Says Glassner, "Brad and I spent about two months in the summer, before we did the pilot, studying the movie, pulling it apart scene by scene, and saying, 'So, what does this mean? What are these guys? What do the 39 symbols on the Gate mean? What are the rules?'" Their research paid off: although the movie and the series differ in significant ways, the original premise behind each is the same, and more than the two main characters carry over into the series. The pilot episode brought back several minor characters, such as O'Neil's friend, the teenaged Skaara, and Jackson's wife, Sha're (albeit with different spelling).

The most striking difference between the movie and the series is the tone. *Stargate* wove a fairly dark tale — the character of O'Neil looked set to kill himself in his first scene, his young son having accidentally shot himself with O'Neil's service revolver; and when we first meet Jackson, he is destitute and living out of two suitcases. The series takes these dark components and spins them into lighter fare, with characters (as well as writers and producers!) who relish a situation's inherent humor.

There were two major differences between the movie and the series: first, the character of Colonel O'Neil; and second, the nature of the Stargate itself. "For Rick [Anderson] to be interested in doing a long running series," said Michael Greenberg, "he [had] to have a much broader range for [the character of O'Neil] to be interesting to him." Accordingly, Dean Anderson's natural energy and humor were allowed a freer reign. Signalling the change, the Colonel adopted another 'l' (O'Neill) and a lighter tone for the series. As Brad Wright pointed out, it wasn't a complete departure since in the feature film, the character of O'Neil had been in a dark place after the death of his son, which the adventure with Daniel Jackson drew him out of.

As for the Stargate, Glassner and Wright knew that the show would have to immediately set up the Gate as a portal not to one world, but to a multitude of different worlds in order for the series to have any room to grow. It would take more research and some well-crafted writing to make that happen. First and foremost, however, was the cast: An extensive series of auditions was held in various cities — including Toronto, Vancouver, New York, and Los Angeles — to find the remaining members of SG-1, actors who could hold their own on screen with veteran actor Richard Dean Anderson.

THE CAST OF STARGATE SG-1

Richard Dean Anderson (Jack O'Neill)

At fifty-five, Richard Dean Anderson has had more career than you could shake a stick at. And if you gave him a stick, most people would probably expect him to fashion a high-tech gadget out of it. But that's what comes of being recognized by most people as the inventive jack-of-all-trades, MacGyver.

Richard (known online by the acronym RDA) was born on January 23, 1950 in Minneapolis. An active, sport-loving child, he had his heart set on becoming a professional hockey player until he broke both his arms — in separate accidents, three weeks apart — at the age of sixteen. Dean Anderson has always had a self-proclaimed love of exploring, which translated into restlessness as a youth. At seventeen, this restlessness led him and three friends to go on a 5,641-mile bike ride across Canada and Alaska; Richard was the only one of the three who didn't quit. The trip became a turning point in his life, offering him a new sense of self and greater confidence.

The eldest of four brothers, it didn't take long for Richard to develop his renowned razor-sharp wit. His father, Stuart Anderson, was a local high school teacher and a talented jazz bassist; his mother, Jocelyn, is an artist, specializing in painting and sculpture. In such a large and varied family, it's no wonder that Richard learned early his love of sports, music, and acting.

In that vein, he went to Ohio State and St. Cloud University where he studied drama, taking time off before graduation to travel. After short stints in New York and San Francisco, Richard finally settled in Los Angeles, where he went through various "careers" as a mime and juggler and as a jester-singer at a cabaret. His fierce love of animals and the environment found expression in his work at Marineland, where he wrote, directed, and performed in the animals' shows. One of his tasks included holding fish in his mouth for killer whales! "I wrote the show, and announced for the killer whales and the high-dive team, and was sure to write myself into a part," said Richard.

During that time, Richard's talent for music led him to sing and play guitar for his friend Carl Dante's rock band, Ricky Dean and Dante. He even fought forest fires in British Columbia one summer, and briefly entertained the notion of devoting himself to becoming a forest ranger, catering to his love of the environment. However, it was his love of acting that followed him through from Minnesota, and he continued to act in plays and live theatre; his first L.A. break came in 1976 when he landed the lead role in the Pilgrimage Theatre production of *Superman in the Bones*. He came to national attention, however, when he was cast as Dr. Jeff Webber on *General Hospital*, a role that he held for five years. In the fickle world of daytime soaps, Dean Anderson's character rapidly became a fan favorite, thanks in part to the actor's good looks, charisma, and fun attitude. A passionate man, Richard has always been invested in perfecting whatever he happens to be doing, and acting is no exception. In 1981, when *General Hospital* started to shift from medical drama to more action/adventure, he decided that he needed to move on from the show in order to grow as an actor. As well as guest starring in various series, he was involved in two television series for CBS: in 1982 he appeared in *Seven Brides for Seven Brothers*, where he played the eldest brother, and in 1983 he played a role in *Emerald Point N.A.S.*

In 1985, however, Richard's life would change: a new kind of action hero was about to be born. MacGyver (whose first name, Angus, was not revealed until 1992) was a character created by Lee David Zlotoff, of *Remington Steele*–producing fame, and was the very definition of a modern-day hero. Resting solidly on the titular character, an ex-Special Forces officer now dedicated to righting wrongs around the world, *MacGyver* would explode the myth of the "man's man." MacGyver relied on mental capacity, not brute force, to get him out of the tight situations in which he found himself in each episode for the series' seven-year run. He refused to carry a gun, was a vegetarian, and preferred finding nonviolent solutions to problems. In an interview with *Parade Magazine*, Dean Anderson said, "That show was the turning point of a lot of the sensibilities of my career. I'd not wanted to be part of the Hollywood mechanism. I was a vagabond and a wandering rogue. Had a Harley. When I went for the audition [for Henry Winkler, who co-produced the show, and his associates], I had long hair, jeans, a leather jacket. I looked like a dandelion." The producers had something very specific in mind for the character, and when Dean Anderson was asked at the audition to cold read a script, he asked if he could use his glasses due to his nearsightedness. Henry Winkler has since said that that unpretentious attitude told him straight away Richard was the right actor for the role. For his part, Richard said, "And since I don't have very good eyes, I asked if I could put on my glasses to read for the part. And when they let me do that, I knew I had the role. They knew I was different."

Although he was far from an unknown, this was Richard's first prime-time television lead. He had taken bit parts here and there, but it wasn't until *MacGyver* that he felt confident he'd found the opportunity he had been waiting for, the chance to play a character who mattered, who was fun, and who would let him develop his skills. "I'd been turning down a lot of things for the last year or so," he said in an interview at the time, letting his enthusiasm for the part shine through. "I'm trying to let integrity be an integral part of my personality. This character has a lot of the qualities that I've been looking for. He's a very physical character, but there's a humanity about the character that is very attractive to me. He's not relying on an underlying vein of machismo to get through all this. I'm going to embellish the hell out of this character. They have no idea how well they cast this."

In later seasons, the series became far more than a mindless action/adventure show, tackling issues close to Richard's heart, including increasing human impact on the environment and social issues such as teenage runaways. This is not merely a youthful passion for Dean Anderson; such socially minded, high-impact issues continue to drive the actor today, and he is involved in many charities and organizations that strive to make a difference in the world.

Richard wasn't mistaken when he said he was the right actor for the role: playing on *MacGyver* shot him into the limelight. He became a household name and face; in fact, twenty years after the show first aired (it's just now finally being released on DVD), it is still in syndication and an internationally popular show. His performance as the low-key ex-special-agent with an agenda and a heart won him accolades from both viewers and critics. One reviewer wrote in a 1986 issue of *TV Guide*, "Besides being terrific looking (our source for this is quite reliable), Richard Dean Anderson is just right as the brilliant, wry MacGyver, who starts his assignments with a knapsack he carries, 'not for what I take but for what I find along the way.' His part doesn't call for much heavy acting, but Anderson, a veteran of *General Hospital* and a couple of brief CBS prime-time series, manages to play it with just the right amount of tongue in his cheek."

The character of MacGyver had an impact with viewers, and with Dean Anderson himself, already a firm ascriber to the "keep it simple" way of life: "MacGyver had a way of thinking that was more logical. He would piece puzzles together with ostensibly things that were available to him. He wasn't into gadgets. The Swiss Army knife was his one and only gadget, which remains to this day virtually the only thing that I have that I kept

Richard Dean Anderson in his earlier acting days. Imagine the field day SG-1 could have had with *that* haircut (SHOOTING STAR)

from the show. But it was a mode of thought, a way of solving problems, regardless of how complicated they might have been. In real life, you know, I have one tool that I take when I'm cycling, and it's called the MacGyver tool, oddly enough." Then he added, with his trademark grin, "And I expect to get a gross of them for saying that."

Throughout and after his career as MacGyver, Richard continued to pursue other roles, making his television movie debut in the 1986 *Ordinary Heroes*, as a soldier blinded three days before returning home from Vietnam. When *MacGyver* ended in 1992, the actor took on a huge variety of roles in movies such as *In the Eyes of a Stranger* (1992), *Through the Eyes of a Killer* (1992 — a creepy role that earned him great kudos from the press), *Beyond Betrayal* (1994), and *Past the Bleachers* (1995). *MacGyver* was far from over, however. Dean Anderson had recently created the Gekko Film Corporation with business partner Michael Greenburg, and they had signed a deal with Paramount Pictures to develop and produce several films and television series. The first such project was the filming, in 1993, of two *MacGyver* television movies, *MacGyver: Lost Treasure of Atlantis* and *MacGyver: Trail to Doomsday*, both of which aired in 1994.

The company's next project, the ill-fated series *Legend*, Richard has cited as his favorite role to date. He was executive producer as well as actor on the action western series. *Legend* allowed Richard to give free reign to his previously untapped comedic potential, and he relished the opportunity to play a double role in the show, as both a dime-novel writer at the end of the nineteenth century and his fictional creation. Despite receiving critical acclaim, the series aired only from April to August 1995 before it was pulled from the air.

In 1997 Richard felt professionally ready to take on another television series, and he signed on to *Stargate SG-1*, although from the outset, the sheer magnitude of the show was daunting. Whereas most series start out with a network ordering four or five episodes, MGM had ordered a full forty-four. It was to air on the U.S. cable channel Showtime. Despite the time commitment, Richard was enthusiastic about the project. "In cable, at least at Showtime, you get large episode orders. This gives you the opportunity to develop your story arcs, character arcs, and so on over the proper amount of time. It allows you to take chances and experiment. On conventional U.S. networks you usually get six to thirteen shows ordered and you could get yanked off the air after just one or two showings without having a chance to build an audience. Financially the large order gives you the chance to amortize expensive sets, props, wardrobe, etc. over many shows. But if you only have six to thirteen shows, everything becomes more expensive. Creatively, in the cable environment, at least that of Showtime, there is very little interference and a great deal of support toward achieving our vision."

Stargate SG-1 would be a very different on-set atmosphere for the actor, who until then had not been interested in pursuing science fiction roles. As an astute business man, executive producer of the series (Gekko Film was hired to produce it), and the lead actor, Dean Anderson was careful to address any concerns he had about the project and his character before signing onto the project. Jonathan Glassner, co-creator of the series with Brad Wright, had had the same concerns as Dean Anderson about the character of O'Neill — how to translate the darkness of the *Stargate* movie Colonel to the small screen and still make the character interesting and entertaining for viewers week after week. "Early in the development process," Glassner says, "Brad and I studied the movie carefully. And one thing we came away with as TV writers was, 'Who wants to tune in to watch that depressing guy Jack O'Neil week after week?' So we decided to lighten him up and give him a sense of humor. If you study the end of the movie, Daniel asks Jack if he's going to be okay, and he says yes. So obviously the whole adventure on the planet, particularly meeting Skaara, has changed him. So that's where we picked up the ball. Then when Richard Dean Anderson became interested in playing the part, the first thing he said to us was, 'I don't want to do this if he doesn't have a sense of humor.' At which Brad and I smiled and realized that this actor-character match was going to be a good one."

And indeed it was. Richard Dean Anderson's steady on-screen presence since 1982 had a hand in making *Stargate SG-1* a fan favorite — and it worked with the rest of the *SG-1* cast. "Having had the amount of experience he's had on series, he really looks out for us and knows when to fight and when not to," says fellow cast member Amanda Tapping of the fatherly side of RDA. "He's sort of our champion of causes; and he's a lovely man, he really is." Dean Anderson has slowly and surely made O'Neill an indelible television presence, imbuing him with an emotional resonance and facile humor that continues to be one of the show's main draws. At the 2004 Spacey Awards, which honor film and television in the science fiction and fantasy genres, Jack O'Neill won second place for Favorite Male TV Character, with twenty-seven percent of viewer votes. He won the same award in 2005, and did his acceptance speech from a swimming pool, dressed in full scuba diving gear and suit and tie.

Dean Anderson's popularity remained high, despite his gradually lessening role on the show. For although the actor has never been far from the public eye for the last twenty years, and his private life has remained just that, private, Richard's life was irrevocably changed by the birth of his daughter, Wylie Quinn Annarose. Born on August 2, 1998, to Richard and then-girlfriend Apryl Prose, Wylie was the apple of her father's eye from the start: "Most elements in my life have changed dramatically since the birth of my daughter. She's taken all my really serious focus and all my serious attention, and my passion is now for fatherhood. I want to be the best dad in the world." That much was obvious, even on set: "I've already apologized to Brad Wright [one of the creators of the show and fellow executive producer] and said, 'Forgive me — I've got some really strong, paternal aspects of life that are pushing to the fore here.' But he told me — 'Listen, I have a family of my own. I know exactly what you're going through. Don't worry about it.' Brad's feelings mirror those of the rest of my co-workers. It's obvious to everyone that I'm just head over heels, consumed by fatherhood and this wonderful daughter . . ."

Wylie's name comes from a story that Richard read to Apryl's belly over the phone during her pregnancy. "I was in Canada for the shooting of *Stargate*, and Apryl was staying in Los Angeles. We called each other every day. I read her fairy tales, while she put the telephone receiver on her stomach so that our baby could hear. One day, while I was telling a story, we found that Wylie, the name of the heroine, was perfect." Richard has a gift for names — his production company got its name from an experience the actor had in Tahiti, when he woke up to find a small green gecko sitting on his chest. The gecko simply looked at him for a few moments and left — Richard decided it was a good omen!

Aside from his role as dad, Richard has kept up his involvement in his other passions, including art, music, sports, and social issues. He continues to play the guitar, and even composed a piece, "Eau d'Leo" that was used in an episode of *MacGyver*. He loves fast vehicles and owns several, including a 1000cc Harley-Davidson Sportster and a black Acura NSX; he let loose his daredevil side when he participated twice, in 1987 and again in 1988, in the Toyota Grand Prix of Long Beach Celebrity Race, a three-day festival where cars race through the streets of Long Beach. His love of sports continued, eventually leading him to co-found the Celebrity All-Star Hockey team.

Rick was recognized by the U.S. Air Force for *Stargate*'s continuous positive depiction of the military (COURTESY U.S. AIR FORCE)

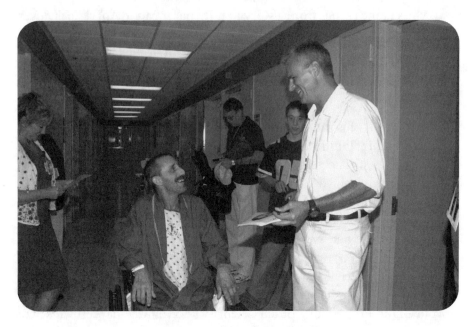

A member of several charities, Rick visits patients at the Walter Reed Army Medical Center (COURTESY U.S. AIR FORCE)

The team is comprised of television and film names who play hockey in NHL cities to raise funds for charity. His devotion to and love of the sport led to him to be two-time honorary captain of the U.S. Olympic hockey team, Team USA, in 1988 and 1992 — quite an honor for a non-professional player.

It's not the only time Richard has been honored by a professional organization. On September 14, 2004, he received the Special Air Force Association Salute at the American Air Force's Anniversary Dinner in Washington D.C. The award, which is rarely given to civilians (in fact, the last one was to James Stewart in 1987), acknowledges Richard's role in the positive depiction of the Air Force in his part as executive producer of *SG-1* and his portrayal of Colonel (later Brigadier General) Jack O'Neill. Pride went into Richard's acceptance of the award, especially as *Stargate SG-1* has taken great care from the beginning in its portrayal of the military, the writers having established a close working relationship with the Air Force. Regular consultation with the organization allows the show to remain, as much as is possible for a science fiction show, grounded in reality. Dean Anderson wrote on his Web site, "The Air Force invited me to be a part of a ceremony celebrating the anniversary of the AF, and the presentation of awards to individuals, retired and active, who have made contributions to the defense industry. It was quite a heady group. Which is why I was a bit confused when General John Jumper was introduced and I was brought on stage with him. He proceeded to launch into the kind of complimentary speech about me that turns me pink. He then presented me with an eagle sculpture, a beautiful medallion from Chief of Staff, United States Air Force, which designates Mr. Richard Dean Anderson an Honorary Air Force Brigadier General, and two silver stars (real!) to seal the deal. Apparently the stars are *never* given out to civilians. I have never been so humbled, I have never been so honored."

Before receiving the award, Richard visited patients at the Walter Reed Army Medical Center in D.C., acting on his belief that it's not enough to say you want to make a difference, you have to actually make one, too. He belongs to the trustee board of a youth organization that promotes constructive outlets aiming to reduce alienation and juvenile delinquency, the Challengers Boys and Girls Club. That organization was founded in 1968, and was the basis for the similar center that was featured in *MacGyver*. In 1995, Dean Anderson was awarded the Celebrity Award from the Make-A-Wish Foundation, an organization that grants wishes to terminally ill children. Many such children have, through Richard, been granted visits to the set of *SG-1*. He supports many other causes, lending his voice and presence when he can. They include the Center for the Prevention of Handgun Violence; Project Literacy U.S.; and the Special Olympics, for which he was one of the key speakers at the opening ceremony in 1991. In December 2004, he was featured in the Vancouver Firefighters' celebrity cookbook, *Pot on the Stove* — a strange outlet to be sure, but the project raises money for the British Columbia Children's Hospital. (For those of you who are wondering, the recipe that Richard contributed to the book is for chocolate hazelnut and coconut cake!)

In a move that perhaps surprised some, in December 2004, Dean Anderson took a stand against pirated autographs. Over the years, he has tried to ensure that any money obtained through the selling of his autograph should be given to charity; in 2004, he took the idea one step further, and, aided by the Legends Memorabilia Web site, came up with a perfect solution. Any autograph sold from that site is guaranteed authentic by Dean Anderson, and all the proceeds are committed to charities.

Still a committed environmentalist, he sits on the board of directors for the Sea Shepherd Conservation Society, an activist organization that aims to protect marine life worldwide. In 2000, he took a rafting trip down Headwall Canyon in British Columbia, which prompted him to get together a small group of partners to create a documentary of the rivers of the world. Sponsored by Dean Anderson himself, the film aimed to chronicle the living rivers as they existed in order to raise awareness of the fragile ecosystems that are today's rivers, and of the importance of water in general. He said in an interview with *Science Fiction Weekly*, "I've recently partnered with Eric Hertz, Steve Mahan, Kate Geis, and Robert Currie. These are people from Earth River Expeditions. I was fortunate enough to be on a rafting trip last summer where I met these guys. The company basically is a rafting expedition corporation that has a calendar of raft trips around the world. Eric approached me and asked if I'd be interested in being part of the documentary film group that would chronicle the great rivers and highlight the more positive sides of rivers that may be at issue with hydroelectric or logging or damming or pollution. Whatever the issue might be. But also to highlight the cultural aspects of the people surrounding any river valleys, the politics of the area, the heritage and basically that's it. I went to Chile. I was on the Futaleufu this last February. I'll be going to Tibet in July for about three weeks. I'll be in Peru, Alaska, Quebec, back to

Chile again. I'll be in Africa at some point in a couple of years. Running all these great rivers. We're loosely calling it The River Project, so we know what we're talking about. Right now it has a bit of a loose form, but hopefully the pieces that we put together will be educational pieces that will throw some light on the situation [as to] what kind of jeopardy may be surrounding our great rivers. So it allows me to travel, I'll be doing that and running these great rivers and doing what I've done [in the past] without much purpose other than for the experience."

He is also a member of Waterkeep Alliance, a grassroots society that acts locally to preserve waterways. In January 2004, Richard could be found at the Celebrity Sports Invitational event, held in Banff, Alberta, indulging his love of skiing. The annual event raises money in support of Waterkeep Alliance by holding sporting competitions with celebrities.

Dean Anderson also actively endorses a number of environmental causes, such as the Charles Darwin Foundation, The National Wildlife Federation, and Greenpeace. In short, he's far from being "just another actor," and is, as all his characters have been, in one way or another, committed to making a difference in the world. His life is as full as it can be — he is a full-time actor (although he has reduced his role on *SG-1* to recurring rather than regular as of the 2005–2006 season nine), a dad, a passionate activist, and a sports aficionado (he regularly scuba dives, skis, sky-dives, cycles, *and* he plays baseball and hockey. Over the years, he's broken both arms, his nose, four fingers, he's had two concussions, three knee surgeries, and back surgery. He's also dislocated his thumbs and shoulders!). In 1997, he even found time to lend his voice to PC game "Fallout" as the character of Killian, alongside Charles Adler and Clancy Brown. "Ultimately," he says, "I guess the sound bite is that if this ever stops being fun then it's time to pack it in, and so far it's still fun."

Christopher Judge (Teal'c)

Christopher Judge is known as the practical joker of the *SG-1* set. Much like his character, Teal'c, he changed his destiny, which at first pulled him toward a career in football, choosing instead to pursue his true passion, acting.

Born Douglas Christopher Judge on October 13, 1967 (although some sources credit him as being a few years younger or older than that), in Los Angeles, Chris is the eldest of two brothers. Information on his early life is hard to come by — about the only things that can be verified are that he has a younger brother, and that he believes in psychic phenomena. In fact, his family apparently bought their first house thanks to Chris' and his brother's psychic ability — their father bet everything he had on a horse that both boys had dreamed about, and it won. In an interview with *Cult Times* in November 2000, he said, "When I was younger I was just so sure of my ability that any subject that was brought to my attention I could almost will myself to dream about. Then, as I got into my teens and people dismissed that kind of thing as weird, I sort of lost that skill. I think extrasensory ability is something we have to believe in and use it or it's gone."

Although he had always wanted to be an actor, and began acting in junior high school, Judge was accepted to the University of Oregon on a football scholarship. He was by all accounts better at baseball, a sport he still harbors a great love for and one that he has always believed was his true athletic calling. Football it was, however, and, playing defensive safety, he was three times selected as All-American, an honorary mention given to particularly gifted players. In his senior year of college, Chris played at Hula Bowl, a college all-star game played in Maui, Hawaii. Although the Hula Bowl is an exhibition rather than a competition game, only the best players are chosen to participate, a testimony to Chris' considerable talent.

He never put acting behind him though: "I always knew I wanted to be an actor. Football was a way for me to make a name for myself. I had always hoped that it would segue into entertainment. Even though I enjoyed the actual Saturdays of football — the game itself — everything else that went into it I didn't enjoy. I didn't enjoy practicing. I could never really put my arms around the single-mindedness that football encourages. I would often get in trouble for questioning a play. One of the marks against me, coming out of college, was that I thought too much. Individuality was discouraged. What made the experience tolerable was that I always recognized it for what it was, a stepping stone to an acting career." At university, Judge followed his heart, changing disciplines until he found the one that was right for him. Knowing that acting would be a tough career choice, he first enrolled in a pre-med curriculum until he discovered that his math skills weren't quite up to par. He then took a philosophy major for half a year before switching to psychology, finally settling on a telecommunications and film major, with a minor in psychology. It is perhaps this training in psychology that has led to Judge becoming one of the most beloved actors on the *Stargate* set. Said co-star Amanda Tapping, "He's charming and he has this great laugh. And he shoots straight from the hip — you can always count on him to say exactly what's on his mind. He's the person I go to when I need cheering up. I absolutely adore that man."

It was in college that Chris got his first break in the entertainment business, when he entered and won a contest being held by a morning radio show in Oregon. Chris presented a five-minute monologue, and won the prize, which was to host the West Coast FOX KLSR Morning Show. Then, in his senior year of college, the U.S. network channel FOX, in their first year of existence and in need of programs, started to host regional contests. After Chris won one such contest, he went on to host, in his words, an "MTV talk show type thing," and got an agent. After that, his career progressed quite quickly.

In 1989, he enrolled at the Howard Fine Acting Studio in Los Angeles, where he studied drama before being cast in his first movie in 1990, *Bird on a Wire*, starring Mel Gibson and Goldie Hawn. Although Judge only had a small part — his cast name read "Cop at a café" — the movie was a box office hit. He had actually read for a different part, but when that part was cut, the producers offered him the role of the cop instead, who chases after Mel and Goldie's characters. Although the extras hired for this scene were all stunt people, one of them froze and Judge had to slam on his brakes, missing the extra by mere inches. In the ensuing nervousness, Chris flubbed his line — at which point Goldie Hawn burst into laughter!

In January 1990, Chris also starred in a fifth-season episode of *MacGyver*, "Live and Learn," in which he played a high school student whom MacGyver tries to mentor and motivate despite negative influences in the boy's life. This type of social issue episode, more common in *MacGyver*'s later years, fit in well with Chris' own personal beliefs, since he's a firm believer that there is nothing more important than children. Fun trivia facts proliferate on the *Stargate SG-1* set, and one is that of the four main cast members, three have links to *MacGyver*. Michael Shanks decided to become an actor when he happened across Richard Dean Anderson shooting a scene from *MacGyver*. (Don S. Davis, who plays the staunch General Hammond in *SG-1* also played in the ubiquitous series!)

In the same year, Judge played in the Martin Sheen movie *Cadence*, where he is credited as Douglas Judge. From 1991 to 1995, Chris honed his skills in different types of productions. In 1991, he landed a part in the comedy *House Party 2*; from 1994 to 1995, he played the character Richie Styles on the television series *Sirens*; and in 1995 he took on a guest-star

Unlike the early Teal'c, Christopher Judge is big on the smiles (but both are easy on the eyes) (ALBERT L. ORTEGA)

role in an episode of *The Fresh Prince of Bel-Air*, starring Will Smith. The episode, "There's the Rub (Part 2)" aired in November 1995, during the sixth and last season of the show's run. Since then, Judge has also guest starred on various comedy series like *Martin*, *Lush Life*, and *The Jamie Foxx Show*; done bit parts in films such as Francis Ford Coppola's *First Wave*; and appeared in TV drama series like *Freedom*, *The Burning Zone*, *Wise Guy*, *21 Jump Street*, *Gabriel's Fire*. He has appeared in two episodes of *Andromeda*, in 2002 and 2003, playing a different character each time — in one, he played opposite *SG-1* co-star and best friend Michael Shanks.

It was in 1997, however, that Chris got his biggest break, when he was cast as the stalwart warrior alien Teal'c on *Stargate SG-1*. On getting the part, he said, "When they conceptualized Teal'c, they really weren't sure what they wanted. I was one of the last guys who read for Teal'c. By the time I came in, I think they were actually starting to stray from the idea of having Teal'c be black." He added, with the laughter that accompanies most of the actor's words, "I don't think that they had met anyone who was definitely Teal'c for them, and I'm not sure they knew what that was anyway." The freedom afforded by the very accepting writers and producers of the show has been a great boon for Judge, who expounds, "So, from day one I would say, 'What do you want? What do you want here or there?' They would say, 'We don't know. That's kind of why we hired you, because to us, you are Teal'c. What you did in the audition, just keep on doing it.' So, from the beginning, I've had the freedom to change lines. They've always been very receptive to me saying, 'I don't think this really works here,' or 'He's saying too much here.'"

Although he was nervous at first about playing an alien slave, with typical determination and courage, Judge took the part and made it his. The personal support he gathered from friends and fans alike also helped him deepen the character he plays. In a 1999 interview, he said, "It has surprised me how much people understand that Teal'c is a liberator. I hate to draw parallels between a real person and a fictional alien, but Teal'c is very much like Martin Luther King, George Washington, or Abraham Lincoln. In the fictional world of Jaffa, he's trying to end his people's enslavement. My friends, down to the last one, have really gotten that. That makes me feel good."

The freedom he experienced at the beginning of the series has also carried through to later seasons: "At the start of every season I've usually sat down with [executive producer] Brad Wright, and this year it was [show runner/producer] Robert Cooper. We talked about what kind of stuff

Teal'c should go through and where we would like to see him become more human." Teal'c's humanization is one of the most important aspects of the actor's portrayal, and he works hard to make that come through in subtle ways. "Teal'c is very much like a human man. Yes, he has certain advanced physical abilities and healing and recuperative powers, but in his heart and in his mind he's very much a man, and he dreams and aspires to things just like human men do."

Judge has a very laid-back view of life, abiding by co-star Richard Dean Anderson's own adage, "life's too short." He also has a very particular approach to acting, and to his role as Teal'c. "I'm habitually late. I get to places at the last possible minute. I don't know how the guys on *SG-1* put up with me. Then there's the whole preparation thing. Shanks and Amanda have a great theatrical background so they tend to break down the whole script and approach the thing like utmost professionals. I usually go to Shanks and ask, 'Should I read the script? How much do I say and how much am I in it?' It's not that I'm lazy or anything like that, it's more that, as Teal'c, so much of my expression is based on surprise, so I like to actually *be* surprised when we shoot."

In 2003, Chris expanded his career by venturing into writing. In the sixth-season episode "The Changeling," he tells the story by focusing on Teal'c's self-identity. This would be Judge's first writing credit, although the story of the fifth-season episode "The Warrior" is credited to him. "The Changeling" is a powerful episode, and shows the firm grasp the actor has on his character. In the audio commentary to the episode, Chris talked about the writing process. "You come up with a pitch, then you submit outlines and outlines and outlines. And to the credit of Brad, he really tries to foster and encourage your creativity. But what happens a lot of the time is he will spoon-feed you the script. And I really wanted to have a genuine assessment of if I had any skill at all as a writer. And so I kind of went about it in a different way: I pitched, and Brad allowed me to hand in the finished draft." As a writer, Judge took a lot of risks, interweaving the narrative thread of the episode within a dream state — a technique that's notoriously difficult. The gambit paid off: the episode was an instant fan favorite, and a turning point for Teal'c within the series.

It is that call of the creative that is so attractive to Chris, who works hard on the development of such skills. He is a gifted photographer, and several of his shots of fellow cast members have become fan favorites. One in particular of Amanda Tapping reveals Chris' very different perspective on people and how they present themselves. Artistically accomplished as well as a successful businessman (he owns two production companies, one in Los Angeles and the other in Vancouver), Judge fulfilled one of his long-time desires during the 2004 hiatus when he recorded a CD; the first single, "We're Going to Take Our Clothes Off," rose in the charts to a stunning number one in Asia.

Chris' writing career was not over with "The Changeling." Later in 2003 he penned the episode "Birthright," and the following year he wrote the follow-up to that episode, "Sacrifices." In 2004, the actor took his career to the next level while on hiatus: he produced and starred in a short feature film, *Hacks*. The movie is about stand-up comedians and their struggle to break into the scene in Los Angeles. Although skeptical about taking on a producer's role ("I don't like [actors], there is no way I want to have to put up with their moods and their 'motivations' and their general attitude") Judge has grown into the role, and has recently gone on record saying he may be interested in moving behind the cameras. In a typically humorous take on life, he suggested that the advantage of being behind the cameras is he could stop dieting and working on his body — something that as an actor, and more specifically as the warrior Teal'c, he can't afford to do. "Honestly, I'm a fat man inside a somewhat-in-shape man's body! The thought of another ten to fifteen years of dieting and working out is daunting. But writing does play to the part of me that is more thoughtful and introspective."

Although he plays the most straight-faced member of SG-1, Chris is well known for his pranks and sense of humor. At one convention, he auctioned off JR Bourne's (who plays Martouf) rear end! "Christopher Judge has a wonderful sense of humor and possibly one of the best laughs I've ever heard," says Amanda Tapping. And he honestly loves doing the show, and everything involved in it — including the fans. Earnest, well-spoken, and with a tremendous sense of humor that leaks out all over the place, Chris was amazed at the fame he had acquired from the show. "I think it was the third season maybe, or the end of the second season, before we got to go out and really see the extreme loyalty and really how people had gotten into the show. It really helps you as a performer to see, this really matters, and I think that's really important."

Judge has taken part in various projects since joining the cast of *SG-1*, including a role in *Stargate* director and writer Peter DeLuise's 2001 television movie, *Romantic Comedy 101*, acting alongside Jeremy London and

Chris smiling Down Under – probably contemplating a prank! (COURTESY PETER FALLON WWW.BOBW.COM.AU)

Tom Arnold. In 2001, he played with Jennifer Beals (of *The L Word* fame) in *Out of Line*. And in 2002, he starred opposite Cuba Gooding Jr. in the Disney production *Snow Dogs*. Judge's distinctively deep, husky voice, as well as his formidable laugh, have led to quite a few voice jobs over the years, in television, film, and other media, such as video games. In 2003 and 2004, he provided the character D-Mob in the video games *Def Jam Vendetta* and *Def Jam Fight for NY*. His other voice credits range from the role of Magneto in 2000 in the television series adaptation of *X-Men: Evolution* to the TV series *He-Man and the Master of the Universe*, where he played Zodak in 2002, and Simon Grey in the series *Action Man*. In 2005, he starred as Nate Wall in the movie *Personal Effects*, opposite such stars as Penelope Ann Miller and Casper Van Dien.

Outside work, Chris remains an avid sportsman, although his passion has turned to golf in recent years — a love shared by many of the cast and crew of *Stargate SG-1*: "Everyone as a whole gets along well and this includes the crew. We have a huge group of golfers on the set and the producers golf with the crew and the actors golf with the crew." In fact, he has nothing bad to say about the atmosphere on the set, and has repeatedly stated that, of all his acting experiences, *Stargate* has been the most positive, especially in terms of relationships between the cast members: "And it's sickening to say, but after some of the other shows that I've worked on, this one's like a big love-in." Like their characters, Daniel and Teal'c, Michael Shanks and Chris Judge have a great relationship. "Shanks and I are best friends. We've seen each other through failed relationships, our kids love each other, our girlfriends get along. The odd thing is that we disagree on everything, but we respect and listen to each other's opinions. I love him to death."

Judge is kept busy by his four children, with whom he spends a great deal of time. Christopher Jordan (who appeared in the episode "The Changeling"), Cameron Justin, Catrina Catherine, and Chloe, are a big part of his life. Chloe, the youngest of the four, was born to Judge and his fiancée, actress/model Gianna Patton in February 2005, and is the couple's first child together. Judge guards his privacy, and so details on his family life are hard to find. It appears that he used to be married and is now divorced, but very little information is available beyond those facts. He speaks openly and often of his children, however, and his devotion to his family definitely doesn't come second to his career. Because the grueling schedule was cutting too much into his family life (Teal'c wears a lot of makeup and so Chris is generally on set much earlier than the rest of the cast), Chris began taking his children to work with him. "The hardest part of this business is the toll it takes on your loved ones. It's difficult to maintain a healthy relationship with a spouse or whoever when you pretty much only have the weekends. Because I happen to be working on several projects at the moment, my weekends consist of Sunday night. I'm up early in the morning and I don't get home until late, so it got to the point where I hardly ever saw my children. Now I bring them to work with me and it's just terrific. I have to get them up at four-thirty in the morning but, thank God, they love it, and I love having them around."

The family devotion started early. When asked by a fan who his inspiration was when growing up, he replied, "My number-one inspiration was my mother. She worked two jobs and had breakfast and dinner prepared. I essentially called my mother 'the lion.' She's fierce and she's proud. I'd like to think some of that rubbed off on me."

Asked whether or not he would encourage his own children to pursue an acting career, Judge responded that he would encourage to be themselves, to find their own way: "[Their choice of career] has to make them happy first," he said sincerely. It's this fatherly, compassionate persona Chris projects that makes him such a great role model for younger viewers. In an online chat with fans, he stated, "I love it when families watch the show. As a parent I also find it hard to watch shows with my kids. For me, being a dad, that's one of the best compliments I can get."

Like most of the cast of *SG-1*, Christopher Judge is active in charity events. He is especially committed to charities that work with children, including the Boys and Girls Clubs of Canada, an organization that provides children and youth with opportunities to develop their skills and interests. "One of the great things about Teal'c is that he's popular with children. I get a lot of requests for autographed pictures and I'm invited to appear at events designed to raise money to help kids. Both *Stargate* and my character allow me to become involved in causes that I don't know if I'd be involved in otherwise. It's certainly one of the most rewarding things about this job. After all, what's more important than taking care of our children?"

Michael Shanks (Daniel Jackson)

When Michael Shanks first enrolled in business school, he would have been stunned to learn that a few short years later, he would be shot to the heights of fan adoration when he took on the role of an archaeologist who steps through an interplanetary portal in *SG-1*.

A native of Canada, Michael Garrett Shanks was born on December 15, 1970, in Vancouver, British Columbia. The youngest of two brothers, he grew up in the then-small ski community of Kamloops in B.C. where he gained a love of sports at an early age. He was given the nickname "Munko" because his brother, at an early age, couldn't pronounce "Michael." He describes himself as something of an overachiever at school: he played hockey (defense) and rugby (fly half, then wing), was on the student council, and participated in the theater group. Although he performed in high school plays (and in fact has been acting in one way or another since he was five years old) — Shanks has named his high school teacher as one of his inspirations, as she encouraged him to pursue acting — his professional interest in acting would not come until much later. In fact, like many Canadians, he grew up wanting to become a professional hockey player — not unlike his *SG-1* co-star, Richard Dean Anderson. Some time before leaving for university, however, he lost interest in playing the sport, citing the fierce competitiveness at that age and skill level. "I think I just lost the sense of fun out of it. Once it gets to a certain level, the parents are up in the stands fighting and the coach is raking you over the coals too hard. Especially in Canada, when you're fifteen or sixteen years old and you're just trying to establish the fun idea of it, and you're being asked to go on the ice and fight and hurt people and stuff like that. I mean the fun aspect of it got lost very quickly. And you start to hang on to your stick a little too hard when you worry about it, because you worry about screwing up. So you start to clutch that stick like it's an axe. You're just afraid to let it go and after a while you stop being able to play, because you're so worried about making a mistake that you can't perform anymore. So once I finished playing it seriously and started playing it for fun again, all of a sudden I found out I was a much better hockey player, because I enjoyed it again, and I was having fun when I was doing it."

Having made the decision to not play hockey professionally, in 1989, Shanks enrolled in a business degree at the University of British Columbia. Needing some arts credits in order to earn his degree, he took up acting. However, upon failing a calculus course, he came up short by a few credits, and changed degrees: in 1994, he graduated with a Bachelor's degree in Fine Arts — an event which he identifies as a turning point in his life. "In terms of my career, a failure of a calculus course forced me to get out of a business major and into acting."

It was during his university years, in fact, that Michael discovered his passion and talent for acting, which he had formerly approached only as a sideline. In another *SG-1* coincidence, Shanks had happened upon a location shoot for *MacGyver* during his first year of university. "Being from a small town in Canada," he said in an interview in his typical down-to-earth manner, "I had never seen a TV show being filmed. I watched Richard work a bit, and it got me excited about the possibilities of becoming a professional actor. I didn't change majors based on that alone — it makes it sound like Richard was the wind beneath my wings!"

Before graduating, Michael performed in a number of small productions for the Frederic Wood Theatre of the University of British Columbia. In 1992, he played the part of an officer in Brian Friel's *Translations*. The drama is set in Donegal, Ireland, in 1833, and tells the story of a land on the brink of change through the intervention of the British Army. Michael's character, Lieutenant Yolland, has come to bring about British law, but finds himself

Michael Shanks, destined for show business (COURTESY MICHELLE)

enchanted by the land instead. Michael has said that of all the characters he's played, Lieutenant Yolland resembles him the most, because, in the actor's own words, "he was searching for perfect happiness." In March 1993, Shanks played up-and-comer Walter Gay in a theater production of Charles Dickens' novel *Dombey and Son*, a social satire that follows the character of Paul Dombey, who is kidnapped and then rescued by Shanks' character. Later that year, in September, Michael played Tereus in a Greek tragedy *The Love of the Nightingale* by Timberlake Wertenbaker. In his first really dramatic role, he portrayed the King of Thrace, who fell in love with his wife's sister, Philomela. When he accompanies her back to Thrace, he pretends to have received news of her sister, Procne's, death, and forces her into a fake marriage. When she finds out and threatens him, he rapes her, cuts out her tongue, and imprisons her. Philomela weaves a tapestry, however, that tells Procne of the crime. To gain revenge, Procne kills and cooks her and Tereus' young son for dinner. When Tereus discovers he has eaten his own son, he flies into a fury and chases the two women. Before the chase ends, all three are turned into birds — Philomela into a nightingale. This harsh and difficult role was instrumental in helping Michael delve deeper within himself as an artist, and the experience has served him even up to his years on *SG-1*, as many episodes often call for him to express fierce emotions and much passion. Just before graduating, in March 1994, Michael performed in Shakespeare's *Love's Labour's Lost*, where he played the part of the Spaniard, Don Armado.

Upon graduating, Michael auditioned for the prestigious Stratford Festival of Canada. Established in the early 1950s, this venue, mainly devoted to the works of Shakespeare, is one of the highest quality theater festivals in North America. Many international actors, performers, and directors have made their debuts at the Stratford Festival, as its standards are world-renowned. Michael played at the theater for two seasons (the Stratford season lasts from about mid-April until the beginning of November), taking on a number of roles, including Lorenzo from *The Merchant of Venice*, Menteith from *Macbeth*, as well as smaller parts in *King Lear*, *The Merry Wives of Windsor*, and *Amadeus*. The sheer variety of roles that Shanks had now taken on were helping him to hone his acting talent and develop a working method, as well as an ability to analyze and work with narrative structure and character motivation. Those skills would stay with him throughout his *Stargate* years as well.

During his university and post-university career, Michael Shanks had begun to take on small parts in various television series. In November 1993, he appeared in both *Highlander* and *The Commish*. In the first, he played a miner's son who dies while trying to get his corrupt father to do the right thing by the workers; in the second, he took on the role of a reckless teenager. In 1994, Michael guest starred on the Canadian series *Madison*, and in 1995 in the short-lived Aaron Spelling series *University Hospital*.

In 1995, Michael also landed his first role in a television movie. *A Family Divided* starred Faye Dunaway and Stephen Collins as parents who begin to suspect their son may have played a part in a gang-rape. The drama also starred fellow *Stargate* actor, Don S. Davis (General Hammond). Hailed as courageous, this television movie brings up questions of morals, ethics, life-changing truths, maternal instinct, and the consequences of our actions — all universal themes that Shanks would eventually channel into the character of Daniel, albeit in a very different way.

It was in 1997 that Michael broke onto the small screen in a big way, when he was cast as Doctor Daniel Jackson in the series *Stargate SG-1*, taking over James Spader's role from the movie. When he went into the audition, he went prepared, and called on his impersonation skills to portray Daniel as James Spader had — not a hard feat for Michael, since he holds great admiration for the movie actor. Because Richard Dean Anderson had taken his own character of O'Neill in such a different direction from the movie's O'Neil, the producers were looking for someone who could make Daniel as Spader-like as possible, to provide some continuity for fans of the movie. Said Shanks, "In some ways, what I had to do was what theater actors do in plays all the time; come in and take over a role that someone else has been handling, and just play it to the best of my ability." In an interview with *IGN FilmForce*, Michael explained his acting choice, and his subsequent efforts to gradually imbue the character with

Michael is a popular figure at conventions

his own personality. "I ripped off Spader left, right, and center, especially at the outset. If you're going to steal from somebody, I'd love to steal from Spader . . . And they were happy with it. It was nice, though, to have the long term benefit to be able to pare away those things and eventually make the character my own and put my own unique stamp."

As it turned out, Shanks's resurrection of the character of Daniel Jackson quickly shot him to fan fame. At twenty-seven, he was the youngest of the core cast, and his golden good looks, coupled with Daniel's gentle humor and friendly nature, endeared him to a large contingent of fans, who, from the start, were extremely vocal about their love of the character, and of the actor himself. "I know that there's a Web site devoted to my feet as well. [See the chapter "No Red Shirts: The Fanchise of *SG-1*" for more on that!] The publicists of *Stargate* pointed it out to me," he laughed in an interview with *SFX*. "Then, in case I thought that was all, there's a phenomenon known as Danny Whumping, which is a law unto itself. One of the producers came to me and said, 'You know there's a contingent of people, fans of the show, who really like to see Daniel get the shit kicked out of him.' I said, 'Whaddya mean, don't they like the character?' And he said, 'No, they love the character!' What the hell is that all about? They like to see the character get beat up! Well, that's an interesting fan demographic there."

Michael took on a number of different roles during his years on *SG-1*, including two guest appearances on *The Outer Limits* in 1998 and 2000. In 2002, he appeared on *The Chris Isaak Show* and on *The Twilight Zone*, and in both 2001 and 2003 he guest starred in *Andromeda* — a fortunate turn of events since it was there that he met his future wife Lexa Doig, who plays "Rommie." He also got parts in quite a few movies, from the 2002 television movie *All Around the Town*, a thriller based on Mary Higgins Clark's novel of the same name and starring Nastassja Kinski, to the 2003 movie *Sumuru*, a futuristic fantasy in which Michael sports a goatee.

Stargate SG-1 was not only a boon for Michael's acting career, it also allowed him to expand his horizons and try his hand at directing and writing. In 2001, during the show's fourth season, he directed an episode called "Double Jeopardy," which featured robot doubles of the SG-1 team, a huge gun fight between the teams and the Goa'uld, and many other large events. Said the actor, "I remember during the first read-through of the script everyone said, 'Oh, my God.' Then the rookie director, me, looked at the script and thought, 'You've got to be kidding.' It was the luck of the draw or just the chips falling where they may, but I ended up with the biggest episode we've done since the series began. It was an overwhelming situation to be dropped into to say the least." "Double Jeopardy" turned out to be one of the season's best episodes, and the directing experience was, according to Michael, wonderful. The rest of the cast and crew were helpful and supportive during this time, and while having to direct people with whom he usually acted might have been a strange initiation into directing, Shanks was also able to draw on his experience as an actor to make the transition smoother for all involved. "Something that a number of television directors do not have is the ability or desire to communicate with actors. You can plan out a scene and know just what you'd like your actors to do, but if you can't express your ideas to them in a 'common language' it's going to make both your jobs a lot more difficult. [. . .] So working with the actors was the easiest part of the job because I was already inside their heads so to speak."

However, in 2002, in the middle of the fifth season of *Stargate SG-1*, things started to turn sour. Citing creative differences with the writing and production team, Michael left the show with the gut-wrenching episode "Meridian." Although his character's ultimate fate was left open to conjecture, fans mourned his passing along with the rest of the SG-1 team. As early as 2001, Shanks had expressed concerns about the direction in which his character was heading. Even in the *Stargate* movie, Daniel had been written as the outsider in the military establishment, and while his expertise and humanist approach to the different civilizations the team encountered were always welcomed by the rest of the team, he was still very much the black sheep — a status that had started to grate on Michael. "Our writers dream up some *great* ideas when it comes to writing Daniel stories, and I've had some excellent ones this year. I relish those episodes as they allow me to spread my wings as an actor. Unfortunately, in group situations they're still not quite sure what to do with my character. I think that's been a common theme since the series began. Daniel is a bit of a loner and an outsider and, to top it off, he's *not* a soldier. So when the fighting starts what do we do with him? We have him crouch behind a rock and leave him out of the action or we don't have him in the scene at all."

When Shanks had signed on for the role of Daniel, he had believed that the relationship between himself and Jack O'Neill would be a major focus of the show, especially as it had been an intrinsic part of the *Stargate* movie. Because the series went in such a different direction from what the actor had expected, it was perhaps no surprise that he had started to feel somewhat underused; after all, if he wasn't working to improve his acting skills, then what was he working toward? It was this that finally led the actor to quit: "Jackson [potentially] had much more interesting things to do than I did. He was a member of SG-1. He was a peaceful explorer, archaeologist, linguist, anthropologist, and a lot more. There were fights with the Goa'uld, with the government. And there were still infinite possibilities and courses to take in developing the character." He added further, "There are lots of things I want to do, including film, theater, and more television if it comes up, but basically I just want to work. I want to feel that I'm not just spinning my wheels. I want to grow as an actor and that desire comes at a price. Even though I could have stayed through season six — Brad [Wright], the show's co-creator, did ask me to stay — I was prepared to take advantage of the question mark of the future rather than carry on in what I knew was going to be a very trying situation. I felt that when feelings were still to a certain degree positive, it was time to move on."

Fan reaction was immediate. Web sites sprang up demanding that the producers get Michael back, petitions were raised, and the studio was bombarded with letters from angry fans. A year went by with only three guest appearances from Michael on the show, and the passion of the fans didn't abate. Finally, in 2003, Michael returned as a full-time cast member, reclaiming his place alongside Richard, Amanda, and Chris for the show's seventh, eighth, and ninth seasons. Because Richard Dean Anderson had decided to reduce his on-set and on-screen time in order to spend time with his daughter, Michael was more confident about the avenues that would be opened up to his character. The additional screen time, as well as the fact that he missed the atmosphere and the people involved, were deciding factors in his return. "One of the main factors contributing to my wanting to come back was the fact that I knew I was going to get the chance to be involved in the individual episodes a lot more." While Daniel would still be portrayed as the humanist of the team, he would no longer be on the outskirts of the action; instead, his experiences during the year away would allow the character to become more involved in the military aspects of SG-1's explorations, and to be more proactive in general.

It is not only the fans who have recognized Michael's talent: critics and award organizers have been consistently supportive of his performances. Since the year 2000, Michael has proven to be one of the most popular stars on television. He was nominated for a Leo Award for best male actor in a dramatic series in 2000 for his performance in the episode "Forever in a Day," a heartrending episode in which Daniel's life is irrevocably changed; he was nominated for the same award in 2003, 2004, and 2005. His performance in the 2004 episode "Lifeboat" — which won him a Leo Award — was a dramatic episode in which Daniel's psyche played host to a dozen different souls and personalities. In 2001 and 2005, he was nominated for a Saturn Award for best supporting actor on television; in 2004, he was nominated for the Saturn for best lead actor.

The reaction to Michael's return to the screen was mixed. While fans of Shanks and his character were thrilled at this return of the prodigal, a year had gone by, and fans of Corin Nemec, who had played the fourth member of SG-1 since Daniel's departure, were angry at the apparent disregard for *their* favourite character. But as Michael took Daniel in new directions and the five-year familiarity and affection between the cast members became apparent, fans' fears were laid to rest and the show went on.

Michael's foray into writing came in *Stargate*'s seventh season, in 2004, with the episode "Resurrection." It was co-star Amanda Tapping who would direct Michael's script, an experience both have described as one of the most fulfilling of their careers. Brad Greenquist, who guest starred in the episode, was very impressed with Michael's work, as were the cast and crew of *SG-1*. Fans immediately latched on to the episode, admiring the sense of tension and the subtle mix of action and character development throughout. "Resurrection" has been hailed as one of the best "first attempts" at writing and directing in the show's run.

Like his fellow *SG-1* cast members, Shanks is actively involved in charities, including the Veterans' Association of Canada, the American Society for the Prevention of Cruelty to Animals, and the Multiple Sclerosis Society of Canada. In May 2005, the Michael Shanks Online Web site

Michael and wife Lexa Doig (ALBERT L. ORTEGA)

launched a charity auction of items autographed by Shanks, the proceeds of which all went to the Multiple Sclerosis Society.

Outside of work, Michael leads a full life; he keeps busy playing sports — hockey, golf, rollerblading, and windsurfing. He is especially devoted to his family. In 1998, his long-time girlfriend Vaitiare Bandera (who played Daniel's wife Sha're on *Stargate SG-1*) gave birth to their first child, Tatiana. Despite the fact that the couple has since split, Michael, who is on location in Vancouver for much of the year, regularly commutes to Los Angeles to spend as much time with his daughter as possible. Tatiana herself has even appeared on *SG-1* — in a way. "Her first acting gig was as a fetus. [Her mom and I] did an episode when she was pregnant. So we call that Tatiana's first acting gig, playing a fetus, as herself."

In 2001, when Michael guest starred on *Andromeda* for the first time, he met and fell in love with Lexa Doig, who played the artificial intelligence of the show's ship. They were married on August 2, 2003, and on September

13, 2004, their daughter, Mia Tabitha, was born. Michael has spent much of the past year outside of work being a doting dad and husband, saying he's happier than he has ever been. He's now a regular on the convention circuit, and is extremely popular there, as his natural charm wins over the crowds. "The fans always surprise me, and it's been wonderful to be more a part of that experience. At a convention, I probably get tired of hearing the same questions, but at the same time I like to challenge myself to find more creative answers to them. I'm always trying to be more creative, you know, find a way to take the same truth and make it more fun."

Amanda Tapping (Samantha Carter)

It seems like Amanda Tapping has it all: she's smart, she's got a husband and baby, and she's the sole lead female role on one of television's most popular series. In the public eye, she has molded her character into a role model for women worldwide, and has quietly honed her talent into something remarkable.

Amanda Jane and her twin brother Stephen were born on August 28, probably in 1965. ("Why I never told my age? I like to keep them guessing . . . so many different ones on the net, I'll let people decide for themselves," said Amanda.) She was born at Rochford General Hospital in Essex (southeast England) because the hospital in Benfleet, where her parents lived, couldn't accommodate twins. The twins were the last addition to the family, who lived in the small town of South Benfleet for three years before relocating to Canada. Amanda was raised with her three brothers (Richard and Christopher are the other two), to whom she was very close; in fact, her first memories involve her and Stephen speaking their "little twin language" together so no one could understand them. In one of those funny quirks of life, Amanda's dad had wanted to call her "Samantha," and when "Amanda" was chosen instead, took to calling her "Sam" as a nickname.

Amanda's mother was originally from Finchley, North London, and her father from southeast London, but her mother's parents and two sisters had all moved to Canada, apparently on a whim, needing to try something different. In 1968, Amanda's family followed them to Toronto. Thankfully, at three years of age, Amanda was too young to feel much homesickness, but even today she feels a strong connection and sense of home in England, and she loves going back there. The only girl in the family, and a self-proclaimed mischievous child, Amanda often fell short of her brothers' athletic expectations; she insisted on playing war with them in the local woods, however.

In Toronto, Amanda attended public school and North Toronto High School. Although she loved school, the high school she went to was out of her district, and populated with children wealthier than she was, so she felt somewhat out of place. Calling herself "one of the misfits," Amanda belonged to a group that called themselves "the group" who drifted from one major clique to another — a difficult high school experience at best. The school did however offer her many avenues to explore. She ran track, tried out for cheerleading (she didn't get in), and she was very involved in her classes, showing a particular affinity for science. She had always been gifted in mathematics, and in high school she developed that facility, as well as taking drama classes. Tapping showed such talent that she won both the dramatic arts award and the environmental science award.

Her parents were very keen on Amanda continuing on to a science career after school (her father was a natural scientist) and Amanda herself had always harbored the idea that she would go into medicine, but as she grew older, she changed directions, going from medicine to marine biology, and finally to acting. As a child, Amanda had loved the television series *Little House on the Prairie*, and the British drama series *Coronation Street*, and according to her mother, she had always held the desire to become an actress alongside her other ambitions. Said Tapping, "I always had this sort of inkling I'd like to be a doctor when I was younger, and then, of course, like everyone else, wanted to be a marine biologist, but acting was always in the forefront." As a small child, Amanda had participated in a school presentation of *The Wizard of Oz*, playing the wicked Mrs. Gulch. In 1983, at age eighteen, her father found out about a professional production of *The Lion in Winter* that was being mounted, and, in an attempt to show her that acting was not really what she wanted to do, took her to the audition. "We got there early, we sat in a little donut shop having a cup of tea and he ran lines with me — he was Henry II — and — just bless his heart — to this day I'll always remember this moment, and he looked at his watch and said, 'Right then, I think it's time for you to go in.'" On the drive home, he preemptively comforted her for not getting the part, despite her conviction that she had done well, and a couple of days later, she got the part. She hasn't looked back since.

Tapping enrolled in and eventually graduated from the University of Windsor School of Dramatic Art in Windsor, Ontario. The prestigious institution is known for its small, personalized classes and teachers who are accomplished theater professionals. After graduation, she trained for another four years in theater and took on several parts in stage productions; at the time, she was firmly set against doing television or commercial work, ensconced as she was in the theater world. "When I left, I swore I would never, oh that word 'never,' do television. I only wanted to act on stage, because I thought that doing television was like prostituting oneself." At the West End Theatre in London, Ontario, the actress played Shelby in a production of Robert Harling's play *Steel Magnolias*, which has since been turned into a hit movie. The lead role of Shelby was a demanding one, and Tapping worked hard to portray the young woman whose pregnancy is threatened by a severe diabetic condition.

Amanda Tapping at a fan meet-and-greet in San Diego (ALBERT L. ORTEGA)

In 1986, Amanda played the part of Alison in John Osborne's controversial play *Look Back in Anger*. The lead female role in a drama about a woman who stays with her angry, violent husband is one that fit in well with Amanda's own ideals. A firm feminist, Tapping believes strongly that women must have a voice, and is committed to exploring that through her various roles. "There is a lack of good role models for women in popular culture, but it's changing. The industry is controlled by men, for the most part, and I think there is an incredible lack of understanding of how to write an equal female character that isn't way over the top — too sexy, or bitchy smart."

While she continued to take on roles in stage productions (she appeared in *Children of a Lesser God* as Sarah, in 1987; in Shakespeare's *The Taming of the Shrew* as Bianca in 1987; in *Noises Off* as Brooke Ashton; and, finally, in *The Shadow Walkers*), she realized that she was completely unprepared for the business side of acting, so she got an agent, and started doing commercials, going against her earlier ideals. Six months later, she appeared in her first commercial, for the Canadian chain Tim Horton's; the money from that one commercial paid Tapping's rent for three months. Several other commercials followed — for the pain relief medication Advil, for laundry softener Bounce, and for the candy bar Choclairs.

With enough money to pursue her dreams once again, Tapping founded Random Acts with friends Anne Marie Kerr and Katherine Jackson. Named after the saying "Practice random acts of kindness," the comedy troupe was formed when Amanda and Anne Marie, who had done a play together, got together over brunch one day. The discussion turned to feminist ideas and Amanda and Anne Marie's desire to found a company, and from there the troupe was born.

The three women wrote a show based on the poetry of Anne Sexton, who wrote of the social anxiety of being a woman in postwar America, and the group traveled a small circuit within Toronto. In an interview, Amanda said, "It was a little getaway, a lifesaver, a creative lifesaver. It was probably the most pure creativity that I'd ever been able to do." While the group didn't start out to do comedy only, Amanda was — and still is — convinced that humor is the way to bring about change and that laughter helps to open the heart and mind. After the Anne Sexton show, Random Acts performed a show called "On Becoming a Woman," which, according to Tapping, "was based on a book written in the fifties about how a nice girl behaves, and how she should greet her husband when he comes to the door. It was a handbook that was put out for young women in the fifties and it just blew our minds. So we did this show and it went off wonderfully and people laughed, which was great, and then this sixty-five-year-old man came up to us at the end of the show and said, 'I had no idea that's what my wife was exposed to. I didn't know.' He was a man growing up in that society and that was just a given. He never knew women were fed all this bullshit, for lack of a better term, about how to behave as subservient members of society. That was one of the most fulfilling compliments we ever received."

Random Acts lasted for several years, until one by one the women moved away from Toronto. In 2005, however, the troupe has been reformed, and is now writing a documentary entitled *Miss Blind River Pageant*. Random Acts is one of the foremost vehicles for Amanda Tapping's comedic talent, an aspect of her talent that is rarely seen on *SG-1*, although in interviews and on stage at conventions she's funny, honest, and has been known to break into different voices (she apparently does a killer Marge Simpson). While taping *The Vicki Gabereau Show* in Vancouver in 2000, Tapping managed to smuggle in a blooper tape from *Stargate SG-1*'s first-season episode "Solitudes," where she lampoons her fellow cast member Richard Dean Anderson's previous role as *MacGyver*. "Don't tell anyone," she said gleefully just before the show ran the clip of her wailing, "I'm stuck on an iceberg with MacGyver!"

Thanks to her comedy shows, plays, and commercials, Amanda Tapping's television and movie career had started to take off. In a 1991 episode of *Street Legal*, she guest starred as a newscaster, appearing in just one scene. Three years later, in 1994, she played McIllroy's girlfriend in an episode of *Kung-Fu: The Legend Continues*. In 1995, she appeared as Dr. Naomi Ross on *Forever Knight*, and got her first movie part playing Mrs. Nicely in the comedy *Rent-a-Kid*, a movie that also starred comic favorite Christopher Lloyd. The same year, Amanda starred in the television movies *Net Worth* and *The Haunting of Lisa*, as well as in the miniseries *Degree of Guilt*. Other guest-star appearances would follow: the children's show *Goosebumps*, *Due South*, a return to *Kung-Fu: The Legend Continues* (all in 1996), and even the ubiquitous *The X-Files*, where she played a dead prostitute. On that role, Amanda said with typical good humor and glee, "I was mostly dead on *The X-Files*, and apparently I give good 'dead.'" She played the part of a prostitute who seduces stern softie FBI assistant director Walter Skinner (played by Mitch Pileggi), "and ends up sleeping with — boy, I'm really proud of this — sleeping with him. And then when he wakes up in the morning, I'm dead and the whole show is about whether or not he killed me." When asked about scenes with the series' stars, she huffed, "I had two scenes with David [Duchovny] and Gillian [Anderson] where I was dead in a morgue drawer and on an autopsy table. Thanks for bringing it up." Mitch Pileggi has since been cast as a regular on *SG-1* spin-off, *Stargate Atlantis*.

Tapping went on to guest star in several other television and film offerings, including *Remembrance* and *What Kind of Mother Are You?* (1996), *The Donor* and *Booty Call* (1997), *The Outer Limits* (1998), *Millennium* (1999), and *Blacktop* (2000). In 2001, she starred in the movie *The Void* as Professor Eva Soderstom, playing opposite Adrian Paul of the *Highlander* television series. Here she was introduced to one of the challenges of acting, the nude scene. Her contract specified a no-nudity scene, and Amanda recalls with amusement being asked to pick a body double for the scenes in which her breast and backside would be visible. She herself filmed a scene with Paul where her back was bared, and she was so nervous about the camera accidentally catching more of her body than she was comfortable with that she kept flinching, until her co-star positioned his arms around her, effectively shielding her. She still remembers the gesture with great affection.

In 1997, like co-stars Michael Shanks and Christopher Judge, Amanda got her first real break when she was cast as astrophysicist Samantha Carter on *Stargate SG-1*. Because the producers were committed to finding just the right cast, auditions were held in several different cities, including Toronto, where Amanda was living at the time with her husband. She auditioned for a casting director in the Canadian city, and left thinking that there was no way she would get the part, believing the directors were looking for a big name, or someone more like a model. When she, along with two other women, was shortlisted for the role, she was flown down to Los Angeles where she met the people who had been shortlisted for the roles of Daniel and Teal'c as well. Strangely enough, she, Michael Shanks, and Christopher Judge were drawn to one another. At a convention, she said, "Christopher Judge, Michael Shanks, and I started talking, and the three of us kind of hung out through the whole day of auditions, because we dug each other. And at the end of the day we were like 'Wouldn't it be cool if the three of us got the parts?'"

The audition was held on a stage, which gave Tapping confidence as it fit directly into her theater training. The other potential Samantha Carters were to read opposite Richard Dean Anderson, who, as executive producer and main star, was present at the auditions. Tapping credits her sense of humor for getting her the part, because despite her nervousness, when Richard asked where she would like him to stand, she said, "Well, a little closer if you wouldn't mind." She continues, "So he stood at the end of the stage, but it would have meant I would have done my whole audition looking down. So I said 'Could you come up on stage, and get a little closer?' — real ballsy, 'cause I was damned scared. So he got up on stage and I went 'Okay, right, um . . . just stay there, don't block my light, and let's go!'"

The scene she was asked to read from was from the pilot episode, and it contained the character's now-famous introduction and feminist rant to Colonel O'Neill. Tapping says she made a conscious decision to use her comedic background to maneuver the character, thinking, "This character cannot be this. She cannot be so one-dimensional. And so when I auditioned in L.A. I decided to give her a sense of humor and said if they go for it then that means that that opens the way up for this character." Later, when she was about to go back on stage for a last audition, she recalls that Brad Wright and Jonathan Glassner, series creators, pulled her aside to tell her that they loved her work, having seen it on several occasions, and that she should continue infusing the character with humor. She did so, and then flew back to Toronto that night.

Two weeks before shooting began, Tapping got the part that would change her life. Her first move when she learned she had been cast as the astrophysicist soldier of the SG-1 team was to delve into research. And her theater training would serve her well, as she probed into Carter's character and learned as much as she could in the two short weeks she had. As she had done her whole life, Tapping threw herself into the experience to find her character and know where to take her. "I talked to a lot of people in the military, and had the wonderful experience of being able to talk to an ex-Navy Seal. Talked to him at great length. And then there was the research with the astrophysics and just finding that I had to make it cerebrally real for myself. I had to truly understand what this woman was talking about and to find it interesting, to find a passion in that. And then it was finding her voice and finding her walk. I had to walk around like her for a while. Had a different pair of shoes and just walked the street . . . cerebrally you can find a character very easily but you have to find that physicality as well. I would put her in situation and see how she'd react, I'd go into a shop and buy a pack of gum as Sam Carter and see how she'd do it. Things like that. I really had to walk around as her. Brush my teeth as her. Go to bed as her. Not to be a method head about it or anything, because I can let her go just as easily, but especially when we started the pilot because I literally had two weeks to pack my bag and get to the set, so that was a pretty intense two weeks, of finding her." Amanda retains that same devotion to her character's authenticity today, even after eight years. She is known to double-check the writers' research, and even verify their equations — only once has she found an error.

Upon getting the part of Samantha Carter, Tapping quickly relocated to Vancouver, where the series is filmed, although her husband, Alan, who owned a Toronto-based construction company, couldn't relocate in time for filming. It was not until several months later that he closed the company and moved west, where they bought a house and started renovating. The house was a mess — wires were held together with duct tape, the kitchen had a fridge but no ceiling, there was no support beam under the roof. It took two years of work before the house was up to standard.

Tapping's development of the character of Sam Carter has been well

Amanda Tapping (ALBERT L. ORTEGA)

documented. "I hated [Carter] in the beginning," she says. "That's not fair — I didn't like her very much in the pilot. I didn't like the fact that she was very linear, one-dimensional, standing on her feminist soapbox, with this raging diatribe about equality that I found really tired and boring. As a woman, I think there are far more interesting ways to present your case." She adds of the early Captain Carter character, "I think she felt very much like a woman in a man's world, always needing to prove herself. Personally, I wasn't fond of playing that dynamic because I think it's sort of tired to keep bringing up the gender war." But she credits smart writing and smart management of the show with fleshing out the astrophysicist-cum-military officer into a more believable and memorable character. "Carter was one of those women you wanted to tell to shut up," she adds, "but now I think it's interesting to hear what she has to say." At the end of the first season, she brought her case to the writers and they hashed out how her character would be developed in the upcoming seasons — a much more three-dimensional character would be the result of that, and today, Carter remains one of the fans' more beloved television characters, and a role model for many women around the world.

Amanda Tapping had been asking to direct an episode of *SG-1* for years before a time slot finally opened up in the show's seventh season. She doesn't like to describe herself as the "actress who always wanted to direct," but she realized that, as a woman in the industry, she needed to start developing a different skill set, because good roles for older women are rare in television and the movies. Although she was slated to direct an episode early in the season, it happened that co-star Michael Shanks' first writing attempt, "Resurrection," was the episode she would shoot. It's an experience that both remember fondly and with excitement. Said Tapping, "It was such a phenomenal experience. The crew was behind me a hundred percent. The cast was behind me a hundred percent. The hardest part about directing is making sure that you're prepared. And because I didn't have a lot of prep time, because we were actually shooting our two-parter season finale while I was prepping, it was a lot of homework on the weekends. But ultimately for me it was sitting down, coming up with an interesting shot list [. . .], and trying to give the show movement."

The episode was such a success that Tapping was nominated for best director award in the 2004 Leo Awards. Although she didn't win for that, she *did* win in 2005 for Best Lead Performance by a Female in a Dramatic Series for the third time in her career (she had also won in 2002 and 2004). Amanda has been showered with praise from fans and critics alike since the series began, having been consistently nominated for Saturn, Gemini, and Leo awards since 2000, and her star continues to rise. In 2005, she won a Saturn for best supporting actress in a television series. She was also recently given the honor of being named "Wonder Woman on Air" by Multichannel News and Women in Cable and Telecommunications in New York.

Outside of *SG-1*, Amanda has worked hard to establish a family. She and her husband Alan Kovacs put off having a child for years, but on March 22, 2005, Amanda gave birth to their first daughter, Olivia B. On her official Web site, Amanda posted the following message: "Hello Everyone!! I am thrilled to announce the birth of my daughter Olivia B on Tuesday March 22nd at 6:29 p.m. She is beautiful and healthy! She weighed in at 9 lbs 4 ozs and was 22 inches long. I am over the moon in love! Thanks to all of you for your prayers and good wishes. Labour and delivery were amazing. With the help of an incredible support team I was able to deliver without any drugs or intervention. I am deliriously happy. Thank you for all of the support and love we have received from you. With love, *Amanda, Alan, and Olivia.*"

With this new chapter of her life beginning, Amanda was written out of the first five episodes of *Stargate*'s ninth season. In her spare time, she is an avid reader, and calls herself "nature girl": she loves to hike, camp, ski, horseback ride, and her newest passion is kayaking with her husband. She's humble through and through, and tries hard not to let her sudden rise to fame go to her head. "I've always said to my friends and family, 'As soon as I start taking any of this for granted, just kick me in the ass, because then I really don't deserve it.'"

And, like all the cast of *SG-1*, Tapping is active in charities and social issues, supporting such organizations as the Multiple Sclerosis Society, Pollution Probe, the Canadian Cancer Society, and the Society for the Prevention of Cruelty to Animals. Her goodwill and enthusiasm shine through in whatever endeavor she supports, and she's an avid spokesperson for the United Nations Children's Fund (UNICEF). While pregnant, she even asked fans who had been sending her gifts for the baby to instead donate the money to help victims of the December 2004 Asian tsunami disaster. She's spent time teaching disabled children to ride horses, and a summer learning American Sign Language and immersing herself in the hearing-impaired community, all in an effort to understand and appreciate other cultures and differences.

And the actress' work on the feminist front continues. Today she is actively involved in mentoring other actors through Women in Film, and through Video Vancouver's "Flash Forward" program, which aims to tutor participants in the vagaries of the industry, focusing on career planning, advancement strategies, self-promotion, and mentoring. Flash Forward teaches students how to survive in the acting business, and Amanda is fully committed to helping others through some of the lessons she's learned in her professional life. It's something she feels very passionately about. "Don't be afraid to stand up for yourself . . . don't let people change your mind. If you have a strong belief, believe in it and stick to it. I spent so much of my time, apologizing for what I thought, and apologizing for having a different opinion, and different opinions are a beautiful thing. Don't focus on the fact that you're a woman, focus on the fact that you're a human being, and that you have something to say. And I think that, if you approach people as an equal — and people will treat us as subservient — but if you approach them as an equal in your mind, if they don't get it, then that's their loss. But, stick to what you have to say, and believe in yourself."

Amanda's relationship with the fans is particularly close, and she's a huge hit at conventions now. Although she was hesitant at first about getting involved in the convention scene, over the last few years, she and co-stars Shanks and Judge have become regulars on the circuit. For Tapping, it's one way to thank fans for their enthusiasm and support over the years. She always sports a huge smile at the events, and finds time to chat with as many attendants as possible. One of the most important events for her is "A Weekend with Amanda," which is organized by Gabit Events. It's a weekend where four hundred fans can gather for a more informal, intimate weekend with the actress, with all the proceeds going to a charity of her choice. Although the 2005 weekend was postponed due to Amanda's pregnancy, it's something that many fans look forward to attending, or reading about.

Tapping's social-mindedness doesn't end with charity. Being involved in a series where the military is such a huge presence has made a difference, and in 2001, Amanda traveled to Qatar in the Middle East on a United Service Organization (USO) exchange. It was a trip that changed her life. "The beauty of it was that it was a handshake tour. We weren't up on stage; there was no publicity. It was beautiful. We walked through these two bases, shaking hands, meeting people, signing autographs, talking to people about why they were there, how they felt, especially after 9/11. It was just like, 'Oh, my God.' The stories that people had to tell us. It was a phe-

Amanda with a sign asking for more Major Davis in season seven (COURTESY PETER FALLON WWW.BOBW.COM.AU)

nomenal experience." She was even awarded a combat bracelet by one of the American soldiers she met on the trip, and refused to remove the bracelet until it started to shred, some two years later.

With many projects on the horizon, and a new role as mother to look forward to, Amanda Tapping really does seem to have it all. But she remains humble: "I would hope that I'd be remembered for being kind. For being a good daughter and a good wife and most importantly a good friend. I'd like it to be remembered that I loved passionately and that I loved a lot and that I cared."

BEHIND STARGATE SG-1

With the cast now on board, *Stargate SG-1* could begin. Right from the start, the writers and producers knew that in order to get and keep viewers they would have to come up with a science fiction show that also had drama — and something else a little bit different: mythology. While most shows in the genre were based on science fiction tropes that had been around since the original *Star Trek* series, *SG-1* took a new tack by basing its premise, at least for its first three seasons, solidly on mythology. It was an interesting strategy, not only because it immediately set the series apart, but also because the stories that could be told through this recast myth were, literally, the stuff of legends. Everyone knows some mythology, whether they realize it or not — Pandora's Box, Prometheus, the myth of Orpheus, ancient Egyptian deities, these are all figures that are in the common consciousness, and the familiarity of these myths combined with different surroundings, characters, and lessons, drew in viewers very quickly.

While the first three seasons took their main story arcs directly from the mythology of the *Stargate* film — set firmly on the foundational myths of Ancient Egypt — in season four, the stories started to shift focus to a more traditional science fiction feel. Earlier seasons explored the austereness of Egyptian and Norse mythologies and delved into how the characters moved around and changed in relation to the stories that were being told. But after season four, a new paradigm emerged for the show: the interweaving of old and new stories, old and new technologies, old and new characters. Myth was still there, but it now had a contemporary flavor. *SG-1* told stories in fragments, in pastiche and parody, while still occasionally jumping back into pulse-pounding action episodes, traditional drama, and unique stand-alones.

Through the different narrative templates, the show was able to delve into issues rarely explored on television, and even more rarely explored in science fiction. Themes like leadership, the consequences of actions, power, knowledge, the power *of* knowledge, the role of memory on an individual and on a planetary scale, the individual versus the galactic — all these were developed in a consistent and thoughtful fashion. This ambitious approach was making the show a fan favorite, one that people could tune in to to watch and be entertained, while considering the questions that the show raised.

An early shot of the cast of *SG-1* (SUE SCHNEIDER/SHOOTING STAR)

The dynamics of the SG-1 team also were a novelty. In a television universe populated with one definitive lead or two-person teams, *SG-1* created the four-person team. Each character was specifically developed for the skill set they would bring to the team, and each character grew and changed as an individual, bringing subtle change to the team. While other shows, like *The X-Files*, *Buffy the Vampire Slayer*, or the newer *Alias* respectively focused on a duo, a quintuplet with a distinct leader, and a solo act, *SG-1*'s dynamic was equitable and balanced. This structure allowed stories to be developed that would showcase each actor's talent within the team as well as individually, and it allowed the reality of the military world within which the characters were operating to come through. No one goes through life alone — and the writers of *SG-1* not only believed that, they illustrated it.

THROUGH THE STARGATE, SEASON BY SEASON

SG-1 began filming in Vancouver, British Columbia in February 1997. Filming took place at Bridge Studios, in part because it had the largest sound stage in North America, which was needed in order to accomodate the large and intricate sets used on the show. When *Stargate: SG-1* finally premiered on July 27, 1997, with the two-hour episode "Children of the Gods" (an episode often split into two parts for syndication purposes), it generated the highest ratings on the U.S. network Showtime for that year, with about 1.48 million households tuning in to watch. Although that number doesn't stand out against some series premieres today, for a science fiction show, the response was phenomenal. Much of the publicity and campaigning around the series had focused on the return of veteran actor Richard Dean Anderson to the small screen; his familiar face and wry humor were the initial lure for many viewers. They came for him, but, while some stayed for him, many also stayed for the intriguing stories and team dynamic, so that gradually, *SG-1* built up the loyal audience it had been hoping for.

Such was its success that half way through the first season, Showtime ordered another forty-four episodes, taking the show to a definite fourth season — a commitment that is still unheard of in the fickle world of television. Said Richard in an interview early in 1998, "[MGM and Showtime] were counting on [. . .] there being a kind of a hub of, or a nucleus of an audience that *MacGyver* would bring along with it, plus the movie that had a kind of a cult following and success as well. And so far it's . . . the highest rated Showtime show that they have."

Highly rated, despite a fairly rocky few episodes following the premiere — episodes that were very much about the show finding its feet and the team getting to know one another and learning to work together, while the actors hurried to smooth out the rough spots of their respective character arcs. However, the first season also presented some of the episodes that are still today the best-loved by fans and actors alike — the dramatic "Solitudes," which was the first hint of unresolved tension between O'Neill and Carter; and "Cold Lazarus," which allowed viewers a glimpse at O'Neill's inner life and tackled the difficult subjects of grief and letting go. In the early days, O'Neill was the most solid character on the show, due both to the backstory from the movie, and to Rick's charismatic and layered performance.

Daniel, too, benefited from the backstory of the movie, and Michael

Shanks spent much of the first season emulating James Spader's perform-ance. His character's forthright and humble disposition immediately endeared him to viewers — the more passionate of them formed a faction known colloquially as "Danielites," who wanted to defend the character from slights and harm.

Other characters had a tougher time getting off the ground, especially Samantha Carter and Teal'c. As the only female member of the team, Carter was immediately saddled with a soapbox-feminist outlook that alienated viewers — and Amanda Tapping herself. Carter spent the first season proving herself as "one of the guys," and was allowed only brief flashes of emotion (and those involved a child in the episode "Singularity," which Tapping singles out as one of her character's turning points). Carter was written as both a scientist and a soldier, but neither aspect was well-developed enough for viewers to be able to grasp the character's person-ality or potential. Aloof and staunchly in control, by the end of season one, Carter still didn't have much direction aside from lending intellectual or military backup to the men of the team. Her history was rarely hinted at and even more rarely shown, and as a result, she floundered. At the end of the season, Amanda and the writers discussed how they could soften the character's edges to make her more human and likeable, paving the way for a much more deeply developed Carter in the second season. "Television is changing for women, a lot, which is great, and it has been over the last decade. Really, creating these strong, wonderful, fully realized women. And so at the end of [the first] season I said: 'Where is she going?' I mean, we're clearly not going to make her a love interest of any member of the team, thank God. Where is she going? What are we going to do with her? Let's not just make her strong and tough. Because she's a human being, so let's give her a sense of humor, and let's make her more accessible. Just because she's a strong, military scientist, doesn't mean she has to be a [bitch]."

Teal'c was afflicted with many of the same teething problems. Unlike Carter, he came fully formed into the team — in Chris Judge's own words, "Teal'c is a rebel in a society that doesn't tolerate rebels." He came with a backstory that was set up in the pilot episode, in one moment of rebellion, and his life outside the military was explored early on in the episode "Bloodlines." Still, the stalwart alien with the unfathomable — and mostly silent — demeanor was less well-integrated into the team than Jack or Daniel, who formed, in the first season, the core of SG-1 — both the team and the show.

Despite the nitpicks, the show did well, and as the SG-1 team explored the galaxy that had been opened up for it through the network of Stargates, so too did *SG-1* explore the people, places and mythologies it posited. In January of 1997 *Entertainment Weekly* ran a small article entitled "The Biggest Gambles of 1997," and put Showtime's newly acquired *Stargate SG-1* near the top. "Our audience loves sci-fi," said Showtime development vice president Pancho Mansfield, whose network airs two other MGM series, *The Outer Limits* and *Poltergeist: The Legacy*.

By the time the second season started airing in July of 1998, the show had developed a core audience, and word of mouth brought in new viewers every week. The fact that Showtime opted to air their seasons in two distinct parts, rather than a full season followed by a five-month hiatus, only added to viewers' fervor. Many complained about the two-month break between December and February when no new episodes aired, but in later seasons, it would allow the writers to have a mid-season cliffhanger, creating anticipation for the show's return.

While season one had set up the characters, their respective roles on the show and the team, and a sense of the vastness of the universe, season two was about taking those characters and placing them at home. Season two focused on each character's sense of home and identity, each character's sense of belonging. Another change from the first season was the increasing friendliness of newly encountered alien cultures. Season one was important in setting up the Goa'uld threat and the sheer magnitude of the enemies that Earth was facing. Season two took the opposite tack, and while its storylines still involved galactic warmongering, the introduction to races such as the Asgard and the Tok'ra, as well as the hardly-ever-heard-of-again Furlings, expanded the team's set of allies. Now SG-1 had to deal with a universe that was not just hostile, but more complex, and had to hone their diplomatic skills as well.

Season two also featured a greater number of political stories, with the emergence of a conspiracy theory that, six seasons later, would rival *The X-Files* in its complexity. Although the NID (who knows what it stands for?) had appeared once in the first season, its scope was expanded in the second — a secret government agency whose intentions and means were unclear, and who thwarted the SGC at every turn. Lessons were learned in the second season, among them one that would need to be learned over and over again throughout the years, that enemies are not just without, they're also within — on Earth, and in ourselves.

Daniel's humanistic approach became important to the team in seasons two and three when the team was slowly learning to walk among the races of the galaxy. The episode "The Fifth Race" turned the show on its head, however, by suggesting that it was O'Neill and not Daniel who would lead the planet to join the galaxy's other four great races. That episode marked a turning point for several characters and for the show's storylines. It was also during season two that the writers introduced more of the Norse mythology that would be the basis for the Asgard civilization: this interweaving of different mythological threads remains one of the show's greatest strengths.

Just as Earth's galactic reputation on the show was growing, so too was *Stargate*'s reputation growing in North America and around the world. In season two we also saw the directing of the prominent Martin Wood, as well as the first episodes directed by Peter DeLuise, who became one of the staples of the series. Between the two of them, they form the directing core for *SG-1*, and they brought a lot of energy with them, as well as a sense of consistency from season to season. While other directors were still involved, the throughline of DeLuise's and Wood's respective styles gave *Stargate* a visual identity from season two on. Suddenly there were more closeups on the characters, more risky shots, more play on light and shadow; the tension and immediacy that visual style brought to the show layered it, gave it depth. Amanda Tapping commented at a convention, "When Peter first came on board he . . . he's got an insane sense of humor, this guy, he's very, very funny. And so he brought with him a real creative urge to do something completely different, and because he brought in the comedy aspect, and because he had been an actor on a television series, he was really great, and he's great with actors. But he brings like . . . it's the yin and the yang watching Martin and Peter direct. They're two completely different ways of doing things."

In syndication in 2000, the second season had reached 3.3 on the Nielsen ratings scale, which represented an eighteen percent increase from the year before — an impressive increase for a small-budget show!

Season three was when the cult began. People had started to catch on, drawn in by the easy humor of the characters and the really big adventures offset by equally big philosophical questions. With Peter DeLuise now on board full time, the show developed a stronger sense of humor; episodes like "Deadman Switch" and the infamous "Urgo" were hugely popular — the latter guest starred Peter DeLuise's comedian father, Dom DeLuise. The season finished strong on ratings, placing second among first-run entertainment shows.

In season three, with their personalities and backstories set up and their team interaction well defined, the actors had by now achieved a rhythm and familiar ease with one another, and the characters were free to branch out on their own personal story arcs, to explore the new terrain that was opening up to them. In much the same way, the *SG-1* writers started to experiment with the mythology that was now theirs. By the end of the season, the

Amanda and Michael always have fun at conventions (SUE SCHNEIDER/SHOOTING STAR)

Goa'uld had been overshadowed by the far more science-fiction-like Replicators, a metallic bug-like race bent on devouring any technology it encountered. That opened the way for more CGI (computer generated image) special effects, something that was increasingly important on the show. Although many science fiction shows play with space shots and the "outer space" feel, *SG-1* took the road less traveled and developed a more fluid and elegant visual play. Said James Tichenor, visual effects supervisor, "I grew up on the computer and am a huge computer nerd; I never was one to build models and practical effects. I was programming computers so my philosophy was that as long as I kept challenging the CG artists, for every five failures, we'd have one resounding success, and it was both the failures and the successes together that would drive the art forward and make for better and more affordable work. I think the effects and the production design and the direction have all been top notch, but more television has top notch production values and most of it fails. I think the only reason the show has succeeded is because the stories have been generally really good."

Besides gentle humor, the third season also featured heavier fare that delved into team members' pasts, opening some doors and closing others. "Jolinar's Memories" explored the consequences of Carter having been briefly host to a Tok'ra symbiote in the second season; "Forever in a Day" irrevocably changed Daniel's life when he witnessed the death of his long-lost wife Sha're, and the human/Goa'uld hybrid child she was carrying was spirited away to hide it from the Goa'uld; "Maternal Instinct" returned to that thread and dealt with the consequences of death in Daniel's life, imbuing the character with new depth, as well as a new mission on the show; "A Hundred Days" stranded Jack on a distant planet (not for the last time) where he falls in love. It's strongly suggested at the end of the episode, when O'Neill finally goes home, that the woman is pregnant, opening up the door for fatherhood and family for Jack. The main arcs of the third season would carry over into later seasons more than those of the first two seasons. Memory became more important, with each team member struggling with that issue at some point in the season. Carter fought to regain the memories of her dead Tok'ra symbiote; Jack tried desperately to hold onto the memories of his life back on Earth before finally putting them behind him; Daniel lashed out each time he remembered Sha're's death.

And it was in "Maternal Instinct" that the thread of Ascension started to weave its web. An intricate and intrinsic part of the *Stargate* universe, the character of Oma Desala and the Ancients' teachings to Daniel only confused him (and viewers), and in typical *Stargate* fashion, everyone would have to wait several years before the enigma that was Oma was elucidated.

Teal'c was the only character who didn't really benefit from the more personal stories that abounded in season three. While Carter's character was far better written beginning in season two, gaining a past, a real personality with quirks and foibles, giving Tapping an opportunity to stretch her acting talents, the same was not true of Teal'c, who seemingly stagnated in the writers' hands in season three. They had already established his devotion to the Jaffa cause, had already delved into the sacrifice of his family, but season three felt like Teal'c spent most of his time bowing his head with a solemn, "Indeed." So it is perhaps not surprising that at the end of season three, rumors began to surface that Chris Judge was thinking of leaving the show. The rumors were quickly and firmly denied, and, no doubt aided by a huge fan contingent — the fierce warrior with an undying passion had become one of the most unusual and beloved characters on the air — the last episodes of season three featured Teal'c in a much more prominent role. The character would also benefit from additional screen time and more interesting storylines come season four.

Another problem was brewing, that of renewal. Although no one at *SG-1* had had to worry about renewal since the series' inception, their eighty-eight–episode run was coming to an end in 2001. As it turned out, in April

2000, MGM and Showtime announced that they were renewing the show, but only for one additional season: the same concern would surface a year later at the end of season five, only at that time, it would be complicated by the departure of Michael Shanks.

Season four marked a big change in the way *Stargate* was viewed, as it relied more heavily on science fiction tropes to tell its stories, mingling within the stories the same mythological elements that had helped *SG-1* stand out from the profusion of other sci-fi shows on television. The existence of the Replicators started the season off, and near the end of the season, the episode "Entity" broke the mold. It was the first time *Stargate* had depicted technological warfare, or rather, technological hostage-taking; it was also one of the first episodes to be filmed entirely within the SGC, with no outside shots. The effect was riveting, and, more importantly, new. The changes that occurred in the fourth season were in part due to two new writers, Joseph Mallozzi and Paul Mullie. This writing team — they are always credited together — became one of the most prolific on the show, and imbued the series with a new enthusiasm and new plotlines. Mallozzi noted, in an interview with the author, "We draw most of our inspiration from the show's rich history — past characters, events, unfinished storylines. More often than not, however, a writer will go into a room with an idea that, over the course of being pitched out, gets spun by the other writers and morphs into a completely different, infinitely better idea that everyone can get excited about." Season four also marked the departure of Jonathan Glassner, who had been gradually handing over more of the executive producer/writer/producer responsibilities to Brad Wright. Jonathan moved on to other projects but remained on board as a creative consultant.

Season four featured some of the best episodes yet, with thrilling alternate universes wherein all the alternate characters die. "2010" was an episode that tugged on heartstrings and garnered massive positive fan feedback for its sheer emotion and scope — and Michael Shanks' first foray into directing, with the ambitious script "Double Jeopardy," featured doubles of all the team members — who also all die! Teal'c's character got a full "Jaffa revenge" arc, pursuing the Goa'uld murderer of his lost love from episode four to twenty-two.

The narratives became more militaristic, with less focus on discovery and more on the technology the team was searching for in order to protect Earth. The galaxy was a scary place, and season four worked to bring that home, and

Chris taking it easy in Pasadena, California (COURTESY VICTOR SPINELLI/WIREIMAGE)

to give viewers a sense of movement within the mythology of the show. The team couldn't just go exploring anymore; Earth faced an imminent threat, and action had to be taken. The new focus on the military meant that the show's producers and writers had to be careful about how they approached the situations they were writing the characters into.

From the start, *SG-1* had taken measures to ensure the realism of the military base for the Stargate program by employing a military advisor. Douglas Thar, the USAF's film, documentary and special events coordinator who has been involved with the series since its third episode, looks over each final script for Air Force content. Although he has no say in storylines or character development, he makes sure the characters are behaving according to military protocol. When he saw the pilot movie, "Children of the Gods," he noticed a couple of instances of unrealistic military behavior and ranking — indoor saluting which, nowadays, is rare; and a sergeant major character (that rank doesn't exist in the Air Force). As Thar said, "What we do look at is whether the characters are being portrayed accurately from an Air Force perspective and proper protocol when talking to a superior officer or to another person of the same rank, that kind of thing. . . . If we look at a script and they are referencing some kind of weapon, say maybe an F15 or an F16, we'll say, 'Well, the most advanced weapon system is the F/A22. Let's change the script from F16 to F/A22.' They're usually very good at looking seriously at the changes that we recommend. It's their call, but over the years they've [. . .] changed most things. . . . They know what they can do and how far they can stretch it, and that's good. It makes for good television viewing, and I think that the people that watch *Stargate SG-1* appreciate our involvement in keeping it as realistic as we can for a fictional show." So fond is the U.S.

Air Force of *Stargate* that in the fourth season episode "Prodigy," the first of two Air Force chiefs of staff features as guest star!

The military realism extended to another facet that became important in season four — the relationship between Sam and Jack. While the writers had toyed with the chemistry between the two since the first season, it wasn't until the middle of the third that Carter first admitted her attraction to her superior officer. In season four, the cards got tossed on the table, and in something of a public relations nightmare, the two ended up having to confront their feelings to prove they hadn't been brainwashed and programed for assassination by the Goa'uld. Convoluted? Yes. In an online message board shortly after the controversial episode "Divide and Conquer" aired (and was there ever an episode more aptly named, given its divisive effect on the fans?), executive producer Brad Wright wrote, "I feel I should reassure those of you who fear O'Neill and Carter will soon be holding hands as they enter the gate. Their mutual affection has been developing since Season One, and it was time to let it become a genuine obstacle in an episode. Their feelings would never have come out were it not for the extraordinary circumstances of the story. Sure they care about each other, and yes, that may occasionally complicate things, but: Carter and O'Neill will not become romantically involved. They are Air Force professionals." Douglas Thar agreed: within the Air Force framework, O'Neill and Carter could not pursue a relationship while serving on the same team, and even though the writers came up with no end of creative ways to explore the potential between the two characters, in their season-four circumstances, there was no way for it to come to fruition.

Season four is still referred to by some as the "shipper" (relationship) season, and with episodes like "Divide and Conquer," "Window of Opportunity," "Beneath the Surface" (the original script for which had Sam and Jack's alternate personalities becoming lovers), and "Entity," it is perhaps not a misnomer. It's also one of the most controversial seasons, because many of those not interested in a potential relationship between Sam and Jack were annoyed by the constant return to the question. It's a season with lots of strengths, but also some pervading themes that caused many viewers to establish a love/hate relationship with it.

Season five was to be no less difficult. It continued the series' move into a science fiction feel, developing the arc of the Replicators and delving into their origin. In a surprise move, viewers learned that Replicators were not weapons conceived by dastardly villains, but instead playthings created by a lonely android girl. The Russian arc, mostly absent in season four, made a comeback, and the season generally took a step back from the galactic gallivanting that had been going on in the previous seasons and offered up more intense and intimate stories. The Jaffa storyline reached a resolution, Daniel befriended a long-lost race called the Unas, Cassandra (the young girl rescued by the SGC in season one) turned thirteen and underwent some drastic changes. The philosophical issues were no less dramatic, either, and Carter, O'Neill, Daniel, and Teal'c engaged in discussions of what it meant to be alive or dead, real or artificial, good or evil.

Midway through the fifth season, *Stargate*'s 100th episode, "Wormhole X-Treme," arrived, and the writers took the opportunity to showcase their capacity for satire and not-so-gentle humor. The episode makes fun of the show, of science fiction, of Amanda Tapping herself, and although some fans regarded it with perplexity, awash in the sea of derision, "Wormhole X-Treme" was greeted with resounding laughter when it first aired and has become a defining episode for the series. While the writers had been incorporating more humor since the third season, the full-on satire marked a departure in tone and flavor that only served to make *SG-1* stand out: it was unlike any other show on television. This was a series so in love with the genre it was representing and changing that it created its own *Galaxy Quest*. Richard Dean Anderson was particularly enthusiastic about the episode and said, "The 100th episode is so anachronistic and so full, it's more of a thank you to our cast and crew and the writers. And everyone who works for the show who wanted to be on camera gets on camera."

Season five also marked a more graceful interweaving of myth and science fiction, with better balance between the two. The thread of the Goa'uld, something of a back-burner thread in the previous season, was brought forward in a big way, and mixed in with the Russians, the Unas, and Cassandra's changes. SG-1 had to cope with not just one threat, but one threat intermingled with many, which infused their jobs and their mutual interactions with tension.

Mostly, however, season five is remembered by fans as The Season Where Michael Left. For five years the cast and crew had talked about the wonderful on-set atmosphere, the friendly get-togethers after work and on weekends, the family barbecues, the family feeling every time you walked on set. In 2002, however, Michael Shanks informed the show's creators and MGM that he would no longer play the character of Daniel Jackson. The writers had no choice but to write him out of the series. When speaking publicly about his departure for the first time, Michael said, "By the start of the fourth season, things seemed to be going in a direction I wasn't comfortable with. I thought that what I was doing on the show was becoming seemingly more confined. And having broached the subject with the powers that control these things, it became clear that the character wasn't important enough to the overall process to warrant an upgrade." It was with a heavy heart that the actor said goodbye to the show, but he tried to console fans by informing them that the writers were leaving the door open for guest appearances in season six. To little avail: Daniel's Ascension to a higher plane of existence was mourned and debated for many months after his final episode aired. Adding to fans' grief was the actor's own feeling that the show's creative department did not think his concerns important enough to address, and that little effort was made to convince him to stay — although all parties were careful to remain as neutral as possible when speaking on record. Whether or not the split was acrimonious, it was hardly harmonious. Daniel's absence irredeemably changed the series.

While this was going on, a behind-the-scenes battle was underway for a sixth season. Late in 2001, speculation began that Showtime would not be renewing the show. As usual, the real reasons were hard to distinguish amongst a slew of rumors. Some believed that MGM was demanding too much money from Showtime in order to air the series; others believed that differences between the show's creative department and Showtime were the cause of the split. Either way, *Stargate*'s future was in serious doubt.

Fans were livid. It seemed to make no sense: ratings were good — in syndication, the series was the top-rated hour-long action show — and nothing had prepared viewers for the possibility that the show would not return. With Daniel's Ascension, panic began in the fandom. Fans rallied to save the show, as well as Daniel's character, and in some arenas the two issues became conflated. Fans started a massive write-in campaign, set up Web sites (the "Save Daniel Jackson" site is one of the better known), sent e-mails, and even tissue boxes (in memory of Daniel's allergies and Jack's message to Daniel in "Children of the Gods"). Thousands of phone calls to MGM were logged and thousands of letters and e-mails as well, asking MGM to find *Stargate* a new home. Hank Cohen, then president of MGM TV Entertainment, publicly thanked the fans for their outpouring of support, but reminded everyone that the show's future was far from secure. Every few days, a different rumor would worm its way into the fan community; one day the show was being renewed, the next it was being canceled, the

Corin Nemec is known to recite his own poetry for fans (COURTESY ELIZA BENNETT)

next it was switching channels. And in fact that's what did happen. The news was made public in an online forum a week before it was official, but the announcement was quickly withdrawn for reasons of propriety. On August 14, 2001, the network channel Sci-Fi announced that it would be *Stargate*'s home for its sixth season.

The relief that spread throughout the fandom was palpable, but relief was offset by trepidation. With network and major cast changes ahead, season six was uncertain. In a season marked by change, the most obvious was the new cast member. Arkansas actor Corin Nemec was known most for his lead role in the television series *Parker Lewis Can't Lose*, although he had had parts in numerous other television series, movies, and features films. On *Stargate SG-1*, Corin played Jonas Quinn, a human from the planet Langarra, who relocates to the SGC to help Earth and his own planet fabricate a weapon after Daniel "dies." From the start, the character of Quinn was distrusted by loyal fans who had watched Daniel grow and evolve over five years, those who had enjoyed the relationship between Jack and Daniel, those who were concerned, with Daniel gone, that the team might lose its moral compass. Amanda Tapping admitted in an interview, "[Corin]'s a very cheerful guy, but to be honest with you, interestingly, by the eighth episode of season one, Christopher, Michael, and me knew everything about each other, because we had the luxury of spending six weeks living in a hotel doing the pilot together and eating all our meals together. We were literally forced to form friendships, in a way. It wasn't difficult by any stretch of the imagination, but we had a much easier road to really establish relationships. It's like being the new kid in school; we're still trying to make [Corin] comfortable, but it's not the same. And we're so established in our routine, we're patterned with each other. I don't envy him, I really don't."

The writers cleverly wrote in the initial resistance to the change, making Jack the most resistant to Jonas' presence. Loyalty and pragmatism warred within the character for quite a few episodes before O'Neill finally accepted Quinn. Richard Dean Anderson said, "The fact that he wasn't accepted right away is just a testament, I think, to my paying attention to what the character is. He's a loyal guy, O'Neill. And he felt in the beginning that this kid was responsible for the loss of one of his friends. But making his peace with that, in a very practical, pragmatic way, O'Neill had to come to some closure about it, or at least an acceptance of what had happened as being the truth. . . . We've had our moment with it, but there's a job to be done. And with that in mind, O'Neill gets on with the job." RDA's sentiments echo those of other fans, who were tired of the drama surrounding the show and just wanted to get back to the drama *of* the show. In some ways, however, Jack's difficulties with Daniel's "death" and Jonas' presence allowed viewers to grieve for Daniel and gradually come to terms with his absence.

For the writers, the challenge was a positive opportunity — this new character opened up new challenges for them. In many ways, Jonas resembled Daniel in his insatiable curiosity and interpersonal skills. Viewers were worried that Jonas would just be another Daniel, but the writers made the shift a subtle one. Said Brad Wright, "As someone who has written a lot of hours of *Stargate SG-1*, I'm looking forward to the newness that will come from having to create a new character and make that character work as part of the team. Whether we're successful enough or not — the fans will have to decide. But I genuinely appreciate the challenge simply because it's new. Very few people in my position even stay on a show as long as I have, so I'm looking forward to the change."

Despite the difficulties major changes presented to the makers of *SG-1*, season six took off in a big way: the first episode ("Redemption, Part 1") was the Sci-Fi Channel's most watched show for the week it aired. Most viewers were enthusiastic about the channel switch, and in the end, season six offered some of *Stargate SG-1*'s most dramatic episodes — some of them featuring Daniel Jackson in special guest appearances. The season took the characters through some major transformations: O'Neill became host to a Tok'ra symbiote to save his life and was tortured at the hands of the "big bad" Baal; later in the season, he's stranded on a planet (again!)

with the pesky Harry Maybourne; SG-1 is captured and experimented upon by the vicious Goa'uld Nirrti; Teal'c loses his symbiote and must learn to live without it, and they all have to deal with the loss of Daniel. Everything changes.

The team dynamic also changes in season six. In much the same way that a group of friends will adapt their interaction to allow room for a new person, the SG-1 team has to establish a new way of communicating and a new rhythm in response to Jonas' arrival. Because the flow had shifted so dramatically, the repercussions were felt even in the kinds of episodes, with a return to more stand-alones that allowed the characters space to get to know each other. Added to all this, the writers and actors had to work around Richard Dean Anderson's reduced schedule. Wanting to spend more time with his young daughter, and seeing that a sixth season was a probability, Anderson asked that his character be made less present — he would appear in nearly every episode, but on a smaller scale, and with a compressed shooting schedule. With this in mind, the writers planned an episode ("Nightwalkers"), one of the only full-on funny ones of that rather sombre season, that didn't feature Richard at all and instead featured Carter, Teal'c, and Jonas investigating mysterious happenings, à la *X-Files*.

Season six was a big one for Teal'c especially, who, late in the season, lost his symbiote in an episode written by Chris Judge himself. It was the actor's second foray into writing. With the introduction of Jonas Quinn, Teal'c was no longer the "Other" of the show; rather, the writers very nicely developed a relationship between the two "aliens" of the team without making it seem exclusionary.

And finally, season six revisited the Replicators, but this time they sported a new, human face; and they would return to plague Earth again and again through to season eight. Along with the slow realization that the show would be returning for a seventh year, (once again, the announcement was made very late in the season), there was one more change coming. In November 2002, the Sci-Fi Channel announced that Michael Shanks would be returning as a regular for the show's seventh season.

With Daniel's return came Jonas Quinn's departure, and the team dynamic was restored to its tried-and-true formula of five seasons, albeit with some adjustments. Rick's schedule was now greatly reduced, and his absence was more marked than in season six. This had the upside of allowing much more screen time for the other three members of the team, each of whom benefited from their expanded storylines. Teal'c became even chattier and more proactive, which in turn changed how Chris Judge approached his character, no longer relying on minute gestures and terse sentences to communicate his character's inner monologue. Daniel became more involved in military storylines. As Michael Shanks noted at the time, "It can't be that Daniel comes back and everything goes back to the way it was before he left, because that would mean the show wasted a year evolving in a different direction without him. It also means the character wasted a year not evolving properly as well. I think there has to be some sort of evolution or change to Daniel when he comes back."

Last but not least, Sam got a boyfriend. Accomplishing this was no small feat on the part of the writers. Over the past seven years, Sam had been wooed by a handful of men — most of them aliens — all of whom had died by the time the episode ended (with the exception of Martouf, whose doom was merely delayed). This unfortunate trend had been dubbed by fans and Amanda the "black widow syndrome," casting her as a woman who had no choice but to be alone since she was a) obviously bad luck for men and b) somewhat attracted to her superior officer. The arrival of Pete Shanahan, played by David DeLuise (director Peter DeLuise's brother), changed that. While many fans hated the fact that Carter was now being dragged into the "cult of true womanhood" (the woman who has it all: good looks, brains, a great job, a wonderful boyfriend), others — including the actress herself — rejoiced that the character was finally moving on and gaining a personal life. In a season focused on issues of belonging and identity, and the difference between team and individual, concerns arose that Carter would lose her autonomy. Said Tapping, "I don't want [Carter] to become that girl who's pining for a boy, or who qualifies herself based on a relationship with a man, whether or not she has one, even though she admits [. . .] that society sort of puts that in question all the time. But I don't want her to become that. I'm really concerned that she stays focused and strong." Not only did Pete not die, but he stuck around through to season eight — the longest relationship any of the team members had maintained since the series began (not including Daniel and Sha're).

Near the end of the seventh season, *SG-1* celebrated its 150th episode. Taking an entirely different tack than for the satirical 100th episode, "Heroes" was sober, somber, and sad, and it marked the departure of one of the most important members of the SGC, Janet Fraiser. Teryl Rothery, who had played the doctor with great passion since season one, was now no longer to be a part of the team, and "Heroes" is still hailed by the fans, actors, and writers as the show's best episode ever. Janet's death under fire was shocking in its portrayal of military life. With no warning, while just doing her job, suddenly a cherished member of the team was gone; the reactions were perhaps not surprising as Janet's demise was the first "real" death of someone close to the team on *SG-1*.

Season seven focused on how the characters worked with the ideas of identity and belonging, and especially in the season's two-part finale, in which O'Neill makes the ultimate sacrifice for the planet, willingly giving up his mind and his identity to protect the planet from the Goa'uld. That episode did more than place a main character in jeopardy; it opened the way for the new franchise that had been on the storyboards and bubbling away on the backburner for more than a year, *Stargate Atlantis*. With the race of the Ancients and their lost city of Atlantis featuring large in the seventh year, the two-parter "Lost City" was to the series what "Children of the Gods" had been — a flashpoint. In the pilot episode, SG-1 had learned that they could travel through the Stargate to many different worlds, not just the planet visited in the feature film; in "Lost City," the way was paved for the Stargate to allow travel not just to Earth's galaxy, but to one far more distant.

The spin-off series *Atlantis* had been given the green light, and it was to start airing in 2004 at the same time as *SG-1*'s eighth year (the Sci-Fi Channel had ordered another season, but only twenty episodes instead of the usual twenty-two). *Stargate Atlantis* (already truncated to *SGA*) was set in the Pegasus galaxy, and used a familiar setup (military characters and the trope the Stargate) so that those following *SG-1* would not be disoriented. A very different color tone was used — the lost city was located under water, giving it a blue hue compared to *SG-1*'s more earth-toned colors. The characters were different, and the facility was run by Elizabeth Weir, a civilian character who had made her first appearance on *SG-1* at the end of season seven and the beginning of season eight. She was not the only *SG-1* character to make the crossover: Rodney McKay, a brilliant, arrogant astrophysicist who had helped Carter with the Stargate several times, also made the leap to *SGA*. O'Neill and Jackson made guest appearances in the spin-off's first episode, which aired on July 16, 2004. Because Teal'c and Samantha Carter were characters that had been specifically created for the *SG-1* franchise, they were not legally allowed to appear in the first episode of *SGA*. As it happened, the producers had no reason to worry about ratings, because, in its first season, *SGA* ranked consistently high in ratings, surprisingly edging out its sibling, *SG-1*.

SG-1 was now in its eighth year, and with a huge mythology behind them, the writers started to tie things together, combining disparate threads. It was a massive endeavor, and resulted in a season full of conflict, drama, and of course, change and adaptation, *SG-1*'s stock-in-trade.

The change started at the top: Brad Wright, a show runner for eight years, handed over the reins of *SG-1* to Robert Cooper, and began to work on *SGA*. While both were creators and executive producers of *SGA*, Wright took on the day-to-day operation of it while Cooper stayed with *SG-1*. Brad noted, "When I see Rob running the show, I have a certain sense of pride in that. I don't covet any of his control over the show, because of my relationship with all of them — and I still feel a part of *Stargate SG-1*. . . . The day-to-day decisions are made by Robert, but when he has a big decision to make, he shares it with me."

Also marked in his absence was Don S. Davis, who for seven years had played the human, hard-nosed General Hammond. Because he had recently married and wanted to spend time with his new family, the actor had decided to leave the series, giving the writers an opportunity to promote both O'Neill and Carter. With O'Neill now a brigadier general, Anderson's even more reduced schedule was no longer a problem, as the character's new duties kept him at the SGC, where less action took place. The team hierarchy was no longer the same, but the interaction *was*, and that was what fans were looking for.

Season eight also saw more use of mythology — the traditional Egyptian mythological arc of the venerable sci-fi series now also included the Asgard and Replicator arcs. Amanda Tapping gave her best performance of the year as both Lieutenant Colonel Carter and Replicator Carter.

In fact, season eight showcased Shanks, Judge, and Tapping admirably, as each got to stretch his or her acting wings. Teal'c, often seen as the most pragmatic and down-to-earth character, was foiled in a virtual simulation that made him repeat endlessly the same scenario. "Avatar," directed by *SG-1* veteran Martin Wood, was a subtle look at confronting yourself and an excellent episode that showcased Chris' skilful use of subtlety, showing how far he had come from the silent, awkward, and stalwart Jaffa from early seasons — especially since it was a nod to season two's "The Gamekeeper." Season eight's Teal'c got out of the base, got a girlfriend (or two), and was gripped tightly in the hand of his people's rebellion. His passion for freedom and penchant for action helped elevate "Reckoning" and "Threads" to mini-epics.

Daniel and Carter had their own arcs to follow: during his second near-

A high point for Chris Judge when not filming is having hair! (COURTESY PETER FALLON WWW.BOBW.COM.AU)

death, Daniel unravels the mystery of his previous Ascension. Knowledge and the power of knowledge once again loomed large as a theme, and Daniel realized how far he had come since season five, when he had thought he could do more good Ascended. The Daniel of season eight knew his own worth, and saw the pointlessness of being all-powerful but impotent against the evils of the universe. As for Carter, she had to watch someone she loved die, and, following that, she made some hard decisions. She realized she needed to be true to herself. In a way, Jack, Sam, Daniel, and Teal'c all grew up.

Mainly, what season eight offered was closure on all of the show's large arcs. The Goa'uld, the Replicators, and the interpersonal relationships, all come to some sort of close during the season. Each character gradually understood that they were their own worst enemy (Teal'c in the virtual reality machine, Carter and RepliCarter, Daniel and his inability to regain his memories from being Ascended), and each made some changes and found peace. Much of this tying up of narrative loose ends by the writers was done on the assumption (until the last minute) that season eight would be the show's last; it was not until the eleventh hour that a ninth season of *SG-1* was ordered, as well as a second for *Atlantis*.

Season nine brought on major cast changes, as Richard Dean Anderson bowed out for good — at least, as much as anyone can truly disappear in a science fiction show. Rumors were already spreading about "guest appearances" when the news broke that Richard would be back in the series' record-breaking year for some of the early episodes. "I've done a couple of scenes for *Stargate* to help launch the ninth season and help make it clear that O'Neill is still alive and that we may see him again somewhere down the line," said Richard. "*May* see him . . . May . . . May not . . . But may . . . But may not."

Filling RDA's shoes was venerable screen actor Beau Bridges. Actor Louis Gossett Jr. and Lexa Doig, Michael Shanks' wife, also signed on. But probably the most anticipated arrival at the SGC were *Farscape* stars Ben Browder and Claudia Black (who returns as Vala).

For nine years, *Stargate SG-1* has been a one-of-a-kind hit in science fiction television, changing the way the genre is viewed and tackling important social, political, and historical issues. In recent years, the show has been garnering nominations and wins at awards ceremonies, ranging from best actor to best series, from awards for special effects to awards for costumes. With an expanded budget (something that had been missing for the previous few seasons), new cast members, and a whole new mythology

A prelude to season nine – Ben Browder and the return of Claudia Black (ALBERT L. ORTEGA)

on which to build, season nine is looking to be one of the most exciting to date. It offers great entertainment, wonderfully three-dimensional characters, intergalactic and Earth-bound adventure, and laughter. It speaks seriously (and sometimes not so seriously) about world events — extrapolated to the limits of science fiction but there nonetheless for the viewing. So when people ask, "Why do you watch *Stargate*?" perhaps the only answer can be, "Why don't *you*?"

Everybody CanCon

Stargate SG-1 in the Great White North

In 2002, rumors started that action star Arnold Schwarzenegger was planning to run for governor of California. At the beginning of the year he pulled production of his latest movie, *Terminator 3: Rise of the Machines* out of its Canadian filming location, sending budgets skyrocketing and tabloids scurrying. While most speculated that it was a politically motivated move on the part of "Arnie," the backlash and subsequent media attention to so-called "runaway films" (American movies that are filmed outside the U.S.) got lots of airtime. The cross-pollination of Canadian and American talent, NAFTA, cable channel pressures, "export production series," creative talent deficit, and nationalism all swirl together in one word — CanCon (Canadian content).

America's neighbor to the north was accused of stealing U.S. film and television production, and jobs. Many of the complaints were about Canada's federal mandates that make explicit that a certain amount of any material produced has to involve Canadian content. CanCon has always sparked debate and discussion. The affable David Palffy, who plays Sokar and Anubis on *SG-1*, is staunchly pro-CanCon. "We must encourage projects that are reflective and indicative of [this] country," he said in an interview. His position was not a hardline anti-American stance, but rather an acknowledgment of the enormity of Canada's southern neighbor.

However, there can be some confusion over the term CanCon, because it refers to either Canadian content as it is broadcast, *or* as it is filmed. The first instance, broadcasting, is controlled by a set of parameters from the Canadian Radio and Telecommunications Company (CRTC), which stipulates that sixty percent of content on Canadian television channels must be considered CanCon, because it aims to foster and protect a national identity that is different from, though related to, the rest of North America's. Both *Stargate SG-1* and *Stargate Atlantis* are CRTC certified, for instance, which means that it can play on Canadian channels and count towards their sixty percent. The second instance is slightly more confusing, because *that* CanCon refers to the Canadian Audio-Visual Certification Office (CAVCO), which houses federal programs that give tax breaks to productions.

In terms of CAVCO, and depending on who you're talking to, *Stargate SG-1* was termed a "6/10" or "export production." That's because CAVCO uses a rating system from 1 to 10 for the amount of Canadian content in productions filmed in Canada. The higher the ratio, the more authentically "Canadian" it is — at least, according to their scoring system. Why was it important? A rating of at least 6 means a show meets the standards set out by CAVCO to allow them certain tax credits, called the Canadian Film or Video Production Tax Credit (CPTC), and it means that "key" creative positions are being held by Canadians. These rated positions include director, screenwriter, art director, and lead performer, among others (directors and writers get 2 each, but there are two slots for lead performer, as well). Without at least 6 points in the rating system, the show just wouldn't qualify for tax cuts. Furthermore, to qualify for the tax program that gives the most tax cuts, the producer has to be Canadian.

This is why people started to yell about lost jobs and revenue — because the scoring system, which allows tax breaks and revenue boons for projects, specifies that Canadian workers are used. With the right number of points, any production could then take advantage of the tax break in its entirety — including non-Canadian workers on location. So, some people referred to *SG-1* as a "6/10" because the series was always intended for American audiences, and was only filming in Canada to take advantage of the tax incentives. Others called it an "export production" because, although it uses Canadian workers in its production, it doesn't concentrate its stories or content on Canadian issues.

Because CAVCO ratings are tied to revenue, a production is not obligated to disclose whether they are using the CPTC. So when irate people call *SG-1*

Representing England and Canada, Amanda and Michael demonstrate the adage, "Can't we all just get along?" (ALBERT L. ORTEGA)

a "6/10," they may or may not be telling the truth. Some evidence suggests that the show uses one or the other of these tax credits, however. Asked if he would ever direct an episode of *Stargate*, Richard Dean Anderson responded, "I have no burning desire to direct. My partner Michael Greenburg and I are the executive producers and we are able to edit the show; also we are not Canadian and that's one of the stipulations." This points to the CPTC tax credit, but it could have been a personal mandate set down by the show runners, MGM, or other powers that be.

The truth is, you don't *have* to have lots of Canadians working on your set. Any production company can film in Canada without using the pool of workers there in key positions. Another program in CAVCO called the Film or Video Production Services Tax Credit (PSTC) was "designed to encourage the employment of Canadians, by a taxable Canadian, or a foreign-owned corporation with a permanent establishment in Canada, the activities of which are primarily film or video production or production services." For that matter, you don't need *any* Canadian workers on your set in order to film in Canada (except for special cases like pyrotechnics) — but not qualifying for CPTC or PSTC means productions will cost more to make.

And that is the real problem, of course — money. As Consul General Colin Robertson explains, "Canada offers tax incentives for those productions that use Canadian talent — onscreen and behind the scenes. This is a public policy decision. We do so because we think it is important that Canadian talent get an opportunity to play on a bigger stage." This bottom-line thinking was what was really bothering most people. Why import American talent when a pool of trained workers already exists ready to work for less money? Canada's CanCon objective was not instituted to deny jobs to Americans; it was meant to "ensure that Parliament's objectives for the development and presence of Canadian content in our broadcasting system are met." But for many Americans, it was a nationalistic, exclusionary tactic that took jobs away from them.

Level heads eventually prevailed. Chairman and Chief Executive Officer of the Motion Picture Association Jack Valenti said, "The U.S. movie industry alone has a surplus balance of trade with every single country in the world. No other American enterprise can make that statement." Acting director of the BC Film Commission Lindsay Allen noted that more than forty states in the U.S. have tax incentives directed at the film industry, including California. If movie companies were heading north of the American border to do business, it wasn't exclusively because of tax breaks. The question then became, why *shouldn't* Canadian law demand certain contingencies to protect its own workforce and creative content, given that American studios were coming north to film?

"We have some of the best cinematographers and crews in the world," noted David Palffy, who has worked in the U.S., UK, and Europe. "That's one of the reasons why major films [. . .] use a lot of talent that happens to be Canadian — because we are good at what we do. But a lot of people don't know about it because we don't advertise it."

A case in point is Bridge Studios in Burnaby, British Columbia. It first opened for official business with Richard Dean Anderson's *MacGyver* series, and hasn't looked back since. They boast North America's largest effects stage at 40,000 square feet. Special effects shots that need lots of room to breathe are excellently situated there. As more work started going to Vancouver, more services became available — everything from craft services to post-production. There are over fifty post-production services in BC alone. Every major American studio — Disney, Warner Brothers, MGM/Atlantis, Morgan Creek, New Line — has filmed either a feature or a series at Bridge Studios. But does filming and using available services in

Vancouver make *SG-1* a Canadian series? That was the debate that raged.

People on both sides of the argument continued to talk. Colin Robertson pointed out, "[I]f production takes place in Canada, the development process, employing accountants and lawyers as well as writers and producers, starts here in Los Angeles. As does the postproduction: the marketing, the distribution, the accounting." Not only that, but usually the "star" of the show is still American. Richard Dean Anderson is American, as is Christopher Judge. Amanda Tapping holds both British and Canadian citizenship. Of the four core team members, only Michael Shanks was born Canadian. Supporting talent like Don S. Davis and Peter Williams are also Canadian, but they were born elsewhere. Like the U.S., Canada is a land of immigrants. Peter Williams (Apophis) was born in Jamaica, Amanda Tapping and David Hewlett (Dr. McKay) in England, Don S. Davis and Corin Nemec in the U.S.

On the subject of CanCon, the actors have various opinions. John Novak, who plays Colonel William Ronson in *SG-1*, recently moved back to Vancouver after several years in California. Actors are used to the lean, mean life of rejection and dubious loyalties, where getting a job is not easier just because of location, or because of cultural content. "You have to be able to put the stuff in the theaters," he said, "and if the theaters are owned by the Americans, then you can try to legislate as much Canadian content as you want, but if it's not good and it's not entertaining, then it's like putting a Band-aid on a gaping wound." A case in point here is *SG-1*. Although it is shot in Canada, it is termed a series "for export," meaning, not intended for a Canadian (or solely) Canadian audience. This means that things like location and decoration must be hidden and/or changed to represent the environment that is being portrayed. Many Canadians are familiar with this phenomenon; shows that are known to be filmed with Canadian locations while purportedly depicting an American city often have less-obvious CanCon intertextuals, such as Tim Horton's donut shops, recognizable buildings, or stoplights and street signs (stoplights hang vertically in most of Canada, and street signs are bilingual).

The debate over whether or not *SG-1* was American, Canadian, or just alien altogether, may also have contributed to the many years *SG-1* went without industry awards. So the folktale goes, in Canada it was deemed "too American" to count, and got ignored in response to its American storylines and tastes by Canadian awards like the Leos, and in America it was called "that Canadian show," a traitorous "runaway production" peopled with Canadians — in response, it got snubbed by the U.S. Emmys, too. Probably the only people who didn't care were Europeans and Australians. To many of them, the whole Canadian/American debate was tiresome and just pointless. The show was good, who cares who made it? Which of course got the debate going again. . . .

Regardless of nationalistic leanings, from a purely bottom-line point of view, you couldn't dispute the fact that the Canadian dollar (also known as a "loonie" in its singular form) is a draw for American productions. With a special-effects-laden show like *SG-1*, millions of dollars (and thousands of hours) are spent on the virtual world, rendering the alien worlds we see each week from studios specializing in CGI effects. An *SG-1* episode budget was, on average, $1.7 million in 2004. "Both Brad [Wright, executive producer] and I were very concerned that there would be enough money to make the show we know audiences have come to expect," said Robert Cooper at the conclusion of season eight. "Last year it was very tight, and with the rising Canadian dollar putting a real strain on our budget we wanted to make sure we could do it right." As *SG-1* rose in popularity, the demands on it also increased. Season eight unfortunately coincided with a slow dollar, and many fans grumbled that too many "Earth-based" episodes (where SG-1 does not go to a different world) were starting to creep in. "Well, going to other planets costs a lot of money," noted Cooper.

Extra room to maneuver with a dollar budget means more room to play. "*Stargate* has really come of age as computer generated and assisted effects came into their own," says James Tichenor, visual effects supervisor. "*SG-1* would never have been able to do what it has in the old analog days — it would have been just too expensive. But as the price of the computer technology has come down, and more people have picked up the tools, there's been more competition and more competent work, which has caused the writers to write more ambitious effects into the show. As we did better, they'd want more — a classic scenario. At the same time, because computers continue to improve in speed and power, we're able use more advanced and intelligent tools."

Since the mid-'90s Vancouver has become known for its science fiction expertise. *Smallville, The X-Files,* both *Stargate* series, *Mutant X, The Outer Limits, Battlestar Galactica* — these are just a few of the series that are filmed there. And you'd be amazed at what can be done in and around the Vancouver area. It's the kind of place where you can sail, golf, and ski all in the same day. Giant redwoods almost rub up against skyscrapers. Sand

All for one – Brad Wright, Richard Dean Anderson, and Jonathan Glassner (SUE SCHNEIDER/SHOOTING STAR)

dunes in the beach areas merge with lush forests on one side and the ocean on the other. Drive in any direction for an hour or two and you come to small towns of every shape and size. While shooting *MacGyver*, Richard Dean Anderson said, "I keep an apartment in Los Angeles, but I feel less at home there than I do here."

Over the last eight years, the large, extremely active crew of *Stargate SG-1* has done an amazing job of rendering the familiar strange. A sulfur pit with its bright yellow sand as the genesis for "Cold Lazarus," a local conservatory for "Gamekeeper," and a university campus for an advanced alien homeworld. And since the show's creators are ever on the lookout for the tongue-in-cheek references, for the episode "Wormhole X-Treme," Bridge Studios themselves stood in for . . . well, a film studio! (Only with a different name, of course.)

In November 2003, the Canadian government made changes concerning the CPTC. They raised the taxable amount of production costs from forty-eight percent to sixty percent; the PSTC, the "foreign" production tax credit, was raised from eleven percent to sixteen percent for Canadian residents on film and video productions on location in Canada. What does that mean? It means that, unlike in the past, *only* Canadian residents get the tax break. American productions can no longer be considered "6/10" productions (that is, making the CanCon commitment in order to receive the tax break), and, since more Canadians were needed to make the tax break lucrative, more creative components (directors, screenwriters, musicians and actors) would be held by Canadians. Canada could no longer be accused of harboring "American" shows under the CanCon label, and the U.S. could no longer say that American jobs were being compromised with the lure of tax incentives.

The funny thing is, *SG-1* never really fell into this category anyway. Martin Wood, Robert Cooper, Brad Wright, Joseph Mallozzi, Paul Mullie, Amanda Tapping, Teryl Rothery, James Tichenor — all of them are "key" creative players, and all are Canadian. In fact, when amendments were proposed to the CPTC, the Writers Guild of Canada noted, "*Stargate SG-1*, arguably the most successful of export series and now in its ninth season, has a Canadian executive producer as a show runner and is predominantly written by Canadians. Canadian Brad Wright was initially hired in the story department and when promoted to executive producer and show runner, he began to use Canadian resident screenwriters."

There are other problems, too, problems not associated with politics. Vancouver is no exception, but true to the vision of the series, ingenious techniques tackled old problems. Rain a lot when you don't want it to? Use lighting tricks to hide it (don't backlight). Need odd-looking buildings? Use sets from other shows ("Beast of Burden" reused the series *Bordertown*'s locations, and "Inauguration" used the remains of the movie set from *X2* for its White House scenes). Running out of options? Shoot the same location from different angles (Tynehead Park, used in the shooting of "Fallen," was also used later in "It's Good to Be King").

While Earth episodes are bound to be easier (it's not hard to make the school in "Learning Curve" look like a school, for instance), making a university campus look like Tollana wasn't as daunting as one might expect. The architecture, raised and streamlined, suited the somber Tollan people. Add some authenticity (real papyrus paper, for instance, on Egyptian sets), and voilà — a temperate zone becomes an arid one.

But there's also the backdrop against which much of *SG-1* gets played. Most of the crew, being Canadian, have a slightly different cultural take on things — even if it's merely, to paraphrase author Will Ferguson, in their not being American. There's a playfulness, a half-earnest, half-smart-aleck sensibility about *SG-1* that we've seen in other shows shot in the same area. Spooky forests, sly madmen, strange, unexplainable things that we laugh at even as we fear them; both British Columbia and its inhabitants help to add a sense of the familiar with a tinge of strangeness. Perhaps that's why the show seems so authentic while remaining not too nationalistic. Canada is a land, after all, of *Rick Mercer's Monday Report*, *The Red Green Show*, *Air Farce*, *This Hour Has 22 Minutes*, all of which are lampoons of current Canadian culture. The same federal mandate that allows *22 Minutes* to operate with tax money also allots the Christian show *100 Huntley Street* funds, too. Canada has a rich history of making fun of itself, and that sensibility also extends to *SG-1*, with episodes like "Wormhole X-Treme," "Citizen Joe," and "The Other Guys."

Landscape isn't just the ground we walk on — it's the people who walk on it too. It's the different cultures and the different viewpoints we encounter. These intersections of culture, politics, and influence go into every minute of airtime that makes up *SG-1*. It could be argued that the epitome of the CanCon experience comes from none other than Richard Dean Anderson, a transplanted American whose seriousness is often belied by a wink, whose exterior seems completely conforming but in reality bubbles with all kinds of frank unapologetic childishness. If you ever ask Richard to sum up his life's accomplishments — his many personal as well as professional goals, the impact he's had on mainstream television, on the youth of today, on the positive military role model he's portraying in the face of so much opposition — his answer is typically Richard Dean Anderson — and typically CanCon: "I thought my life was complete when my name was a clue in the *TV Guide* crossword puzzle."

Like the clues of a crossword, the land on which *SG-1* is filmed offers a meeting place between American, British, and Canadian cultures — an American heroic story told using a more European aesthetic, with a Canadian sense of character. And just as the series seamlessly blends traditional sci-fi lore with Egyptian mythology, branching out into different cultural landscapes as the show progresses, so too does the backdrop for the series bring together different civilizations and people. As a new-world land with an old-world history and mentality, Canada is an ideal setting for a show that melds ancient and new worlds, stories, and storytelling.

Coding the Wormhole

An Interview with GateWorld's Darren Sumner

Google anything to do with "SG-1" and eventually, inexorably, you'll come across GateWorld, arguably the most comprehensive *SG-1* site out there. While other guides will often include an interview with one of the show's stars, I chose to put my cast interviews into the guide itself and offer instead this . . . well, comprehensive, look at the show from one angle — as a fan. Like a lot about this series, GateWorld is a hybrid of officialness and enthusiasm. Darren Sumner's overview of the show includes many aspects — from acting to lighting to writing — and his genuine love for the series seeks out the best the show has. You can visit the site at http://gateworld.net.

How did GateWorld come about?

I have a nasty habit of creating Web sites for topics that really interest me, and as I'm a sci-fi fan from the womb, *Stargate* was a shoo-in. I enjoyed the series from the early days and got into it more and more. What I came to appreciate in particular is the writers' terrific ability to interweave elements from past episodes into new stories, so that there is a tapestry of continuity that most shows do not maintain.

The site is more than five years old now, and we've been truly blessed with success and with generous contributions from other fans.

Can you give us a brief overview of the function and layout of GateWorld? A mini "walking tour," if you will.

GateWorld's home page is designed to be the one-stop info site for the *Stargate* universe, which we hope you'll want to visit every day! It has the latest *Stargate* news, flanked by today's episode listings and bigger, more mainstay site features like interviews, special articles, and so forth.

Once you get past the home page, the site is divided into several interconnected sections. The heart of the site will always be the episode guides: every episode of every season of each *Stargate* show has its own home base with a synopsis, deeper analysis, and notes on what we learned in that episode, photos, reviews, line-by-line transcripts, comments from the cast and crew on that episode — and, of course, spoilers for upcoming episodes.

The episode guides are interlinked with The Stargate Omnipedia. If the episode guides are the heart of GateWorld, the Omnipedia is the lungs (or maybe the brain — I haven't figured out the best analogy yet). We are growing it into an exhaustive, searchable encyclopedia to the canonical *Stargate* universe — an entry for every character, species, planet, piece of technology, et cetera. It already has hundreds of entries, and we are working to add hundreds more to make it truly comprehensive, up to the most recently aired episodes — from Abu to Zelenka.

Beyond that, GateWorld has articles, regular interviews with actors and crew members, an active fan fiction archive, a thriving discussion forum with thousands of fans participating, and an online store. We also have sections that track the broader *Stargate* franchise, beyond the television shows, including comic books, video games, fan conventions, and more.

GateWorld is not an official site for *SG-1*, but it is an extremely comprehensive overview of the *Stargate* universe, from canon to "fanon." Can you outline some of the differences between your site and the official one hosted by MGM?

The differences between any fan-created site and a site created by a marketing department are usually going to be like night and day. They are different animals, they have different advantages and disadvantages, and they really exist for different purposes. MGM's official site is intended to support and supplement the syndication series, and is generally going to attract more of the crowd who watch the show on Saturday afternoons and don't surf the Web for comprehensive, fan-made sites. As an official site, they also have the inside connections to get behind-the-scenes material, interviews from the set, and the like. (In the interest of full disclosure, I myself have been a contributor and consultant for MGM's official sites since 2003.)

Fan-made sites will be more in tune with the latest developments and new episodes, the intricate minutiae about the show's universe, fan-created fiction and art, and so forth. Fan-run sites have also tended to rely on "official" sources for news and information.

GateWorld has made great strides in bridging that gap, though. We have developed a strong network of resources and placed such a high premium on reliable news and information that we're now the ones breaking many of these stories. We don't have to wait for MGM or the network or *TV Guide* to give us the goods on the future of the franchise. Sites like GateWorld and other film and television news sites are the ones breaking news, in large part because (unlike a magazine, or even an official Web site) we can publish a breaking story at the drop of a hat.

I avoid calling GateWorld a "fan site" anymore, because there seems to be a stigma attached to that in the industry. It makes it hard to be taken seriously when we are approaching actors, agents, and studio executives seeking an interview or comment on a news story. So we are trying to define a new category, in many ways: GateWorld is a professional news and entertainment Web site, like SciFi.com or Cinescape.com, and not a "fan site."

What *is* the appeal of *SG-1*? Do you see this appeal also working for *Atlantis*, or do the two series have fundamental differences?

As with any show, I think there are different elements that appeal to different viewers. For some it is the cast and the character development; for others it's the classic sci-fi elements and visual effects; for others still it's the well-told stories and production values. For most, it is some combination of all this and more.

Again, I personally love the show especially because of its sensitivity to its own past continuity. And because that's what I love most about *Stargate SG-1*, I think that *Atlantis* absolutely has the ability to run with that same appeal. It is set in the same universe, it follows the same rules of continuity. It is building its own mythology, yet that always remains connected to what we long-time viewers have come to know from a feature film and eight years of *SG-1*. That attraction is built in to the show; so all it needs is a good cast, character development, well-told stories, and high production values. And I think it has those in spades.

How important is fan input to the site? How important are fans to the show?

Without fan support there is no site, just as without fans there is no show. GateWorld is entirely a fan endeavor, and after all the success and attention it is still a hobby. When it stops being fun, I have other ways to spend my free time.

But my own fandom aside, *Stargate* fans are awesome and have made the site what it is. They write content, participate in the forum on a daily (and, for some, hourly) basis, upload fan fiction, vote in polls, and e-mail in suggestions and comments. Without them, there is no GateWorld – not only because no one would be there to visit, but because no one would be there to create it.

Fandom's participation in GateWorld is what has made it a success. We've only been able to define this new category of what a fan-run site can do, land big-name interviews, even host special fan events, because fans of the show have put our site on the map. For good or for ill, MGM, licensees, publishers, and even the producers of *Stargate* know that they can communicate with a lot of people through this site.

Do you think items on your site can or are used by TPTB (the powers that be) for the show's direction or reference?

We have been told on a number of occasions that the show's writers, producers, cast, even executives use GateWorld. In the absence of an up-to-date show bible, new writers are often pointed to GateWorld for a crash course on the mythology so far and to become acquainted with the types of stories that they tell (and that have already been done). When they want to stand quietly at the back of the room and hear some fan response to an episode or a decision, they will often lurk at GateWorld Forum.

The Stargate Omnipedia is really the most ambitious thing we've ever undertaken. Our goal, as I've explicitly told Robert Cooper, is to turn it into the definitive *Stargate* information source that, together with the episode guides, will replace the show bible altogether. When a writer five years from now needs to remember what the Ashrak assassin's ring weapon is called, it will be online at his or her fingertips; no need to pop in the DVD for "In the Line of Duty" and try to find the brief reference to the device. (It's a "hara'kesh" by the way!)

What is the hardest part of your job as Site Administrator/Webmaster? What is the easiest?

Right now the hardest part of my job is keeping up with the workload, especially with two *Stargate* series on the air. When new episodes are airing and next season is in production, we publish news stories, spoiler reports, new photos, episode reviews, summaries, analyses and transcripts, interviews and special features, ratings data, updates to existing sections, TV listings, a new poll — all in any given week. (I also have a "real" job, a marriage, and am finishing a master's degree.)

So our immediate goal is to launch a new back-end content management system, which will allow all of the site's various contributors to work on their material and publish it without a word from me. Then you'll really see something!

The easiest part of the job — most days, anyway — is keeping up the enthusiasm to do all of those tasks. They are still making new episodes of my favorite shows, and I love playing in this universe. I get a jolt from being able to share news, info, and photos with other fans and saying, "Cool! See what's coming?"

How time intensive is it to maintain GateWorld? Are your staff members volunteers, or paid employees?

My hobbies have the habit of becoming addictions! [GateWorld] has taken up progressively more of my time over the years, and now it's easily a part-time job. I typically spend at least twenty hours per week on the site, though quite often much more. It's rather intensive at present, because the entire site is still hand-coded HTML — so all new content, even if it's created by someone else, must go through me to be published. We're hoping to solve that little bottleneck soon.

We have a number of volunteers on the site who write articles and episode reviews, and moderate the forum. Only our assistant editor, the inestimable David Read, is regularly compensated with more than love and warm fuzzies — but he's still a volunteer at heart.

Is this labor of love worth it? You were recently seen in the official *Stargate SG-1* magazine, and you're now a "professional" *SG-1*'er. Do you still approach the work after all these years as a fan?

Like I said, when all of this stops being fun I'll stop doing it. I'm absolutely having a blast. I get a jolt out of publishing new content on the site, and then seeing other fans talk about it.

As a writer and editor, GateWorld has also opened up some remarkable doors for me professionally. I am working with MGM on their official sites, I am responsible for reviewing and editing every *Stargate* comic book for continuity with the TV shows, and now I am serving as the news editor for the official *Stargate SG-1* magazine. We do six pages of news at the top of every issue that is "in association with GateWorld.net" — it's a great privilege.

As much as I do it all as a fan, though, it is greatly satisfying to see GateWorld being recognized as something other than a run-of-the-mill "fan site" done by a kid in his basement with too much time on his hands.

What do you see in the future of *SG-1*? Another spin-off, a movie, a tenth season?

Stargate fans are riding the crest of a wave that is truly the next great, long-term science fiction franchise. Thanks to MGM and The Sci-Fi Channel, right now the sky is the limit. *Stargate SG-1* shows no signs of stopping, and it will be interesting to see whether season nine's major cast changes help or hurt the ratings. If it helps, there really may be no end in sight.

With the ability to replace cast members and still keep telling interesting stories that hold on to viewers, the show could go another ten years. Of course that is hard to predict, as no genre show has ever done it before (with the exception of *Doctor Who*, which never aired much in the U.S. outside of public broadcasting). That's where we are at now: The original series is testing the waters to see if it can change the kind of show it is, from a one-cast series that goes eight years to a revolving cast series that will go on until people just stop watching it.

Another spin-off and a movie seem inevitable at this point, but it is very difficult to launch a feature film with significant dollars behind it based on a TV series. *Star Trek* really only did it successfully because it had been seeping into the national consciousness through syndication reruns for more than a decade after it was canceled. *Babylon 5*'s recent attempt at a feature film was aborted, but other shows like *Firefly* may set precedents on the big screen that will encourage the studio to take a risk on *Stargate*.

Our show certainly has the advantage of having been a feature film originally, and quite a successful one at that. I think it'll happen eventually, but probably not while the series is still in production.

Regardless of what form it takes, the future of *Stargate* is truly bright. And GateWorld will be along for every twist of the ride!

Out of the Blue
The Franchise of *SG-1*

"So, are there any indigenous lions, tigers, or bears I should lie awake at night worrying about?" – Sam Carter, from "The First Commandment"

It's odd for some people to think of a television show as a "franchise," but in the case of *SG-1*, it's very apt. Any fan of the movie *Spaceballs* knows of the hilarious sequence where Mel Brooks lampoons franchising, pointing out the lunchboxes and toilet paper all with the *Spaceballs* logo on it. But the fact remains that people who love a particular movie, series, character, or book often feel a strong kinship with it that they wish to expand and solidify. *SG-1*'s franchising has some interesting entries, both old and new, and is continually looking to branch out. The franchiser of *Stargate SG-1*, MGM, contracts out certain unique items to franchisees, who then have the "official" stamp of approval (and hopefully some backing) from the media corporation.

Officialness has its good sides, and its bad sides. On the one hand, holding a franchise licence means much easier lines of communication with MGM and, more often than not, with the cast and crew. Production values are higher, whatever the merchandise, due to MGM's awareness of public image, and it's easier to find memorabilia thanks to networked marketing. On the other hand, it sometimes removes the community element. Savvy fans have not missed this aspect. "I have not much nice to say

"Official" conventions are a popular option for many fans. Amanda, Chris, and Michael attend one in Burbank, California (COURTESY MICHELLE)

about [MGM licencing]," said *SG-1* fan Denise in an interview. "For years, it was sad that there was nothing out there. MGM did have some licenced stuff, but it was lame. Then, the show moved to Sci Fi [from its original home on Showtime] and all of a sudden, MGM cares. Now we have 'official sites', 'official conventions', 'official magazines' and what I as a consumer feel is that I'm being 'officialed' to death and, in many ways, the *Stargate* fandom is becoming one where only the rich count." There's an added problem in that, once a licencee acquires a product, there is a concentrated effort to remove "unofficial" copies, because they are in violation. For instance, MGM recently licenced "official" SG-1 and SGC patches with Creation Entertainment. The result was that many fan-run sites that offered similar, though unofficial, patches, were told to stop producing them, as they were in copyright violation. New fans just arriving on the scene might miss the backstory shift from unofficial to official, unless they come across a fan whose been watching for a long time, or surf old forum topics. The Web site GateWorld is as good a place to start as any, and since it's a hybrid of unofficial and official, it also has a unique perspective (see, "Coding the Wormhole").

While it is much easier now to acquire memorabilia and souvenirs for fans who want more of *SG-1* in their lives, that very opportunity seems to be changing aspects of the fandom, drawing money lines in the sand, so to speak. Both sides have salient points to consider. For more on the "fanchise" aspect of *SG-1*, see "No Red Shirts: The 'Fanchise' of *SG-1*." For more homegrown *SG-1* swag, see "Resources."

Here are some of the officially franchised items available, listed alphabetically:

BOARD GAME

http://www.fleetgames.com/ Developed by Fleet Board Games, *Stargate SG-1* the board game is a strategy-based game that resembles the board game "Risk," with three factions — human, Goa'uld, and Asgard — battling it out across the two-dimensional universe of the board. It won a 2004 Seal of Excellence from *Creative Child Magazine*. The national U.S. magazine is dedicated to nurturing creativity in children, and the award was high praise for the game.

COMICS AND CARTOONS
AND TRADING CARDS, OH MY!

There is an enormous amount of paraphernalia (more positively known as memorabilia), surrounding the series *SG-1*. Hats, T-shirts, bobblehead figurines, drink coasters, trading cards, calendars, toques (beanie hats), a mobile phone game (believe it!), and soundtracks to the show are all available — and that's just for starters. While these items appear most often at conventions, there are other franchised areas you can explore if you have the inclination (and the cash).

Cartoons

Stargate Infinity aired for one season (2002–2003), in conjunction with MGM, DIC, and 4 Kids Entertainment on the FOX network. The series was set thirty years in the future, and does not use any of the original *SG-1* cast. In it, the *Stargate* program is firmly established. A veteran Gater, four cadets, and an alien are kept from going back to Earth by a traitor. The series received lukewarm reviews, and *SG-1* producer Brad Wright said that it should not be considered official *Stargate* canon.

Comics

http://www.avatarpress.com/stargate/ From Avatar Press/Pulsar, *SG-1* goes to the colored printed page in the form of comics. Like the licenced novel tie-ins, the comics retain the universe of the Stargate, but use their own storylines, narrative techniques, and antagonists as well as already established characters (such as Aris Boch of "Deadman Switch"). James Anthony Kuhoric, who pens the stories, is happy to be adding to the franchise in new ways. "The major benefit to comic books as an entertainment medium is that you can do things that simply can't be done on film," he said in an online interview with GateWorld. "You are not hampered by a budget to create the special effects for any scene. If the writer and artist can imagine it, it can happen."

Mobile Phone Game

http://game.skyzonemobile.com/ You're Colonel O'Neill, and you get to run through four missions in this action game. The game is supported by most carriers in the U.S./Canada and some carriers internationally.

Trading Cards

http://www.digitalheroes.com/Stargate/Stargate1.asp Rittenhouse Archives has been making *Stargate SG-1* collectible cards since 2000, and have seasons one to six available. Collect-A-Card issued a set of cards for the movie *Stargate* in 1994. Packs include costume cards, set cards, character cards, and usually one autographed card. Available online at the above URL, on eBay, or through your local hobby/comics store.

Conventions aren't just restricted to North America. Colin Davis, Corin Nemec, and director Peter DeLuise attend one in France (COURTESY ALINE REINHARD)

CONVENTIONS

Although not an "item" per se, conventions are immensely popular, they are a great place to party, and it's worth attending at least once if you can. They cement franchises because they can be a veritable feast of consumables, offering a one-stop shopping spree. Conventions usually have question-and-answer periods with the various actors on the show (some principles, like Chris Judge or Michael Shanks, as well as supporting characters like Tony Amendola or Teryl Rothery), where fans can satisfy their thirst for knowing how exactly Chris deals with wearing a gold tattoo on his forehead as part of his day job. Conventions are often made fun of in popular culture — think of the movie *Galaxy Quest*, where conventions are lampooned — but as Peter Wingfield (who plays the Goa'uld Tanith) says, "The weirdest part of [the *Stargate*] fandom is that everyone is so normal — surprisingly." In addition to meeting fans from all over, there are autograph sessions, chances to swap stories (oral or otherwise), and buy memorabilia galore.

The two biggest convention companies are the Wolf convention series and the Creation Entertainment series.

Creation Entertainment

http://www.fansofstargate.com/ Creation Entertainment is marketed as *The Official Stargate SG-1 and Stargate Atlantis Convention Tour*. A newer convention, Creation Entertainment has hosted numerous previous tours for *Xena*, *The X-Files*, and *Star Trek*. They also wholesale licenced merchandise. Most of their conventions are in the U.S.. Tickets range from just getting in the door to packages that include personally signed autographs from the actors, and photos. Other attractions are videos, costume and trivia competitions, auctions, parties (which guest cast and crew attend), and charity fund-raising. They recently acquired the licence for and added Vancouver to their roster which had, until 2005, been the site of the Gatecon convention.

Wolf Events

http://www.wolfevents.com/php/index.php Wolf Events is the older convention holder, focusing mostly in Europe, especially London, England, but also in Scotland and Germany. They title their events a little more breezily, although their "core" *Stargate* conventions are simply called the "Wolf SG" series. "Wolf SG-8," for example, was their eighth installment and ran from November 5–7, 2004, to a sold-out crowd. They also run conventions for *Alias* and the series *Dead Like Me*.

Both convention franchises allow online ordering over a secure network, as well as mail, phone, and fax options for ordering tickets.

Gatecon

http://www.gatecon.com/ For five years Gatecon was *the* convention to attend. It was held in the Vancouver area, which meant more actor and crew member participation, it was a friendly family atmosphere, hosted charity events, and brought people together from the four corners of the earth, all in support of *SG-1*. Denise wrote, "Gatecon is a gathering of friends. There are people that make the yearly trek just to see each other, the actors are incidental. I've been in the lobby of the Best Western and seen folks running across the hall to hug each other and greet each other like long lost friends . . . and that's just what they are."

In 2005, MGM started requiring licences for conventions, and Creation Entertainment licenced the convention for the Vancouver area. Gatecon proper eventually moved to the UK, and the Vancouver version morphed into Timeless Destinations http://www.timelessdestinations.com.

FICTION/NOVEL TIE-INS

Novel tie-ins are books that spawn out of the universe created by a movie or series, but which have their own storylines. They conform to established parameters such as characters and sideplots (like the Tok'ra and Goa'uld arcs), but are not direct continuations of particular episodes. Unlike the cartoon *Stargate: Infinity*, they do follow established canon. In contrast to the *Stargate* comics line, there are no graphics.

Unfortunately, officially sanctioned novels have not done as well as other aspects of the franchise. Unlike the voluminous *Star Trek* novel tie-ins, there are only two limited series of books available for *SG-1*. One was brought out by the Penguin/Putnam imprint Roc, but this series is hard to get ahold of and was disappointing to most fans. One fan's bulletin board post read, "I will read anything on any topic but this was rubbish," in response to the novel *The Morpheus Factor*. There was some speculation that the author, Ashley McConnell, had not watched the show and had worked from scripts, basically a writer-for-hire.

Roc also released a second series of *Stargate* novels by Bill McCay, but this series does not follow the *SG* universe as it is portrayed in the television series. Most fans of *SG-1* are not fans of this series.

There is a current series in print from a UK-based independent publisher called Fandemonium. While some fans loved the attention to detail and the fact that the writers were also fans of the show, others were disappointed that its availability was limited outside the UK (and terribly expensive for a paperback book), and, as one fan commented, "The book is riddled with grammatical and punctuation errors and typos." It's a shame that this potentially lucrative area of the franchise is such a letdown, especially since there is such a proliferation of good stories being written from the *Stargate* universe.

The Roc novels are available (if not out of print), online at Barnes and Noble and Amazon, or at Indigo/Chapters in Canada. You can also order them at your local bookstore (I didn't find any on the shelves of several "bricks and mortar" bookstores). Fandemonium books are only available in the UK from Amazon or directly from the publisher.

ONLINE AUCTIONS FOR PROPS

http://www.stargateprops.com Legends Memorabilia has acquired the licence to sell props from the set of *SG-1*. Their preferred vendor is eBay, and they have a wide variety of replica props to satisfy the power-hungry Goa'uld within. They also have costumes, set decorations, limited editions, and studio art up for grabs. Want to dress up like an Argosian from "Brief Candle"? Feel like swinging around a staff weapon like you saw in "The Warrior"? Donning the rubber suit of the aliens from "Foothold"? Well, now you can. Each piece of memorabilia comes with a Certificate of Authenticity from MGM Television too.

Another place to look for on the Legends site is the Stargate Autograph Web site. http://www.stargate-autographs.com/ is a site that sells autographed pictures of the cast. How is it different from the other stuff Legends sells? All the money goes to charity. The official Web site acknowledges the recent spate of falsely autographed photos, and in conjunction with MGM and Legends, created a site that ensures that the autograph you pay for is the real thing. Richard Dean Anderson endorsed the site personally, stating, "My arrangement with Legends is a clean, straightforward proposition that deposits *all* monies collected into the hands of several charitable organizations I have supported over the decades." (See cast biography of RDA for which charities he endorses).

ROLE-PLAYING GAME

http://www.stargatesg1rpg.com/ From Alderac Entertainment Group. Based on the rule set created for the venerable role playing game "Spycraft." For those who like role-playing models, creating a personalized universe for others to explore (the original manual also has ten worlds already mapped out for ready-to-play action), and generally geeking out, this game is for you. Unfortunately, in 2005, Sony, who had recently acquired MGM, did not renew the licence, although Alderac hopes to maintain support of the game through its online forums.

No Red Shirts

The "Fanchise" of *SG-1*

In my interview with Teryl Rothery, I asked her to sketch out a perfect Janet Fraiser episode. Amazingly, she quoted a complete story from beginning to end — and took absolutely no credit for it. The story was given to her by one of her fans, who went by the name "Meesh." "God bless them all," she said with her characteristic enthusiasm. "I love them. I totally embrace fandom. I think they're the most supportive, caring, loyal, wonderful people around."

And it's true; fans are what makes *SG-1* as good as it is — because they demand the best. So, along with Meesh, for this book, seven members of the *SG-1* community were interviewed: all of them write fan fiction and are involved in the online fan community. Some watch every episode, and some watch only occasionally. They are students, professionals, family members. To ignore the presence of viewers and their opinions, or not look closely at what evolves from that presence, is like ignoring the thumb on your hand.

Fandom always has its particular jargon, its own way of speaking. Catchphrases, memorable lines, and other tags, whether they are common or unique on the show, make it into instant message conversations, forum discussions, and even everyday language usage. In this book, for instance "Parlez-vous Gate?" notes some of those lines and snippets of dialogue that have become standards for fans, but every fandom has them. In *Star Trek*, it was the infamous "red shirt," a (usually) unnamed member of the crew who got killed in the same episode he or she appeared. *SG-1* even alludes to this (sort of a cross-cultural sci-fi homage line), in "The Other Guys":

FELGER: You are not going to die, Coombs.
COOMBS: Oh, come on, Felger. We might as well be wearing red shirts.
FELGER: I don't get that . . .

Playing on both the lineage of science fiction and the difference between *SG-1* and the *Star Trek* franchise, Felger and Coombs' interaction sums up the tongue-in-cheek-ness of the show that draws so many fans in. Fans identify with the character of Felger, and so, when he saves SG-1 from imminent demise, they too have a sense that they are not "red shirts" — an expendable component in the enormous entirety of the series.

There are no "red shirts" in the fandom of *SG-1*; each fan has an opportunity to make his or her voice heard in any number of ways — and many take it. *SG-1* fans are intelligent, personable, community-minded, and passionate. People devote time to this show, to the fan fiction, to maintaining Web sites, contributing to spoiler sites, making music videos, going to conventions. "[The fandom] broadened my horizons," writes Denise, who helps moderate the GateWorld forum in her free time. "I went on my first trip out of the country to go to a convention, Gatecon, because of folks I met in the fandom. I now have friends all over the U.S., Canada, the UK, Australia, Germany, France, and the Netherlands. These are people that I talk to, interact with, and know."

The "fanchise" of *SG-1* has an amazing presence. Hardly surprising, since the film *Stargate* had the first official Web site for a movie, way back in 1994, starting a trend that's become big business. While it's debatable whether or not fans' interaction with producers and the channels which air the show have direct consequences, their contribution does make the powers that be sit up and take notice. And they're still listening. The Sci-Fi Channel's press release for *SG-1*'s ninth season states, "In response to overwhelming viewer demand, Sci-Fi Channel has ordered new seasons of its highest-rated and most successful original series, *Stargate Atlantis* and *Stargate SG-1*, from MGM Television Entertainment." As already noted in our chapter "Making Myth," the departure of Daniel Jackson sparked a huge fan controversy which may have contributed to the actor's return.

Alexis Cruz's character Skaara is one of the few characters to transition from the movie to the series. Here he is making one fan's day (COURTESY TRICIA BYRNE)

TV culture is so much about a passive audience (it's not called the "idiot box" for nothing), but *SG-1* fans are an example of *active* watchers. Darren Sumner, the mastermind behind what is arguably *the* Web site for the series, is a perfect example. "So GateWorld started on October 22, 1999 — the night that Apophis stepped into the light and revealed to the world that he'd been brought back from the dead ('Jolinar's Memories'). The site has always been my big fat 'thank you' to the writers, cast, and crew for creating such an intricate and engaging universe, and for taking science fiction fans seriously."

SG-1 fans are intelligent, if occasionally a little overzealous. Suz Voy, like many fans, started watching the show after hearing about it through word-of-mouth rather than through an ad campaign. "It was the second season episode 'In the Line of Duty' that got me hooked," she said. "A friend of mine loved it so much that she convinced me to watch, so I went out and bought the first DVD I could find. That was pretty much it. Then it was the mass buying of DVDs, etc. (grins)" Tricia had much the same experience. "A friend who knew me from another fandom told me that he thought the series was just up my alley and I should check it out (I think he now regrets that decision)." For five years *SG-1* told stories to a medium-sized audience on Showtime. They were never the worst-rated show — nor the best. But fans kept quietly appearing, and with the fans came the fervor.

From the humble beginnings of word-of-mouth, *SG-1* has generated a plethora of fan-based Web sites, consumer awareness, a community of Web journals, newsgroups, lists, forums, and Web rings, and recently, general and academic discourse. From BenBella Books comes *Stepping Through the Stargate*, a general look at the *Stargate* universe from various viewpoints — science fiction writers, scientists, and some cast and crew takes. Academic publisher IB Tauris prepared a critical look at *Stargate SG-1* for 2006 called *Reading Stargate*, dissecting and deconstructing various aspects of the series, from individual episode analysis to the cultural impact of the series as a whole. Julie, a Masters in Education, is very clear on the importance of this aspect:

"I think the wild popularity of *Buffy* in the academic community has had a big impact on examining genre shows in this manner. I'm not too surprised to see people starting to look at *Stargate* in that manner, since it too makes that cross into mainstream, and has that sense of immediacy in setting. While very simplified and written for dramatic effect, there's a lot of sociopolitical stuff going on in the *Stargate* universe [like] the NID and the role of the U.S. and foreign governments in the Stargate project, and in the SGC's relationship with its various enemies and allies."

These sorts of analogous threads make *SG-1* not only an escapist adventure series, but also a kind of mirror. The thirty-one-year-old science fiction fan and sometime fan fiction writer sees that, too. "Given the social and political upheaval in the U.S. over the last few years, and all the sociopolitical ramifications of the U.S. foreign policy and foreign relationships, I think *Stargate*, like *Buffy*, can be seen to act as a metaphor for things going on in the modern sociopolitical sphere. Add to that *Stargate*'s emphasis on exploration, of moral choices in dealing with other cultures, and you get a scarily accurate picture of so much of what's going on in the world today. It makes *Stargate* ripe for cultural analysis."

The inclusion (some might say intrusion) of the Internet in our lives has led to a way of looking at television series that has never before been possible. The traditional watercooler talk of TV shows has expanded to everywhere that can be accessed by the Internet. "Some of my closest friends I have met through this fandom," notes Lab_brat. "I am sure many other people have too. We all live in different parts of the world, but we

It's amazing what you can get online these days . . . two fans in France go all out for their favorite show (COURTESY ALINE REINHARD)

are given an opportunity to meet face-to-face through conventions and other gatherings."

Gathering together holds lots of appeal for fans because it gives them an opportunity to exchange viewpoints. "The show encompasses lots of different aspects — the U.S. military, the team, the civilians; the aliens giving it a wide-ranging appeal," says fan fiction writer and *SG-1* viewer Tricia. "From fans who adore the mythology, to the science and technology fans, to the fans of the military aspect. There are so many different types of people who enjoy the show for different reasons. You can find people who normally you would never interact with (different ages, jobs, locations) and you find you have something in common, half the time you don't even talk about *Stargate*, yet you seem to get on with people like you've known them much longer than you have!"

Fans aren't restricted to official conventions. In 2004, *SG-1* fan A.J. started what quickly became known as "Squee Con," a gathering of *SG-1* fans from all over the world. After inadvertently posting a public rather than limited notice to her blog about having "a few" people over to watch *SG-1* for the weekend, she decided to leave the invitation open to everyone. "I arranged to pick people up/have people stay with other nearby fen [fans]. Then I suddenly had 15 people coming to visit me and to camp in my living room, eat, watch, and be merry."

An amazing group assembled, some from as far away as Australia! The weekend was not as rigidly defined as an official convention, but it did involve a lot of watching *SG-1*, video and music video clips (a subset of the fandom, where music videos are montaged to short clips from the show), a sharing of fan fiction, and most especially, talking about the show.

"It's really a very interesting experience because some online friendships are really very intimate," she noted, hastening to add that *intimate* doesn't necessarily mean sexual. "However, for the most part, people are meeting for the first or second time in person. Squee Con is as much a reason to watch television as it is to have a safe environment to meet the people you've been talking to within fandom boundaries." The gathering of fans to meet, discuss, and expand their respective fandoms was a huge success, and Squee Con was a go for July 2005, as well. As with most things *SG-1* related, it's branching out to other ventures. "It seems to be spawning a lot of similar-type get-togethers," said the part-time graduate student. "At least two of the original Squee Con attendees are putting out feelers about hosting their own weekends."

And it's not just the fans who get together. The approachability of the actors, from their appearances at conventions to their charity work, fosters a sense of community and family. "Film stars always seem to be complaining about the media, how their privacy is always being invaded," said Snarkhunt, a freelance editor, "and how the very people that pay to see their movies are somehow lesser copies of 'real fans' that exist in some vacuum (apparently in their mind). But the *SG-1* cast, and the crew too, and all the people involved at conventions, always embrace the fan contingent. They listen, they answer questions, and sure they sometimes aren't at their best but regardless, they don't treat a fan like a freak if [that fan] derives pleasure out of the show."

Carmen Argenziano, who plays Jacob Carter on the series, agrees that it's not just about working as an actor. "The appreciation from the fans is quite moving and it reaffirms why I wanted to be an actor in the first place," he said. The stories that *SG-1* tells are entertaining and didactic, and they *do* make a difference. "I see that happening," says the veteran method actor. "I see that in the faces of the people at the convention. It's very supportive and it makes me feel good."

A lot of crew members incorporate the Internet into their lives, as well. James Tichenor and Joseph Mallozzi both have blogs, and Richard Dean Anderson's official Web site, rdanderson.com, boasts an extremely comprehensive look not only at the actor, but also at the show itself. Amanda Tapping took much the same route as Anderson did, allowing a fan who had previously run an "unofficial" fan site to host her official one, instead of paying someone to do it (Anderson's site is maintained by a long-time friend). As is typical with most *SG-1* cast members, Tapping's aware of the impact technology has on her life, and the devotion that viewers have for her character, and her show. The opening page of her Web site (www.amandatapping.com) reads simply, "Welcome to my website. Thank you for your interest and support. I really appreciate it." The site still maintains its homey, fan-based feel, but now has the advantage of having updates by Amanda herself on her life, her career, and the projects she supports.

E-mails, live chats, instant messages, and a host of technology like online journals and forums allow people to interact and discuss, love, or hate their favorite shows. Fan fiction was born, and although it has been labeled a giant "vanity press," where everyone who has access to a keyboard can make their voice heard, it has also become a moderated forum (in varying degrees) for worldwide discussion of its cultural relevance. "Writing lets me ponder the motivations of these borrowed characters, and lets me speculate on the things we as an audience aren't shown. Yes, there is an aspect of wish fulfillment to it, but not on any visceral level. Not to me anyway," says A.J., a self-styled "rabid" fan, and a veteran of ten other fandoms. "I know what I'm talking about when I say that the *SG-1* fandom houses some of the most long-term, hugely obsessed fans on the planet. Some of these people put the (original series) *Trek* obsessives to SHAME." Sometimes, writing is a way for a fan to work out his or her own ideas. A.J. says, "I guess you could say that fan fiction is my way of discussing a show over the watercooler with myself."

The online community allows the freedom to voice individual opinions on the cultural relevance of Teal'c's hair change in season eight, the reason why Jonas didn't die and Daniel did (sort of), when exactly O'Neill got that scar on his eyebrow and whether or not that makes him an even more likeable hero. There are forums on large, entertainment-based sites such as GateWorld and the SG1archives, and there are also Internet newsgroups of

These three fans (Lindsay Booth, Laura Aitken, and Vicki Pryke) were horrified when a certain cast member met with her demise (COURTESY ELIZA BENNETT)

every denomination on Yahoo!, from those who are Sam/Jack aficionados to groups dedicated to fan fiction postings. In between there are "slashers" — groups devoted to same-sex pairings in the *SG-1* universe; spoilme's — groups that concentrate on amassing every scrap of information, rumor, or scandal attributed to or from the series; and e-zines — electronic magazines, to choose from as well. The largest Yahoo! newsgroup, *sg1fans*, boasts over 3000 people, and there are hundreds of groups to choose from.

While some circles dismiss the "real world" relevance of these fans, their close examination of and immersion into the series, is "deconstruction," even if they don't call it that. It also shows that contrary to the opinion that television is mind-numbing, fans are active, political, and engaged. "I think the writers have done a great job in trusting the viewers to make the show what they want it to be," maintains Julie. "I, as a viewer, make my own connections and links. All that empty narrative space that the writers left is why I *started* to write fic for this show."

Fans also reflect a typical attitude of contemporary times (and the show) as well, because right after discussing how the SGC simulates, cross-pollinates with, and encapsulates the U.S. military, don't be surprised if a fan also has a fervent argument for or against the question of whether Sam and Jack are ever going to just give it up and (as the euphemism goes) "go fishing." "I really, really, really hope there will be a positive resolution," said Denise, in an interview at the beginning of the show's eighth season. "I mean, what will it hurt? Fans have been strung along for years and, unless they want a repeat of the final episode of *Forever Knight* or *Quantum Leap*, I think the powers that be really need to have some sort of positive resolution . . . unless of course, they like ticking thousands of people off."

Fans of *SG-1* are well aware of their own interconnectedness with the show, the characters, and the actors. They are interested in how a given actor portrays a character, what kinds of choices he or she makes, and how that reflects not only the show, but the world in general. Science fiction no longer exists in a vacuum of the fanciful, but rather is an extrapolation of the here and now. "Science fiction in general is hugely popular now," explains Tricia. "The fact that *Stargate* is the most popular science fiction show on television only brings that much more attention to it. I think, in a way, that Don S. Davis said it best himself when he explained that the 'heroes' that are available for the youth of today are dwindling. Most of the ones that do exist are shrouded in scandal."

The characters of *SG-1* are not omnipotent or flawless, but they react and change like we do, on an everyday basis, sometimes making mistakes, and sometimes doing the right thing from sheer luck. The four characters that make up SG-1 reflect different aspects of our lives, and they're led by a person who acts as a common denominator. "I don't know if O'Neill's presence changes the way we write certain episodes," said writer Joseph Mallozzi, "as much as it affords us the opportunity to attack scenes differently.

"Specifically, he allows us to deliver necessary exposition, scientific or technical background (which, let's face it, can be pretty dry) in more interesting ways. He's the 'everyperson,' who like many of our viewers may not necessarily get all the backstory babble and question Sam, Daniel, or Teal'c on what they're saying." Jack O'Neill himself is an everyday kind of hero. Not the towering hero type of *Star Trek*, or the silent but brooding hero from *The X-Files*, or the flippant and cynical hero of *Farscape*. If he *was* in a *Star Trek* episode, he'd probably be wearing a red shirt; but this is *Stargate SG-1*, so he's not. He's like us, and we love him for it.

It's from this portal of everyperson that fans stretch out their intellects and admire, critique, question, and occasionally have hissy fits about the universe of *Stargate* — just as, on the show itself, the characters do. And new communication technology allows these people to connect in ways they've never been able to before.

The wide open interaction with and between viewers allows *Stargate SG-1* to be more than just a one-hour fix of action/adventure television per week; it allows the cast, crew, viewers, and fans to interact and contribute. From the writer comes a character, and the actor who portrays that character inspires a viewer to write another story, and that story changes its readers, who tell the producers and the directors, who take those ideas back to the show's writers — somewhere down the line, the actor and the writer of the fan fiction meet, exchange ideas, and come away changed. "It's a fandom where everyone can be involved in some context or another," says Meesh, "no matter whether they are a writer, reader, vidder, or someone with strong opinions on the mythology or politics of the show. " But perhaps Denise says it the most succinctly. "It's widened my scope of knowledge," she said. "I've been exposed to different countries, different people, personalities, and behaviors. My world isn't just one town in the Midwest, it's got tendrils to the four corners of the planet."

And beyond, you could say.

Stargate SG-1 Episode Guide

This episode guide contains "spoilers" for each episode — since this series has been running since 1997 I'm assuming most fans have seen at least to season four; if you don't want the story ruined for you, don't read an episode until after you've seen it.

This is an episode guide that delves more deeply into what's known in some circles as "deep story structure" — that is, what myths and narrative structures are in the background, contributing to what you view — as well as (I hope) satisfying our inner geek with tidbits of science and other arcane areas.

I've avoided two things on purpose. The first is delving too often or obviously into the Sam/Jack subtext of the show — although there are arcs that deal with their relationship, I've stayed away from seeing romantic Sam/Jack moments where they aren't an integral or obvious part of the story. The other thing you won't see much of is nitpicks; if you want to know every gaff and goof of production and/or continuity, see Keith Topping's *Beyond the Gate*, which goes to season six. I do mention some annoying moments, but most of the time, one part willing suspension of disbelief and one part compassion for the large and intricate machinations of a television series lets me sail over things like the shadows of boom mikes appearing, and/or props occasionally disappearing.

Each episode lists at its conclusion some odds and ends of information to round out the view of the story. **Gods & Scientists** explains some background on the myths operating in the episode. Sometimes the motifs are traditional versions of what we call a myth — deities like the Goa'uld, the Asgard, or the Ancients — and sometimes they are contemporary motifs, which we call science or science fiction. Both are used to explain aspects of the universe, which is why they're placed together; it gives two sides of the same narrative coin, so to speak.

Interesting Fact adds something about a location, actor or backstory/production problem that's not necessarily well known. **Why We're Space Monkeys**, a catchphrase that originated in the season-two episode "The Serpent's Lair," highlights the difference between *Stargate SG-1* and other popular shows that have a science or fantasy feel to them. Because *SG-1* is a meld of fantasy and science fiction and treats its material with both humor and seriousness, the series is set apart from other traditional genre shows such as *Star Trek*. Jack O'Neill sums up that attitude in "The Serpent's Lair" when he affectionately calls Daniel Jackson a "space monkey," marveling at and making fun of the archaeologist's ability to escape death. Finally, **Parlez-vous Gate?** is a fun capture of some of the wittier dialogue or scenes that pepper this great series, lines that Gaters often use as shorthand when speaking to each other. (Ya think?)

Below are listed the regular cast members from seasons one to eight.

CAST LIST

MAIN CAST:
Richard Dean Anderson (Rick or RDA) as Jack O'Neill
Michael Shanks as Daniel Jackson
Amanda Tapping as Samantha Carter
Christopher Judge (Chris) as Teal'c
Corin Nemec as Jonas Quinn (season six)

SUPPORTING CAST:
Tony Amendola as Bra'tac (season two)
Carmen Argenziano as Jacob Carter (season two)
JR Bourne as Martouf (season two)

Ronny Cox as Senator Kinsey
Vince Crestejo as Lord Yu (season three)
Alexis Cruz as Skaara
Colin Cunningham as Major Davis (season two)
Don S. Davis (Don Davis) as General Hammond
David DeLuise as Pete Shanahan (season seven)
Neil Denis as Rya'c
Gary Jones as Walter Davis/Technician/Sgt. Harriman
Tom McBeath as Colonel Maybourne
Michael Palffy as Sokar/Anubis (season three)
Anna-Louise Plowman as Sarah/Osiris (season four)
Teryl Rothery as Janet Fraiser
Dan Shea as Sgt. Siler
Cliff Simon as Baal (season five)
Peter Williams as Apophis

STARGATE SG-1 — SEASON ONE
"At the edge of the universe lies a gateway to adventure."

101. Children of the Gods

Original airdate: July 27, 1997
Written by: Jonathan Glassner, Brad Wright
Directed by: Mario Azzopardi

The Stargate program is resurrected after a member of the military is kidnapped by an alien with glowing eyes who appears through the Stargate. Colonel Jack O'Neill is recalled to active service, and, along with Major Kawalsky and Captain Samantha Carter, goes through the Stargate again — hoping to find Daniel Jackson still alive on the other side.

Stargate SG-1 is a television series that developed from a movie. In a way, *SG-1* is exactly like the title of its pilot: a "child" of its godlike parent. But children often differ greatly from their parents, and this pilot episode signals that while the nut didn't fall far from the tree, it definitely had its own growth pattern.

Peter Williams in his favorite T-shirt

The pilot was quite shocking compared to the PG-rated film; nudity on prime-time television! While it was brief and tasteful, the nudity was nonetheless there; ears immediately perked up.

Science fiction and fantasy have always been fringe areas where things like nudity were tolerated — precisely *because* they are on the fringe — but *Stargate SG-1* is more than a purveyor of nudity. It starts out with a bang, not a whimper (and let's hope it ends that way too!), signaling right from the first minute that the writers are going to be tackling large, contentious issues, and they're not necessarily going to do it quietly, either.

The pilot opens with a group of military people playing poker. The line "jack gets a box" — was it on purpose? — resonates strongly on multiple levels. Jack, as in Jack O'Neill, gets handed a Pandora's box in the shape of the Stargate, and whether or not he chooses to open it, and how he chooses to view and implement the contents inside, is up to him and his team. For now, General Hammond relays the military mandate: "to perform reconnaissance, determine threats, and if possible, to make peaceful contact with the peoples of these worlds." The first team, designated SG-1, is headed by Colonel O'Neill. Richard Dean Anderson's Jack O'Neill is not the same as the O'Neil in the movie. Besides the spelling, this Jack is less emotionally tortured, and more easygoing — at least on the surface.

We immediately notice also the makeup of the military, starting with the female Sergeant who was abducted, the female staff populating the control room — and, of course, Captain Samantha Carter. The movie had an almost all-male cast in terms of active military servicemen; the introduction of women into these roles not only portrays the military today more realistically, it also allows developers Brad Wright and Jonathan

Glassner to engage a demographic not often addressed in science fiction, and only stereotypically addressed in fantasy. That demographic is women, aged eighteen to forty-five. It's a demographic that earns a living, expects equal treatment on the job, and successfully negotiates the tougher choices of the working life, whether it be in academics or the Air Force. It's a demographic that has strong ties to feminism — and loyalty to brands and shows that perceive, maintain, and actively assert this reflection in the media. This is another keynote of the difference between *SG-1* and other sci-fi shows.

Daniel Jackson, played in the series by Michael Shanks, literally jumps onto the scene in a memorable moment, defusing a possibly hostile situation with grace and intelligence. It's a personal mandate that he follows very closely throughout the first few seasons, although he, like all the members of SG-1, undergoes some painful growth and change. In the pilot, Shanks does an uncanny impression of James Spader's Daniel Jackson in the movie, but as the series progresses, Shanks wisely leads his character down other avenues, making him seem more human and less a James Spader caricature.

The next big thing we learn is done so neatly and succinctly it's almost overlooked — always a sign of great writing. In a nutshell: the Stargate goes to multiple worlds, not just Abydos. In one sentence, Sam Carter places the entire Stargate universe within reach. She explains, "According to the expanding universe model, all bodies in the universe are constantly moving apart." By leading us up to that point with enough information to make the conclusion ourselves (something which the writers do very well in season one especially), when Captain Carter reveals that crucial piece of information it's all that's needed to get everyone excited about the possibilities of Gate travel — to almost anywhere. The Stargate overcomes entropy.

In the role of Apophis, Peter Williams is stellar. By the time SG-1 learns that the Goa'uld are not one but many, and Daniel Jackson realizes that they are living their lives "right out of the Book of the Dead," the stage has already been set far ahead by Williams' great portrayal of a guy we really love to hate. His pleasure at other people's suffering, his mixed horror and fascination at the messy, fragile human bodies the Goa'uld use as hosts, and his complete arrogance in the face of danger, make for an antagonist worth his weight in gold — even if he does look a little over-the-top in *his* gold lamé number. But Apophis' motivations are clear — he is not omnipotent, he is not a god. He merely possesses superior technology, a ruthless, unquenchable desire to conquer, and a casual disregard for all life but his own.

Closely linked to that idea is the newly faceted life of the Goa'uld's guardsmen. There is unrest and even dissension in the ranks of the guards, and while only Teal'c has the courage to act on this mutiny, we know now that the Jaffa are not mindless, loyal servants, but enslaved like all the other races the Goa'uld have come into contact with.

While a newcomer can wriggle their way into the *Stargate* universe without watching the first episode, it's a shame to miss this great pilot. Viewers may get a little squeamish at some parts, especially the scenes involving Daniel's wife Sha're, who is abducted and then used as a host for Apophis' Goa'uld bride. Even on the second viewing I closed my eyes when the "slime scene" commenced! But it's well worth watching more than once to see all the pieces put into play. And it certainly whets the appetite for more.

Gods & Scientists: We learn that Ra (from the movie *Stargate*) is not a one-of-a-kind alien, but rather a member of a race called the Goa'uld. The Goa'uld are parasites who incubate inside Jaffa until they are mature, then move into human hosts and take them over physically and mentally. This episode introduces us to Apophis, the God of the Underworld, who was Ra's mortal enemy.

Interesting Fact: The original Stargate used in the movie was too damaged when it came to shooting the series (it was stored badly), so a new one was built — but some parts of the old one were incorporated.

Why We're Space Monkeys: Amanda Tapping lives up to her character's ethos by getting the writers to add the line, "It took us fifteen years and three super-computers to MacGyver a system for the Gate on Earth," a tongue-in-cheek reference to Richard Dean Anderson's long-running hit show, *MacGyver*.

Parlez-vous Gate?: Sam geeking out in a totally enthusiastic way, oblivious to Jack's annoyance, is the beginning of a beautiful friendship (and a great deal of angstship, too!).
CARTER: My God . . . look at this. The energy the Gate must release to create a stable wormhole is — is astronomical, to use exactly the right

word. (Reaches out to touch it.) You can actually see the fluctuations in the event horizon.

(Annoyed, O'Neill shoves her through the wormhole, then steps through himself.)

102. The Enemy Within

Original airdate: August 1, 1997
Written by: Brad Wright
Directed by: Dennis Berry

Major Kawalsky battles Earth's newest enemy from the inside instead of heading up a new SG team. Teal'c comes under scrutiny as an alien — and a possible threat.

"The Enemy Within" sets out two of the major problems that plague and occasionally surprise the SG-1 team throughout the first season; one is the Goa'uld, driven (and, according to them, destined) to conquer any and all inhabitable planets they find; and the other is the United States government — in particular certain bodies of it, which undermine and devalue from the inside the work that the SG teams do, seeking to control all aspects of Stargate Command (SGC) for their own shadowy purposes — much as the Goa'uld symbiote attempts to take over and control its host human. It's a nice use of irony by the writers, as the very people shouting the loudest about the Goa'uld threat are the ones who act as the same sort of device within their own government; subversives who answer to few and do as they please, regardless of things like dignity for their fellow humans or the advancement of peace for all beings.

The Goa'uld, we learn, rule by force. An early scene highlights their egotistical and maniacal nature as the queasy sound of bodies hitting the protective iris of Earth's Stargate prompts Jack to observe, "Like bugs hitting a windshield." There are also some upfront, tongue-in-cheek nods to narratives that seem fantastical. Colonel Kennedy acts as the viewer when Jack says, in response to Kennedy's comment on the Chulak mission, "Thanks. What was your favorite part?", again playing up the idea that the fantastical settings and places beyond the Stargate *seem* unbelievable to the modern, scientific mind, but are nonetheless real.

The Jaffa Teal'c's guiding ideology is put up front, as he narrates the plight of the worlds which have been used and then abandoned by the Goa'uld. His moral fortitude shines as he relates how he feels, and the viewer does not hesitate to sympathize with what must have been a terrible decision for him, to leave all that he has known behind for an idea of freedom. His staunch loyalty and personal code endear him to O'Neill, who says, "Teal'c, I saw you stand up to a God. . . . I learned everything I needed to know to trust you." Teal'c's individualistic stance is also typically a reflection of American ideals, that one person can make a difference.

Richard Dean Anderson very clearly sets up in O'Neill the kind of hero television viewers can instantly recognize — a moral man inside the boundaries of an establishment that doesn't necessarily abide by its own code of conduct. This antiestablishment, antiauthoritarian character type is prevalent in many modern stories; the "good cop in a corrupt system." RDA is constantly and quietly building his character's motivations until we start to expect — before he even does or says anything — a trustworthy if not always communicative leader for his team.

Jack O'Neill is a military man, but the most significant difference between this Jack and the Jack from the movie is that Rick brings out more of his character's humor. There is still a strong link between the movie and the television show, however; in both, the colonel's son has been killed by his own service weapon, a tragedy that prompted Jack to quit the Air Force in the first place. So when O'Neill returns to active duty, he is very much a man who has seen the worst that life can offer, a man unwilling to play the political game that threatens to hurt or, worse, cloud what the SGC is trying to do. He's lived quite happily without the Air Force in his life, and his return will be shaped by he himself, and not by games: Jack takes care of his team first, and everything else afterward. A brief but important scene highlights this: when his friend Kawalsky is given his own team to lead, he passes by O'Neill and the two men exchange a smile, one that delivers in a second the background story of two men who've devoted their lives in service to their country, who have bonded in war as well as peace.

The least used character here is Daniel Jackson, who, except for his initial scenes explaining the Dial Home Device, only ever appears to moon over Sha're. A bit clumsy; but in later episodes Daniel picks up, thankfully.

While Jay Acovone, as Major Kawalsky, has one of the most ignoble dramatic scenes I've ever seen on television (strapped face down on a table with his boxers showing — compared with the superb acting

Acovone did, switching seamlessly from human to repulsively egotistical Goa'uld symbiote, it seemed very undignified and almost condescending), this episode puts most of the main characters of the *Stargate* universe into play in a way that is both exciting and full of dramatic tension. If the Goa'uld can infect any human, what are the chances that any member of the SGC going through that Gate can get infected? The use of emotion as a conduit for the Goa'uld symbiote is both chilling and suggestive of what happens when we "lose our cool," allowing a sort of monster to appear. There are other questions as well — how will the SGC cope with the new information they've received? Will Colonel Kennedy attempt revenge? If there are as many Goa'uld as Teal'c says, how often will they encounter them? All these story questions and more are clearly outlined, and

Jay Acovone's character Kawalsky made the jump from movie to series, if only for a few episodes (ALBERT L. ORTEGA)

although the next couple of episodes stumble out of the block, eventually the season gets its feet back under it and moves along with good stories and pacing.

Gods & Scientists: We learn that there are many Goa'uld, not just Ra. Teal'c was a member of the honor guard for Apophis before turning against the wishes of his master and joining the humans in their fight for freedom from slavery and domination. Teal'c tells Jack and General Hammond that Jaffa legend tells of a "first world," where the descendents of all the worlds the Goa'uld dominate came from. The descendents are called the Tau'ri. Colonel Kennedy deduces that, since life evolved on Earth (according to Darwinian theory), their planet must be the famed place of legend.

Cosmogonic myths (also known as creation myths) serve to distinguish between the sacred and the mundane, and they exist in almost every culture. They are the defining line between the known and unknown, and are used as the yardstick for reality. Some creation myths use patterns of emergence (creation that comes from within the earth over time), others a supreme being (usually put above or outside the earth), and still others assume cosmic parents (a combination of both earth and sky). By positing Earth as the seeding ground for the evolution of humans on thousands of planets, *SG-1* partakes of its own creation myth based on the idea of emergence, the transplantation of humans.

Interesting Fact: We learn how to spell Teal'c's name. "That's Teal'c, with an apostrophe - T-e-a-l apostrophe c," says Jack imperiously to the stenographer accompanying Colonel Kennedy.

Why We're Space Monkeys: Of all the people in the complex, it is Sam Carter who seems to be the most aggressive in securing the SGC against the Goa'uld's attacks — and she's not afraid to get physical about it, either. The writers nicely showcase the strength and intelligence of all the team members here.

Parlez-vous Gate?: On the whiteboard behind Sam and Daniel in the first scenes you see the words "Dial Home Device," or DHD as it's known afterward. The squat, round pedestal with a red centre is the recall device used to power and direct the Stargate. It is because Earth did not have one of these devices that the Gate remained inoperable for so long, and why the Goa'uld did not return, since they could not leave once arriving and it took too long to get there by ship to make the trip worthwhile, apparently.

103. Emancipation

Original airdate: August 8, 1997
Written by: Katharyn Powers
Directed by: Jeff Woolnough

SG-1 encounters a race that resembles Earth's ancient Mongolians. Carter is in danger when she refuses to abide by local custom.

You know that feeling you get when you're in the middle of a very embarrassing moment, like tripping on the way to the bathroom on a first date? Welcome to "Emancipation." This episode completely veered off the Goa'uld threat thread, intending, one would surmise, to show that it's not all about fighting the bad, snakey aliens. This episode is the Ford Edsel of *Stargate*'s first season. As one online fan remarked, "It's a good thing this wasn't the first episode I saw, otherwise I doubt I would have continued watching it." Most fans of Stargate place this episode in the we-don't-talk-about-it category.

The writing in this episode is dismal, which is a surprise, given the writer, Katharyn Powers, whose other *SG-1* offerings, like "Thor's Chariot" and "Crossroads," are much more evenhanded and less . . . well, cringeworthy. Powers is also the executive story consultant for all of season one.

After trying so hard to make a fair, equitable impression with characterization, situation, and interaction, this episode fails miserably to move anything forward as it staggers over every single tattered, sexist cliché known in an effort to . . . what? Develop the character of Samantha Carter as super soldier with a heart of gold? Show that the other members of SG-1 are so horrified at the thought of sexism in the world (which apparently they never encounter on Earth), that they fail to see its repercussions *every single time* it comes up? And then there's the fact that this inane episode is kluged together by about three sentences at the beginning and end, ostensibly as the team searches for a miracle anaesthetic to bring back to Earth. It's hard to believe that one episode could alienate feminists of either sex, science fiction fans, and martial artists all in one go.

Any martial skill involves hundreds of hours of training, dedication, and commitment. Sadly, this is glossed over quite regularly on television. "Emancipation" is no exception. The "to the death" knife fight at the end of the episode (did no one think to ask the rules in a society that has done nothing but boast of its bloodthirsty ways since the beginning?), was another teeth-gritting moment, as it brought to mind another of my pet peeves in television — the badly choreographed and executed fight scene. Camera angles were used so sloppily that the three gaping feet between the actors were clearly visible, ruining the dramatic tension of the moment and making the actors seem clumsy. That clumsiness wasn't helped at all by the execution of movements by Cary-Hiroyuki Tagawa and Amanda Tapping. It would be better to see a stunt double who knows what they're doing rather than a clearly struggling actor with minimal physical training who, at one point, almost falls on top of her opponent after foot-sweeping him. That kind of awkwardness pulls me right out of the story — which in this case I was working really hard to stay in anyway.

There was one glimmer of redemption, something which makes us, as viewers, feel sympathetic; it was raining. As in, raining the way it might do in everyday life; not for furthering the plot or as an effect, but raining because hey, it rains when military people go on missions, and they have to slog through and deal with it and meet their objective anyway. We wait for the bus in the rain, why shouldn't SG-1 have to negotiate peace or settle clan wars in the rain?

Gods & Scientists: We don't meet any new Goa'uld here, although they may be obliquely mentioned by Moughal when he speaks of the "old laws" that were put in place to protect women against "the demons" who brought the Shavadai to the planet. Sam refers to her tent as a "yurt," which is the Russian word for the ingenious collapsing tent that the ancient Mongolians devised — the Mongolian word was *ger* (pronounced gair). The tent was collapsible and light, because the Mongols were a nomadic tribe, and the tent doorways, as depicted in the episode, were brightly colored and always faced south.

Why We're Space Monkeys: One funny line from the almost entirely silent Teal'c stands out: "What is an Oprah?" he asks, as the writers poke a little fun at modern English's penchant for turning proper nouns into common nouns.

Parlez-vous Gate?: (As the rest of the team enters her tent to find Captain Carter "suitably" attired):
CARTER: Daniel, find me an anthropologist that dresses like this and I will *eat* this headdress.

104. The Broca Divide

Original airdate: August 15, 1997
Written by: Jonathan Glassner
Directed by: William Gereghty

SG-1 travels to the "Land of Light," where the divide between light and dark can also mean life and death.

"The Broca Divide" is the next stumble out of the block mentioned in "The Enemy Within," but it contained enough good dialogue, usually involving Jack, to make it worth watching once or twice.

One of the greatest themes in the Western literary canon is the narrative of the constant battle between dark and light, good and evil. "The Broca Divide" picks up this thread of how both dark and light reside within us, as they do outside us. The title, taken from the name of Pierre Paul Broca, a surgeon (although Carter identifies him as an anthropologist), seems also a pun-like homophone: "broca" sounds very close to "broken," and it's a nice allusion to the broken alliance between the Touched and Untouched.

Daniel aptly compares the Touched to a colony of lepers; much of our lives are spent either ignoring or banishing the parts of ourselves we wish we didn't have or don't want to admit having to a dark place — whether it be hidden in the subconscious, projecting it on to someone else, or channeled into activities where they can be safely released. When they arise in situations that aren't necessarily socially acceptable — like Sam's attempt to seduce Jack in the locker room — the results can be dangerous or even have violent repercussions. But it's oh so fun to watch Jack's wide-eyed *wuh?* expression as he plays the innocent bystander with satiric zeal.

Jackson says with disgust that the Untouched abandon members of their society when they become Touched, but Teal'c reminds him that they have done the same thing to infected members back on Earth — including Carter and O'Neill, who, once judged "not fit for duty," were summarily locked in isolation.

Teal'c, whose symbiote protects him against almost all illnesses, is a further refinement of the idea of the divide or interplay between light and dark — because he houses darkness (a kind of Touched) within him in the form of the Goa'uld symbiote, he is immune to the pathogen. But those members who strive to live in "The Light" at all times, like Carter, O'Neill, and even General Hammond, are not immune. Daniel Jackson succumbs eventually to the virus, perhaps pointing out that even those most loyal to the light are vulnerable, while Dr. Fraiser's immunity could be explained by the fact that she deals with death (and thus darkness) every day.

Scientifically, this one can get you into some rather heated discussions, depending on your view of physics. For instance, it seems extremely improbable to have a biosphere in operation that allows for a dark/light divide as sharp as it is on P3X-797 (although some speculative fiction writers, such as Dave Duncan, have tackled this issue as well). But as far as recasting and reimagining myth, "The Broca Divide" doesn't hesitate to take on large questions and then showcase different facets of an ancient, pervasive problem through different characters.

Gods & Scientists: While we don't meet any new gods, we are told of the Hylk'sha, translated by Teal'c as the Gods of the Underworld, or evil gods. There are many versions of underworld gods in mythology, from Pluto of the Greek pantheon to Hel of the Norse gods. An underworld association did not necessarily equate evilness, however: Pluto merely drew straws with Zeus and Poseidon for rule over the sky, seas, and underworld.

Why We're Space Monkeys: Jack's tussle with Sam was the start of much "shipper" action (fan discussion of a possible relationship between two characters). The kiss that started it all — and, unlike many other sci-fi shows, it's the woman who starts it. O'Neill's lip-locked dialogue with her in this scene is hilarious, even if the tanktop worn by Sam is eye-rollingly obvious.

Parlez-vous Gate?: Jack asking Teal'c to let him out of isolation calling, "Lucy, I'm home!"
O'NEILL: No, no, no, I'm fine. I'm back to being myself. Just open up.
TEAL'C: I cannot be certain that you are back to being yourself. You referred to me as "Lucy."

105. The First Commandment

Original airdate: August 22, 1997
Written by: Robert Cooper
Directed by: Dennis Berry

After the SG-9 team fails to return from a mission, the SG-1 team is sent to retrieve them.

In terms of story arc, the writers in "The First Commandment" start to attend to background stories, fleshing out the characters of *SG-1* without pandering to any one character in particular. One of the reasons people enjoy *SG-1* is that team dynamic, which is carried from episode to episode, especially in the early seasons. There are the occasional episodes that focus more specifically on one character; the "Jack" or "Daniel" episodes (see "Cold Lazarus" and "Fire and Water" from the first season), but SG-1 is most often treated as a team, and each member's story is interwoven with his or her teammates'. In these early episodes, the writers often thread in this information within the mission itself.

In "The First Commandment," we again are given tidbits of information about the main threat to Earth — the Goa'uld. We learn that after enslaving the peoples they relocate, the Goa'uld abandon them (Teal'c mentioned this in "The Enemy Within" as well) once their usefulness has come to an end. On some planets, the Goa'uld use their slaves as miners, sending them down into dangerous, inhospitable places. On worlds like the one shown in this episode, once the mineral they are searching for is tapped out, the Goa'uld leave. The casualness with which the alien race uses others for its purposes has been alluded to in several episodes by now, without us ever having seen a Goa'uld since the pilot. It's an excellent use of suspense: when we finally do meet another Goa'uld that is not immature or within the body of a Jaffa, we are sufficiently versed in their traits that we do not underestimate what otherwise looks like a steroided version of an inchworm.

Meanwhile, some serious Carter background is being snuck in through snippets of conversation. Already the camera is highlighting some Sam/Jack subtext, such as when Sam and Daniel converse about her past and she mentions that her taste in men isn't always the best, at which point the camera cuts quickly to a shot of Jack. More telling than that, though, is the calm, cool way in which Captain Carter acknowledges and doesn't shy away from her past and her relationship with Jonas Hanson.

Although they are not well drawn, the ideas in this episode are played out against the people of the planet, simply called the Cave Dwellers. Like the people in Plato's allegory of the cave, they exist only to name shadows. In this case, the shadows they name are false gods — whether Captain Hanson or the Goa'uld.

Jonas, the leader of SG-9, seems almost casually insane. At several points, especially when he's talking with Carter, he seems to drop the persona of insanity, in an earnest plea for the people he feels honor-bound to protect. This "means to an end" idea is seen in daily life as well, from child-rearing to warmongering, and "The First Commandment" seems to suggest that, regardless of the ends, willingly encouraging others in false beliefs is more often the result of egotism than altruism.

Unfortunately, there is little Daniel interaction except when he acts as a foil for other characters; it's particularly fun to watch him tell Teal'c to smile and look friendly, and even funnier if you have ever seen an interview with actor Christopher Judge — he is *always* smiling! Perhaps because the movie was so heavily based on the character of Daniel Jackson, these early episodes seem to be concentrating more acutely on Jack, Sam, and Teal'c. It's not until "The Torment of Tantalus" and "Fire and Water" that we get to see more of the Daniel Jackson as Michael Shanks portrays him.

The episode is sprinkled with biblical allusions, and it's a good place to start questioning the idea of "having none above him." "The First Commandment" plays with the idea of blasphemy: if the Goa'uld are not gods, and if Jonas is not a god . . . then what is a god? Who decides what a god is? Religions of all denominations abound with stories of gods who demanded sacrifice and tested their followers, all for a larger cause. If people are happy at the end, and life made easier — is the cause of that happiness then the unwritten first commandment?

While the writing in this episode, especially the use of metaphors, causes some confusion — are we happy or sad that Jonas failed in his attempt to "better" the Cave Dwellers? — this episode was worth watching mostly for background information on Sam, the insight into the mind and habits of the Goa'uld, and the potential extent to which Teal'c's past privileged position could be used.

Gods & Scientists: It's the Christian god who is mentioned in this episode; no Goa'uld gods are mentioned by name. A truncated version of the story of Abraham is told, where Abraham nearly sacrifices his son to show his devotion to God. Abraham is known as the first man of faith in Christianity.

Interesting Fact: Roger C. Cross (who plays Lt. Conner of SG-9), also appeared in season two's "Spirits," and worked with Amanda Tapping again in 2001 in the movie *The Void*. He was also in the canceled television series *First Wave*, which ended in 2001.

Why We're Space Monkeys: Sam was engaged to Jonas Hanson but broke off the engagement. She self-deprecatingly refers to herself as having a "soft spot for the lunatic fringe." For better or worse, this is the beginning of Carter's so-called "black widow syndrome," in which every man she gets involved with eventually dies, usually in the same episode that she meets him.

Parlez-vous Gate?: The ubiquitous military food poke:
DANIEL (eating his rations): This tastes like chicken.
CARTER: So what's wrong with that?
DANIEL: . . . It's macaroni and cheese.

106. Cold Lazarus

Original airdate: August 29, 1997
Written by: Jeff King
Directed by: Kenneth J. Girotti

SG-1 returns from a planet with crystals to study, unknowingly bringing with them a duplicate of Jack O'Neill.

"Cold Lazarus" is a poignant episode that is one of the best showcases of Rick's talent from season one. It opens with SG-1 doing a recon of a planet where they come across what Daniel assumes is a place of celebration. What he realizes later in the episode is that it is in fact a burial ground — from which a different O'Neill, resurrected from his own past, emerges to travel back to Earth with the rest of SG-1 in an attempt to heal certain aspects of himself and his past. This play on the biblical story of Lazarus, whom Jesus revived four days after death, is a strong backbone, which once again shows the cast and crew are not afraid to tackle heavy subjects on a galactic scale.

Writer Jeff King (who has also written for *Due South* and *The Outer Limits*) approaches the idea of emotional healing by introducing an alien who masquerades as Jack — like one side or facet of a crystal. Is it an accident that behind the alien Jack in his son Charlie's bedroom there hangs a poster about crystals?

Sam, when she is surveying the crystals, mentions that they are not volcanic in makeup — in other words, they didn't form through heat, but rather pressure. Crystals usually break along particular planes — this is called "cleavage" — because of the way they are formed. The use of crystals is a great way to allude to Colonel O'Neill, as his usual persona is flip and sarcastic, and not as serious and heated as, say, Daniel's; but when he does break, it's usually over the same few things. And one of those things is the violent, accidental death of his son, for which he blames himself — it is a 'cleavage' in his life.

The idea that Jack O'Neill is reluctant to show emotion, or hides his emotions behind a mask of flippancy, is reflected in the title of the episode. Brad Wright agreed and supported Richard Dean Anderson's decision to develop this side of the character. "What we've done is we've covered the fact that the Jack O'Neill character has had that experience; it's a dark part of his past that actually helps define why he is kind of a fun, happy-go-lucky kind of guy all of the time." Rick said in an interview, "As portrayed by Mr. Russell [Jack] was a little more stoic than I think I could endure over a long period of time." This is not to say, however, that Jack is *always* happy-go-lucky, and episodes like "Cold Lazarus" are foils to the more often seen smartaleck Jack O'Neill.

Another long story arc that begins in "Cold Lazarus" is the idea of energy as a life force that doesn't necessarily only exist in a physical form. We don't see this thread taken up again until season three, in the episode "Maternal Instinct," so I won't delve into it more than to say that a second viewing of "Cold Lazarus," in light of later seasons, will give fans a definite shock of recognition.

Gods & Scientists: No Goa'uld are named in this episode, but they are, once again, referred to as destroyers of a civilization. The entity within the crystal refers to itself as "the Unity" — crystals are derived from a set of atoms called a unit cell, which is repeated exactly throughout the material. Just as creation myths attempt to make sense of reality and how it came about, myths of annihilation or destruction try to look forward to the end of reality. Luckily, many destruction myths and stories often point to motifs of rebirth, such as the biblical story of the Flood.

Interesting Fact: Dan Shea is something of an all-round man in the *SG-1* universe. In addition to playing the character of Sgt. Siler, he also works behind the scenes as the stunt co-ordinator, and he's RDA's stunt double.

Why We're Space Monkeys: Teal'c, sturdy warrior that he is, does not hesitate to drop the macho image in favor of some firepower. After watching television in his quarters, he embarks for the first time to the world outside the SGC (through a regular door rather than a Stargate), where the Jaffa warrior calmly tells General Hammond that he's taking his staff weapon because he's quite sure he'll need it.

Parlez-vous Gate?: Sam and Daniel, looking very guilty in the Gate room after being asked what they're doing:
TEAL'C: You received permission for me to fire my staff weapon in the Gate room?
CARTER: Oh, yeah.
DANIEL: Absolutely.

107. The Nox

Original airdate: September 12, 1997
Written by: Hart Hanson
Directed by: Charles Correll

SG-1 goes in search of stealth technology, and learns that ordnances have many forms.

On the surface, this episode seems a little on the light side, almost like a breather after the heavier fare of "Cold Lazarus" and "The First Commandment," especially since the opening scenes seem to almost mimic a children's show, with simple, fantastic sets and lilting music. And the . . . hair . . . of the Nox is somewhat disturbing to watch. But "The Nox" is much more than its surface appearance, and anyone who comes away from this episode without the larger implications of the story might be one of the "young ones" that Anteaus refers to.

Apophis makes an appearance; it's the first we've seen him since "Children of the Gods." We learn that he has a new First Prime named Shak'l, and that he usually has a personal guard of three to four Jaffa with him.

The forces that have brought both Apophis and SG-1 there are large, and dangerous. Apophis seeks technology that will aide him in defeating other Goa'uld and conquering more planets, while SG-1, after being harangued by Secretary of Defense David Swift, are in a crisis themselves, determined to find *some* technology to help in the fight against the Goa'uld — and to keep them going through the Stargate.

When Anteaus tells SG-1 to leave, and "take [their] ways with [them]," a complex series of events is set in motion. Even when they work together very well as a team, SG-1 still manage to make more of a mess of things than be a help. They blunder through simple problems by advancing com-

Armin Shimerman, minus the hair from "The Nox" (ALBERT L. ORTEGA)

plex solutions; when Daniel mentions that a surefire way to stop the Goa'uld from infiltrating the planet is to bury the Gate, the response is stunningly simple. It would stop the Goa'uld from coming — but then they would also know that there was something there worth coming for.

SG-1's persistent belief that the Nox are not capable of defending themselves against the Goa'uld seems altruistic. Teal'c, feeling the most culpable, knowing well the ways in which the Goa'uld enslave, tells Anteaus, "It is our way that the strong defend the weak."

Apophis looks more paranoid than lethal and cautious when we first see him, but he dispatches the SG-1 team with brutal efficiency, and displays the kind of sneering confidence and domination we know and hate in the Goa'uld. Apophis is a good example of the template we will come to expect of that alien race. Actor Peter Williams' ability to create a really hateable villain is evident. (He's still a popular guest at conventions all over the world; lately he's even being DJing some of them.)

A few details rankled: Lya has something that looks suspiciously like bananas in her basket — sort of out of place in beautiful British Columbia (pardon me, the planet of the Nox). And fashioning a short bow, even in the space of an hour or two, seems more than a little miraculous. But perhaps the adage "necessity is the mother of invention" is put to good use here. Certainly, as Daniel notes, the rash acts and leaping to conclusions that humans seem to be really good at are the same traits that would make them lousy Nox. But the message is clear — weakness isn't necessarily merely a physical trait, and neither is strength.

Gods & Scientists: The Nox, perhaps loosely connected to the ancient goddess Nyx, Nox being the Roman transformation of that name, are a fairy-like race of beings. Nyx was portrayed as winged — much like the creature SG-1 was hunting in this episode, whom they mistakenly believe to have the ability to become invisible — and is said to have traveled on a two-horse chariot drawing darkness across the sky. Like the Nox of the *Stargate* universe, this goddess was very ancient and wise — and she was the daughter of Chaos. "Nox" also means "night" in Latin.

Interesting Fact: Terry David Mulligan is familiar to many Canadians as a former veejay on the national music channel, MuchMusic.

Why We're Space Monkeys: The character of Teal'c is fascinating throughout the series, but this episode is where he is first denounced publicly for turning against Apophis, who calls him "shol'va," or betrayer. He replies "Dal shakka mel" — "I die free." Teal'c's battle as First Prime to Apophis comes up again and again, as the former servant of the gods faces his past. Spock never had to do that.

Parlez-vous Gate?: Teal'c explains their quarry to the rest of the team.
TEAL'C: They are most vulnerable when they hover.
DANIEL: Hover? You mean like a hummingbird?
TEAL'C: . . . with teeth.

108. Brief Candle

Original airdate: September 19, 1997
Story by: Steven Barnes
Teleplay by: Katharyn Powers
Directed by: Mario Azzopardi

On Argos, Jack discovers that life is definitely too short.

While "Brief Candle" is one of the most roll-your-eyes episodes of the first season, it's still important in terms of long-term story arcs. In retrospect, it seems almost as if the love interest in this episode was thrown in to sell the technology talk and the idea of humans as lab rats. On repeated viewings, the idea of the replicators, nanotechnology, and the use of races as science experiments definitely stand out — a story arc that comes up more than once in later episodes. In "Brief Candle," the Goa'uld have tried to pull a fast one on nature by attempting to cheat death and fabricate better, longer-lasting hosts: in the end, the experiment is thwarted.

The title (an obvious metaphor for life's brevity) is an allusion to Shakespeare's *Macbeth*, another tale of an extremely arrogant man who thought he could get away with anything, including making unwitting men do his bidding: "And all our yesterdays' have lighted fools / The way to dusty death. Out, out, brief candle!"

Rick does a good job going through a process of rapid aging, although his voice modulations are a little grating at times. After his initial, err, mis-judgment with Kynthia, he does his best to be an honorable man, answering her direct, embarrassing questions as honestly as he can, while also trying to minimize any damage to her feelings. This is a part of Jack O'Neill that never goes away; while he can be a right bastard to Goa'uld, Replicators, and nasty government types, his personal dealings with people who are doing nothing other than living their lives is warm, caring, and oddly humanistic — I say oddly because he's often seen deriding Daniel for having the very same instincts.

For the first time we see a worshipper directly addressing an absent deity, also known as "apostrophe." While we've gotten lots of 'I am your god' stuff so far in *SG-1*, this is a more personal look at the individual con-fronting his or her beliefs without the intermediary of a sneering Goa'uld. Sadly, it's also an illustration of the blindness of the people of Pelops, and a strong case against the Goa'uld. The alien parasite just doesn't give a damn about anything other than itself and its power base. A Goa'uld is more concerned with the power games played among other Goa'uld than about its so-called subjects.

It's also the first time we see nanotechnology, which is very important later in the series. Nanotechnology is more than just a buzzword; it's a very new technology that uses incredibly small (*nanos* is Greek for "dwarf") particles. Objects that are said to be nano are much smaller than the width of a hair, for instance. Because of their smallness, they can exhibit different properties than larger material. "Brief Candle" definitely invokes a science fiction ideal here because it posits this new technology working within a human body, although Trekkies may be familiar with it already from the "nanoprobes" that the Borg use.

One of the reasons this episode may be hard to watch is that the writers seem to be working out some continuity issues. For instance, at the end of the episode — when the team knows all they need to know about the threat the nanotechs represent — why do they come through the Stargate as if they're expecting nuclear war, and then in the next scene they're lounging casually on the steps? Still, we do get more chilling background on the nature of the Goa'uld, and their ability to play not just one set of gods, but many — whatever they need to achieve their megalomaniacal ends.

Gods & Scientists: The planet's people worship the Goa'uld god Pelops. The descendent of a Greek half-god, Pelops was the son of Tantalus. Up until now, the Goa'uld gods have all been taken from Egyptian mythology; here, the writers expand the pantheon to include other mythologies. This same lineage is taken up in the later episode, "The Torment of Tantalus." According to the Greek myth, Pelops was killed by his father and served up to the gods for his arrogance in having tried to cheat them.

Why We're Space Monkeys: Contrary to most of the sci-fi canon, it's Daniel who delivers the baby, not Sam. Also, Jack's foray into the realm of physical pleasure actually has consequences instead of being a merely titillating dalliance. It's pretty funny to see Jack's bashfulness when the rest of the Argosians traipse in to go to sleep and he remembers he's naked.

Parlez-vous Gate?: Jack makes an extremely ironic statement in light of the rest of the episode.
O'NEILL: Yeah, sure, have an apple. What could happen?

109. Thor's Hammer

Original airdate: September 26, 1997
Written by: Katharyn Powers
Directed by: Brad Turner

SG-1 travels to Cimmeria, where Teal'c and Jack are abducted by a mysterious device called Thor's Hammer. Sam and Daniel attempt to rescue them with the help of Gairwyn and Kendra.

In "Thor's Hammer" we see the show really start to come together, especially in terms of character development — human and nonhuman. This episode starts to delve into the group dynamic in earnest, and tackles what happens when SG-1 gets split up — how do they work together when not physically together? It also pairs the team off in a way that hasn't been done before; one military personnel with one nonmilitary.

Daniel Jackson identifies two main factions of what he refers to as "star gods" — tyrants who use their advanced technology to enslave people, and what Daniel characterizes as "culture bearers," those races who use technology to benefit humans. The two races, the Goa'uld and the Asgard, respectively, take the forms of two different mythological streams, and employ different strategies. The Goa'uld co-opt the Egyptian mythology (as seen from the movie *Stargate* onward), concentrating on tyranny, while the Asgard use Norse mythology, preferring a more benevolent, protectorate role, with minimal influence on the societies they oversee. In particular, the Norse god Thor, in legend a warrior god, is used by the Asgard as their symbol for protected peoples among the planets they rule.

"Thor's Hammer" is a great episode in that it points out the ways in which myths can be interwoven, even though we think they are "worlds" apart. Norse mythology sets the Etons as their mortal enemy; Daniel suggests that the Etons are merely the Norse personification of the Goa'uld.

Jackson also suggests that the Goa'uld are merely using the Stargate and did not, in fact, build it. This parallels ancient Egyptian nobility historically as well, who in antiquity used slaves to build what they needed, and often imported technology from other societies. The Goa'uld are not builders or explorers by inclination; but they are warmongers and in that sense are extremely . . . dedicated to their cause.

"Thor's Hammer" accomplishes a great deal of excellent character development as well. The dynamic of SG-1 learning to cope as a team is stressed by their separation. Each member has a strong driving force behind them: Sam and Jack maintain the original military mandate; Teal'c is still struggling with his sense of guilt at having served the Goa'uld for many years; and Daniel is focused on any and all means to find and save his wife Sha're.

This episode also revises some stereotypes, reversing a few of our own present-day myths — like the myths of beauty and gendered roles. Early on Sam and Daniel encounter a woman named Kendra, who was taken as a host by the Goa'uld, although she uses Thor's Hammer to rid herself of her symbiote when she first comes to the world. When Daniel asks her what her childhood was like, Kendra replies sadly, "I was beautiful." The myth of beauty is reversed — a beautiful appearance can be a bad, not a good, thing. Later, another turnaround occurs, when Sam and Daniel are arguing over continuing to allow Kendra to guide them to the entrance of the labyrinth, where Teal'c and Jack are trapped. Sam's concern is that Kendra is deceiving them. Daniel says heatedly, "Haven't you ever had a feeling that made absolutely no logical sense, and it turned out to be right?" Sam's answering look is skeptical. Again, the usual script — that women are somehow more intuitive than men — is reversed, since Sam is shown to be the linear thinker, while Daniel follows his intuition.

A poignant moment (but too quickly glossed over) is when Jack hands Daniel Teal'c's staff weapon to disable Thor's Hammer so that Teal'c can get out alive. Daniel, who is excited because of the Hammer's ability to remove Goa'uld symbiotes (and thus possibly save his lost wife), is torn between his hopes and the reality of the situation. He asks Jack, "Do you know what this means?" Jack sums up the moment very succinctly when he says, "Teal'c is here now." It seems unnecessarily mean of Jack to make Daniel fire the weapon that destroys the Hammer (he could have done it himself, or asked Carter to do it). But when Daniel hesitates, aiming the staff weapon at the Hammer, Jack says, "Come on," under his breath in an almost pleading tone, as though, by pushing Daniel past his immediate, all-consuming thought of saving his wife — as painful as that moment will be — Jackson will become a better team member, and see the bigger picture in the fight against the Goa'uld. Colonel O'Neill may often seem ruthless, especially in the early seasons, but this scene highlights his dedication to a team that is strong and cohesive — mentally as well as physically.

Gods & Scientists: The term "System Lords" is used for the first time, to refer to the collection of Goa'uld who have divvied up the galaxy with the Asgard. The Asgard are introduced, in particular Thor, who is the supreme commander of the Asgard fleet. The Asgard and the Goa'uld apparently have some sort of understanding about Cimmeria. Thor is probably the most well-known of the Norse gods.

Interesting Fact: The voice for the Unas is provided by James Earl Jones, who was also the voice of Darth Vader in the *Star Wars* trilogy. Gairwyn's greeting of Sam and Daniel near the beginning of the episode may be an oblique in-joke to this end: after a long assessing look at the two SG members, she says, "You're a little short for gods." James Earl Jones also played the main villain in *Conan the Barbarian*, the first *Conan* movie with Arnold Schwarzenegger — who, incidentally, turned into a giant snake for the climax. Conan the character is known as "Conan of Cimmeria," as it was his home land.

Why We're Space Monkeys: When SG-1 comes through the Gate they are greeted by laughing Cimmerians who look rather obviously more primitive than the SG team — sort of an odd welcome for heroes. Once again the preconception of who is superior gets dumped on its head. The Cimmerians are happy, and do not see their civilization as inferior. Quite a change from the usual posturing — take us to your leader, we're here to save you — normally associated with science fiction shows.

Parlez-vous Gate?: (while regarding the Unas as it advances on them):
TEAL'C: Are you considering the same tactic as I?
O'NEILL: Teal'c, the cliché is, "Are you thinking what I'm thinking?" And the answer is yes.

110. The Torment of Tantalus

Original airdate: October 3, 1997
Written by: Robert Cooper
Directed by: Jonathan Glassner

Daniel's desires are thwarted when SG-1 explores a world not shown on the Abydos cartouche. One of the instigators of the Stargate program, Catherine Langford, gets a surprise.

This is an episode about torment. I know, you're thinking, "Really? It's not like it's in the *title* or anything." But in the *Stargate* universe, the title is a great way to approach episodes — they'll give clues as to which mythology you're working with (usually Egyptian, but also Mayan, Incan, Norse, and Native American), and help to round out less obvious themes. Tantalus, as explained by the elderly Dr. Ernest Littlefield when they rescue him, was a Greek king — in fact the son of Zeus. Tantalus' son, Pelops, has already been seen in "Brief Candle."

Daniel's observation, "It's hot in here," is a key to this episode —

everyone has their own private anguishes, things that make them, literally, hot under the collar. "The Torment of Tantalus" isn't just about the torment of Catherine, who worked for years on the Stargate program through miles of red tape, ignorance, and misogyny, only to have it wrested from her once the military deemed it worthwhile. It's also a torment for Sam, who is unable to figure out how the DHD works, saying that it would take years to figure out — and we get the feeling that she would love to spend her time doing so, but it never seems to be top priority.

Every time O'Neill walks through the Gate, he's hoping to see something worth taking back to help in the fight against the Goa'uld; instead he always seems to find people who need help, and/or tantalizing technology that's broken or can't be figured out. Daniel constantly reaches into the future (or the past), skimming history for brief seconds before it's snatched right out of his hands — as in this case, when the power source for the Gate is destroyed (which, interestingly, leaves dangling wires much like those left from Ernest's lifeline the first time he went through the Gate in 1945), and they try to use the power of the pedestal that houses what could be "the common language of the universe" instead. Although this scheme doesn't work and they are instead saved by Jack's Benjamin Franklin–inspired idea (can anyone say *MacGyver*?), the end result is that Daniel, standing in for the mythological figure Tantalus, learns to be content, or at least *more* content, with the knowledge he brings back, knowledge that he is able to share. In this way he is unlike Ernest, who spent fifty years stranded in Heliopolis learning secrets of the universe that he could never share.

The relationship between Jack and Daniel in this episode is superb; Jack's patience is at an end as Daniel refuses to see the danger of his situation, but the colonel still tempers his sense of 'getting things done' with understanding how important the chamber of language is to the archaeologist. Daniel's desires seem so often to be thwarted — at times he can get a bit whiny, but thankfully, Michael Shanks does a good job making sure that, while Jackson is still impassioned and driven, he's not blind to reality. A particularly great moment is when Jack, who's under pressure to get Daniel back to the Gate, just grabs him and starts to haul him bodily back to the Gate. Both men's motivations are strong here, so strong they crackle like the lightning Sam and Teal'c are trying to call down in the Gate room.

Some elements of this episode are groan-worthy — calling Catherine's fiancé Ernest was a little too blatant, with the play on his earnest nature and ambition to make the Stargate work. And he seemed a little unrounded — one moment he can hardly speak, the next he's flipping out pearls of wisdom, Shakespearean style. Was the intent to make him appear mad so that Daniel couldn't depend on him for information? After all, he *did* spend fifty years there; you'd have thought he'd learned a little bit about what was going on.

Interestingly, in the original myth there is a time when Tantalus forgets his thirst — when the Greek hero Orpheus visits Hades, where Tantalus is imprisoned, to free his true love, Eurydice. Foreshadowing for another visit to Hades? See "The Devil You Know" and later, "Abyss."

Gods & Scientists: We are introduced to the idea that there are four races and a sort of United Nations of the gods. This planet is outside the Abydos cartouche, which means that the Goa'uld may not be aware of its existence. Daniel is excited by this news because it suggests that it may not be the Goa'uld who built the Stargate. Teal'c says the Goa'uld are scavengers. Ernest Tantalus likens Daniel to Tantalus. A true child of the gods, Tantalus angered them by killing his own son Pelops and serving his body to them, thinking himself smarter than they. The gods punished him by placing him in Hades where he was doomed to stand for eternity in the scorching heat, his feet in a puddle of water; each time he reached down to drink the water evaporated, only to return when he stood upright again. His name is the origin of the word *tantalize*.

Interesting Fact: Heliopolis is also the name of a repository of *SG-1* fan fiction (see "No Red Shirts") on the Internet. The name means "city of the sun."

Parlez-vous Gate?: Jack's response to Captain Carter's query:
CARTER: Where's Daniel?
O'NEILL: Oh, Ernest was showing him a new toy.
CARTER: Really? What?
O'NEILL: Some fancy lightshow that might be the key to our existence or something like that.

111. Bloodlines

Original airdate: October 10, 1997
Story by: Mark Saraceni

Teleplay by: Jeff King
Directed by: Mario Azzopardi

A vision while under anaesthetic convinces Teal'c to travel back to Chulak to stop Rya'c's religious rite of passage.

Like the heart line or the head line in palmistry, the idea of a bloodline indicates the passage of time — the change from year to year, and generation to generation.

"Bloodlines" watches two threads simultaneously — the immediate story of Teal'c and his family, whom he left on Chulak when he pledged allegiance to Earth in the fight against the Goa'uld, and the larger story of an enslaved people, the Jaffa. Thus far, we've seen the losses that Daniel Jackson and Colonel O'Neill have suffered, and to a lesser extent we see trials that Sam Carter undergoes as a woman in a traditionally male role, but Teal'c's history and feelings only ever get oblique reference.

This episode is an excellent illustration that, with Teal'c, silence does not equal aloofness. He hardly betrays a flicker of emotion, unless he is alone or with trusted friends like Jack and the rest of SG-1, but when he does, the fullness of his life and the evidence of his hardships appear to us, rich and layered. Teal'c's reaction to seeing the brand of a traitor on his house made by his own people, and the fear that they had taken out their aggression toward him by killing his wife and son, seems almost surprising in its emotional intensity — but not unrealistic. Christopher Judge has worked hard to bring the character of Teal'c out of the realm of the stereotyped silent but deadly sidekick and into a living, breathing entity whose struggles and fears, though set on a different world and in a different culture, are as easily recognizable as our own. This is one of the main reasons that *SG-1* has become as popular as it is with fans. The developers, producers, actors, and writers strive hard to make all the characters in the show first-rate and to give equal weight in terms of backstory and character development even if it does not translate directly into airtime.

"Bloodlines" is a good example of this sort of backstory, the holes in which we can fill in. With a few well-chosen lines between Teal'c and his wife Drey'auc, we are brought up to date on their lives so far, and where those lifelines, and bloodlines, could lead. Teal'c is very much opposed to continuing to serve as a slave for the false gods, starting with wanting his son to never feel the taint of the Prim'ta (which is both the name of the rite of passage on Chulak, and the name of the immature symbiote that is carried within the Jaffa). However, Rya'c has contracted scarlet fever. Teal'c desires above all to have his son live free — but when it looks as though his son will not live at all, Teal'c sees the terrible irony of the situation: this same rite which he hates so much could save his child's life. Teal'c sees, weighs, and makes his decision, all in the space of a few moments. More than any other member of SG-1, Teal'c's inner wrestlings cause us to sit up and pay attention to what is happening, lest we miss some subtle moment, some glimpse into this enigmatic character.

This episode also highlights the difference between Rya'c's religious rite, where priests perform a functional ritual that furthers the enslavement of a people, and Teal'c's paternal "right" to implant a Prim'ta within his son to save his life. While the writers skirt some dangerous waters here (O'Neill's monologue on deities gets hastily drawn away from whose-god-is-better to at-least-they're-not-alien-snakeheads), the real emphasis is on Teal'c's conviction that freedom from the Prim'ta is the first step toward freedom for all Jaffa. This arc is long and starts slowly, but its eventual transformation into a new, exciting one starting in "The Changeling" is worth the wait.

Except for a few "what were they thinking" moments — you abort the dialling sequence of a Stargate with the Escape key? I hope it's XP compatible! — this episode was great for further developing the character of Teal'c without compromising the identity of the Jaffa as a strong, thoughtful people not afraid to fight for what they believe in.

Gods & Scientists: In its larval stage, the Goa'uld needs a Jaffa host to incubate in. This implantation has been interwoven with the Jaffa religion so that it is seen as a rite of passage for young Jaffa. Once implanted, the Jaffa's own immune system ceases to work, effectively making the Jaffa a slave in body as well as in mind and spirit. As we see in "Children of the Gods" and later in "Hathor," a Jaffa cannot live long without a Goa'uld symbiote. Think Jaffa is a weird name? It's actually the ancient port city that is now Tel Aviv, in Israel.

Why We're Space Monkeys: Daniel Jackson may be idealistic, but he can hold a grudge. As much as he holds all life sacred, he still kills a large number of Goa'uld larvae, even after Sam points out to him that by doing so, he is no better than the alien race itself.

Parlez-vous Gate?: Bra'tac's grinning line, "Not bad for a man of a hundred and thirty-three," after dispatching several Jaffa with apparent ease.

112. Fire and Water

Original airdate: October 17, 1997
Story by: Brad Wright, Katharyn Powers
Teleplay by: Katharyn Powers
Directed by: Allan Eastman

SG-1 returns without Daniel, and General Hammond and Dr. Fraiser work with the team as they deal with the fact that he's dead — even if they don't believe it.

A very Daniel-centric episode, "Fire and Water" shows us a bit more of the grandeur and seriousness with which the military treats its people — enlisted or not. The scene of Daniel's memorial is poignant, and the fact that it's treated as seriously as it is before cutting to a scene of Daniel, very much alive, speaks to the gravity with which the writers treat the dangers and consequences of real Air Force staff life.

Nem's alien nature is set up very well. A strange-looking creature who can walk under water, he can read minds, sense the presence of the Goa'uld, and is thousands of years old — not to mention he's got pointy teeth and blue skin. Oh, and gills. So SG-1 is faced with a creature who can breathe on land and underwater, and who possesses superior technology. At first, when we learn that Daniel is alive and meet Nem, all these elements work together to distance us from such an obviously different creature — and yet, by the end of the episode, we have come to understand exactly what motivates this strange and strangely gentle creature. Like Jack, like Daniel, like anyone with a dangerous vocation or a missing beloved, he is waiting for word on someone who might not come back. In this case, Nem waits for over four thousand years to hear the fate of his beloved.

Fire and water are also primary elements, and, like the cuneiform language that Daniel identifies, were used as symbols by primitive cultures. Fire and water were symbolic for cleansing, and many cultures still use them in rites to signify a passage into a new place, either within or without.

Daniel, consumed by fire, is renewed by salt water, a powerful image of rebirth, after undergoing a painful rite to unmask memories that Nem needs. Nem also suggests the human race retains all the memories of its history within each individual — this idea has already been put in play in the *Stargate* universe through the Goa'uld, each of whom are born with the genetic memories of all the Goa'uld imprinted in them. Is Nem suggesting some sort of genetic memory for humans, too? It's unclear since, in the next few scenes, after Nem retrieves the memories he wants, Daniel says, "That's all I know," which seems to counter Nem's earlier suggestion. Or perhaps, going back to what the Nox said about the human race, the culture of Earth is still too "young" to have developed a tie with its own history, as the Goa'uld and other, older races have.

"Fire and Water" offers a graceful interweaving between military might and cultural importance; Dr. Fraiser, who has only been seen a couple of times so far, is already someone we look forward to seeing — her no-nonsense approach to the safety of the people around her, regardless of the fact that she, too, is a member of the military, is clear when she stands up to (albeit a few inches shorter than) General Hammond, a man used to giving orders, not taking them. Probably the only thing that rankled about this episode is the trend that seems to be developing that makes General Hammond seem less in control of his own command than he should be. In "Bloodlines" he capitulates to Teal'c, in "Fire and Water" to Jack, and in "The Torment of Tantalus" to Daniel. For a guy in charge of a top-secret military program, who has the ear of the President of the United States on a regular basis, he sure can be easily swayed.

Gods & Scientists: The god Belus is referred to by Daniel and Nem. Belus is Latin for Baal, a Goa'uld whom SG-1 meets in later seasons, although the two names may be coincidental. Suffice it to say that Baal is not a nice god.

Interesting Fact: Amanda Tapping participated in the USO's "Operation Starflight" in 2001, flying overseas to visit allied troops stationed in the Middle East. As a memento she received a 'Combat Bracelet,' made by the troops to reflect their bonds as service members. And does he look familiar? The character of Nem (big alien, pointy teeth) is played by actor Gerard Plunkett — who also played High Councillor Tuplo (big alien, pointy hat), in "The Broca Divide" and "Enigma."

Why We're Space Monkeys: *Stargate SG-1* has strong ties with the U.S. military — though they occasionally spoof even *that* relationship (see "Wormhole X-Treme").

Parlez-vous Gate?: Occasionally some real groaner lines infest the script — one of my all-time favorites is Captain Carter's, "I've had some experience with hypnosis in an undergrad psych course; let me take a shot at it." Okay, I took undergrad courses in psych too — and other than reading about hypnosis, nothing happened during those three-hour lectures that would make me more or less a candidate for it, unless you count my uncanny ability to win at Hangman.

113. Hathor

Original airdate: October 24, 1997
Story by: David Bennett Carren, J. Larry Carroll
Teleplay by: Jonathan Glassner
Directed by: Brad Turner

Archaeologists uncover an Egyptian sarcophagus in a Mayan temple, and discover the mother of all Goa'uld — still alive.

Unfortunately, even though *SG-1* moves far ahead in terms of its representation of women as members of the military, scientists, and doctors, and though they are often portrayed as emotionally strong, every time some aspect of traditional "feminine wiles" is trotted out, viewers' teeth grit and online bulletin boards light up. "Emancipation" was one example — women as fragile, protected chattel; "The Broca Divide" another — women as (titillatingly attired) sexual predators; and this one, which manages to squash a third annoying stereotype in there, the fury of "women scorned" (in this case, by another woman, Hathor, looking really bad in a red wig and an English accent — uh, English accent? English wasn't even a *language* when Hathor was alive). In particular, many fans resented the implication that Daniel's DNA specimen (acquired through his semen), was so flippantly gathered. The scene of Hathor and Daniel *does* amount to rape, and its callous treatment in the episode, coupled with the suggestion that it is a female prerogative, is sad.

Squashed between Colin Cunningham and Chris Judge – there could be worse ways for Suanne Braun to go! (COURTESY PETER FALLON WWW.BOBW.COM.AU)

If this was supposed to be a spoof on or satire of the "women behind bars" movies, it fell flat . . . on its face. Dr. Fraiser looked ridiculously out of place in greens so new they still had creases, although to her credit, Teryl Rothery's portrayal of her character was as gutsy and practical as always — just now with a strangely incongruous submachine gun in hand.

And what is it with story lines that continue to portray archaeologists as bumbling, middle-aged treasure hunters who wander into cool places and then put their paw prints all over stuff? Archaeology is a science, and as such has trained professionals who I doubt very much would be mauling a newly discovered sarcophagus without proper documentation and the appropriate authorities nearby. When the sarcophagus is found, a lot of attention is paid to brushing off sand, but then one of the scientists simply grabs the shiny object in the center? *Tsk tsk.* As one fan (who is also a student of anthropology) put it:

". . . usually that sort of thing [opening a sarcophagus], is done post-field in a lab under controlled conditions. Especially because if you do make the find of the century [. . .] you're not going to want to give your colleagues any more ammunition to claim you're a nutbag than necessary by opening it in the field and possibly contaminating your find and thus destroying any credibility of your analysis. You're going to box it up, ship it home, x-ray it, and then open it in front of trusted colleagues."

For its obvious groping (pun intended) after the male demographic here, "Hathor" gets firmly placed in the "please vanish" category. It did little positive besides furthering the idea that the Goa'uld, as a race, are egomaniacs, bent on total domination. It did a lot that's negative by implicitly giving the nod to sexual tactics as a means to an end, a sort of postmodern "lie back and think of England." I'd rather have watched "Emancipation" again.

Gods & Scientists: Hathor is the Egyptian goddess of fertility, the goddess associated with the living queen in Egypt. Sam mentions that Hathor was sent by Ra to destroy mankind — they supposedly became enemies due to his capriciousness, but this is actually the goddess Sekhmet (see "Resurrection" in season seven), who is sometimes seen as an aspect of Hathor, and sometimes seen as a goddess in her own right. Sekhmet was known as the "Eye of Ra," and meted out his punishments to mortals. Ra once sent Sekhmet to destroy Pharaoh's enemies, but Sekhmet started to kill the Pharaoh's army as well, and Ra could only stop her by getting her drunk. In the *Stargate* universe, Hathor is a Goa'uld Mother; that is, she can birth Goa'uld larvae imprinted with all her knowledge, after acquiring the DNA (life code) of the species she is attempting to blend with.

Interesting Fact: Most of *SG-1* is filmed in the Vancouver, British Columbia area (see "Everybody CanCon"). But the set decorators do a good job with the Mayan temple, making it really seem like a desert and not, say, an old-growth redwood forest.

Why We're Space Monkeys: I hate to say it, but this one screamed *Star Trek*. However, the concept of the woman with the pheromone-releasing-power was later done on both *Mutant X* and *Smallville* — in both cases, the pheromones were released as a colored mist from the mouth. Hmm.

Parlez-vous Gate?: Carter, after knocking out General Hammond. "Yeah — my career is over."

114. Singularity

Original airdate: October 31, 1997
Written by: Robert Cooper
Directed by: Mario Azzopardi

An alien girl is used as a time bomb for the Goa'uld, and Carter must deal with the consequences.

"Singularity" is one of those episodes in which particular moments help to define a character. Just as O'Neill's character is defined when he tells Teal'c he can "stay at [his] place" after helping to rescue the team in "Children of the Gods," and as Daniel's encounters with an alternate reality renew his faith in doing the "right thing," so in "Singularity" we get to see shadings of a Sam Carter that might not be shown otherwise. As the title suggests, a singularity is a defining moment, an event that can change the course of all the events that come after it. For example, the fight with the Goa'uld is taken to a new level when the Goa'uld, by killing an entire planet in order to achieve their aim of destroying Earth, choose to acknowledge Earth as an enemy — and reveal that they think humans are more dangerous than they originally suspected.

The cliché being revised in this episode is that Captain Carter is a career woman — an officer in the military with no husband and no children, having chosen this life in order to focus on her work. In the 1980s this choice was often lampooned in television and movies as improper or misandrist (discriminating against men). Only selfish women who wanted power chose their jobs over a relationship with a man, and their lives were usually portrayed as lonely and bitter, with no emotional content other than an unquenchable thirst to be better than men.

Unlike "Hathor," "Singularity" shows a strong female character without also introducing tired stereotypes. Sam chooses to stay with Cassie, who's implanted with a Goa'uld bomb, under emotional duress; but not without clarity; rather, she loves Cassie, and hates what the Goa'uld stand for. She realizes that, if she leaves, she will be behaving no better than the Goa'uld who implanted the girl with the bomb in the first place. In this way she follows her own moral imperative, seen in "Bloodlines," where Daniel wants to destroy the Goa'uld larvae and Sam attempts to stop him.

All of Sam's actions are believable; from her concern about her team to her conviction that, sometimes, you have to give up everything, if that action proves to be the more honorable choice. This is not a woman with a revenge complex, driven to become an officer in the military only to show up friends, family, the world at large. This is a sensitive human being with the strength of her convictions. There is no sexist game going on here; as a role model Sam is neither too girly nor too macho.

Gods & Scientists: We are introduced to the Goa'uld Nirrti, and to the idea that naquadah, an element found in the alien Goa'uld, is also in the Stargate. Someone with naquadah in their blood (as seen in "Hathor") can sense the presence of the mineral when it is nearby. This will be important in later episodes in detecting the presence of Goa'uld. Nirrti is a slippery eel, and we see her in almost every season of *SG-1*, although in her first incarnation Teal'c refers to Nirrti as "he." While the episode describes a singularity as a single event or defining moment, it is also the mathematical term used to define the point at which a structure, surface, or equation degenerates to the point of change, usually to another state — like the shielding wall inside the bomb inside Cassie. She herself houses a mathematical singularity. A little heavy? Check out season eight's "Moebius"!

Interesting Fact: Katie Stuart, who plays the role of Cassandra, was also in the movie *X2*, as Kitty Pryde, one of the young mutants in Professor Xavier's school.

Why We're Space Monkeys: All of SG-1 abides by Sam's decision to stay at the compound where Cassie has been brought to die. This speaks highly of their cohesion as a team, despite the fact they are four completely different individuals with four very different characters.

Parlez-vous Gate?: Cassandra, trying out the name of her fake place of birth (and perhaps a little tongue-in-cheek reference by Vancouverites who are tired of people from Ontario making like it's the center of the universe):
CASSIE: I know, the Stargate is a secret and I was born in a place called . . . Toronto?

115. Cor-ai

Original airdate: January 23, 1998
Written by: Tom J. Astle
Directed by: Mario Azzopardi

Teal'c comes face-to-face with his past, and Jack can't persuade him to abandon his guilt.

This episode makes good use of the terminology of law and the idea of justice, and, from a writing point of view, an excellent use of revelation to heighten tension; we ourselves don't know exactly what has transpired between Teal'c and Hanno's father. Hanno also raises some interesting questions, about impartiality and the weight of present actions which cannot, in some ways, ever repair what has happened in the past.

At the outset, we still hold to the view that Teal'c is an honorable character, regardless of his past. But when that past behavior rears up and shows a human face to both Teal'c and the rest of the team, we are confronted with the knowledge that, while Teal'c did not *like* what he did, he still *did* it. And so, when he is confronted with his past, all he can do is accept it and offer whatever recourse he can. In this case, if his death will appease those wronged, then so be it.

Another well-written piece, where both sides of the argument, the Byrsa and SG-1, each have powerful motivations. Although the idea of guilt is originally a Christian one, the idea of remorse and reflection on one's past actions is more universal. Especially well done is when Hanno asks Teal'c for *his* forgiveness for having acted in anger. It's clear that these are a people who are compassionate and aware of their own past actions, and it mirrors Teal'c's own dilemma — he cannot take back what he has done in the past, but he can ask for forgiveness and feel remorse for those moments.

Some really great moments in the episode: the scene between Hanno's father and Teal'c, though wordless, is extremely emotional; the tension between Jack and Daniel; and again between Jack and Teal'c. Daniel's impassioned plea to all of the Byrsa seems out of place until he is reminded that it is only Hanno who can judge. And General Hammond's comparison of Teal'c to a war criminal is strong, but also apt. Jack's retort, that he too would be considered a war criminal, shows the real balance of tension in this episode.

Teal'c's line, "I would save those who deserve to live," is wonderfully layered, one that speaks not only to Teal'c's hard-won moral code, but also to his earlier lines about why he chose Hanno's father for a victim (albeit obliquely); death had to be dealt, but he would rather choose the lesser death (and by extension the lesser evil), in any situation — Hanno's father over Hanno, or his fellow Jaffa over the Byrsa. An excellent, well-acted, and poignant episode.

Gods & Scientists: Although the Cor-ai seems weird to us, it has an historical precedent. In Athens, early forms of trials were not presided over by a judge, as they are now (that came about in the Middle Ages), and there were no lawyers; any citizen could prosecute, and the defendant *defended* himself. They did have a jury, however — between 200 and 500 people!

Interesting Fact: David McNally, who plays Hanno, also appears in "Demons."

Why We're Space Monkeys: Teal'c's stalwartness in the face of judgment is partly what makes him such a favorite role model among young viewers. And Jack is told he is being "antagonistic" rather than the perfect, all-knowing team leader.

Parlez-vous Gate?: Teal'c and Daniel's interaction is pretty amusing here:
TEAL'C: The Goa'uld visit here regularly. It is one of their favorite places to harvest hosts for Goa'uld absorption.
DANIEL: You know, I wish you wouldn't say "harvest." We're talking about human beings, not Brussels sprouts.

116. Enigma

Original airdate: January 30, 1998
Written by: Katharyn Powers
Directed by: William Gereghty

SG-1 rescues the Tollan from their dying planet — much to the Tollan's dismay — and then almost lose them to their own governmental machinations — much to SG-1's dismay.

Lya (Frida Betrani) of the Nox makes a reappearance (COURTESY JO STORM)

Right out of the gate (pardon the bad pun), this one makes us sit up and watch. We have a wonderful opening scene — it looks like it's snowing, but when we look closer, we notice the volcanoes in the background and realize it's ash. Such a beautiful scene that reveals so much death; it really is an enigma.

"Enigma" is defined in the Oxford English Dictionary as, "a person or thing that is mysterious or difficult to understand." It's also the name given to a cipher machine used in World War II — the Enigma machine coded messages so that only those with the correct code key could read them. The Tollan's version of this, used to send a message to the Nox, speeds through time and space in a way that seems easy to decipher (Daniel marks it as a laser beam), when, in reality, it is a complex message that tells the complete story of the Tollan's technological advancement — an advancement that only a few can read. When Daniel tries to puzzle out the meaning of Omac's analogy (with a stick no less), Omac smiles at him very much like a fond uncle and says simply, "No. You wouldn't understand." He's not saying it condescendingly, he's simply stating the facts.

Omac, the Tollan leader, is a great synthesis part, and played well by Tobin Bell. He's not malicious, but he is mean; he's not kind, but he can be empathetic. This sort of enigmatic behavior helps to distance Omac from the Earth humans, and to highlight the notion that just because someone thinks they've done you a good turn, don't expect it to be acknowledged. As Daniel points out to Omac, when the Tollan are given back their supplies and equipment, their scientists "didn't know what they were," a point which Omac takes to indicate the inferior technological state of Earth and thus their inability to be allies or even acquaintances.

Omac's behavior and personality have parallels in Earth's governmental activity, with its need-to-know policies, and one person speaking for all, regardless of their personal feelings. As well, Omac's reluctance to divulge information that might jeopardize another planet's population (as well as neighboring planets, as happened with his own planet of Tollana), harkens to some of our own experiences with technology used for applications that are not peaceful — the invention of dynamite by Alfred Nobel is a well-known example.

"Enigma" is another chapter in the "black widow syndrome" book for Sam (see "The First Commandment"), as Sam meets Narim, played to the hilt by Garwin Sanford. A cat is exchanged and wham!, Sam's in love. Sam does not however, have any . . . relations. Sam *never* has any . . . relations. Jack gets relations ("Brief Candle"), Daniel gets relations ("Children of the Gods" — inferred), and Teal'c has relations-by-proxy, in the form of his ex-wife. But not Sam.

Interesting Fact: Tom McBeath (Colonel Maybourne) and Garwin Sanford (Narim) also worked together on a 1989 Canadian film called *Quarantine*. Last time I saw it on eBay, it was going for $3.97. Canadian.

Why We're Space Monkeys: Earth is not the only place to find technology or cool people. Omac treats General Hammond and Colonel O'Neill like annoying younger brothers, not people to whom he should be grateful, much to their annoyance. Who says that alien races have to be your friends or your enemies? Species like the Nox and the Tollan are great because they show that the universe doesn't revolve around the humans.

Parlez-vous Gate?: Daniel's "Whoops!" when he interrupts Narim and Sam kissing. Another great one is Daniel being overjoyed that he remembered his college physics, only to have Omac tell him bluntly that he's wrong.

117. Solitudes

Original airdate: February 6, 1998
Written by: Brad Wright
Directed by: Martin Wood

Jack and Sam get separated from the rest of SG-1; Teal'c and Daniel try to save them before they are categorized as MIA.

"Solitudes" is one of this show's amazing episodes. It's the first one in which we see Martin Wood and Brad Wright working together, and the quality of this episode is a clue to the beginnings of this great team that lasts for eight years. Other writers and directors are added to the mix, and each brings their unique talent to the table, but Wright and Wood have a vision of *SG-1* that pins the series together for the long haul.

"Solitudes" is jam-packed with information about the Stargate system, contains threads that are used in later episodes, and has that hint of danger right up until the end when the cavalry, in the form of General Hammond, Teal'c, and Daniel, comes roaring in to save the day. But first and foremost, this episode is about the different kinds of solitude we all experience. The poet John Donne said, very famously, "no man is an island"; we all belong to the larger continent of beings. He was speaking specifically of humans, but probably wouldn't quibble about including Jaffa. The team of SG-1 is a perfect example of this idea of a continent founded on trust and developed over time, each member bringing his or her expertise to different situations and learning to rely on each other.

But what happens when they are separated? "Solitudes" is the first episode where we see the team split in such a way that they cannot be brought together by a simple horse ride or a Gate hop. Suddenly, each member feels separate and alone, and how they deal with this makes for one of the better episodes of season one.

There is, most obviously, the military/nonmilitary split. Whereas Daniel and Teal'c are quite happy to continue searching for Sam and Jack for as long as necessary, General Hammond must call off the search because of other concerns — cost, effectiveness, the reality of military life. So Daniel and Teal'c are separated from the rest of the SGC as well as from their team. Even within their solitude as nonmilitary members, Daniel and Teal'c each deal with the loss of their team members in different ways. Teal'c, the man of action, continually wants to embark through the Gate, regardless of his fatigue or the cost to others. Daniel, as a scientist and a scholar, wants to use the vast resources at their disposal to rescue people whom he believes are worth saving, regardless of the cost.

From their icy predicament, Jack and Sam battle their own sense of solitude. Even though they are together, and their sense of camaraderie is strong, built from both being in the military and from their time as teammates, eventually they, too, must each realize and overcome a sense of despondent aloneness. Jack's isolation comes from his rising feeling that he, at least, will not make it through the mission. Even though he may, in moments of adoration, admit to having feelings for Sam that are not strictly comradely, still he knows he must keep on the straight and narrow, for her sake, since keeping her alive trumps his personal desire to feel loved. This military bearing that Jack maintains is evident through the whole episode, and I think the writers and RDA did a great job skirting this intensely scrutinized thread in the SG-1 team: Jack is first and foremost a military man, and his job is to get his team safely home, not waste time worrying about feelings — or what his body is doing.

Sam's battle is much the same as Jack's, with the added component of not being able to "fix" the situation, something that she has already begun to internalize. As a scientist and a trained military officer, she feels as though nothing is beyond her means. When she is confronted with an impossible situation, her own sense of aloneness — not having an answer, not having a commanding officer on whose authority she can fall back, not knowing where the rest of her team is — threatens to overwhelm her. Solitude threatens to overwhelm them all, in fact, and each member has a poignant moment when they realize that they may not be getting out of this one.

It's this sort of strong, thorough look at each character that pulls us into the world of *SG-1*. The stakes are high — life and death — and each character's development and portrayal is measured out equally well, thanks to both the writers and the actors.

Gods & Scientists: Daniel reminds us that the Gate system was not built by the Goa'uld, but by another race. He reasons that a second Stargate could have been placed on Earth earlier than before the one the SGC is currently using. This thread reaches far, far into future episodes, and even into the spin-off *Stargate Atlantis*.

Interesting Fact: Amanda Tapping, who appeared on the Vancouver daytime talk show *Vicki Gabereau* in December 2000, smuggled in a hilarious blooper tape from this episode. Stuck on the glacier with the Colonel, Tapping ad-libs a whole series of lines which make fun of colleague Rick's past series *MacGyver*. At one point she quips, "You've got a belt buckle and a stick of gum — build a nuclear reactor!" much to the amusement of fellow cast and crew.

Why We're Space Monkeys: Jack has broken ribs and a broken leg, but that doesn't stop him from trying to help. However, when things get too rough, he does stop. And even though Sam's quite clearly distraught, freezing, and worried over her commander's health, she still focuses on the task at hand. No whining sissies here.

Parlez-vous Gate?: Jack and Sam, as they lie huddled together on the frozen ground, a million miles from anything they know, facing death:
CARTER: Colonel?
O'NEILL: It's my sidearm, I swear.

118. Tin Man

Original airdate: February 13, 1998
Written by: Jeff King
Directed by: Jimmy Kaufman

SG-1 wakes up on a planet and is greeted by a strangely effusive host. They soon find out they may not be who they think they are.

With its allusion to the movie *The Wizard of Oz*, "Tin Man" is great fun after the heavier episodes of "Solitudes" and "Singularity." Jay Brazeau, who plays the happy-go-lucky Harlan, is funny and endearing — a true mad scientist with a heart of gold. Like the man behind the curtain, Harlan does try to finagle things without anyone being the wiser, like not telling the team of the truth that lies behind the façade. But once evidence of the team's "realness" comes into question, Harlan continues to act as the humorous foil to some serious questions, without detracting from their importance.

In *The Wizard of Oz*, the Tin Man lacked a heart, but the opposite is true in this episode. Harlan's effusiveness hides a large, lonely heart. The contemporary retelling of the story, however, is not that the *heart* is replaced — instead, Sam theorizes that their *consciousness* has been swapped. Jack rather pointedly states that they don't really count as human anymore because they've lost their physical bodies. His Cartesian outlook is more like the stalwart O'Neill we know; who cares about his brain? Those are not his . . . *appendages*!

The synthetic SG-1 cannot stop being themselves any more than the real

SG-1 can stop. Teal'c's sudden transformation into someone we don't know is spooky, and when we learn that it is caused by the incompatibility of the two minds in one body, we are reminded of the ruthlessness of the Goa'uld. It's an excellent way for the series to "stay on track" without including a direct story line. This episode raises some interesting questions about what it means to be human — indeed, what it means to *be*. This sort of ontological question is often addressed in the sci-fi world, but it is Jack's horror about being a robot that makes this episode interesting. Other questions, like what it might be like to live for thousands of years, or what a consciousness is, are not addressed as much as alluded to, and their answers left open by the writers, since the story is really about a decaying civilization.

Consciousness has come a long way from Sigmund Freud and his theories. The counterpart to this episode, "Double Jeopardy," is another excellent look at the literal doppelganger of SG-1.

"My least favorite moment," said Teryl Rothery (Dr. Fraiser) of working on *SG-1*, "would be behind the scenes in the episode 'Tin Man' where take after take after take I was supposed to put this needle into Rick's arm. What we had in there was a tube, it was a special effects tube, so that when I put the needle in — it was a real needle — I'd get a blood sample. And take after take I broke the needle, and I was sweaty, I was getting *so* worried now, I was thinking, 'Oh dear God, I'm taking up valuable time and money' and Richard's getting — you know, he's being very gracious, but I can tell he's starting to think, 'Come *on*, lady, get this bloody needle in.' This was in season one, so at this point I was not a season regular, I was just a guest who kept recurring. Well, finally, I got it in, and we were filming, cameras were rolling, and Richard gave this reaction, and I remember in the moment thinking, 'Wow, that was the best reaction that I've ever seen Rick give.' And the director yelled cut and he went, 'You stuck me!' And I'm thinking, 'Yeah, I did, I did!' He went, 'No my *arm*!' I was sick. I thought, 'That's it! Fraiser is *gone.*'"

Interesting Fact: This set is used quite often for *SG-1* episodes, including "Cure," from season six. And if you watch the beginning closely, you'll see the team standing in the glow of the ring, awaiting their cue to jump through.

Why We're Space Monkeys: *The Wizard of Oz* gets some repeated play in the series — see "Seth" and "Tangent" for other examples.

Parlez-vous Gate?: Harlan, pinned against the Gate by a pissy Colonel O'Neill:

HARLAN: You are . . . damaging me.

119. There But for the Grace of God

Original airdate: February 20, 1998
Story by: David Kemper
Teleplay by: Robert Cooper
Directed by: David Warry-Smith

Daniel Jackson encounters an alternate reality — one in which he doesn't exist, and Earth is in peril.

This is the first multi-part episode we've seen since the pilot, "Children of the Gods," and includes the next three episodes. It's fitting that the word God also appears in this title as well; the pilot episode referred to the Goa'uld, who pose as gods to the civilizations they enslave, ensuring complete devotion — if only through the use of fear. In this multi-episode, the god referred to is the Christian God, as indicated by the title, "there but for grace of God (go I)." This expression is generally sourced to clergyman John Bradford, when he saw criminals about to be executed (he himself was charged and burned for heresy in 1555). The tension between the two ideas — gods as benevolent beings and gods as dictators, is rooted in many cultures, including Christian cultures. The Bible describes moments of divine wrath (mostly in the Old Testament), but also focuses on Jesus, who is benevolent and gentle. The idea of duality is not only Christian, however, and can be seen in, among others, Egyptian mythology (Isis, for example, is known as both a goddess of creation and of destruction), and Aztec mythology (Ometeotl is both male and female, light and dark, positive and negative).

The multi-parter is also a great way for the writers to be able to put forth ideas that may not be amenable to a larger, season-long story arc, but can be toyed with nonetheless in smaller chunks. A popular example among them is the relationship between the alternate-universe (AU) Sam and Jack. In this episode, because AU Sam is nonmilitary, the rules of fraternization do not apply, and hey, guess what? They get to be engaged! And hug each other! Longingly! Humor aside, it's a very tender moment when Jack gestures almost roughly to Sam and then they share a long, close hug, accompanied by Daniel's 'huh?' look. And, as the science shows later in "Point of View," with only one Daniel in the picture, there's no risk of two entities in one spot. So, while each character does get to maintain a certain amount of his or her original flavor, they are all allowed to stretch their abilities in new ways — with great results from the actors.

Possibly one of the most interesting and fun performances was AU "Colonel" Hammond — we get to see that Texas backbone, the unswerving devotion to a cause, and the balanced, thoughtful strategizer — but then he picks up a gun and we see a Hammond who can do the dirty work just as well as any other soldier. His anger and hatred of the Goa'uld is much sharper in this other reality, untempered by bureaucracy and a position of authority, and when he finally falls for his country, he takes more than a few Jaffa with him.

And, much like the pilot episode, "There But for the Grace of God" held more of the flavor of the movie; a little darker, a little more tense. Apophis is shown much as he has been lately — nonexistent except for his actions, cruel, vengeful, and ruthless. His Jaffa minions are silent except when they are firing their staff weapons. And Daniel's scene where he repeats, "This can't be happening this can't be happening" like a mantra was great — he was shocked, frustrated, and just a little pissy. He couldn't curl up in a ball and wait for it all to go away. Jackson's emotional reactions highlighted the man we've all come to know — flighty, sure, but when the chips are down he doesn't hesitate to use any means at his disposal to ensure the fight against the Goa'uld continues (although I found his "Help me save my people in my reality" leap a little hard to swallow).

Gods & Scientists: Real-life astrophysicist Stephen Hawking recanted on his black hole theory (he postulated that black holes were something that made material in the universe disappear utterly, leaving no trace of its existence), in July 2004. Hawking also said he no longer believed that black holes were portals to alternate realities, either. "There is no baby universe branching off [inside a black hole], as I once thought," he stated. "I'm sorry to disappoint science fiction fans, but if information is preserved," — and not, as he earlier thought, decimated completely — "there is no possibility of using black holes to travel to other universes." *Farscape* fans everywhere were devastated . . . okay just kidding. Besides, he was wrong once. . . .

Why We're Space Monkeys: Teal'c is not the good man we see in "our" reality. This is not just a Jekyll and Hyde case, either, unlike *Star Trek*'s "The Enemy Within" with the evil Kirk. This is a Teal'c who lived his life out in service to Apophis and his only moment of weakness is not in going back to his life with the Goa'uld (see season five) but rather in being tempted by the reality that General O'Neill lays out for him. Judge does a great job of making us believe both his versions of Teal'c.

Parlez-vous Gate?: Daniel, staring at the large red dots on the map that denote obliterated cities, placing his finger on where he would be:
DANIEL: Uh-oh — I think I'm dead.

120. Politics

Original airdate: February 27, 1998
Written by: Brad Wright
Directed by: Martin Wood

A U.S. senator arrives to find out whether or not the SGC is worth the tax-payers' money. SG-1 relives their recent efforts.

Darn, the flashback (or clip) episode. Season one was really starting to cook, and then "Politics" arrives. Although it's part of a mini-arc (four episodes if you count season two, episode one), all the other episodes except this one seem to be able to still stand on their own, whereas "Politics" really labors, especially in the middle.

There are three ways to look at this episode: first, it was a discreet use of cost-cutting measures — no sets except the permanent one of the briefing area and the command room, and the rest of the story told in flashbacks. Second, it was a recap for old and new viewers alike, a way to remind everyone of past events, as well as a nice way to update us on particulars (for instance, that the Chosen from "Brief Candle" are hale and hearty).

The third option though, is that this episode is, in subtle ways, a microcosm for the entire season, a synopsis and synthesis of the overarching ideas behind the series: that is, the making of myth, and how it shapes and even directs our history.

Throughout "Politics," three distinct elements are entwined: the Greek myth of Pandora's box, the Egyptian myth of Ra, and allusions to the Hebrew god. All three of these master narratives have been seen throughout season one, and what better way to highlight how stories ground us and give us metaphorical footings than to allude to three very separate ideologies? Even Colonel O'Neill, directly after he professes to "not talking in metaphors," then uses a metaphor to make his point — that something has been done, and so one can only make the best of it, not pretend that nothing has happened.

Ronny Cox plays a mean diplomat on the show, but in real life plays a mean guitar!

(COURTESY MEESH)

Metaphor is one of the strongest and most common tropes we use in English. Some readings of mythology point us to the idea that myths and stories are merely long metaphors in action — like fairytales or other stories with a moral. And "Politics" points specifically to the idea that the political arena, like the mythological arena, cuts across racial, cultural, and economic boundaries.

And, as in any political narrative, especially those written after the resurgence of the antihero, we have the nefarious element. Played by actor Ronny Cox with real style and panache, Senator Kinsey is a guy you love to hate; just hearing his sanctimonious voice ringing through the SGC is enough to make the hair on the back of your neck rise. It's a good introduction to the thread (and threat) of the NID.

Meagre as those twenty-five minutes or so of new material may be, they do have some real-life implications. How often has the word "superconductor" been thrown around, not to mention the myriad times Sam has commented on how much energy it takes to power the Gate? Does the SGC have its own personal power grid? How much does it cost to start up and shut down this thing, anyway? The American political system is supposed to make the actions of most of its branches accountable to the people, so it's not inconceivable that someone would be sent to make sure that the sGC isn't a money pit, or worse, a money-laundering site.

Gods & Scientists: As mentioned above, the writers make use of the myth of Ra, and especially his love of vengeance. Also highlighted is the Greek myth of Pandora's box; Pandora was the first woman on Earth, whom Zeus ordered Hephaestus to create in order to punish Prometheus for having stolen fire from the gods, and humans for having accepted the gift. Pandora was given in marriage to Prometheus' brother, Epimetheus, and Zeus gave her a jar (or a box, the stories differ), which he ordered her not to open. Having been endowed with curiosity, Pandora opened the jar, and all the evils in the world were released. Hope alone remained. Just as that moment is said to mark the end of the Golden Age of easy living, so too does this episode mark the end of the complacency of the government in the face of the Stargate program, and the realization of outright war with the Goa'uld.

Why We're Space Monkeys: Kinsey struts down the stairs to the briefing room as though he owns the place, and his bearing and rapport with everyone in the room is that of someone used to power and not afraid to wield it. As a setup for the more abundant appearance of the NID in later seasons, they couldn't have picked a better mouthpiece.

Parlez-vous Gate?: A bittersweet moment between General Hammond and Jack, where they discuss the futility of resisting the shutdown of the Stargate program. It's nicely acted, and gets the helplessness of the moment across:
O'NEILL: How about a bake sale? Yard sale? Garage?
HAMMOND: This is what I look like when I'm not laughing, Colonel.
O'NEILL: Car wash?

121. Within the Serpent's Grasp

Original airdate: March 6, 1998
Story by: James Crocker
Teleplay by: Jonathan Glassner
Directed by: David Warry-Smith

Daniel convinces the rest of SG-1 that a Goa'uld attack on Earth is imminent. The team transports onto a Goa'uld ship against orders, in an attempt to save the planet.

We've sure come a long way from first discovering that the Goa'uld are still out there. The first season finale is an interesting and fast-paced episode that ends on a cliffhanger and reminds us that whatever else happens, the four members of SG-1 are travelers not only in space but also in their own lives. "Within the Serpent's Grasp" shows us how far SG-1 has come since the first episode — both on an individual level and as a team. The voyage they've each made to get to the point where they stand together and consciously decide to disobey direct orders is pretty astounding.

Teal'c's journey is the most obvious — not only has he had to adapt to a new planet and way of life but he's become one of the strongest warriors in the fight against those whom he once served. Although he still serves under a military command, his situation has changed enormously, and the writers have started to use the character more frequently and in better ways, giving him some great parts and story lines. He's no longer the silent onlooker and backup to the rest of the team; Teal'c's evolution and integration is one of the most interesting aspects of the first season.

Sam Carter has evolved since "Emancipation," and even "Hathor": she's more disciplined now, and more confident in herself and her place in the team. When we met her in "Children of the Gods," she very quickly rose to what she perceived as bait thrown out by Jack and through the first few episodes, we see her fighting to prove herself as an equal. Her comment to Janet Fraiser in "Hathor" about feeling that she doesn't fit in with "the boys," seems a thing of the past now; she stands her ground, parries easily with Jack, and seems to really have grown into her role in the team.

Jack's made some changes, too — a far cry from the closed man we first saw in the movie and the first episode. He's had a couple of opportunities this season to open up, to grieve for his past life and his son ("Cold Lazarus," and even "Solitudes"), and this episode highlights how he's opened up to his team, as well. He's still very much in command, but his friendship with Teal'c, his respect and affection for Carter and Daniel despite their fields of expertise, have given him the chance to see other options. He's more trusting now, and a better leader for it.

Daniel Jackson's journey is a bit of a twist — he's not looking to find something new, he's trying to regain what he's lost, and he never lets us forget it. He started out the series happily married on Abydos, but in the first episode, his wife and home were taken away. In some ways, Daniel represents the general population. His approach has never been military, unlike the rest of the team, and we can imagine that his reaction at having his life as he knew it stripped away from him would be much the same as any one of ours. Several episodes this season have raised the question of how the world would react to finding out about the Stargate, alien life, and the Goa'uld threat. Daniel's personal crusade to find Sha're keeps the team's link with the "common person" alive.

This episode showcases teamwork — nothing is done solo, every decision is talked through and carried out together. A great season ending.

Gods & Scientists: It's the first time we've seen Klorel — the Goa'uld inhabiting Skaara's body. Klorel is eager to earn the respect of his father, Apophis, and his fervor to do a good job destroying Earth makes him a startling contrast to the Abydonian he's enslaved. There's some very good acting here on Alexis Cruz's part. Klorel will come back in other episodes — his need for domination is an excellent, and chilling, example of the Goa'uld mentality. Possession is a theme that we see repeatedly in *SG-1*. Using the idea of the Goa'uld possessing or taking over a host's body is reminiscent of Christian ideology that asserts some possessions to be the result of an evil, transcendental being. Contrary to popular belief not all possessions are viewed by the Christian church as evil or needing to be cured by exorcism. In the secular realm, science views possession as a psychophysical manifestation that responds to medical treatment of the body and mind.

Why We're Space Monkeys: While Daniel can occasionally come across as a bit whiny, Shanks' character choices are usually strong, and they get stronger as the seasons progress. At times he seems like the only true individualist in the midst of an army of like-minded military combatants (including Teal'c), but Daniel's naivety about the reality of war up close and in person is still striking and believable.

Parlez-vous Gate?: When SG-1 comes out of hiding on the Goa'uld ship, Daniel asks Teal'c about the big ball they're looking at:
TEAL'C: It is a long-range visual communication device. Somewhat like your television. Only much further advanced.
O'NEILL: Think it gets Showtime?

STARGATE SG-1 — SEASON TWO

"The danger's coming home again."

201. The Serpent's Lair

Original airdate: June 26, 1998
Written by: Brad Wright
Directed by: Jonathan Glassner

Trapped on board a Goa'uld ship, SG-1 must save the Earth — and then worry about saving themselves.

Although this is billed as a two-parter, this mini-arc really encompasses four episodes, starting with "There But for the Grace of God." The episode (and season) starts off right in the thick of things — with the Stargate program shut down, SG-1 gone AWOL, Earth about to become a pile of dust. It's a great analogy for SG-1's predicament, a serpent's lair. Apophis, the god whose symbol is a serpent, is like a snake too; every time SG-1 gets their hands on him, all they find in their hands is a shed skin. Okay, so a Ha'tak attack vessel is quite the skin, but you get the gist.

Skaara is trapped inside Klorel, SG-1 is trapped in the Ha'tak of their worst enemy, Earth is trapped in the sights of a vengeful Goa'uld, and Hammond is trapped in a nightmare thanks to the actions of a bean counter (Samuels), whose ladder-climbing urges obliterate his common sense; a lair indeed.

Meanwhile, on Earth, Daniel's worst nightmare is coming true. As the Tollan predicted in "Enigma," the very first use of an alien substance — naquadah — is in a military application, the "Goa'uld Buster." You can almost hear Daniel sighing, can't you? Season two really has some shining Daniel moments; his intense motivation to save Earth from a terrible fate comes across clearly, without him resorting to waving his hands about and looking like a displaced banshee.

There are many uses of the snake analogy. Goa'uld shock grenades cause temporary blindness. And when a snake sheds its skin, the oil that is secreted under it, facilitating its removal, causes a temporary, partial blindness in the snake; the film evaporates once the skin has been shed. This metaphor of shedding skin/renewal has been used in many different cultures for a variety of reasons (even, believe it or not, for circumcision), and shows here that, even in the lair of the enemy, renewal is possible.

Cue Jack's great line, "We're just having a bad day." Even in the depths of the enemy's stronghold, the team, who goes through their own temporary blindness — figuratively, in not believing Daniel's alternate reality prognostication, and literally, because of the shock grenade — eventually emerges renewed, the film of disbelief gone from their eyes; they understand the stakes. Their lives for Earth's, as Bra'tac eloquently puts it, seems a justifiable trade. Even Jack, whose quips, as always, lighten the somberness of the moment, nevertheless makes decisions without remorse, having been through some tough times in season one. Once again, he's willing to give his life for the greater cause.

Klorel is not named in the usual pantheon of Egyptian gods and goddesses. In the episode, Klorel tells Jack that Apophis is his father because he "seeded" the Queen Mother, Hathor. In the pilot episode "Children of the Gods," we saw Skaara taken away by a different pair of Goa'uld, ostensibly to act as their "son." Perhaps Apophis saw Skaara and took him? Or perhaps all of the Goa'uld there that day choosing "children" were also progeny of Apophis (who, as the second most powerful System Lord and at least as old as Ra, would be really, really old), and thus Klorel would still be, technically, his son, in a sort of intergalactic fostering?

Interesting Fact: See that scene where Klorel and Apophis ring out at the last second? Klorel looks a little . . . odd, doesn't he? That's because it's an inserted image of Alexis Cruz from other shots. Originally, the episode ended with Cruz's character dying, but fans were so taken with the character he had to be "revived" in postproduction from earlier shots; literally cut and pasted into Apophis' last-minute escape scene.

Why We're Space Monkeys: This is where it all starts, people. When Daniel returns to Earth, Jack greets him with a warm hug and an enthusiastic "Space monkey!" — a nickname that spawned many a chuckle and fandom in-joke. RDA's (ad-lib) delivery of the line is perfect — he infuses it with "We missed you," "You just never die, do you?" and "We won!" simultaneously.

Parlez-vous Gate?:
O'NEILL: We've been in worse situations.
TEAL'C: Not to my knowledge.

202. In the Line of Duty

Original airdate: July 3, 1998
Written by: Robert Cooper
Directed by: Martin Wood

SG-1 send the Nassyans through the Gate and back to Earth, fleeing from a Goa'uld attack, but what they don't know is that there are Goa'uld among them already — and one's in Captain Carter.

The word "duty" connotes actions performed regardless of their cost, or for a larger cause. This is a recurrent theme in *Stargate SG-1*, and once again, in this episode, two conflicting worldviews collide, both of which have validity. The consequences of this episode extend far into the future, from an uneasy alliance with the rebel Goa'uld ("The Tok'ra," Parts 1 and 2), to inborn knowledge of Goa'uld technology thanks to the genetic imprint of the symbiote on the host (see "Seth" for an example).

The "shipper" aspect of this episode is almost completely downplayed; all that is suggested is that Jack O'Neill has just lost a trusted and valued comrade (Major Kawalsky, in "The Enemy Within"), and does not want to lose another. Jolinar does take advantage of Sam's knowledge when she can, however, as she cries, "Jack!" repeatedly at one point, but Colonel O'Neill refuses to allow that kind of emotional ploy to work. The appearance of a new race, the Tok'ra, opens up the universe of *SG-1* in a way that hasn't been seen thus far. Taking our comfortable impressions of the galaxy — these are the bad guys, these are the good guys, draw lines in the sand here and here, start battling for galactic domination — writer Robert Cooper throws in some interesting questions: who are the Tok'ra, really? Can we trust them? Does an ideological difference count?

An excellent small moment, before the episode really starts in earnest, is when SG-1 is doing the humble and necessary job of trying to relocate the Nassyans. It's not glorious or heroic, it's the everyday fallout of a job that involves integration, exploration, and sometimes, bloodshed. *SG-1* tackles this theme over and over again during its run, and it's always fresh, because it's always different. Something happened while the team was off planet, and they do their best to repair the damage they may have caused (although in this case they didn't do it).

Captain Carter gets a whole lot of story pummeled into her in one episode. She's taken over by a symbiote (Tok'ra aside, it was still hostile in the beginning), and now carries naquadah in her blood. As Dr. Fraiser notes, naquadah could be not only a mineral but a reactor for sensing symbiotes. Cassie's reaction to Carter certainly tells us there's *something* up with that whole implanted-with-Goa'uld thing — even if it's not technically a Goa'uld.

The music gets pummeled as well, however; a little over-the-top for this episode, with the heavy original themes running throughout. The CGI more than makes up for the sense of threat and jeopardy, so the music was an unnecessary touch. The opening scenes of the episode especially are awesome: the sudden appearance of a haunting, totemic item that's swept by the shadow of the Goa'uld ship is flawless, and the firefight and village in desolation are excellently set up to mimic a truly alien world. The totemic item is especially interesting in that it suggests, long before we realize it, that the Tok'ra and the humans could form a bond. While totemic emblems are normally animals or part-animal, part-human, in this case it is a blending of alien and human spirits. It's the rift between the two spirits that is painfully evident when Carter, under the power of the Tok'ra says, "Let me go. I must go." Only when the two spirits in collusion are ready to understand each other can they work together, and the rest of the episode plays that out. When Jolinar finally gives her life, it's in the true spirit of her ethics, and Carter must now carry this totem with her for the rest of her life. As with many life-altering events, at the end of the episode you get the sense that it's going to take Carter a while to come to terms with her experience.

Another great performances here is Michael Shanks'. Season two really lights up for Shanks. All the pain and torment, the sleepless nights and the pacing — all that subtext of loss and grief is flashed in a single sad smile to Talia, the Nassyan woman who has lost her husband. Shanks plays this episode low key, and it works. Dr. Jackson, like Talia, has burns of his own now, on the inside. The world is not quite the happy-go-lucky place it was when we first met him; he is losing his naivety.

A reverse of this situation is that it is Cassandra who tells Sam, "It's going to be okay," at the end of the episode. She is echoing Sam's own words back to her — the ones Sam told Cassandra when the young girl first came to Earth ("Singularity"). Suggesting a return of sorts, this scene is a great reminder of the strengthening of bonds that happens between two people (military or nonmilitary) when they've been through an ordeal together and not only lived through it but learned from it. That Sam would look to this young girl — as Cassie looked to her last season — is a wonderful use of that relationship; it also harkens back to the various threads in *SG-1* about "being young." Youth does not necessarily always mean naivety, as Cassandra amply shows. Grown up too fast, this girl is also prepared to do what her duty demands when she is asked.

There are Goa'uld who do not necessarily masquerade as gods. As Daniel says at the beginning of the episode, "We still understand very little about their society." Up to now, all the Goa'uld we've met have been big guns, but in this episode we meet the Ashrak, an assassin who is also a Goa'uld. He apparently retains some of the cooler aspects of being a Goa'uld (as when the Ashrak rips open the cell that Sam/Jolinar is in — hey, can they *all* do that?), but does not command legions of followers.

Gods & Scientists: The Goa'uld within can take over immediately (unlike the pilot episode where Kawalsky's absorption by the symbiote took some time, though later we find out this is because his symbiote was not yet mature), and can manipulate the voice of the host if they choose. We see this later in the character of Hebron ("Crossroads"). This gives the show room to grow and change, much like Egyptian mythology, which, because it evolved over thousands of years and was mostly oral in tradition, had a fluidity to its stories, since they grew and changed also. Many stories that we see today as narratives started out very differently, changing over time accordingly to place, teller, and the political climate of the period.

Interesting Fact: Does that technician who handed Jack the phone look familiar? Blue garb, looks pregnant? Her name is Tracy Westerholm, and she's in at least ten episodes of *SG-1* (once uncredited). She never has the same role more than twice. The official credit listing for "In the Line of Duty" says "Technician #2." However, last time you saw her was in "Enigma" — except she was an airwoman. She was also in "Hathor" — but that time she was toting a submachine gun. Last but not least, she is Amanda Tapping's stand-in (along with Jacquie Janzen). Phew.

Parlez-vous Gate?:
TEAL'C: I have seen many Goa'uld strategies revealed and certain victories lost because of Goa'uld arrogance. It is the Goa'uld's greatest weakness.
O'NEILL: (sighs) Yeah.
TEAL'C: Colonel O'Neill. When you speak to her, do not see your friend.
O'NEILL: How do you do that?

203. Prisoners

Original airdate: July 10, 1998
Written by: Terry Curtis Fox
Directed by: David Warry-Smith

After inadvertently aiding and abetting a murderer on a mission, SG-1 is imprisoned on a penal colony. Carter devises an escape plan, helped by one of the prisoners, but they find out too late that they let valuable information fall into the wrong hands.

As Jack notes of Hadante, the penal colony where SG-1 finds itself trapped, "Any place like this has its own set of rules, and they don't have to make sense." Perhaps a sly allusion to organized institutions in any form, "Prisoners" watches the interplay between different moral aspects of cultures — law, responsibility, ownership of one's fate or destiny — and comments subtly. Especially telling are moments such as when Linea tells Sam very calmly, "Do not think that I am innocent," or when the Taldor, speaking to General Hammond, blithely states, "Our law is immutable."

Besides the obvious reference to Dante Alighieri's *The Divine Comedy: Inferno*, this episode touched on some of the most endearing aspects of myth and the reason for mythology, without ever naming any deities or religions.

"Prisoners" is about the result of wanting. In a reversal of the previous episode, where SG-1 helps the Nassyans because it's the right thing to do, here they are penalized for the exact same behavior. Similarly, when Carter and Linea begin talking about what needs to be done to power the Gate to get them out, Sam's desire to obtain the new technology that could open the door for the Stargate and the rest of Earth blinds her to the possibility of deceit. Daniel is also a prisoner of Jack's command to go home, as his initial impulse to stay on the planet and explore was vetoed. Daniel is often seen on the receiving end of a military "no" in seasons one and two, and it seems as though he's always one step behind his personal desires.

The web of deceit is implied right from the start, as the team heads past a spider spinning away on a giant web. Linea is also like a spider, patiently waiting for the right circumstances and the right prey to enter her trap, so that she can gain the means to go home. She is waiting for a particular set of people who fit her needs as Vishnor fits her need for physical protection. The organic ropes around the Stargate also mimic a spiderweb — thin, ethereal-looking, but ultimately holding death, as they transport the very lethal Destroyer of Worlds back to a place where she can do her best — or her worst, as the case may be.

SG-1 often tackles the theme of justice. The objective, law-abiding view is not necessarily the right, or good, or even true one. While many other shows use law as a background, it is usually seen as being above everything else, and "immutable," as the disembodied voice at the beginning of the episode says. *SG-1* takes this theme and expands it by showing not only this side of the law but also the other side(s) — the difference between guilt for a crime and culpability (as when SG-1 helps a murderer). Can their ignorance be termed a crime? If so, should it be punished? Is punishment always tied to suffering, and is death always the way to end it? And did we need smoking boots to really help us understand that?

Sarcasm aside, in religious or secular texts, one of the largest concerns of mythology is how to make sense of suffering. Mythology was, until recently, often derided as something only "primitive" societies indulged in. Now, mythology has been placed alongside, as opposed to beneath or completely discarded by, Western rationalism. Scientific exploration still can't tell us what love or suffering *feel* like. They can explain the physical processes or the cause-and-effect nature of them, but not what it's like to experience them. As Linea explains bluntly to Daniel Jackson when he protests that what the prisoners are doing by standing in front of the event horizon is dying, not saving themselves, myths are needed that explain the imperfect, unfair state of the world — which evolve because there is suffering that cannot be explained by pure reason alone. Myths that illuminate and work to alleviate suffering are found in almost every culture. "It was his life [to throw away]," she says.

Interesting Fact: When the nuclei of two atoms are fused at a cool temperature, it's called cold fusion, and it's one of science's Holy Grails. Sam's excitement at finding a possible organic source of fusion was probably actually toned down. Although it's so far pure theory — despite one discredited claim of success in 1989 — it's still a major area of research in nuclear physics, since achieving cold fusion would provide huge amounts of energy very easily. *Fusion* refers to energy created by combining atoms, as opposed to *fission*, which creates energy by splitting atoms.

Why We're Space Monkeys: If you'd like to see Amanda Tapping talk more about cold fusion, check out her 2001 movie, *The Void*, where she goes on (and on and on) about it.

Parlez-vous Gate?: Jack using Teal'c as a battering ram:
O'NEILL: Teal'c, look scary and take point.

204. The Gamekeeper

Original airdate: July 17, 1998
Story by: Jonathan Glassner, Brad Wright
Teleplay by: Jonathan Glassner
Directed by: Martin Wood

SG-1 is trapped in a virtual reality; Jack uses his super black ops powers to not hit the Gamekeeper, a man with a bad tan and a wandering accent.

Season two is much more about exploration than the first season was; we see a lot more stand-alone episodes that don't tie in with the larger Goa'uld arc or the upcoming NID arc, even though we do meet another important cast member in this season, and we've already touched on the Tok'ra in "In the Line of Duty." Stand-alone episodes are writer Joseph Mallozzi's preferred kind. "To be honest, as much as I love working on arc-driven episodes, nothing beats the conciseness of a one-off," he said in an interview. "One of my favorite episodes over the past couple of seasons was season seven's 'Revisions,' a story with no back-references to the show's mythology or past events. It was a simple 'team goes off-world, encounters a sci-fi problem, saves the day, and goes home' tale."

As far as stories go, "The Gamekeeper" is fairly straightforward, unlike the more subtle offerings that opened the season. Because hey, who doesn't have a half dozen things they'd like to do over? Unfortunately, unlike video games or other virtual reality scenarios, we can't rewrite history, and so, right from the start, Colonel O'Neill's pragmatic outlook is what we cling to. That, coupled with his black ops penchant for suspicion. . . . One of the funniest moments of the episode comes when O'Neill pats the top of General Hammond's head, sure that he is still in the virtual world. In a great setup line for the episode, the Gate technician notes that

P7J-989 has an ideal temperature before the team embarks. Like many aspects of our lives, it always looks perfect before we get there, but the reality is quite different: job in Paris? Great! Oh wait, my French isn't as good as I thought it was, and they smoke in bars. Heavily. It's the details that really get us in the end.

Teal'c and Captain Carter are left out of the "game" due to their unique circumstances — Teal'c's symbiote and the remnants of Jolinar within Carter act as blocks to their minds. (But we do get to see a reenactment of the same principle with different parameters — with Sam in season seven's "Grace," and with Teal'c in season eight's "Avatar.") "The Gamekeeper" is another example of Teal'c's and Sam's backstories being built up over the season. While both Jack and Daniel have the feature film behind them, neither Teal'c nor Sam were present. Occasionally, these two SG-1 team members seem little more than corollaries to the action, both acting as informants in their respective fields: Sam in the area of science, and Teal'c in the area of alien or Goa'uld intelligence. But it's not as though they're being completely left out of the loop — check out Carter's "love what they've done with the place" line when first entering the dome that houses the Watchers. It's small continuities like this that built up steadily over time and weave characters together. As we learn later in "One False Step," Carter not only likes plants, she actually talks to them!

We also learn that Daniel has not been immune to tragedy, having lost his parents in an accident when he was young. Again, Shanks really steps up well in the scenes where he has to watch their death reenacted repeatedly. The sense of loss and tortured anger at an accident he couldn't have prevented shows clearly on his face and in his actions. RDA also does a great job — at first, the urge to make amends for past actions, a chance to save lives and friends, has him revisiting his history, and there is a real yearning on his face for things to work out right. Later, when he realizes what is happening, he literally digs in his heels and refuses to play. Where Carter would try to fix it, Daniel to talk it out, and Teal'c to blow it up, O'Neill's reaction seems the most petulant, but in the end his way works the best.

Sometimes sandbox rules really *are* the way to go.

Gods & Scientists: It has to be asked: *is* there a logical theory for time travel? And wouldn't the Keeper still age, as he was not hooked into the machines as the residents were? He looks pretty good for a guy who is 1,022 years old.

Interesting Fact: The Gamekeeper's domed structure is actually the Bloedel Conservatory, located in Vancouver, BC.

Why We're Space Monkeys: Dwight Shultz, who plays the Gamekeeper, is probably well known to *Star Trek* fans as Reg Barclay, but older fans probably always see the patina of Madman Murdock from *The A-Team* about him.

Parlez-vous Gate?: SG-1 doing its best to tick off the Gamekeeper and thwart his plans:
THE KEEPER: Go where? Where would you like to go? I can take you any-where you can remember, anywhere you can imagine.
O'NEILL: Okay, we want to go *free*.

205. Need

Original airdate: July 24, 1998
Story by: Robert Cooper, Damian Kindler
Teleplay by: Robert Cooper
Directed by: David Warry-Smith

Daniel becomes addicted to the effects of a sarcophagus, while the rest of SG-1 endures hard labor on a planet where the ruler poses as a Goa'uld.

"Jack, I need to try." Daniel's statement near the end of this episode reflects the basic premise of this episode: needing something. It seems we need a lot of things, and while the highlight of "Need" is Daniel's psychological and physical dependence on a Goa'uld sarcophagus — an addiction — this episode is also about the other needs we have in our lives. And although many of us use the word "need" and "money" interchangeably, financial need is the one facet of this emotional pattern that is not addressed. Even when talking with King Pyrus about the mining operation, the dialogue focuses on the glory and the prestige, rather than fiscal rewards.

While the Tok'ra have been seen now in "In The Line of Duty," a small but crucial piece of information is imparted to us: the Tok'ra do not use sarcophagi. By refusing to prolong their life artificially, the Tok'ra bypass the need that the sarcophagus develops in its host and in the symbiote. A nice allusion to the idea that those who talk the talk should also walk the walk. It makes sense that the Tok'ra would be ideologically against everything that the Goa'uld stand for, and if the need for domination and control is literally bred in the bone as the symbiote and host lie in a sarcophagus, the Tok'ra's refusal to use them fits in well with this new race's mythology. There is no real need for the sarcophagus to be used at all, and so desire is explored once again in the *SG* universe, and with interesting results.

Both Shyla and Daniel feel a need to find a mate and achieve a sense of completeness in the world — the need to make a difference, if only to one other person. Though this need is cast in the romantic, chivalric tradition (somewhat improbable on P3R-636), the quest for "the one" stretches way back on Earth — in the Western tradition it started with Plato. Shyla's need to

Amanda is known as one of the happiest people on set, as well as off (COURTESY MAUREEN THAYER)

fulfil her destiny — that is, to lead her people with the help of a king — makes her do things she would not do otherwise. In a means-justifies-the-ends confrontation, she lures Daniel into an addictive state, hoping that his natural goodness will compensate for the more unhealthy aspects the sarcophagus metes out. And although Daniel resists Shyla's advances, as the effects of the sarcophagus take hold, that need within him also rises up, warped now into the form of desire for Shyla, and for power.

Daniel tells Sam that he doubts she's known what real love feels like, which might be a reference to what Sam needs, or, perhaps, some foreshadowing to later episodes, especially "The Tok'ra" mini-arc where we meet Martouf, Jolinar's mate. Even Jack alludes to his own need, telling Daniel in the depths of Jackson's "withdrawal" that he understands what it feels like to want something so badly you'd do anything for it. He could be referring to his son, or he could be referring to the aftermath as well; substance abuse often occurs with people who have lived through extremely traumatic circumstances.

Shyla's preoccupation at the beginning of the episode about her "destiny" also brings back the ideas brought out in "Prisoners." Most people (human and nonhuman), in the universe of *Stargate SG-1* demonstrate a deep-seated need to be *doing* something, whether for good or evil; there must always be a sense of movement toward something. In this episode King Pyrus, the ruler of P3R-636, defeats an unnamed Goa'uld and takes his place, using the dead Goa'uld's sarcophagus to prolong his lifespan and keep him in perfect health. This unnamed Goa'uld ruled the peoples of the planet and enslaved them in a naquadah mine; the mineral was then transported somewhere else. Even though he continues to mine for nothing, the act itself creates meaning for Pyrus. This long-held narrative of progressing toward something is a foundation for most stories, oral or otherwise. Unless you're a strict academic of semiotics or literature, you want your story (and, by reflection, your life) to *mean* something. It's almost like an addiction.

Gods & Scientists: Often, people take drugs to enhance aesthetic experience, whether that enhancement comes through extrasensory stimulation or a deadening of the senses. Psychedelic mushrooms were called "God's flesh" by the Aztecs. Addiction is a state wherein a person cannot live without the drug from a physiological point of view without going through withdrawal, because his or her body has adapted physiologically to a particular substance. Daniel's body gets used to the effects of the sarcophagus, and the changes in his body make its removal from his life physically painful as his body readjusts.

Why We're Space Monkeys: While sci-fi shows generally tackle the issue of addiction (*Andromeda*'s "It Makes a Lovely Light," *Star Trek: The Next Generation*'s "The Game," for just two examples), *SG-1* does so in a much more emotional way. While the writers of *SG-1* often bring to its episodes a sturdy tongue-in-cheek component, it's not above dropping that rhetorical device in favor of good, linear storytelling.

Parlez-vous Gate?:
DANIEL: Look, I just wanted to let you guys know I was okay. And I'll talk to Pyrus tonight at dinner.
CARTER: You get dinner?

206. Thor's Chariot

Original airdate: July 31, 1998
Written by: Katharyn Powers
Directed by: William Gereghty

The team returns to Cimmeria after learning that the Goa'uld have invaded. The team feels responsible, since on their previous visit they destroyed Thor's Hammer, the planet's instrument of defense against the Goa'uld. Later, they make some remarkable discoveries.

Up to now we've mostly seen "SG-1 vs. The Universe," with SG-1 usually doing okay. But it's nice to get a little helping hand now and then, and this episode delivers help. At the beginning of the episode, General Hammond echoes a central premise/problem for the SGC: how much should humans interrupt or change the course of a civilization's history? Is it ethical, not to mention safe, to go meddling in the history and course of events for any given civilization? At the end of the episode, after struggling with the consequences of past actions, SG-1 meets a tentative new ally who, even in their advanced technological state, still wrestle with the very same questions — illustrating that there's no neat and tidy solution.

One of the major differences between *Stargate SG-1* and the *Star Trek* series is their treatment of what is called in *Star Trek* terminology, the "Prime Directive"; that is, it is forbidden to interfere with other civilizations under any circumstances. *SG-1* is a newer show, and as such it reflects the growing understanding of cultural factors in any civilization. The early seasons of *SG-1* worked with this problem very well. Modernity, with its ideas of rationalism and neutrality, gives way to a more postmodern viewpoint — by even viewing something, you are changing it. As soon as you make contact with something, it has necessarily changed; neutrality is not an option.

Daniel is especially aware of the implications of changing a society just by coming into contact with it. This viewpoint sounds out more adequately the real questions of first contact. Exploration and interaction is an ongoing process by which both the SGC and its teams give to and take from those they meet. Rather than try to dissect cultures from the outside, placing an arbitrary value system on them, characters like Daniel and Teal'c show how the exploration and acceptance of difference and diversity is not threatening but helpful.

A good example of this is a silent but telling Teal'c moment, after he relates to Colonel O'Neill exactly how the Jaffa who are hunting them go about capturing prey. "It is an old Jaffa technique," he finishes, and then a flash of emotion crosses his face — something very like respect. This moment plants a seed which is later developed more fully as Teal'c realizes that the size and skill of the Jaffa people could be the most important factor of all in the fight against the Goa'uld, and that their tightly knit, highly disciplined lifestyle is not a sign of a rigid people, but a sign of strength.

In this continuation of season one's "Thor's Hammer," SG-1 persuades General Hammond to let them go, because, since they mucked up the planet's defense system in the first place, they should be the ones to fix the problem. This theme is seen often in later episodes as SG-1 deals with the consequences of their actions (or inactions). The episode also explores the question of what happens when we unleash power that we don't understand or can't control (which we see also in "Touchstone").

So much of speculative fiction writing on television can come off as clichéd or pat, but "Thor's Chariot" shows why *SG-1* is so popular. When Sam puts on the ribbon hand device she finds at the gravesite of a former Goa'uld host, her expression is one of confusion — as though she isn't quite sure *how* she knows what she's doing. The hand device is usually used by the Goa'uld and Sam is shocked when she concentrates and fires the device, leaving a smoking hole in the ground.

Some great work by Amanda Tapping, who really works to let the viewer see Sam's mixed reaction of horror and fascination at the knowledge she's discovered. Goa'uld devices are designed for one thing only — inflicting pain and maintaining order through fear. Sam's character, thus far as upright as Dudley Do-Right, has a real chance to expand here, and Tapping does a great job of revealing emotion without letting it slide into a wibbly moment of girlishness. In fact, these two episodes, "Thor's Chariot" and the earlier "Thor's Hammer," feature several strong female characters who fight, decide, and judge alongside their male compatriots.

Gods & Scientists: We physically meet the Asgard for the first time, who, like the Goa'uld, also coopted human gods and used them as masks; but they use the Norse gods. They are technologically superior to the Goa'uld, but also benevolent, only interceding when one of their planets (under the Protected Planets Treaty), is threatened. As Sam reports, the Asgard look like "Roswell greys," the same aliens made popular by the television series *Roswell* and *The X-Files*.

Interesting Fact: Due to budgetary restrictions, Thor's voice was originally provided by Michael Shanks — modulated so that it is masked, but if you listen closely you can hear the overtones of it. The voice has developed something of a cult following since then, and other members of the *SG-1* cast also did Asgard voiceovers in later episodes. Also, you can see the rocks placed as the actors' markers in the ending sequence when SG-1 is standing on the road, watching the Asgard dispatch the Jaffa hordes and Heru'ur.

Why We're Space Monkeys: It's the second time you hear the "you're too young" parable that bugs Jack so much, first seen in the episode "The Nox." It's nice to see SG-1 humbled.

Parlez-vous Gate?: Daniel gets to make fun of the rational, scientific mind when Sam tries to explain how the holographic image of Thor works: echoing Gairwyn's confused expression, he says blithely, "Oh yeah, if you say so." On the flip side, we learn Daniel isn't good with heights, and Sam gets to do the dangerous stuff usually reserved for manly men in manly shirts.

207. Message in a Bottle

Original airdate: August 7, 1998
Story by: Michael Greenburg, Jarrad Paul
Teleplay by: Brad Wright
Directed by: David Warry-Smith

SG-1 retrieves an orb that Sam and Daniel speculate may be a time capsule, a trap, or a power source. It turns out to be all three, and SG-1 must figure out how to remove the item from Earth — and from Colonel O'Neill himself.

"Message in a Bottle" is a return to season one in some respects. There's a lot more team interplay, and the character advancement is well paced — though sometimes a bit too convincingly. Maybe the writers were scrambling to throw in a more "human" element after the last few episodes, where SG-1 explores planets with Earth-like human elements; sort of a "Hey, remember it's us and them?"

This is another difference between *SG-1* and other sci-fi shows. We are not met constantly by humanlike entities (okay, so thus far in season two we mostly *have* been, but this is an anomaly!), but instead confronted with entirely alien species that it is SG-1's job to figure out, without resorting to the ethnocentric idea of laying human values over anything they encounter. The name of the bomb, "Wildfire," is also perhaps an allusion to *The Andromeda Strain*, a book written by Michael Crichton that was later made into a feature film of the same name in 1971.

Another reason for the highlighting of human relationships has to do with a word in the title — message. By not using a textual message, while alluding to it in the title, the writers suggest a comparison we might not otherwise make. A message in a bottle is written — the text is passed from writer to reader without spoken words. There are several scenes in this episode — at the beginning between Sam and Daniel, in the control room between Hammond and Fraiser, and in the Gate room between Jack and Teal'c — all showing us the power of unspoken communication.

For instance, how does Dr. Fraiser relay her pain at seeing the needless suffering of infected patients thanks to the lockdown ordered by Hammond? Without words. Daniel, perhaps making up for his behavior in "Need," has a touching moment with Sam at the beginning of the episode, noting Lt. Simmons' crush on her. When they're overheard, the two share a long, silent look of understanding, love, and compassion. And Teal'c remains wordless, at Jack's side (more like at his knees since Jack's hanging five feet off the ground), throughout the colonel's ordeal.

And most interestingly, it is Colonel O'Neill who is chosen by the entity to be its mouthpiece, rather than Carter, who would be the most intelligent, Daniel, who would be the most empathetic, or Teal'c, who would be the most used to encountering different technologies, races, and ways to communicate. There are other reversals, too. At the beginning of the episode, O'Neill asks Captain Carter for a threat assessment. It is typical of O'Neill (and we see this quite clearly when situations are reversed in season four's "Entity") to get rid of any threatening technology brought home to Earth. In this episode, it is Carter who recommends — somewhat nervously, too — removing the device and placing it back on its original planet. Even when almost completely taken over by the alien species, O'Neill's character remains pragmatic and consistent — he cares to save his world, and he wishes to live; beyond that he lets the fates decide. Still, when his loyalty is won, he will go to extraordinary lengths for friends and allies. Even though he must be in terrible pain, he manages to console Teal'c by recognizing that the Jaffa has made an "Earth" joke.

Interesting Fact: "Don't give Rick a prop," notes Michael Shanks, in reference to his cast mate RDA. "[You're] always going to get some sort of buffoonery." Thankfully, in this episode there's little for Rick to play with, since most of the time he's hanging five feet off the ground.

Why We're Space Monkeys: Sam is right, then she's wrong, then she's maybe both: not once does she say "Told you so," "Well, what did you expect?" or "It's not my fault." Carter is a military officer who values intelligence and perseverance. Right or wrong, she just wants the job done. No egos, please.

Parlez-vous Gate?: Sam's very quick but very funny reaction shot after Teal'c's "booby" query makes me laugh every time I see it. On a more serious note, General Hammond stands tall when he tells Captain Carter, "Damn right they won't [take the SGC without a fight]," pointedly looking out the window, complete master of the moment. Some fine veteran acting there. And only Teryl Rothery can make lines like, "Tetracycline. It's kept the infection at bay in the colonel and it seems to work prophylactically with everyone I've been able to get a shot into," sound not only easy to say, but also all sciencey and stuff. But the last word is Teal'c's:
TEAL'C: Undomesticated equines could not remove me.

208. Family

Original airdate: August 14, 1998
Written by: Katharyn Powers
Directed by: William Gereghty

Teal'c's son Rya'c is taken hostage by Apophis as revenge for Teal'c's defection. Teal'c must return to Chulak with his mentor and the rest of SG-1 to rescue him.

Family is an important thread in Teal'c's life. Even though he has willingly given up his immediate family in order to help Earth, Teal'c still has a

Tony Amendola as Master Bra'tac

strong sense of honor and commitment to his past. Not that he would let the past interfere with his present duties, but it would be unwise to say that Teal'c is someone who burns his bridges as he goes — this is a man with a sense of responsibility, and his conduct almost always reflects the conflict between his desire to do the right thing and his desire to do the necessary thing (sometimes the two are mutually exclusive), and it's in these tensions that we find Teal'c's best (and hardest) moments.

"Family" is about the changes that can occur in a unit bound together. The idea of family is not restricted to the traditional bonded pair and children (the nuclear family); this episode highlights both traditional and nontraditional types of family. Teal'c's family is defined both by blood and marriage (Drey'auc, Rya'c, and Bra'tac), and by bond (the Tau'ri, and in particular, the members of SG-1). As General Hammond notes, it was Teal'c's fear of being made vulnerable that led him to withhold information about his family to the SGC. But his plan backfired. His family *did* make him vulnerable — to Apophis, not the NID.

This episode also rewrites some aspects of the idea of family. When Teal'c confronts Drey'auc suggesting she has abandoned him, she replies quickly and strongly that she had to take care of her family in the ways she felt most appropriate, as Teal'c himself was taking care of the family in the ways he felt appropriate. Brook Parker does a great job of making Drey'auc a strong, authentic woman. "How dare you judge me and dishonor Fro'tak in his own house after what you have done?" she says, challenging Teal'c right back. It makes sense that Teal'c's chosen would be as demanding and honorable as Teal'c himself, for he would not respect anyone in his life who was not courageous and disciplined, as well as intelligent. Which is why lines like, "Woman, be silent," sound very odd coming from him; Teal'c respects and honors women as equals.

And guess what? Apophis isn't dead. At the conclusion of "The Serpent's Lair," as his ship is being destroyed, Apophis escaped with Klorel (this fact is unknown to SG-1 at the time) by using the same Stargate that Daniel Jackson used aboard Klorel's ship.

Although cultural influences can make intelligent people say and do silly things, in this case Teal'c's immediate retreat into he-man mode is not really believable. This anomaly of the *SG-1* universe comes up quite a bit nonetheless. Whenever we meet people from Chulak, there seems to be a discrepancy between what they preach (equality and justice) and what they practice (misogyny and ownership). Later in the series ("Birthright") it gets even more uneven when a tangential Amazon-clone civilization is brought in, primarily (it seems, anyway) to get Teal'c some nookie.

Gods & Scientists: Revisionist mythmaking is seen a lot more these days, from television shows like *Stargate SG-1* to poets like H.D. (Hilda Doolittle); telling the side of the story which, until now, has been spoken and transcribed by men.

Interesting Fact: In online discussions, one of the monikers for Apophis is "Pops."

Why We're Space Monkeys: Recasting mythology and incorporating different perspectives (especially a feminist one), is part of the reason *SG-1* is so popular. "[In the beginning] I think [Carter] felt very much like a woman in a man's world," noted Amanda Tapping, "always feeling that she needed to prove herself. Personally, I wasn't fond of playing that dynamic because I think it's sort of tired to keep bringing up the gender war, and the writers, to their great credit, really fleshed her out and gave her a lot less of a didactic message." The writers could have been merely responding to Tapping's own consistent resistance to lines and situations which she felt were not reflective of how women act — in the military, or at all.

Parlez-vous Gate?: Jack as he comes into Fro'tak's house, looking a little stiff in a Serpent Guard's uniform, including huge headdress.
O'NEILL: No wonder these guys are always cranky. Get me out of this thing.

177 ✧

209. Secrets

Original airdate: August 21, 1998
Written by: Terry Curtis Fox
Directed by: Duane Clark

Everyone has a secret to keep, and a reason to keep it.

"Secrets" is one of those episodes that says a whole lot in a really short time — much like the title. The subtext of the word *secret* can spin off into a completely new world — or several hundred, if you're talking about a secret that's in the form of a big, grey spinning ring. The stakes in this episode are as high as they ever get. Daniel finds, and then loses, his wife. Teal'c's secret — that it was he who supervised Sha're's symbiote implantation — is revealed. Sam can't tell her dad that she's doing something far more important than applying for the NASA program, and Jacob Carter has kept the secret of his cancer from his daughter. Finally, Jack O'Neill gets tagged by a reporter and must deny any knowledge of the Stargate program.

What are the costs of all these secrets? The reporter dies, Jacob is crushed by his daughter's refusal, Teal'c lives with guilt that he cannot overcome, and Daniel comes within sight of resolving his struggle, but hope is whisked away again. Secrets can tear lives apart, make situations impossible, and make people shift from caution to paranoia. The first seed of doubt is sown in O'Neill's mind; even as he receives a medal honoring his loyalty he questions the rightness of saving a country whose government kills whenever it wants. Who, in the end, is O'Neill saving? Killers? General Hammond's firm statement that the reporter's death was an accident does nothing to appease the colonel, whose black ops training gives him firsthand knowledge of how "accidents" can happen. RDA's glittering, hooded eyes and carefully blank face are hallmarks of this character actor. He doesn't have to say a lot to get his message across.

Another interesting thread that is picked up later on in the season is the relationship between Jacob and Sam Carter. Carmen Argenziano, who plays Jacob Carter, said in an interview with *Cult Times*, "[The executive producers] told me that Jacob Carter was probably going to lose his bout with cancer. However, upon further consideration they changed their minds and, much to my delight, I became a recurring character." While some online fans disliked Jacob's tough exterior, especially when it was directed at his daughter, the portrayal of a military man who settles for nothing less than the best reveals a telling aspect of Sam's own need to succeed. Fortunately, Sam is intelligent and mature enough to know that living her father's dreams, while admirable, will not satisfy her. It's an interesting and tricky interplay here between the two family members who are also military; imagine telling *your* father, "Sorry, it's classified"!

But perhaps the most ardent displays of secrecy and the power it has to corrupt come from Daniel and Teal'c's journey back to Abydos to see Kasuf, the "Good Father" of Sha're, so that Daniel can tell him he has not found his wife. One secret after another is shotgunned into Daniel — his search was in vain, for his wife was on Abydos all along, impregnated by the hated Goa'uld Apophis. Of all the characters in the *SG-1* universe, Daniel Jackson is the most open and truthful, trying to live his life as well as he can. Seeing him constantly beset by lies, deceit, and cunning is like watching someone tear the wings off a fly — it's heartbreaking. But somehow Daniel continues to perform actions according to a "do unto others" code. When Sha're cannot look at her husband for shame and fear, he soothes her and explains he understands what has happened to her and places no blame on her shoulders. A rare man, on any planet.

Gods & Scientists: We learn that Sha're's symbiote's name is Amonet. "Amoret" is Spenser's faerie queen, who has, among other things, the ability to remain invisible to humans; and the Egyptian deity Amun (also spelled Amon) was, as Amun-Re (Ra), connected with the god Ra, and known as king of the gods. Amunet was his female counterpart. Amun mean, "The Hidden One," and he was the god of those who felt oppressed. When they are shown together, Amunet usually has the head of a serpent — a perfect fit with Apophis. And, speaking of "The Hidden One," what we learn later about Sha're's child becomes more symbolic; he is hidden from the start of his life, and for good reason, as we learn in "Forever in a Day." We also see a return of Heru'ur, whom we saw in "Thor's Chariot."

Interesting Fact: Even though his character dies in season four (which aired in 2002), Douglas H. Arthurs' portrayal of the Goa'uld Heru'ur was very successful; as of the time of writing, 2005, he still attends conventions.

Why We're Space Monkeys: Executive producer Jonathan Glassner: "Most sci-fi shows take place on one or two main sets each week, usually a spaceship. *Stargate SG-1* will take viewers to strange new worlds each week, with different costumes and sets for each show. It's much more demanding and costly to do, but we're very excited about the challenge and the rewards of presenting a unique environment and adventure with each episode."

Parlez-vous Gate?: Jack, upon meeting Captain Carter's father:
O'NEILL: Carter? As in . . .?
CARTER: As in, my father sir, yes.
O'NEILL: Get outta town. Sam's dad? (Extends his hand for a handshake with a big grin). I've heard nothing about you, sir.

210. Bane

Original airdate: September 25, 1998
Written by: Robert Cooper
Directed by: David Warry-Smith

On BP6-3Q1, Teal'c is infected by an alien bug, and the NID *want him as a study subject.*

Originally, the word "bane" was used to refer to a murderer. Nowadays it's been downgraded to mean a cause of stress or strife. It's also a DC Comics character.

"Bane" delivers on all three of these ideas. Poor Teal'c is just a patsy in this one, although his interaction with Ally is sort of nice to watch — sometimes too cutesy, perhaps. It's hard to believe a child of that age would be running around in the slums and have no more serious problem than getting yelled at. On the other hand, her concern for the Jaffa is real, and reflects what a great many younger viewers think; that Teal'c is a gentle giant. "When we first meet Teal' c, all he is concerned about is freeing his people," said Christopher Judge in *TV Zone*, "but as the show has progressed he has come to appreciate the complexities of personal relationships."

Dr. Harlow and Colonel Maybourne are both great villains, like the DC Comics character Bane — although Harlow functions more as a sidekick than a true villain. Maybourne's effortless sneer when he meets Ally is astonishing to watch. Actor Tom McBeath really dredges as much muck out of himself as he can in portraying this seedy NID agent. "When it comes to Maybourne," said McBeath in an interview, "I try to think about what makes him tick. He's a tight little knot who sees his work in a very narrow way. His attitude is, 'Let's just get the job done, no matter how many people die.' Those aspects of the character are more important to me than the military ones."

"Let none admire / That riches grow in hell; that soil may best / Deserve the precious bane," wrote John Milton in *Paradise Lost*. Accumulating "riches" is Maybourne's ultimate goal — money, knowledge, and power. Some for him, and some for his government. The pursuit of these has Maybourne neither caring nor even thinking about the impact his actions will have on the SGC, SG-1, or poor Teal'c. Lurking xenophobia? Who can say. Egomania, for sure. It's sort of a reversal of the Goa'uld situation: Teal'c, with his symbiote inside, becomes a throwaway object for the humans, much as the Goa'uld use humans as hosts, not caring about what happens to the mind within.

Seeing Teal'c suffering physically after a season and a half of good health is powerful stuff. Again, his personal strength of character and his desire to maximize the safety of the people he protects become starkly clear.

Interesting Fact: Colleen Rennison, who plays Ally, took over the role of Cassandra ("Singularity") in season five, when the original actor was not available.

Why We're Space Monkeys: Who uses water guns to parody their own show? While the "little kid who saves the day" theme is occasionally overdone in *SG-1* (among others, "Singularity," "Bane," "Show and Tell," and "Fragile Balance"), it's usually pulled off due to the hard work of the young actor involved, and the attention paid to making the character seem real, despite the unreal situation. Ally swears, is sarcastic, and hides a heart of gold, but she never does anything that seems uncharacteristic, especially when she's talking back to Colonel Maybourne.

Parlez-vous Gate?:
ALLY: Peanuts and caramel. Pretty good, huh?
TEAL'C: Can you get more?
ALLY: Maybe. What's in it for me?
TEAL'C: Peanuts and caramel.

211. The Tok'ra (Part 1)

Original airdate: October 2, 1998
Written by: Jonathan Glassner
Directed by: Brad Turner

SG-1 travels to a planet Sam Carter thinks is the base of operations for the Tok'ra, but the Tok'ra are not as eager to form an alliance as Earth is. Jacob Carter's cancer is worse than it appears, and he is hospitalized.

"The Tok'ra" is still one of my favorite mini-arcs; director Brad Turner ("Thor's Hammer," "Touchstone") does some really great things with these two episodes, utilizing camera angles and pacing to set off important moments. So many things come together, and at just the right time. Thus far, it's seemed that, while there are some good elements out there in the galaxy (the Nox and the Asgard, for example), none of these races are pitted directly against the Goa'uld. Then we meet the Tok'ra. This mini-arc introduces the yin to the Goa'uld yang, which serves to give the humans a helping hand in an otherwise vast, cold universe. While it's fine to have superior technology but withhold it due to moral codes (the Nox), or due to a belief of benign intervention (the Asgard), it's nice to see people who aren't afraid to get down and dirty with the Goa'uld — even if the Tok'ra use mostly subterfuge and infiltration to achieve their ends.

Of course, it's not an easy alliance. The same characteristics that make the Tok'ra valuable in a fight — tenaciousness, vigilance, intelligence — can also make them a bit haughty and paranoid. But in this case it only serves to highlight SG-1's drawing together as a team. Witness the beginning of SG-1's encounter with the Tok'ra on their planet; Daniel, who usually does the negotiations with new races, parlaying and playing diplomat, says nary a word — either his ways are rubbing off on the rest of the team, or they're rethinking their "shoot first, ask questions later" MO.

Perhaps the only thing that rankled in this arc was the profusion of weak lines from Carter. For a person who normally tries to understand something, if not scientifically, at least with some depth, she sure says, "It's just something I have to do," a whole lot. While Carter's serious, intellectual side is shown to dominate in most instances, it's not as though she doesn't feel things. "Singularity" is a good example, as well as her concern for fellow team members ("Message in a Bottle" and "Gamekeeper").

While the cognitive functions of emotions are not well understood, you would think a series that delves so well into other areas of turmoil — like what it means to have, leave, or reunite with family, or how to deal with past actions in the present — would not stoop to generic hero rhetoric like, "It's just something I have to do."

Certainly, when an opportunity presents itself for Captain Carter to take action and find a solution (by using her father to save both the SG teams, the alliance with the Tok'ra, and her father), she doesn't hesitate to clearly explain her thought processes. But every time she is asked to explain how she knows what she knows, she merely shrugs and we are left to guess. It's unclear whether this is a pointed reference

Don S. Davis, in full civilian regalia (ALBERT L. ORTEGA)

to the fact that we don't know that much of how our emotional and mental phenomena (like memory) work or tie together; either way, it's very uncharacteristic of Sam, and makes an otherwise amazing episode seem incomplete.

Gods & Scientists: Jack likens blending with a symbiote to a "Faustian deal." Based on one or two actual figures of history, Faust was a German astrologer (or necromancer, or both, depending on the source), who sold his soul to the devil in exchange for power and immortality. The historical Faust was well-travelled and well-known for his evilness. After his death the myth was resurrected by various people in various forms, including *Doctor Faustus*, a novel by Thomas Mann in 1947, and *Faust*, a popular blank-verse drama by Johann Wolfgang von Goethe in 1801.

Why We're Space Monkeys: The Goa'uld, as a race, are not all bad guys — but they and the Tok'ra are not exactly opposite sides of the same coin, either. The Tok'ra possess many of the same traits as the Goa'uld, including a very diverse and codified set of internal rules and occasionally, a slight superiority complex. They are also proud, and savage when roused (witness Garshaw's reaction to Cordesh's defection). But the Tok'ra, by not using the sarcophagus, keep these character aspects in the manageable background of their lives. One of the real reasons the relationship between the Tau'ri and the Tok'ra is so interesting to watch is because of this clash between the two races.

Parlez-vous Gate?:
O'NEILL: You know, in some galaxies, this is called loitering. How long do ya think we can keep it up?

212. The Tok'ra (Part 2)

Original airdate: October 9, 1998
Written by: Jonathan Glassner
Directed by: Brad Turner

Sam has an idea that could save both the alliance with the Tok'ra and her father's life, but while she's on Earth making preparations, the Goa'uld attack, and SG-1 must decide whether to abandon the Tok'ra, or stay and fight with them against impossible odds.

One of the most brilliant shots of the series is in this episode — it's where Sam and Martouf are on the dune behind the Stargate, with Sam sitting and Martouf a little ways off, standing. Both are still within the circle of the Stargate, though just barely. This shot is incredibly poignant because it encapsulates so much of the series in a single picture: the Stargate, so close and so alien, through which anything is possible. People meet and lives are changed, but the tentativeness of relations, the impact that interaction with others has on our own lives, also has an effect which cannot be taken back. Director Brad Turner and director of photography Peter Woeste do a stellar job again with camera work, integrating special effects with strong character interaction.

Again, with the exception of Sam's occasional, "just have to do this, sir," this episode is one of the best of the season. The Selmak and Jacob blending scenes are powerful and touching, and timed with humor to lighten the heavy themes of death and rebirth. Joy Coghill is amazing as Saroosh, accepting her death and maintaining a wise, no-nonsense attitude. It makes the tough scenes of Saroosh's death (and Jacob's imminent demise unless he gains a symbiote) manageable, as the two humans exchange banter which sends them both off into a coughing fit, tickled pink at their respective predicaments, telling the other they look terrible. There's great chemistry between Argenziano and Coghill, both veteran actors who are comfortable in any role. Coghill especially lends a sympathetic dignity to the Tok'ra elder Selmak, and this goes a long way to repairing the more astringent personalities of other Tok'ra. Garshaw also does some healing in that vein, as she becomes almost warm with Teal'c after he makes a gesture of friendship. And her kissing O'Neill's cheeks stuns both him and the rest of the team; O'Neill's little throat-clearing afterwards is hilarious. For once, he has nothing witty to say.

Actor JR Bourne as Martouf has some serious sex appeal. Those crazy blue eyes and full mouth; no wonder Sam is smitten. The trouble that Sam has with Martouf, once she realizes who he is to Jolinar, is understandable. It's hard enough to deal with our *own* emotional content, never mind adding the consciousness of a whole other person (for lack of a better word). Add to that the fact that the Tok'ra, though they don't live as long as the Goa'uld, live significantly longer than humans, and you have a whirligig of memories. As Jacob notes, "I have a headache the size of Kuwait," from the sudden infusion of knowledge.

Gods & Scientists: Sam undermines a lot of the work we've done in understanding how the Tok'ra and host blend by incorrectly labeling it as "schizophrenic." This is a common mistake, equating schizophrenia with compartmentalized areas of the brain having more than one consciousness, which is actually called "dissociative identity disorder."

Why We're Space Monkeys: Mushy moments. You know, where we get teary-eyed. While *Stargate SG-1* does tend to add to its repertoire more humor than other series, it doesn't shy away from heavy-handed subjects. The truth is, there *are* millions of people on Earth dying from diseases; if they had a new lease on life, would they take it? *SG-1* doesn't just throw away opportunities like that with a few lines. The entire blending procedure is taken seriously from both sides, necessary levity notwithstanding.

And people we love do die, and we have to go on. O'Neill lost a good friend in Kawalsky ("The Enemy Within"), and has continued, and Martouf has also lost someone, and tries hard not to overwhelm Sam with his sense of need as he also struggles to continue in his life.

Parlez-vous Gate?:
CARTER: Well, believe it or not, we need your help, Dad.
JACOB: What? The Pentagon wants me to deliver a message to God when I get up there?
HAMMOND: Not exactly.
JACOB: Well, I don't plan to see the other guy.

213. Spirits

Original airdate: October 23, 1998
Written by: Tor Alexander Valenza
Directed by: Martin Wood

Sam leads her first solo mission with the rest of SG-1, after Colonel O'Neill is injured by an arrow, fired from the same planet where SG-11 has gone missing.

While we do learn some Jaffa lore (for instance, they don't believe in ghosts), this was a less-than-satisfying episode. Thus far, director Martin Wood's offerings have been well done — "Solitudes," "Politics," and "In the Line of Duty" in particular — effectively matching pacing with story, and throwing in the odd cool camera shot or Foley effect. "Spirits" has great costumes, but lacks a bit in story; it's hard to recast any kind of native mythology without getting caught in the trap of making it look "primitive" in the meager sense of the word. Writer Tor Alexander Valenza, who also wrote one of the other funniest episodes in *SG-1* history, "Urgo," is skilful with jokes; not so good on incorporating a breathing mythology into a story. His other offerings, including "Holiday," "Legacy," and "Past and Present," work better because they're not rooted in actual mythology.

But few episodes made me laugh out loud as much as this one did. The Sam/T'akaya interaction, with Sam mimicking Tonané's actions — which you would swear he was doing just for fun — had me laughing for a while. But actor Rodney Grant's portrayal of Tonané was just a little too sweet, and made his clincher lines like, "How does it feel to have met the wind, Sam?" more eye-rolling than wise. Colonel O'Neill's environmental concerns were valid, and expose an aspect of his character that we see more often in later seasons (in addition to any and all references to his beloved fishing expeditions).

As well, Wood's direction incorporated some very nice moments of team cooperation. Season two is very much about the gelling of SG-1 as they "leave the nest" so to speak, exploring the galaxy. One telling scene of team cooperation is when O'Neill, in the midst of giving orders and filling people in, opens the armory and grabs a gun, and hands it to Captain Carter without breaking his narrative off. She takes it, flips off the safety, and cocks it, handing it back to the one-armed colonel. The whole sequence takes less than ten seconds, but is very important; a glimpse of the team in an "off" moment, preparing, strategizing — cooperating almost unconsciously.

Aside from those few moments of team cohesion and the fun factor, however, this episode was a mediocre treatment of a powerful way of life that could have been dealt with much more sensitively.

Gods & Scientists: Several American Indian tribes seem to have been lumped together under the one heading of Flatheads here — pretty much like calling Canadians Americans. The Flatheads lived in what is now Montana, and their religious beliefs were focused on guardian spirits with whom they communicated through visions. One of their particularities, shared with the Plains Indians, was that they would touch their enemies in combat to shame them.

Interesting Fact: Alex Zahara, who plays Xe'ls, is another regular figure on *SG-1* — you just never see him, since he's usually under makeup. This talented actor has a huge range, everything from the hippy Michael in season two's "1969" to the extremely proper Warrick in season seven's "Space Race."

Why We're Space Monkeys: Jack doesn't stand for any monkeying around, and calls a spade a spade, regardless of rank or privilege; but even he is subject to the rules. It's nice seeing him dress down the NID (even if they're not there), with a simple sentence. "You mean steal it?" SG-1's actions stand up behind closed doors as well as in front of the people they meet, but they are restricted to their chain of command. As O'Neill says to Teal'c in "Cor-ai," "There are a lot of things we do that we wish we could change and we sure as hell can't forget, but the whole concept of chain of command undermines the idea of free will. So, as soldiers, we have to do some pretty awful stuff. But we're following orders like we were trained to." This truthful portrayal of military life comes up in this episode, too, when SG-1 is ordered by a frustrated General Hammond (who is also following orders) to deceive the Salish.

Parlez-vous Gate?: When SG-1 encounters T'akaya in her wolf form, Tonané imparts diplomatic wisdom to a long-suffering Carter:
TONANÉ: T'akaya, my friend. My, your coat shines beautifully today. (He looks sideways at Sam.) A little flattery couldn't hurt, Sam.
CARTER (after a moment): My, what big eyes you have.

214. Touchstone

Original airdate: October 30, 1998
Written by: Sam Egan
Directed by: Brad Turner

SG-1 must rescue a weather device that has been stolen from the planet Madrona — by its own people.

One thing that comes out of this episode: you would have thought that the Ancients who built the Stargate would have had some sort of redial! Daniel goes running to the truck that houses the DHD in Area 51 (just in time to see it go out, of course). Considering the things that Carter has already done with the Stargate, we might think that she would consider perhaps looking into that problem with the DHD — does it have a recovery system? Surely it must have all the available coordinates available within (see, "The Other Guys"). She's already thought of resetting the DHD's memory ("Solitudes"), so the SGC must be aware that the DHD keeps a log of sorts housed within it. A "redial" would seem like a natural thing to think of. But it would also ruin the story, which must be why it's glossed over.

Overall, this episode looked quite a bit like *The X-Files*: the overhead shots of the team as they enter the hangar where the second Stargate is kept, the discovery of the "ruse" Stargate, the informant, the dark lighting, Colonel Maybourne's presence — it was a little heavy-handed. Later episodes in this arc ("Chain Reaction," "Smoke and Mirrors") are more discreet and concentrate more on the issues surrounding the Stargate, not the conspiracy itself. Whether or not "Touchstone" was a nod to *The X-Files*, which filmed in the Vancouver area for five years, the resemblance is uncanny. Maybourne starts to look cheaper by the minute, although his parting shot to O'Neill, "Every day is a new day," and that signature smirk indicate that, if the Goa'uld are ever defeated, there's lots of stuff at home that can be cleaned up, too. And a three-tier back-up system? That's a lot of time and effort. O'Neill's quip, "No more smoke and mirrors?" is an excellent set-up for a later Area 51/O'Neill confrontation in season six ("Smoke and Mirrors"). While it is nice to see the team working on their own world, the anti-hero subtext just doesn't work as well as it could have.

The real let-down is the premise — the planet Madrona didn't appear or feel real for one second. The sets were very plastic-looking (the fake Stargate looked way better), the indigenous people looked out of place (did anyone realize that Roham was blind at first?), and the science was extremely iffy. We have a meteorological device that changes the weather on a terraformed planet, in use for 900 years, and it takes four days to completely destroy? That's one shaky ecosystem. It was also never explained how the device worked. Writer Sam Egan (better known for his work on *The Outer Limits*) seems to have kluged this one together, which is too bad, since his *Outer Limits* offerings were so good.

Gods & Scientists: The "NID" keeps being mentioned, but never by their full name. It's never expressly stated on the show, but fans speculate that it stands for either National Intelligence Department or National Intelligence Division. Martin Wood says very adamantly that it means nothing. Fraternal societies like the NID are groups of people who band together because of similar political, ethnic, or economic interests. Secret societies are the third type of fraternal society, the other two being benefit societies, like the Polish National Alliance, and service clubs like the Rotary Club or Kiwanis. Secret societies, also called orders, are by far the oldest of the three types, and the most elusive (obviously), but they include NID prototypes like the Freemasons and the Knights of Malta who started in 1070.

Interesting Fact: How the weather device works, while never properly explained in the episode, nevertheless got message boards ruminating on how it might. Some dismissed it as impossible, since a device that did not allow for seasons would prove more disastrous than not. Others speculated that the device affected not the planet but perhaps another body close to the planet — such as a moon or sun — and manipulated the weather through that instead.

Parlez-vous Gate?: As always, Jack offers up some great lines for the Luddite in all of us:

O'NEILL: Carter wants to get a closer look with some of her specialized doohickeys.
HAMMOND: Doohickeys?
O'NEILL: I believe that's a technical term, sir.

And General Hammond gets pissy with someone in a way that only he can:
HAMMOND: No, I need to talk to [the President] now. Son, do you know what color this phone is?

215. The Fifth Race

Original airdate: January 22, 1999
Written by: Robert Cooper
Directed by: David Warry-Smith

SG-1 explores a new site, where Jack gets the entire repository of the Ancients downloaded into his noggin.

"The Fifth Race" is a good example for the series: in terms of mythology, this is a powerful example of mythmaking in action. The writers have gone the next step in the creation of this series — they are developing their *own* mythology now. By suggesting that the humans are on their way to becoming (or at least have the ability to become) the fifth race of benign, advanced species, and by showcasing this evidence in the person least likely to be chosen (I mean, really, who would choose Jack over Daniel or Sam for important intellectual stuff?), the writers are alluding to the very fabric of humanity. As Jack says to Thor, "We're out there, now." And although humanity may differ slightly person to person, the fact that Jack could be a repository for a knowledge base so intricate and developed speaks to the advancements of humans in general.

And frankly, only Richard Dean Anderson could have pulled off this sort of role this early in the show's run. Many people were still watching *SG-1* because of him, and it was his steady characterizations and rhythms, as well as his confidence and experience as a seasoned television actor, that brought together much of the show's cast and story lines. He has a great knack for making Jack O'Neill seem vinegary but approachable, humble but provocative. As an everyman, O'Neill's appeal is indisputable; and yet he can still hold his own next to the sharper renderings of intellect and morality (represented by Jackson and Carter). While *SG-1* draws on mythology as a basis for its story lines, there comes a point when myths and legends move out of the

Rick at the premiere of *Man on the Moon* in Hollywood (ALBERT L. ORTEGA)

past and apply to the present. Myths, whether they are based on fiction or half-fact, still hold a fascination for us. These days, many of the stories in science fiction have now entered the culture as bona fide myths. The possibilities of science are as rich and varied as are the stories of the gods that every culture on earth has seen fit to pass on. The myths of science are what the Western world is leaving as its legacy.

So, we learn the Stargate is not limited to a seven-chevron configuration, but, with access to more power, can add an eighth chevron as well. Captain Carter likens it to an area code, and while imperfect, the analogy serves as indicator of just how far the Stargate system *could* go. In this respect the Stargate is also an allusion to humanity itself; new things are always being learned about the Stargate, just as new things are always being learned about human nature, even though both are age-old.

Gods & Scientists: The Romans were typified as "the builders of roads," which they claim they learned from the Ancients (we know them as the

Etruscans). Daniel surmises that Latin may be based on the language of the Ancients — a thread we see popping up again and again. Eventually, Daniel starts to search for a lost city of the Ancients ("Full Circle"), and when he does, he again uses Latin to translate the Ancients' text. There is a flaw in this roping together of the Earth peoples and the Ancients, however; the earliest estimate of the establishment of the Roman Empire is 753 BC. But the Stargates are thousands and thousands of years old. So, either the Ancients waited around for a few thousand years for the Romans to appear, or they left and came back, found the people who would eventually become the Romans, and taught them road building. Also, the Roman Empire was founded on slavery, and their roads were instituted to allow easier access for military applications and the movement of slaves and goods; is this a suitable way to allude to the superiority of the Ancients?

Interesting Fact: *TV Guide* columnist G.J. Donnelly isn't a fan: "*Stargate SG-1*'s biggest asset is its accessibility. Since its 1997 inception, the series has provided meat-and-potatoes escapism with a dash of intelligence and plenty of action. But despite occasional flickers of inspiration, it's merely a mediocre adventure with better-than-average production values."

Why We're Space Monkeys: The meaning of life stuff, though it's almost always tongue-in-cheek, is nevertheless brought up incessantly. Michael Shanks notes, "The additional sentiment that you can add [by incorporating into the base of the show the fabric of myths and legends] the avenues you can explore in human relations, in moral issues, things like that — just to touch on it, not to go too far and tell you how it's supposed to be, just to say 'what if'; I think that's as good a reason as any to show how we could look at things differently, if presented with them again."

Parlez-vous Gate?:
DANIEL: You just said there's nothing "cruvus" with you.
O'NEILL: I did not.
DANIEL: Yes, you did.
O'NEILL: No, I didn't.
DANIEL: Yes, you did.
O'NEILL: Didn't.
DANIEL: Did.
O'NEILL: Didn't.

216. A Matter of Time

Original airdate: January 29, 1999
Story by: Misha Rashovich
Teleplay by: Brad Wright
Directed by: Martin Wood

SG-10 is trapped on a planet near a black hole, and the wormhole established to rescue them is sucking in the SGC, and eventually the whole Earth along with it.

If there's one thing this episode reflects, it's that the SGC is learning some harsh lessons about exploring the galaxy. The universe, it seems, is not benign, and traipsing about from planet to planet poses risks that sometimes cannot be foreseen. O'Neill's characteristic "let's go save 'em" attitude is addressed here. It's a strong code in the colonel, who takes very seriously the credo "Never leave a man behind," and in this episode we find out why. Left behind by *his* team on a mission, he sat for four months in a prison (also alluded to in "Prisoners") before getting out. His team's abandonment marked him deeply, and it explains his seemingly overzealous attitude. We see it again in season six's "Abyss"; in fact, the plot hinges on that central idea in the later episode.

"A Matter of Time" is also a chance to see some more urban myths go down the drain. More than once, O'Neill informally dresses down Captain Carter — in a reversal of the "conventional wisdom" that women are too emotional for the military life, Carter's enthusiasm for the science of what is happening makes her appear extremely callous. In this episode, Sam seems almost oblivious to the fact that four people are going to die quite horrible and painful deaths, slowly ripped apart by the force of the gravitational pull from the black hole. In a nice bit of character movement, by season six, Carter will have eased so far from that egg-headed coldness that when she's faced with the repeat situation of having to leave someone to die ("Unnatural Selection"), she is neither nonchalant nor cold-hearted; instead she reacts with remorse and reluctance.

What doesn't go down the drain is the science; instead it's a great vehicle to foster endless debate about the circumstances set in motion in the episode. Black hole theory is fairly new, and not a lot of it has been scientifically proven. It's a great place for science fiction writers to wade around, deploying this story or that. The idea of time slowing down, the effects of the event horizon, and the notion that time is not a static, immutable entity but an elastic point of reference are all phenomena that have been developed in the last hundred years. In terms of the series, however, the continuity of the show is solid, as throughout the episode, each time we see the monitor that is watching SG-10, their time has only elapsed a few second, even though three times that amount of time has elapsed in the SGC.

And, as the iris was destroyed with the force of the gravitational pull, it was replaced with a trinium-enhanced one. Trinium was the mineral found in "Spirits." Apparently, either there was enough lying around for this, or SG-1 managed to negotiate a deal after all.

Gods & Scientists: In physics, matter is described as anything that has mass (this can be solid, liquid, or gaseous in nature). The "stuff" of time is also measurable, in seconds, minutes, hours, etc., but it has no spatial dimension. The matter of time becomes an interesting paradox when it encounters Einstein's special theory of relativity (later expanded to the general theory), which says that physical laws and measurements change when considered by observers in various states of motion. If time has no spatial dimensions and we can't see time, we can only see the effect of time — on matter. Thus, we see the effect of the gravitational pull on Major Boyd and SG-10, but we never actually "see" time.

Why We're Space Monkeys: "Think of something." Carter, far from being a pretty prop, or eye candy for the traditional sci-fi audience of eighteen- to thirty-year-old males, is relied on frequently to find ways out of the fixes SG-1 finds themselves in. This episode is a perfect vehicle for showcasing her expertise in physics, and astrophysics in particular.

Parlez-vous Gate?:
CARTER: Keep your distance, Lieutenant. Sir, for some reason, the warping of our space-time seems to be in advance of the gravitational field rather than as a result of it. It's probably a lensing effect generated by the Stargate itself, but I can't be sure.
CROMWELL (to Colonel O'Neill): Don't even pretend you understood that.

217. Holiday

Original airdate: February 5, 1999
Written by: Tor Alexander Valenza
Directed by: David Warry-Smith

Ma'chello, a man wanted by the Goa'uld for his anti-Goa'uld fighting, escapes the confines of his planet and body and has a little holiday on Earth.

What SG-1 does for a living is dangerous, has large, long-reaching consequences, and often involves things like saving worlds and/or civilizations. Pretty heady, hardcore stuff. But this is also a science fiction show, and one thing the writers know about science fiction fans is that they're smart. And smart people really appreciate irony. Irony is Richard Dean Anderson's stock-in-trade, and he can trade on it admirably. But until now, you don't really get to see any of the other actors get a hand in. "Holiday" is their opportunity (with the possible exception of Sam).

More than a treatise on what it would be like to inhabit someone else for a bit, "Holiday" has many layers of meaning. Ma'chello gets swapped with Daniel, but Daniel gets swapped with Jack too, at least for a bit. Teal'c gets swapped with Jack, then . . . in fact, there's so much body-swapping going on near the end, it's mind boggling. How Carter manages to keep straight who's who is probably one of the reasons she was left out of it — well, that and the obvious desire on the part of the writer to avoid that kind of low-brow titillation. But there's another layer; series characters are notorious for always being the same person, from beginning to end; detractors say that the members of SG-1 are merely updated stereotypes: Teal'c, the stalwart warrior; Daniel, Mr. On-A-Mission-To-Save-Everyone; Jack, the acidic-antihero-leader; and Sam, the sexy tomboy.

While narrative structure insists on characters we can recognize from week to week, *SG-1* does not hold to the charge that they must be two-dimensional pawns in a space soap opera. By now, each character has had a piece of their history excavated; meanings behind actions (such as O'Neill's firm commitment to the team, and Daniel's ideological outlook on life), have been established, and most importantly, the characters have either moved on from those early motivations, or are incorporating them less. In short, they're human, learning as humans do. The series *Farscape*, for instance, has been described as a series that delves more deeply into character because its characters change more rapidly and those changes have a greater impact on how they react to situations from week to week.

But honestly, how quickly *do* we change? How many, for instance, New Year's resolutions are made and broken each year because we *don't* integrate change fully into our lives? The members of SG-1 reflect the slower pace at which most of us develop — we adapt, sure, but sometimes we drag our heels — sometimes, we positively dig our heels in.

And writer Tor Alexander Valenza again draws the most humor he can find out of this episode, while simultaneously interspersing bits of wisdom that don't point so much as vaguely gesture in the direction of a moral. What's more, his tongue is firmly planted in his cheek — as the title suggests, not only a vacation for the characters of *SG-1*, but also for the actors. Witness the fun that Rick, Michael, and Christopher have as they swap and swap again, parodying (but not maliciously) each other's characters.

Gods & Scientists: Dr. Fraiser states, "Our personality, our memory, our conscious selves are derived from unique networks of neurons in the cerebral cortex." Within the central nervous system (discussed also in "The Broca Divide"), the reticular formation (a section of the brain) seems to act like a conduit, passing along and perhaps modifying or even codifying the vast network of interconnections between the cerebral cortex and other regions of the brain. It's this unique melding of sensory experience that we call consciousness.

Why We're Space Monkeys: It's nice to see that Teal'c has some surprising characteristics, even though in early seasons he does resemble the strong silent type. As a former First Prime to Apophis, he has seen and done unusual things. It seems logical that he would be a source of information about the Stargate universe. It adds a dimension to his character when we discover he not only knows who Ma'chello is but explains his history with the man. The fact that he failed in this mission also demonstrates that the Jaffa is not infallible, nor too proud to admit it.

Parlez-vous Gate?: Ostensibly showing the slightly daft nature of the old man, there's a fun tongue-in-cheek reference to the fact that Ma'chello is also played by actor Michael Shanks.
DANIEL (in Ma'chello's body): Ask me anything, something only Daniel would know.

CARTER: Okay, who's Cassandra?
DANIEL (in Ma'chello's body): She's a twelve-year-old girl we found abandoned on P8X-987.
O'NEILL: P8X . . . ? (looks at Sam)
CARTER: . . . 987, yeah.
O'NEILL: All right, lucky guess.

218. Serpent's Song

Original airdate: February 12, 1999
Written by: Katharyn Powers
Directed by: Peter DeLuise

Apophis, beset by the System Lords, asks SG-1 for help.

This is director Peter DeLuise's first episode. Along with Martin Wood, he is one of the most regular directors, especially in later seasons. Son of Dom DeLuise (whom we see in the hilarious "Urgo"), DeLuise's strengths as a director are not readily apparent in this episode, but we can see hints of his ability to move tense scenes along with the right amount of lightness and joviality.

Although there are technical glitches near the beginning (Sam has a weird, tinny voice from a wrongly placed mike or ineffective postproduction procedures), for the most part "Serpent's Song" is a solidly told tale with no unexpected camera angles, utilizing basic cinematography and relying on the actors to carry the momentum of the story. Unlike some directors we've seen, DeLuise doesn't linger too long on reaction shots (see Rodney Grant's smile while behind Sam in "Spirits" — it looks like he's *really* waiting for that "Cut!"), and he stays with safe medium shots and closeups when applicable — although he does a nice marine-cam sequence, following a guard as he races to the Gate room for an unauthorized wormhole.

"Serpent's Song" is an episode that raises questions about criminals, punishment, and revenge. SG-1 might start developing ophiophobia (fear of snakes), since Apophis just won't die. At the end of this episode, Martouf reveals that Sokar has a sarcophagus at his disposal, and so he can revive the dead Goa'uld to torture him as often and for as long as he pleases (also a foreshadowing for "Abyss"). Unlike the Earth contingent, Sokar is not troubled by a conscience and he doesn't care about the fate of the host, or worry about the rights of another being, prisoner of war though he may be. But when O'Neill says, "That's why we're the good guys," the pain that comes through in his voice speaks to the effort that is needed to counteract a seemingly natural instinct to hurt back when we have been hurt. Although at the beginning O'Neill, Teal'c, and Daniel are all ready and willing to pull the plug (or the trigger, as the case may be), they still refrain from acting on these impulses.

This is not to say that the SG-1 team doesn't feel anger and disgust at Apophis' continued existence. Of all of them, Teal'c seems the least perturbed by the pain that the host is going through. The Jaffa seeks revenge and exhibits a merciless use of mental torture on the bound and helpless Apophis. The smile of happiness that Teal'c holds throughout most of the episode is almost feral — a nod to the dangers lurking in revenge. Christopher Judge turns in a stellar performance as the vindicated former First Prime, gloating and lying to the deposed Goa'uld, telling him that he is nothing, that no one on Chulak still worships him. It's tough to see the normally restrained Teal'c give free reign to feelings of revenge and hatred — but it's not unjustified, and part of us wants to be right beside him, sneering too. Teal'c's battle with, and submission to, revenge is one of the reasons this episode is worth repeated watching.

Peter Williams, as always, puts in an amazing performance, both as the ancient, harried Goa'uld Apophis, and as the thousands-of-years-old host he inhabits. Williams switches like lightning between the arrogant, haughty Goa'uld — amazingly, still chilling and threatening, even strapped immobile to a gurney — and the terrified, uncomprehending, and terribly sad host (helped along by excellent work by Michael Shanks, whose character truly has empathy for the ancient Egyptian scribe).

Gods & Scientists: Sokar, also known as Ptah or Neph, was the chief god of Memphis (an ancient Egyptian center), and was often depicted as a mummy. He was, in later incarnations, an artisan of the world, creating the sun and moon and earth; he held the world in his hands, and was complete master of it. Some theorize that Sokar (as Ptah) may have been "invented" as a theological concept, since he did not carry the usual characteristics of a mythological figure and has a very convoluted history. He seems instead to possess the attributes of all the gods, subsuming them as his figure became better known and followed. This is an uncanny foreshadowing of the Sokar we meet in later seasons, a powerful and dangerous villain who consistently keeps one step ahead of SG-1. On the online message boards, there are occasional rants against this type of supervillain who always seems to come back; but as his mummy-like figure suggests, since he is never truly alive, he has nothing to fear from death. And, if he's been invented and imbued with the aspects of many other mythological figures, his resources are vast indeed.

Interesting Fact: A painted canvas iris is sometimes used when the iris on *Stargate* needs to be backlit, but since the individual tines are painted on, no camera can be moved when filming it because it destroys the illusion.

Why We're Space Monkeys: SG-1 isn't always right, but when they're right, they occasionally hate it. When Jack is told that Apophis is dying, he says shortly, "Good — when?"; and Daniel, in a threatening and coldly appropriate manner, leaves Apophis to suffer instead of killing him as he had just threatened to do.

Parlez-vous Gate?:
O'NEILL (when he sees it's Apophis he's pointing his weapon at): "Holy buckets."
A sweetly ironic opening line in an episode that deals very much with the antithesis of holiness — hell and damnation. And later, Jack is positively gleeful, having finally captured an honest-to-goodness bad guy with no chance of his escape. You can almost hear him saying, "Sweet!" every time he looks at the wasted carcass that houses the Goa'uld.
O'NEILL: What do you want?
APOPHIS: To live.
O'NEILL: Can't help you out there. That's between you and your God. Oh wait a minute. You *are* your God. That's a problem.

219. One False Step

Original airdate: February 19, 1999
Written by: Michael Kaplan, John Sanborn
Directed by: William Corcoran

When the population of PJ2-445 begins to fall ill after SG-1's arrival, the team races against time to save the aliens.

"We just can't keep trampling through the galaxy with no regard for the damage that we can do." Sam's line to General Hammond sums up the premise of this episode — a promising one, but one that really didn't come across well in the execution. "One False Step" brings back one of the important themes of the show: the damage wrought by humans as they traipse across the galaxy and their responsibility to the civilizations they're affecting. This idea was first — and more subtly — explored in "Thor's Chariot," but here it falls flat, from the quirky music to the leotard-clad aliens, to the Stargate personnel's improbable behavior. Any doctor worth her degree would have initiated immediate quarantine measures when confronted with this situation — yet Janet Fraiser blithely states that the damage is "probably already done," and on goes business as usual.

Some good points though — a cute Sam moment when she confesses to talking to her plants. It's always exciting when we get a glimpse of the non-SG side of the team, and Sam seems to be more remote than others in that respect. We're reminded, too, that she won't hesitate to stand up for what she believes in when she berates General Hammond for his complacency toward the possible extinction of a population. In a shift from the team interplay we've been privy to all season, this episode shows SG-1 at less than their best. The scene between Jack and Daniel is particularly effective, and the alien's distress — and Teal'c's — at the sudden turn in their usually amiable (if not always on the same wavelength) relationship mirrors our own bewilderment at what we're seeing. Also, Teal'c's symbiote apparently doesn't protect him from everything: even he is not immune to the effects of the plants' ultrasonic vibrations, and it's kind of interesting to see him brought down by a headache.

It's an interesting approach to have the aliens look so human but be constituted so differently they completely stump Fraiser: not everything is what it appears to be. It's one of the leitmotifs of season two, that there is unknown in everything, even in that which seems to be known — and it's something that SG-1 has to face repeatedly throughout the season. The unknown with a familiar face — most spectacularly with Sam's father in "The Tok'ra" — the same person on the outside, but very different inside. In this episode, that idea is shown also through the cause of the aliens' illness — all the obvious causes turn out to be irrelevant, the damage had in fact already occurred by the time SG-1 sneezed, bled, or put new materials in the path of the native population.

Interesting Fact: Sam may have been on to something; for some tips on how to make your garden grow, The Gardener's Network (www.gardenersnet.com) has some clues: "Those of us who cannot sing can turn off the plants' growth and development with our off-tune attempts to promote growth, and result in stunting all growth. Sad songs and slow elevator music can also result in reduced production. Slow music can put your plant to sleep. An upbeat, fast tempo is the preferred choice." Let's hope Sam sings on key.

Parlez-vous Gate?:
DANIEL: Déjà vu.
TEAL'C: I am unfamiliar with that term.
DANIEL: Um, it means I feel like I've been here before.
TEAL'C: That is correct, Daniel Jackson. Yesterday, when we first arrived on this planet.
DANIEL: Right. What was I thinking?

220. Show and Tell

Original airdate: February 26, 1999
Written by: Jonathan Glassner
Directed by: Peter DeLuise

A strange boy comes through the Stargate to warn SG-1 of an imminent danger.

"Show and Tell" had some interesting, thought-provoking moments, but there is a serious lack of jeopardy, especially at the end when the SGC is invaded by *five invisible, angry aliens bent on the destruction of the whole planet.* A breathing space between the more lamentable "One False Step" and the more tailored "1969," this episode is nonetheless enjoyable thanks to the enthusiastic camerawork by Peter DeLuise.

This is the first time we see a TER (Transphase Eradication Rod — couldn't they have come up with a better name?), but we'll see it again, through to season seven ("Fair Game," "Death Knell"). And Colonel O'Neill's hair transformation is complete. Oh, you missed that? Jack's hair, which started out a rusty brown, has gradually become its now standard salt-and-pepper with greying sideburns.

Dr. Fraiser, whose character's growth is remarkable over the series' run, culminating in two of the best episodes in *SG-1*'s history, (season seven's "Heroes," Parts 1 and 2), is calm, methodical, and pragmatic as always. But the glimmers of fire we've seen in previous episodes (such as "Serpent's Song" when she is adamant that the rights of the patient trump the punishment of a war criminal) are also evidenced here, even if in small doses; whether the child has been grown or cloned, her concern is genuine.

Is this the "mothering" instinct in operation? Hardly. "It's like Mother Nature put him together in a hurry and got everything just a bit wrong," she admits to O'Neill. The concept of mothering is a volatile subject for many feminists, who object to the stereotype of mothers as universally good, and motherhood as an inborn trait of woman. Tied in with that is the idea that goodness is somehow connected with beauty. Thus, when the Reetou is finally "seen," her ugliness surprises the team, because they had assumed that, even though she was an alien, she would somehow be — well, not ugly. By showing Mother, the creators of *SG-1* show us how mother's nature and the myth of Mother Nature collide. Mother Nature is often depicted as a nymph or woodland creature, beautiful, surrounded by flowers. She is not green, squat, and possessing multiple appendages whose functions are not readily apparent. And when Mother is shown, what do the members of the SGC do? They react in terror at the difference between themselves and the alien.

Another step in of the long arc of "bringing danger home," for season two.

Gods & Scientists: That reticular formation is getting a lot of airtime lately — more than the omnipresent Gate technician, even! In this episode, Dr. Fraiser states that a consciousness was grafted onto Charlie's brain. His reticular formation is twice the size of normal humans. She then speculates on theories of ESP (sorta) — the extra size of the reticular formation could account for the ability to see things "out of phase."

Interesting Fact: Director Peter DeLuise, like movie director Alfred Hitchcock, always tries to have a cameo appearance in the episodes he directs, usually as nondescript military personnel (or making fun of his dad, as in "Urgo"). In this episode, he very clearly comes from behind the big gun (a clever allusion to a camera, perhaps?) and looks inquiringly at the small boy who's come through the Gate. (Can you spot him in his first episode, "Serpent's Song"?)

Why We're Space Monkeys: O'Neill doesn't always live up to his "stiff-upper-lip" image. He encourages emotional displays in Charlie, carefully making them into a list so as not to look condescending to the sensitive boy. Jack is determined not to make the same mistakes he made with his own son; or perhaps he sees an opportunity to right a few wrongs, cultur-ally — even galactically, one might say.

Parlez-vous Gate?: While not actually dialogue, this is a great moment between Jack and Daniel. The two SG-1 members crouch outside the infir-mary and Jack signals Daniel to go in with guns blazing. When Daniel mimes "people," Jack's exasperation (civilians, geez!) is hilarious.
O'NEILL: ("On three — one, two . . . what?")
DANIEL: ("There are people in there.")
O'NEILL: (glaring and mouthing, "I know!")

221. 1969

Original airdate: March 5, 1999
Written by: Brad Wright
Directed by: Charles Correll

SG-1 gets thrown off course and ends up on Earth, thirty years into the past.

We're nearing the end of season two, and *SG-1* is hitting its stride. This series has a knack for pulling the final three or four episodes of each season tighter in terms of drama, slowly heightening tension for a (usually) spec-tacular cliff-hanger ending.

The supporting cast for *Stargate SG-1* is competent, commanding, and original. Since their introductions, characters like Dr. Fraiser, Sergeant Siler, the "Chevron Guy" (who was officially named Sgt. Walter Harriman), Colonel Maybourne, Jacob Carter, and Master Bra'tac consistently turn in excellent, well-tuned performances. They are the reality against which the explorations of SG-1 are set, people with complex personalities, personal agendas, moral codes that do or do not accord with the SG-1 team, and the intelligence to ask questions and make decisions.

At the forefront of these supporting characters is General Hammond. Don S. Davis brings out his character's actions and motivations with the confidence and thoughtfulness that only a professional of many years can. The opening scenes of this episode are perplexing, but Hammond's choice to behave as though nothing is wrong is perfect, and believable. With the stakes as high as they are, all this competent general can do is set up things as advantageously as he can. For all his spouted bottom-line pragmatism, George Hammond has climbed the ladder in the military by being shrewd, intelligent, and possessed of a long vision. Who else could wait thirty years for something to come about?

Nineteen sixty-nine brought a summer of change for a large portion of the Western world — the moon landing, a contested war in Vietnam — the world changed, but those changes, in retrospect, seem insignificant to the team when placed beside the Stargate. But as Carter remarks, it is the nature of things like solar flares (and life) that you can't predict precisely what will happen. It is only afterwards, upon reflection, that we can make sense of something. We see that Hammond's life, which is fairly routine for a military man, is touched by world events like everyone else's. But we never know when chance happenings in our life can return in a meaningful way. Hammond completes a mission he started thirty years ago (although in season seven Hammond is described as having been in the military for thirty years, it would have been more than that since he was already a lieutenant in 1969). The image of "69" is also an allusion to the solar flares themselves, arcing around the sun in the two positions which take SG-1 back, and then forward, in time. Again, the only connotation of 69 that's *not* alluded to in this episode is the sexual one. With the cultural reference already in place, there's no need for the writers to hammer on that, thankfully.

Aaron Pearl does an amazing job as the younger George Hammond, right down to the slight head tilt and speech lilt. And although the older Cassandra was a bit confusing (*SG-1* is inundated with a profusion of wise, older women: Cassandra from this episode; Catherine, the older woman from "Prisoners"; Saroosh/Selmak), she got quickly to the point (well, after she made fun of Daniel's hair) when she said, "Your journey's just

Don S. Davis (COURTESY JO STORM)

beginning." Such a positive message leaves us feeling good, somehow, about all the strife and grief that cannot be fixed; the good people lost, the situations that cannot be changed, the stumbles in relations.

Interesting Fact: Although he's well known as a character actor, Don S. Davis is not averse to doing comedy, or improv. He had a chance to flex both those muscles in the 2000 feature film *Best in Show*. A dark comedy that looks at the world of dog shows and the people who love them, *Best in Show* was based very much on improv. "All we were given was a scenario for each scene," said Davis. "We weren't given scripted lines. And it was fun." *Best in Show* also had another *SG-1* cast member in it — Colin Cunningham (Major Davis); he played a butcher.

Why We're Space Monkeys: O'Neill makes fun of the science fiction genre whenever he can, an ironic sensibility that's fun for us, too. We know we're watching TV, and Rick, in letting us in on the joke, breaks the "fourth wall," an actor communicating directly to the audience. And parodying himself by comparing himself to two of the most recognizable figures in science fiction — James Kirk and Luke Skywalker — is part homage, and part nose-thumbing.

Parlez-vous Gate?: There are so many great lines in this episode; the quip by the older Cassandra about Daniel's hair, Teal'c's annoyance at having to thumb a ride. And this:
O'NEILL: Or . . .
CARTER: I can't think of an "or" at the moment, Sir.
DANIEL: No "or"?
O'NEILL: There's an "or."
DANIEL: There's an "or"?
CARTER: Sir, you can't just will something to happen because you want it to be a certain way.
O'NEILL: Captain . . . where there's a will, there's an "or" . . . way.

222. Out of Mind

Original airdate: March 12, 1999
Story by: Jonathan Glassner, Brad Wright

Teleplay by: Jonathan Glassner
Directed by: Martin Wood

Each member of SG-1 awakens to find themselves catapulted into the future where they are interrogated about past missions.

As always, the title gives us a good clue about the episode. While the most obvious phrase to come to mind is "out of sight, out of mind," there's always "out of my mind." The removal of the possessive ("my") is an allusion to the universality of the idea of mind; what arises out of mind? What dangers lie within the mind?

Season two was about the consequences of bringing danger home. But as it explores the reaches of space, SG-1 must also deal with the fact that new enemies come with new information — literally speaking, they are bringing home the good with the bad. The mind is not inherently good or evil, it just is — and this episode emphasizes that idea of neutrality; it is up to whomever is controlling the mind to decide its direction. In this case, the members of SG-1 are not controlling their own minds, and even though the knowledge that may be arising from the experience is inherently good, it can be used for not-so-good purposes. We can also tie this into season two's "A Matter of Time"; the "matter" that arises from the mind has different purposes at different times.

Once again, danger has sought out SG-1 — in "Serpent's Song," Sokar tried to come through the Stargate seeking revenge; in "Out of Mind," the Goa'uld are coming through the gate of the mind, consciousness. With no iris other than military training, it's up to SG-1 to push past the barriers of what they see as reality — to go "out" of their mind — in order to perceive the danger.

Unfortunately, the premise got sort of bogged down by the use of flashbacks; budgetary restrictions and special effects aside, many directors, from Peckinpaw to Hitchcock, have created tension without the use of flashback effects. Of course, the flip side of the coin is that movies are not television, and a series that runs for several years has to incorporate some flashback material.

This is the second season's "clip show" (although it's fairly light on clips and heavy on story), but it serves to remind viewers of what has happened over the season, while weaving in some new story material. SG-1's forays into the galaxy don't come without a cost: in a series like this, it's actually nice to see where the team has gone and what they've done, compressed into a short segment. Over the weeks, as we tune in, it's sometimes a little like watching the show in a vacuum — team goes out, team does things, team comes back. So episodes like "Out of Mind" serve to reinforce not only the continuity that the writers, producers, and actors are implementing, but also the notion that this is a team that works together day in and day out. In this case some hard work was necessary to fit two different types of show (season finale, and clip show) into one while keeping it fresh. It's the new content that saves the day here. Throughout its history, *SG-1* has always tried to push the envelope in terms of clip shows, from the tense "Inauguration" to the extremely whimsical "Citizen Joe." Just another reason why the series stands out.

And, still playing both side of the fence, the writers have incorporated a nice "shippy" moment between Jack and a naked Sam. And hey, a new haircut for Daniel!

Gods & Scientists: Society usually exists in strata; from ancient times, societal myths have been used to define group limits and explain why those limits exist. Originally myths explained the stratification by use of divine law — defined by the gods, and thus immutable. In this episode, the underlying mythic structure can be seen in a contemporary sense when SG-1, at various stages, comments on the unusual combination of Horus and the Serpent Guards.

Interesting Fact: While most people know Peter DeLuise makes an appearance on each episode he directs, fewer people know Martin Wood does, too. Look for him usually standing beside Sgt. Siler and/or holding a giant wrench. He calls himself "the Faithful Companion."

Why We're Space Monkeys: Jack very gradually comes to the realization that something is amiss, but there's no melodramatic waiting between the moment he figures it out and the moment he gets up, disables his captor, and walks out to figure out what's going on. Jack's black ops military training is never really portrayed as either heroic or paranoid, it's woven into the fabric of his life. He is constantly vigilant and follows his gut instinct.

Parlez-vous Gate?: When Jack and Sam find Daniel and explain the situation to him, the danger of their position becomes clear to all of them and they don't waste time over technicalities.

DANIEL: So this is all a . . . hoax?

O'NEILL: Big hoax. I'd say so.

DANIEL: I have more questions, but that can wait.

STARGATE SG-1 — SEASON THREE
"Alone in the future."

301. Into the Fire

Original airdate: June 25, 1999
Written by: Brad Wright
Directed by: Martin Wood

Trapped on Hathor's ship, SG-1 fights to free themselves from her while Teal'c fights to free the Jaffa from their dismal fate.

The return of Hathor — we tremble in our boots. A mediocre opening for season three; season two ended on a high note, with lots of tension and disparate threads being woven into the story, but here it fizzles out like the sheen on Suanne Braun's bad wig. Even the Teal'c story line seemed like vapid shouting most of the time — Christopher Judge should never shout, his voice goes up about three octaves and he sounds less like the heroic warrior we've come to love and respect and more like a teenager.

On the upside, we do see a return to human military tactics. We get to see several SG teams working in cohesion. Colonel Makepeace puts in a good performance as Mr. Military Man. But if this was the fire of the title, it was more like a lighter than a bonfire. Hathor's meant to be the queen of the Goa'uld — why is she traipsing around without an army? And if she is picking up Jaffa from other deposed Goa'uld, what's going on in the minds of the Jaffa who obey her? It seems highly improbable that they would do so, especially since Teal'c has worked so hard to portray the Jaffa as intelligent, free-thinking beings. The disparity between these so-called free-thinking beings and the automatons walking around obeying the whims of the first Goa'uld who comes along is a bit hard to swallow. Since the writers have already drawn a religious analogy with the Jaffa (see "Bloodlines"), it would be like a Christian accepting that his God is dead and attending a mosque the next day.

On a more lighthearted note, Daniel's hair has changed with nary an eye blink; and General Hammond gets to be on the front lines — something that would hardly ever happen in a real military situation.

Season three is pretty uneven, with some brilliant stand-alones: "Foothold," "Urgo," and "Shades of Grey," as well as "The Devil You Know" and "Point of View," which are both good continuations of previous arcs. However, these are counterbalanced by some pretty dull plotting ("Crystal Skull"), "shipper" offerings ("A Hundred Days"), and more child-prodigy acts ("Learning Curve").

This episode is like a microcosm of the whole season; the team works well together, everyone's motivations are strong, but they're bogged down by badly thought-out science and needlessly convoluted subplots. We're still watching primarily for the team interaction, not for the over-the-top baddies or the special effects.

Gods & Scientists: As is common with Egyptian mythology, the goddess we see as Hathor is actually an amalgamation of a lot of different deities. One of the reasons Egyptian mythology is so rich is that, unlike Greek myths where you know exactly who did what and to whom, the gods and stories in the Egyptian pantheon move around and change. In that postmodern respect, Egyptian myths are really fitting for the *SG-1* universe, as they allow a lot more room to play, parody, and posit questions.

Interesting Fact: The "briefing room," as it is known, is where a great deal of exposition goes on. Since the room is used so often, directors and camera operators often find it difficult to portray the room in new ways while maintaining a sense of continuity so that it feels familiar to us. One of the ways they avoid making the room seem static is by projecting moving pictures onto screens in the background behind General Hammond — on the computers, which show the status of the Stargate, or on the larger screen, often used to flash looping playback of conception art that was used in the episode.

Why We're Space Monkeys: We're space monkeys because we're willing to watch large dangerous threads, like Teal'c's fervent desire to free the Jaffa.

At best, the Jaffa show a reflection of the innate desire of all beings to be free, but this subplot runs the danger of becoming mere soapbox moralizing. Still, the writers tackle the issue in almost every season in some form or another, and they allow it to change the way that a real freedom fight would change.

Parlez-vous Gate?: Two quotes stand out in this episode.
The first is Teal'c's description of the being he used to serve:
TEAL'C: False god. *Dead* false god.
And Daniel has a fun line when Colonel Makepeace asks him if he's okay despite being injured:
DANIEL: It's just a deep bleeding gash, but it'll be fine.

302. Seth

Original airdate: July 2, 1999
Written by: Jonathan Glassner
Directed by: William Corcoran

The Tok'ra take a Goa'uld census and request SG-1's help in finding one who may still be on Earth.

The universe of the Stargate is growing. The movie was based on the premise that there was only one Goa'uld (see "Making Myth"). Ra was the last of a dying race; but SG-1 learns that there are in fact several thousand Goa'uld (which does not mean they're *not* a dying race) and, of those, perhaps a dozen System Lords, those who rule over other Goa'uld and anyone else they can find. This episode highlights the Tok'ra's reliance upon reconnaissance and infiltration as their offensive weapons; while they don't engage the Goa'uld face-to-face like the Tau'ri do, they know where every System Lord is, which puts them at an advantage over the Tau'ri, who just fight them wherever they see them, without regard for the impact. The season finales of both season one and two emphasize this: SG-1 encounters a Goa'uld and dispatches it only to have their actions come back and bite them.

Season three takes the Goa'uld stereotype built up over season one and expands on it. The Tok'ra are less haughty and seem to be more blended with their hosts, allowing for an emotional range that the Goa'uld don't have. And the Goa'uld, while they're still shown to be mostly about power-mongering, can also use their intelligence for things other than procuring power. "Seth" is a good example. In this episode, we have a Goa'uld hiding out on Earth on purpose, not rushing about the galaxy trying to strangle his competitors.

As for the humans, they're not just blindly racing around trying to procure technology that they don't understand: they're becoming better, too, adopting the Tok'ra's reconnaissance stance and turning the Goa'uld mentality to their advantage. They're also relying on their own technology when they can. In "Seth," human technology is used to cause an electric charge that disrupts the effects of the brainwashing.

SG-1's movement as a team is very well coordinated — perhaps as a result of the fact that they're finally able to focus on just one Goa'uld, in a specific place, at a specific time — a known battle, of sorts. Coming after the season opener, which seemed so big and loose, "Seth" is a return, literally and figuratively, to closer communications.

There are also some funny moments — downplayed for sure but if you're watching for them, you get to see some "behind the scenes" team action. The funniest is when Sam tests the ear device on everyone except herself.

There were a couple of gaps in the episode that were very strange. At the beginning, for example, the iris is covering the Stargate *before* it's engaged. It opens, and *then* the wormhole is established — how do they know who's coming in, since the wormhole has to be in place before a signal can be sent? Besides the funny moments and the expansion of the Goa'uld hierarchy, however, these gaps were negligible.

Gods & Scientists: According to the *Pyramid Texts*, a collection of ancient Egyptian writings gathered from the insides of pyramids, Seth dismembered his brother Osiris and then denied doing it. In this episode, Daniel refers quite significantly to the fact that Seth always kills his followers — perhaps an allusion to this aspect of Seth's story. The *Pyramid Texts* tell how Seth and another god, Horus, fought, and Seth's testicles were torn off (one wonders how he handles a harem — and the irony of course is that Daniel alludes to Seth castrating his own people, when in mythology, he himself has been castrated). This Egyptian myth is in direct contradiction to the Western notion of the charismatic person as being sexual (or sexualized). Even Seth's leather coat, a garment traditionally denoting virility, is worn over — yes, you saw that correctly — pyjamas in the episode.

Interesting Fact: Ancient Egyptian burial rites took seventy-two days — innards were removed (including the brain, by a hooked pick), but the heart (which Egyptians thought was the seat of intelligence) was left in the body.

Why We're Space Monkeys: Sam kills Seth — and it's her job, she doesn't make a big fuss over it. Another *Wizard of Oz* moment — "Hail Dorothy!"

Parlez-vous Gate:
CARTER: So, Daniel, you feel pretty certain that if we get caught he'll turn us into one of those zombies rather than kill us?
DANIEL: Well, we're more valuable to him that way.
CARTER: Why? How do you think he'll use us?
DANIEL: Well historically, he used women as a harem. They catered to his every whim and as a result they were well cared for.
CARTER: Super.
DANIEL: And the men outside the main court were used mostly as warriors and guards, protecting his compound, pretty much doing his bidding.
O'NEILL: Dare I ask about the men inside?
DANIEL: They were turned into eunuchs.
O'NEILL: Eunuchs, as in snippidy-do-da? Sweet.

303. Fair Game

Original airdate: July 9, 1999
Written by: Robert Cooper
Directed by: Martin Wood

The Asgard and the Goa'uld meet on Earth to decide the fate of the Tau'ri.

What is the ontology of benevolence? What constitutes benevolence, and what is limited benevolence? In other words, what constitutes a fair game? These issues are all key to this episode. Jack accuses the Asgard of refusing

Martin Wood and Peter DeLuise, two guiding lights for *SG-1* (<small>COURTESY ZOE BENNETT</small>)

to help defend Earth from imminent destruction because their benevolence is limited. The subtext is that each society takes care of itself, and that a truly selfless being (or race) is rarer than rare; despite their posturing, the Asgard are still, debatably, just like everyone else — looking out for themselves.

"Fair Game" also emphasizes the sacrifices inherent in politics. There comes a point when any advantage or skill, whether it be yours or the enemy's, is fair game if it can be used to achieve what you want. In this case, the humans are up against a system of politics that they have never before encountered, literally on a galactic scale.

There's an interesting play on the contrast between self-determination and fair game: is it fair game that the Asgard are playing, divvying up planets and people like chattel, based on a bluff? The crux of the problem is that the Asgard, who have superior technology to the Goa'uld, don't have the resources to back up their claim. How much self-determination do the Tau'ri really have if they're under the yoke of a bluffing, albeit benevolent, Protectorate? In this way, the people from Earth mimic the Jaffa situation, as traditionally the Jaffa are seen as fair game for the Goa'uld in terms of slave labour and in terms of being hosts. In that respect, the episode turns the question of good and evil on its ear — can any particular race be defined as truly good when each is playing their own game with their own stakes?

"Fair Game" made use of a lot of knowledge from seasons one and two; Jack makes use of intel in his own bluff to delegate Yu about Nirrti's intentions. Although the episode that first named Nirrti (season one's "Singularity") casts Nirrti as a man, this could easily be explained by Nirrti having taken another host for whatever reason. This is another example of the fluidity seen in the original Egyptian mythology, where storytellers had enormous licence with the particulars of the story, as long as the characters exhibited the same characteristics as Nirrti does here. Nirrti's character always seems to be thrown into the mix and then vanishes again without a trace, which is a shame because she has a lot of potential. She does, however, reappear in a big way in season six's "Metamorphosis."

Gods & Scientists: Nirrti is the Hindu goddess of death. Her name, meaning "destruction," says it all. She is said to live in the south — which is itself the land of the dead. She is mentioned in the *Rig Veda*, the oldest book of hymns in the Hindu religion.

Interesting Fact: Like many people we see in *SG-1*, Ron Halder (Cronus) also appeared in *MacGyver*, in "Blind Faith" and "The Ten Percent Solution."

Why We're Space Monkeys: Sam gets promoted, but it's not treated like it's a big deal. Most series would use their token female officer as a bandwagon with which to wave the feminist flag, but Sam becomes a major and it's business as usual. Season three does a pretty good job as a rule, of blending Sam in with the rest of the SG team, making her no different in behavior or treatment than any other member. The writers do, however, pause to make fun of the whole thing in the later episode, "Deadman Switch," with one of the funniest lines of the season, and again in season eight's "Reckoning."

Parlez-vous Gate:
TEAL'C: I mean no disrespect. But I give my allegiance to you, the SGC, and to the people of this world, freely. I will, however, not see to the petty needs of these Goa'ulds.
DANIEL (half raises his hand): I'll see to the petty needs of the Goa'ulds, sir.

304. Legacy

Original airdate: July 16, 1999
Written by: Tor Alexander Valenza
Directed by: Peter DeLuise

Daniel gets to go crazy. The rest of SG-1 gets to stand by and look skeptical.

A dismal Ma'chello add-on pack, this episode delivers exactly what you'd think it would — basically, nothing. A rogue faction of Goa'uld called the Linvris are discovered by SG-1. Daniel goes crazy, and we find out that Ma'chello's devices from "Holiday" are actually anti-Goa'uld devices, which in this case hunt the wrong people, since the Linvris are anti-Goa'uld (but no one seems to acknowledge that). The *clever irony* here, that the legacy of Ma'chello is counteracted by the legacy of the Goa'uld marker left in the host's bloodstream, is about as subtle as a night at a strip club.

The writing is tired, the characters seem tired, and even Jack has no patience for crazy Daniel. Poor Sam looks tired of being the one to find all the answers, and even the stalwart Dr. Fraiser looks apoplectic, not delusional, saving the day. In one scene that makes absolutely no sense, she starts to take her clothing off (which became fodder for some interesting fan fiction).

Again there is an allusion to beings who do not exist on the material plane but are beings of energy, foreshadowing season three's "Maternal Instinct" and the end of season five. Michael's reprisal of this role under different circumstances in season seven's "Lifeboat" garnered him a Leo for best performance by a male, and you can see the germination of that role here.

One of the legacies dealt with implicitly in this episode is the long-term effects of the Gate. For three seasons we've seen team after team depart through a gate that demolecularizes them and then reconstitutes them billions of light years away on distant planets where they encounter unimaginable forms of life. The team lives in a high-stress environment even when not off-world, as the SGC is the frontline for anything that comes through the Gate that's not friendly, and they must meet, deal with, and attempt to understand technologies and beings for which they have absolutely no point of reference. When it's all put down in black and white like that, no wonder so many of them have headaches!

But the fact is that the Gate has serious consequences, and "Legacy" points readily to this.

Gods & Scientists: Used usually in terms of the law, a legacy is something that is left by will or testament from one person to another. While this episode deals in individual legacies, it also alludes to the collective legacy that the Linvris leave for the Goa'uld. That's the thing with legacies: the person receiving may not necessarily *want* what they're getting. A popular motif in Victorian novels was for someone to leave a legacy behind them to an illegitimate child or undeserving relative. For instance, Jane Austen's *Sense and Sensibility* is based on this idea.

Parlez-vous Gate: A line by Daniel that is supposed to be funny but actually ends up just being irritating:

DANIEL: Teal'c said the Linvris were being hunted by the System Lords, right? Now what if they used some sort of technology that transformed their bodies into . . . I don't know, energy or something.

O'NEILL: Energy?

DANIEL: Or something. I don't know exactly how — Sam can figure that part out.

305. Learning Curve

Original airdate: July 23, 1999
Written by: Heather Ash
Directed by: Martin Wood

The SGC participates in a peaceful exchange of technology and information with the people of Orban, until they realize that the Urrone children harbor nanotechnology within them.

SG-1 tends to delve too often into the realm of children-as-plot-development, but somehow, they always seem to pull it off; perhaps this is partially due to the series being a family show. In any case, this episode is no exception. It starts out a little slow and, in all honesty, boring (watching Daniel dust off the carefully broken pedestal plates is just annoying), but picks up about halfway through the episode, as SG-1's "learning curve" for the

Urrone and the Orban civilization gains momentum. Strong throughout the episode is O'Neill's insistence on children's rights, which he champions with the same hotheadedness we saw for Tonané's people in "Spirits." Normally, it would seem out of place to have a military man, with black ops training no less, be so fervent about ecological and sociological factors. But O'Neill pursues Merrin's freedom with the same driven energy that makes him denounce his own people (in "Spirits"), or fire on the enemy.

SG-1 is at first eager to share and trade technology and information, then they have an about-face as their own moral codes come into play, when they learn that Urrones, who have undergone an "Averium" procedure, are reduced to the neural level of a newborn when the nanites are removed. The team is understandably wary of nanotechnology (see "Brief Candle"), and part of their learning curve involves understanding a technology they had previously labeled dangerous. But they slowly become aware, through repeated contact with Merrin and the adult Kalan, that there are other ways to pass along knowledge besides the traditional human one. It's also a nifty allusion to the theme of genetic memory, an idea we've seen already with the Goa'uld (each Goa'uld is born with the cumulative knowledge of all its brethren, much as the citizens of Orban all share the same knowledge). But while the Goa'uld use the information for personal gain, the Urrone use it to benefit their entire society.

The mythology of the *Stargate* universe is branching out; in "Fair Game" we saw Chinese and Hindu mythology, and in "Learning Curve" it's Aztec mythology being used. While it's nice to see the writers incorporating other mythological figures and historical data, somehow none of the mythologies showcased in this series have the punch of the Egyptian mythology. They lack the austerity, and the dangerous lilt that was set up in the movie. The svelte emotions of the Goa'uld go well with the formal, ceremonial mind of the ancient Egyptians. Still, to hold up another mythology as a counterpoint — as is seen in "Learning Curve" — highlights those very differences for the viewer and makes the return of the Egyptian thread that much more stark. How we love to hate those false gods, the Goa'uld.

"Learning Curve" had a great premise, and yet the writers used children as the focal point when they could have used any element of society whose rights we take for granted (the ill or the handicapped would have been an interesting choice, but perhaps kids get paid less?). In the end, the episode bears repeated watching: the learning curve on this episode is tricky and somewhat steep.

Gods & Scientists: A "learning curve" is a two-dimensional representation of the rate at which a person learns or acquires a new skill. At first, the "output" for the skill is high and the return or reward is low — think about learning to throw a ball, for instance. As the person practices, the output becomes smaller — concentration, muscle control, and so on — and the reward bigger. But the people of Orban do not have this learning curve, except in the Urrone. To an adult Orban, there is only knowing, and not-knowing.

Interesting Fact: Laara Sadiq, who is credited as some variation of "Technician" in at least fourteen episodes on *Stargate SG-1*, is also a stage actress. She was nominated for a Jessie Richardson Theater Award in 2005 for her role in *Crime and Punishment*.

Why We're Space Monkeys: This episode really speaks to you on an emotional level; when SG-1 leaves the planet, things aren't perfect, they haven't accomplished everything they wanted to, and you get to see that there are real emotional repercussions of what they go through on their missions.

Parlez-vous Gate?: Hammond gets very few great lines, but this is definitely one of them:
HAMMOND: In the future, Major, before you activate any device that includes the word reactor in it, I would appreciate it if you'd notify me.

306. Point of View

Original airdate: July 30, 1999
Story by: Jonathan Glassner, Brad Wright, Robert Cooper, Tor Alexander Valenza
Teleplay by: Jonathan Glassner, Brad Wright
Directed by: Peter DeLuise

An alternate universe Sam and Major Kawalsky appear through the quantum mirror requesting asylum at the SGC when their world is destroyed by Apophis.

When this episode started off with yet another *X-Files*-ish feel (big, spooky warehouse, low lighting, creepy music), I was concerned that season three had bogged down again. Far from scraping the bottom of the barrel, "Point of View" delves into some hefty subjects and offers some strong opinions. Space and time may bisect at a million different points, each with their people and stories, but as Teal'c sums up so succinctly, "Ours is the only reality of consequence." Picking up where "There But for the Grace of God" left off, SG-1 continues to puzzle through difficult situations in very postmodern terms; there is no one way to do things, so there is no one truth, and no universally applicable framework in which to exist. Yeah, that's some heady stuff for a television series to tackle.

Point of view is one of the most basic components of telling a story — who tells the story, and why? However, this episode also plays on the pun of the words — Daniel's use of the quantum mirror is pointing his view toward different realities, searching for the one he wants; in this case, the point of viewing is to get back to the reality they know.

As with every venture into the land of "shipdom" (season four's "Window of Opportunity," for example), the writers' dilemma is pretty thorny. On the one hand, they know that if they introduce the relationship aspect into a series, they have to continue it (see "Making Myth"); on the other hand, they know that military protocol discourages fraternization; since the Stargate program is military-based, they can't go bending the rules, especially since viewers' suspension of disbelief for any science fiction show relies on its plausibility. Nonetheless, this show has always been concerned with fan response, and the fans wanted to see the shipper aspect explored. This episode plays with the idea by positing the possibility of romance within an alternate universe. This could suggest that the creative team don't truly believe Sam and Jack belong together, or they could be suggesting that, in "our" reality, they're just not going to be. Either way, the possibility is left up to the viewer's own point of view. Enmeshed in science and drama, "Point of View" is worth rewatching.

Gods & Scientists: Doctor Fraiser notes that AU Kawalsky *is*, for all intents and purposes, Kawalsky. In terms of physics, this poses the problem of "entropic cascade failure." Entropy is defined as a thermodynamic measurement that dictates the extent of randomness in the universe — in concrete terms, AU Sam cannot exist in our reality because her molecules are already being "used."

Interesting Fact: Many visual effects are incorporated into today's film and television shows, most without our even noticing it. Like a good paint job, "FX" are noted by their absence rather than their presence. Everything from matted stills of cities ("Children of the Gods" and numerous others), to matted textures (the lake behind O'Neill in "Fifth Man" is not actually there, it was added in postproduction), to full-motion CGI models (most notably, the Asgard and their interactions with SG-1). Often Richard, Michael, Amanda, and Chris will spend many days acting in front of a large green plate, onto which computer graphics and images are generated in postproduction. When the actors are actually being filmed however, instead of seeing what we see — the bridge of an alien ship, or an alien talking to them — they see X's, which mark where they should be, where their computer-generated companion will be, and if they're lucky, a stick with a can on top that they act to. "I stood in an area where everything was green except for me," said Dom DeLuise of his own green screen experience for the episode "Urgo." "They took some shots of me as Urgo that made him appear three inches tall. It's been a while since I was three inches," joked the veteran actor.

Why We're Space Monkeys: No other science fiction show makes fun of its own hairstyles as much as *SG-1* does. The plethora of hair jokes between the two Sams is fun, and really, when confronted with an alternate version of yourself, it must be pretty damn hard to know what to talk about — hair is a great option. Plus, it's a great opportunity to see what the hairstyle you were thinking about going for would look like.

Parlez-vous Gate?: As Sam stares at a living, breathing version of herself:
CARTER: Oh my God. This is too weird.
O'NEILL: Yeah. How about that hair?

307. Deadman Switch

Original airdate: August 6, 1999
Written by: Robert Cooper
Directed by: Martin Wood

SG-1 gets caught by an alien bounty hunter and tries to negotiate their way out of bondage. But somebody, somewhere, has to die . . .

Season three takes quite a few risks — moving away from the centrifugal plotline of the Goa'uld for a while, opening the possibilities of the universe that SG-1 is exploring, and inserting more stand-alone episodes. The writers of this season are embracing the possibilities that multiple worlds with multiple personalities can offer, and, with the continued presence of Peter DeLuise as a director, allowing more of the humorous tones to come out. There's more banter, especially on the part of Jack and Daniel (Richard Dean Anderson is notorious for ad-libbing his lines), and more cohesion to the team as a whole. Again, this is a reflection of a real-life team, be it military, office, or creative. With the addition of history, certain things become background noise — like Sam's ability to come up with insane but workable solutions; Jack's stance on the mistreatment of anything, human, animal, or vegetable; Teal'c's straight-guy attitude as a setup for humor.

"Deadman Switch" doesn't move plot along so much as alleviate some tension that follows from a stronger story arc — in this case, the AU arc. The previous week's offering was hard to watch, emotionally, but one of the great things about SG-1 is the writers' habit of lightening the mood between thematically "heavy" episodes with more ironic fare. They clearly realize that, for all the narratives of consequence that are being shown, this *is* a television series, and a science fiction television series at that. Sometimes people just want to unplug, sit back, and listen to someone tell them a funny story.

And that's what this episode delivers. Some of the funniest lines in the whole season come up here, and honestly, if you don't laugh at least once, you need to go outside more. Sam J. Jones (he was a *Playgirl* centerfold in 1975, can you believe it?) plays the smart-aleck alien. Aris Boch is cunning, and yet never loses sight of the fact that life is just a big ball o' fun. His grumbling as he returns, wounded, to his ship, the one eye opening after he cagily allows himself to get shot with a zat gun — all remind us of a burly but benign bear. Definitely one of my top five episodes for humor, making fun of itself, the premise, and the genre in general.

Interesting Fact: Isn't that the *same* wash we saw SG-1 slide down in "Children of the Gods" and later in "Thor's Chariot"? Add a few trees, change the camera angle; they get a lot of use out of that valley.

Why We're Space Monkeys: The priceless moments between characters that don't even involve dialogue. SG-1 has something like a reverse soap-opera effect here; instead of long-suffering looks of angst and wanton-but-repressed lust, they glare, raise eyebrows, smirk, and otherwise twist their facial features in wordless answers much like the ones real people use every day. One of the best of these comes after Sam mentions that Aris isn't a Goa'uld, to which Jack quips, "And? But? So? Therefore?" Sam's answering shrug is absolutely priceless — half exasperated, half annoyed — and speaks so well to another facet of teamwork, those it's-been-a-long-day moments that we rarely see on the small screen.

Parlez-vous Gate?:
ARIS: Dr. Jackson, if you don't mind . . . (looks at Daniel's confused face) treating my wound.
DANIEL: I'm an archaeologist.
ARIS: I know, but you're also a doctor.
DANIEL: . . . of archaeology.
ARIS: Never mind. Captain, you must have some medical training.
CARTER: Actually, I'm a Major now.
ARIS: Oh! Well, how very important. I'll inform the galaxy. Can you get over here now and help me, Major?
And a little later:
ARIS: O'Neill, you're considered . . . well, you're a pain in the mik'ta!
(Jack looks at Teal'c)
O'NEILL: Neck?
TEAL'C: (pause) No.

308. Demons

Original airdate: August 13, 1999
Written by: Carl Binder
Directed by: Peter DeLuise

SG-1 encounters a civilization still stuck in the Dark Ages, and tries to rescue them from the clutches of an Unas.

Sam notes that this is the first time that SG-1 has encountered a Christian settlement in their hundreds of missions; while this is not strictly true ("The First Commandment" was based on Christian beliefs), it is certainly the first time the writers of the series have delved deeply into the arena of Christian ideology.

Keith Topping, who wrote the book *Beyond the Gate*, notes that this episode is a "good attempt [. . .] at something conceptually tricky and ethically dangerous." While the first part of the statement rings true, the second does not. There is nothing ethically dangerous in portraying the Christian value system, any more than there is in portraying any system of belief or mythology — professionally dangerous, perhaps, but not ethically. That statement presupposes that the Christian tracts are the only truth. "Demons" demonstrates once again that *SG-1* is willing to tackle contentious issues. If mythology can be defined by the inclusion of acts of a deity or deities (gods and their actions for or against humans) as a means to explain, validate, or warn, then Christianity, by strict definition, could fall under the heading of "mythology." Where it gets tricky is when mythology is perforce debunked as "untrue." Since it is maintained that "truth" itself can be open to interpretation, this episode won't be looked at in terms of ethical treatment of Christianity as a religion, but rather as a codified set of parameters, embodied (rather obviously) in the character of Canon (played by Alan Peterson). The character's name suggests strongly that he is the living embodiment of those parameters.

As a character, Canon is the most interesting we meet in this episode. Simon, played by David McNally (who seems to be really good at being the "wronged guy" — witness his performance in "Cor-ai"), is less subtle than Canon, at least until the end of the episode when it flattens out into a bad-guy-gets-his type of thing. Alan Peterson's portrayal of the spiritual leader of the village is varied enough to make us harbor, if only once or twice, some sympathy for the man. Medieval times were characterized by a very superstitious view of the world. Whether or not this outlook was brought about by the church of the time is not our debate here — instead, there are moments when Canon seems weighed down with the responsibility of looking after his village the only way he knows. You can imagine that, like Simon, Canon started out with a real spark of altruism, which, when in combination with his ring, the passage of time, and the rush of power that came with his station, turned him into the ugly, misshapen version we see.

This is the problem that can come about when anything is rigidly codified. The clever pun of "Canon" that the writers use here is an allusion to the very fabric of mythology (and religion, perhaps) itself. Only when things become dogmatic do we see an establishment of a "canon," a rule set that is used to judge.

Gods & Scientists: Although derived from Greek, where it meant "rule" or "standard," the word *canon* was seen mostly in Christian thought. It has since wended its way into more popular vernacular — for instance, a particular director or author's works or subsection of works attributed to them can be called their "canon"; within an oeuvre of works by a particular author the best representatives together are often called their canon; in works of antiquity where the author can be questioned, only texts verified as authentic are referred to as that author's canon.

Interesting Fact: "Fanon" is a term adopted by Internet groups and fans to speak of those things which are well established in the fandom but not necessarily made explicit in the show, and is an amalgamation of the word "canon" and "fan." For instance, we never are told explicitly about Sam Carter's "black widow syndrome," but it was picked up through inference and then replicated by fandom writers and message posters. The whole *fanon vs. canon* debate gets murky though, since, with the plethora of material for *SG-1*, lines get blurred between who said what, to what purpose, and when. Amanda Tapping, who plays Sam Carter, has herself referred to the black widow syndrome — but this is the actor talking, not the character. And yet, how Tapping approaches the role — whether her opinion of Sam's black widow syndrome changes her choices *as an actor* — does affect how the fannish canon reacts, and vice versa.

Why We're Space Monkeys: Continuity is, as always, pretty darn good in this episode. Okay, okay, sometimes it's terribly lacking — but this is the episode where Jack gets his eyebrow scar.

Parlez-vous Gate?:
O'NEILL (as SG-1 is carted off to die): Carter, if I ever get the urge to help anybody again, feel free to give me a swift kick.
Then later:
O'NEILL (as SG-1 is carted off *again* to die): Major, next time Daniel gets the urge to help someone, shoot him.

309. Rules of Engagement

Original airdate: August 20, 1999
Written by: Terry Curtis Fox
Directed by: Bill Gereghty

A group of unknown SG teams turns their guns on SG-1, who later learn that these are not members of the SGC, but trained infiltrators of Apophis.

"Rules of Engagement" is a return to honest, full-out, nonstop action with a bone of the Jaffa life thrown in for good measure. After the heavy fare of "Point of View" and "Demons," and the fluffy "Deadman Switch," director Bill Gereghty gets back into the nitty gritty (literally) of grenades, lots of dirt, cool facial makeup, and guns. Lots of guns.

The beginning of the episode is very well done, and, in true action style, has lots of slow-motion camerawork as the unknown SG team (gasp!) turns its guns on SG-1 (gasp!). It's hilarious to watch the hapless sergeant continually frustrated by the talking "dead" SG-1. Poking a little fun at the military itself, suggesting it's merely a collection of young boys with guns (nary a woman in the ranks besides Major Carter), this episode doesn't serve very much in terms of larger story arcs, but it's darn fun to watch. With Apophis dead, the fallout of his reign will be felt for a while, and it was smart thinking on the writers' part to use the idea.

It's a little sketchy in places, though — why would watching a video monitor, once, suddenly change the mind of a man who had spent the entire episode fiercely loyal to Apophis? Even Jack's trademark quips fall a little flat in this episode, though, as always, his presence as military officer is well executed. SG-1 is a unique team in that its ranks are not exclusively military (or human, for that matter). The fluidity of command, such as when Teal'c assumes leadership when they realize they are dealing with followers of Apophis, is great, and alludes to O'Neill's comfort level with his command in general; he trusts his team to do the right thing at the right time, and the unspoken respect that they have for him reflects in how seriously they take their job — even if they have a little fun with it. I loved Teal'c's face when he called O'Neill, "underling."

There is a bit of Jaffa lore thrown in to the mix as well, broadening

Christopher Judge (ALBERT L. ORTEGA)

the background of this people, but again handled somewhat unevenly. Why are there no women, when on Chulak women are clearly in the ranks? Kyle seems as easy to brainwash as he is to deprogram, so why was he left in charge? Are the others worse? Perhaps it is a comment on his youth, that he can be so easily swayed, and thus by extension, a comment on the military (and conscription) in general, commandeering young men and molding their minds as they see fit. Take a look at the flip side of this equation in "The Other Side."

Interesting Fact: Born out of the Hague and Geneva Conventions of 1907 and 1949 respectively, which set out the international rules of war, the term "Rules of Engagement" (ROE) is used to describe the set of parameters that American military personnel abide by while under conditions of war. While based on the international war laws, the ROE for American military is actually more stringent, reflecting the original ideals of the American people. You often see these rules in operation in the background of *SG-1*. Guns are loaded but are on safety at all times unless threat is imminent, for instance; and the use of force is a last resort, used only to accomplish immediate goals of a mission, ceasing when that objective is completed. While the ROE are more of a guideline and change depending on the situation (political, social, and military), their most basic tenets are almost always followed, including the allowance for nonmilitary personnel in war zones (medics and the Red Cross, for example — see "Heroes").

Why We're Space Monkeys: Daniel's revenge. Daniel is slowly morphing from the geeky, clumsy Daniel Jackson of the movie into a mature man who has seen a great deal. He can handle a gun (though he still hates to), and isn't quite so quick to save everyone all the time. But he's still human, as we see when the sergeant calls him "four eyes" (see "Upgrades" for the next instalment on this subject).

Parlez-vous Gate?:
ROGERS: I will reveal nothing. You may begin torturing me.
O'NEILL (waving a tuna sandwich around): Oh, I've already begun. This is the infamous tuna torture.

310. Forever in a Day

Original airdate: October 8, 1999
Written by: Jonathan Glassner
Directed by: Peter DeLuise

Daniel Jackson must come to terms with the death of his wife, who is killed by Teal'c.

It was good to see this opening: for the most part when we encounter the Goa'uld they're either secreted in some giant ship (which may or may not get the giant erase-o treatment from the Asgard), or they are surrounded by only a few Jaffa. The apparent ease with which SG-1 dispatched Apophis and Hathor was making the Goa'uld seem a little too easy to kill. The beginning of this episode helps eradicate that by bringing in the old-fashioned "hordes of bad guys." It's truly a moment of fear when what looks like hundreds of Jaffa come streaming over the hill. You understand much more clearly the odds against which these four-person SG teams pit themselves when they encounter the enemy.

Three things are happening in the moment that Amonet is attempting to kill Daniel. For Daniel it's a moment of communication/communion with Sha're, his long-vanished wife. For Sha're it is a last ditch struggle against all that the Goa'uld represent — everything that has been taken from her in her life. For Teal'c, it is a choice between acting as a warrior and acting as a friend. In all three cases, what transpires takes only a few seconds, yet those few seconds, once released from the constraints of time (and this is shown really well in the episode, using analepsis, or flashback, as the story mode), contain the seeds for so much more. Daniel's movement through the different places of grief and loss, Teal'c's battle with his choice to kill or spare Amonet and his subsequent pain over not being forgiven by Daniel, and Sha're's desire to allow her "real" self to emerge, even momentarily, makes for compelling watching.

It is a terrible and intriguing choice on Teal'c's part to kill Sha're rather than disable her. Teal'c, who is still wrestling with his overt hatred of the Goa'uld and what they have done to his people, reacts in a way that is unfortunate, but not unmitigated. For decades, this Jaffa has seen the worst that the Goa'uld can do — can we really blame him for literally shooting from the hip in a moment of crisis? We often hear stories of people doing things they might not if given more time to reflect, but "Forever in a Day" reverses this idea. In the heat of a battle (and Teal'c's reaction to Amonet can be seen as another battleground in the middle of his personal war), judgments and decisions must be made in the blink of an eye. It is the aftermath and the consequences that are stretched out for Teal'c to deal with. While Daniel's foray into forever happens within the moment of being tortured by Amonet, Teal'c's stretches out across the rest of his life, as he must forever deal with the consequences of his actions. Which forever, in that case, is worse?

This episode gives us a new Daniel: his main quest has ended. While he remains the most forgiving of the team, and in some ways the most intelligent, especially in matters of the heart, he now has to move on from his original intentions. His character development plays out more fully later in the season (see "Maternal Instinct"), and is the groundwork for a much later development as well (see "Ascension" and "Threads" in particular).

And let's not forget the technical aspects of the episode. The grainy, dull-to-golden-brown quality of the sand adds to the sense of timelessness and gives an almost restful quality to the scenes between Daniel and Kasuf. The shot where Amonet/Sha're reveals her face past the hand device is stunning. Once again we are transported into the world of the Goa'uld, who care nothing for Daniel except that he can be used and then disposed of.

Gods & Scientists: Amonet and Apophis mated (that is, their hosts procreated), which resulted in a Harcesis child. This child was born with the genetic memories of both its parents — a human with the knowledge of a Goa'uld. The Goa'uld, obviously, are not keen on humans possessing their knowledge, and so they hunt them down and kill them. The Harcesis could prove to be a very important factor in the fight against the Goa'uld — and that, along with his emotional attachment to the child, brings Daniel back to the SGC. Many religions include a savior or supra-child in their writings, from the god of light Mithra in the Iranian pantheon to the idea of the rebirth of the bodhisattva ("Buddha-to-be") in the form of the Dalai Lama.

Why We're Space Monkeys: Teal'c's emotional life is powerful. Christopher Judge pulls out all the stops, and even though he is a supporting character in this episode, he steals scenes all over the place. When the shroud for Sha're is pulled back, ostensibly it's Daniel for whom we should feel the most sympathetic, but it's Teal'c's barely withheld tears that get the most heartstring action. Same with Teal'c's absolute refusal to let things lie, as happens so often in our own interactions with each other. He wishes things to be cleared up, and his constant attempts to confront Daniel, who so obviously wants to avoid confrontation, are powerfully wrought.

Parlez-vous Gate?:
O'NEILL: Give it a week. You'll miss me.
DANIEL: Yes, all the salty, bad-tempered insults, all the illogical arguments.

311. Past and Present

Original airdate: October 15, 1999
Written by: Tor Alexander Valenza
Directed by: Bill Gereghty

SG-1 tries to help an entire population afflicted with amnesia, and comes face-to-face with the consequences of previous actions in the form of an old enemy.

We are halfway through season three, and *SG-1* seems to really struggle through this one, despite some great moments. Jack, Sam, and Teal'c are reduced to the status of bystanders, we're subjected to some incredibly irritating mannerisms on the part of Megan Leitch (Ke'ra), and although the team's circumstances are pretty grim and humbling, the episode is strangely slow-moving. This contrasts sharply with the pacing of the last episode which, while it also dealt slowly with contentious issues, had better tension and pacing.

"Past and Present" brings back Linea, the Destroyer of Worlds, whom we first encountered in season two's "Prisoners"; she, along with her victim population of choice, has lost her memory — and her age — while trying to concoct a potion for eternal youth. In this episode, SG-1 has to deal with the consequences of their carelessness in "Prisoners," when they inadvertently gave Linea information that allowed her to escape through the Stargate.

Memory is one of the more encompassing themes of the show, and of the third season. In "Learning Curve," the memories of the children are wiped as soon as they have served their purpose; in "Jolinar's Memories" we'll see how the memories of the Tok'ra symbiote and Sam's own are integrated; in season two's "Gamekeeper," memories were used as a trap for SG-1; and in season one's "Fire and Water," Daniel accesses memories he didn't know he had. The Goa'uld have genetic memory, the Tok'ra have memory-amplification/exhibition devices. Who are we without our memories? How does memory loss affect us on an individual level, and on a societal one? How much of who we are is shaped by our personal memories and the stories passed on to us by our elders? The importance of myth and history in our beliefs and identities is explored really well through the characters of Mayris and Orner especially — without even basic knowledge of who they are and what their lives were like before the Vorlix, they represent the difficulties of not-knowing. Knowledge is a weapon and a defense, it's identity and direction. "Past and Present" shows effectively that not-knowing promises more than just irritation — it's dangerous. And even though the end of season two told the story of what happens when knowledge is turned against you, in the end, not having it is the greater of two evils.

Unfortunately, the impact of Ke'ra's character is lessened by her annoying mannerisms — the eyelash fluttering, the stilted speech, the too-earnest, doe-like eyes. She's an amalgam of two stereotypes: the damsel in distress and the perfect woman who lives just to help others. One can see why Daniel would be drawn to her. She has the same innocence he found so intriguing in Sha're — but frankly none of the charm. Appearances are deceiving, a lesson SG-1 has to learn over and over.

"All you have to do is forget." Daniel's plea to Ke'ra is heartfelt and telling; he's just lost Sha're, for good, and he doesn't want to lose her, too. Shanks delivers the line in an understated way, with real grief and pleading in his voice — he, too, would like to forget and go back to being the person he was before Sha're was taken from him.

Gods & Scientists: On one of his expeditions, fifteenth-century Spanish explorer Juan Ponce de Léon learned from native Indians of an island on which there was a spring that granted eternal youth; this is the origin of the Fountain of Youth mythology in Western culture. The legend has been transformed and used in many stories — even in *Indiana Jones and the Last Crusade*! — and its supposed properties vary from healing wounds and curing illness to giving eternal life. See another version of this myth in season seven's "Evolution."

Interesting Fact: When Ke'ra talks about dargos, a pesticide that caused fertility problems in the Vyans, Daniel refers to DDT. The pesticide known as

DDT (dichlorodiphenyltrichloroethane) is a synthetic insecticide that acts by affecting the nervous system. It was first made in 1874, but only realized as a potential pesticide in 1939 by a Swiss chemist. Because many insects rapidly developed an immunity to the agent, the compound built up in birds and fish — both human food elements. The general use of DDT was banned in the United States in 1972 due to the potential danger to humans.

Why We're Space Monkeys: SG-1 is responsible for the whole debacle on Vyus, but there's no melodramatic holding of heads, no long speeches expositing dismay, beyond the initial recognition that SG-1 messed up. They observe the problem — and its cause — then work diligently and without complaint until they fix it.

Parlez-vous Gate?:
O'NEILL: Linea is dead, right?
CARTER: Well, if those two bodies that Ke'ra found really were the Vian elders that Linea was experimenting on . . .
O'NEILL: Don't say it, Carter.
CARTER: Sir, we wouldn't recognize her even if she walked in the front door.
O'NEILL: Don't, don't . . .
(Puts his hands over his ears and starts singing.)

312. Jolinar's Memories

Original airdate: October 22, 1999
Written by: Sonny Wareham, Daniel Stashower
Directed by: Peter DeLuise

Jacob Carter is imprisoned on a hell planet by Sokar; SG-1, accompanied by Martouf, try to infiltrate the prison with the help of Jolinar's memories.

"Jolinar's Memories" is a great example of everything that makes *Stargate SG-1* unique: jam-packed with action, full of dramatic and emotional tension, and offering a nice segue into more team-oriented episodes, after the last couple of Daniel-centric ones ("Forever in a Day," "Past and Present"). It's also a showcase for some subtle acting on Amanda Tapping's part. She lets a lot of Sam Carter's facets shine through — the devoted daughter and the consummate professional, the emotional and the military melding, neither one overtaking the other. Her grief at having to relive receiving the news of her mother's death is heartwrenching, and you get pulled into all the battles she goes through in this and the next episode ("The Devil You Know") — physical and emotional.

Here again, one of the main issues is knowledge — this time in the form of Jolinar's memories, which Sam hopes to access with the Tok'ra memory device we first saw in "Out of Mind." In reliving the memories — both Jolinar's and her own — she also relives the emotions attached to those moments, showing us the double-edged sword that is memory, and toeing the line between the useful and the dangerous. We learn that Sam experiences flashes of Jolinar's memories, sometimes in dreams; dreams have typically been seen as one of the ways through which the mind releases what has been pent up, so it seems logical that that's how these memories would be revealed.

The bond between Sam and Martouf strengthens, despite some tensions and differences of opinions. As with any real-life relationship, however, things aren't smooth and easy, and unfortunately for both of them, their emotions are entwined with those of and for Jolinar. This makes it difficult for Sam and Martouf to figure out exactly what's going on between them.

The Goa'uld Sokar is also a revisitation of a type of Goa'uld we don't see too often — but when we do, it's worth the wait. As with Amonet, Hathor, Apophis, and Nirrti, the ideology of the Goa'uld is simple, but their ways of implementing it are as varied as cruelty can be. Hathor favored deception and subterfuge while amassing an army to take on the System Lords. Nirrti prefers experimentation to promote her agenda and gain the freedom of immortality, at which point she can more leisurely attain dominance over the galaxy. Apophis uses a combination of explosiveness, charisma, and cunning to achieve his goals. There are two common threads we see in all: disregard for any life but their own, and a fatal underestimation of others. Okay, usually it's SG-1 who bests them, but as the series moves along, this particular weakness has serious repercussions.

Other themes are visited, too. The death imagery is ironic and clear when the team and Martouf take the life pods, which look fairly coffin-like, to Ne'tu. *Stargate SG-1* often does "descents" — descents to different mind states, to hell realms in different circumstances, or to different timelines where things have gone wrong — but "Jolinar's Memories" is perhaps the most blatant use of the motif.

The episode ends with Apophis alive, if not entirely well, having taken SG-1 and Martouf captive; in the show, as in reality, threads and people return throughout our lives and we have to deal with them repeatedly, in different forms and ways. Seeing Apophis alive — again! — could come off as more irritating than it does. Once again, Peter Williams makes his nine-lives trick seem realistic rather than redundant.

Gods & Scientists: Ne'tu, the hell that Sokar has constructed in "Jolinar's Memories" is based on myths of hell in the *Book of Am-Taut*, a guide of sorts to passing through the otherworlds of ancient Egypt. It's a fairly typical image of hell, with fire and smoke and eternal suffering, and one that's been taken up throughout the ages in many cultures — including Christianity and Dante Alighieri's *Inferno*. In that book, the poet-protagonist had to journey through the nine circles of hell in order to attain paradise; each circle was reserved for a specific brand of sinner — from the unbaptized to traitors — and each had an eternal torment assigned to it. In much the same way, SG-1 (and in particular Jacob Carter, played almost monotonously by Carmen Argenziano) has to suffer through the torments of Ne'tu in order to regain Earth, guided by Martouf and Jolinar who, despite her memories, remains an elusive character.

Interesting Fact: When asked in an interview with *Cult Times* what his favorite episode was, Carmen Argenziano replied: "As a viewer I had a lot of fun watching "Jolinar's Memories" and "The Devil You Know," but as an actor there was more I wanted to do with my character. I thought my performance was very one-note. Even though Jacob/Selmak was near death, most of the time I should have animated him somehow or given him more energy. So I was a bit disappointed with myself, but in the end I decided to look upon it as a learning experience."

The set for this episode took a couple of months to build, and cost almost as much as the pilot "Children of the Gods." "Jolinar's Memories" and the second part, "The Devil You Know" were filmed together as one episode.

Why We're Space Monkeys: Sam has some wonderful moments in this episode that show she's truly got it all down — she's not perfect, but she keeps her professional, military behavior while still showing emotion about her father being captured. Rather than being all one, or all the other,

her character has grown to such a degree that she combines both really well. When she remembers Jolinar's association with Bynarr, she expresses sincere regrets to Martouf, but she doesn't dwell on it — there's a time and a place for everything.

Parlez-vous Gate?:
MARTOUF: As soon as you are ready. If you are sure, you are *all* sure you understand what you are volunteering for.
DANIEL: You said hell, right?
O'NEILL: Well, I'm going to end up there sooner or later. May as well check out the neighborhood.

313. The Devil You Know

Original airdate: October 29, 1999
Written by: Robert Cooper
Directed by: Peter DeLuise

SG-1 is stuck in hell with Jacob Carter, and must escape before the newly risen Apophis and his army clash with Sokar.

The writers of *SG-1* often use a humanistic slant in their episodes, and "The Devil You Know" is no exception. The humanist premise is again raised here as mythological entries to heaven and hell, retribution and remorse, are played out on a different plane — or planet, in this case. Starting with the title, the very fact that the devil can "be known," moves it from a scenario involving the acts of a deity (an evil one) to the realm of choices which humans can understand and relate to. Normally the concepts of hell and devils are placed in the category of the "unknowable," since we have to die to see if they are real. But the notion of hell (and hell states) is strong in most Western religions. Eastern religions such as Buddhism have a slightly different take on it; hell is not a separate place to which the soul travels to, it is here and now, operating through the senses with things like lust, greed, and ill-will. The very postmodern writers of *Stargate SG-1* are incorporating both ideologies here, to form, once again, that great meld of science fiction and fantasy. SG-1 travels to a hellish place, but as they are still alive, they feel the nature of hell immediately.

Again, this reflection of our current reality is strong — the world can seem to be a very hellish place these days, especially if you are an avid CNN watcher.

Bedevilled by memories (a similar situation to "The Gamekeeper"), SG-1 is like us, feeling out of control in their own lives and at the mercy of an entity who cares nothing for *them*, only for what they can bring. Thankfully, SG-1 is far and away a different team than they were in season one — this team is now familiar with the kinds of technology that can be leveled against them, and they refuse to submit to the insidious demands of Apophis, even when drugged, because they are prepared

Peter Williams as Apophis, or "Pops" as he's known online (COURTESY JO STORM)

to meet their worst fears. Jack, Daniel, and Sam have all been to the depths of their past and come back from it whole. It will take more than a clever devil to undo this team.

Gods & Scientists: The word "devil" is from the Greek "diabolos," which means "slanderer," or "accuser." It is a spirit or power of evil. "The Devil" generally refers to the most important evil spirit in a given religion, and it can take many forms. The main difference is between monotheistic religions and religions with multiple deities. In Western theology, the devil's main task was to tempt man away from God. Many religions, including Christianity, Islam, and Buddhism, have stories or fables that include a prophet who is tempted by a devil, a necessary obstacle they must overcome before becoming purified. Also, in Greek mythology, the tale of Orpheus has an interesting parallel in SG-1's journey. Orpheus travels to Hades (the underworld) to rescue his love, Persephone, braving all the horrors that mortal man is not supposed to be able to stand.

Interesting Fact: Actor David Palffy, who plays Sokar, also plays season six's Anubis. A great bad guy, with that steely eyed, ruthless, Goa'uld glare.

Why We're Space Monkeys: Teal'c makes no bones about his loyalties, or his methods. He tries the talking route with Aldwin, but when he's shut down, bides his time until the best moment and then calmly shoves the Tok'ra into a holding cell until he accomplishes his mission. And while he genuinely apologizes to Aldwin afterward for his treatment, we have no doubt that he'd do the same thing again in an instant.

Parlez-vous Gate?: At the end of the episode, a very satisfied Teal'c comes into the Ring bay where the rest of SG-1 and Martouf are collapsed, barely alive, and states the obvious:
TEAL'C: We have escaped.

314. Foothold

Original airdate: November 5, 1999
Written by: Heather Ash
Directed by: Andy Mikita

The SGC is overrun by an alien race who are determined to take over Earth, right after they take care of Teal'c and Sam.

This is a great episode! It's fun, has crazy aliens, great team moments from Sam and Teal'c, and again from Jack and Daniel, but there's enough tension in the plot to keep it from seeming too flippant. Plus it has my all-time favorite line from Carter. And Janet Fraiser's turn from concerned doctor to mad scientist experimenter is stunning. Even when seen side by side with Christopher Judge or Richard, Teryl Rothery brings them all down to size with her pure talent. It must have been great fun to have been the subject of O'Neill's reluctance as she was lying in Major Davis' arms and Jack had to partially disrobe her; you can almost see the smirk she's holding back.

Unfortunately a couple of early gaffs stick out — if the Stargate only moves within one galaxy, why, at the beginning, do the aliens characterize the Goa'uld as the "dominant parasitical species of *this* galaxy"? The implication is that these aliens are from a different galaxy, which would seem to contradict *Stargate* mythology as it has been presented thus far. And geez, I know Carter's a good shot, but firing a gun in an airplane? Colin Cunningham as Major Davis does a crazy alien scream that still creeps me

Colin Cunningham auctions off an *SG-1* script for charity (COURTESY ROBIN BENNETT)

out, even after repeated viewings. It's also nice to see an episode based on revealing information rather than the usual setup of problem-posed-then-fixed. This reflects a real foothold situation, where people don't know what's going on and make judgments accordingly, as Colonel Maybourne's actions indicate when Sam calls him.

Heather Ash's script is otherwise well written. Science fiction fans really liked this one (it made sense when O'Neill woke up after his double had died), and it had cool alien technology. It's almost a shame that it was a stand-alone, especially given that the ending is left open (the aliens who escaped are now in possession, or so the SGC believes, of a lot of sensitive material about Earth). The episode also reverses the standard of exploring — what happens when other races come exploring on *Earth*? And the development of Colonel Maybourne's character is also well worth watching — he's not just a powermongerer after all, or so it seems. Ruthless and highly intelligent, "Harry" is seeing firsthand what happens when the missions come home. Up to this point he's been in charge of the pillaging aspect of the Stargate in Area 51. This episode, he was nose to nose — well, nose to *something* — with an alien.

Interesting Fact: Alex Zahara (who plays the alien leader) takes a long time to learn his lines to perfection in his various roles, but the most arduous of them all was when he played an Unas in season seven's "Enemy Mine." Said Zahara, "Iron Shirt was huge — lots of lines in English, translated to Unas, and then performed, so lots of work, there. I had the animal thing going on myself, so not too much prep was needed." According to Zahara, while filming "Foothold," an extra passed out while wearing the heavy alien suit. Zahara himself was the alien who got shot in the shoulder by Maybourne on the plane.

Why We're Space Monkeys: Siler gets beat up — again. That poor man gets thrown down the stairs ("Upgrades"), electrocuted ("A Matter of Time"), and punched almost every time there's a scuffle. Thankfully, since he's also the stunt coordinator for the show, he doesn't mind too much.

Parlez-vous Gate?: My favorite line of the whole series (well okay, top five, anyway, see "Deadman Switch"):
CARTER: Maybourne, you are an *idiot* every day of the week! Why couldn't you have taken just one day off?

315. Pretense

Original airdate: January 21, 2000
Written by: Katharyn Powers
Directed by: David Warry-Smith

The Tollan invite SG-1 to participate in a Triad, a court of sorts, at the request of Skaara/Klorel, who is on trial.

Law, the function of law, and courts are often seen in *SG-1*. From *Hill Street Blues* to *The Practice* to *CSI*, TV shows about law invest us. "Pretense" picks up this idea and puts it in an alien context. As with other stories in the Goa'uld arc ("Fair Game," "Children of the Gods," "Serpent's Song"), the duplicitous nature of the Goa'uld symbiote is the focus here; Klorel and his counsel Zipacna play to perfection the sneering, domineering Goa'uld; their complete disregard for any rules but their own is a militant stance we see reflected in some nation-states in our world. And the use of civil law to mask military intentions has many despicable precedents in human history.

"Pretense" struggles with some real issues. The Tollan cannot or will not undo what has been done (Klorel being implanted); they can only deal with circumstances as they have arisen. And Klorel does lengthen Skaara's life, as well as preserving it in circumstances where he would normally die; an interesting look at autonomy over shared resources. While the outcome is fairly predictable (of course the Goa'uld are going to tamper with the Tollan's technology), Alexis Cruz does a great job as Skaara/Klorel, switching back and forth between the two identities with real panache and talent. Who'd have known this secondary actor from the movie would have had such a long run in the television series? And Zipacna, in all his nail-regarding glory, is so easy to hate it's almost sinful.

The scenes between O'Neill and Skaara are excellent. Skaara almost doesn't trust himself anymore, as he has been a prisoner of the Goa'uld symbiote for some time, but when he does speak, it is with disarming simplicity. Jack certainly doesn't trust the Goa'uld inside Skaara, but warring with distrust is his deep love for the young man — the tempest of hate and anger toward the Goa'uld and love for the boy make for high tension, heightening the alien courtroom drama. And it's always nice to see the Nox; this particular arc is well thought-out; the fairy-like creatures are not just put into a stand-alone episode and then tossed aside as ethereal aliens. They may look little, but the Nox's wisdom is portrayed as deep and abiding, not a television version of a fairytale.

There is great computer-generated art in this episode, too; you can see the budget of *Stargate SG-1* expand as the show gained momentum and viewers. And pay attention to O'Neill's barbs about technology, a setup for the later "Shades of Grey." Teal'c defies orders (he does that a lot in the early seasons, doesn't he?), but again his intentions are loyal — and Lya is just so *cute* and childlike, but completely believable as the earnest, nonpartisan member of the Nox contingent.

Gods & Scientists: Early Egyptian law was not codified as clearly as modern Western law is. Societal myths, which were constructed orally over time, were applied explicitly or implicitly as evidence or a precedent when needed. From there myths became rooted in the tradition of rules that eventually became the law — but the law, like the myths themselves, was

Alexis Cruz (ALBERT L. ORTEGA)

very regional and fluid. Stories about divine wisdom revealed to seers, prophets, or the Pharaoh himself were used as baselines. More emphasis was placed on harmony and balance within the nation than on the individual — and individual rights only fell within certain boundaries. For instance, slavery was acceptable. An Ancient Egyptian would have no trouble seeing both sides of the Klorel/Skaara argument.

Why We're Space Monkeys: The Nox. They rock. Wish we'd see them more. It's nice to see other familiar races coming back, especially benign races like the Tollan and the Nox.

Parlez-vous Gate?:
DANIEL (explains to Jack): So the seeker is the defendant and the archon is the attorney.
O'NEILL (snarkily): I got it. (To Travell) So Skaara is our . . . (pauses and looks at Daniel)
DANIEL: Seeker.
O'NEILL: Seeker.

316. Urgo

Original airdate: January 28, 2000
Written by: Tor Alexander Valenza
Directed by: Peter DeLuise

SG-1 travels to an alien paradise and comes back bugged — literally.

A great deal of sci-fi canon deals with two things — humans in other places, and the importance of the personal, subjective experience. Contact with aliens, machines, giant glowing minds, cyborgs, and talking clouds (see season eight's "Grace" for more on talking clouds), has always brought up the same questions: what does it mean to be alive? What constitutes living, awareness, subjectivity? The word "person" is adapted from the Latin "persona," which, ironically, was used to denote the masque worn by an actor when performing a play. Later, "persona" was adopted by the Jungian psychological school to note the different identities we have throughout our lives — sibling, lover, friend, parent. Each persona has its own unique aspects that are shown only in their particular instances. A further refinement of this in linguistics by Ferdinand de Saussure also attaches a particular way of talking to each persona, called a "parole."

Oh, who are we kidding? "Urgo" has a hilarious plotline (my favorite of Tor Valenza's by far), and Dom DeLuise's treatment is delicious — so much fun, so many great lines, the whole "me, me, me, meeeee" thing that makes me laugh until my sides hurt every time — but the impact of the story is still as deep as ever. Going all the way back to personalism's forefather, René Descartes, this episode expands lines that were begun in "Pretense" — what does it mean to "be"? In this episode, Daniel scales it down rather drastically to "self-awareness" and leaves out a ton of philosophical cant, basing most of his rhetoric on fear of death. A little thin, but we'll take it, mostly because we're still laughing. "Yes, as in dead. They're gonna kill ya. They'll open your brains with a big, giant can opener, and then they scoop me out with a big scoopy thing. That's how it works. It's death or me. Me or death. You have to decide. Me . . . or death." And Urgo's fear of his own twin, the "brain sucker" . . . his Jaffa melding with Teal'c ("Teal'c? Help. Kree! Jump him. Give him a double Jaffa-Jaffa kick. Go on!") . . . the list goes on.

Basically, if you're having a bad day, stick this in, and by the end of the episode, everything will be all right again.

Gods & Scientists: "Urgo" is a homonym for the word "ergo," which means "therefore," and was most famously used by René Descartes: "cogito, ergo sum" (I think, therefore I am). An allusion to the whole premise of the episode, with a clever twist on the 'ur,' since the German prefix "ur" denotes "original" or "proto."

Interesting Fact: When Urgo changes into someone he thinks SG-1 is looking for (the implication is "dull"), he morphs into none other than Peter DeLuise, director of the episode and Dom's son.

Why We're Space Monkeys: Director Peter DeLuise gets to make fun of his dad and let his dad make fun of him — and he gets paid for it, too! Eventually all the DeLuise boys make their way onto the SG-1 set — Dom, Peter, Michael ("Wormhole Extreme"), and David (who plays Pete Shanahan in later seasons). To a man they're all fun, funny, and endearing.

Parlez-vous Gate?: Every line. Woof.

317. A Hundred Days

Original airdate: February 4, 2000
Story by: V.C. James
Teleplay by: Brad Wright
Directed by: David Warry-Smith

Jack is a farmer, Sam is a genius, Teal'c is determined. But then again, we already knew that. And where's the archaeologist again?

Few episodes thus far have caused as much controversy in the *Stargate* fandom than "A Hundred Days," especially amongst the shipper faction. The episode is far from perfect, resorting to some tired clichés and plot devices, and it seems condensed, too tightly packed for the time allotted it. Even executive producer Brad Wright believes the episode should have been a two-parter, and that O'Neill wouldn't have given up so fast — echoing the sentiments of many a fan. Since Jack does give up and starts to accept his life on Edora, his reaction when he is finally rescued must have been quite a shock to the rest of his team. But Jack is human, and therefore adaptable — he's trained his mind to believe that he's stuck there for good and to make the most of the situation. Confronted with a situation he had buried — much like the planet's Stargate — he has a lot of ghosts to deal with before being able to move forward.

We have the idyllic setting — but really, there are only so many times you can pan to a shot of a calm, pristine lake or a quiet field before it gets old. The message that life is simpler on Edora is not so much shown as it is thrown at you. What could have been a lovely setting for a compelling episode becomes a deterrent to the story, because the idea *is* compelling — Jack stranded on a planet, unable to get home, having lost everything and everyone he knew. What do we do when we've lost it all? In some ways, "A Hundred Days" puts a character we've come to know and love in the position of the populations that the SG teams usually help. Through the eyes of someone we trust, we see the lack of direction that comes from losing your home and your livelihood. It's a promising idea, and Richard does a fantastic job of showing us the quiet desolation he's feeling. And, like in "Into the Fire," Jack comes face to face with the fact that he may be facing the future alone. In those circumstances, who wouldn't try to put the past behind them and move on?

Playing the devoted dad is Rick's favorite role (JIM SMEAL/WIREIMAGE)

But the writers' best intentions keep getting thwarted by cloying annoyances. James and Wright use convenient plot devices to move the story along — the old cliché of the teenage kid getting people into danger through heedless actions, the oh-so-convenient timing of Laira hearing the voices on the radio. The whole episode can seem like a forty-two-minute wait just for Sam's reaction when Jack moves over to Laira to say goodbye after Sam has slaved for three months to get him back.

"A Hundred Days" is built on moments; like a string of pearls, each follows another, each with a different sheen but forming a whole. Ellipsis is a huge factor in the episode — not only in time, but in what remains unsaid. Each moment has significance, and it's on these increments that a story is constructed. It's an effective way to show as many facets of a character as possible — it allows us a fuller view of Jack, Sam, and even Teal'c, whose determination is a driving force of the episode. Jack puts it best when he happily shouts, "Teal'c, you are one stubborn son of a bitch!"

Gods & Scientists: Sam takes the idea of the particle beam generator from Sokar ("Serpent's Song"). After the twentieth-century discovery of subatomic particles (like electrons, neutrons, and protons) came the discovery that they were much more complex than originally thought. A particle accelerator does just that — makes subatomic particles accelerate to the speed of light — and then causes it to collide it with another particle. Particle accelerators are colloquially referred to as "atom smashers," but you probably have one in your house right now — a television set or computer monitor, which, if it has a cathode tube, acts much the same way, speeding up particles and then smashing them onto the back of a screen.

Interesting Fact: According to an interview given to *TV Zone Magazine*, Richard Dean Anderson would like to revisit the Laira story line: "There was an episode in our third season in which we gave every indication that O'Neill had fathered a child. Earlier this year [season five], I asked Brad Wright if he'd ever consider doing a story in which O'Neill goes back to that planet and discovers he's got a child. If we did, I'd like it to be a daughter, only because he's already had a son. I'd love to see a relationship like that unfold in front of the cameras."

Why We're Space Monkeys: We know it's not going to last past the end of the episode, and we know there are reasons it can probably never be, but seeing the raw emotional sparks between Sam and Jack — or rather, from Sam toward Jack — is gut-wrenching. As Rick stated in an interview, "As much as he has his moments of adoration for Carter, he's still aware of the propriety involved in keeping feelings at bay."

Parlez-vous Gate?: When Sam and Jack experience the asteroid's near-miss:
O'NEILL: Whoa . . . Carter, how close was that?
CARTER: Close, Sir.
DANIEL: How big?
CARTER: Big.
DANIEL: Thought so.

318. Shades of Grey

Original airdate: February 11, 2000
Written by: Jonathan Glassner
Directed by: Martin Wood

Jack steals technology from the Tollan and ends up working for Maybourne in a covert operation.

Once again, the title of the episode offers an entry point into the episode. "Shades of Grey" is about the delineations between good and evil, and the expanses in between. The rogue team is almost an anti-SG-1 group, with the ultra-military man's man lead and the female engineer mirroring Jack and Sam — a glimpse at SG-1 gone slightly off. The threat of the Goa'uld hasn't been this present since "Deadman Switch." Season three has a lot of stand-alone episodes, but here, the major threat is brought back in a way we haven't yet seen, and asks some hard questions about how prepared Earth is to meet a potential attack.

There's a real conflict between the means-to-an-end attitude of the rogue teams and the more ethical stance taken by the SGC regarding technology. What the episode does really well is draw the viewer into the battle — we're hard-pressed not to agree, at least partly, with Maybourne's concern that Earth is putting itself in danger by not taking every opportunity available to it. And, playing into the themes brought up in "Fair Game," no one will care how morally upright the SGC is if it leads to the imminent destruction of Earth. The Asgard, the Nox, and the Tollan were ready to cut all ties with Earth following the theft of their technology. The Tollan are still adamant about not giving any technology to the SGC, but at the end of the episode, diplomatic relations are stronger than ever. As the series progresses, the SGC must learn to negotiate with better clarity their relations in the galaxy (with the Tok'ra, the Asgard, and even the Goa'uld), or risk alienation from everyone, which would leave them very much alone in the future. O'Neill himself faced that aloneness in the previous episode, "A Hundred Days."

After the emotional turmoil of "A Hundred Days," Jack's character makes a complete turnaround — no longer sensitive or emotional, he's gone back to the Jack O'Neill from the movie, cold and hardened. More than that, he's deliberately cruel to his friends, with perfectly targeted barbs designed to hurt. You can really see his military training at work here — he's clearly thought about how best to go about alienating Daniel and Sam, and he does so with calm efficiency.

The acting in this episode is wonderful. Some subtly funny moments lighten up the tension — in particular at the end, as O'Neill is trying to make nice with his team after having snubbed them so thoroughly throughout the episode, and Teal'c raises his eyebrow and cocks his head — expressing his disapproval in exactly the way Jack had described earlier. Sam's look of betrayal rings true, and Daniel's disbelief at Jack denying their friendship comes through loud and clear.

The moral at the end of the episode is as subtle as a sledgehammer — usually *SG-1* is really good at seamlessly weaving in ethics and action ("Learning Curve," "Urgo"), but Jack's heavy-handed line, "We don't need their *stuff*, Makepeace; we need *them*," far from being inspiring, is just cringe-worthy. But the characterizations in this episode really help to show the many shades of grey within which the SGC operates.

Gods & Scientists: Although it's often sort of thrown in to movies, films, plays, and books, computer hacking is neither as simple nor easy as it seems. There are multiple language codes, multiple protocols, and endless variations within those. The term "hacker" actually predates computers, referring to electronics enthusiasts before it was connected with interrupting or otherwise modifying computer codes for personal or malicious use.

Why We're Space Monkeys: Sam's passed over for heading up SG-1 when Jack leaves, but she accepts Hammond's choice of Colonel Makepeace without making waves. And despite the turmoil they must be going through, Sam, Daniel, and Teal'c keep their heads down and keep at their job. The writers don't make any bones about showing both sides of the coin — Maybourne and his rogue team may well have a point.

Parlez-vous Gate?: Jack's observation on Teal'c's disapproval:
O'NEILL: To be fair, General, I did it. Carter and Daniel protested. And Teal'c, well he really didn't say anything but I could tell he was opposed to my actions by the way he cocked his head and sort of raised his eyebrow.

319. New Ground

Original airdate: February 18, 2000
Written by: Heather Ash
Directed by: Chris McMullin

SG-1 find themselves trapped in the middle of a religious war between rival continents on P2X-416.

"New Ground" is a complacent offering for the end of season three — unfortunately there are several of these in quick succession (although "Nemesis" more than makes up for them) — but it does cover some interesting, well, ground.

The Bedrosians believe their founder to be Nefertem — although they do not believe in his Goa'uld origin. Forced to cover "new ground," albeit unwillingly, some citizens counter with more resistance than others. This episode is open-ended, and we are left to assume that the Bedrosian society will be completely upturned by the events that have just occurred. Rigar says, "I will not allow our people to have their faith attacked in such a cynical way." In an ironic linguistic turnabout, although today the word "cynic" denotes negativity, or skepticism of others' motivations, it originally comes from the Greek "kunikos," or "doglike," and refers to a branch of philosopher from Ancient Greece who believed that virtue was the only good, and self-control the only means through which to achieve it.

In a nice use of metaphor, Teal'c is blinded in his fight with the guard — an embodiment of the blind fanaticism that's running rampant on Bedrosia. In a very real way, the Bedrosians are blinded by their own beliefs — that which they believe gives them insight into their origins has, in the way of religious wars in the real world, been turned into an organized manhunt for dissenters. The writers again show that they've got the guts to go with the glory by taking on subjects as thorny as religious wars and by showing how defensive a faith can be when attacked.

It's a good example of other ways in which SG-1 affects the civilizations they meet — they don't merely have physical impact (as in "One False Step" and "Thor's Chariot") but their arrival also brings with it cultural implications; this is the first time we've seen that aspect fully explored, and it's interesting to see how lackadaisical the team is about it — even Daniel who, while the most sensitive to the Bedrosian's upheaval, doesn't hesitate to inform them that their beliefs are wrong. And we can't really blame him — being manhandled, threatened, and locked in an electrified cage would take a toll on anyone's tact. In that respect, though, there's a parallel drawn between SG-1 and Christian missionaries who dictate their truth regardless of the consequences on the society to whom they're preaching.

Gods & Scientists: We learn that the Goa'uld Nefertem probably brought the Optricans and the Bedrosians to their planet. In Egyptian mythology, Nefertem was a minor deity, the god of the sunrise, bringing the sun to where Ra was. He was said to have sprung from a lotus blossom, and had no formal following. His mother was Sekhmet, whom we see in season seven's "Resurrection."

Interesting Fact: While the feature film shows only one shot of the Stargate *whooshing* open, the television series has several. The effect was created with a 180 mph jet engine and a big pool of water.

Why We're Space Monkeys: One of the most important factors of exploration in *Star Trek* is their noninterference policy when in contact with other civilizations. Still, *Star Trek*'s characters weren't usually involved in a galactic-scale war to save Earth. In "New Ground" (and in many other episodes), SG-1 doesn't hesitate to gather every possible ally in the war against the Goa'uld, even when it means being undiplomatic. Also, they go through incarceration and great physical discomfort without giving up Teal'c.

Parlez-vous Gate?:
O'NEILL (touches the bars of the cage he's in and receives an electric shock): That hurt.
DANIEL: Well, this day just keeps getting better and better.

320. Maternal Instinct

Original airdate: February 25, 2000
Written by: Robert Cooper
Directed by: Peter Woeste

Aided by Bra'tac, SG-1 finds the location of Kheb, where the Harcesis child is hidden, and sets off to find it.

"Maternal Instinct" rounds off the Daniel arc, resurrecting and concluding story lines from "Children of the Gods" and "Forever in a Day." His quest has changed — no longer searching for his lost wife, he's moved on and is now looking for the Harcesis child she bore. And in this episode, Daniel finds him — only to have to give him up again in a terrible but necessary parallel to his wife.

The episode offers an interesting character study of Daniel: his parents are dead, as is his wife, her child has been hidden away, and he's a pariah in his professional field (see season four's "The Curse"). He is alone in the universe, the members of SG-1 his surrogate family. One can only imagine that he has his own personal reasons for wanting to find the child — not just to help the fight against the Goa'uld or a promise kept to Sha're, but also to ease some of the loneliness he must feel. So when he turns around at the wall, holding the boy, and gives him back to Oma Desala, it's a heart-breaking moment, and one whose importance can't be overstated for Daniel's development as a character — and it will come back in a big way in season five.

The metaphor of Mother Nature echoes the traditional feminine principle of the creative. We've seen another version of her in "Show and Tell." In Western society, the stereotype of Mother Nature posits creation and inspiration as female figures — and the force of nature is shown to full effect in "Maternal Instinct." Oma Desala is a deadly force. The fact that she destroyed the Goa'uld, who did not put down their weapons, alludes to a Buddhist belief that anger and hatred lead to self-destruction. This allusion further complements the Eastern feel of this episode.

"Maternal Instinct" also allows us to see a different side of Bra'tac: he's getting closer to the age where he can no longer bear a Prim'ta, and he's tired of fighting the good fight. It's the first sign of relenting we've seen in him, and it affects us on a visceral level when he tells Teal'c that he's ready to pass on the torch. Tony Amendola does an amazing job of mingling pride and stubbornness in with obvious exhaustion, and hope and faith with despair. Bra'tac is a very human character, with layer upon layer of emotional wealth. His relationship with Teal'c is one of the most touching in the show, a father/son bond that's very different from the one between Sam and Jacob Carter.

Another of the themes of "Maternal Instinct" is the removal of barriers — barriers of the mind, of the body (when Daniel and Bra'tac take off their shoes to talk to the monk), and of emotions. Daniel has to push past his preconceptions of what would be best for the child in order to perceive a greater truth; Jack has to forego his military instinct and blindly trust Daniel when he tells him to put his weapon down; Bra'tac has to keep searching, despite his exhaustion; they all have to rely on their instincts.

Gods & Scientists: The monk in the Kheb temple speaks in Zen koans. Zen is a Japanese branch of Buddhism in which the mind is considered the greatest obstacle to *satori*, the Zen word for enlightenment. Koans — somewhat similar to parables only more enigmatic and usually quite short — are a way to train the mind to achieve the state of *satori*. In getting Daniel to think in koans, the monk is trying to get him to push his mind past normal thinking processes so he can perceive something more. The Zen practitioner believes that *satori* cannot be achieved through rational thinking alone. The mind must be able to encompass the "unknowable" and "unspeakable" as well.

Interesting Fact: Tony Amendola, who plays Master Bra'tac, spent the first twelve years of his career as an actor almost exclusively in theater. No wonder he has such a commanding presence.

Why We're Space Monkeys: What other science fiction show so seamlessly blends cultures, religions, and worldviews? In this episode alone, we have two kinds of Buddhism, Western images of Mother Nature, the American cult of the alien, and ancient Egyptian culture, all coming together in a single narrative.

Parlez-vous Gate?:
MONK: Because it is so clear, it takes a longer time to realize it. If you immediately know the candlelight is fire, then the meal was cooked a long time ago.
DANIEL: Right, well, I . . . I have no idea what you're talking about.

321. Crystal Skull

Original airdate: March 3, 2000
Story by: Michael Greenburg, Jarrad Paul
Teleplay by: Brad Wright
Directed by: Brad Turner

Daniel finds an artifact that sends him to a different plane of existence where the rest of SG-1 cannot see him.

Continuing the thread of Daniel-as-orphan, this episode holds up a tantalizing glimpse of what could be for Dr. Jackson, only to whisk it away again (this seems to happen a lot to the poor guy). Apparently, Daniel comes from a long line of anthropologists — his parents, and now a long-lost grandfather too. Perhaps it was this sort of trauma that pushed the idealistic Daniel toward archaeology — to avenge his grandfather's work and be remembered as having made a difference in the world. Certainly Daniel's family all seem to come from the same place — idealistic, positivist people who believe in the goodness of humanity. Ah, innocence . . .

It seems the writers of the show — who dip again into the well of Daniel Angst — want to push the idea of Daniel up against the odds while maintaining at least a modicum of moral conscience in the face of unremitting evil and Galactic Meanness. Teal'c, Carter, and O'Neill are more aware of the neutral aspect of the universe; Teal'c and Jack because of their personal confrontation with a grinding reality, and Sam mostly due to her objective, theoretical outlook.

While these three members of SG-1 don't hesitate to try to fulfil a personal objective, Daniel works almost as a moral doppelganger, asking the hard questions when silence would better allow the job to get done. But it's these hard questions that make the team more aware in the long run, and we can see its effect as the seasons progress. When Daniel is not there, they ask themselves the questions he would most likely be posing. In a sense, a part of Daniel is now inside the team's conscience. The transparency of his actions as a fundamentally good person are like a crystal skull — his actions are hardly ever hidden (except in extreme cases like the one we saw in "Forever in a Day"), and his intentions are good.

Gods & Scientists: The science in this one is a little questionable (the writers even make fun of it themselves in the episode "Wormhole X-Treme"). Quetzalcoatl was the benevolent god of the Aztecs (who are not exactly the same as the Mayans, although Daniel ascribes the myth to them), often depicted as a white, bearded god and inventor of the arts. Unfortunately, when the Spanish landed in what is now Mexico in 1519, they were white and had beards. The indigenous people thought it was the Quetzalcoatl of myth. For their part, the conquistadors thought that the Indians were part of *their* mythology — a lost tribe of Israelites.

Interesting Fact: This was *SG-1*'s first "virtual set," where the majority of the set is actually a giant "greenscreen" (see "Point of View"). Christopher Judge's voice gets a lot of airplay: he was the voice of Quetzalcoatl, and the voice of the Unas in "Demons." The other cast members voice the Asgard (Michael Shanks is Thor, Teryl Rothery is Heimdall, and Peter DeLuise is Loki). Judge does the more obscurely modulated voices — the technique used is called "flanging." Originally, flanging was done using two reel-to-reel tape decks which recorded sound to one track — the modulation of voice was done by holding a finger on one of the reels, slowing it slightly, which altered the sound of the voice. The two reels together on one tape produce the "flanged" voice.

Parlez-vous Gate?: Sometimes the writers pack more tongue-in-cheek references into six lines of dialogue than entire episodes of other series whose name we won't mention but which involve red shirts . . . Carter is a major, and Jack is dense. Get it?
CARTER: This is a major find. I have to see this.
O'NEILL: You too?
CARTER: Well, look at these readings. Sir, these are leptons.
O'NEILL: Get out.
CARTER: Well that means something inside this pyramid is slowing down neutrinos. Normally neutrinos pass right through ordinary matter no matter how dense. I mean something like five hundred million billion just passed through you.
O'NEILL: No matter how dense?

322. Nemesis

Original airdate: March 10, 2000
Written by: Robert Cooper
Directed by: Martin Wood

His ship infested with an alien enemy, the Asgard Thor tries to fend off an invasion of Earth, but fails; it's up to SG-1 to save the day/planet/galaxy again.

Wow. When *SG-1* does a season ending, it *really* does a season ending! All the classic elements of fiction and science are here: a foreign, creepy enemy who seems unbeatable, odds that are longer than a Canadian football field, an impossible situation, cool alien technology, and a mistake.

I love the title. Having just seen the Replicators for the first time, in all their steely, machiney, alien glory, this arc setup was well done. Remember Carter's line from "Brief Candle," when she says that "machines replicate"? There's no doubt in our minds that these little buggy things are *bad* for us. And the humorous thread of Jack again being transported right in the middle of talking to (or about) Carter is carried on. The episode is a cleverly disguised action mini-arc, and introduces so many new elements — we learn that the Asgard are not perfect, that the Replicators are conquerors who make the Goa'uld look nice by comparison, and that Jack likes fishing (like, really *really* likes fishing). How could it go wrong?

Some excellent small moments of tension — Teal'c, outside the ship, must push off the hull in order to be rescued, much as SG-1 must let go of their own ideals to win against the Replicators ("Nemesis"). And the idea to take the Stargate from the SGC is great, showing Robert Cooper's flexible storytelling style. And it makes for Don S. Davis' best nonspeaking moment, staring out the window of the control room at the big hole where the last three years of his life were.

Rather than stuffing the episode with too many visual effects, "Nemesis" worked CGI in as a support to, not an overthrow of, the story. The ending of the season finale escalates nicely, thanks to the evenhanded direction of *SG-1* veteran Martin Wood. His familiarity with the cast and the feel of the show shines through. The final shot is classic, with a Replicator climbing across an Asgard symbol on the hull of the destroyed ship; it sends shivers down the spine — and sets up a serious thirst for season four.

Gods & Scientists: Neutrinos are a type of fundamental particle with no electric charge and very little (or no) mass. They are part of the lepton family (remember the leptons from "Crystal Skull"?), and the most penetrating of subatomic particles. The first type of neutrino, associated with the electron, was discovered in 1930 by an Austrian physicist named Wolfgang Pauli.

Interesting Fact: Michael Shanks really did have his appendix out at the time the episode "Crystal Skull" was being filmed — he thought it was food poisoning from the Thanksgiving dinner he'd had the night before. Both Daniel and Jack have had hairdo changes, which went unmentioned until this episode ("Did you get a haircut?" asks the newly shorn Dr. Jackson to a now completely grey O'Neill). Their new looks were commented on so much on the online boards the lines were probably added to appease viewers.

Why We're Space Monkeys: The ubiquitous Sam/Jack interest is still around in this episode; however, while flirtatiousness generally makes the "shipper" faction gleeful, Sam's reaction to Jack's invitation could be read as her being truly touched at being let into the "inner circle" of his life, and finally being "one of the guys" (see "Hathor"). This is a problematic reading, though, because we never really get a sense that Sam feels left out in any way, except when something occurs out of the blue — like the invitation.

Parlez-vous Gate?:
O'NEILL: Yeah sure, y'betcha.

STARGATE SG-1 — SEASON FOUR
"Question every assumption."

401. Small Victories

Original airdate: June 30, 2000
Written by: Robert Cooper
Directed by: Martin Wood

Teal'c and O'Neill attempt to save Earth from the Replicators, while Sam does the same for the Asgard.

What an entrance into season four. This first episode highlights what will be one of the main themes of the season — opportunity. In "Small Victories," SG-1 is given the opportunity to, among other things, deepen team bonds (Sam and Jack) and to save Earth and the Asgard home planet. How they respond to these challenges makes for one of the most enthralling episodes to date — enthralling enough to make us forget that nearly the exact same premise was used in "Nemesis."

Season four includes some of the funniest episodes of the series, and also some of the best team moments. "Small Victories" is especially big on the Sam/Jack dynamic, continuing from "Nemesis," and we're treated to some awesome grins from RDA and Amanda Tapping, as they toe the line between fraternal teasing and downright chemistry. Tapping in particular is given some comedic opportunities, and her horrified face when she tries the Asgard "food" is priceless, as is her attempt at backtracking when she realizes the faux pas.

Michael looking cool and classy, as always (ALBERT L. ORTEGA)

There are some cool Thor moments as well. And, in an ironic twist, the Asgard's "you're too young" tirade finally works *for* SG-1 — in a manner of speaking. Because they're not as technologically advanced as the Asgard, Thor believes they might be just dim-witted enough to hit the Replicators where they least expect it.

Again, *SG-1* turns commonly held ideas on their heads. We're taught very early that "advancement" is always good, right, and beneficial. But in "Small Victories," being *less* advanced forces humans to think resourcefully, creatively, and independently, while the Asgard, the Tollan, and the Aschen are restricted by their own superiority. In fact, the closest "kin" to the humans are the Goa'uld and Tok'ra who, because they scavenge, must also think outside the box, so to speak.

In the otherwise comic background looms the theme of salvation —

what it costs individually and as a team, or as a nation, and the strange forms in which it appears. For all their technological savvy, the Asgard are incapable of saving themselves and face the very real threat of extinction in "Small Victories." In an ironic twistback from season three's long theme of "alone in the future," the Asgard are threatened with isolation now, *because* their advances allowed them to stop cultivating diplomatic relationships. At the end of the episode, the Asgard are on the brink of annihilation, and now have to rebuild their society and their numbers.

SG-1 has to fight gargantuan odds, while separated. Daniel is relegated to spectator status, and Shanks lets us see how much that rankles. We also find out how much Daniel's military mind has developed, compared with season one's "Thor's Hammer." He's placed in the difficult position of having to order the destruction of a submarine, knowing O'Neill and Teal'c are on board. He hesitates, but in the end he gives the order and watches it carried out. Jackson's never shirked his duty to the team or to Earth, but that moment speaks to how far he's incorporated the harsh realities of military duty.

Interesting Fact: Those are real Russians on a real Russian Foxtrot submarine in the first scene of the episode, and they're speaking real Russian. So you may have missed a joke between the two sailors: when asked by his comrade what the noise is, the second sailor replies, "Maybe it's one of the bugs from the other episode!"

Why We're Space Monkeys: At the start of the episode, Daniel has been brought down by a mundane case of appendicitis — nothing extra-planetary, just a plain old Earth ailment. Jack and Teal'c's singlemindedness in the face of what they believe to be death is perfectly *Stargate*-esque — no heroics, they just get the job done, no matter what it takes. This "everyman" side of Jack's personality is one of the main reasons he's so loved on the small screen.

Parlez-vous Gate?:
DANIEL: Wait a minute — are you actually saying you need someone *dumber* than you are?
O'NEILL: You may have come to the right place.
CARTER: I could go, Sir.
O'NEILL: I don't know, Carter. You may not be dumb enough.

402. The Other Side

Original airdate: July 7, 2000
Written by: Brad Wright
Directed by: Peter DeLuise

SG-1 is contacted by a people who offers technology in exchange for help in fighting a long-lasting civil war. However, their past is shadier than SG-1 suspects.

"The Other Side" doesn't so much make its point as beat you over the head with it — and although the topics it deals with are important and well worth treating, the foreshadowing was more like a giant neon sign than a shadow. The title refers both to the different points of view that clash in this episode (Daniel and Jack, as well as the humans and the Eurondans) and as to the proverbial "two sides to every story" — or perhaps more subtly, the three sides to the truth. According to that adage, there are three sides to the truth — yours, mine, and the truth. What this episode highlights very well is human lack of moderation — each person believes their position to be The Truth, and there is no room for compromise. Everyone simply pushes on blindly for what he or she thinks is right. In that respect, "The Other Side" is a study of excess, and also an indirect reference to the audience. *We* also think we know the truth, about what's happening, and who the Bad Guy is — but do we? Who's telling the story? What would happen if the Nox told this story? Or a Goa'uld?

Stargate SG-1 is four seasons in, and by now we're used to seeing Jack and Daniel at opposite ends of the philosophical spectrum; but until now we've never seen Jack outright ignore Daniel and refute his point of view so thoroughly. We've also never seen Daniel turn his passion on Jack quite so fully, rebuking him in front of the people they're there to help. The clash between military and humanist thought processes is clearly drawn, and it's not until Alar finally makes his intentions clear (Teal'c is "not like us") that Jack realizes his error and asks Daniel to investigate further. This is a nice upping of the ante we saw raised in "The Torment of Tantalus."

The twist in "The Other Side" is that Alar doesn't go out of his way to deceive SG-1 — he's honest right from the start about his people's needs and intentions. It's Jack who willingly blinds himself — a human trait that has been written about for centuries, from Etienne de la Boétie's 1548 *Discourse on Voluntary Servitude* to George Orwell's *Animal Farm*. And when Jack voluntarily shuts the iris on Alar, there is the cold and chilling realization that he's just killed someone — the first time we've seen him do so outside of a combat situation. We're reminded that O'Neill is more than a witty leader; he's first and foremost human — and then military. The lines have never been more formally drawn, as evidenced by Carter's reflective look. She doesn't know what to think of her commanding officer's actions, and her moral compass visibly wavers.

The acting in this episode is tremendous — from Jack and Daniel's firm convictions to Alar's blind belief in the civil war he's been fighting since he was a boy to Carter's horror at discovering the truth behind the Eurondan war. Plus we get to see Teal'c and Jack play in virtual reality planes. Sci fi at its best. Also, the writers make a very Swiftian version of words "European," "American," and "Canadian" into the hybrid "Eurondan."

Interesting Fact: The underground set is only one floor: the illusion of two levels was made by filming the same set at different angles, and then tiling the frames together and painting a little floor between them.

Why We're Space Monkeys: It was his character's low profile in seasons four and five that prompted Shanks to leave the show at the end of season five, but you don't see that in this episode; in fact, the Daniel/Jack relationship is showcased. They don't pull any punches in their arguments, and as soon as Jack realizes his mistake, he apologizes — a pretty rare occurrence — all of which reveals the care that goes into making the characters and their relationships real.

Parlez-vous Gate?:
O'NEILL: So, what's your impression of Alar?
TEAL'C: That he is concealing something.
O'NEILL: Like what?
TEAL'C: I am not sure . . . he is concealing it.

403. Upgrades

Original airdate: July 14, 2000
Written by: David Rich
Directed by: Martin Wood

A Tok'ra representative asks SG-1 to wear alien armbands that increase their strength and speed exponentially. Dr. Fraiser is dubious about Anise's wardrobe — I mean, methods.

This is a fun episode, especially after the seriousness of "Small Victories" and "The Other Side." We get to see SG-1 (minus Teal'c, whose symbiote protects him from the fun) as superheroes. And we get to see what's important to them — when the armbands are activated, Sam goes straight to writing a book on the science of the Stargate, Daniel heads straight for his bookcases, and Jack heads straight to the pacing, itching for some action. The writers show us very clearly that the trio remain themselves, even through their descent into difference. Another instalment in this season's theme of opportunity, each makes the most of his or her upgrade.

Anise/Freya is set up to be the *femme fatale par excellence* — sultry looks and Wonderbra firmly in place. You don't know whether or not to trust her; and, with her scientific symbiote clearly interested in Daniel while her more sympathetic host makes eyes at O'Neill, in this first appearance, she's quite the cliché. It's been a while since the ignominy of "Hathor" and "Emancipation," but the stereotypes of women haven't stopped flying. Can't we just have a woman interested in O'Neill or Daniel who's *normal*?

General Hammond has some wonderful moments, his frustration with O'Neill finally coming to a head. The fine line that actor Don S. Davis treads between professionalism and camaraderie with the SG team — especially with Jack — is always spot-on, and his exasperation at what amounts to babysitting his star team is perfectly played.

Another theme here is the introduction of a stranger into a close-knit group, how each member reacts, and how the change affects the relationships that have already been set up. The interesting thing about this episode is that it is a two-parter with "Divide and Conquer," but it was neither treated nor aired as such. It's not until the second part that we get to see the ramifications of this episode — which reflects real life; things that seem unimportant in the moment take on a whole new aspect over time.

Pay attention to the lighting in this episode — Anise/Freya is nearly always seen in a criss-cross of light and shadow, Sam writes her book in the dark and is shocked by the light poured over her by Janet Fraiser, and the muted yet fluorescent glow of the force shields emphasize and conceal what you're not sure you're seeing between Jack and Sam.

Gods & Scientists: The newest addition to the Tok'ra family, Anise/Freya has a less than clear agenda. In Norse mythology, Freya was the goddess of love and fertility, the most beautiful of the goddesses. An archetype of sensuality, she wore a necklace as well as a cloak made of feathers allowing her to transform into a falcon — much like Anise's own transformation into and from Freya. And we learn that Apophis is assembling a new and powerful battleship. We might be surprised, but Apophis has more lives than a cat. A charmed cat.

Interesting Fact: You don't see it in the episode, but Amanda Tapping sank all four balls on the pool table — not once, but twice, during rehearsal and during filming. She was meant to be replaced by an extra for that shot, but there was no need. Too bad the shot was cut!

Why We're Space Monkeys: There's a powerful mixture of humor and seriousness in this episode, very much dependent on the actors' descent into their character's changes. And SG-1's sheer easygoing nature and the blithe way in which they disobey direct orders isn't something you'll see very often on television. Especially not for a steak!

Parlez-vous Gate?: Teal'c's morality gets a serious "upgrade" at the end of the episode when the rest of the team apologizes to Hammond.
O'NEILL: Even so, I . . . I'm sorry.
CARTER: Me too.
DANIEL: Me three.
TEAL'C (looking smug and very pleased with himself): I have no need to apologize.

404. Crossroads

Original airdate: July 21, 2000
Written by: Katharyn Powers
Directed by: Peter DeLuise

Teal'c's old flame claims to have learned to communicate with her symbiote. This could turn the war against the Goa'uld around, but is it too good to be true?

If we were ever in doubt about the pure evilness of the Goa'uld, "Crossroads" lays all that to rest. Another of the main themes of season four, along with *opportunity*, is *choices* — how we make and implement them, and their consequences. Along with that is the rapidly maturing SG-1's determination to question all assumptions — too often in the past, their blindness and guesswork based on "normal" human assumptions have landed them in hot water. This episode emphasizes those themes — choices are made throughout it that will have long-lasting repercussions for all characters — especially Teal'c and the Tok'ra. "Crossroads" marks a changing point in several aspects of the show: from this point on, relations between the humans and the Tok'ra are more tumultuous, most intensely shown by O'Neill.

Quite often, episodes end with shots of Jack. He's the everyman character whose reactions guide our own. In "Crossroads," however, we finish with the silent showdown between Tanith and Teal'c — Jack is nowhere to be seen. This departure, along with the palpable tension between the two characters, foreshadows events from now to season five ("Exodus," "Between Two Fires," and "48 Hours"). The unfinished business here requires neither words nor interpretation through another character.

"Crossroads" is a vehicle for some of the best Teal'c moments of the entire series, rivaling even later Teal'c gems like "The Changeling" and "Avatar." This episode shows us a new side of Teal'c, one that chooses to love and to believe, despite all he has been taught. Christopher Judge's acting is superb here — he's mastered the art of saying everything with a look, and he has some moments where he says nothing, but expresses worlds of emotion, ranging from joy at seeing Shan'auc again, to grief at her death, to pure hatred for Tanith.

In ancient Egypt, the priests and priestesses carried sacred knowledge about creation and they communicated with the gods. They also kept society in order, maintaining it for future generations. Because Shan'auc is a priestess, she is privy to certain rites (such as kel'no'reem) and knowledge that would make her believe she's learned to communicate with her symbiote. The delusion she lives under eventually kills her: she falls victim to one of the mainstay themes of *Stargate SG-1* — there is nothing more dangerous in this universe than false beliefs. A good episode for showing the consequences lurking in opportunity.

Gods & Scientists: We were led to believe that only Hathor could produce Goa'uld larvae, but now we learn that there is more than one queen. The

Tok'ra were spawned from Queen Egeria who broke from the Goa'uld two thousand years ago. She tried to stop the Goa'uld from taking humans as slaves and hosts, but was found and supposedly killed by Ra. In Roman mythology, Egeria was the goddess of fountains and childbirth. In *SG-1*, her offspring became the Tok'ra. See also season six's "The Cure" for more on Egeria.

Gods & Scientists: Teal'c's father was killed by System Lord Cronus ("Fair Game"). In Greek mythology, Cronus was one of the twelve Titans who reigned supreme. Born of Uranus and Gaia, he is said to have castrated his father with a sickle, and with his wife began a "Golden Age" reign, until he was defeated and banished by his own son, Zeus.

Interesting Fact: For those wondering what happened to Drey'auc from "Bloodlines," the first draft of the script had Teal'c divorced — or the Jaffa equivalent thereof.

Why We're Space Monkeys: This episode shows grief that will have long-lasting effects on Teal'c's actions. As always, the writers don't hesitate to incorporate emotion, including those human ones like revenge and hatred. Teal'c's determination to descend as far as possible into a state of kel'no'reem, even knowing the risk to himself, in order to perhaps uncover a weapon against the Goa'uld, is a bold move.

Parlez-vous Gate?:
O'NEILL: Bra'tac! You've . . . done something with your hair!

405. Divide and Conquer

Original airdate: July 28, 2000
Written by: David Rich
Directed by: Martin Wood

Sam and Jack may be under some form of Goa'uld mind control; the Tok'ra set out to find out the truth.

Let's call a spade a spade: "Divide and Conquer" is like fan fiction gone wrong. The whole episode plays like a manipulation to get to the scene where Sam and Jack finally admit they have more than professional feelings for each other. Other than that, it serves virtually no purpose other than to kill off Martouf. Because, of course he has to die — he loves Sam!

It's not clear how the Goa'uld perform their mind-control experiments. Up until now, the Goa'uld have only used physical methods — taking hosts, using zat guns — and this more psychological technique is new in their arsenal. It's interesting to see that the Goa'uld, too, evolve over the show's run, giving SG-1 a worthy enemy. It's a smart move on the writers' part, never letting the Goa'uld become old hat — they're always one step ahead, and that's what is so scary about them. The doubt is always there that perhaps the Goa'uld might win the war.

"Divide and Conquer" fills in the subtextual blanks from "Upgrades," but it gets snagged when it tries to extrapolate a plot. The writers have set it up as a character study of sorts, but it fails in that respect as well; the relationship issue comes up so quickly, it feels almost forced. Richard Dean Anderson and Amanda Tapping's scenes are riveting though; their chemistry is at its best.

Anise is much more sympathetic in this episode (mostly because she appears as her host, Freya), so you genuinely feel for her when Jack turns her down. It's the best acting Vanessa Angel turns in on the show, but the stereotypical female-as-man-hunter image is still in full force. Thankfully, it's one of the last times we see it, because the show grows out of it. Up until now, *SG-1*'s female characters have been somewhat unevenly drawn, representing the same archetypes that are seen throughout mythology. In that vision, men fight and are mortal (Martouf, Kawalsky), women don't and are sexual — which is perhaps one of the reasons Sam is subjected to the "black widow syndrome" (and Anise to her really bad leather outfits).

Myths and stories are one way in which that representation of women has been passed on for centuries, stories traditionally told by men and thus imprinted with their viewpoint; even the *Stargate SG-1* writers sometimes fall into the pattern of portraying women simplistically. However, as evidenced in discussion boards on the Internet, the show's viewers are unwilling to accept that kind of characterization — in fact, "Divide and Conquer" and similar episodes that value women only through their sexuality, rank extremely low in terms of fan preference. And from here on, the writers make a real effort to portray more skilfully drawn female characters. Carter and Dr. Fraiser benefit the most from this turn-about — see season seven's "Grace" for one example of how Sam's character evolves. "Divide and Conquer" is an absolute favorite of fans interested in the Sam/Jack dynamic however, and makes good use of the theme of opportunity we see in season four — but for the writers, not the characters, who take advantage of the opportunity to showcase some character development in a romantic way.

Gods & Scientists: Martouf is dead, the victim of Goa'uld mind-control technology. The Goa'uld have upgraded their weaponry to include psychological warfare. Mind control is the term used to define behavior modification techniques — through drugs, hypnosis, and neurological influencing devices (for example electromagnetic). It's an important tool in military and intelligence operations.

Interesting Fact: "I knew as soon as Brad and Robert started to tell me the story of 'Upgrades' and 'Divide and Conquer' that it was going to be a pot-boiler," noted director Martin Wood. "I added a few things to heat up the force-field scene like the fact that Jack and Sam were nose to nose — neither Rick or Amanda felt comfortable being that close together and saying lines (they love each other, don't get me wrong, it's just weird to be talking to someone with your noses almost touching) I had to keep reminding them 'there is a force field between you, it isn't weird.'"

Why We're Space Monkeys: Not too many shows would term sleeping with a handsome leading man "suffering"! The Anise/Freya split is interesting because it gives us a chance to see how the Tok'ra are different from the Goa'uld — in this situation, the host wins out, and the symbiote takes second place; not so in Goa'uld society. And the fact that O'Neill turns her down is truly representative of how the show has evolved over the last four years — a far cry from "Brief Candle."

Parlez-vous Gate?: As Jack waits to go crazy:
FREYA: You are probably not happy to see me.
O'NEILL: Well, if you're not here to tell me it's all a big mistake, I might be a little glum.

406. Window of Opportunity

Original airdate: August 4, 2000
Written by: Joseph Mallozzi, Paul Mullie
Directed by: Peter DeLuise

Jack and Teal'c are stuck in a time loop, with some interesting consequences.

In some ways, "Window of Opportunity" seems inevitable; from the very first episode, there has been a play on the opportunities that present themselves between Sam and Jack — their camaraderie has always been tinged with . . . something else. Not exactly an uneasiness, but an acknowledgement of tension, which is something some fans looked forward to. That tension naturally leads to story lines like this one.

But not all fans — or even crew — think so. Amanda Tapping admits that, in the first few seasons, she had some reservations about her character. "I didn't dislike her in the beginning, but I wasn't fond of her," said the actress, noting that her own repeated insistence that "women don't talk that way" helped to get the character of Carter onto a more even keel. Some fans don't like the Sam/Jack dynamic at all, and they deride its presence in season four. "We're all going to see something," notes an online fan. "The diehard shippers are going to see [particular moments] as hope for something to happen between them. You call it chemistry. Personally I have never seen any chemistry between the two."

The constant angsty tension was used in endless variations in fan fiction and personal observations on *Stargate* boards worldwide, but it can be a thorn in the side of more literal, pragmatic viewers. The Sam/Jack thread is especially volatile because, unlike many other science fiction couples, neither of the two primary people in the unacknowledged relationship is "other," that is, an alien in some way or another. That facet of alienness relieves the lovers (and the audience) of much of the guilt they feel about acknowledging a 'wrong' but needed union, like Aeryn Sun and John Crichton from *Farscape*, or Buffy and Angel from *Buffy the Vampire Slayer*.

Which brings us to the other side of the argument: in some ways, "Window of Opportunity" seems completely unnatural, and for many of the same reasons. It presupposes (not without canon to back it up, mind you), that both people are single, heterosexual, and interested in each other. It places both these people in a professional situation where they constantly and consistently break the rules of conduct for their jobs (at least those concerning fraternization). From a storytelling point of view, it is a constructed narrative that allows the writers to play with possibilities It's almost like a workshop that people perform informally in their minds, changing the ending to see what happens. For instance, you've had an unpleasant confrontation, and two hours later you're still mulling it over, concocting the perfect comeback line, changing the argument so that it persuaded the other person and simultaneously made you look really, really smart. These sorts of memory and time-loop games are ones that we play all the time. In academic circles, this trend toward playfulness in the construction of reality has been onerously dubbed postmodernism. "Window of Opportunity" acknowledges the potentially annoying nature of this sort of play, too, when Jack tells Teal'c that if he doesn't get out of the endless time-loop soon, he's going to go "wacko." Similarly, postmodernism concerns itself with the idea that there are no universal truths; but that causes most people real discomfort, because we seem to have a deep-seated need to see causal relationships in life.

This is the first episode attributed to the writing team of Joseph Mallozzi and Paul Mullie, and it's a fitting title for their entrance as well, since this episode was their window of opportunity into a very long writing gig — a rare thing in television.

Whatever side of the argument you end up on, or even if you tend to waffle somewhere in between these two poles, "Window of Opportunity," arriving as it does near the middle of season four, is one opportunity to mix things up that the writers couldn't have, shouldn't have — and certainly didn't — ignore.

Gods & Scientists: Malakai uses electromagnetic interference to initiate the time loop, which ties in well with Einstein's special theory of relativity (no doubt Einstein would get a kick out of that). That theory is mostly concerned with electric and magnetic phenomena, and could be an explanation for the time dilation factor.

Interesting Fact: Juggling was one of Richard's many earlier careers (see "Making Myth"). Also, Joseph Mallozzi and Paul Mullie have written (as of season eight) more than thirty episodes. The "M&M" team has a huge whiteboard on which they sketch out the acts and scenes of an episode, and apparently have a separate board which keeps tabs on who has written the really good — and really, really bad — lines that appear in the show.

Why We're Space Monkeys: All science fiction shows eventually do the "time loop" episode, but tradition has it that it's either one person or everyone caught in the loop — and it's generally boring, too. *SG-1* takes that convention and turns it on its head by having only Jack and Teal'c caught, and it's a credit to the writers' talent that "Window of Opportunity" ends up being entertaining. Plus, where else would you see an alien from Chulak juggling while learning Latin?

Parlez-vous Gate?:
O'NEILL (at Janet shining a light into his eye): I ask you: what could *possibly* be in my eye to explain this?!

407. Watergate

Original airdate: August 11, 2000
Written by: Robert Cooper
Directed by: Martin Wood

The SGC discovers the Russians have a Stargate. SG-1 steps in to help them when their secret experiments end in disaster.

"Watergate" is different from other *Stargate SG-1* episodes in at least one way: rather than an action/adventure story, this episode plays like a mystery, with all the elements inherent to that genre. It starts with a problem — the Stargate won't engage — which is quickly solved, uncovering a deeper issue: the Russians have a Stargate that they've been concealing, and it won't shut down. Russian scientist Svetlana Markov provides us with all the unanswered questions — what has happened and why? where is the underwater crew? — and along the way, other puzzles come up. When the solution is finally presented, it's the last line of the episode, but many of the other issues that were brought up are left unresolved — another interesting part of this episode's storytelling technique.

It's refreshing to see SG-1 play detectives rather than action figures. We don't get to see this very often — they're using their brains more than their brawn in this episode, which changes the slant of the show. There is more dialogue, and more character development, all of it against a backdrop of water, the universal metaphor for change, movement, and the subconscious. It's both subtle and effective, and acts as a good starting point for the ebb and flow of the characters' interactions.

The title is an obvious allusion to the Gate's underwater location, but it also refers to the political scandal in 1972–1974 that led to U.S. president Nixon's resignation. The term has entered the popular lexicon to denote a disgraceful event, usually leading to someone's demotion. Here, the Russians experience their own catastrophic event, similar to those we've seen through SG-1's eyes for four years, only this one is compounded by the weight of international secrecy. The theme of knowledge, from season three, how it's kept and used, and its place in a power struggle, makes a comeback in "Watergate"; the reference to the political espionage of the Watergate scandal provides a framework within which to view the episode — not just mission, or mystery, but also political minefield. Jack's blatant distrust of Svetlana doesn't seem as out of place as it could, given his age and career history — he's lived and worked through the worst of the Cold War, and retains a certain distance with the Russians throughout the series ("The Tomb," "48 Hours," "Lockdown").

On a more lighthearted note, it's always fun to see Sam geek out with a fellow scientist. Unfortunately, there are some scenes in the sub where Svetlana is relegated to the role of narrator, as she blandly relates her every move — it doesn't exactly make for compelling drama, and the character should have had a lot more going for her than that. But a chance to see brainwork rather than things being blown up is a nice change of pace, as is character interaction without heavy innuendo.

Interesting Fact: Director Martin Wood, visual effects supervisor James Tichenor, and director of photography Jim Menard have commented on the limitations of only having a little more than forty minutes to tell a story: "People have to make these giant leaps of logic," notes Wood. "Suddenly we've got [a character] saying, 'okay, here's a problem,' and then *eight seconds* later, Daniel Jackson is able to figure it out." Special effects supervisor Tichenor chimes in that the audience didn't have time to wait the two weeks it would take Daniel to figure it out. Menard noted dryly, "Work[ed] great in the feature."

Why We're Space Monkeys: When Jack isn't around, Daniel takes up the slack in the dry comeback arena. Michael Shanks said in an interview, "Fortunately there were some humorous scenes inside the mini-sub with Marina [Sirtis], Amanda, and myself. That's another facet of my character I'd love to see the writers explore more. I have a very dry, sort of subtle sneak-up-on-you sense of humor that I think would suit Daniel in the appropriate situations."

Parlez-vous Gate?:
SVETLANA: If you're implying that everything Russian-made is of poor quality, actually . . . the sub is Swiss.
DANIEL: So they occasionally catch fire, but they keep perfect time . . .

408. The First Ones

Original airdate: August 18, 2000
Written by: Peter DeLuise
Directed by: Peter DeLuise

Daniel is captured by an Unas, and must learn to communicate with him. The rest of SG-1 have their own problems as they try to rescue their teammate.

This character episode — Daniel's — is one of many stand-alones in season four, which is much lighter on arc episodes than other seasons. "The First Ones" is a bit uneven, because while it gives us a chance to breathe between scenes, it also serves to separate action and communication. These two facets have been all-important throughout the series, and they are nearly always used in conjunction ("Urgo," "Shades of Grey"); here they're firmly divided, and while each facet achieves its objective, the separation feels unbalanced. Daniel doesn't take advantage of any of the military skills he's picked up over the years, for example. The argument can be made that he is, at heart, a humanist interested in communication and culture, but it seems like he's taken a step back. And unlike "Watergate," where action was not an option, here it could have been.

Chaka is undergoing a rite of passage in which he has to bring back a "beast" for his tribe to eat, thus proving his virility; however, he's not the only one undergoing transformation in the episode, physical or mental.

Daniel is facing his own rite of passage — this is suggested as he transcribes chalk markings on the cave wall with words spoken into a recorder, and as he attempts to find a common ground with a creature by all appearances entirely different from himself. Hawkins and Rothman similarly undergo a transformation when they're taken as hosts by symbiotes.

The Unas were deemed a primitive species by the Goa'uld, and used as their first hosts. The two evolved on the same planet, and many Unas are still hosts or slaves to the Goa'uld. They have developed methods to avoid being taken as hosts by the Goa'uld, specifically necklaces around implantation areas. They are very strong, and have a tribal social system. In the feature film, Ra is described as "the last of a dying race," and when he finally dies we see the body of an Unas superimposed under the skin of his human body. Presumably this was an Unas (within which was a Goa'uld?). It gets a bit complicated, but this is about the point when the producers start saying things like, "Hey, it's a TV show, lighten up."

Rites of passage are part and parcel of society's hierarchy — today they take different forms, but in ancient times they were usually a physical ordeal that had to be endured without comment. In ancient Greece, one such ritual often included elements of cross-dressing to ensure a firm gender identity — we see this updated ritual in the full military get-up that Daniel wears in this episode (he's rarely seen in camouflage); face-painting was also a frequent aspect — reminiscent of Chaka swiping the severed symbiote's blood over Daniel's face.

Other myths and parables are used in this episode as well. The scene in which Daniel removes the bullet from Chaka's hand alludes to Aesop's fable, "Androcles and the Lion." In the fable, an escaped Roman slave comes across a lion with a thorn in its paw. He removes the thorn, much to the lion's relief, but is soon found by soldiers and thrown to the lions, one of which is the one he had helped. In return for his kindness, the lion refuses to eat Androcles. Androcles is pardoned and the lion is set free. Aesop's fables were well-known in ancient Greece for providing models of behavior and ethical guidelines; the contemporary Daniel is often the moral compass for SG-1.

Gods & Scientists: The pose struck by Chaka as he leaves the scene at the end of the episode is a replica of that of Bigfoot, taken from archived footage. This is a deliberate duplication on Peter DeLuise's part, as he weaves together Earth mythology and *Stargate* mythology. Again, mythologies are not static pieces of literature that are told exactly the same way each time. DeLuise demonstrates mythmaking in action; not only is he using North American mythology, but he's also using Egyptian. King Unas, a ruler in Egypt in the fifth or sixth Dynasty, was given the "Ba" (soul) of the gods, achieving their powers. *Stargate* mythology revises and mimics Egyptian mythology, as the Unas were given the powers (and corporeal body/soul) of the Goa'uld, who masquerade as gods.

Interesting Fact: "I do big episodes, but Martin [Wood] does even bigger than mine," noted Peter DeLuise, who directed this episode. In his usual joking style, "I mean, he did the finale, and he usually does the season cliff-hanger and the opener. I tend to think my strength is character-driven sto-ries, but I love doing action stuff."

Why We're Space Monkeys: Jack and Sam offer no arguments when Teal'c says they have to be tied up in order to hold the unknown Goa'uld host captive. They realize that in order to accomplish their mission, they have to be effectively retired from it, and they don't hesitate to make the necessary sacrifice. Daniel's determination to keep a record of his experiences shows real bravery and an archaeologist's mind — he's consistent even in the face of danger.

Parlez-vous Gate?: The first moments of Daniel's recorded message: DANIEL: I met a wonderful new friend, and he's taking me on a long journey to see his planet. At the moment, my main concern is that my new friend is an aboriginal Unas in its unGoa'ulded state, and that I'm the evening meal. (At Chaka's growl.) Shut up? I understood that. We're communicating.

409. Scorched Earth

Original airdate: August 25, 2000
Written by: Joseph Mallozzi, Paul Mullie
Directed by: Martin Wood

SG-1 relocates a population to a planet that isn't as available as it first seems.

Who do we become when we no longer have a place to call home? How do we recreate a sense of community, a social structure, a life and livelihood when our roots have not only been severed, but have vanished? "Scorched Earth" examines these questions and places at the center of the debate the choices we make when we're faced with an unwinnable war. This is another episode that forces SG-1 to look at their assumptions — in this case, that the world in question was "uninhabited."

Free will is one of the more encompassing themes in *Stargate SG-1*, one that's been examined in a lot of different ways ("Thor's Hammer," "Tin Man"). It's a topic that's widely debated in scientific, religious, and philosophical arenas, as well — whether the universe is governed by laws of causality or hazard. Season four takes the question of free will and approaches it from a different angle — the episodes are more clearly about how we act when free will is taken away ("Beneath the Surface," "Entity") and how the characters enforce free will when there appears to be no choice. Decisions are made in this episode, regardless of Lotan's irrevocable claim that the lot (perhaps the origin of his name?) of the Enkarans is decided. The choice Jack makes, to save the Enkarans at the expense of a technologically superior race, is an expression of free will; the choice Daniel makes, to try to save Lotan is his expression of the same idea; the Enkarans choose to stay and fight for the land that they're claiming as their own; and finally, Lotan takes on an identity and chooses to make a life on the planet — he chooses a home. Home is not merely a physical location, it's primarily a choice; the writers make sure that nothing is taken for granted in this episode — food, relationships, land, or life.

We get some, well, scorching moments between Jack and Daniel, who as always play off each other in remarkable ways, and a great guest appearance by Brian Markinson as Lotan, whose rationality and implacability ratchet up the tension several notches each time he speaks (also raising the frustration level, giving us a sense of what it must be like for SG-1 to try to negotiate with people they know nothing about). However, we never get a sense that the Enkarans are in real danger. The polarity between Jack and Daniel is as powerful as its been since "The Other Side," and Sam gets a bitter reminder of the difficulties of her job when her choice is taken away from her by the chain of command. The effects in the episode are excellent, however, with some vast shots of Enkaran life, and the idea of a sulfur-based life-form is intriguing. We see again the ruthlessness of the Goa'uld, who kidnapped the entire population of Enkarans generations ago and made them serve as slaves.

Interesting Fact: According to Joseph Mallozzi, the original ending to the episode was very different. "Rather than the (what I felt was too convenient) solution at the end of the episode, the original script had Lotan deciding to stop the terraforming process, thereby dooming the civilization he had been programmed to seed. The closing scene ended with Daniel in his office, listening to a snippet of alien music, a parting gift from Lotan and the final memory of a distant civilization now extinct."

Why We're Space Monkeys: Everyone in this episode makes difficult decisions, from Jack to Daniel to the Enkarans. Each one stands up firmly for his or her beliefs, making for compelling character drama.

Parlez-vous Gate?:
O'NEILL: Chemical warfare?
CARTER: I don't think so, Sir. Take a look at this.
(O'Neill looks into the microscope)
O'NEILL: Oh, yeah . . . Little . . . fuzzy orange things.

410. Beneath the Surface

Original airdate: September 1, 2000
Written by: Heather Ash
Directed by: Peter DeLuise

SG-1 are enslaved underground and their memories wiped. With no memory of their former lives, how will they escape?

Much as the workers are buried beneath the city, so too are the emotions of the SG-1 team members buried beneath the surface of their consciousness. In particular, "Beneath the Surface" explores some of the feelings expressed by Sam and Jack in "Divide and Conquer" by taking away the one thing preventing them from embarking on a relationship — their respective military ranks. RDA and Tapping glow (literally, it's sweaty down there!) in their scenes together, and the lighting department does a fantastic job throughout the episode, giving everything a heated, brown/orange tone, bringing out the grimy underground atmosphere as well as the hidden, subconscious feelings between all the team members. The episode shows barriers brought down — physical (jobs), psychological (conscious vs. subconscious, true vs. false) — and emotional, and is in that respect very reminiscent of season three's "Maternal Instinct."

It's also reminiscent of the scenery in "Jolinar's Memories" and "The Devil You Know": inferno-like — and much like those episodes, there's no reprieve in sight, only a lifetime of unending labour. Peter DeLuise purposefully injected apocalyptic overtones into the episode. In Christian and Jewish literature, the Apocalypse (from the Greek, *apokalypsis*, meaning revelation) is a revelation of hidden things by God; in the apocalyptic religious literature, such revelations are usually made through dreams or visions, in much the same way as each character experiences in "Beneath the Surface" as the lives they've lost are gradually revealed to them in dreams.

But why does Janet Fraiser volunteer for the search-and-rescue mission? As she herself so quickly pointed out in "Hathor," she's a *doctor* and hasn't touched a weapon since first enlisting in the military. Why fail to look for better candidates for a mission that's likely going to be fairly dangerous? It's an annoying pattern that's repeated in episodes like "2010." Are they just trying to squeeze in quality Teryl Rothery time? The good doctor, like Daniel Jackson, had a very fervent group of fans who could be quite vocal when they wanted. A shame to mash in this great supporting character in such odd circumstances.

Even when SG-1 is living under their new identities, their seamless interaction, the result of years of habit, comes through — when the machine's pressure is building, they work together effortlessly to save the facility. Sam's new name, Thera, Greek for 'wild,' reflects the wildcard element to the episode: in a reality where barriers no longer exist, anything can happen.

Interesting Fact: The idea of the unconscious mind originated in ancient time, was foreseen by such philosophers as Leibniz and Schopenhauer, and was brought into the collective knowledge base by Sigmund Freud, who believed that dreams were one of the most direct routes to the unconscious. He further divides the subconscious into two parts — the *id* and the *superego*. The *id* is instinct, the baser aspects of human personality, while the *superego* acts as the moral agent. The set used for the underground city is the same set used in "Watergate" and "Tin Man," and the original version of the script had Thera and Jonah as lovers.

Why We're Space Monkeys: Although *Stargate SG-1* is an intelligent show, sometimes it's just really nice to gawk at sweaty, topless men glowing in perfect amber light. Chris Judge's muscles bulge impressively, and the sheer number of half-naked bodies in the underground city makes for some eye-candy moments. Yeah, it's shallow — but hey, I have one word in retaliation: Anise.

Parlez-vous Gate?:
O'NEILL: Would it mean anything if I told you I remember something else?
CARTER: What?
O'NEILL: Feelings.
CARTER: Feelings?
O'NEILL: I remember feeling . . . feelings.
CARTER (smiles): For me?
O'NEILL: No, for Tor. [Teal'c]

411. Point of No Return

Original airdate: September 8, 2000
Written by: Joseph Mallozzi, Paul Mullie
Directed by: William Gereghty

A paranoid stranger approaches Jack with startling knowledge about the Stargate, and he claims to be an alien.

"Point of No Return" is one of those episodes you can't really hate but can't really love either. There are some pacing problems in the episode, moments when it lags where it should speed ahead, and others when it speeds ahead where some explanation would be appropriate. Willie Garson does a good job with Martin, but his mannerisms can be somewhat irritating to watch.

Cowriter Paul Mullie noted that the episode grew out of the plethora of *Stargate* sites on the Web, some of which actually claim that the Stargate program is real and the show merely a cover — so if the premise seems a bit unbelievable, that's why. Somewhat alarming however, is the way in which SG-1 blithely overlooks civil rights in the name of national security — there's not a blink or a hesitation; they oh-so-easily break, enter, and take what they need. While it's understandable that national security is pretty damned important, it's still a bit discomfiting to see Jack, Sam, Daniel, and Teal'c take on such (self-)important and covert roles. Still, the "M&M" team likes to play with viewers' assumptions about the characters and the actors, and "Point of No Return" is a tongue-in-cheek reference to that.

Martin's sentiment that he just doesn't belong on Earth is one that we've all felt at some point or another — the feeling that we're out of place, unfulfilled, unfulfilling. Each of the characters displays a facet of otherness in "Point of No Return" — SG-1 is well outside of their comfort zone (Teal'c especially), and Martin really *doesn't* belong on Earth.

The episode is worth watching just to see SG-1 in full Earth daylight and in civilian clothes — such a change from the usual drab-but-necessary military garb. And they all look like they're having a lot of fun with the script. Daniel and Sam have a very fraternal bond that always plays well; they're obviously comfortable with each other and their joking under interrogation serves both as a classic deflection/defense mechanism and a reminder that they're not going to cave under pressure. (For another great moment like that, check out season eight's "Endgame.") It's a nice way to make sure we remember they're professionals, despite their getup. It's amazing how much they get across in short bouts of dialogue and a couple of sideways looks.

On the other side of the team, Teal'c gets to enjoy life above ground, and discovers the joys of vibrating beds and changing headgear — in a very funny turn of events, he's the biggest fashion guru of all of them, and Chris Judge hams it up as much as he can.

The lighthearted tone of the episode is enchanting and carries you along for (most of) the ride, and it's repeated in the show's 100th episode, season five's "Wormhole X-Treme," and again in the controversial "Citizen Joe" of season eight.

Interesting Fact: Does Martin look familiar? He should — he's a great character actor who's played in pretty much every series out there, including *Friends*, *The Practice*, *The X-Files*, *Sex and the City*, and *NYPD Blue*.

Why We're Space Monkeys: It's usually the humans arriving on other planets — not aliens landing on Earth, but the writers — and actors — are totally invested in the cliché-fest. In keeping with that theme, there's a real

X-Files feel running through the episode — from lighting to music to composition (different angles, leg and object shots, the motel set). Everyone's clearly having a lot of fun in this representation of the aliens-among-us story line.

Parlez-vous Gate?:
MARTIN: You think I'm making this all up. Look at this. (Hands Jack a toothpick.)
O'NEILL: Yes. It all makes sense now.
MARTIN: I propped it up against the inside of my door. When I got home, it was on the ground, meaning someone was there.
O'NEILL: If you prop it up against the inside of your door, how do you get out?
MARTIN: Through the window! You think I'm so stupid I go out my own front door?

412. Tangent

Original airdate: September 15, 2000
Written by: Michael Cassutt
Directed by: Peter DeLuise

Jack and Teal'c are marooned in an aircraft in space with no way home.

This episode has suspense, humor, emotion, and a deep-space ring rescue. We get some wonderful dialogue between Jack and Teal'c. It makes reference to *The Wizard of Oz* again, even (see "Tin Man"); there's just no denying it — "Tangent" is a pretty cool episode.

We see a new arrogance in Jacob Carter, a melding of his consciousness and his symbiote's, which is apparently allowing him a different viewpoint on the humans' "infantile" status. We've come to expect that from the Tok'ra, but coming from Jacob it's a real cold shower — a nice touch on the part of writer Michael Cassutt. It gives rise to the first signs of true friction between Jacob and Sam since he became a Tok'ra, adding a more realistic facet to their relationship — parental conflict is something a great many of us can identify with. It's also nice to see Jacob again — a rare occurrence in season four despite the increasing focus on the Tok'ra and their relationship with Earth.

In the rarely seen–character category, "Tangent" offers actor Colin Cunningham a chance to flex his acting muscles as Major Davis. His character makes a welcome change to the usual military personnel who step into Cheyenne Mountain bent on the program's closure. He reflects the viewers' reactions, and as such, his genuine desire to do good and save the SG-1 members is heartwarming, and pulls us into the drama. He is also an example of season four's long theme of challenging assumptions. Until now, the government was almost always *bad*. Major Davis makes SG-1 look again at the people who pull the strings in the government.

Apophis is one cunning and vengeful foe — and his hatred for Teal'c knows no bounds. He's apparently rigged his death gliders to direct themselves back to his homeworld in case Teal'c ever gets in one again.

Colin Cunningham addresses his fans
(COURTESY ELIZA BENNETT)

Not surprisingly, the Goa'uld are hot on the tracks of anyone who intrudes on their territory — one of the things that's so threatening about them, and that makes them such powerful enemies, is that they pay attention to both the larger picture (planetary wars and universal domination) and the small events (one small ship in space). Sort of like a terrier, with big honkin' guns.

Although the death glider prototype is "lost in space," it still marks Earth's first successful attempt at retrieving and using significant alien technology; it's taken four years, but the SGC has finally secured technology that could help in the fight against the Goa'uld. "Tangent" has an ominous feel to it that foreshadows "The Serpent's Venom" and carries through to "Double Jeopardy" and "Exodus." The Goa'uld are not to be underestimated.

Interesting Fact: This is one of only a handful of episodes where the Stargate isn't used.

Why We're Space Monkeys: When the going gets tough, the tough say their goodbyes in a manly man's fashion, but with real emotion. O'Neill and Teal'c don't ignore the fact that they're in all likelihood about to die; instead they express a sincere sentiment (albeit in their particular styles) and don't hide their affection for one another. And only *SG-1* can so seamlessly mix humor with near-death situations.

Parlez-vous Gate?: Second place for best line ever goes to Daniel:
DANIEL: Mak tal shree! Lok tak. Mekta satak Oz! Mok tal Oz kree! I don't think they bought my act.
JACOB: Who'd you say you were?
DANIEL: The Great and Powerful Oz.

But first place goes to Jacob, earlier in the episode:
DANIEL: Um, well, we were kind of hoping you could, like, beam them out.
JACOB: Beam them out. What am I, Scotty?

413. The Curse

Original airdate: September 22, 2000
Written by: Joseph Mallozzi, Paul Mullie
Directed by: Andy Mikita

After Daniel's former mentor dies, he discovers a canopic jar thousands of years old, containing a Goa'uld symbiote.

Okay, how awesome does Teal'c look in shorts? He tries so hard to fit in to Earth life but he stands out no matter what he does. He and Daniel Jackson have a lot in common: they are both pariahs in their respective communities. When Daniel attends his former mentor's funeral in "The Curse," he's pulled back into his old life — old haunts, old girlfriend (we assume), old rivalries. The pained look he sports in several scenes reveals the disorientation he feels at this revisitation — and rightly so; when you've come as far as Daniel has, it's hard to go back and look at where you were before.

We've always assumed that Daniel's pariah status in the archaeological field must have been hard for him to bear, but this episode offers the first real glimpse at how it's affected him. And we also see how far the discovery of the Stargate has taken him — when he's offered the chance to get his reputation back, he refuses, because he knows that what he's doing is more important than any personal pursuit could be. It's much the same way, in fact, that Teal'c gives up his family — both make sacrifices for the "greater good." One of the messages of *SG-1* concerns sacrifice — personal lives, reputations, relationships, all fall under the circular shadow of the Stargate, and what each person can do in the name of the greater good.

This is another in a long line of Daniel-centric episodes. Despite the fact that he bows out at the end of season five, Michael Shanks gets a heck of a lot of airtime in seasons four and five. "M&M" do another great job writing genre episodes that

The beautiful Anna-Louise Plowman (RAY MICKSHAW/WIREIMAGE)

also incorporate good characterization, allowing Daniel's backstory to come alive so that he doesn't exist in some sort of geeky archaeological vacuum.

We discover that Osiris is alive and on Earth, having vowed vengeance — we'll see more of him in later seasons. It may be somewhat confusing for viewers that Osiris is a male god but has chosen a female vessel. Either way, Isis is dead, her stasis jar having been damaged in transport.

"The Curse" is a truly creepy episode — what is it about museum archives that just spells spooky? — with some wonderful acting by both Anna-Louise Plowman (Sarah) and Ben Bass (Steven), although Steven is far more three-dimensional than Sarah. She seems the paragon of the Western woman — ethereal beauty, intelligence, lilting English accent. Her motives and emotions are never delved into, though, and so the episode seems a bit skewed in favor of the men of the show. Also, despite its great use of props, atmosphere, and music, the episode is hardly unpredictable — it's not much of a surprise when the Goa'uld turns out to be the perfect woman. And check out her wardrobe change from this episode to "Summit." Yeesh.

Gods & Scientists: Osiris was the Egyptian god of the underworld, married to Isis. He was killed by his brother, Seth (see season three's "Seth"), who locked his body in a chest and threw it into the Nile. Isis retrieved the body, and Seth later dismembered it and scattered the pieces throughout Egypt. In pity for the grief of Isis and her sister, Nephthys, the gods Anubis and Thoth mummified Osiris and put his body in a lion-headed bier. Isis changed into a kite (a bird) and gave breath to him. Revived, Osiris was not allowed to stay on Earth, and instead was sent to the underworld to serve as king and to judge the souls of the dead.

The scientific procedure used to date artifacts is called carbon dating, or radiocarbon dating. It uses the presence of a naturally occurring isotope, carbon 14, which disintegrates at a set rate over millennia, to calculate the age of fossils and other artifacts of interest to scientists.

Interesting Fact: Not many shows rewrite plot points to be environmentally safe. In the DVD commentary, Joseph Mallozzi noted that in the original script for this episode Jack pulls the battery out of the cell phone and throws it on the ground; however, when the scene came to be shot, this was deemed to be environmentally irresponsible and the battery was thrown into the lake instead. (Perhaps because the lake had been described as having no fish in it.)

Why We're Space Monkeys: Daniel accepts his status of pariah with equanimity. This thread has been carried straight from the movie, and although Michael Shanks makes Daniel seem angrier than James Spader did, both actors do a great job of infusing Daniel Jackson with verve and passion.

Parlez-vous Gate?:
TEAL'C: Daniel Jackson. We have caught nothing. We are fishing.
DANIEL: Right. Um, listen, I need a little help with a translation. I've got a line here that reads "Hako thra terak shree."
TEAL'C (slaps a bug on his neck): Banished to oblivion.

DANIEL: Right. Okay, uh, thank you.

TEAL'C: If you require assistance, I would be more than happy to return to the sgc.

DANIEL: No, thanks. I think I can take it from here.

TEAL'C (looks disappointed): Are you certain?

414. The Serpent's Venom

Original airdate: September 29, 2000
Written by: Peter DeLuise
Directed by: Martin Wood

Three members of SG-1 are sent on a mission with Jacob Carter while Teal'c attempts to negotiate an uprising on Chulak.

"The Serpent's Venom" sees a return to one of the longest story lines in the *Stargate* universe — the battle with Apophis.

Like some kind of snake antivenom, Teal'c, who was once part of the poison of Apophis, has turned into the antidote for his fellow Jaffa. Teal'c preaches revolution and uprising against the false gods the Jaffa serve, and although he's starting with Apophis, he hopes to free all Jaffa from their slavery, no matter which Goa'uld they follow. This episode is a great vehicle for Chris Judge — he spent much of it hanging from chains, and for once his physical prowess as a warrior was less impressive than his stalwart refusal to give in under torture. His tolerance of the Goa'uld's lies and deceit is utterly gone and he is now a passionate and dangerous enemy who threatens their very existence. As such, he is hunted with much conviction by the System Lords, especially Apophis.

When Heru'ur finally brings Teal'c out as his trump card in negotiations, preceded by the insane Terok, we are already three-quarters of the way through the episode. Writer Peter DeLuise did a great job of keeping the two story lines (the Tok'ra operation and Teal'c's abduction) separate enough to make the audience keep asking, "Yes, but *how* do they fit together?" This heightened background tension plays well against the science fiction edge of big special effects in space — minefields, mother ships, space travel. And as for bad guys, Terok takes the cake. Actor Paul Koslo gives us a chillingly real bad guy, a Goa'uld who is neither powerful nor

285

Christopher Judge on the set, in costume as Teal'c (COURTESY JO STORM)

willing to play by the rules — a recipe for insanity. Since the Goa'uld live for such a long time, it's surprising that we haven't seen more of the madness that could creep into their personalities. Director Martin Wood says he was actually scared of the actor when he auditioned — which is exactly what he was looking for, so he cast Koslo immediately.

The one person who has no chance of being saved from the poison of Apophis is Heru'ur. Since he is inured in the very system which gives Apophis his poison (in the shape of hataks and mother ships and tyranny), he cannot denounce Apophis without also drawing attention to himself. And, as a Goa'uld, he's too blinded by his own power to feel endangered by a rival. This middle-of-the-season epic battle spruces up season four after the touchy-feely mini-arcs devoted to Sam and Jack. It's as though the entire ensemble of *SG-1* took a step back and a deep breath and said, "Hey yeah, we're out there fighting bad guys."

Gods & Scientists: Heru'ur (or Heru-ur), means "Horus the Elder." Horus is the son of Isis and Osiris (see "The Curse"), but he is also considered in some myths to be her brother, and all three are the offspring of Geb and Nut (the earth and sky, respectively). Horus embodied the living pharaoh as well, tying him to humanity, and tying humanity (in the form of the pharaoh), to a direct lineage of the gods. Thus when the pharaoh spoke or decreed law, it was understood he was speaking with the gods' authority, and could not be opposed.

Interesting Fact: The elevator used on the set doesn't actually move. In this episode we see a tricky shot where the camera follows Jack, Sam, and Jacob into an elevator, then follows them from one floor to another, where the door opens to a view of Daniel Jackson. The movement was one continuous shot except for one brief moment, when the camera pans to the unopened doors of the elevator, where postproduction effects did their job, making it look as though the camera (and the characters) had changed floors.

Why We're Space Monkeys: Teal'c does "stalwart" really well. He makes resisting torture look like what it is — excruciatingly hard to combat, and only defensible with an ironclad will to live and see justice.

Parlez-vous Gate?: A classic Jack O'Neill look, when Jacob tells him to come pilot the ship — in the middle of a minefield, with alien technology and a live mine inside the ship itself. That, "What, me?!?" look always manages to appear both put out and innocent at the same time.

415. Chain Reaction

Original airdate: January 5, 2001
Written by: Joseph Mallozzi, Paul Mullie
Directed by: Martin Wood

General Hammond resigns his post abruptly, and while Colonel O'Neill searches for an answer, the rest of SG-1 must deal with General Bauer, the SGC's replacement.

The American military depends quite heavily on chain of command. A superior officer is legally accountable for any actions he issues to lesser ranks. "Chain Reaction" sets up an interesting dichotomy between the military's chain of command and the rebel NID faction's reactions to those commands. Because the NID stands outside the military and thus military law, it behaves much like the naquadah element on the test planet to which General Bauer sends his new bomb — it magnifies the blast to such an extent that the damage cannot be measured at first. The only thing we instinctively know is that their reaction (like the devastation on the planet) is very, very bad.

The execution of this episode is at times rocky (what is with the Warren Beatty lighting on Richard Dean Anderson in the jail cell?), and there were some downright boring moments. The aptly named cloak-and-dagger stuff Jack mentions is one of the least explored areas of the *SG* universe at this point, seen only occasionally ("Touchstone," "Shades of Grey," and "Watergate").

Lawrence Dane, who plays General Bauer, starts out well. He is volatile, driven, and much more the military man we saw in the early days of General Hammond. He's pragmatic and authoritarian — a leader, in other words. However, halfway through the episode, after one mistake, he seems to deflate utterly; this change is hard to believe in a man who has worked his entire life in the military. The other incredible aspect is Sam's reaction to the situation; she's positively pouty, when in similar circumstances she merely bends her head and fixes the problem. On the other hand, the low-

Don S. Davis always seems to have Dr. Fraiser looking over his shoulder (COURTESY TRICIA BYRNE)

key performance by Don S. Davis seems perfectly in tune with the later revelations that the NID is ushering him out the door by blackmail. Rather than risk the rest of his staff as well as his family, Hammond tries to exit quietly, which must go against all his blustery Texas background. As a veteran actor, Davis made good choices about his role in this episode. (You'll see this same technique used much later in season eight by Davis' real-life friend, Teryl Rothery, in "Heroes," to much the same effect.) And Ronny Cox is as slimy and hateful as ever.

Perhaps it's actor Tom McBeath's unfamiliarity with technology, but the scene where he exposits on how cunning and well-kept the secrets of the NID are (with redundant technobabble like, "firewall protected floating server") is completely deflated in one line when he adds the throwaway quip, "I'll try to hack in through the back door." That sort of silliness assumes the ignorance of the audience and is meaningless in itself. In the midst of such a great character-driven story, this small deflation dents an otherwise great episode.

Gods & Scientists: The NID is a secret operation within the U.S. that apparently everyone knows about. In terms of the purpose of the acronym, director Martin Wood swears it was made up by developer Brad Wright. A chain reaction refers to a self-sustaining sequence of events (in chemistry and physics) set off by a single event. They are volatile and can follow each other with extreme rapidity (like nuclear fission). A popular movie by the same name with Keanu Reeves delves into this phenomenon.

Interesting Fact: The inside of General Hammond's house, with its view of the backyard, is the same house as the one used later in the series for Senator Kinsey's mansion. Originally, the sequence between Jack and General Hammond was scripted for outdoors, but it rained the day of shooting and so it was moved indoors to the kitchen area; the two grandkids still had to play outside, though.

Why We're Space Monkeys: The cast and crew often refer to the fact that the set of *SG-1* is friendly and homey. This sense of camaraderie is one of the underpinnings of its popularity — from the ubiquitous Sgt. Siler and his Faithful Companion, to, in this episode, Oscar the dog — who's actually Richard's own dog, Zoë.

Parlez-vous Gate?:
TEAL'C (to Hammond): On Chulak, when a great warrior retires from the field of battle it is customary to sing a song of lament. (Pause) Fortunately, we are not on Chulak.

416. 2010

Original airdate: January 12, 2001
Written by: Brad Wright
Directed by: Andy Mikita

It is 2010 — Senator Kinsey is the President, disease has been wiped from the planet, and everything's peaceful. Of course Jack O'Neill smells a rat, and when he's right, the team tries to enlist him to make it all "right" again.

Although "2010" plays with several interesting ideas, my first reaction to watching this episode was, "Okay, the whole thing is stemming from cloak-and-dagger *gynecology*?" Although the subject matter (women's reproductive choices, the desire for a family) is treated very seriously (women speaking to women, in very believable dialogue, so kudos to Brad Wright), and though this is a good premise for an episode, Janet's conspiracy theory was a little too radical a departure for her character, since she is usually much more methodical and pragmatic. Again, as in "One False Step," Dr. Fraiser gets saddled with the plot-moving moments, when the writers need someone to make logical leaps a mile long.

Gary Jones as Technician, err, Walter Davis, err, Chevron Guy, err, Sgt. Harriman, err, himself . . . (COURTESY TRICIA BYRNE)

On the upside, Janet and Sam's onscreen time is wonderful. These two strong female characters are friends and share private moments that aren't weepy or overdone, even though the subject matter is tense and of deep importance to Sam. Although she's portrayed as a career woman, Sam breaks out of that stereotype as often as possible. Brad Wright is aware that just because a person has brains doesn't mean that he or she is not interested in having a family and bonding with others. Given his other scripts ("Out of Mind," "Abyss," and "Prodigy"), Wright's strengths lie in his understanding of the intricacies of character and character interaction, even if I do disagree with his choices occasionally.

In a larger sense, SG-1 must challenge the assumption that one good leads to more good — the Aschen's one "good" act turns out to be a means to a very bad end.

Where the episode really bogged down was the inevitable moral stand taken by Jack O'Neill. It seemed a little heavy-handed and obvious. Jack doesn't seem to be the gloaty, "I told ya so" type; at least not with his team. O'Neill is aware of the fallibility inherent in being human — of how we all want things to be easy and carefree. It's part of his personality, as integral as is his silence on his past. So it seems too over-the-top for him to go prancing around an obviously distraught Dr. Carter, going *nyah nyah* — when you'd think he would be overjoyed at the opportunity to fix things. However, as the best representative of the everyman, he has a deep distrust of theoretical principles like moving through time, and usually is satisfied with the here and now.

In that way, "2010" also gets to play — in true postmodern style — with parody, the narrative of time, and pastiche. *Stargate* is already futuristic, and Brad Wright plays gleefully with the idea that this episode is set "in the future" of the future. Sam mentions that they have already gone back in time (she's referring to "1969" — interestingly all episodes in this arc are named numerically — "1969" in season one, "2010," and "2001" in season five). But the show was aired in 2001 — and shot in 2000. In the episode, SG-1 is looking back in time (which is actually our present, albeit in a fantastical world), and trying to make things right for "the future" — a future that cannot be theirs, since all the characters as they exist at that moment will cease to exist once that little piece of paper goes sailing through the Gate. Perhaps it's that conundrum that prompted Brad Wright to kill each member of the team at the end of the episode. This provides a double duty — it both avoids a "superman" mentality that has been cropping up of late (it's been four whole seasons and SG-1 is, apparently, impossible to kill), *and* it allows for the characters to return to life in a way that makes sense.

In the gaff department, watch the first scene closely — is it a thing now, to swipe cards upside down (see "In the Line of Duty")?

Gods & Scientists: The Aschen are neither gods nor Goa'uld. They are an alien race who are advanced enough to help the human population, but like the Goa'uld, they have their own interests at heart.

Interesting Fact: The blue curtain you see when the team is descending to the room where the Gate stands had to be put there to discourage tourists, who shuttled back and forth past the set on a tour of the JR Reed Terminal in Vancouver where the episode was shot. Director Andy Mikita didn't think it would be very realistic to have thirty people in the background peering into the window and saying, "Hey what's that?"

Why We're Space Monkeys: Janet Fraiser. Period.

Parlez-vous Gate?: A great ending line for the episode, one that encapsulates all the threads of the episode:
O'NEILL: You gotta wonder.

417. Absolute Power

Original airdate: January 19, 2001
Written by: Robert Cooper
Directed by: Peter DeLuise

SG-1 locates the Harcesis, and the boy teaches Daniel Jackson a life-changing lesson.

Much like the earlier episode "Beneath the Surface," this episode can be seen as a large wrestling pad for the subconscious. There are two very obvious foreshadowing lines at the beginning of the episode that seem almost like throwaway lines. Only near the end of the episode do they wrap around again and become important. This circularity is a tool used by certain meditative techniques, most especially by Buddhism — and Shifu's robes and haircut make this connection overt. The technique involves watching each thing that enters the mind, whether it is a thought, emotion or sensation. No thought is too small, no smell too slight, to be reflected upon.

From this perspective, the two lines — one by General Hammond stating that all information about the Goa'uld must be shared with their allies, the Tok'ra; and the other, Shifu's statement to Daniel that his reckoning with Sha're at her death was "like a dream" — seem slight, but they are in fact the shell beneath which (like the subconscious) everything else rests. Refusal to look closely at them results in exactly what happens to Daniel in the episode — he lives the dream as though it were reality, and the consequences of his actions are not truly understood until it's too late. Unfortunately, though the ending was softened by Daniel's morality fix and a little sleight of hand with cool CGI effects, this is still a dreaded "it was all a dream . . ." episode, a trope that is frankly tired and empty. The SGC and the Tok'ra blithely accept Daniel's private vision (and yet they were hell-bent against the real phenomena he had encountered in "There But for the Grace of God"), and Shifu goes sailing off into the blue event horizon. Shifu, by the way, is a close derivation of *sifu*, or "teacher," in Chinese.

From a continuity angle, if the episode is being told from Daniel Jackson's POV, then why do we see scenes he's not in? Does he see them too? They could have been taken out without lessening the tension of the story — in fact, they would heighten the tension, since a story told from strictly one point of view makes us ask more questions and is often more powerful. And Carter as the feminine intuition/voice of reason crossover is just boring. Jack would have twigged to it far sooner than she, given his suspicious mind. However, the interplay between Jack and Daniel is great, with the two actors sharing some screen time alone in a way they haven't done in a while.

Why We're Space Monkeys: Daniel does a good descent into madness. He's at his best when playing a man in the grips of something alien — in this case, an alien megalomania (see also "Need," "Legacy," and season seven's "Lifeboat" for more cases . . . I mean instances).

Parlez-vous Gate?:
HAMMOND (grabs intercom): All personnel, this is General Hammond. A . . . glowing energy being . . . is headed for level 28.

418. The Light

Original airdate: January 26, 2001
Written by: James Phillips
Directed by: Peter Woeste

A powerful addiction affects SG-5 and Daniel Jackson. When SG-5 dies suddenly, and Jackson slips into a coma, SG-1 returns to the planet to find out why.

Is it just me, or is Daniel in a heck of a lot of comas these days? He just came out of one in "Absolute Power" — okay, it wasn't *technically* a coma, but almost — and here he is again, out like a light. Considering the stress involved in being in a comatose state, that's one resilient man they've got on the team. Ever notice it seems to be O'Neill who gets physically injured, while Daniel gets psychologically injured?

With less emphasis on the Sam/Jack relationship, the writers are returning to more of season one's banter and camaraderie. While Jack's outward relationship with Daniel is often antagonistic, there is an under-current of true friendship that Daniel is not only the moral compass of the team but also the human bridge between all three team members.

The lightness of the beginning of the episode makes the inexplicable death dramatic enough to put us on the edge of our seats — and the credits haven't even rolled yet. This is Peter Woeste's second time in the director's chair. He's more often credited as a director of photography, "Maternal Instinct" being his first attempt at directing. But by this time the cast and crew of *SG-1* is operating smoothly, so it seems he might merely have to put the camera on them, and yell, "rolling!" Of course the addition of two excellent supporting characters — in true *SG-1* style, one human, and one machine — helps to keep the plot engaging and tense. And in "The Light," the lush, thick set pieces make a truly alien environment seem "natural." It's easy to suspend disbelief in sets like those.

Interestingly, although the focus is on light in this episode, it is the *sound* of the device that really draws us in. Watch the episode muted at the points when the device is shown, and you'll find the effect drops off. However, light is a major concern in *SG-1*, and it is often wedded to the idea of "rightness" or "good."

"The Light" is very much like season one's "Torment of Tantalus," with its special effects (although a reversal from Daniel/Ernest to Jack/Loran). It also allows us to see once again that even the seemingly undefeatable SG-1 team is human, and that striving for the "light" can be addictive.

Gods & Scientists: The Goa'uld are immune to addiction; we saw this earlier when Daniel got addicted to a sarcophagus in "Need." Addiction itself has been characterized as a defense mechanism; people retreat into an addiction to combat other, stressful aspects of their lives. Addiction may depend on certain neurotransmitters (like a chemical courier) such as dopamine.

Interesting Fact: It is a common practice on sets for makeup artists to apply glycerine to an actor's eyes before a scene where they are required to cry, to lubricate the tear ducts. Kristian Ayre (Loran) doesn't need them — he can cry on cue. Peter Woeste notes that the entire scene between Jack and Loran was only shot twice, and most footage was used from the first take. It could be helped along by the fact that Kristian, though he's playing a fourteen- to fifteen-year-old old boy, was actually twenty-three (if the episode was filmed in 2000 — Kristian was born in 1977). Check out his tongue-in-cheek line to Teal'c, "You don't look that old," in response to Teal'c informing him he is 101.

Why We're Space Monkeys: Teal'c's character arc is often subtle, but those few glimpses are enough to satisfy us that he is, in fact, a fully integrated member of the team — even if he doesn't usually get as much screen time. In "The Light" there are two moments when we see this in particular — when he uses a computer and in his short scene with Loran, where he refers to the episode "Bane" and his young cohort's penchant for playing with water guns. "It's fun," replies Loran simply. A great moment.

Parlez-vous Gate?:
CARTER: Be a good excuse for you.
O'NEILL: Huh?
CARTER: To do nothing for a while.
O'NEILL: What?
CARTER: Forget it.
O'NEILL: That would be forget it, *Sir*.
CARTER: Oh please, you think I'm keeping that up if we're stuck here forever?

419. Prodigy

Original airdate: February 2, 2001
Story by: Brad Wright, Joseph Mallozzi, Paul Mullie
Teleplay by: Joseph Mallozzi, Paul Mullie
Directed by: Peter DeLuise

Carter takes it upon herself to show a young cadet her future if she persists in the Air Force. She takes her to a planet where O'Neill has found energy beings that can pass through solid matter.

If you ever wanted to see women working in a male-dominated job, *as seen by men*, this is the episode for you. Elizabeth Rosen (Hailey) and Amanda Tapping are both given roles that may on the surface seem pretty sterling — but when you get right down to it, they're playing a man's game in a man's way. The clichés fly fast and loose, from the typically misunderstood genius who gets into fights, to female rivalry in the workplace; "Prodigy" manages to offend even as it pretends to boost women. Hailey and Carter are both the protagonists of this particular episode and its victims. The argument put forward by the writers that women are competitive in the same way that men are is undisputed; that they experience workplace rivalry just the same as men do is also undisputed; however, that they resort to what amounts to name-calling and rank-pulling is reverting to stereotypes that are beneath the writers of *SG-1*. This episode is really out of character. In four years, we've never once seen Sam so obsessed with being right that she outright rejects a colleague's — even a younger colleague's — theory. Sure, there are some subtle moments of vanity and pride in her work when she's lecturing, or one-on-one with her former professors/mentors, but that at least seems true to Sam's character — she's always demonstrated a need to gain the approval of her superiors. The vicious streak she exhibits when talking with Hailey, however, comes as a shock to the system. And we already know that Sam is pretty darn cool — does she have to save the world one person at a time as well? Doesn't she have enough to do?

The other moment of dismay comes when, with just a few short words of wisdom from a man (O'Neill) — "It doesn't matter who's right, cadet," — Hailey's worldview is changed, as though the previous half hour in close contact with Sam had done nothing. As an added insult, you never really get a sense for the cadet's character throughout the episode (which is unfortunate since she takes over as the episode's protagonist); she goes through rapid personality changes, moving from withdrawn rebellion to wide-eyed wonder in the time it takes for one of those energy beams to pass through her.

The executive summary? It's a shame the writers didn't focus more on the off-world plotline — it has a lot more going for it, and at least it doesn't pretend to be about women. "M&M" usually do a good job with character, but this one falls short, a fact which they're aware of. "I've always preferred the character-based stories," said Joseph Mallozzi, "although 'Prodigy' is a bad example as it doesn't rate as one of my, oh, top seventy-five *SG-1* episodes."

Gods & Scientists: A major branch of physics is mechanics, the study of matter; a subsection of that is dynamics, or matter in motion. Other branches of physics include solid state (it has to do with transistors, diodes and photoelectricity or light), plasma physics, cryogenic physics, and cosmology (or astro-) physics. So, when Sam Carter is described as an astrophysicist, the term places her very specifically within a branch of physics that studies the physical properties and interaction of celestial bodies and events. Not that she wouldn't necessarily know about televisions — but the study of physics is a huge and complex subject.

Interesting Fact: That's the real General Michael E. Ryan, former chief of staff of the United States Air Force, appearing in this episode. He retired in 2001. "Prodigy" was his first acting role, and he did it as a long-time fan of science fiction. In a quote on Richard Dean Anderson's Web site he said, "The ideas that come out of science fiction are often more science than fiction."

Why We're Space Monkeys: The idea of establishing a research facility off-world is a neat idea, and one that brings us back to the roots of the SGC, one that we haven't seen for a while. Remember their mandate? To find and analyze new technology. It seems strange that Sam and Janet wouldn't have been involved in checking out the site for such a project though, given their scientific backgrounds. See more on off-site projects in season seven's "Death Knell."

Parlez-vous Gate?:
O'NEILL: I'll never complain about mosquitoes again.

420. Entity

Original airdate: February 9, 2001
Written by: Peter DeLuise
Directed by: Allan Lee

Sam is taken over by an alien entity. Jack, Daniel, and Teal'c struggle to find the best way to save her.

"Entity" is one of a handful of episodes shot entirely in the SGC. One of the most enduring aspects of these episodes is their claustrophobic feel — the walls of the mountain seem to press in on characters and viewers alike ("Foothold," "Divide and Conquer"). Form and the content mix really convincingly; not only are the SGC members under quarantine and trapped underground, Carter is trapped within her own mind, taken hostage by an alien entity, and the entity itself is cornered in one spot after the other. Visually, this claustrophobia is reflected in the sets — a small hospital cell; a small, locked room filled with electronic paraphernalia; the control room gone haywire. It's a really effective use of physical location that brings out the episode's theme of survival.

As can happen in any series, season four has uneven moments — it's got some amazing episodes that you can watch over and over, but it's also a departure from the three previous seasons, with less mythology, more CGI, and new-and-improved alien cultures. That's not a bad thing. We've been introduced to a lot of advanced civilizations this season: energy beings ("Prodigy"), water aliens ("Watergate"), Replicators ("Small Victories"), and, here, a digital being. But there has been far less emphasis on the original myths the show has so far been based on.

One possible reason for this shift is the arrival of a batch of new writers and directors who are working to fit their ideas into the framework of the show. These new faces also reflect the long arc of challenging assumptions. Writers in particular often excavate other writers' works, asking "why?" to unchallenged ideas — like, for instance, that the Goa'uld are always ruthless, or the Tok'ra always benign. In "Entity," as with "Prodigy" and "Watergate," we get the feeling that the SGC is in over its head in terms of alien life-forms — not only does the facility have to deal with the ever-looming threat of the Goa'uld, but it is now thwarted from every corner of the universe, or so it seems, alien entities seeking to harm them.

"Entity" takes a good look at the Jack/Daniel as well as the Jack/Sam relationship, with varying degrees of success. Much like in "Scorched Earth," Jack and Daniel find themselves on opposite sides of the spectrum, Jack pushing for a military coup against the entity's home world and Daniel for communicating with it. Unlike "Scorched Earth," however, where Jack was concerned with justice and helping the Enkarans, his concern in "Entity" is entirely focused on his teammate's safety.

In terms of the relationship between Sam and Jack, however, season four is beginning to look excessive. The entity states that it chose to inhabit Sam because it knew she was important to Jack (and to the SGC). How did it know? It had been observing them for all of a couple of hours at most —

and it's unlikely there would be anything in their personnel files regarding their feelings for each other. The whole thing seems really forced, from Hammond's "I know that Major Carter means a lot to you" to the showdown forcing Jack to shoot Sam with the zat gun (although that moment is a very nice allusion to the scene in "Thor's Hammer" where Jack makes Daniel destroy the Hammer to save Teal'c, despite what it means to him personally). This is one assumption that Peter DeLuise chose *not* to question. On the upside, the episode contains some thought-provoking undercurrents of universal vs. personal theory, rejoining the theme of sacrifice that we've seen so often on the show.

Gods & Scientists: "The human brain is capable of storing terabytes of information." For the non-computer people out there, a terabyte is the equivalent of one trillion, or to be exact, 1,099,511,627,776 individual bytes — that's a *lot* of information! The workings of human memory are still only partially understood, but three types are generally distinguished: sensory, short-term, and long-term. As well, there are three processes of memory: encoding (forming the memory), storage (maintaining a memory), and retrieval (recovering information from memory). While the analogy of a computer system is in some ways deficient when talking about human memory (things like creativity, physiology, and psychology are stripped away), it is often used as a comparison.

Interesting Fact: This was Allan Lee's second episode as director — he was often the show's editor during seasons one, three, four, and five. TV editors are heavily involved in how the episode turns out — they view film that's already been shot, alongside production personnel, to analyze what scenes need improving or reshooting; they edit specific scenes to specific lengths, arranging them so that the story and the effect is emphasized; they edit music and effects; they select stock shots (like shots of the wormhole) where necessary to incorporate them into the episode. Along with the director, editors are an unseen but incredibly important final part of a show's production.

Why We're Space Monkeys: For all of Sam's fortitude when she's injured in the control room at the beginning of the episode, she's not able to fight off this intruder. Amanda Tapping does an amazing job of looking alien. Her blank, unblinking stare makes your "awww" button go off.

Parlez-vous Gate?:
HAMMOND: What's it doing?
CARTER: Flying, Sir.
O'NEILL: MALPS can't fly.
DANIEL: Apparently they can.
O'NEILL: Shouldn't there be a memo on this stuff?

421. Double Jeopardy

Original airdate: February 16, 2001
Written by: Robert Cooper
Directed by: Michael Shanks

SG-1's "Tin Man" counterparts rescue a planet from System Lord Cronus; SG-1 rescues their "Tin Man" counterparts.

The second-to-last episode of season four, "Double Jeopardy" satisfies the action cravings in us, much like "Small Victories" and "Tangent" did.

The term "double jeopardy" is a clause included in the Fifth Amendment to the American Constitution; it's a legal term referring to the fact that once you have been prosecuted for a crime, you cannot be prosecuted for it again. The irony in the episode's title is obvious once the action gets started — the people of Juna are suffering for the same "crime" twice — once for Heru'ur and once for Cronus. Of course, having two SG-1 teams running around only adds to the irony; it's an interesting revisitation, and the "Tin Man" story line comes full circle as each member is killed off in turn.

It's hard to not notice the fact that "Double Jeopardy" is directed by Michael Shanks: if you happen to miss one of the closeups of Daniel, there's a plethora of others sure to catch your eye. I can understand that it's probably a lot easier to direct yourself than other people (a fact Shanks himself points out on the audio commentary to the episode), but a couple of the pans seem a little out of place and self-indulgent.

Although there's apparently meant to be some backstory between Cronus and his First Prime, Hira, it seems forced — Hira comes out of nowhere as the sneering counterpart to Cronus' evil smirk, with nothing to indicate her background or give her any texture as a character except the fact that she's evil.

Regardless of these nitpicks, "Double Jeopardy" is still fun to watch, and you really get your SG-1 quota; there are a lot of really difficult postproduction elements — like Daniel getting his head shot off, or Jack wrestling with himself — that are seamlessly edited into the episode and make it a pleasure to watch.

Never mind what could be a slight production goof — when Harlan sends the message through the iris, it says Comtrya, not Comtraya. Either it's spelled phonetically, or those darn Stargates have a mind of their own.

Even though the people of Juna buried their Gate after SG-1 led them in a rebellion against Heru'ur (last seen in "The Serpent's Venom"), Cronus came back by ship and took control of the planet (Teal'c speculates that he was unwilling to leave the planet alone for strategic military purposes). With Cronus now dead, the balance of power between the System Lords will have shifted dramatically. Season five should be spectacular if the indications from writing, CGI, and directing are any sign.

Interesting Fact: John DeSantis, the tall, square-looking Jaffa warrior from the beginning, was first discovered at a gas station in Duncan, BC. He was one of the warriors in *The 13th Warrior* and also plays Lurch in the *Addams Family* movies.

Why We're Space Monkeys: The cast of *SG-1* has been given the opportunity to write and direct at various points. Although Amanda Tapping had expressed an interest in writing/directing an episode for a while, and although she had the most experience of anyone on the cast (having written and directed stage productions), she had to wait until season seven to get her chance — by which point Michael had directed, and Chris written, several more episodes.

Parlez-vous Gate?:
HARLAN: The beginning, yes. They were not happy, they could not stop being you. The portable power pack you invented.
CARTER: The robot me?
HARLAN: Oh, it was ingenious. Even Hubald would have been impressed. I have one in my chest now; would you like to see it?
CARTER: Yes!
O'NEILL: No! You can show her later.

422. Exodus

Original airdate: February 23, 2001
Written by: Joseph Mallozzi, Paul Mullie
Directed by: David Warry-Smith

SG-1 and the Tok'ra join forces to eliminate Apophis once and for all — and they're taking an entire solar system along with him.

"Exodus" has so much going on, it's hard to find fault, but this season finale has a few disappointments. This mini-arc, comprised of "Crossroads," "Double Jeopardy" and this episode, begins *in medias res*, but the backstory, due to its enormity, is not filled in. So if you're a new viewer of the series, you're bound to be confused. Perhaps hoping to counter this, the makers added massive CGI content to the episode. Even more than the Replicator arc, this arc uses mattes, generated effects, and a multitude of postproduction painting to give the illusion of a lush and rich alien (but not too alien) topography.

On its most basic level, the story has a gaping hole that even those fans who happily turn a blind eye to most of the science find glaring: the beginning of the episode has Jacob Carter telling SG-1 that the Tok'ra are using Cronus' mother ship to move the Stargate to another location, "not currently on the Goa'uld map." According to other episodes ("Children of the Gods," and season seven's "Avenger 2.0" in particular), the Gate system talks to itself like a network; so then wouldn't the Gate, wherever it is placed, relay its information to other computers? (Would the Tok'ra use a DHD? If not, then this wouldn't happen. But we aren't told either way).

On another level, while the Goa'uld are seen as the *most evil ever*, the writers are walking a fine (and dangerous) line between ridding the universe of evil, and partaking in genocide. When Jacob says to Jack that the Tok'ra's way of doing things involves allowing the Goa'uld to fight amongst themselves until they (the Tok'ra), have found a way to deal with them, "once and for all," it smacked a bit too much of genocide and "final solution" to me.

Standing out in a different way are the two polemical positions of the allies. While the Tok'ra's ideology is more communal in nature (and/or dictatorial? who can say?), the humans' more individualistic (and definitely American) pattern of taking on one Goa'uld at a time means the two factions will constantly be at loggerheads. This is a great tension-building device that's used more effectively in seasons seven and eight. Ideological oppositions are one thing that *SG-1* always does well.

In her summary of the devised plan (and the weakest justification for CGI ever), Carter mentions that the entire solar system they are working in is "abandoned and barren." Let me say that again, just so you don't miss it; an *entire solar system, abandoned and barren.* Does the word xenophobia mean anything to anyone? On the other side, (perhaps to balance out the galactic implications of Carter blowing up stars), there is the single-minded vengeance motif that Teal'c embodies, which, in essence justifies murder (since it's an alien who's doing it, it's okay?), bringing home the message that, while SG-1 does save the universe (at the expense of the occasional solar system), they still must grapple with frightening and often terrible consequences.

Jacob's arrogance, seen most recently in "Tangent," has toned down a bit as the Tok'ra/human meld continues. It's nice to see Argenziano's choices as an actor as his character is developed. He's still a little hard-nosed, but now seems more in line with his human military personality and less like an overwrought, superior symbiote. Of all the characters, it seems Jack's is the most underused in this episode. At times, he is just the gag-line guy, and this trend toward saying nothing but quips can get a little irritating after awhile. Mostly, Richard chose to look baffled and sort of dragged along by events in "Exodus," instead of displaying the leadership skills he normally does. There is a great synchronized moment, however, when Jack and Daniel are across the table from "the Carters," and their summation of the plan echoes the two big brains themselves: "Ambitious."

Gods & Scientists: Tanith's symbiote's name was Hebron. Hebron is one of the six cities mentioned in the Bible where a criminal could go (in particular someone who had murdered another), to seek asylum without fear of reprisal from the murderer's next of kin. In ancient times "blood vengeance," or retribution killing, would be condoned by the society. Oh, the irony. . . .

Interesting Fact: A lot of the desert scenes in *SG-1* are shot in the Richmond sand dunes area just outside Vancouver. The feature film *Mission to Mars* was also shot in this location.

Why We're Space Monkeys: Who else blows up solar systems? How cool is that?

Parlez-vous Gate?: Another nonspeaking moment that's just hilarious is when poor Daniel is left at the helm of the captured mothership while "the Carters" go off to fix things and be geeky. A little spooked by the giganticness of it all, the archaeologist does a great parody of the Goa'uld, standing in a self-conscious jaunty pose (great shot of his . . . profile, though!).

STARGATE SG-1 — SEASON FIVE
"Do what you have to do."

501. Enemies

Original airdate: June 29, 2001
Story by: Brad Wright, Robert Cooper, Joseph Mallozzi, Paul Mullie
Teleplay by: Robert Cooper
Directed by: Martin Wood

While Teal'c is brainwashed into loyalty to Apophis again, SG-1 must escape from Apophis — again.

Apophis is dead. No, I mean it! Yep, really and truly this time. Season five's beginning seems like an ironic counterpoint to its title. Five seasons for a science fiction show is already a pretty big coup, and here we see the writers coming to terms with the fact that all arcs must eventually be wrapped up. This can be a scary thing for a show because the writers might discard components that drew people to it in the first place. *Stargate SG-1* is in its fifth year, and even though real-life wars often last a lot longer than that, the reality of a TV show is that timelines have to be compressed in order to stay compelling to viewers.

The end of season four and the beginning of season five see a change in the flavor of *SG-1*, away from the stronger mythological ties to a more hardcore science fiction element. There are lots of big explosions and CGI, but sometimes the writers' treatment of the mythological components of the show seems to be cast out, rather than wrapped up. Apophis has been resurrected a number of times, but the writers seem to be unable to join that kind

Despite being *SG-1*'s nemesis, Peter Williams is still a favorite with the fans (COURTESY TRICIA BYRNE)

of science fiction and mythology together when Apophis dies "for good."

You have to give them credit — in mythology, most gods *don't* die, so the writers had to work within a situation that was less than optimal. For four seasons, there's been a balancing act between the fact that the Goa'uld portray gods and the fact that they are not gods. This tension between science and mythology leads to a fork in the road: when Apophis finally dies, the writers have to choose, and the only road open to them is the science fiction one — Apophis is human, therefore his death has to be treated as both human, and evil. In Western canon, the death of an evil human is usually ignoble, and so now we're faced with a character who has been quite convincingly portrayed as a god, but who dies without a final great story.

In the same way, the Teal'c thread at the end feels tacked on, and lacks the vigor it could have had. The writers disregard their own show's bible when Teal'c is shot with a zat gun while brainwashed and nothing happens (see "Family" and "Seth" for more on how electric jolts have counteracted brainwashing on the show). That kind of deviation doesn't help when the episode's story line is already weak.

In terms of storytelling, when we watch a show, we are implicitly agreeing to a set of conventions, one of which is the forward movement of the story. Apophis is dead and keeping Teal'c brainwashed for the next few years will not move the story forward, so we *know* it's just a matter of time before he's back to normal. And in a series that works so hard to give us unexpected events, that's a bit of a letdown.

On the other hand, the inclusion of the new emphasis on science fiction in the shape of the Replicators is a nice metaphor for where the show is going in general. The season four/season five bridge is, in retrospect, pretty clear as we see the show move out of strict mythology — and Egyptian mythology in particular — to a more twentieth-century mindset of the fantastical (the Ascended) versus the scientific (the Replicators). A new enemy, a new tension.

Gods & Scientists: Most cultures have at least one story of overcoming death — in Christianity, Jesus revived Lazarus (see also "Cold Lazarus" from season one), and himself rose from the dead.

Interesting Fact: The scene on the ship where the lid of the box disintegrates is all real; visual effects supervisor James Tichenor explained that there were props people spraying gasoline onto styrofoam out of view of the camera, causing the lid to crumble.

Why We're Space Monkeys: The interaction between Jack and Jacob (see below) is wonderfully true in this episode. The casual banter reminds us of the family atmosphere —on the set and off.

Parlez-vous Gate?:
O'NEILL: Excuse me. I distinctly remember someone saying "We're not going to make it!" I think we made it.
JACOB: I'm sorry, I overreacted. At the time it seemed we weren't going to make it.
O'NEILL: Yes! Well, next time, maybe we'll just wait and see.
JACOB: And blow the last chance I'll ever have of being right?
O'NEILL (at Sam's smile): What?
CARTER (following Jacob): Welcome to *my* life!

502. Threshold

Original airdate: July 6, 2001
Written by: Brad Wright
Directed by: Peter DeLuise

Teal'c must go to the brink of death to recover from being brainwashed.

This episode explores each character's threshold. One question is, how much pain can one person take? In a lot of ways, the episode echoes the motifs we saw in "Need." It troubles the idea of what we assume pain to be, and highlights the different types of pain that we endure. Besides the purely physiological pain, we have psychological pain, as SG-1 has to stand by helplessly, and also the pain of integrity that comes from thwarting your own desires. In "Threshold," Doctor Fraiser's integrity, her code of ethics, demands that she alleviate immediate physical pain, but, because she has to follow orders, her personal integrity is overlaid by the dictates of military law/moral code and she is unable to perform her functions as a medical doctor.

The normally laconic Teal'c gets a lot of lines in this one; how Chris Judge chooses to interpret these lines shows us how close to the threshold Teal'c is. In an interview given to *Xposé*, Chris says: "Combined ['Enemies' and 'Threshold'] really deal with my character's whole backstory, and [they] lead in from and tie up directly with the show's pilot episode. In 'Children of the Gods' there was basically no development as to why Teal'c chose to help SG-1. So what 'Threshold' really does is kind of deal with my life and how I came to feel like I did about the Goa'uld; why I was teamed up with Bra'tac and about my training with him. It also focuses on my life as a young warrior before I was Apophis' First Prime."

Because Teal'c's lines are usually delivered with very little emotional flourish, it would be easy to fake emotional depth and drop a cheap clue for the audience. Instead, Chris uses more subtle modulations and trusts that the audience will pay enough attention to pick up the clues. For five years we've had to watch Teal'c closely to understand what he's going through; in "Threshold" we watch even more closely, feeling his pain intensely.

Brainwashed or not, Teal'c is still himself: stoic, determined, and loyal. Because Jack knows that Teal'c is these things, he also knows that Teal'c's capacity for following those traits does not conform to our set of ethics. Teal'c's threshold for proper social conduct does not lie where ours does;

For Michael, Amanda, and Tony, three is never a crowd (ALBERT L. ORTEGA)

he doesn't draw the line at lying, even though lying is inherently unethical, because loyalty is more important to him. It is this that makes O'Neill so suspicious of a Teal'c that would be so easily disloyal — or unbrainwashed.

The flashbacks from Teal'c's life as First Prime of Apophis and his training with Bra'tac sow the seeds for the character's development throughout his SG-1 years. As the instigator to Teal'c's inner rebellion, Bra'tac will always be held close to Teal'c's heart and his cause — he'll grow old and they'll still fight together, united against a common belief in the Goa'uld's evildoing. The moment of realization that Apophis is no all-knowing, all-seeing god is devastating to watch; we're not seeing a pathetic alien determined to take respect not owed him. Instead, we're watching the annihilation of a lifetime's worth of faith and service. The ritual through which Teal'c is taken is similar to hypnosis, which in some circles is thought to aid in recovering memories. Here, he is forced to relive painful experiences until he comes to a point where he can accept who he is, who he has become. The alienation Teal'c has lived with over the past four years can't have been easy for him — the refutation of his and his people's way of life, the relocation to an alien planet, the slow development of a new set of friends and allies. In some ways, being brainwashed was probably easier on his psyche, a relief to the system, to stop fighting and just go with the flow, follow the leader and forget about defeating an awe-inspiring enemy. Reliving pain that he propagated through his fear and uncertainty is undoubtedly something that Teal'c needs in order to let go of his guilt and come to a conscious, and subconscious, realization that he is where he belongs, where he is meant to be, and that he's fighting the good fight.

Daniel is particularly sympathetic in this episode, again perhaps alluding to his own experience in "Need" — he knows what it's like to fight for your life, feeling alone and betrayed by everyone, against an enemy you're not even sure *is* an enemy (or there, for that matter).

Gods & Scientists: In scientific terms, a minimum threshold is the least amount of stimulus required to provoke a sensation. A maximum threshold is the most amount of energy that an element can withstand. Different animals have different thresholds; dogs have a much higher auditory threshold than we do, for instance.

Why We're Space Monkeys: *SG-1* doesn't hesitate to show the ugly, personal side of a war, down to the inhumane lengths to which people go when they care about someone. The scenes where Teal'c is near death are difficult to watch, but the emotions that are being dealt with are real, and very powerful.

Parlez-vous Gate?:
O'NEILL: Uh, just out of curiosity . . . how do you feel about . . . ?
TEAL'C: Apophis is a false god . . . a *dead* false god.

503. Ascension

Original airdate: July 13, 2001
Written by: Robert Cooper
Directed by: Martin Wood

Sam gets an alien boyfriend other people can't see. Jack, Daniel, and Teal'c are concerned for her sanity.

"Ascension" follows the same basic setup as season one's "Enigma," in having an alien fall in love with Sam, only the twist is revealed later in the episode, indicating how different the storytelling techniques now are this far into the series. While "Enigma" begins *in medias res*, "Ascension" offers up the relationship, and its context, before giving us a clue about how we as viewers should feel about the situation. It's an effective way to tell the story — one the writers have become adept at over the years.

This is definitely a "black widow syndrome" episode, despite some excellent acting from Amanda Tapping and Sean Patrick Flanery. The problem with "Ascension" may be the fact that the writers seem to be saying that Sam can't have it all — in fact, she would have to be literally insane to have a guy as well as a cool job, or a guy as well as a happening social life with her friends and co-workers. The episode neatly sets up season seven's boyfriend, Pete, who first appears sweet and innocent, and then stalks Sam. It also parallels season one's "The First Commandment" where Sam says, "I seem to have a soft spot for the lunatic fringe."

If Sam did have it all, the writers would have no tension to work with, and no way to draw the viewers in — no one really wants to watch a show about someone with a perfect life, you can't identify with that. So episodes like "Ascension" make the best of a difficult situation by bringing in a (short, thin) string of suitors who promptly kick the bucket or leave — but it offers us the possibility of seeing Sam in a different context, of seeing her emote on a personal level rather than a professional one.

"Ascension" was written because fans on the Internet were asking to see more about the characters' personal lives — specifically Sam's. There was a scene between Janet and Sam that was later cut in which Sam realizes that her psych evaluation has come back clean but no one has called her back in to work — and she infers that they still don't trust her. Amanda was very disappointed about the cut: "That was the pivotal point for me, where I actually sort of flip to the dark side, if you will, and decide that I can go against my superior officers. It's the scene that sends me over the edge."

In some ways, "Ascension" brings Daniel and Sam closer than ever, because, like Sam, Daniel has had a run of bad luck, with people and things he loved being taken away from him (see season four). Jack and Teal'c have lost their families; Daniel his career, his wife, and her child; Sam any chance

Richard receives an award at the USAF Association's 57th Annual Air Force Anniversary Dinner for *Stargate*'s continuous positive depiction of the U.S. Air Force (COURTESY U.S. AIR FORCE)

of a love life beyond her career — and her multitude of vehicles (and how cool are they!?). It seems almost like a comment on the rigors of military life, where the military becomes one's family, one's life.

From a feminist perspective, however, Sam has virtually no control over her life; it's hard to imagine that, in the same situation, Jack or Daniel would have been given the same treatment — suspected of insanity and spied on in their own home. Season five studies the issue of otherness quite a bit, and in "Ascension," it's nearly impossible not to see that Sam and Teal'c are clearly "other" — one a woman, the other an alien, their positions immutable and irrefutable. So, despite the writers' efforts to bring Sam in as "one of the boys," to include her, seamlessly, as we saw in season four, this episode places her on the outskirts of her own life.

Gods & Scientists: "The Ascension" in Christianity refers to one of the main celebrations in the Christian religion; it commemorates the ascension of Jesus to heaven, forty days after his resurrection from the dead. In *SG-1*, ascension is a phenomenon we'll see a lot more of after "Meridian."

Interesting Fact: Amanda thought that the house they set up as hers in the episode had way too much "stuff" in it to be in character for Carter — so she played the part on the assumption that the house was her father's, and that she had taken it over once he went off to be a Tok'ra.

Why We're Space Monkeys: How cool is Sam? Amanda Tapping agrees: "I drive an amazing car. It's sweet. You know what? I think Carter is very cool. She has a 1940 Indian motorcycle; a 1961 beautiful, mint, vintage Volvo; and she's got a Harley in her garage that she's working on, too. How great is that?"

Parlez-vous Gate?:
CARTER: Take it easy?
O'NEILL: Yeah. You've been a little tense.
CARTER: Tense? Me? I'm not tense . . . am I? When did you first notice?

504. The Fifth Man

Original airdate: July 20, 2001
Written by: Joseph Mallozzi, Paul Mullie
Directed by: Peter DeLuise

SG-1 is compromised off-world by an alien entity who is passing himself off as a member of their team.

Season five, already unsteady out of the starting block, wobbles again in this episode. In fact, season five is very reminiscent of season one — lots of heady, interesting ideas that get lost in techniques and devices. As well, it seems as though season five doesn't know where it's going — again, much like season one. The transition from mythological fare (like "Thor's Hammer" and even — shudder — "Hathor") to a more keenly edged science fiction ideology is basically what season five is about. Although Peter DeLuise's penchant for big explosions and war-like atmospheres in his episodes plays well when it's needed, it's not really needed here.

The ambivalence of the long arcs in this season is reflected as early as the title. Perhaps an oblique allusion to a novel by Graham Greene called *The Tenth Man*, or the 1949 film *The Third Man* (also collaborated on by Greene), "The Fifth Man" does have some of the same ideas — but only vaguely. In *The Tenth Man*, men captured in wartime must draw lots to see who will die. It is decided that the tenth man will face execution. When lots are drawn, it is a wealthy man who loses. He tries to bargain his way out of death. While the Reole are being hunted to extinction like the characters in the novel were, the sense of urgency that Greene's protagonist, Louis Chavel, displays is not reflected in Lt. Tyler. It is instead reflected more in O'Neill, who displays his military skills to great advantage. Always near a weapon and on alert, it's clear that the Colonel is in his element, and that he takes his military responsibilities seriously. When he discovers Tyler is not who he claims to be, he doesn't stop protecting him.

In the film *The Third Man*, a naive writer goes searching for answers in the mysterious death of his friend, who was involved in the black market. Again, the Goa'uld involvement in testing and attempting to use the Reole's natural abilities could be seen as a black market tactic. The episode seems to move sluggishly between these two ideas, and while the photography is great (the night scenes have an authenticity to them), and Richard gets to play soldier boy to the hilt, and no one does explosions like Peter DeLuise, the episode fails to really push any buttons other than the "wow, cool CGI!" one. Lots of Jaffa are shot, zatgunned, and generally spend most of their on-screen time in a horizontal pose.

The character traits that we see exhibited in Carter and Fraiser, however, make it worth watching. Whether or not it's the effect of the Reole chemical, Sam's near-insubordination (when she's told that no rescue team will be sent in for O'Neill and Tyler until the SGC figures out what's going on) borders on alarming. Always the "good soldier" of the team, her anger is thrilling to watch. Her motives or reasons aren't clear, and they're almost not important. Some fans speculated that she was being so adamant because it is O'Neill in the field, but that doesn't stand up with what we know of Sam's character. Here, her loyalty melds with a fierce passion we haven't often had the opportunity to see.

John de Lancie as Colonel Simmons brings us a new baddie, working for Senator Kinsey (although this is never said explicitly). The "M&M" writing team had originally written in a new character for this episode, but decided to instead bring in an established character. Although John de Lancie is somewhat hampered by the immediate reaction, "Hey, look it's Q from *Star Trek: TNG!*" he does a great job as the human face of corruption. His motives are shadowed beyond the obvious one of getting what he wants — and whatever that may be, you get the distinct, creepy feeling that it ain't good.

Gods & Scientists: Tyler uses a chemical substance to insinuate himself into SG-1, using it in effect as a sort of camouflage. There are several examples in nature of animals that can change their exterior appearance to blend in with their background — chameleons are the most obvious example. Many mammals change their fur or feather color to blend in with the earth tones of spring and summer, and the starker colors of fall and winter. It's not known exactly how the change occurs, but it is mostly attributed to shifts in temperature or light that trigger a hormonal reaction. In reptiles and amphibians, the process is somewhat different because their color is determined by biochromes in living cells (as opposed to mammals and birds, whose color is determined by dead cells, and they must therefore produce a whole new coat or layer of feathers in order to camouflage themselves). In these reptiles and amphibians, the biochromes, or cells which control color, are located in the skin's surface, or at a deeper cellular level — these cells are then called chromatophores. By constricting the chromatophores of a certain pigment and relaxing those of other pigments, some animals can change the apparent color of their body.

Interesting Fact: Exterior shots for "The Fifth Man" were actually filmed outdoors, instead of on a soundstage, as usual.

Why We're Space Monkeys: Rick's ability to take long, complicated esoteric thoughts and compress them into one-liners, such as, "That may be the way they are. They're the way . . . we are, so . . . there you are. Get some sleep."

Parlez-vous Gate?:
O'NEILL: Well, I wasn't gonna let you die, Lieutenant — it's like, a *ton* of paperwork.
TYLER: Paperwork?
O'NEILL: It's a joke. It's my way of deflecting attention from my obvious heroism. You'll get used to it.

505. Red Sky

Original airdate: July 27, 2001
Written by: Ron Wilkerson
Directed by: Martin Wood

SG-1 accidentally dooms a planet. When the Asgard refuse to help them, the team tries to help, despite the population's resistance.

Visually, this episode is stunning. The grainy tone, the all-red hues that contrast with the harshness of the landscape, the colors that blend in perfectly with the episode's themes — religious zealotry, remorse, guilt, faith. These are all vague, intangible aspects of human experience, and the graininess really works well here to reflect that ambiguity.

The power of "Red Sky" resides primarily in the all-too-human attempts by SG-1 to fix what they've broken; but many of the scenes with the villagers fall a bit flat. The characters are stereotyped — the religious fanatic; the curious, understanding middleman, the throngs of unheard masses.

Between Teal'c's lurking on street corners, Carter's launching of rockets into the sun, and O'Neill's aggressive sense of helplessness, it's no wonder that the people of K'Tau seem more at home with Daniel. His Daniel-ness is pushed to the extreme in this episode (something that we're reminded of when, two episodes later in "Beast of Burden," he suddenly deals in arms with the Unas and rallies for war), but, while it makes for some interesting interaction between him and Jack, his attitude can sometimes seem holier-than-thou.

There are some great scenes in "Red Sky." When two members of SG-6 are killed in the explosion O'Neill's rage is huge and intense — RDA does a great job of making us believe he really is ready to kill Malchus, taking us with him, right to the edge of reason. His resistance to the population's beliefs is in stark contrast to Daniel's respect for those same beliefs, and this contrast is reflected in the lighting when they face off, again and again, throughout the episode.

"Red Sky" focuses on difference and contrast. The SGC expected that overriding the Gate dialing protocols would help them, not doom planets; here, they're faced with a seemingly hopeless situation that they've caused. The difficulty the team has accepting that there's nothing they can do to right the wrong they've brought about is seen through the visual effects — this episode is a wonderful example of form reflecting content. The bleak exterior mirrors the bleakness of the planet's future; the growing red of the sky mirrors the growing anxiety, rage, and helplessness felt by the team; the calm ambiance that reigns on the planet, the tranquil way in which the deadly sky overtakes the episode mirrors the quiet faith of the planet's population.

Some interesting themes as well — the introduction of one small element poisoning an entire sun, in the same way that invasive species on Earth slowly take over and destroy entire ecosystems. We're so used to seeing the Goa'uld play the role of invasive species that when we see SG-1 in the same position we're shocked. Although malice was not intended when the team overrode dialing protocols and dialled K'Tau's Gate, the fact remains that their ignorance had far-reaching repercussions, and not for them. The episode nicely posits the idea that causing harm to others is more difficult to accept than harm you've caused yourself.

Following in the same vein as "Thor's Hammer" and "Thor's Chariot," K'Tau culture is based on Norse mythology — from Ragnarok to the "eye of Odin" to the worshipping of Freyr. Ragnarok, Norse for "destruction of the powers" (powers here being the gods) is the Norse equivalent of the Apocalypse; it is said to start with three consecutive winters, at which point conflicts will break out and morality will vanish. The sun and moon will be swallowed, and a massive battle will take place between the gods and the evils, risen from hell. The K'Tau people believe that the gods — the Asgard, purporting to be gods in this case — want them dead; "Red Sky" brings back the theme of free will versus determinism, recalling season four's "Window of Opportunity" and "Scorched Earth."

Gods & Scientists: In Norse mythology, Freyr is the god of sun and rain, a god of peace, and the ruler of the elves. He is called the "god of the world," and rides a chariot pulled by a golden boar. He owns a ship that always goes directly to its target — and can be small enough to fit in his pocket — and a sword endowed with the power to autonomously inflict carnage when so desired (much like the Asgard ships and technology — powerful and potentially dangerous). Freyr belongs to the Vanir race of Norse gods, as opposed to the Aesir, to which Odin belongs.

SG-1 are compared to elves in this episode. Elves first appear in Germanic folklore, originally a race of minor nature and fertility gods. Norse mythology recognizes light, dark, and black elves — and some speculate that the Vanir are in fact light elves — so Freyr would have been an elf god. Norse elves are of human size.

Interesting Fact: To get the visual effects in this episode, the crew built an Amish-like village on-set so they could control all aspects of the lighting. Any on-location shots were done so with filters and blue screens, and then put through a bleaching process to make the toning more stark and compatible with the episode's feel and themes.

Why We're Space Monkeys: When SG-1 messes up, they try to fix it — even when it really irritates the people they're trying to help. Their desperation leads them to consider improbable solutions, and they're not afraid to risk failure.

Parlez-vous Gate?:
O'NEILL: I have great confidence in you, Carter. Go on back to the SGC and . . . confuse Hammond.

506. Rite of Passage

Original airdate: August 3, 2001
Written by: Heather Ash
Directed by: Peter DeLuise

When Cassandra falls ill, victim to Nirrti's experiments, Janet and SG-1 fight to save her.

"Rite of Passage" plays on our fear of solitude and of being misunderstood. Cassie is the last survivor of her people, and more than that, she's a teenager, with all the hormonal and emotional trials that implies. This episode brings Janet face-to-face with her worst fears as a mother — losing her daughter. "Rite of Passage" is Teryl Rothery's episode; she goes through the whole spectrum of emotions, from frustration with Cassie's adolescent snit to terror at her being taken away to fierce determination when she confronts Nirrti. Her beatific smile at the end is clunky and really obvious, but it gives us the essence of the episode — it's all about emotion.

Adolescence is a period of intense transformation, physical, psychological and emotional, so it's no wonder the writers chose to approach that phase of Cassie's development through the theme of transformation. Nirrti's experiments are literally transforming her; Cassie's words, "I'm changing into something and there's nothing you can do to stop it" reflect her feeling of being out of control in her own body and mind — in her life, even — a feeling common in adolescence.

And just as common in parents is feeling helpless. Janet Fraiser faces a metaphorical brick wall from both the maternal and the medical side of things; she's clearly unable to get through to Cassie, and the knowledge she's used to save hundreds of people throughout her career is of no use to her for her daughter.

Aloneness pervades the SGC — and as with many rites of passage, Cassie's must be done alone. On her home world, the affected teenagers were sent into the forest alone. (In many Earth cultures, adolescents go through a rite of passage to become men and women.) Other SG-1 members undergo solitary transformation as well — Daniel in "Need," Teal'c in "Threshold," and Jack in "A Hundred Days," — but the inclusion of Cassie makes the idea of a rite of passage more than just a hero motif. It's a rite that almost everyone at one time or another comes up against.

There's a nice moment between Sam and Janet when Janet expresses how useless she feels — Sam responds, "What are we going to tell her?" The use of "we" brings Janet out of her isolation and reminds her that as always, the SGC are in this together.

Gods & Scientists: Far from being dead, as everyone had assumed, Nirrti is still alive — and now she's free. She infected the children of Cassie's home world with a Goa'uld retrovirus to speed up their transformation into super-beings. She then cured them, so that each generation would pass on the changed genes. Because she was unable to get a sample of Cassie's blood, she has to start her experiment over again — and she's free to do so.

Interesting Fact: The hand-holding scene in the corridor between Daniel and Janet got many a shipper's heart going pitter-patter. The Daniel/Janet relationship is one of the most closely watched amongst fans, although they're not as vocal as the Sam/Jack shippers. When asked what he thought Daniel would do if he had been stuck in a time loop, à la Jack in "Window of Opportunity," Michael Shanks replied, "I don't know . . . If Dr. Janet was lurking about, you'd have to see!"

Why We're Space Monkeys: "A mother's love knows no bounds." The adage is certainly true in Janet's case, as she goes above and beyond the call of duty — and even bypasses it to threaten Nirrti. A number of science fiction shows have conflated the maternal and the professional — Doctor

Crusher on *Star Trek: TNG* springs to mind — but Janet's frightened fierceness was characteristically *SG-1* in that it was intense and realistic rather than watered-down and merely there to move the episode along.

Parlez-vous Gate?:
JANET (to Cassie): Fine! Invite him in . . . I'm sure he'd like to have a piece of birthday cake that Sam went to all the trouble to . . . bake.
CARTER (softly): Buy.
JANET (loudly): Bring!

507. Beast of Burden

Original airdate: August 10, 2001
Written by: Peter DeLuise
Directed by: Martin Wood

SG-1 follows an Unas and his captors back to their homeworld to try to free Daniel's friend, Chaka.

"I would rather have a root canal than watch this episode," said one online fan. A dismal, soggy set, a dismal, soggy performance by most of the cast (except Dion Johnstone, who plays Chaka, and Alex Zahara, who plays Unas), and a dismal, soggy script. What they really needed was a giant anvil in the center of the town with a huge placard reading, "Plot: slavery is baaaad."

A throwaway episode that makes us impatient to get back to a real story, "Beast of Burden" sags, slack-jawed, in the hands of its own narrative. Yes, slavery is bad. Yes, things are not as easy as we want them to be. Yes, Burrock's logic skills are in top form when he argues an eye for an eye. To quote O'Neill: "And? But? So? Therefore?" It's a shame, a third of the way through the season, to make viewers sit through a story that might have better been told in the show's first season, when the characters were less defined and their backstories less ingrained in the audience's mind. In the fifth year of a show, however, when there are far more enthralling story lines available, whose depths have barely been plumbed (the Ancients, the Jaffa rebellion, a boyfriend for Carter who doesn't die), to revert to a people and a plot that's really just filler is disappointing.

The Unas are an interesting population, there's no doubt about that.

They're complex, they have ties that go way back with the Goa'uld, and they're capable of learning, interacting, and communicating. "Beast of Burden" does make you think about what exactly constitutes a beast. Here, it is quite obviously the Unas' outward appearance and their inability to speak as humans that has them labeled as beasts. Scaly and knobbly, they don't exactly look like bright figures of the galaxy's future. They are, however, inextricably linked to the galaxy's past, and it is partly for that reason that Daniel finds them so interesting. And *SG-1* always takes care to look beyond the surface — it's one of the reasons the show does so well.

Some plot devices chafe, nonetheless. Would Teal'c just drop everything for no apparent reason and run back to "rescue" his teammates? Although he often disobeys orders, it is always a personal choice, and not thrown in as an obvious plot device to get the divided team back together. Carter has been left in charge. Why would a man like Teal'c, trained his whole life in service, in hierarchy, who understands the chain of command and feels incredible guilt when he disobeys it (see "Cor-ai"), just up and leave his *commanding officer* because he doesn't *like* where he is and what he's doing?

And this episode has more closeups of Daniel Jackson than anyone else. In fact, Michael Shanks' appearance in the many Daniel-centric episodes of season five ("The Tomb," "Beast of Burden," "Red Sky," "Summit," and "Last Stand") belie his feeling that the character of Daniel Jackson was underused and mishandled. The one glimmer of hope in this episode is a true moment of character change for Daniel. In "Beast of Burden," he has an abrupt turnabout on his usually pacifistic modus operandi, and it is not unwarranted. Jack points out that they won't be able to "talk" their way out of a situation, and Jackson responds tiredly, "For once, I'm not asking us to." This is a Daniel who has seen the red tape trotted out one too many times. His own relativistic moral code gets booted around so often that he finally gives in to more "primitive" reason — he just wants something he thinks is important to happen, for once.

The difference between Jack and Daniel is once more highlighted in this episode. They manage to find some common ground, but on either side of this lies their strongly opposed views. Daniel is focused on the here and now, wanting desperately for something good to come of his interaction with Chaka, and wanting it *now*. Jack is militarily trained; he knows, probably firsthand, exactly what a revolution will entail, and he's therefore less inclined to prod the movement along. Revolution means weapons, hardship, death — not just for the Unas, but also for Earth should they decide to help them. It's a fiercely wrought story line. What price freedom? Daniel is willing to pay the asking price, in the present time; Jack is looking at inflation, wondering if it will be worth it *in the end*. Neither man is right or wrong, they just look at the situation from different timeline perspectives.

Interesting Fact: The set for this episode is actually the set used in the series *Bordertown*, another Canadian/American export that did better in Europe than at home. Chaka is played by Dion Johnstone, who we've also seen (with less makeup) in "The Fifth Man."

Parlez-vous Gate?:
DANIEL: I'm Daniel Jackson, this is Colonel Jack O'Neill.
BURROCK: Colonel?
DANIEL: Yes, it means he's our head . . . trader.
O'NEILL: Head trader?

508. The Tomb

Original airdate: August 17, 2001
Written by: Joseph Mallozzi, Paul Mullie
Directed by: Peter DeLuise

SG-1 and a Russian Stargate team attempt the rescue of another Russian team.

"The Tomb" is more standard fare for the fifth season. The evenhanded directing by Peter DeLuise hits a couple of gaffs (the silly, completely backlit scene with Colonels O'Neill and Zukhov comes to mind), but for the most part it's a tense episode, thanks to some intertextual nods — the creepy alien à la Ridley Scott's film *Alien*, the creepy lighting à la adventure movies from all over, and the creepy bug theme à la *The Fly* and *The Mummy*.
    One area of confusion is the confrontation of the Goa'uld Marduk with the humans. Zukhov throws the Goa'uld a grenade, which he catches. It seems unlikely that a hand grenade going off within five feet of O'Neill and Zukhov would result in only one of them getting buried under rock. The whole sequence is a little confusing, since there is no cut shot, and then we get the rising hand of Marduk a little later — it is to signal to us that the

hand grenade did not go off, the roof just fell in. Unfortunately a lot of viewers thought the hand grenade went off, in which case, they wondered, how the heck did Marduk stay alive? He was holding a live grenade!

Some of the camera shots are hard to follow, which detracts from the tension. The plot of the episode would be a chilling horror movie, but the shifting from one segment of the teams to another, never lingering long enough to get a sense of the jeopardy they're in, really diminishes the edge-of-your-seat factor. Carter and Teal'c are woefully underused in this episode, with the former bringing out her "sense the Goa'uld symbiote" party trick for an instant before the story moves again.

One hasty exit offers Daniel a chance to do his "But this is a ziggurat worth studying, don't blow it up" lecture, but curiously he remains silent. It's especially odd since he started out at the tomb with such praise of the architecture and the story of Marduk. "The Tomb" does offer up some great archaeological fare, a theme that hasn't been explored in quite a while. It's sometimes easy to forget that the stories *SG-1* are following are rooted in galactic history; episodes like "The Tomb" do a good job in reminding the team, and viewers, of the intricate link between past and present. One of Daniel's main roles on the show, from the feature film onward, has been to tie the two together, to study the past so that the team (and Earth) can better understand the present. Translating history for present-times causes and consequences is an extremely important aspect of his job, and one that's glossed over far too often in seasons four and five.

The niggling flaws are a shame because the episode is *really* good. It's tense, the plot moves along well, and it gives the Russian arc a chance to spread its wings, which it hasn't done since last season's "Watergate." The show's Russian arc offers up some of the most effective dramatic episodes of the series. Thanks to American/Russian history (and once again the impact of the past on the present is of import), the relationship between Russian Stargate team members and SG-1 is particularly interesting to watch, full of push-and-pull, and really challenging the boundaries of trust and deceit. These episodes are usually seen through the eyes of O'Neill, who's the right age to have lived through the Cold War and whose sense of distrust is robust at the best of times.

The episode does give out some creepy vibes, the likes of which we haven't seen since "Watergate," "Foothold," or just about any time the Replicators show up. Being trapped in a sarcophagus that revives you continuously only to be then consumed again by your nemesis? Wow, that's nasty. And look for the Eye of Tiamat to pop up again in season six ("Fallen"). Neither the Russians nor the Eye are done with yet. Joseph Mallozzi and Paul Mullie are adept at long arcs, and this is one that comes back in a big way.

Gods & Scientists: Mythically, Marduk is a Babylonian god who later became known as Bal, or simply "Lord," in the Semitic language. By defeating the monster of chaos, Tiamat, he became known as the god with fifty names, each name representing a different aspect. In this way he is similar to the Egyptian mythological gods. A ziggurat differs from a pyramid in that it is stepped and does not have the same smooth look that an Egyptian pyramid does, has no interior chambers, and none have survived until today in their original sizes. Marduk's ziggurat in Babylon has been associated with the biblical Tower of Babel.

Interesting Fact: Peter DeLuise's picture tells us he is one of the Russian soldiers who went missing at the beginning of the episode. So is director of photography Peter Woeste.

Why We're Space Monkeys: Even though he's occasionally annoying as heck, you gotta love the salty-dog routines of Jack O'Neill.

Parlez-vous Gate?:
DANIEL: They sealed him in the sarcophagus, and placed something in there with him. There's no direct translation for the word, but I assume it's the reference to the creature that ate him.
CARTER: Are you saying he was eaten alive?
DANIEL: The sarcophagus would have done its best to continuously keep him alive, so it probably would have taken a while.
O'NEILL: Okay — that's officially the worst way to go.

509. Between Two Fires

Original airdate: August 24, 2001
Written by: Ron Wilkerson
Directed by: William Gereghty

The Tollan offer to give Earth advanced technology in exchange for trinium. SG-1 investigates the Tollan's sudden change of heart, prompted by a warning from Narim.

An interesting episode that delivers some nice, tense storytelling and an ending that is sad but feels right, despite its blatant addition to Carter's "black widow syndrome."

Usually people associate the adage "out of the frying pan and into the fire" with moving from one bad situation to a worse one. In this episode, the most direct reference to being between two fires is not, for once, SG-1, but rather the Tollan. Chancellor Travell and the Curia of Tollana are caught between their ideals, nicely alluded to in the fire of Omac's remembrance flame and the fire that the Goa'uld Tanith and his unnamed master stand for — the imminent destruction of the Tollan. By setting up the episode from a long shot, directly above the head of Chancellor Travell, director William Gereghty suggests that while we are outside the politics of the Tollan, we are nonetheless going to see both sides of Travell's problem — to be between the two fires with her. Gereghty uses some great shots in the episode to highlight both the odds that the Tau'ri are up against and their sense of being larger than life by using shots that are canted upward. Look for these especially as SG-1 moves from ignorance into knowledge; the corresponding camera shots work from a level of almost no knowledge (low, looking up), to one where the team knows what's going on (level shots).

As the episode progresses, it's harder for us to be unsympathetic to Travell's plight. While she and Narim may, in the words of Jack, be, "trying to save [their] own ass," it would be a dilemma most people wouldn't want, choosing between one's own company, which is immediate, known, and intimate, and the larger view of other planets, other people. Another great and subtle play is that Omac's fire is small; he represents the more altruistic ideal, while Tanith is all about being big — big explosions, big sneer, big shoulder pads.

The passing references to *Star Wars* (from the "ion cannon" to the Princess Leia hologram schtick by Narim) are not too annoying but they make one think "Okay, and next?" And the end shot of angsty Sam is too predictable. So too is the homophobia present in the Teal'c/Jack holding-hands scene. They've worked together for five years now — surely they can get past that sort of silly stigma. The scene looks ad-libbed (RDA is famous for it), and honestly, untruthful to either character.

This is one of a handful of times that SG-1 is within arm's reach of achieving their original mission, that of procuring technology to help protect Earth. The possibility that looms so close and how it is reflected in each character is one of the great dramatic boons of the episode. Jack and Daniel, in a change from the last couple of episodes where they've been on opposite sides of a debate, cooperate here, bringing the best of what they each have to offer (Daniel's diplomatic skills and Jack's business sense and hard-nosedness) to get what they want. While Teal'c wreaks havoc during the Goa'uld attack, Carter is somewhat distanced from the process as she is trying to keep an even keel during a personal affront. She has a soft spot for Narim, and the difficulties that he's going through affect her on more than a professional level; she keeps up a professional front at all times, courtesy of her training and her own work ethic, but it's clear that she's having a tough time. She too is caught between two fires, wanting what's best for Earth and for someone she may potentially have feelings for. Although always brief (at least until season seven), the crushes in Carter's life serve to flesh out her character. Carter being vulnerable and tremulous, shyly confident, isn't something we're used to seeing, and it opens up a whole new aspect of her.

The end of this episode is particularly harsh: the destruction of a whole people in service of doing the "greater good" is what Earth might face. The Tollan and the Tau'ri are two populations that are not so dissimilar — the fate of the Tollan could have been, and could still be, that of the Tau'ri. A daunting, haunting prospect.

Gods & Scientists: The convention of naming or even refusing to name a god, is a feature in all religions and mythologies. Some members of the Jewish faith, for instance, write "G-d," based on the tenet that the name of god should not be erased or defaced. Thus if they write "God" they are responsible for that act of writing. This respect for the sacred is also shown in the Christian faith by capitalizing His or Him when referring to God or Jesus. In Egyptian mythology there is the story of Isis who learned the "true name" of Ra, which granted her great power. Secret names that hold power are another cultural motif. By leaving his master "unnamed," Tanith indicates his master's power, and we are left to imagine exactly how bad this new Big Bad is.

Interesting Fact: Does Tollana look a little institutional? It's actually

Simon Fraser University in Burnaby, British Columbia. Although this is the last time we see Garwin Sanford in *SG-1*, we do see him again in the *SG-1* progeny *Stargate Atlantis*, though not as Narim.

Why We're Space Monkeys: Even the good guys make bad decisions. Although SG-1 lands a little heavily on the side of "I told you so" (Jack, Daniel, Sam, even Teal'c's raised eyebrows), the Tollan, and in particular the chancellor, really are caught between two urgent needs. Travell's decisions could be argued — and they are by the chancellor herself, who points out to Jack that politics are always driven, in some way, by selfish motivations, the implication being that she understands as well as anyone that the Tau'ri's happiness at getting an ion cannon is at least part of why they are there.

Parlez-vous Gate?:
O'NEILL: Give us more than . . .
O'NEILL & DANIEL: One.
COUNCILLOR TRAVELL: How many would you require?
DANIEL: Thirty . . .
O'NEILL: . . . eight.
DANIEL: Thirty-eight.
O'NEILL & DANIEL: Thirty-eight.

510. 2001

Original airdate: August 31, 2001
Written by: Brad Wright
Directed by: Peter DeLuise

SG-1 and the Aschen hash out a treaty between their two worlds. But Daniel and Teal'c discover that Earth is on the verge of making a catastrophic decision.

"2001" is a great prequel to "2010," even though, chronologically, it comes after. There's some fantastic teamwork, very cool technology, frighteningly calm enemies, and good plot movement. The tension is very well measured out in this episode, with a mix of slower- and faster-moving moments, and we're breathless by the time the resolution comes. It also helps that we've already seen "2010," so we know more than the SGC does about what's at stake. It's like watching a train wreck in slow motion, hoping for it to right itself at the very last second.

The Aschen's veneer of social grace makes them all the more scary, and with all the politics in this episode, you can't help but make the comparison between the Aschen's hypocrisy and political hypocrisy in the real world. The theme of politics comes up a lot in season five ("The Tomb," "Between Two Fires," "Desperate Measures," "48 Hours," "The Sentinel"), and we're frequently reminded that danger comes not only from other planets and peoples but from within. The political thread, which started all the way back in season one's "Politics," starts to weave through the story lines more strongly in season five, and it will have repercussions through to seasons seven and eight. But for this season, the political upheaval reminds us of one long thread: do what you have to sometimes, regardless of the consequences.

The technology offered by the Aschen is pretty nifty — the harvesters especially, because it's one of the first examples of the Stargate being used for something other than the transportation of people. In "Prisoners," food was delivered via the Gate, but "2001" develops that idea more fully, illustrating the potential of the Stargate to contribute to the economic development of a planet. It's also a nice allusion to the idea of the Stargate feeding us with stories.

Daniel's loquaciousness plays off Teal'c's quiet resolve. As in "2010," each member of SG-1 fights the battle on their own ground — Jack through politics and force, Daniel by looking at the past, Sam with science, and Teal'c with commitment. Peter DeLuise redeems himself in this episode after the fiasco that was "Beast of Burden."

Gods & Scientists: Biological warfare involves the use of a natural organism (bacteria, viruses, toxins) to weaken an enemy. Before the twentieth century, it took the form of poisoned food and water supplies, or infected blankets and corpses, among others. The Aschen have managed to program their bioweapon to attack only a certain race of beings — a targeted genocide machine.

Interesting Fact: Peter DeLuise noted that the original pronunciation of "Aschen" was a little bit too "on the nose," given their pale complexions. It was therefore changed to be pronounced with the accent on the second syllable. And, joining the ranks of *SG-1* actors doing Asgard voices, Dion

Luther, who plays Molum, also does the voice for one of the Asgard council members in "Red Sky" and "Fail Safe."

Why We're Space Monkeys: Daniel gets to save the day! Even Peter DeLuise concedes that most of the time, it's Sam's scientific know-how that saves the day: "The way that it works in the formula is that Carter will probably build something, or decipher something scientific, but only be able to figure it out or make it work [. . .] in the fourth or fifth act, at the last moment. And it's also a given that Daniel will have to read something, or decipher something, and that will contribute to it." It's a real change of pace, and "2001" puts Daniel and his skills in the spotlight, to great effect.

Parlez-vous Gate?:
O'NEILL: Just when you think you're not in Kansas anymore, turns out you are.

   And a fun visual gag when he calls after Senator Kinsey, "That's O'Neill! Two L's!" — holding up three fingers.

511. Desperate Measures

Original airdate: September 7, 2001
Written by: Joseph Mallozzi, Paul Mullie
Directed by: William Gereghty

Carter gets kidnapped, Jack gets shot, Teal'c and Daniel skulk, and Colonel Simmons is Bad.

The most interesting part of this episode is not the immediate action or its consequences; rather, as with many things in the *Stargate* universe, it is the longer arc picked up later. Two things the writers and directors of this show are good at are mining past episodes, and thinking long-term when they write stories. For instance, while Alexis Cruz's character was already in the movie, his popularity in the television series prompted his character Klorel/Skaara to remain on the show even though he was to be killed off (see "The Serpent's Lair"). We saw it again in the characters of Jacob Carter, Colonel Maybourne, Senator Kinsey, the Replicators, Colonel Frank Simmons, and now in the form of Adrian Conrad. When a character catches the attention of the viewers, that character usually becomes a survivor. Joseph Mallozzi and Paul Mullie, who write episodes more frequently as time goes on, are very good at integrating older threads of the show into newer episodes, drawing on unexpected characters and situations.

"Desperate Measures" examines the theme of the fear of death — not something that's commonly looked at on the series. The Goa'uld may be completely egomaniacal and close to immortal, with their sarcophagi, but we rarely see any real examination of their process of dying. It's left to the human faction of the *SG-1* universe to delve into that. And that seems fitting; after all, fear of death is one of the most prevalent fears among humans, and this show has never held back when it comes to looking at things that may cause discomfort. In "Urgo," SG-1 concludes that Urgo is sentient based in part on their realization that he has a fear of death. While "Urgo" was a comedic look at the idea of dying and death, "Desperate Measures" is more somber.

Adrian Conrad is dying: he's rich, and he's powerful, in both money and knowledge (and, once again, *Stargate* demonstrates how a little knowledge can go a long way to warping minds). Conrad is scared. In that situation, it's hard to say what one might be driven to do. Not everyone has grace under pressure, and it can be good to be reminded of that. The members of SG-1 operate with so much grace under pressure that it's almost painful sometimes. Would Daniel, Sam, Teal'c, or Jack cave under the fear of dying, kidnap someone, and implant an alien into themselves to keep on living? Unlikely. But what about the everyday non-hero? Who's to say? It's also worth noting that when Jack is placed in a similar situation in season six, he *does* get implanted — the circumstances are, of course, different, and no one else is harmed, but it's still an interesting turnabout of the situation.

"Desperate Measures" is a return to an idea we haven't seen since season two's mini-arc "The Tok'ra" — the lure of becoming a host to a Goa'uld if one has an incurable or debilitating disease. "Desperate Measures" tackles this idea from a different viewpoint — necessitated by ego and fed by greed, in contrast to Daniel's more altruistic idea of cancer victims given a new lease on life — but the initial premise is the same. It could have been a vehicle for excellent psychological drama, but in "Desperate Measures" it's reduced to a lifeless (pardon the pun) "bad guy gets his" scenario, complete with almost every human Big Bad we've come across thus far in the *SG-1* universe: Maybourne (who's more sleazy than bad now), Colonel

Simmons with the shady NID behind him like an elongated shadow of ick-iness, and the new Adrian Conrad. But the situation is believable, especially in a nation, the writers argue, where money and power can get you pretty much whatever you want; human experiments (in the form of Carter) without fear of reprisal (in the form of Jack, Daniel, and Teal'c). The love interest for Adrian Conrad is also believable, but the two geeky scientists are not. Conrad is excellently Goa'ulded at the end, and another story question goes unanswered, fueling our desire for a return. Is this the end of the Conrad arc?

Gods & Scientists: In a surprising move, to date we never learn the name of the symbiote that eventually takes over Adrian Conrad's body (see "48 Hours," "Prometheus"). Actor Frank C. Turner, who plays the homeless man O'Neill barters his *National Geographic*s with, also "writes icons," according to movie sources. Icons, which are paintings of revered Christian saints and other holy figures, are said to be "written" rather than painted because their structure is like a poem, rather than a picture. Each pictorial representation corresponds to a "word" in the biblical canon.

Interesting Fact: If you look closely at the monitors in the episode's hospital bed scene, they spell out "BG" — an homage to William (Bill) Gereghty, who directed the episode. He's apparently a very popular director on the *Stargate* set.

Parlez-vous Gate?:
HOMELESS GUY: Well I'm just a crazy old guy with a shopping cart full of cans.
O'NEILL: I'm just a cynical Air Force guy with a closet full of *National Geographic*s.
HOMELESS GUY: Can I have 'em?

512. Wormhole X-Treme

Original airdate: September 8, 2001
Story by: Brad Wright, Joseph Mallozzi, Paul Mullie
Teleplay by: Joseph Mallozzi, Paul Mullie
Directed by: Peter DeLuise

The 100th episode, with all the fun that entails.

One hundred episodes in, and *SG-1* has really grown. Like the mythology it's based on, the show is not always about heavy moralizing, it also provides entertainment. "Wormhole X-Treme" is one of the all-out funniest episodes of the show, with a carnivalesque atmosphere that's as fun as cotton candy.

"Wormhole X-Treme" is set up as a *Galaxy Quest*–style spoof on *SG-1*; all spoof, all the time. The 100th episode is a huge landmark for any TV show, and they nearly all — from *The Simpsons* to *Buffy the Vampire Slayer* — celebrate the moment in some way or another. This episode reflects the entire evolution of narrative, from oral (hearing the story) to written (writing the stories down in their various forms). Writing leads to the codification of stories — because they are now in written form, they're less subject to change than are oral narratives. Codification becomes canon, an intrinsic, understood, part of a culture, which in turn leads to parody. "Wormhole X-Treme" is very much an example of that kind of narration.

The crew of season five solidifies around certain groups of writers, directors, directors of photography, and arcs, and because of this the episodes and storytelling techniques gradually become much more unified, leaving behind the dabbling exploration of previous seasons. The content of the episodes reflects this as well; we see less emphasis on mythology, less exploration — the team's mission has become clearer and more direct. Like Egyptian mythology, the transition from oral to written culture, the stories of *SG-1* become more codified when they are set down, weighted by their own history and the fixedness of form.

"Wormhole X-Treme" isn't the same kind of fun as "Urgo," but Peter DeLuise is definitely "large and in charge" in these kinds of episodes. He's at his best when being completely irreverent and allowed free reign. It's not the kind of fare that would be enjoyable week after week, but it celebrates the show in a big way. In the tradition of "Tin Man" (season one), "Deadman Switch" (season two), "Urgo" (season three), and "Window of Opportunity" (season four) "Wormhole X-Treme" is season five's fluffy offering, a delightful, vacuous, and expensive-looking treat. There are loads of in-jokes and "guest appearances" by crew members. There's also trash talk about the show's own science gaffs; Amanda is known for going through the scripts to make sure the science that's presented is correct, and "Wormhole X-Treme" makes fun of the folklore that has arisen from it. Even (or maybe, especially)

Peter DeLuise makes fun of himself — actually, it looks like he makes fun of his whole family. A ton of fun, don't miss it.

Interesting Fact: The prop that Martin picks up, asking "Do you have any idea what it costs to make one of these?" was the prop used in "Urgo" — according to Peter DeLuise, it cost about five thousand dollars.

Why We're Space Monkeys: I think it's fairly obvious why we're space monkeys on this one (spray-painted kiwi).

Parlez-vous Gate?: One of many in-jokes from the episode, this one pokes gentle fun at Peter DeLuise's "alien" fruit in season four's "Beneath the Surface."
MARTIN: Okay, scene twenty-three takes place on another planet. You think aliens eat apples?
PROPS GUY: Why not? They speak English.

513. Proving Ground

Original airdate: March 8, 2002
Written by: Ron Wilkerson
Directed by: Andy Mikita

A group of young cadets is pulled into a combat situation at the SGC when Colonel O'Neill, their training officer, is wounded. It's up to them to save the world from an alien incursion.

In military jargon, a proving ground is a space for testing new ideas or technology and equipment. It's not generally used as a term for testing *people*, but it works well in this episode to bring together the location, the characters, and the plot under one term. The cadets are being tested, but so are SG-1 and the SGC, for their training abilities. Everyone must provide proof here — of courage, quick thinking, skill, intelligence.

"Proving Ground" is one of those episodes that can only really be enjoyed if you can accept the idea that one of the most important — and expensive — military facilities in the world would shut down to play war games with potential recruits, or that the military would be hiring new recruits fresh out of the academy for a top-secret government program. What's more, these recruits are annoying — it's a pleasure to see O'Neill dress them down.

If you can get past that, though, the episode can be a lot of fun — mostly thanks to SG-1's moments alone, when they reveal the plot that's afoot. Sam and Jack's covert hand movements and eyebrow communication, as well as Jack and Daniel's hilarious phone conversation, show a side of SG-1 we don't often get to see — the team having fun with each other. It's also nice to see O'Neill in a leadership role that isn't in the field. He has paperwork to do, evaluations to write up — even Stargate colonels have to do the paper-pushing thing every now and then.

SG-1 play their parts in the deceit with an ease and a delight bordering on mischievous, while never forgetting the serious application of the training they're providing. They're almost like kids let loose in a candy shop (if a military base can stand in for a candy shop), and the actors look like they're having a ball. The boundaries between the four teammates aren't as strict in these circumstances. Wee see casual talk between Carter and O'Neill in the cafeteria as he completes the evaluation forms for the cadets and this moment is particularly off-the-cuff and welcome. Season four was apt to focus too strongly on the bonds between Sam and Jack; season five tends to overlook the relationship entirely, focusing instead on team interplay and the Jack/Daniel dynamic.

Elisabeth Rosen reprises her role from season four's "Prodigy"; unfortunately her character appears to have gone from one stereotype (obnoxious reclusive) to another (socialized smiling), but she's much more enjoyable to watch this time around. You get a sense from the cadets of the pressure they're under to perform above and beyond expectations — a reminder of just how elusive and demanding a placement in the SGC is. SG-1 so comfortably does what's required of them in each and every episode that it's easy to forget how skilled they are.

One of the things "Proving Ground" does well is to showcase the steep learning curve that military cadets must go through. *SG-1* makes a concerted effort to bring out contemporary and real-life issues in their episodes, even when they are somewhat shrouded by metaphor and visual artifice.

Jack's outrage at and complete intolerance of the fact that Elliott would leave a teammate behind — through carelessness to boot — resonates strongly. Although *SG-1* often emphasizes the need for personal and professional sacrifice for the "greater good" ("Divide and Conquer," "The

Curse," "2010" for example), the sacrifice of a teammate is one that should never be made, no matter what the circumstances. We've watched SG-1 develop as a closely knit family, and we see the same thing develop over the course of this episode between the cadets. Seeing the dynamic of the team in miniature reminds us of why we keep coming back, season after season.

Interesting Fact: Courtenay J. Stevens appears in the sixth episode of *Stargate Atlantis* as a twenty-four-year-old about to kill himself for the greater good of his people. He also reappears in season five of *SG-1* in the two-parter "Summit" and "Last Stand."

Why We're Space Monkeys: The cadets are not the only ones being toyed with here. SG-1 takes time to have fun with and goad each other in this episode — Sam provides the cadets with a reason to stun Jack (granted, she was put on the spot), and Jack "forgets" to tell the cadets to take Daniel prisoner rather than shoot him. And given the chance to play The Leader for a day, who wouldn't enjoy that chair?

Parlez-vous Gate?:
CARTER: Uh, Sir, if you don't mind, your wound is getting all over my lab.

514. 48 Hours

Original airdate: March 15, 2002
Written by: Robert Cooper
Directed by: Peter Woeste

Teal'c gets trapped in the wormhole. With forty-eight hours before his energy pattern is erased permanently, the SGC turns to unlikely sources for help.

"48 Hours" accomplishes a lot in its forty-odd minutes. It brings together threads that until now have been kept separate, puts Teal'c in jeopardy, ties up a lot of loose ends — and all before a deadline. The deadline is a smart move on the writers' parts; it raises the tension a *lot* — there is a sense of urgency in the interaction between the various characters, the political hagglings, and the technological dealings of Sam and Dr. McKay.

David Hewlett, who will reprise his role as McKay in season six

David Hewlett chows down — let's hope it's not lemon chicken! (ALBERT L. ORTEGA)

("Redemption") and gets a regular part as the same character in *Stargate Atlantis* (although he's definitely more sympathetic there than on *SG-1*), does an excellent job of making us seethe with indignation at how he treats Sam. He's funny in that obnoxious, arrogant way that we've so far really only seen in the politicians on the show. But he does bring up an important fact that hasn't been focused on yet: the SGC has been running the Stargate program a bit willy nilly, disregarding security protocols and putting things together as the need arises. It's understandable, given that the U.S. Gate doesn't have a DHD, and that the possibility of Gate travel was a fluke in any event, so they weren't as prepared as they could have been — but the fact remains that Earth has a greater margin of error than probably any other planet because of its disregard for Gate protocol.

"48 Hours" weaves together the Russian, Tanith, Colonel Simmons, and Colonel Maybourne threads, and succinctly puts an end to quite a few of them. A nice echoing of season four's "Exodus" when Jack groans, "It's a damn Jaffa revenge thing." The episode takes the SGC to new places by making the characters find unlikely allies — from the Russians to a Goa'uld to McKay to Maybourne. Finding trust in unlikely places — it's a huge step in the SGC's development (and more specifically Jack's and Daniel's).

More than that though, when Daniel finally wins over the Russian colonel, he does it by appealing to his emotions — he lost a friend, Daniel is in danger of losing a friend. The negotiations until then have been the U.S. vs. The World (or rather, vs. Russia), but by bringing them onto the plane of human sensibility, Daniel — always the humanist — reminds us that whatever else happens, it's about the people involved.

One of the things that makes "48 Hours" so effective is the way SG-1 functions as a team. SG-1 works together toward a common goal, despite being in completely separate physical locations. They each take their area of expertise and work with that (Jack on the military side of things, Sam on the scientific, and Daniel on the diplomatic) in their respective spaces (Jack at the Goa'uld holding area, Sam at the SGC, and Daniel in Russia). But there's a real sense of solidarity between them. They touch base with one another and they work on the problem wholeheartedly, in concert, to bring the team back together.

And, Teal'c finally has his revenge — Tanith is dead.

Gods & Scientists: Teal'c's "Jaffa revenge thing" is not unheard of in history, mythology, or literature. Many great stories contain at least a hint of something resembling vengeance, and the gods of the Greek pantheon were especially vicious when it came to revenge. Seth, for example, killed his brother, and then was involved in a long fight with his nephew, Horus, who sought to avenge his father's death. In another myth, Procne married Tereus, king of Thrace, who seduced Procne's sister. To get revenge, Procne murdered Tereus' son and served him up as dinner to the king. To get *his* revenge, Tereus chased after the sisters and tried to murder them. They were all turned into birds as a punishment. In literature, perhaps one of the most famous revenge motifs is seen in the play "Romeo and Juliet," wherein clan member takes on clan member until the tragic ending.

Interesting Fact: The crew loves working with Amanda Tapping and Teryl Rothery. Director Peter Woeste and director of photography Andrew Wilson praise Amanda highly for her abilities with techno-jargon lines: "Amanda is incredible when she has to read these lines. She actually knows this stuff, it's not like she's reading lines. And she's the only one who can just rattle it off like this [. . .] And if she ever flubs a line [. . .] she's just beside herself. [. . .] Our dreams for Friday afternoons are to have Teryl and Amanda with long scenes, just the two of them . . ." And in terms of the sets, the house that appears in this episode was apparently recently bought by Kurt Russell and Goldie Hawn.

Why We're Space Monkeys: Richard does his own stunt at the beginning of this episode — scrapes along the ground and gets a bunch of dirt in his eye, just for the heck of it.

Parlez-vous Gate?:
CARTER (to McKay): Go suck a lemon!
And for sheer rarity of lines, Siler's should be put down for posterity:
O'NEILL (to Sam): Hey, you sure you want to be in there for that?
SILER: Not really, Sir.

515. Summit

Original airdate: March 22, 2002
Written by: Joseph Mallozzi, Paul Mullie
Directed by: Martin Wood

The Tok'ra ask Daniel to run a dangerous mission that they think will mean the end of the Goa'uld System Lords, but complications arise when Osiris arrives and a new Goa'uld player is revealed — one who's been dead for a thousand years.

This ambitious mid-series arc could only have been handled by two veteran *SG-1* behind-the-scenes-teams: the writing team of "M&M," and director Martin Wood. The word "summit" in the contemporary news lexicon refers to a meeting of the heads of governments, thus alluding to the System Lords convening in order to ascertain their new enemy's identity while keeping an eye on old ones under the guise of partisanship. But a summit is also the peak of a hill or a standard. "Summit" brings together a big kettle of fish. In less than fifty minutes we see new technology from the Reole ("The Fifth Man"), the Tok'ra's driving ideology, a sardine tin crammed with Goa'uld, the return of Osiris, a new Big Bad in the form of Anubis, the Sam/Martouf aborted love story, and lots and lots of cool costumes, sets, and lighting.

There's so much going on that at times it's hard to keep all the threads straight; it takes careful watching to follow everything. Season seven's "Heroes" vies with this mini-arc for ambition of story and character; but while this arc concentrates on multiple stories for multiple characters, "Heroes" concentrated on the effects of a single character on multiple lives.

System Lord Yu represents an older Goa'uld type. Cronos and Apophis, both also of the old school of Goa'uld, are gone, and Nirrti is *persona non grata*; now, only Yu is left to contend with the upstarts. He is much more inclined to use partnership to achieve an end, and despises the "younger"

Goa'uld's crass scrambling for power. It's almost funny to see the levels of despicableness amongst the Goa'uld, and the "M&M" team do a good job making us waveringly sympathetic to Yu. A good setup for the later "The Warrior."

Zipacna's role in this episode is both bothersome and unnecessary. At times he's just a Sneering Lip sent in to leer at Osiris and throw around the weight of the unseen Anubis. The second stage of this two-parter, "Last Stand" leaves his fate unknown, however. He just slithers off into the background with nary a line, which is a letdown considering the degree to which his badness was played up in this episode. Zipacna operates much like the bounty hunter Aris Boch, apparently selling his services to whomever wants him. From lowly lawyer to right-hand man, Zipacna's revival could have been used more effectively (also like Aris Boch).

The episode leaves us holding on to lots of reins — SG-1 is trapped, Osiris is alive, she knows who Daniel is, and Daniel's mission is compromised. Great episode.

Gods & Scientists: We have not seen the Goa'uld Baal since an oblique reference to him as "Belus" waaay back in season one's "Fire and Water." Certainly, the description of him from that episode fits this Baal. He uses whatever means are necessary to achieve his ends, including treachery, spying, and espionage. He and Yu have a long-lived enmity. Both are intelligent and cunning. But Yu still holds some personal honor in his dealings, while Baal cares only for himself.

Although the word "baal" was originally a Semitic word denoting "husband" or "lord," the god Baal was a Canaanite god of storms. He was fierce and chaotic and usually depicted as a bull. Historically, the Israelite prophets denounced Baal, who was a fertility figure, because of his association with the sky, which was the domain of the their god Yahweh.

Why We're Space Monkeys: "Little joke?" Sam's sense of humor gets made fun of. Because let's face it, she *hasn't* been very funny thus far; the writers have been very conscientious about keeping Sam fairly literal. So when she does make a joke, it flies right by us, until it's pointed out by her, and then Jack's response is the real humor.

Parlez-vous Gate?:
JACOB: Just don't jab yourself with it.

DANIEL: Why?

JACOB: Actually, I don't know exactly. That in itself should scare you.

516. Last Stand

Original airdate: March 29, 2002
Written by: Robert Cooper
Directed by: Martin Wood

The System Lords vote in Anubis, who promises to destroy Earth as a signing bonus.

Through Osiris, Anubis promises to destroy Earth and those pesky Tau'ri so that the Goa'uld may return to their (*Star Trek*, anyone?) "Grand Principle." Yu's refusal to acquiesce to Anubis has more to it than just indifference. The only member of the System Lords who was around when Anubis committed these "unspeakable" atrocities, Yu's reticence could also be because he has seen Anubis' work and doesn't want to be a part of it.

"I think this episode probably ranks up there for bringing together the most elements from previous episodes in the *Stargate* universe," noted Robert Cooper, who penned the second of this two-parter. Thankfully, we've shed the "Hey that Goa'uld is dead — no wait he's not" trope that got so tiresome with characters like Hathor and Apophis.

Echoing a large theme from season five, both Sam and Daniel must "do what they have to do" when confronted with specters of their past. But while Carter leaves Lt. Elliott to certain death, Daniel refuses to complete his mission, choosing one life over many. Both threads of this motif are well drawn, and while they may be a little stale (Carter almost always chooses the military, and Daniel almost always chooses the humane), the fact that both are included in this mini-arc makes it at least a balanced staleness.

In "Summit" I suggested that this episode has a great many threads going on simultaneously, and compared it to the season seven mini-arc "Heroes." Another difference between the two is that, unlike "Heroes," which uses more universal themes so that viewers can enter the *Stargate* world without knowing precisely what is going on, in "Summit" and "Last Stand," I doubt very much that a new viewer would have even an inkling of what is happening. This is an unfortunate but sometimes necessary occurrence in television. Long-time viewers demand continuity, but since the show is always looking for new viewers, it must also make the series available to those who have never seen it before. At this point in season five, *SG-1* is carrying around quite a bit of baggage, and it culminates here, a chancy but perhaps wise decision on the part of the writers and producers. Since season five is already moving away from arcs of single Goa'uld confrontations into the larger areas of the System Lords, the Replicators, and the Asgard, it seems prudent to tie up loose ends, risking a slight alienation of new viewers who happen to tune in to that particular arc. Perhaps to make up for this lack of background information, the "Summit" arc has more effects, eye candy, gilt-covered props, and beautiful, half-clad men and women than we've ever seen.

One thing that did stand out was the story's refusal to divulge why exactly Anubis had been banished in the first place. We've already seen treachery, murder, cannibalism, and bad taste in clothes — how "unspeakable" are these acts? If this is a nod to an older technique of allowing the audience to imagine the worst, then it seems like a cop-out. Since the story was being developed when the future of *SG-1* was unsure (at the time, season six was not guaranteed, and Brad Wright and Robert Cooper were looking to segue from the series back into a movie — or two), there was some hasty replanning when it was renewed for a sixth season. Perhaps this accounts for the jumbled feeling to the character of Anubis, but still, most viewers do not care about the mechanics behind the world: they just want to see the world in a cohesive, understandable way.

Gods & Scientists: Interestingly, in Egyptian mythology Anubis is sometimes said to be the son of Osiris. In the movie *Stargate*, Anubis is First Prime to Ra, and is subsequently killed. However, he was revived for the fifth season, and makes an excellent antagonist with long-reaching consequences for the team.

Interesting Fact: The original intention of the Sam/Martouf thread in this mini-arc was to have actor JR Bourne, who played Martouf, appear. Unfortunately, Bourne was unavailable and the script had to be rewritten using Lt. Elliott instead.

Why We're Space Monkeys: Robert Cooper is an executive producer of *SG-1* as well as a writer for the show. Part of *SG-1*'s ongoing popularity is due to the very familiar and family-like atmosphere created by the actors — but also created by the directors and producers, the directors of photography, and the crew in general, as well. While credits are sometimes misleading (for instance, while Mallozzi and Mullie wrote the first part of this arc, it was originally Robert Cooper's conception), the give and take on set and in the creation process helps to streamline the show. Plus, as Cooper joked, as an executive producer, "You can [pass on the whole script] and put all the good parts in your episode."

Parlez-vous Gate?:
CARTER: That's it. I'm done.
O'NEILL: How do we know it's working?
CARTER: I guess if someone comes to rescue us.

517. Fail Safe

Original airdate: April 5, 2002
Written by: Joseph Mallozzi, Paul Mullie
Directed by: Andy Mikita

SG-1 works as a team to divert an asteroid on a collision course with Earth. As usual, they don't get fan letters thanking them afterward.

"Fail Safe" is a nice stand-alone episode after the heavy offerings of "Summit" and "Last Stand." These "one-offs," as they are called by the crew, serve to readjust the picture of the universe back to a focus on SG-1 and its workings. Another series that pretty much always runs with this idea is *Star Trek*; the conclusion of each episode deals not with *will* the protagonist get out of a particular situation, but with *how* they get out of it. *SG-1* takes a different tack and brings to the screen a universe as diverse as Earth itself is, with themes, ideas, cultures, people, and emotions that encompass a vast spectrum. While some themes are revisited many times (consequences of actions, knowledge, memory, belonging), they are nearly always trested in fresh ways.

Here, *SG-1* tackles the familiar threat of the destruction of the planet. While the problem itself is hardly new in the series or in the larger framework of storytelling itself, it's the team play that makes it feel fresh. The last few episodes have seen the team split up and/or working with other races or other SG teams. "Fail Safe" returns to the four-member unit that works effectively to solve the problem at hand. When the team does split up, it is nice to see Sam and Daniel together — we haven't seen this in a while, and the comfort of the two with each other counteracts the episode's tension and makes it a lot easier to watch. Still, it's the four main characters interacting that we're watching for, and the sheer amount of screen time given to this dynamic is wonderful.

Jack's wry comment, "It's a great story, isn't it?" brings into focus the idea of the Stargate feeding the audience stories. The Gate does indeed feed us, with the characters, with their universe, with their adventures. Their enemies become ours through the portal of the Gate; their allies, too. The Stargate gives viewers a chance to become involved in lives not their own — as we see more literally in season eight's "Citizen Joe." Unlike SG-1, the Stargate cannot fail — it is the gateway to a different universe for both the characters and their viewers, a giant, grey fail-safe in and of itself.

True to form, the suits that Jack and Teal'c wear are much closer to actual space suits than the ones we usually see on television, which are more aesthetically pleasing and make the actor look less like they have teeny tiny arms and a huge head. Kudos to the art direction on that one.

The word "fail" comes from the Latin root "to deceive." While the fail-safe of Earth has been passed, SG-1 also deceives the Goa'uld, thwarting them. The Tau'ri are becoming very thorny annoyances these last few episodes. But mostly, "Fail Safe" is a nice, light shower after the downpour of "Summit" and "Last Stand," and a good segue into the heavier fare of "The Warrior" and "Sentinel," and the much ballyhooed *sturm und drang* of the end of season five.

Gods & Scientists: The asteroid is to be destroyed by taking it out of phase with Earth and passing it through the planet. The term "out of phase" refers to a scientific pattern wherein two or more signals, defined as a sequence of information, are altered in some way so that their usually identical frequencies are not synchronized. In science fiction terms, let's take the example of a person in a room. Usually, the frequency of the person is identical to that of the room. If the frequency emitted by the person is somehow changed, the patterns will no longer match and the person may be able to walk through the wall. That's the theory, anyway. . . .

Interesting Fact: Although it seems as though there are as many actors as trees in BC, *SG-1* often recasts actors for different parts. David Bloom, for instance, was a background character in season two's "Prisoners." He was upgraded to "talky" (a minor actor who has lines) for "Fail Safe."

Why We're Space Monkeys: *SG-1* is often described as a "classic" show because it uses traditional camera techniques, traditional storytelling techniques (story A and a sideline story, or stories A and B, which tie together at the end of the episode), and traditional archetypal scenarios (the "time anomaly" episode, the "mistaken identity" episode, the "altered consciousness" episode). However, *SG-1*'s uniqueness comes out because of the *way* that it handles these traditional elements. Even stand-alone episodes become part of the backstory, the canon of the show, and are referred to in subsequent episodes. For example, when Sam is told in "Ascension" to take some time off, Dr. Fraiser lists the reasons for her medical advice: a Tok'ra symbiote, memory stamping, and Sam's entire consciousness transferred into a computer and back again — "and that's just for starters!" While none of those episodes have any bearing on "Ascension," they provide a layered-reality effect that makes the more fantastical moments of the show more compelling — say, landing on an asteroid and then pulling said asteroid *through* the Earth in the very "out of phase" trope that the writers themselves made fun of in "Wormhole X-Treme."

Parlez-vous Gate?:
CARTER: It's good to go, Sir. If it comes right down to it, we can detonate it right here. What's our position?
DANIEL: Well, personally I'm against it.

518. The Warrior

Original airdate: April 12, 2002
Story by: Christopher Judge
Teleplay by: Peter DeLuise
Directed by: Peter DeLuise

A charismatic Jaffa forms an army of Jaffa warriors to overthrow the Goa'uld. Teal'c's loyalties are put to the test when SG-1 considers an alliance with the warriors.

What exactly *are* Teal'c's loyalties? For five seasons now, he's been all gung ho about SG-1 and how they're fighting the good fight. But each time the Jaffa come into play, it's like SG-1 was just a pastime. Not that Teal'c has ever hidden that his main interest in defeating the Goa'uld is the freedom of the Jaffa, but his attitude can sometimes rankle — and it does in this episode. Teal'c seems content here to be led around by the nose by the first person who comes along, and Chris Judge doesn't seem to know how to play this one — he wallows in Zen-like half-smiles for the whole episode.

The title, "The Warrior," is a play on character — exactly who is the warrior in question, Kytano or Teal'c, is unclear — but the question

Tony Amendola is very amiable at Q&A sessions (COURTESY PETER FALLON WWW.BOBW.COM.AU)

of identity is inherent in all the characters' interactions. Teal'c's identity is Jaffa, but his life over the past five years has been with the SGC; Kytano appears to be a charismatic leader, but he turns out to be not who he pretends, as happens so often on *SG-1*. It's a nice twist on the usual idea of a Goa'uld pretending to be a god here, with a Goa'uld pretending to be a Jaffa in order to achieve his aims. While the first couple of seasons focused on the Goa'uld as a threatening specter, the reality of their altercations with SG-1 showed them to be a warlike, presumptuous race. In later seasons, the writers have concentrated on showing specific Goa'uld who have foresight and strategy, effectively upping the ante and making the threat they present more tangible and realistic.

"The Warrior" offers viewers an interesting concept, but we can't help but feel cheated when Mr. Melodrama comes along and, on the strength of Teal'c and Bra'tac's blood, sweat, and tears over the past half a decade, gathers an army. If the Jaffa were that easy to convince, surely someone would have thought of creating some sort of workers' union or something before now. The ease with which they are brainwashed diminishes Teal'c's struggle. Hasn't he been trying *hard* enough to rally the Jaffa? It makes for an episode that's sometimes hard to watch, because the character jumps through so many hoops. Just as Teal'c's loyalties are put to the test in this episode, so too are the viewers' — can we stick by Teal'c even when he willingly blinds himself, when he disowns his friends? And that's maybe how the writers wanted us to experience "The Warrior"; to see how hard it is to watch someone we know and love make the wrong decision time and again and be unable to stop him.

So, while the episode had its downfalls (the *Matrix*-style fighting, Kytano's big soulful eyes), it definitely makes us see things through SG-1's eyes.

Gods & Scientists: Imhotep, whose name, in an ironic twist, means "the one that comes in peace," was one of the most well-known commoners in Ancient Egypt. He is known as the world's first named architect, having designed the first pyramid, and was also a doctor, priest, scribe, poet, astrologer, and vizier to his Pharaoh. The name "Imhotep" has become infamous from use in many mummy movies — for example, *The Mummy* and *The Mummy Returns*.

The fighting technique used at the Jaffa camp is a form of capoeira, a combination of dance, ritual, and martial arts that developed in Brazil. It grew from the Portuguese trade of African slaves to Brazil, and was illegal there until the 1930s. Unlike the Jaffa warriors' technique, however, capoeira most highly values strikes that do not result in actual physical contact.

Interesting Fact: The camera shot used in the fighting sequences of the Jaffa warriors on the platform was achieved by mounting a camera on a steel rod underneath the platform and rotating the rod 360 degrees.

Why We're Space Monkeys: Not only does Sam carry wounded men way bigger than she (see "Last Stand"), but she has really impressive weapons skills. Jack gives the order and she very calmly does what's asked of her. And that little smile she gives at the end of her demonstration to the Jaffa warriors, like she's saying "Oh yeah, I did that, but good," is just too cute.

Parlez-vous Gate?:
KYTANO: I see you are one who speaks your mind, O'Neill.
O'NEILL: Yes, which is why I don't say much.

519. Menace

Original airdate: April 26, 2002
Story by: James Tichenor
Teleplay by: Peter DeLuise
Directed by: Martin Wood

On a decimated planet, SG-1 comes across an advanced robot who holds the key to the origin, and the destruction, of the Replicators.

"Menace" is a good example of an episode revolving around team play. It's also a good example of how effective pacing can make an otherwise mediocre episode that much more exciting. "Menace" provides us with some answers about the Replicators. We've only been exposed to them in a handful of episodes, but already we're well aware of the threat they present; the plot elements of "Menace" do a good job of doling out information little by little, making us wait for the answers.

Reese — whose childlike and petulant presence throughout the episode is intriguing, if a tad irritating — is a perfect analogy of what can happen when things exceed our grasp. Here, a seemingly innocuous child's "toy" becomes a galactic threat. And while most people have probably never had that *exact* thing happen to them, humans are well versed in events spiraling out of control, from personal catastrophes to political ones.

The final ten minutes of "Menace" in particular highlight the efforts that went into pacing. The action is split into three on both a physical and a psychological level, and the back-and-forth between each "scene" ratchets up the tension until the final climax. Sam and General Hammond (we finally get to see a non-alternate-universe Hammond in camouflage and carrying a gun — Don Davis plays the part with a lot of guts and gusto) barricade themselves in a small room and deal with the ramifications of a very visible countdown to self-destruction. Meanwhile, Jack, Teal'c, and the airmen crouch outside the Gate room and try to break through to save Daniel, the SGC, and Earth (no pressure there). On the other side of the Gate room, Daniel rips through layers of Reese's emotions to control her toys — and her mind. The intensity of the scene between Daniel and Reese is a showcase of the actors' skills; the strength of their connection pulls you in. The narrative technique here is very effective; Reese's sudden death, and O'Neill's immediate reaction after taking in the situation in one glance, bring out the vagaries of human connection. Sometimes you put laborious effort into making a connection with someone, only to have that connection ripped apart in a moment. It must be particularly difficult for Daniel — the character has had so little with which to work this season in terms of forming a "human" bond, in terms of simply relating to another, that to have that shattered just as he was making progress and about to gain something full of import for the planet, the answer to the Replicators' destruction, would have been devastating, and angering. That scene also underscores the harshness of the world these characters inhabit, where tough decisions have to be made on a daily basis.

The ending leaves an even more bitter taste in the mouth when Daniel points out that Jack may have just destroyed the one chance they would ever have of stopping the Replicators. It's a chilling moment; the Goa'uld are certainly a threat, but there's never been any doubt that there is *hope* they can be destroyed; to have that hope for the Replicators pretty near demolished is a sad and frightening note on which to finish the episode. The Replicators are the result of a child's toy gone wrong, and their creator, Reese, is now dead, leaving open the question of whether or not they are now invincible. Also, the "human face" of the Replicators is seen later in "Unnatural Selection," and the two-part "New Order." "Menace" is a great episode worth rewatching.

Gods & Scientists: They are called Replicators because they replicate, rather than reproduce. Self-replication is the process by which something makes a copy of itself. It's found in the human body in cells, which, given the right conditions, replicate by dividing. In research in the early twentieth century, scientist John von Neumann established some common denominators for artificial self-replication.

Reese is a "gynoid" — the female form of android. The term, which is defined as a robot designed to look like a human female, is fairly recent (first used by science fiction author Gwyneth Jones in the late twentieth century) but the concept abounds in history. From the year 600 BC, storytellers told of women figures coming to life. Such an event occurs in the *Iliad*, for example.

Interesting Fact: The solemn atmosphere surrounding this episode isn't entirely due to the script: parts of it were shot on September 11, 2001, and it shows. The beginning scenes where SG-1 is on the planet and find Reese were shot very shortly after news broke about the World Trade Center attacks.

Why We're Space Monkeys: O'Neill and Jackson have their issues, and they don't hide behind pettiness or sniping, they speak their minds directly and with real anger. *SG-1* has always been extremely good at portraying friendships and working relationships in all their complexity, and the bond between Jack and Daniel is one of the more complicated and intimate on the show. Many fans felt the loss of this dynamic when Michael Shanks left. "Menace" gives us some good moments between the two characters. They have real respect for each other, but their differences can be stark, so when they come up, both men passionately express their views.

Parlez-vous Gate?:
O'NEILL: Has it occurred to anyone that that thing may have been lying around that planet for, oh, quite some time, and that maybe it's broken? Or perhaps it never worked right in the first place?
CARTER: So, you think we should just shut her down?
O'NEILL: Oh, I don't know, let's just ask the man who just had his head cracked open.
DANIEL: I don't think she meant to hurt me. I just don't think she liked what I was saying.
O'NEILL: I don't like most of what you say. I try to resist the urge to shove you through a wall.

520. The Sentinel

Original airdate: May 3, 2002
Written by: Ron Wilkerson
Directed by: Peter DeLuise

The NID's rogue operatives have messed something up on another planet and now they, along with SG-1, have to fix it.

Another example of a "one-off'" episode that uses backstory to fuel the tension. Colonel Grieves in particular is an effective doppelganger for Colonel O'Neill. His adamant stance on obtaining technology to defend earth before "the Goa'uld finally decide to stomp on us," is a darker shading of O'Neill's own choices. Unlike O'Neill's however, Grieves' sense of ethical responsibility does not extend to other races. Or perhaps he reasons that six billion to several hundred thousand is worth the risk. Either way, it is interesting to see how he is used in the *SG* universe. It's hard to paint a man like Grieves as truly evil. We've already seen Maybourne's persuasive tactics ("Desperate Measures" and "Shades of Grey"), and we've seen him petition O'Neill directly to join the NID. Grieves and O'Neill are not as far apart as they might seem. This is definitely suggested at the end of the episode when Grieves does "the right thing" and sacrifices himself for the people of Latona.

Jack's leadership skills are often underplayed and it is usually up to the viewer to make sense of his strategy. It is key to his character that O'Neill can circumvent a traditional chain of command without losing either face or respect. This is seen in his talks with Marul, played by actor Henry Gibson, who did a good job as the leader of this utopian society but after a while he sets your teeth on edge with his wide-eyed . . . everything. When O'Neill's comments and advice are backed up by Lt. Grogan, O'Neill doesn't even acknowledge that the other man is speaking, but allows his voice to be added to the sum of his own argument and even takes his cues from the tone and diction of Grogan. As usual, RDA's understated characterization of the colonel might land a more immature actor in the land of the upstaged, but every time the camera cuts back to O'Neill's face we realize that we're waiting for him to speak. We also get some good team tactics, as Sam and Teal'c square off against the Jaffa, acting as the sentinel for Daniel and the NID operatives. It's not often that we see Teal'c and Sam together, and their work as a team is quietly effective.

Gods & Scientists: For those of you conversant in Romanian, the word *sfarog* ("torrid") is attributed to the Slavic fire god Svarog, who was associated with the Greek Hephaestus, god of the smithy. In the *SG-1* universe, Svarog has been seen in "Summit" and "Last Stand" — he was the guy in black leather with the big, blue stripes on his face. Whether or not he gets killed by the Sentinel is not established in the episode.

Interesting Fact: Christina Cox, now mostly known for her role opposite Vin Diesel in *The Chronicles of Riddick*, as well as the Canadian film *Better than Chocolate*, has already appeared in the *SG* universe — as usual, under makeup, so you won't recognize her. She was T'akaya in "Spirits."

Why We're Space Monkeys: Daniel appears to have perfect pitch and the ability to discern harmonial chords by ear. Only Danny could do this and still look remotely studly.

Parlez-vous Gate?:

GREAVES: I'll say this again. I don't like the thought of going into this unarmed.

O'NEILL: And I don't care.

KERSHAW: I feel better just knowing there's an archaeologist watching our back.

DANIEL (holding up his knife): Um, yeah, which end do the bullets go in again?

521. Meridian

Original airdate: May 10, 2002
Written by: Robert Cooper
Directed by: William Waring

Daniel disarms a dangerous experiment gone wrong. But several people have died, and the alien civilization that he saved condemns his actions, demanding that he stand trial for his "crimes." While the debate rages as to what to do about the situation, the rest of SG-1 stands aghast at the real truth of the matter — Daniel has received a lethal dose of radiation, and is going to die.

An episode that spawned a lot of controversy, backlash, navel-gazing, and tremendous emotion, "Meridian" puts into play everything that *SG-1* has in its arsenal over the last five years, in one episode. Fierce debates raged over whether this episode was sentimentalized to the point of being unwatchable, or was instead a subtle handling of an impossible situation.

This episode is part Greek tragedy, part Zen Buddhism 101, part Humanism as the Great Equalizer, and part team story. Greek tragedies were performed for the communal custom of "catharsis," the relieving of builtup emotion through the actions of another. Greek tragedies seem to us today to be full of intrigue, espionage, seductions, and betrayals (I might make a sly comment about "reality television" here), but they served a real purpose to the Greeks. By expunging excess emotion in public, alongside their partners, family, and friends, theatergoers came away feeling empty, and ready to face new challenges. "Meridian" works in the same vein, adding a dose of calm, cerebral Zen koans to both indicate the new challenges ahead and tone down the overzealous emotional handwringing that could otherwise take over the episode.

The word "sentimental" as we know it (overly emotional), came to us during the Victorian era. The newly created class of the bourgeoisie, with increased free time on their hands and more education, demanded more entertainment. A multitude of novels arrived, and were rushed into print, gleefully overexposing the emotional lives of characters without equally developing qualities of intellect (or even logic). The "deathbed scene" — mimicked in soap operas to this day — is a staple of the genre. Prior to that, the word sentimental was used in reference to a state that goes beyond mere emotion and approaches the sublime, and was used with much effect in the Romantic period by both poets and prose writers. In "Meridian," you can see writer Robert Cooper moving between these two aesthetics as he weaves a very postmodern tale full of references to other cultures, blending them all into a large humanism that really illustrates what Daniel Jackson stands for, and opens up a space for new character Jonas Quinn to enter (played by Corin Nemec).

Although he's set up right from the beginning by O'Neill's quip, "He's a nerd, sir; he and Daniel got along great," the character of Jonas Quinn had a hard row to hoe. As Nemec said, "These folks have worked together for five years, and I'm just walking into the party. I had to work hard to stay relaxed, but by the end of the second day of production, I felt like I was hitting my stride."

As of the end of 2004, a little more than sixty percent of viewers responded to a GateWorld poll saying they thought the episode was "Outstanding." While it does bog down at times, especially in the "my government says," "well, *my* government says" section, which was really kind of kindergarten politics, the dialogue is paced well enough that we are not bogged down in emotion for too long. Robert Cooper does a good job allowing feeling to work out naturally by having an emotional segment (such as the Jack/Daniel interaction when Daniel asks Jack to let him go) followed by a non-emotional one. In this way, Dean Anderson's understated style does a beautiful job of allowing us to project onto his carefully neutral face our own thoughts and feelings. This is a contemporary catharsis, more befitting our contemporary psychology.

"Meridian" uses humanism to great advantage. Jackson's firm belief that his life is no more valuable than anyone else's is a quintessential humanist ideal; he believes in fostering human virtue above all things. Further explorations of this theme in season six are interestingly taken up by the alien Jonas Quinn. The Jaffa Teal'c, a comfortable and valuable asset in terms of his "Other" viewpoint, remains almost always on the side of the "way-of-the-warrior crap," as Sam so eloquently puts it in "Revelations."

Unfortunately, there is one continuity error that was sailed over so blithely that it was an annoyance for many a fan: in the beginning of the episode Sam states that Daniel received over seven grays of radiation to his whole body from the radiation that had flooded the room. If both he and Jonas were in the same room, why weren't they both hit with the radiation? Jonas seems to be the same smiley guy they met at the beginning of the episode, while Daniel talks about drowning in his own blood and racking convulsions of pain.

Also, one has to wonder why, of all the directors that could have been chosen (DeLuise, Wood, Warry-Smith, Gereghty), William Waring drew the straw. Only directing three out of a possible 175 episodes (give or take, for eight seasons), it seems an odd choice to give such a momentous task to the poor guy. His resumé does include a number of movies — but as a camera operator, not a director. Even as a second-unit director (which is not credited, so we never see it), his responsibilities would have been different, far more technical and less artistic.

"Meridian" is both bold and traditional, postmodern, egalitarian, a little maudlin, a little escapist, a little moral, a little easy on the eyes with soft lighting and CGI — and definitely worth watching.

Gods & Scientists: Although we think of radiation in terms of its unhealthy aspects, we are in fact always being bombarded with radiation of some form or another. The electromagnetic spectrum includes x-rays, gamma rays, and microwaves. Radiation can travel at the speed of light or slower. The biological damage done to tissue when exposed to abnormal amounts of radiation (called "dose") is measured in the "gray" unit. So, when Sam mentions that Daniel absorbed "eight to nine grays" to his hand, she is using the standard measurement.

Interesting Fact: If you are a fan of *Stargate Atlantis*, there is a seed planted here regarding Ascension that is further defined in episode three's "Hide and Seek." In *SG-1* the emotional component of ascension is highlighted, but in *Stargate Atlantis*, another facet of this process is revealed.

Why We're Space Monkeys: Despite his idiosyncrasies and his penchant for talking faster and faster as the seasons wore on, Michael Shanks always does his job with a seriousness that makes it hard to ignore. His total earnestness with O'Neill when he says, "I think I can do more this way," coupled with that one flashback to his first appearance in "Children of the Gods," which was nicely done inside a frame, are powerfully felt. Although his reasons for leaving may have been debated endlessly, once the cameras were rolling, Shanks dropped everything and played the character.

522. Revelations

Original airdate: May 17, 2002
Written by: Joseph Mallozzi, Paul Mullie
Directed by: Martin Wood

The Asgard Freyr contacts the SGC and asks the Tau'ri for help in extracting a stranded Asgard scientist along with his research. SG-1 learns that Thor has been captured by the Goa'uld Anubis.

"Revelations" is a dramatic departure from "Meridian," and with good reason. The team seems exhausted, wrung out, and distant. Completely believably, a very smart Colonel O'Neill requests, against Sam's almost belligerent disapproval, that the team remain on active duty. The team is embroiled in a galactic war again, perhaps the only thing that can remind them of the things that Daniel Jackson fought and died for. Each actor works hard to make their character's choices seem authentic, and they do a great job.

It's also a return to a motif that Jackson himself cherished, that every action, even a small one, can make a difference, from the death of an individual (Daniel) to the defection of another (Jonas) to a small infiltration team (SG-1). The team soon realizes that their mission is far more important than they at first realized. The entire future of the race of Asgard depends on the research being conducted by the feisty Heimdall.

Although Carter accuses Teal'c of following in the footsteps of Colonel O'Neill with "that way-of-the-warrior crap," he quickly but compassionately reminds her that sorrow is as much a cultural manifestation as a personal one. For her part, Sam is the most outwardly touched by recent events, a strong contrast to her usual controlled persona, proving that she too, has learned from Daniel's absence. In "Meridian" she does a good job revealing that she understands her own limitations emotionally, without making it seem like a "shippy" moment at all, and O'Neill's wall of coldness rivals the glacier he and Sam had to chip their way out of in season one's "Solitudes."

We meet the Goa'uld Anubis for the first time. Unlike the rest of the Goa'uld we have encountered, Anubis' face is not human; it is a shifting plane of blackness. He states with a sort of savage satisfaction that many things have changed since his return. Banished for a thousand years, we are left to wonder what he got up to in the interim. The Goa'uld Yu is harassing Anubis' fleet, and Osiris — as always at her sneering best — works between ridding the galaxy of that pesky but tenacious System Lord and retrieving Heimdall and his research, which is what Anubis really wants.

The title could be an allusion to the last book in the Bible, since Revelations finishes the Bible just as this chapter in the lives of SG-1 finishes the fifth season. It could also be an allusion to the quiet disclosure that occurs during the episode. Carter's conversation with General Hammond, which is wonderfully heartwarming, shows us Sam's difficulty in accepting Daniel's departure. She can't fathom what has happened, and the uncertainty plagues her. She wants closure, and she must gradually come to the realization that the answer just isn't there. She is quickly pulled into another Asgard adventure in "Revelations," a fact that emphasizes her character's need to have something to work on, a problem to solve. Unlike Carter's intellectual life, where she is offered a problem and must come up with a solution, her emotional life is vague, unclear. It's fitting that the problem the team has to solve is the future of the Asgard race; at a time when they're unsure what their own future holds and facing the death of someone they loved, concentrating on perpetuating another's life, another's future, can only be a positive thing.

Unlike every season in the past, season five does not end on a cliff-hanger, in deference to the fact that "Revelations" marks the last episode to be broadcast on Showtime, the channel that had hosted the series since its inception. As of the next season, SG-1 would be aired on the Sci-Fi Channel, and the writers and producers thought it would be disrespectful to Showtime viewers to leave the channel with a cliff-hanger. Instead, the season ends with the establishment of a new antagonist, an almost unutterable rift in the team, and the probable death of a powerful ally. SG-1 is once again the underdog, and the breath of Daniel follows them, suggesting that his presence is still with them even in their darkest time.

Gods & Scientists: In Norse mythology, Heimdall is the god of light, and was said to be born of nine mothers at the end of the world. He was variously called "White-god" and "Golden-tooth" because, fittingly enough, of his golden teeth. Endowed with very keen senses, he was the guardian of the gods, stationed at Bifrost (a bridge, and the only entrance to Asgard, home of the Norse gods). He owned the Gilliar Horn, which he would blow should danger approach Asgard. His duty was to protect Asgard from being besieged by the giants. Requiring very little sleep, he could see up to a hundred miles around. It was said that at the final battle of Ragnarok (the end of the world), he killed his archenemy Loki (see season seven's "Fragile Balance"), but then died himself of his wounds. It is also said that Heimdall created the three races of mankind: serfs, peasants, and warriors. So it is perhaps not a coincidence that it's Heimdall in this episode who is responsible for the laboratory that is working on the perpetuation of the Asgard race.

Interesting Fact: Teryl Rothery was used as the stand-in for the computer-generated Heimdall, as well as providing the voice. Suited up in a black leotard and later painted out, she provided the face of the Asgard Heimdall, placed at a height that the actors (Rick, Chris, and Amanda) could work off while taping. Unfortunately, that height was in a conspicuous place (the Asgard are rather short, after all), somewhere between her neck and her belly button. If you watch carefully, you can often see the cast members acting slightly off-pitch; almost as though they were trying not to laugh. Amanda Tapping in particular, who has the most eye-to-"eye" contact with Heimdall, wears an almost pained expression.

Why We're Space Monkeys: Teryl Rothery as Heimdall. Some of the best lines of the episode are hers, and that cheeky verve is something we've not really encountered with the Asgard; seeing the primness made fun of, simultaneously making fun of the Tau'ri, is very satisfying. And Carter's face, watching O'Neill's butt as he pretends to talk to Thor via the Asgard's nifty space illusion, is hilarious.

Parlez-vous Gate?:

HEIMDALL: For nearly a thousand years, we have been physically incapable of achieving cell division through meiosis.
O'NEILL: Hmm?
CARTER: Sexual reproduction, Sir.
O'NEILL: A thousand years?
HEIMDALL: It is not something we usually discuss with other races.
O'NEILL: That I understand.

STARGATE SG-1 - SEASON SIX
"We're just going to have to learn to live with it."

601. Redemption (Part 1)

Original airdate: June 7, 2002
Written by: Robert Cooper
Directed by: Martin Wood

Teal'c journeys to the side of his dying wife, and then cannot get back to the SGC because Anubis has attacked the Tau'ri through the Stargate, rendering it inoperable.

"Redemption" is a huge two-parter that picks up season six and throws it into the gaping maw of its new home, the Sci-Fi Channel. Two things are immediately clear. First, there's no Daniel Jackson, and the reverberations of his absence are going to be felt for a while. Second, they've got a new budget, and it looks big. Very big. This two-parter was actually shot all at once and has a feature-film flavor to it because of that. The thread with Teal'c and his son is given room to breathe and not wrapped up neatly at the beginning of the first episode. Instead, most of Part 1 is spent setting up the tension between father and son, in preparation for the redemption they undergo in the second part, as both absolve themselves of past errors.

Enter Jonas Quinn. His effusiveness is always watchable, and actor Corin Nemec walks a fine line between peppy and preposterous. Nemec works hard to make both his alien identity and his sympathy for the Tau'ri seem believable. He is idealistic, like Daniel Jackson, but his reasons for joining SG-1 are not as personal. Jonas feels responsible for the death of Daniel Jackson to a certain extent, but he also has a very strong tie to his people. Daniel was on a very personal mission at first to save his wife, and later to end the threat of the Goa'uld. Jonas does not want to fill Dr. Jackson's shoes, but he does want very badly to contribute in his own way to the fight.

"It [couldn't have been] that easy," noted Amanda Tapping about the inclusion of Jonas Quinn in season six. "If you think about how the group dynamic changed and grew over five years, to suddenly introduce a new element and expect [SG-1] to replace the person that was there before is . . . is wrong." Of all the members of SG-1 it is Carter who has the most difficulty here with Jonas' bright-eyed, bushy-tailed enthusiasm, telling him point blank that she just doesn't see him joining SG-1. Carter is extremely loyal, and she feels there has not been a long enough period of mourning for Daniel. To pick up and move on as though nothing had happened strengthens that "way-of-the-warrior crap" that Daniel helped her see past. In "Meridian," Carter says to Daniel, "I don't know why we wait to tell people how we really feel." But, as Jack keeps SG-1 on active duty, the team is forced to continue to function and live with the new dynamic. All they can hope for is redemption in their future. They have a new weapon to use in the fight against the Goa'uld, the X-302, which is the result of six years of hard work and team effort. That it is a new team that becomes its first user is perhaps not a surprising irony in the world of *SG-1*, where things rarely turn out the way you'd expect and everyone is aware of the inevitability of change. Change is a necessary part of life, and that's something that *SG-1* expresses in many different ways, both subtle (as in the X-302) and the not-so-subtle (the arrival of Jonas).

Gods & Scientists: The X-302 uses the new naquadria mineral that Jonas procured for the Tau'ri before he defected from Kelowna. The X-302 is also the first machine to be engineered completely by the Tau'ri — no retrofitting old, broken-down gliders anymore. This shiny new addition to the Air Force is capable of interstellar travel, but its hyperspace drive is still faulty. The SGC wants so desperately to have ships capable of moving through space so that they don't have to rely on the Stargate to get around, in case of imminent Goa'uld attack.

Interesting Fact: While it looks as though the X-302 is a big plane, the actual model used on set sat on top of a box that was draped in a green sheet and later painted out with a "greenscreen" effect. The wings were also added later using computer-generated effects.

Why We're Space Monkeys: Jack, Teal'c, and Sam do not act like stalwart heroes all the time. Teal'c misses his family and almost starts crying when talking to Rya'c, Jack makes fun of his own penchant for burying emotions, and Sam is positively snippy to poor Jonas. This is not Captain America and his team of stalwart sidekicks. It's a military team under a lot of pressure and doing the best they can.

Parlez-vous Gate?:
JONAS: How do I know what color to wear?
CARTER: (as she is leaving) We call each other every morning.

602. Redemption (Part 2)

Original airdate: June 14, 2002
Written by: Robert Cooper
Directed by: Martin Wood

With the Stargate still under attack, Carter cannot think of a way to save the planet. Teal'c, Rya'c, and Bra'tac embark on a dangerous mission destroy the Goa'uld weapon, and things look grim. But Jonas has an idea . . .

The second part of this mini-arc is a nice showcase of special effects. "*Stargate* has really come of age as computer generated and assisted effects came into their own," noted James Tichenor, explaining how the series evolved from its early episodes with fewer effects to later ones like "Redemption." "The price of the computer technology has come down and more people have picked up the tools; there's been more competition and more competent work [available], which has caused the writers to write more ambitious effects into the show — as we did better, they'd want more. A classic scenario." Compare, for instance, the force field we see in season four's "Upgrades" with the one in this episode.

Anubis has procured technology far beyond the usual range of the

Dr. McKay (David Hewlett) made the jump to *Stargate Atlantis* in 2004 (ALBERT L. ORTEGA)

Goa'uld. There is speculation that he has obtained Asgard technology from Thor, whom he imprisoned in "Revelations," and perhaps has some idea of Ancient technology. His shifty, unknown face (does he even have a face?), and chilling arrogance outdoes even the most arrogant Goa'uld. A fitting replacement for Peter Williams.

The beginning scene between McKay and Carter is hilarious, with McKay mimicking what everybody else is thinking, really: I mean, c'mon, what kind of Galactic Bad Guy says, "Prepare to meet your doooooom," like that? McKay is like an amalgam of every geek and nerd we've ever met (or been, for that matter). Completely cynical — but only after the fact. In the moment he's as captivated as anyone else. His flirtatiousness with Sam is characteristic, and Carter's response to it characteristically Carter-like. The kiss she gives him after explaining that having a crush on her is really unhealthy (a reference to her long-standing "black widow syndrome") is almost like a kiss of death — and very much the "it's not you, it's me" deal that plagues so many relationships. In this case, it really *is* her: her syndrome, and her attraction, albeit mostly unspoken and hidden, to O'Neill.

Jonas comes through in a big way in "Redemption," and it's clear he's been observing from the sidelines as he was doing his research into Earth, the SGC, and SG-1. His too-innocent questioning of how the Stargate was placed inside the mountain is a subtle way of letting Carter take the initiative for the idea to save Earth, and also of showing viewers that Jonas isn't out for the glory. He's in a tough position, but you can already see the glimmers of determination in him. And it was a nice idea from the creative department to shoot Jonas' scenes mostly one-on-one with an SG-1 member. The last shot of the episode is the first of the full four team members since Daniel's death, and it's fitting that it should come now rather than earlier, when Jonas was still cautiously edging into his new territory.

True to form, writer Robert Cooper hones in on the character arcs, using the effects as frames within which SG-1 struggles. A good example is Anubis' ring itself. Mimicking the Gate network, it adds power from one stone to another, but we're not quite sure ourselves how it works. Neither, it seems, is Anubis. Relationships are like that, working when we least expect them to (like McKay and Carter), working when we don't want them to (Rya'c refuses to be sidelined by his father, and in the end, his stubbornness wins the battle), working despite all the odds (Jonas' idea being used even though he's an outsider, and seen by some as the catalyst for Daniel's death). All that energy flowing around; it seems ultimately mysterious, and yet it works. Add to the mix the still nebulous form of Anubis, who puts fear into us for the first time in a while. The Goa'uld, while strong, had started to be relegated to "pest" status, but the appearance of Anubis ratchets up the tension between good and evil. Let round six begin!

Gods & Scientists: O'Neill tries to fly the Gate far from Earth with the X-302, but fails. The attempt to escape Anubis' plan is reminiscent of the Greek myth of Icarus. Icarus was imprisoned in a tower in Crete with his father, Daedalus (see "Revisions"), by King Minos. Because the sea was under constant surveillance, Daedalus decided that he and Icarus would escape by air. He devised a set of wings for each of them, made with feathers held together with wax, and when they were done, he warned Icarus to stay close to him and not fly too low, or too high. Icarus failed to heed his father's advice, however, and flew up toward the heavens. Too near the sun, the wax that held his wings together melted, and Icarus plummeted to the sea, where he drowned. The island and the sea were named after him (Ikaria).

Interesting Fact: Corin Nemec (Quinn) had never actually seen *SG-1* when his agent called. In "Meridian," he felt in awe. Not only was he replacing a very important character, but his first introduction to the world of sci-fi was a little . . . restricting. "[The Kelownan costume] was kinda like wearing a corset," he said in at a Gatecon convention in September 2003. "The vest thing that they had me in was made out of like real firm, yet spongy material. It was alien, I'll tell ya that. And it squeezed me really, really tight. So I didn't have freedom of movement like I normally am used to."

Why We're Space Monkeys: There's a real sense that O'Neill's tired, that *he's* not even sure why he's fighting anymore. Daniel is gone and there was absolutely nothing he could do. More than that, O'Neill was the one who had pretty much allowed it to happen. To carry the responsibilities for so many lives and then to have to stand helpless time after time while other people save the planet has got to get wearying. Anderson does a great job injecting a sort of tired humor into his scenes. In older episodes like "Cor-ai" we see this less often, but look for it again in season seven's "Abyss." And check the irony of O'Neill's "fall to Earth," in the next episode, "Descent."

Parlez-vous Gate?:
CARTER: Maybe he wanted to make sure it was going to work.
McKAY: Yeah, that would be embarrassing, wouldn't it? (Imitating Anubis' voice) "Nothing can stop the destruction that I bring upon you!" Then the Gate shuts down. "Oops, sorry, never mind."

603. Descent

Original airdate: June 21, 2002
Written by: Joseph Mallozzi, Paul Mullie
Directed by: Peter DeLuise

SG-1 investigates a mother ship orbiting Earth's atmosphere. They must free the disembodied consciousness of Thor, and then escapes before the ship is destroyed.

"Descent" is a return to an older storytelling style, and an older style of *SG-1* episode, like season three's "Past and Present," and season four's "Beneath the Surface," for example. The episode starts with a question — why *would* Anubis abandon a ship? — and spends the rest of the story delving into why. The "M&M" writing team use a classic narrative device when they leave this question open so that the audience can develop their own ideas — is it a booby-trap, a red herring, or a Trojan horse?

Another problem the writers address is how to jump-start Jonas on a team that has worked together for five years. In this episode, both we and Jonas realize that something has to happen to make him — and us — feel like he's earned his place there. Jonas himself explains that when the chance arose to prove himself on a more-than-intellectual level, he froze — he's well aware of the fact that he has a long way to go before he's fully accepted. The writers, too, know that they have to work Jonas in in a way that's different from Daniel's role but that doesn't make him stray too far from the team's dynamic.

As the Big Bad, Anubis is kind of an ironic twist on season four's "Upgrades" — except now it's the Goa'uld who's been upgraded. He's got technology from the Ancients, the Asgard, and the Goa'uld, making him the most threatening foe to date, but he still retains recognizable features, like the flanged voice. What's chilling about Anubis is that he has a hint of the Asgard/Ascended mentality, too. He is far more calm, less blustery, and willing to wait until the odds are stacked in his favor before attempting something. He's not the egomaniacal scavenging type that the Goa'uld have been descending to.

Another reminder the writers succinctly bring us (in one line, actually) is O'Neill's assertion for the reason for SG-1's existence. There have been a lot of really huge, interesting arcs on the show, and Jack's words, that the team's standing orders are to procure technology to aid in the fight against the Goa'uld, come as a stark reminder of the underlying mission.

We also get to see Major Davis, whom we haven't seen since "48 Hours." He seems to have picked up a lot of Goa'uld information, and he believes that the noise they hear on the ship is patterned. He's come a long way from the annoying sycophant he used to be.

The title of the episode is, as always, apt. The ship is descending, Jack's relationship with Jonas is on a descent thanks to his continued stonewalling, and Teal'c seems to be descending from the heights of unapproachable warrior (see also "Nightwalkers") — it could be suggestive of the larger arc that we see culminate in "The Changeling" where Teal'c loses his symbiote.

Gods & Scientists: The Ancient Greek myth of Orpheus is often used as a metaphor for the poet. One of his first mentions is by Pindar, a lyric poet from the fifth century BC. Here it is given a modern treatment in the irreverent Jack O'Neill. Orpheus was a hero who married Eurydice, and who saved the Argonauts from death by Sirens (sea creatures, part human, part bird, who lured sailors to death with their songs; a kind of evil mermaid). Eurydice died after being bitten by a snake, and was transported to the underworld. Orpheus descended to reclaim his love. After many trials, he was granted permission to take her back, but only on the condition that he not look back. Unfortunately, when Orpheus emerged into the sunlight, he looked back in joy at Eurydice, who was still in the dark — she promptly vanished. Unlike Orpheus, Jack never looks back in his attempt to save Thor — he chooses his line of attack and follows it through to the end.

Interesting Fact: Peter DeLuise and others have dubbed the model from this intro sequence "the cross-eyed sphinx," but season's six's intro is a favorite among the crew.

Why We're Space Monkeys: Jonas and his imperturbable smile. There was a huge kerfuffle in fandom over the character of Jonas, but anyone who's that peppy and enthusiastic deserves to be given a chance — and kudos to Jack O'Neill for giving him one.

Parlez-vous Gate?:
JONAS: Thanks, Teal'c! I really appreciate that. I mean, those of us not originally from the planet Earth have to stick together, right?
TEAL'C: Are you suggesting an alien conspiracy?

604. Frozen

Original airdate: June 28, 2002
Written by: Robert Cooper
Directed by: Martin Wood

A woman is found frozen in Antarctic ice. SG-1 discovers that she may hold the key to the Stargate's origins — and carry a deadly disease.

"Frozen" is one of those episodes that seems good but innocuous, until the last ten minutes, when it sends you reeling with the implications and repercussions. It's a fabulously acted episode — especially the work of Ona Grauer, who makes more than the most of her 0.5 lines and manages to move us through facial movement alone. In fact, all the guest stars here do an incredible job of fitting in with the SG-1 members, and the added numbers bring an interesting tension to the episode.

Season six has so far shown us a lot of changes in the characters' lives;

"Frozen" does a very good job of showing the disorientation they're feeling, without making it blatant, as they learn to live without Daniel. Jonas is settling into his own in the team now, and his interactions with Ayiana provide the only real warmth of the episode. The scenario of "Frozen" is fixed so as to clearly mark the distinction between isolation and intimacy. The setting is much like season one's "Solitudes," where we saw a growing intimacy and camaraderie between Sam and Jack. Here, however, the characters — from Sam to Jack to Janet to the scientists — all go about their jobs without breaking the pace to interact on a purely human level. That aspect is left entirely up to Jonas, in an attempt perhaps to remind the audience of the necessity of a fourth team member, one who can connect, human to human (or, in this case, Kelownan to Ancient).

Ona Grauer looks pretty different when three-quarters of her body is not encased in an ice block (ALBERT L. ORTEGA)

It's the first time Jonas is given the chance to expand his involvement in the team, and it works well.

Almost every interaction the characters have is marked by some sort of barrier between them — at first, the ice barricading Ayiana from the rest of the lab's inhabitants; the quarantine suits when Carter asks O'Neill to take on a Tok'ra symbiote; and the use of monitors throughout the episode to enable communication — these offer a very different feel from face-to-face communication. They all have the effect of distancing the characters from one another. And the final scene of Jack being carried through the Stargate, from the coffin-like quarantine pod to the six "pall-bearers" who carry him through, makes clear that in its extremist form, isolation from communication can lead to death.

The symbology of the last scene, which mirrors the first one so well, is striking. The episode opens with the shot of the ice block within which Ayiana is frozen, and it ends with O'Neill being transported in a quarantine unit, firmly sealed. This is the start of a major transformation in O'Neill's character; from here on, he'll be irrevocably changed; he'll have seen the other side of the symbiote issue, something he's been crystal clear and decided on since the beginning of the series. His distrust for the Tok'ra, blended as they are with the "snakes," as he calls them, is going to be challenged and altered — how can it not be, after all?

Gods & Scientists: Much is made in "Frozen" of the possibility that humans could have evolved from the Ancients; Janet puts Ayiana as having been frozen some 50 million years ago. As Jack pithily says, "Darwin would be crushed." In 1859, Charles Darwin posited that human beings evolved on Earth thanks to a process he called natural selection. Because the growth of species' populations exceeds the natural resources available to them, there would be a constant struggle for survival — only the "fittest" would survive to pass on their genes. This theory of "survival of the fittest" was hotly contested — and is still stricken from some school curricula, despite scientific consensus about the theory's validity.

When Ayiana cures people, she does so by laying hands on them. In some religious traditions, the laying on of hands can be a part of prayer, or the invocation of a higher power to perform acts of healing. In England and France, kings and queens were said to have healing powers, carried out through the laying on of hands. You'll also notice that Ayiana's placement mimics (or is the original of?) how the Tok'ra use their handheld healing device, most recently seen in "Meridian."

Interesting Fact: The actress who plays Ayiana, Ona Grauer, has appeared in quite a few television series, and she, like much of the cast of *SG-1*, has a *MacGyver* link: her mother was a caterer on the *MacGyver* set.

Why We're Space Monkeys: Continuity. Although it seems like Ayiana is a throwaway character, appearing in one episode never to be heard from again, the first scenes of the first episode of *Stargate Atlantis* prove that there's much to be said for continuity. In that scene, two Ancients are watching the demise of their home, Atlantis — and one of them is Ayiana. Not many shows pay that much attention to continuity, but the *SG-1* writers have always made an effort to keep threads and characters consistent.

Parlez-vous Gate?:
O'NEILL (throws up his hands): D'oh!
TEAL'C: What is it, O'Neill?
O'NEILL: I forgot to tape *The Simpsons*. (Teal'c looks at him.) It's important to me.

605. Nightwalkers

Original airdate: July 12, 2002
Written by: Joseph Mallozzi, Paul Mullie
Directed by: Peter DeLuise

When a scientist who may have had ties to the Goa'uld dies under mysterious circumstances, Carter, Teal'c, and Jonas investigate in a town full of people acting very strangely.

One of the most striking things about this *Stargate* episode is its very un-*Stargate*-like feel. From the tinkling music to specific shots to the conspiracy theory plot, "Nightwalkers" plays like a suspense movie pastiche. The beginning shot of Sam, awoken and rumpled in bed; the presence of the seedy motel; the Mulder-like diatribe from Jonas in the diner about the townsfolk's strangeness — all bring to mind the eerie atmosphere of *The X-Files*. The empty night streets, the closed, claustrophobic air of the sheriff's office, and the meeting place for the Goa'uld remind us of horror and suspense films like *Psycho* and *Deliverance*.

Of course, there is a definite *SG-1* twist. The Goa'uld are not easily categorized and keep cropping up in unexpected places. In this episode, the Goa'uld symbiotes were looking merely to leave Earth, and their MO is very different from what we've seen before. It's a good move on the writers' part, because it serves to make the Goa'uld more menacing — they're capable of change and adaptation.

The episode also marks a nice return to the mini-arc of Adrian Conrad, from season five's "Desperate Measures." It's been a while since the writers introduced a mini-arc, and this one fits well within the context of the beginning of season six, where everyone is trying to get their bearings within a new team dynamic and figure out where to go from there. This holds true not only for the members of SG-1, but for the cast and

Corin Nemec's smile is infectious (MIKE GUASTELLA/WIREIMAGE)

crew, whose move to a new channel no doubt brought about a lot of changes.

Fear of the dark is a powerful motivator in this episode; only when the villagers are sleeping do they fall victim to the Goa'uld's mind and body control. *Stargate* has always been very good at taking clichéd plotlines and weaving their unique mythology into them to create something original ("Crystal Skull," "Window of Opportunity," "Beneath the Surface").

A *lumbricus terrestrius*, known as a night crawler or walker, is a type of worm that usually comes to the surface when the earth is cool or wet, and is used as fishing bait. "Night walker" also refers to someone — generally a burglar or a prostitute — who plies their trade at night. In this episode, Sam uses herself as bait for the townsfolk, and is then used as bait for Jonas and Teal'c. Most of the scenes are lit darkly — from the bar to the arrival of the cavalry — but even daytime scenes are pretty stark, with a bleaching effect that never warms but makes us uneasy instead.

There's some great interaction between Teal'c and Jonas, a continuation of what we saw started in "Descent." The writers are treading very carefully here, as they clearly want to avoid an aliens vs. humans scenario within the sGC; but they're also not avoiding the fact that Teal'c and Jonas share an otherness that Sam and Jack don't.

Speaking of Jack, the only lack in "Nightwalkers" is the throwaway setup at the beginning of the episode to tell where he is. A little more integration of that story line would have brought "Nightwalkers" more closely into the season.

Gods & Scientists: Stem cells are embryonic cells that can be developed into specific and useful kinds of cells. Stem cell research is a very controversial scientific arena, as the immature cells are taken from human embryos. The aim of the research is to treat disease, but it can also be used to further research on cloning — as we see in "Nightwalkers." By cloning the Goa'uld symbiotes, Immunotech was creating genetically identical symbiotes — all formed from the same parent genes.

Interesting Fact: "Nightwalkers" got director of photography Peter Woeste nominated for a Gemini Award for Best Photography in a Dramatic Program or Series in 2004. "Nightwalkers" really does stand out, cinematographically. There are a lot of unusual camera movements, and the atmosphere of the episode — nearly all shot in the dark, fittingly enough for the title — is striking.

Why We're Space Monkeys: Sam in leather pants. She rides motorbikes, picks locks, and wears leather pants — and manages to save the world every other week. "Nightwalkers" lets us see many sides of Carter, flawlessly merged — the scientist, the woman put on the spot when Jonas interrogates her about Jack's feelings about him, the detective. And the impish sheepish look on her face when she admits to being in control when she slapped Jonas is pretty damn cute too.

Parlez-vous Gate?:
SINGER (to Carter): You worry too much. The humans have no idea what's going on here.
CARTER (pulls out a zat gun): Oh, I wouldn't exactly say that. (zats both men) You guys aren't nearly as smart as you think you are.

606. Abyss

Original airdate: July 19, 2002
Written by: Brad Wright
Directed by: Martin Wood

Colonel O'Neill has gone missing from the Tok'ra base along with his symbiote, Kanan. Daniel Jackson makes an appearance, trying to save O'Neill, but his Ascension proves to be a handicap this time, instead of a help.

Much to the fans' delight, Michael reappeared in season six for several guest spots (SUE SCHNEIDER/SHOOTING STAR)

"I'm not you." An incredible, heart-wrenching episode that begins and ends in the scenes with Jack and "special guest star" Michael Shanks. The Tok'ra/Tau'ri alliance is fraught with suspicion and miscommunication. Each is, as Sam puts it, "a passionate race," and their continued problems (see "Allegiance" and "Death Knell" in particular) are being fleshed out as the seasons progress. This is a wonderful, multilayered story line that writers like Robert Cooper, "M&M," and Brad Wright use efficiently and with great results. Exploring the idea of allies and what constitutes alliances, allegiances, and the spaces between makes for great storytelling.

Brad Wright walks a fine line between drama and melodrama; in a new type of love triangle, Jack's blending with the Tok'ra Kanan mirrors Sam's problem in the earlier seasons with Martouf. Shallan is, annoyingly, too close to Sam, and the implicit Sam/Jack relationship is a bit heavy-handed and angsty. And Jack's ex-wife, whom he still loves, is present in her features too. That's a lot of women; we already know he's a sex symbol, no need to beat us over the head.

A more interesting love thread was the one between Daniel and Jack. Both were intensely passionate, driving hard with their personal code for what they wanted — but the gulf between them is never more apparent than now. At this point the Ascended Daniel Jackson plays very strictly by the rules, and quite correctly asserts that were he to intervene, "play God," as he says to Jack, he would be no better than the Goa'uld. An interesting visitation, which brings up the theme of power that Daniel wrestles with again and again.

There are interesting additions to the *Stargate* universe. Janet mentions that while the symbiote can effectively take control of the host's body, it does not work in reverse; Colonel O'Neill cannot take control of his body without the consent of the symbiote inside him. This is obliquely contracted in earlier episodes, "Forever in a Day" and "Within the Serpent's Grasp," but both these incidents presented extreme duress and emotional turmoil so the connection wasn't as clear. In addition, both Sha're and Skaara sort of bend the rules rather than break them; Sha're works subliminally, and Skaara's moment of lucidity was due to the shock of the zat gun's blast.

We've seen Baal before, mostly in "Summit," but here he makes an awesome, oily appearance. Tall, dark, and handsome (Peter DeLuise thinks he has a great chin), Cliff Simon as Baal picks up where Seth left off. This prototype of a bad guy is still very appealing to audiences.

Gods & Scientists: A revisitation of the Orpheus myth we saw in "Descent," Jack descends to hell to rescue his beloved. This updated version of the myth has cooler CGI, but still basically tells the tale of the warrior poet who risks all for someone (or in this case, something), he believes in so utterly he'll defy the gods to do it.

Interesting Fact: All scenes with Rick were shot in four short days, before he went on holidays. In particular, the set where Baal tortures O'Neill is actually three separate sets that were later put together in postproduction. While shooting, Cliff Simon (Baal) spoke his lines to RDA's stand-in, and Rick also was filmed without the benefit of Cliff Simon. It's a tribute to the skills of these television actors, whose craft is very different from that of the more traditional theater actor, that these scenes play so naturally.

Why We're Space Monkeys: O'Neill. Rumpled, in bad clothes (I mean really, a smock?), and black slip-ons, O'Neill has a dignity that not even multiple deaths can dim.

Parlez-vous Gate?:
O'NEILL: What good's the power to make the wind blow or toss lightning around if you can't use it to spring an old friend out of jail?
DANIEL: I would if I could.
O'NEILL: You can't do that stuff?
DANIEL: I can. I just . . . I can't.
O'NEILL: Well, thanks for stopping by, then.

607. Shadow Play

Original airdate: July 26, 2002
Written by: Joseph Mallozzi, Paul Mullie
Directed by: Peter DeLuise

The Kelownans open up fresh wounds when they approach the SGC for help in an impending war. Jonas must choose between his home planet and his adopted one when his old professor asks him to join the Resistance.

"Shadow Play" deals with two of the most painful things to have occurred over the past five seasons — the death of Daniel and Jack's implantation of a Tok'ra symbiote and subsequent torture at the hands of Baal. Daniel's death is recalled explicitly, through the presence of the Kelownans and through Jack's angry lashings at the planet's delegates. It's hard not see that each time he looks at Jonas, he remembers his friend's death, and the presence of additional Kelownans — Kelownans who are asking for his help to boot — only adds insult to grievous injury.

The second event, which concluded only one episode ago in "Abyss," is much more subtly handled through Rick's portrayal of Jack. In this episode, Jack doesn't fiddle, doesn't pace, doesn't get jittery. He exhibits two moods — complacent and mad. It's a real contrast to the Jack O'Neill we're used to — in command, ever-moving, and throwing witticisms around. After being tortured for who knows how long, O'Neill raised some thick psychic walls. We come out of "Shadow Play" somber, reminded that all is not well in the world of SG-1.

This episode also wrestles with the lack of control that each character feels over the events that affect them so deeply. It's not limited to "Shadow Play," but echoes a trend that we've seen several times in recent story lines: Jack lost control of his mind and body when he was implanted with the Tok'ra symbiote ("Frozen," "Abyss"), as did Sam ("In the Line of Duty"); Teal'c lost control of his mind and body during Apophis' brainwashing; Daniel lost control of the situation and consequently died ("Meridian"); Jonas has lost control of his profession, lost his home planet, lost control of much of his life; Dr. Kieran has slowly been losing control of his mind over the last twenty years. "Shadow Play" shows what can happen when scientific experiments go awry. The idea that when you seek to control something it slips from your grasp is really effectively shown throughout the season ("Cure," "Unnatural Selection," "Paradise Lost").

The themes in "Shadow Play" are reminiscent of those that come into play throughout the whole series. Dr. Kieran tells Jonas that they didn't know what they were creating, they were merely "pursuing knowledge." With that, he enunciates one of the ideas nearest and dearest to the show, the dangers of knowledge if it's in the wrong hands. Uncontrollable, unforgettable, knowledge can destroy lives just as easily as it can improve them. The thread of the power of knowledge is one that we've seen before, from "Thor's Chariot" with the Goa'uld hand device that Sam finds and discovers she can use, to Daniel's struggle with being Ascended, from Jack's gradual loss of sanity in "The Fifth Race" to later seasons — particularly "Reckoning" — it's a theme that comes back repeatedly.

A "shadow play" is a type of theater performed with puppets, most likely originating in China, where the action is expressed by shadows projected through a screen — literally, a play made by shadows. Pay attention to the lighting in this episode, it's an integral part of the story: the scene between Jonas and Velis is especially striking, as the entire scene is shot in semi-darkness, with shadows streaked across their faces.

There's also a play on the concept of death, real and metaphorical. Jonas has to come to terms with the fact that he is "dead" to most of his people. Dr. Kieran isn't even aware that his mind is slowly dying, while we (and the characters) are all too aware of the very real absence of Daniel. "Shadow Play" takes a lot of strings and pulls them together and it does so effectively, and with emotion. As an aside, it's interesting to see how Teal'c has grown since he first relocated to Earth, when he counsels Jonas on the changes he's going through. A nice episode, made especially poignant by RDA's subtle rendering of O'Neill, in pain but pushing on.

Gods & Scientists: Schizophrenia, from which Dr. Kieran is suffering, encompasses a group of mental disorders the symptoms of which include hallucinations, delusions, and withdrawal from reality. Four main types of schizophrenia are widely recognized, and it would seem that Dr. Kieran suffers from paranoid schizophrenia: it's characterized by delusions of persecution and grandeur, hallucinations, and illogical thought processes. Are the writers redressing their earlier *oops* from "The Tok'ra"?

Why We're Space Monkeys: Sometimes, SG-1 doesn't have the last word. Velis' line when SG-1 are trying to convince him to make the Stargate public knowledge — "Of course, if it were that simple, I'm sure the existence of the Stargate would be public knowledge on Earth as well, isn't that right, Colonel?" — makes a sharp point that Jack can't help but concede. And it's a subtle move on the writers' part, reminding us that while the politics of the episode are certainly all about shadow play, not even SG-1 is all black, or all white.

Parlez-vous Gate?: The last scene adds to the episode's bittersweet flavor, and it sums up the episode's theme of the struggle between the truth and the good thing.
JONAS: That's good, Professor. They couldn't have done it without you.
KIERAN: Do you really think so?
JONAS: I know so. You saved the world.

608. The Other Guys

Original airdate: August 2, 2002
Written by: Damian Kindler
Directed by: Martin Wood

SG-1 is captured by a Goa'uld in the service of Anubis, and an anti-Dynamic Duo of scientists sets out to free them — whether they want it or not.

Three episodes in season six stand out as comic relief: "The Other Guys," "Nightwalkers," and "Sight Unseen." While "Nightwalkers" had suggested tongue-in-cheek references to horror and camp classics, and "Sight Unseen" the effects of CGI (which actors react to but don't actually see), "The Other Guys" offered by far the most physical humor of any episode to date.

"Peter [DeLuise] usually gets the funny scripts," commented director Martin Wood. And boy, this is one funny script. This one-off, a necessary breather after the "Redemption" mini-arc and most especially after "Abyss," was an episode that is exactly what it purports to be — a giant rollicking good time that every sci-fi nut wishes would happen to them . . . and probably, like Felger, occasionally daydreams about.

There are many homages to the *Star Trek* franchise in this episode — behind the Goa'uld Khonsu, for

John Billingsley gives great geek! (ALBERT L. ORTEGA)

instance, is a Klingon sword. Coombs' and Felger's little interchange near the beginning of the episode and Coombs' later "red shirt" reference pay homage to that massive shadow that every science fiction television show must work under. But as usual, both writers and actors work to update the traditional science fiction tropes. Patrick McKenna in particular, an excellent physical actor, among other things, really adds to the difference between SG-1 and "The Other Guys" with his awesome gracelessness. Anyone who's seen *The Red Green Show* knows that Patrick McKenna does nervous like nobody's business, and here he uses that screwy energy with small, jerky gestures and eye movements without compromising the intelligence of the character. Sure, he's flighty as heck, but he's also smart as heck, too. And John Billingsley's scruffy-haired nerd (or is it geek?) is picture-perfect.

"The Other Guys" allows an injection of humor partway through a tumultuous season, continuing the series' penchant for making fun of itself without sacrificing the integrity of the premise. Seen from the outside, SG-1 *is* a little mythical in stature. How many times have they saved the planet? (Eight, according to Teal'c, who's apparently keeping count.) How often have they come out of situations that no one should survive? How real *are* they?

Contemporary viewers don't get caught up so much in the "realness" of a given show, the way that audiences have in the past. In Elizabethan times for instance, drama was an escape, a place for the common man to live the lives of others who are powerful and get the girl at the end. Greek dramas were cathartic, written to perform a social function, and they almost always had a didactic message. But *SG-1*, with its contemporary flavor, assumes the audience already has background knowledge when they sit down to watch. It's one of the reasons I think that highlighting of the *Star Trek* series is so amusing. Captain Kirk took himself *way* too seriously; Colonel O'Neill *never* takes himself seriously. Again, the antihero thread is highlighted here, not only with the character of O'Neill, but also in the characters of Coombs, Felger, and Meyers. Meyers, who gets less airtime than the anti–Dynamic Duo, nonetheless adds his own flavor — he is the prudent scientist. All three have wonderful scenes that get us laughing at them, and ourselves through them.

On the down side, the ending was just a complete groaner. We slide from tongue-in-cheek to just silly as Felger gets a new set of parameters with which to daydream. Perhaps this element of fantasy is a sly reference to a certain set of fan fiction writers? It's handled even worse in "Avenger 2.0." In fact, put side by side, "The Other Guys" is the better episode.

Gods & Scientists: We saw Khonsu way back in the pilot as well, as a Goa'uld in Apophis' fortress, although he's not named. The mythical Khonsu was son of Amon and Mut. He was sometimes depicted with the head of a hawk, and sometimes as a naked boy. In Khonsu's palace in "The Other Guys," you'll notice the jackal heads on either side of his throne. This is to signify that Khonsu is in the service of Anubis, and not a powerful Goa'uld in his own right. However, his Jaffa are loyal to him until Anubis explains he is not a Goa'uld "god" but a Tok'ra. The details are a little sketchy here — where exactly is the proof that Khonsu is a Tok'ra? How then do they differ from the gods the Jaffa worship?

Interesting Fact: Commenting on her hat during the filming of this episode (which is much more like the one we saw Daniel Jackson wear in earlier seasons): "I figure you oughta be cute while you're killing things." She also comments, "I especially like the ending, where I get to smooch somebody and he doesn't die." And remember those other hats SG-1 used to wear? Chris Judge told participants at a recent convention that the reason for the change was because Amanda had "hair issues."

Why We're Space Monkeys: Jonas smiling through every single new thing he encounters, including being incarcerated. Man that guy is peppy and optimistic!

Parlez-vous Gate?:
COOMBS: Jay . . . are you sure about his?
FELGER: Think about it, Simon. What would Colonel O'Neill do if he was here now?
COOMBS: You want me to shoot you?

609. Allegiance

Original airdate: August 9, 2002
Written by: Peter DeLuise
Directed by: Peter DeLuise

An invisible enemy creates tension between the Jaffa and the Tok'ra at the SGC's off-world base.

"Allegiance" takes three of the main races and puts them together in a tense situation to see what comes of it — a bit like adding block after block to a tower to see how long it takes for it to crumble. For any building to stand firm, its foundations have to be strong; "Allegiance" gives us the first signs of fissure in the three-way alliance between the Tok'ra, the Tau'ri, and the Jaffa.

In a continuation of the Jaffa arc in season five's "The Warrior," this episode is a great illustration of how an allegiance is built — and, fittingly, architecture plays a central role in it. Sam comments to Malek about the Jaffa operating as a fifth column within Goa'uld ranks. A fifth column is a term that dates from the Spanish Civil War in the 1930s describing a group of subversives who try to undermine the enemy from within — sort of a humanized Trojan Horse. The military's architectural structure is also displayed: the term refers to columns of troops. Structurally speaking, a column is a supporting element — it holds things up; in "Allegiance," the Jaffa warriors acting as subversives within the Goa'uld army are supporting the actions of the Tau'ri, the Tok'ra, and the other Jaffa — they are an additional structure to bolster the fight against the Goa'uld.

The funereal structure that's holding the three dead Tok'ra is also reminiscent of architecture — it looks almost like scaffolding — and the circle of people, divided neatly into the three factions surrounding the bodies creates perfect geometrical symmetry. This rule of threes is repeated later on in the episode when the factions have drawn together to find their invisible enemy, and split up into groups of three — one from each group.

"Allegiance" is a solid episode that offers some real insight into the characters and different races that form the *Stargate* universe. The conversation between Jacob and O'Neill is particularly moving; it's the first time we've seen O'Neill talk about his experience with Kanan, and the intimate, confiding air between the two is surprising, and very touching. Sam and Jolinar were blended — all Tok'ra hosts are blended with their symbiotes — but Jack and Kanan were not, and it creates additional difficulty for Jack because he cannot sympathize with the Tok'ra. The idea of blending, however, adds another architectural metaphor — the blending of different minds, different cultures, to forge a strong allegiance.

The Jaffa in this episode hold up well. They are an enslaved race thirsting for freedom, built on loyalty and used to being used by others. The tricky portrayal of the Jaffa as being under a yoke without suggesting victimization is accomplished through choreography — by the stance of all the Jaffa in the episode. They're loose, aware, but hands always at the ready for a weapon. Much better than the more uneven Jaffa stories like "Bloodlines."

Gods & Scientists: The word "allegiance" (as distinct from "alliance") comes from the Old French, *liege*, a sovereign in feudal law, and indicates a loyalty or obligation of loyalty to another person, nation, or cause. The title of the episode doesn't make clear which race has pledged allegiance to which, putting all three on the same footing — equal in the fight against the Goa'uld, despite their differences. It's almost an ironic use of the word "allegiance" since there is no real leader among the three races.

In Western symbology, three is known as one of the sacred, or perfect, numbers. It appears throughout history and literature — Christianity's Holy Trinity; Dante's *Divine Comedy*, entirely written in "third rhyme"; the adage "bad luck comes in threes." Seeing things in terms of threes, rather than "us vs. them" often allows a more even, balanced approach to an issue, and that's what we see here — the gradual formation of an equitable team, the putting aside of differences, and the construction of solid foundations.

Interesting Fact: At a recent convention, Peter Stebbings, who plays Malek, revealed that he had never seen the final product of any of his *SG-1* appearances (he also appears in the next episode, "Cure"), and didn't know the producers had done anything with his voice (they flanged his voice to get the voice of the Tok'ra symbiote) until a friend asked him how they'd made him sound so different.

Why We're Space Monkeys: Sam finally shows some impatience with Jack's questions when she's trying to work. For six seasons we've watched her answer and explain her technological jargon patiently. "Allegiance" is the first time we've ever seen her interrupt him. The snappish, stressed-out tone Tapping puts into her voice is perfect for the moment — after all, frustration with a coworker is something everyone has to deal with every now and then.

Parlez-vous Gate?: Another in a line of somber episodes. One line particularly stands out:
MALEK: Many Tok'ra have died in recent days. To lose another of our number in a place that we had thought was refuge . . . it is difficult.

610. Cure

Original airdate: August 16, 2002
Written by: Damian Kindler
Directed by: Andy Mikita

A planet offers SG-1 a miracle cure for pretty much everything — but discover that it's made from Goa'uld symbiotes that are being spawned by none other than the queen of the Tok'ra herself.

This is Damian Kindler's second writing credit after "The Other Guys," although he shared story line credits for season two's "Need." He has lots of backstory to deal with here, with several large arcs being drawn — that of the Tok'ra queen, Egeria, the tritonin created from her offspring, and the difficulties of Tok'ra/human relations. (We'll see it again in "The Changeling," which marks a huge change for Teal'c, and for the Jaffa as a race.) "Cure" creates a complementary pastoral background to the rather dark story of experimentation and a population's imminent downfall.

The queen of the Tok'ra, whom we heard mentioned in season four's "Crossroads," makes her first and only appearance in this episode. Although the Tok'ra had long believed that Egeria had been destroyed by Ra, we discover that she had been placed in stasis in a canopic jar (much as Isis had in "The Curse") on Pangara. Shaq'ran, a Goa'uld who had driven Ra from Pangara, had set up a stronghold directly on top of his temple on Pangara; Egeria was found by the Pangarans in the ruins of Ra's city, and experimented on for fifty years. She mutilated her off-spring's genetic memory, bringing them forth as blank slates. Freed finally by Kelmaa's sacrifice, Egeria dies in a bittersweet scene, having seen the great race she engendered.

The pace tends to plod along a bit at times, but "Cure" makes up for it with a few intense moments — a particularly bitter one is when we realize that instead of thousands of blank symbiotes being used for the miracle drug, there could have been instead thousands of Tok'ra descendants — an army ready to take on the Goa'uld. The Tok'ra and the humans continue on their rocky road to an alliance, and the Tok'ra continue to be an unknown factor. The blatant hypocrisy of their reactions to the queen's situation is a bit disconcerting — if they're okay with torturing a Goa'uld for fifty years, are they any better than the Goa'uld themselves? Even Jack — who of all the members of SG-1 has always been the most vocal in his hatred for the Goa'uld — exhibits more empathy than the Tok'ra do — especially surprising given his recent experiences at the hands of Baal (in "Abyss").

The Goa'uld and the Tok'ra seem to have a matriarchal social system, which is ironic considering how few of the Goa'uld we've seen with any power have been women. Hathor was a queen, but she was running around the galaxy with no entourage — certainly not reigning over anyone that we could see.

Gods & Scientists: The Tok'ra all spring from Queen Egeria. Although this is not the same thing as their having a matriarchal society, it is reminiscent of that. Matriarchy is a tradition in which social and economic power lies with the women or mothers of a society. Matriarchal societies are rare today, and it is disputed whether many have in fact existed in history. There are, however, many known cases of matrilineal societies, wherein children are known through their mother rather than their father. There is some dispute as to whether Japan was a matriarchal society before becoming patriarchal upon contact with other countries.

Interesting Fact: The name of the planet Pangar had to be changed when the crew realized they had accidentally named it after Buzz Lightyear's (of *Toy Story* fame) homeworld.

Why We're Space Monkeys: The look of pure smug glee on Teal'c's face every time he gets to tell someone that the "false gods" are dead. Nothing gives him more pleasure.

Parlez-vous Gate?:
TEAL'C: A Goa'uld offspring is born with the intellect and knowledge of the queen who bore it. Normally, the fully developed personality would emerge, allowing the symbiote to control the host immediately upon blending.
O'NEILL: Glowing eyes, cliché behavior, evilness, that kind of thing.

611. Prometheus

Original airdate: August 23, 2002
Written by: Joseph Mallozzi, Paul Mullie
Directed by: Peter Woeste

A plot hatched by Adrian Conrad and Colonel Simmons leads to the U.S. Air Force's new spacecraft Prometheus *being stolen, along with SG-1 and a news reporter.*

While the SGC's relations with the press are never easy or open (take "Secrets" or "Heroes," for example), "Prometheus" opens the issue up by tackling it only tangentially. For the first fifteen minutes it seems that the journalist will be a main focus of the episode, but the plot abruptly shifts, a shift marked by O'Neill's outburst to Major Davis (whose first name,

Colonel Simmons (John de Lancie) gets his in "Prometheus" (ALBERT L. ORTEGA)

we learn, is Paul). It's also an allusion to the myth of Prometheus, as Conrad and Simmons steal the ship from the government, much as the mythical Prometheus stole fire from Zeus.

It's an interesting take on the idea of concealment; generally speaking, the SGC is forever having to hide — hide the program, hide the Stargate, hide from politicians, the press, the world, the Goa'uld. Here, Jack makes no attempt to conceal his rage (some excellent acting from both Richard Dean Anderson and Colin Cunningham in this scene, tension and powerlessness tangible in the air around them). "Prometheus" takes the theme of secrecy — seen a lot in the *SG-1* universe ("Secrets," "Politics," "Watergate") — and adds a twist, so that it's no longer a clichéd trawl through press and military relations, but a game of hide-and-seek and cat-and-mouse through the X-303 as well as the labyrinth of the U.S. Air Force's hierarchy.

"Prometheus" concludes the mini-arc of Colonel Simmons and Adrian Conrad, whom we've followed for a whole season now. This small arc got a lot of attention and played an integral role in how the politics of the SGC played out. John de Lancie plays a wickedly good bad guy, and his comeuppance is almost movie-like in its dramatic flair. Simmons and Conrad allow the writers to draw a parallel they haven't been able to before; side by side, there's not much difference between the human and the Goa'uld. A scary realization, and one that brings back the theme of power and its effects that we've seen throughout the series' six seasons ("Politics," "The Serpent's Venom," and "Desperate Measures," for example). *SG-1* goes to great pains to demonstrate the effects of power mongering, through all the races, from the Asgard ("Red Sky") to the Tok'ra ("Crossroads") to the Tau'ri in this episode.

While most technology SG-1 gets their hands on somehow gets snatched from them during the course of the episode or soon after, the *Prometheus* sticks around for a bit — all the way through to season eight's "Prometheus Unbound." We'll see it a couple more times in season six as well. And look for the continuation of this thread (the world that Adrian Conrad and Simmons were going to) in "Smoke and Mirrors."

Jack O'Neill and Michael Shanks (no wait, Shanks just does the *voice*)

(COURTESY JO STORM)

Gods & Scientists: Prometheus was the Greek god of fire, known for playing pranks and for his intellect (his name means "Forethinker"). According to the poet Hesiod, there were two main legends relating to Prometheus. He tricked Zeus into eating bones and fat instead of meat, so Zeus hid fire from humans; Prometheus stole it back, and here the stories vary. We most often hear of him being punished by being chained to a mountain top where an eagle ate his liver every day, and every day it regrew. An eternal damnation, until Hercules killed the bird. The other legend, however, has Zeus creating Pandora as a punishment to humans and as a price for the gift of fire. See "Politics" for more on Pandora.

Why We're Space Monkeys: The SGC doesn't hesitate to pull strings and resort to borderline bribery when it has to. While we're used to seeing General Hammond and SG-1 as stand-up sorts of people, we're not allowed to forget that when the chips are down and things go against the program's best interest, they'll stalwartly if not happily go behind people's backs and get the job done.

Parlez-vous Gate?:
DAVIS: Did he say anything to you?
TEAL'C: He was uncharacteristically silent for a Goa'uld.

612. Unnatural Selection

Original airdate: January 10, 2003
Story by: Robert Cooper, Brad Wright
Teleplay by: Brad Wright
Directed by: Andy Mikita

When the Asgard make a grave error in judgment, Thor asks SG-1 to save the galaxy from the Replicators. When they arrive on the planet, they find that the Replicators have assumed a surprising form.

"I have a theory why you lost the war." Jack's not-so-gentle reprimand of Thor sums up this episode nicely; not only does "Unnatural Selection" tackle the fight against the Replicators, it also shows us what makes *SG-1* so interesting — the battle between members of the same team, and against oneself.

This episode sees a return to team play, and to a lighter tone (at first), after the darker feeling of the last several episodes. It's been a while since there were a bunch of laugh-out-loud lines to enjoy, and this episode offers up a gaggle of them — strange, considering how sad it is. There are some wonderful team moments, notably between Carter and O'Neill, and then between O'Neill, Teal'c, and Quinn — where else are you going to see three grown men sitting around eating ice cream? The camaraderie between all four team members is really evident in this episode, and it comes as something of a relief to see that Jonas has managed to make his way into the team despite all of O'Neill's (and our) misgivings.

This is the last Replicator episode we'll see for a while, and the way in which it's handled is original, but bittersweet. There's a lot of that sentiment in season six ("Frozen," "Abyss," "Cure," "Metamorphosis," "The Changeling" for just a few examples), perhaps as a result of all the changes that the series has been adapting to. "Unnatural Selection" pitches SG-1 against a whole new form of Replicator, and the question arises — how do form and content mix in the *Stargate* universe? How much are the Replicators still Replicators, despite their outward appearance? The character of Fifth is intriguing, although Sam and Jonas are the only ones to realize that he's different and to try and fill in the shading between black and white. It's also a return to the idea of the fifth column, which we saw in "Allegiance," but this time it's inverted. Fifth is the "fifth column" for the humans, acting as their subversive operative against the Replicators.

In a nice cinematographic move, the bleakness of the planet — filmed in shades of sepia, which really brings an air of isolation and separateness to the atmosphere — reflects the bleakness of the galaxy's fate at the hands of the Replicators. To O'Neill, the Replicators always have been and always will be machines. His stance on this is a slight departure from the usual sympathetic Everyman character. While Quinn, Carter, and Teal'c grow and change, O'Neill generally does not. The startling rigidity from a character we've come to like and respect is a great way to show *us* the shadings of an otherwise black-and-white Jack.

The danger that SG-1 willingly walks into is made very clear, and we're once again brought face to face with the fact that these characters are willing to give their lives for a greater cause. And that, perhaps more than anything else in the episode, contrasts sharply with the decision Jack enforces at the end. No doubt that's the reaction the writers were looking for, the shock and heartache we feel when the episode closes with Fifth's slow-mo'd betrayal.

An important, interesting, and a well-executed episode on everyone's part. Amanda Tapping in particular is wonderful as she tries valiantly to save SG-1 and Fifth, and as she unwillingly obeys her commanding officer in condemning Fifth to death at the hands of his peers, as is Chris Judge's portrayal of Teal'c's calm acceptance of O'Neill's final command. And although we've seen them in a handful of episodes by now, the Replicators never fail to send a shiver up the spine — they don't *look* all that threatening, but the sound they make is frankly creepy.

An awesome episode whose great story line will be picked up again in season eight.

Gods & Scientists: The episode's title is a play on the scientific process of natural selection, according to which a species adapts to its environment by genetically transmitting selected changes that will allow it to survive (see "Frozen"). Unnatural — or artificial — selection, on the other hand, is a biological procedure through which certain characteristics are reproduced or eliminated by artificially controling certain factors. This process, practiced by First in this episode, allows him to remove the flaw that was reproduced from Reese's programming ("Menace") — and then plan to put it back in when Fifth does not live up to expectations.

Interesting Fact: Don S. Davis on fellow cast member Tapping: "Amanda; the myth they created for Doris Day, that *is* Amanda. She is warm, the camera loves her, and she can take a scene that really should never be in public and make it ring like a diamond."

Why We're Space Monkeys: The ice cream scene. Teal'c, Jonas, and Jack camped out in the food storage locker, with Jack and Teal'c fighting wordlessly over ice cream. Great tension releaser.

Parlez-vous Gate?:
O'NEILL: No. No. We full well expected the other shoe to drop eventually.
THOR: We can only hope this will be the last footwear to fall.

613. Sight Unseen

Original airdate: January 17, 2003
Story by: Ron Wilkerson
Teleplay by: Damian Kindler
Directed by: Peter Woeste

People are seeing things: head for the hills!

The third goofy instalment for season six. The writing team of "M&M" wrote "Nightwalkers," while Damian Kindler penned this and "The Other Guys." All three are cited by fans as low points in season six, one-offs that do little more than alleviate tension from larger, more dramatic episodes and arcs. This trend has been followed throughout *SG-1*'s development. The harder-edged, "sciencey" episodes are muted or else contrasted with the more whimsical, fantastical episodes. Season one's "The Nox" is an early example of this fantastical element.

However, unlike "The Nox," later whimsical pieces did not carry a didactic message, and they lack the heart that we saw in season one. In "Nightwalkers," the premise of immature Goa'uld and human intelligence trumping alien arrogance — as Sam put it so unsubtly, "You guys aren't nearly as smart as you think you are" — was silly and just thrown in alongside the "Goa'uld as Goth" element. Very much in the vein of the feature film *Men in Black* and perhaps *Evolution*, "Sight Unseen" flaunts its CGI, overdoses on paranoia — but not a heck of a lot else. The team doesn't seem to be too concerned that Jonas may be going nuts from his exposure to naquadria (the other Kelownan scientists all did), and this lack of tension (like the absent Jack from "Nightwalkers") ruins any character continuity.

Thankfully, we're already clued in to the idea that this is a whimsical episode thanks to the music, an often overlooked element of this series in particular, but even it has an inauthentic feel, almost like it's parodying itself — which would be fine, but I would have preferred more, well, *heart* in this one. As it is, at the end of the episode, besides the sly Sam and Jack innuendos, I couldn't help but say, "So what?" The region 2 DVD from France translated this episode to "Hallucinations." In that vein, let's just chalk this one up to a bad trip, and leave it at that. See season eight's "Citizen Joe" for a better outing of whimsy.

Gods & Scientists: Not unlike this episode, humans are covered in weird-looking things that we can't see — scientists call this our "normal flora." Our skin and our digestive and breathing systems are literally covered in bacteria. They are helpful bacteria though, because they take up microscopic space that might otherwise become the breeding ground for disease. In fact, in this context, scientists refer to the individual human body who carries the bacteria as the "host." Eerie, n'est-ce pas?

Interesting Fact: Peter Woeste notes that there is, actually, more than one director per episode — it's just his name at the top. Second and sometimes third units will often film simultaneously, which is one of the reasons an entire episode can be shot in about a week.

Why We're Space Monkeys: Jonas Quinn is fun, you can't deny it. And he makes the most of seeing weird, glowy, slimy things (which in reality are little black boxes later matted over). Still trying to fit in, despite his almost Sam-like ability to save the day, his infectious smile and heartfelt camaraderie is welcome as the team continues to struggle with the loss of Daniel Jackson.

614. Smoke and Mirrors

Original airdate: January 24, 2003
Story by: Katharyn Powers

Teleplay by: Joseph Mallozzi, Paul Mullie
Directed by: Peter DeLuise

Senator Kinsey is shot and killed, and all the evidence points toward Colonel O'Neill as the assassin.

"Foothold" was a great episode, and it's nice to see a thread revisited in a totally new way. Gone are the strapping, tentacled aliens; instead we only have inferences. This is a great way to keep both seasoned viewers and newer ones interested. Long-time viewers have a sense that the *Stargate* universe is continuous, while newer viewers are not lost in the backstory shuffle.

From a continuity angle, this episode draws threads together nicely. We keep hearing about the dreaded Area 51, but to see Sam Carter and a technician enter a secure area and actually handle objects suggests that artifacts just aren't just collected and then shut away forever like something out of *Indiana Jones*. Numerous mentions are made to the testing of alien technology, and, more importantly, we are brought into an extremely contemporary framework with the capitalist ideal of buying technology to reproduce it commercially for an unsuspecting public. Ten new patents had been traced directly to technology procured by SG teams and housed in a supposedly secret area. The commercialism of contemporary America gets a wink here as SG-1 has to fight not just the Goa'uld, but its own organizational structure.

Also nicely done here are is the way the writers show the general level of paranoia that can result when working under such secrecy. Jonas Quinn refers specifically to O'Neill's work in "Shades of Grey" when he alludes to O'Neill's past missions, which the rest of SG-1 weren't always privy to. Agent Barrett, first seen in "Wormhole X-Treme," reappears as the stalwart, gold-hearted operative in an otherwise seedy operation. Unfortunately, actor Peter Flemming looked more sad than stalwart during this episode. We keep waiting for him to double-cross Sam. That, coupled with the other niggly things really lowered the value of an otherwise excellent story. From the beginning of *SG-1*, the NID were characterized as "rogue operatives," a few really bad guys who acted out of desperation and with extreme cunning. Now suddenly, they have offices, secretaries, respectability, and they handle contraband weapons operations like they were corner stores?

"Smoke and Mirrors" makes some good advances in the characters. Whereas in "Ascension" Jack, Teal'c, and Daniel all suspected Sam of going insane when she told them about her invisible, alien boyfriend, here, there's no suspicion that Jack actually did shoot Kinsey. Instead, the team rallies to prove his innocence, never doubting him for an instant. While the title of the episode refers to the use of trickery to create a false spectacle, the episode itself is all about trust; trusting Jack, trusting Agent Barrett, trusting that they'll make it over the hurdle without serious upset, and, in the end, trusting Senator Kinsey to keep his side of the bargain with Jack. It's a nice turn-around, and good to see how the team has grown over the last year, even without Daniel. They're moving on, and "Smoke and Mirrors," more than any episode so far this season, marks the fact that they now have new enemies, new challenges, new team dynamics.

Gods & Scientists: The first recorded patent was in 1421 in Florence to Filippo Brunelleschi, an architect and engineer; he got the patent because he claimed he had invented a new way of transporting goods up the Arno River, and he would not develop it until others were prevented from stealing his idea. He walked away with the right to exclude all new means of transport on the river for three years! Thankfully, things have changed somewhat since then. A patent is a government sanction to an individual or group for the exclusive right to make, use, or sell an invention. Patents usually have a time frame (twenty years, for instance), after which period they must be renewed or they fall into the public domain. Some countries even patent new forms of life developed through genetic engineering.

Interesting Fact: "Smoke and Mirrors" is also the name of a production company used by special effects supervisor James Tichenor for postproduction work on *SG-1*.

Why We're Space Monkeys: A competent character actor, Colin Cunningham (seen recently in Showtime's *The L Word*) is, as always, ready to tackle his parts in exciting ways. Although he has only three seconds of airtime in a fight, his was the best piece of choreographed fighting in the series; authentic, brutal, and very, very short — like real fights tend to be. The more colorful training sequences that we see in "The Warrior" and even season seven's abysmal "Birthright" are what viewers are more used to, but they lack a certain intensity that's present in "Smoke and Mirrors." It's hard to come back from *one* direct blow to the face, never mind ten or twenty, à la Arnold Schwarzenegger or Bruce Willis.

Parlez-vous Gate?:
JONAS: How'd you learn to drive?
TEAL'C: It was Daniel Jackson that instructed me.
JONAS: When was that?
TEAL'C: I believe the year was 1969.

615. Paradise Lost

Original airdate: January 31, 2003
Written by: Robert Cooper
Directed by: William Gereghty

Harry Maybourne and Colonel O'Neill are trapped on an alien planet with no way home, and as time passes they become increasingly paranoid about each other's motivations.

The setup for "Paradise Lost" is intriguing, but really unnecessary. The beginning of the show has many cut shots of the Harry/Jack relationship — Harry as bad-guy-with-good-intentions, and Jack grudgingly liking him. Ultimately, this first sequence fades into the background as the two actors do more than an adequate job of revealing their history with one another, keeping the stakes high, and their interactions true. Both men are hard-hitting, unscrupulous, and quite used to doing whatever is necessary to get the job done. Both are also a little paranoid, even *without* mind-altering substances in their bodies. The writers could have chucked the whole beginning sequence in favor of more airtime between the two men and not lost a thing in backstory.

This episode, which looks at how language, and lying in particular, can mold our lives, is an oblique revisitation of an earlier episode, "A Hundred Days." The Utopian thread is carried in that earlier episode as well as in this episode; a simplistic but somehow advanced society, a common bonding of morals and ethics, and a remote location inaccessible to the uninitiated. Also revisited is Sam's obsession with saving Colonel O'Neill, but as always, the writers twist it a bit so that her motivation is to avoid losing another team member, rather than the dreaded specter of the Sam/Jack relationship.

There were two spots that didn't really track in "Paradise Lost": one was Sam's extreme, almost tantrum-like reaction to Dr. Lee when she sees him packing up; the other was the sudden appearance of Teal'c in the women's changeroom. While they are a close-knit team and have shared a great deal together, I don't think Teal'c would ever step over protocol like that, especially on base. As for Dr. Lee, is he not under the direct command of a superior officer, as Teal'c and Jonas are? Would that make him under *Major* Carter's authority?

The Furlings are mentioned, one of the races first alluded to in "The Torment of Tantalus." We've heard very little about them, and Jack's observation that anything with a name that sounds like a furry little animal seems a little suspicious resonates with this viewer, at least.

"Paradise Lost" is named after the 1667 book of the same name by John Milton. A ten-book, blank-verse epic poem, *Paradise Lost* tells of the origin of evil itself. It begins in the Christian hell, then moves on to Heaven, and then to Earth. Many believe that Satan is the protagonist of the book, as he struggles to accomplish his goal of corrupting mankind, but the narrative features main personages from the Bible. In much the same way, although it seems like the episode "Paradise Lost" focuses on Harry Maybourne, as he fights to regain his sanity and make sense of the world he's now living on, Harry is just one of many protagonists. Jack, Sam, and even Teal'c, in an understated and tender way, also vie for the story. "Paradise Lost" is not so much about the origin of evil as it is about the difficulties inherent in trusting someone, or about survival. Evil has no place in the episode — Harry is far too complex a character to be merely "evil," and the episode nicely showcases the two men as they deal with a situation neither had expected and forge a new existence, however temporary.

Watch the early crane shot of Harry and Jack as they find themselves in this "utopia" for the first time — it's the same style of shot we see in season seven's "Fallen," when Daniel comes back. The crane shot suggests omniscience and it works very well in these two instances, showing how these views change when they are seen from a more removed point of view. Another great idea was turning the film to high contrast, documentary style, when O'Neill is in the grips of the substance's hallucinatory effects. Not only does it borrow from movies like *Black Hawk Down* and *Apocalypse Now*, but it gives a nod to wartime photographers with their handheld sequences and close, bobbing shots. When the effects of the plant wear off, the film goes back to its normal color saturation; a nice storytelling technique that shows a great deal without having to tell us anything explicitly.

Gods & Scientists: Utopian texts have been around for a long while. From Plato's *Critias* (see "Lost City"), to Thomas More's aptly named *Utopia* in 1516, to Harriet Perkins Gilman's more contemporary *Herland* in 1915, utopias and utopian societies are often represented in books and films. One of the most famous utopias that is still read widely today is Jonathan Swift's *Gulliver's Travels*, where the hero Gulliver wanders about the world, going to strange places where the people are very big, very small, or they are . . . talking horses.

Interesting Fact: Bill Dow, who plays Dr. Lee, started out as a bit character who kept coming back, right into season eight's "Avatar." He's also well known in another Canadian television series, *Da Vinci's Inquest*.

Why We're Space Monkeys: Richard Dean Anderson still earns all his stripes every time he steps in front of the camera. While he may be quip-prone and occasionally even annoying with the ad-libs (see "Birthright" for my least favorite ad-lib ever), he is still a character actor who delves deeply into his work and makes us believe, even six years later, in O'Neill's personal code of ethics.

Parlez-vous Gate?:
O'NEILL: What are you doing here?
MAYBOURNE: I can't drop by an old friend's house for a little barbecue?
O'NEILL: Well, there's that treason thing.

616. Metamorphosis

Original airdate: February 7, 2003
Story by: Jacqueline Samuda, James Tichenor
Teleplay by: James Tichenor
Directed by: Peter DeLuise

SG-1 moves to stop the Goa'uld Nirrti, who has again been experimenting on a population.

Although credits for writing, directing, photography, stunts, makeup, and a host of other production elements usually carry one name (or, as in the case of "M&M," two) after them, the truth is that television series involve more collaboration than people may think. As James Tichenor noted in his blog, "Like 'Menace' [the first episode he wrote for *SG-1*], my outline lay on the table when I went into the story meeting. And that's where it stayed. We started from scratch, me and all the writers, and we came up with a completely new story, brand new." This story was a "pay-off" for "Prophecy" and "Singularity," both concerning the Goa'uld Nirrti and her experimentation on humans.

Quite a few people have the idea that writers live and work in dank, basement apartments, pounding away on typewriters, drinking gin straight from the bottle; it's an image that just keeps going, for some reason. The truth is, writing, like any other art, is about collaboration, renewal through constructive criticism, and above all, experimentation. In some ways, "Metamorphosis" handles all the problems that writers face, and places them in a science fiction setting with DNA, explosive and uncontrollable powers, and death scenes that still chill me, even on repeated watchings.

Experimentation, and its companion, creativity, are hallmarks of humanity. Usually the Goa'uld are shown as scavengers, parasites who live off the work of other people. "Metamorphosis" sees Nirrti using technology she has found that was originally in the hands of the Ancients. And she doesn't scruple to use any and all available means (including live test subjects Wodan and Eggar) to achieve her ends. The actress who plays Nirrti, Jacqueline Samuda, mentioned in an interview that she thinks of her character as a scientist and an explorer, in some ways. Taken in that light, it's interesting to look at the episode "Metamorphosis" and see the different paths a theme can follow from one character to the next. Jack O'Neill is an explorer, but his methods of exploration take on decidedly different aspects than Nirrti's; Carter is a scientist, and the comparison between the two women is starkly revealing. While Carter is all heart aided by the mind, Nirrti is all ambition served by the mind. The two are determined, focused, intelligent — but their means are so different that their ends cannot help but be different also. The cold twinkle in the Goa'uld's eye in every scene reveals a frightening sanity. She has knowledge, and she desires more of it; and she's set in her ways — she'll do everything within her considerable power to gain the knowledge she craves. In some ways, Nirrti is an interesting character study of what threat the members of SG-1 could pose if they ever turned to the "dark side."

The character of Wodan is really interesting, and indicative of the kind of revisionist mythmaking that *SG-1* continues to explore. Both Wodan and Eggar possess psychic abilities. While Eggar has one eye, the other being misshapen to the point of obscurity, Wodan has an extra eye. This suggests that the two characters (played by real-life friends Dion Johnstone and Alex Zahara) have mutated into each other; Wodan's "third eye," associated in Buddhist faith with inner perception, feeling, the pineal gland, and the brow chakra, is bound up closely in his relationship with Eggar, who can see the thoughts of others but always looks to Wodan for leadership and advice.

Nirrti's attempt to construct a hok'taur (from the two Goa'uld words "hok," which means advanced, and "Tau'ri," which designates human), is a new addition to the mad scientist cliché, which is usually male, and usually completely nuts. Here Nirrti is chillingly in control, only giving in to the kind of pleading we've seen in other Goa'uld like Apophis and Hathor at the very end. A nice, strong portrayal of a complex antagonist, renewed by the actor, and a strong entry into revisionist mythmaking by James Tichenor (with the help of experimentation and collaboration).

Finally, kudos to the postproduction people who made the complete cellular decay of affected subjects so intensely terrifying to watch. There's something just . . . wrong about watching a person become water, and the two people who succumb to that grisly end really heighten the drama of Sam's predicament. In this case, the CGI effects were well worth it.

Gods & Scientists: Nirrti's been a veritable thorn in the side of SG-1, but her death, unlike Hathor's, is not cheesy. Okay, it's not *quite as* cheesy. By the time Wodan (perhaps an allusion to Woden, the Norse god often depicted with one eye) does his telekinetic grip of death on the ruthless Goa'uld, we really, really hate her. Jacqueline Samuda does a wonderful job as a heartless, power-hungry Goa'uld. She uses sex on Jonas as dispassionately as she uses the gene-altering machine on Sam, quite a difference from Hathor's "sex goddess" role.

Interesting Fact: Raoul Ganeev, who plays Lt. Colonel Sergei Evanov in this episode, was also in the episode "Desperate Measures," although as a different character. In "Desperate Measures" he spoke entirely in Russian.

Why We're Space Monkeys: The women characters are changing. No longer quite so easily slotted into the templates of harlot, black widow, or nice grandmother, the female characters are becoming more complex, with conflicting emotions that are truer to contemporary women than the jaded, patriarchal stereotypes we saw in "Emancipation" and "Hathor." This is a return to characters like Linea from "Past and Present" and Selmak from "The Tok'ra."

Parlez-vous Gate?:
O'NEILL: Originally we came here to rescue you, but as you can see we've run into a bit of a snag. So, if any of you can bend steel with your bare hands, or happen to be more powerful than a locomotive, just raise your hand, identify yourselves, let us know where you are.

617. Disclosure

Original airdate: February 14, 2003
Written by: Joseph Mallozzi, Paul Mullie
Directed by: William Gereghty

In this season's clip show, General Hammond and Major Davis battle it out with four other countries for control of the Stargate program.

Ah, the inevitable clip show for season six. We haven't had one in a while, so it was overdue. And as clip shows go, "Disclosure" is far above par; the story line actually matters in the grand scheme of the show, and the pacing is extremely well executed.

"Disclosure" is the first — and so far only — episode in which no members of SG-1 appear outside of flashbacks. The anchor for the episode is General Hammond, and Don Davis carries the honor gracefully and with authority. You really get a sense of just how experienced an actor he is as he puts his all into this performance, and you can't help but be persuaded by his arguments. Usually Don gets unfortunate lines like, "My hands are tied," or, "There's nothing I can do," but not in this episode.

There are some slyly funny moments — how politically correct the ambassadors are, mingling and making nice with cups of tea in hand, for example. And it's the first time the idea of an international allegiance on Earth has been followed up on; "Disclosure" is almost a mimicry of "Allegiance," set on Earth. While the three ambassadors, who are only just now learning of the Stargate's existence, are embedded in their notion of national security, only General Hammond and Colonel Chekov see the bigger picture — and on behalf of the viewers and of the people working at the SGC, they fight the good fight with words, the only weapons at their disposal. Who would have thought Chekov would become such an ally after his first few appearances on the show? Just one example of how the writers on *SG-1* really work to portray realistic human relations, where the stakes — and friends — can change.

The episode focuses on General Hammond and Major Davis finally disclosing the existence of the Stargate to the political giants of the world, but it's really a sort of evaluation of the show itself. The episode asks not only how far the SGC has advanced toward fulfilling its mandate of gaining technology to protect the Earth against the Goa'uld, but also asks how effective the show has been in making us care about its characters and its story lines. "Disclosure" is very effective as a best-of clip show that serves to inform newcomers to the series about ongoing story lines and character interaction, and also to up the international and internal tensions we rarely get to see outside of SG-1's involvement. In fact, as Senator Kinsey grudgingly admits to General Hammond, it is "well played."

Interesting Fact: We love to hate Senator Kinsey, but actor Ronny Cox's gruff voice is pretty versatile — in fact, he's a folk singer with four CDs out. For that matter, Don Davis has been alternately a carver, a painter, a sculptor, and an army captain in Korea. Oh yeah, and he has a PhD in dramatic theory and criticism, too.

Why We're Space Monkeys: Where else will you see a grey — sorry, brown — alien beaming into the middle of a political meeting? Thor's sudden appearance finally pays back some of what we've seen SG-1 do for the Asgard over the last six years — and it's a lot of fun to see him chastize Senator Kinsey, raising his . . . index (?) finger to make his point. A very fun moment that works a minor miracle in terms of the Stargate program.

Parlez-vous Gate?:
THOR: Senator Kinsey, O'Neill suggested I send you to a distant planet for your actions here, but I am reasonably certain his statement was in jest.
KINSEY: I'm sure it was, Commander.
THOR: *Supreme* Commander.

618. Forsaken

Original airdate: February 21, 2003
Written by: Damian Kindler
Directed by: Andy Mikita

SG-1 finds a crashed ship on a planet they are visiting, but helping the stranded crew is more hazardous than they expect.

One of the long arcs for season six is learning to live without Daniel Jackson. In this episode, we miss one of his aspects in particular: his lack of xenophobia. Of all members of SG-1, Daniel was the most even-keeled in his attitude. The big mistake the team makes of trusting the first people they find because they're nice and *look human* might not have been made had Dr. Jackson been there. He would have been more suspicious of the initial story Aiden Corso gave, whereas it takes a while before Colonel O'Neill gets suspicious.

The three penal escapees rely on their own tactics as a team to achieve their ends. Pendell, Corso, and Reynard are separated from one another for much of the episode. Both Corso and Reynard use sex and sexuality as a way to bait their "marks"; Reynard may look like the one who uses her sexuality more cynically, but this cultural representation of women has been seen in other episodes as well, most notably in "Hathor." Corso uses his charm and sexual appeal just as coldly and calculatedly as his fellow prisoner, even suggesting that Reynard is a lesbian so that he can bond better with Sam — oh, pity him. Only Pender uses the "less talk, more action" approach so beloved in action genres in Western culture. In a way, the team of Corso, Reynard, and Pendell act like the mythological figure of Cerberus (their ship's designation is the *Seberus*), guarding against Warrick's escape from the hell that they landed on. In addition, the three-person escapee team acts as a doppelganger (in this case, a negative double) of SG-1. Still grappling with the loss of Daniel, the three remaining team members often tighten their bonds, leaving Jonas Quinn to either make light of the situation, or save the day at the last instant — and usually, by himself. SG-1 has been in many similar situations where they were split up and had to complete their mission objectives without knowing how their teammates were faring. Corso's team is just as closely knit and just as fierce in gaining their objectives, until they are undone by greed.

In the end, "Forsaken" is a little morally heavy-handed. Sam's protests that SG-1 isn't in it solely for the technology and other goodies they can retrieve just rings false no matter how many times I watch it, and Corso's team is too easily duped into the "riches beyond our wildest dreams" thing. But there's some great chemistry between Sam and Corso, and again between Reynard and Jonas. And Dion Johnstone's Warrick is no wilting alien in need of rescue, either.

Gods & Scientists: Cerberus (note the extra "r") figured in Greek and Scandinavian myths as the guard dog to the underworld — literally, a hell-hound. Cerberus would allow spirits (or "prisoners") to pass by, but would not let them leave again. In Greek mythology the hero Aeneas descended to Hades and lulled the dog to sleep with specially prepared cake. Yep, cake. O'Neill would be so jealous.

Interesting Fact: Dion Johnstone (Warnck), whom we've recently seen in "Metamorphosis," is replaced in season seven's "Space Race" by actor and friend Alex Zahara.

Why We're Space Monkeys: The bad guys are human, the good guys are aliens. Go relativistic writing!

Parlez-vous Gate?:
O'NEILL: Lots of interesting nebulous things going on?
CARTER: Yes, Sir.
(Jack stoops and squints into the telescope)
O'NEILL: I don't see squat.
CARTER: You wouldn't, Sir, during the day.

619. The Changeling

Original airdate: February 28, 2003
Written by: Christopher Judge, Brad Wright
Directed by: Martin Wood

Teal'c awakens from a dream where he is a human firefighter. But is it a dream that he's awakening from, or reality?

An excellent instalment in season six, written by Christopher Judge, who really shows that he thinks deeply about his character, Teal'c, delving into his past and future — or in this case, alternate lives.

"The Changeling" tells the familiar story of dream worlds and dreaming in a new way. Couched in the disorienting world of dreams and delivering a bittersweet ending, the real meat and potatoes of the plot is in the *middle* of the episode, when we learn, in a short sequence of shots, what's actually happening to Teal'c. Each dream world that Teal'c inhabits feels very real — so real, in fact, that neither the Jaffa nor the viewer can discern what *is* real. Often, this sort of attempt merely frustrates the viewer, as they believe the story is merely playing with them to no purpose. While some fans did find this episode a little confusing (one online fan noted, "I'm a pretty linear person and all that jumping around from 'dream to dream' made my head kind of hurt"), careful watching reveals everything we need to know.

What a showpiece of work from Christopher Judge! After six years, it's so *nice* to see free emotional play in his character. The movement from Teal'c's rhythmical speaking cadences to the contemporary speech of "T" is excellently done, and what a shock for the viewer! On the downside, it was such a complete departure from the show, it sometimes indicated an eagerness to impress: it's a space opera, after all — where's the space? And the other element that irked, which we've also seen in "Need," is that this is *Teal'c's* dream — why do we have a scene between Bray, Shauna, and O'Neill in the hallway? Michael Shanks' appearance, his first since "Abyss," shows yet another side of this versatile actor. Rather than the confrontational, antagonistic stance he took with Jack, Daniel uses a softer, less abrasive approach with "T." Note especially the ending, which feels a great deal like "Abyss," but again with a softer feeling.

As the title suggests, "The Changeling" changes many familiar and expected elements in *SG-1*. With much less obviously sci-fi CGI and more attention to the story, this episode tips its hat to older seasons. Again, this is not because effects are not used, it's because they are seamlessly employed in service to the story, not in service to the cool factor. In particular, the panning shots that move from one Teal'c's life to another are extremely tricky to do, but the final product is quite smooth. We move from life to life with nary an eye blink: even Judge was surprised at the end product. Kudos to James Tichenor and his department on that.

Mythology still plays a role in "The Changeling" — the loss of a piece of one's self, in this case Teal'c's symbiote, parallels the rites of passage many men enact. By acknowledging that he is not indestructible, Teal'c moves beyond dualistic notions of warrior/weakling and becomes changed. Some interesting contemporary psychomachy (battle for the soul, or between vice and virtue) here as well.

Gods & Scientists: According to European legend, a changeling is the child of a creature such as a fairy or an elf, left secretly in exchange for a human child. The legend came about to explain mental or physical retardation in medieval times, and earlier. In order to get a troll to take back its change-ling child, the human mother would sometimes resort to all sorts of dis-turbing actions — up to and including placing the child in an oven, so that the "real" mother would retrieve it to avoid its being treated cruelly. In the episode, Teal'c is transposing his existence into various personas, living out a different life as "Teal'c" in each.

Interesting Fact: Coquitlam (the town name painted on the fire trucks) is a town in British Columbia. The boy in the car who Sam checks on at the beginning of the episode is Chris Judge's son, and that firefighter sliding down the pole at the beginning of the episode? That's Amanda's husband, Alan Kovacs. They do claim it's a "Family" show, after all . . .

Both Teal'c and Jack have now seen Daniel since his Ascension. Of the original team, only Sam has not seen Dr. Jackson. In the season finale, "Full Circle," a scene between Sam and Daniel was cut which would have redressed this imbalance. Unfortunately, it makes Daniel's appearance in that episode, especially his reactions to Sam, seem flat and unnecessarily cruel.

Why We're Space Monkeys: Taking risks with story lines. Television serials are usually shown in the format of a problem that needs to be solved (the "reveal"), or events which culminate in a "natural" ending (the "pay-off"). This episode buttresses the story on either side of its pivot point, allowing the story to unfold in a much less linear fashion. Mimicking this technique of storytelling, director Martin Wood does not use a great many quick shots, which would ultimately make us think we were being tricked or led by the nose. Rather, he uses steady, simple shots and lets the story and the pathos of the characters do his work for him. It's great when a director has enough con-fidence to know when to get out of his own way and let the story tell itself.

Parlez-vous Gate?:
O'NEILL: Bray, you old fart, you still alive?

BRAY: Chief, you sorry excuse for a human being. When are you going to get the message and stop visiting me?

620. Memento

Original airdate: March 7, 2003
Written by: Damian Kindler
Directed by: Peter DeLuise

The Prometheus *suffers damage and must land on a planet; the indigenous population has deliberately buried its past, and may not have the ship's crew's best interests in mind.*

"Memento," Latin for the imperative form of "remember," is the latest entry in the episodes focusing on the theme of memory and the importance of remembrance. Unlike other episodes in that vein, however ("Past and Present," "A Hundred Days," and "Beneath the Surface," for example), "Memento" is based on the idea that the people of Tagrea don't want to unbury their past. The thrust of the episode is that to live a full life in the present, we need to know our past; ignoring it leads to blindness, which can ultimately become lethal. "Memento" focuses not on the history of a particular person, but rather that of an entire population where each person has made the conscious choice to ignore their past — people willingly walking into their own trap.

"Memento" includes a wonderful montage where the Stargate on Tagrea is uncovered, with scenes and music that remind one of the uncovering of the Stargate in the original movie. Similarly, the music that plays when Tarek shows Jonas and Teal'c the etchings is also reminiscent of the music in the movie, and we get the sense that the Tagreans are, like the Abydonians, about to enter an entirely new phase of existence.

While it's easy to dislike Kelfas, it's also easy to forget that he's doing his job, using all the knowledge he has at his disposal. There lies the crux of the story, because his actions are determined by a unilateral past he in fact knows nothing of, and he is therefore blinded to the possibilities of his planet's present. Fear of change is omnipresent in this episode — what happens when you admit you have made a mistake, when you seek to retrieve something you voluntarily lost? From that standpoint it's easy to understand Kelfas' reluctance to take his followers down that road.

The episode has some good team play, and a twist on the usual schema of SG-1 in command; the *Prometheus* is commanded by another team, and we get to see the issues of command through their eyes as well as through SG-1's. Jack takes Colonel Ronson's rebuke with grace, and it coalesces suddenly how much more sedate Jack is this season — both easier in himself and more tolerant of differences of opinion. A consequence of being Tok'ra'd, tortured to death time and again, and having lost Daniel, perhaps? His acquiescence to another point of view both here and in the earlier episode "Shadow Play" is striking, and is another example of how the writers of the show work to create growth and movement within the characters.

Interesting Fact: Ever wondered how science fiction shows achieve that sleek, unlined look under the space suits? According to director Peter DeLuise, he had all the actors in *Prometheus* crew suits to go *sans* underwear under their jumpsuits!

Why We're Space Monkeys: Ring travel in an Earth ship — finally. Six years later, Earth has alien technology that works (some of it, anyway . . .), SG-1 fulfilling its mission in at least one regard.

Parlez-vous Gate?:
CARTER: The hyperdrive was fitted with a buffer, like a surge protector. It was designed to modulate extreme fluctuations in the energy coming from the naquadria. This shouldn't be happening.
TEAL'C: Yet it is happening.
O'NEILL: Yet it is!

621. Prophecy

Original airdate: March 14, 2003
Written by: Joseph Mallozzi, Paul Mullie
Directed by: William Waring

Jonas starts having visions of the future. In the meantime, Jack and Teal'c are captured by the Goa'uld Lord Mot and must avoid a Jaffa ambush to return home.

"Prophecy" is an interesting episode; it's got a great premise and wonderful underlying concepts. There are a few long scenes of circular conversations, but again the writers experiment with notions of continuity and the premise of *SG-1* dealing with the consequences of their actions. Unfortunately, we never really learn anything new about Quinn's visions throughout the episode, aside from the fact that they may have been brought about by Nirrti (see "Metamorphosis"), and although this may have been deliberate on the writers' part — admittedly, precognition *is* a mystery — we're left wanting something more at the end.

"Prophecy" is a bittersweet offering as SG-1 struggles to live with the reality of their situation: living without Daniel, and now possibly, without Jonas. Janet Fraiser's words to Jonas, "You might want to consider the possibility that you're valuable enough already," and Carter's at the end of the episode, "I knew he'd warm up to you eventually," speak volumes about how far the characters have journeyed over the last twenty-one episodes. It's taken a while, but Jack has finally fully accepted Jonas into the fold of SG-1.

The word "prophet" comes from the Greek *prophetes*, for an interpreter of God's will. In Ancient Egyptian society, prophets were especially revered because they helped the Pharaohs make decisions that affected the everyday lives of people — still today there are murals depicting their collaboration. The high priest to the Pharaoh was also known as the First Prophet, but prophets as we understand them today were rare at the time, because Egyptian gods were neither omniscient nor singular as some other gods are.

In "Prophecy," Jonas discovers the problem with having that sort of knowledge: once he has a vision, everything he does from that point on is different than it would have been had he not had the vision. The question of determinism is an important one in the *Stargate* universe, and it is explored in various ways ("Gamekeeper," "1969," "2010," "Window of Opportunity"). Here, as in other episodes, the question remains open, but the writers do a great job of opening up the complexities for us — this debate is not only philosophical, it also incorporates quantum physics, science, religion, folklore, and personal beliefs about identity and the universe. No wonder the issue stays unresolved.

In the nitpicking category, what surgeon takes the time to lock eyes with someone to claim victory *while still operating*? We understand that it's meant to heighten the tension, but Jonas is on an operating table, dying — the scene is plenty tense already.

On the upside, some very nice camera/lighting effects from director of photography Peter Woeste. The blurred, misty overexposure that characterizes each of Jonas' visions reflects how unclear the future appears to be.

Gods & Scientists: Mot was the Egyptian god of death and sterility, and the arch enemy of Baal, fighting him each year for control of the fields. Baal announced that he no longer recognized the authority of Mot, and cut him out of his life, attempting also to restrict Mot to the deserts of the Earth. Mot reacted to this challenge by inviting Baal to his home (the Underworld), where he was vanquished. Upon his death, his sister Anat, brought the corpse back for burial, and when Mot refused to resurrect Baal, she attacked him with a knife and dismembered him (a lot of that going on in Egyptian mythology). In "Prophecy," Mot is shot by Natania and we presume him to be dead.

Interesting Fact: The Heisenburg uncertainty principle, also called the indeterminacy principle, was proposed by German physicist Werner Heisenburg in 1927. As Sam explains, it states that one cannot know the position *and* the velocity of an object simultaneously. This only has validity for very small items — such as electrons — because any attempt to measure its position will automatically affect its velocity as the object is pushed around in space.

Why We're Space Monkeys: The in-jokes. They're almost a prerequisite in any medium now, but some of them are more subtle than others. Here for example, if you freeze-frame on the book Jonas picks up halfway through the episode, *Precognition*, it's actually a fake cover that was made up by the props people. As an in-joke, the author is credited as W. Waring, and the director's photograph is on the back cover.

Parlez-vous Gate?:
MOT: You are the Tau'ri of Stargate Command.
O'NEILL: And you are Lord Mot, come to punish us for our insolence, et cetera, yadda, et al.
MOT: That is correct.
O'NEILL: Yeah. Well, Mr. Mot, we're onto you. We know what you've got planned and we've informed the Tok'ra. If we don't report back on schedule . . . they're going to rat you out. They're going to tell your boss. They'll snitch on ya.

622. Full Circle

Original airdate: March 21, 2003
Written by: Robert Cooper
Directed by: Martin Wood

Anubis threatens to destroy Abydos unless he acquires the Eye of Ra, and SG-1 is called in to save them.

Not a cliff-hanger! *SG-1* changes the rules again. Well, it's not *technically* a cliff-hanger, although Sam's line about Daniel near the end is more than enough to keep us going to next season. A big, pyrotechnic episode (putting the action back into action show), "Full Circle," brings us back — back to Abydos, where it all started, back to Daniel Jackson's most fervent wish, and back to a crazy team of four saving the universe, one day at a time. It's even back to a happy-go-shippy attitude between Sam and Jack, when he wonders with some suspicion if he's asking her out on a date to Skaara's wedding until she puts his mind at rest.

The wonderfully layered interior shots full of rich colors really dump us into the sand planet of Abydos. The sanctimonious Herak reappears — do these guys have sneering contests? The Eye of Ra becomes integral, as does Daniel's understanding that the Ascended *are* the Ancients. This episode was originally written as a segue back into a feature film format, but once again *SG-1* was picked up by the Sci-Fi Channel at the last minute.

O'Neill's rather flat reaction to Skaara's death suggests that even he's not buying the idea that Skaara is actually dead. How many times has Skaara been resurrected, anyway? (Director Martin Wood joked that every time Skaara showed up it was just to die again.)

Most importantly, "Full Circle" brings us the return of Daniel Jackson. Probably Daniel's finest moment is over in a split second, as he realizes that everything he's doing is not only being watched by Oma Desala (from "Maternal Instinct" and "Meridian"), but most likely being judged as well. There is an instant transfiguration on Daniel's face as he decides a course of action that will change his whole existence — again. Daniel comes full circle when he decides to act rather than stand by watching events he could change. Although his actions have severe repercussions for him in season seven, you can't help but wonder what might have happened if he hadn't done anything. Would all of Abydos have been wiped out rather than

Ascended as they so graciously (and geez that's getting old) were? Wasn't it his very passion for helping that brought Oma to where he was? And hey, how come *she* can Ascend a whole planet while Daniel can't even stand up to one bad guy?

While Anubis is the biggest bad guy yet, he has some issues, not the least of which is his highly flappable cowl. Director Martin Wood thought that not seeing his face was a bit of a setback in terms of the story, but others disagreed. If Anubis' face is blotted out, it must be blotted out for a reason, and no CGI-inspired death mask is going to be more frightening than what we can conjure up in our own heads. What is annoying, however, is that every time we see Anubis on his throne, it always looks like he's slouching due to the constraints of his headdress (more men wear headdresses in this show than women, ever notice that?), never mind the fact that his throne is sloped like a black diamond ski hill.

Gods & Scientists: Daniel confirms that Anubis is not a Goa'uld — or not all Goa'uld, anyway. We see his "face" for the first time. Look for eerie replications of it in season seven's drone warriors. Mythologically, the Eye of Ra (which was first mentioned in the feature film *Stargate*) referred to aspects of the god Re (Ra). In particular, Hathor and Sekhmet (whom we meet in season seven's "Resurrection") have been connected to the Eye of Ra — Hathor as his daughter, and Sekhmet as the bringer of his wrath.

Interesting Fact: Sean Amsing, who plays Tobay (the guy beside Teal'c in the trench), harkens all the way back to "Children of the Gods." And the cool pyramid blowing up? It was achieved with a model and a whole lot of Ping-Pong balls, according to special effects coordinator Wray Douglas.

Why We're Space Monkeys: The same passion that led Daniel to Ascend leads him back to Earth. Regardless of the political machinations surrounding the show, writer Robert Cooper still managed to put Daniel in a position where he responded authentically to a situation. Anubis really *would* destroy a planet to get what he wanted, and Daniel really *would* do anything to stop him.

Parlez-vous Gate?:
DANIEL: Is that my stuff?
JONAS: You weren't using it anymore.

STARGATE SG-1 — SEASON SEVEN
"Everybody has an agenda . . ."

701. Fallen

Original airdate: June 13, 2003
Written by: Robert Cooper
Directed by: Martin Wood

SG-1 tries to eliminate Anubis once and for all, with the help of System Lord Yu. And Daniel is found on a distant planet, stricken with amnesia.

When, in the first five minutes of "Fallen," the camera goes from Daniel's figure on Vis Uban to Jonas' on Earth, the very effective juxtaposition provides the main focus for this episode. The major problem of Anubis and the cooperation between SG-1 and Lord Yu seem almost sidelined compared to these character crises.

Many of the personal difficulties faced by the characters are shown through camera shots and character groupings; when Jack, Sam, and Teal'c go back to Vis Uban to persuade Daniel to return with them, Jonas never appears — a clear indication of rising conflict, and a reminder of "how things used to be," bringing back the Fabulous Foursome.

Throughout the season, there will be quite a few episodes dealing with identity and belonging — "Homecoming," "Orpheus," "Lifeboat," "Grace," and "Lost City," for example. It's one of the larger arcs of season seven, dealing with how we choose and define who we are. Daniel's amnesia in "Fallen" is just one aspect of the constant struggle between knowing one's past in order to live the present more fully, and refuting one's past history in order to move beyond it. English philosopher John Locke wrote the *Essay on Human Understanding*, which set out the principle of the *tabula rasa*, or blank slate. According to Locke, humans are born with minds as empty as blank slates, and it is not until the empirical experiences of life begin to etch themselves on the slate that one's character can form. Daniel's amnesia in "Fallen" provides him with exactly that blank slate — and most people can identify with his desire to choose his own life, to not be bound by the ties of the past. He wants to make a clean start. In regaining his memory, however, Daniel also regains a sense of purpose, and attachment

Breakfast with Michael in Sacramento (COURTESY MICHELLE)

to his life — while it is freeing, his lack of memory ultimately seems to be detrimental to the planet, and to himself.

A very subtle piece of dialogue targets the sense of alienation Daniel is feeling. When he calls after Sam, "Samantha Carter?" on Vis Uban, it's instantly reminiscent of Teal'c, the resident alien on the show. In two words, the writers lay out the depths of Daniel Jackson's isolation and alienation — he is, literally, not himself, and no longer has any points of reference for his comrades or himself.

"Fallen" is very good; Michael Shanks does a great job, and the interaction between his character and Corin Nemec's makes for some wonderful development. Daniel and Jonas each have a chance to expand on their previously unexplored relationship — a really smart move on the writers' part, to ensure that neither fan faction has too hard a time accepting Daniel's return/Jonas' departure. It's a bittersweet episode because we know what's coming for Jonas; but it's also an important one, showing the team going back to their roots and coming together in a new but familiar way. And since bittersweet has been a major motif for Jonas Quinn in season six, it's a fitting homage to him here as well. The Daniel and Jonas scenes are also important because they make reference to the Lost City of the Ancients, and set the scene for *Stargate Atlantis* — an arc that will be revisited at the very end of season seven and that carries over to the spin-off series.

In a season opener as good as "Fallen" is, it's too bad one thing sticks out so blatantly: exactly why is Daniel allowed to participate on the mission to destroy Anubis? He's just come back from being "away" for over a year — he's calling Jack "Jim," he can't be in the best physical shape in the world (do Ascended beings exercise?), and there's no reason for General Hammond, or indeed the rest of SG-1, to trust that he's up to the task. And then they pair him up with the (relative) newcomer to the team? It's obvious that the writers are trying to reestablish the original SG-1 team dynamic, but it really doesn't ring true, and it does a disservice to everyone — including Daniel.

In a nice combination of form and content, there's a great debate about the phrase "the Lost City" versus "the City of the Lost"; while Jonas and Daniel debate the issue on a linguistic basis, thematically, the debate reveals the ray of hope that underscores the show. Daniel may very well have lost his memory — but what is lost is not dead, and it can be regained. A wonderful way to open the season.

Gods & Scientists: The title of the episode suggests a reference to Lucifer, of the Christian religion. Although the story is not told in the Bible, one version relates that Lucifer was the highest archangel in heaven, before he became consumed with pride and greed, and led a rebellion against God. For this, he was cast out of heaven, and became known as the original fallen angel — Satan. According to Christian doctrine, fallen angels are doomed to roam the Earth until Judgment Day, when they will be eternally banished to hell. The name "Lucifer" springs from the Latin *lux* and *ferre*, meaning "light-bearer," and this could be an additional reference to Daniel's ability to shed light on various cultures and problems, as well as an allusion to how his character will change throughout seasons seven and eight. No longer simply the "light-bearer" or moral compass of the team, Daniel's return raises more questions about what it means to be the good guy, year after year.

Interesting Fact: Michael Shanks has mentioned in interviews that filming buck naked in British Columbia in the middle of winter is not as fun as one might expect . . .

Why We're Space Monkeys: The proverb exchange between O'Neill and Shamda serves two purposes — to amuse, and to promote a cultural discovery, small as it may be. Oral cultures in particular are proverb-oriented, and while some proverbs are riddles (dancing monkeys, anyone?), many provide concise statements about life in a specific society. The fact that the writers rely on proverbs to bring together the contingents from Earth and Vis Uban offers a more in-depth perception of Vis Uban life than if they had used traditional cinematic techniques like "the village shot" or storytelling techniques like exposition.

Parlez-vous Gate?:
DANIEL: Besides, who am I going to tell? I mean, I don't, uh, I don't remember anybody, right?
O'NEILL: Good one.
DANIEL: Thanks, Jim.

702. Homecoming

Original airdate: June 13, 2003
Written by: Joseph Mallozzi, Paul Mullie
Directed by: Martin Wood

Jonas' homeworld is threatened by Anubis; Jonas is captured by Anubis; SG-1 attempts to destroy Anubis. It's one big Anubis-fest.

As a follow-up to the season opener, "Homecoming" does its job, although it's not as exciting as it could be, or as the leadup suggested it would be. It does serve the purpose of bringing Daniel Jackson back into the fold, though, without making waves out of ripples. The rapport between Jonas and Daniel is amicable, easy, and they approach the difficult subject of each other's presence with grace and aplomb. The writers do a good job of bringing out the strength and maturity in both characters without resorting to melodrama or to inane quips that would take the viewer out of the carefully ratcheted tension.

The chemistry between the actors is undeniable — say what you will about Michael Shanks' controversial departure and reappearance on the show (and it's all been said), he brings a quirky, human, unpredictable dimension to Daniel that just isn't found in any other character. And while the comparison was made between Jonas and Daniel, Jackson's return and his interaction with Jonas can only clear up doubts about the interchangeability of the two — they're very different characters in this episode, with separate agendas and emotional landscapes, elements which each actor portrays very powerfully.

The title of the episode refers to the various homecomings that are occurring on the show; while Daniel is returning to his home — both physical (Earth) and psychological (his memory, his mind) — Jonas has to question whether or not he still belongs at the SGC, his new home. This episode, more than any other in the series, pushes the idea that home is defined by a conscious choice, an idea we saw earlier in "Scorched Earth." Physical and psychological location become tinged with the reverberations of "home" when *we* choose or adapt to them. Like the first year on campus at a university, or moving to a new job in a different city, things are strange, but if we're prepared for change, then we quickly adapt and don't remain alienated by our circumstances. "Homecoming" could have easily allowed either Quinn or Jackson to fall into this sort of trap, but the strong choices made by the actors indicate that each character is continuously fighting for what he wants.

That idea is tied into the concept of coming full circle. Daniel tells Jonas "I owe you one," to which Jonas replies, "Call it even," and Jack's final words to Jonas — "You earned it" — these moments really bring out how far the characters have traveled. While Daniel died saving Jonas's planet, Jonas is now moving on from helping to save Daniel's planet and trying to heal his own; and Jonas finally gets to let go of some of his guilt through Jack's acceptance and well-earned praise. "Homecoming" offers some extremely touching moments from unexpected sources, and the actors get it right every time.

Interestingly, when Jonas first joined SG-1, he did so as a bridging factor — there was one too few members on the team, and Jonas had to bridge the gap. Similarly, in "Homecoming," Jonas Quinn returns to Kelowna as a bringer of peace and harmony — a unifier of the three nations of his homeworld. In each case, he represents a link between three separate entities. It's a wonderful way to say goodbye to the character.

Gods & Scientists: Kelowna is a real place in British Columbia, mostly known as a haven for bicyclists, skiers, and retirees.

Interesting Fact: After seven years on set, what's Chris Judge's biggest dream for Teal'c? "Hopefully," he said in an interview in 2003, "when this is all done, I *will* have hair."

Why We're Space Monkeys: The space monkey factor is almost literal this time: according to Joe Mallozzi, the original script called for Jack to call Daniel "space monkey" again, but the line was passed over in the final version.

Parlez-vous Gate:
O'NEILL: What's your situation?
DANIEL: I'm hiding. What's yours?

703. Fragile Balance

Original airdate: June 20, 2003
Written by: Damian Kindler
Directed by: Peter DeLuise

A teenage clone of Jack O'Neill shows up at the SGC; SG-1 investigates, and discovers that the Asgard may have had a hand in it.

When "Fragile Balance" aired, it quickly became a favorite among fans — mostly due to the fantastic performance by Michael Welch, who manages to get O'Neill down so perfectly that it's hard to believe it's *not* Jack O'Neill himself at a younger age. The episode toes the line between fun and out-right self-parody, and it does it well, delivering laugh after laugh as Young O'Neill bulldozes his way through the SGC, thwarted at every turn. The poor guy can't even buy himself a beer.

On a more serious note, "Fragile Balance" revives the themes of second chances and revision that we see so often in *SG-1*. "Fallen" and "Homecoming" each presented Daniel and Jonas with an opportunity to change the direction of their lives; in this third episode, O'Neill gets a chance to literally live his life over — only, as always on *SG-1*, there's a proviso — it's his clone who gets to live life over, not Jack himself. Jackson and Quinn both had to give up something in order to live out their new opportunities, and Jack must do the same.

The resurrection of the reproductive problems of the Asgard is gracefully written into the episode, neatly tied into Earth's traditional alien-abduction lore. One of the strengths of *SG-1*'s writing is the way new and old are seamlessly linked together — Ancient Egyptian mythology with current sci-fi tropes, for example — or here, alien-abduction stories with the Asgard's cloning experiments. The idea of the Asgard performing experiments on humans is chilling, and the episode serves as a reminder that although the Asgard are willingly allied with Earth for the purposes of fighting the Goa'uld, when it comes down to it, humans are still fodder for experimentation. The other things we see are the particular agendas of individuals, races, and political factions. Loki does what he does and the Asgard punish him for it. But what if the humans had never caught on? Would the Asgard have punished Loki, especially since it looked like he was getting somewhere with his research?

All in all, "Fragile Balance" gives us a glimpse of some of the show's greatest strengths — new takes on old stories, the theme of redemption as mini-Jack gets a chance at life, and some wonderful acting and laugh-out-loud scenes. It's also worth noting that this episode sets up the idea of advanced genetic makeup, which is what launches the Atlantis project in *Stargate Atlantis*'s first episode where we learn that it is only those people who are directly descended from the Ancients who can manipulate their technology.

Gods & Scientists: Loki is one of the main gods in the Norse pantheon, and is often called the Trickster. He had the ability to change his sex and shape, and was included in the tribe of gods known as the Aesir. After he played a part in the death of another Aesir, however, the gods punished Loki by chaining him to three boulders and setting a poisonous snake above him.

Interesting Fact: To play the part of a younger O'Neill, Michael Welch was given tapes of three episodes by the production crew. He says, "I rewound them a hundred times, and I was up all night studying this guy. Because, I've got to tell you, that was very challenging. Rick — he is so original. I don't think there's ever been an actor quite like him before. So it was really challenging, but a lot of fun." Director Peter DeLuise also helped the young actor along by giving him point-to-point directions on how RDA might do a certain scene. DeLuise not only directed this episode but also "starred" as the voice of Loki — a fitting choice for the comedic actor/director.

Why We're Space Monkeys: The casual atmosphere on set extends even to guest stars, who pretty much all rave enthusiastically about the cast's fun and easygoing attitude, even if some (like Chris Judge) are more prone to teasing than others. In an interview, Michael Welch laughed about when Judge teased him by yelling out, "That's a wrap on Corey Feldman!" at the end of a day of shooting.

Parlez-vous Gate?:
HAMMOND: In the meantime, I suggest we try to make him as comfortable as possible.
CARTER: I'll go set up a PlayStation.

704. Orpheus

Original airdate: June 27, 2003
Written by: Peter DeLuise
Directed by: Peter DeLuise

SG-1 launches a rescue mission to save Bra'tac and Rya'c, while Teal'c struggles to regain his confidence when he is wounded, with no symbiote to heal him.

Another retelling of the myth of Orpheus (see "Descent") but this time with a different character, Teal'c, who in this episode must descend to the depths of his own personal hell to retrieve the most important people in his life, Bra'tac and Rya'c. The episode has wonderful pacing, and some very poignant moments, starting with Teal'c in the infirmary — something neither character nor viewers are used to, given his six-year run of extraordinary health and healing powers. It's a great way to open the episode, giving Chris Judge the opportunity to really plough through some emotional terrain as Teal'c works through the loss of his symbiote.

In a similar fashion, "Orpheus" takes Daniel down a rocky road. It's been a while since Teal'c and Daniel interacted in any real way, and the fact that despite their differences — Teal'c being the most military-minded of the team, and Daniel the least — they battle some of the same demons in this episode, adds some much-missed buddy bonding to the mix.

The acting of Neil Denis (as Rya'c) and Tony Amendola especially hit the mark. Bra'tac looks seriously unwell and Amendola draws a sense of urgency out of his character's situation without it ever appearing melodramatic. Rya'c, too, is taken to a new level of maturity, and while he's been stuck in the adolescent phase for a while, "Orpheus" brings out his affection for Bra'tac, and you can see how far he's come over the years. Neil Denis does a great job with his new, young adult role, and makes Rya'c a more three-dimensional character. It also helps that this is the first episode where Rya'c is really center stage, rather than an appendage to Teal'c's character, and the shift in focus shows. The camera plays up the bond that Rya'c has formed with Bra'tac, very much a father-son relationship, with a lot of one-on-one scenes, and the dialogue between the two is both subtle and poignant. Much like the myth of Orpheus, there is a lot going on beneath the surface in this episode.

There is also an awesome shot of the three Jaffa warriors — Rak'nor, Teal'c, and Bra'tac — lining up and firing before the screen fades to white, a shot that really emphasizes the strength in unity of the Jaffa people, and Teal'c's own renewal of faith in himself. But really, it just looks damn cool. Three generations of Jaffa — the past, present, and future — is a great hint at the Jaffa story line and where it might go over the rest of the season.

At the end of "Orpheus," both Daniel and Teal'c have moved past feeling that their jobs are done, and realize that there's still work to be done — it's a big galaxy, and if they can help, they must. And finally they realize that they belong, even though they've had to give up something that made them special in order to get to that point.

This is a wonderful revision of the Orpheus myth. In the myth, Eurydice gets snatched away from Orpheus and the poet sings endless laments, stuck in his grief. In "Orpheus," both Teal'c and Daniel look back — but then they continue on, strengthening their resolve instead of forever lamenting. It's a point that's made subtly by the writers, who give us a thoughtful, insightful look at two of the lead characters, and show us something we didn't know about them, even after seven years. That's just one reason *SG-1* has held its core audience for so many years — it manages to surprise, even seven seasons in.

Gods & Scientists: In the Greek pantheon, Erebus was the son of Chaos, who also sired Nyx (night). Erebus was the father of Aether (the bright upper atmosphere) and Hemera (day), and is also said to be the father of Charon, who ferries dead souls across the River Acheron in Hades. In later myths, Hades is said to be split into two parts, one of which is Erebus, where the dead have to pass immediately upon dying. Erebus is often used as a metaphor for Hades — or hell — itself.

Interesting Fact: At a recent convention, Neil Denis revealed that he refuses to watch his own performances, because he's his own worst critic. And in the audio commentary of "The Changeling," Chris Judge noted that it's actually quite hard to lie perfectly still on a hospital bed, as he does in this episode as well.

Why We're Space Monkeys: All shows have in-jokes, but *SG-1* really takes the cake. Due to RDA's reduced shooting schedule, director Peter DeLuise wrote in an *in absentia* scene for him involving Jell-O, the food of choice for SG-1. Jell-O has appeared in a number of episodes already, including "Urgo," "Ascension," "The Changeling," and season eight's "Lockdown."

Parlez-vous Gate?:
TEAL'C: Colonel O'Neill has officially informed me that I have my "mojo" back.

705. Revisions

Original airdate: July 11, 2003
Written by: Joseph Mallozzi, Paul Mullie
Directed by: Martin Wood

SG-1 visits a climate-controlled bubble in the middle of a planet devastated by toxic waste to find the population linked in to a central computer — that seems to make streets and people vanish.

The first stand-alone of the season, "Revisions" is a spooky episode. Every guest star is perfectly cast, each with a hint of untrustworthiness. Check out the creepy way Pallan stares at Carter when they're at the dome's computer console — during filming Amanda Tapping actually had to ask actor Christopher Heyerdahl to stop staring at her like that because she couldn't concentrate! (Although he's a one-time guest star in *SG-1*, Heyerdahl has gone on to play recurring character Halling in *Stargate Atlantis*.)

It's also the first episode of the season with a substantial Richard Dean

Anderson presence, and you can really feel the difference in how the team interacts. The comfortable chemistry between them gives a sense of cohesion and unity, even when they're separated, as they are for much of the episode. The interaction flows smoothly, and the actors all look genuinely happy to be working together. Rick is noticeably absent from the final scene, however, and that marks one of the striking differences between earlier seasons' stand-alones and this one.

One of the season's through-lines, that of revision, is tackled very literally in this episode, where revision is going within or without a thing, place, or situation to see it in a different way. Throughout the episode, the townspeople are forced to see their existence differently, while SG-1 enters the Dome and sees the planet very differently compared to how they had first seen it — as nothing but a toxic wasteland. In much the same way, season seven offers viewers a chance to re-vision SG-1's team interplay, to alter their vision of the show. While many fans had difficulties getting used to RDA's reduced presence, the extra effort put in by cast and crew to establish a different ambiance that retains that *SG-1* blend of humor, sci-fi, myth, and effective storytelling, pays off as season seven offers some really good episodes.

Daniel and Carter have the most prominent roles in the episode, each doing what they do best. How long is it since we've seen Dr. Daniel Jackson surrounded by books? Putting him a musty library for a good part of the episode was an inspired choice; it makes Daniel's return feel more real, more everyday — he's no longer separate, or a new-but-old member of the team, he's just Daniel. And there's a comforting familiarity in that, especially in a season with so much change.

Gods & Scientists: The town in this episode is almost labyrinthine, with its changing streets and disappearing citizens. The oldest known examples of labyrinth designs are small petroglyphs, or stone carvings, some 3,000 years old, found throughout the world from Syria to Iceland. Probably the most well-known labyrinth was the one constructed by the Greek inventor Daedalus (father of Icarus) for King Minos, and was designed to house the Minotaur.

Interesting Fact: The cast hates those red isolation suits — with a vengeance. Michael Shanks talks about the "puddle of sweat" that would accumulate in the bottom of the suit on warm days. When they had to wear the suits, they made sure that director Martin Wood was wearing one too — at least they weren't suffering alone.

Why We're Space Monkeys: Consistency is one of the keys to *SG-1*'s success, and they work hard to maintain it. The writers don't abandon threads halfway through. Although it is a stand-alone episode, "Revisions" interweaves themes from the series' major theme arcs, such as memory and constructed/deconstructed reality. It tackles this through the use of the Link — a not-so-subtle allusion to the potential dangers of excessive reliance upon technology — and through the metaphor of the changing, labyrinth-like town — an entirely constructed reality, but it is something in which the population believe wholeheartedly.

Parlez-vous Gate?:
NEVIN: You wear strange clothes.
O'NEILL: You caught us on a bad day.

706. Lifeboat

Original airdate: July 18, 2003
Written by: Brad Wright
Directed by: Peter DeLuise

Daniel's mind is taken over by over a dozen dead souls when SG-1 finds a crashed alien spaceship full of frozen bodies.

"'Lifeboat' was a story that Brad wanted to tell last year," said Joseph Mallozzi, "but because of the type of story it was, it only worked with the Daniel character, which was why when Daniel came back, Brad dusted off the pitch and wrote the script. This is another fun stand-alone, and sort of a tour de force for the Daniel character."

Only a character like Daniel would be able to house so much potential within him. Teal'c is quite used to housing more than one entity in his physical body, but several would probably prove to be too many. Jack is fine with entire downloads of civilizations and their achievements into his noggin — as long as it's in another language so he can cheerfully ignore it. And Carter — well, Carter might be a little too interested in controlling any personas that got into her instead of understanding them. But Daniel, as an anthropologist specializing in ancient civilizations, is the best at seeing other points of view, at brokering lives, as it were, to make as many people happy as possible, while still maintaining a sense of dignity and truthfulness.

"Lifeboat" is one of Teryl Rothery's favorite episodes, and it's easy to see why — she and Michael Shanks hold the story together. Janet Fraiser's scenes with Daniel have an emotion and strength that remind us at each turn why she's such a core member of the team. If you're not a Daniel fan, admittedly, the episode might tend to be dull — an inherent risk in any single-character-story. Without Shanks' skill at bringing out the different personalities, "Lifeboat" would be, pardon the pun, lost at sea.

Fortunately, Shanks puts in an great performance (it garnered him a Leo), so while the plot does drag on at times, the scenes in which Martice is the dominant personality are riveting. It's an interesting choice of story line for Daniel, who has just returned from being Ascended and who has been questioning his place in the team, trying to regain a sense of self and belonging throughout the season so far. It's especially interesting because we don't get to see Daniel's reaction — his character is being put through an extremely distressing event, but since his identity is absent, we have no cue on which to base our reactions.

The story choice is relevant in terms of the other characters, too — they've just got Daniel back after thinking him gone for good, and the prospect of losing him again is obviously unthinkable for them. The gung-ho determination with which they go after a solution is touching — the "team member in distress" story line always serves to bring the team spirit into the foreground and remind us that, no matter what else is going on in the SGC and the galaxy, the characters are there for each other.

Gods & Scientists: The multiple personalities in "Lifeboat" can be seen through the lens of myth as well as that of science. In Egyptian mythology, many gods were in fact amalgams of different, older gods, different aspects of various deities cohabiting the same body. In scientific terms, multiple personality disorder is a rare mental affliction where two or more distinct and independent personalities develop within the same person. There is commonly one dominant personality that is unaware of the other personalities' existence. The condition is thought to be brought about by trauma resulting in dissociative mental processes — a means by which feelings, thoughts, and memories split off into a separate consciousness.

Interesting Fact: The cryopods that contained the frozen bodies posed some problems for the guest actors: one was claustrophobic and had an anxiety attack, while another fell asleep!

Why We're Space Monkeys: Any episode that can rehash aspects of its own story lines ("Holiday," "Entity") and make it entirely different has got to be given kudos. There's not a moment when you worry that you're in for the "same old thing" — it's all new and very well developed. The show's writers are also adept at weaving moral questions in with questions of mere survival — we're constantly torn between concern over the disembodied souls who would be condemned without a host body, and our desire to see Daniel return.

Parlez-vous Gate?:
DANIEL (as Martice): Just find the small woman and tell her that what she gave me is not good enough!

707. Enemy Mine

Original airdate: July 25, 2003
Written by: Peter DeLuise
Directed by: Peter DeLuise

Earth tries to mine a naquadah vein located on Unas sacred ground. When the indigenous Unas become hostile, SG-1 turns to Chaka for help.

"Enemy Mine" is a welcome return to Daniel-the-archaeologist. He's been missing for quite some time now. After Daniel's absence and his difficulties readapting to life as part of the SGC, it seems almost a relief (to him as well) to see him back in familiar intellectual territory, playing to his strengths. This is a very dialogue-heavy episode, however, and it's hard not to glance at the clock during the long sessions of Daniel translating grunts that we had already understood. Added to that the hardheaded colonel who can't see anyone else's point of view and the tribes of Unas suddenly appearing over the crest of the mine and "Enemy Mine" begins to feel like a rehash of season two's "Spirits."

This episode does play the continuity card well — Chaka's story line is a followup from season five's "Beast of Burden"; reference is made to the

Prometheus, last seen in "Memento"; and when Daniel gives the Unas his lighter, it's a direct play on the scene from the *Stargate* movie, when Colonel O'Neil made the same gift to Skaara. Both Daniel and Jack have now played the role of the Greek god Prometheus, handing down fire to a "less advanced" people. In fact, in O'Neill's absence, Jackson takes on a lot of his characteristics — he becomes impatient and hyperaware of his environment, for example. In this episode, they're very much an old married couple, with some very funny give-and-take.

Although Carter and O'Neill usually have a very chummy and respectful relationship, sometimes Jack can be a tad . . . insensitive. In this episode, he manages to belittle his teammate's scientific expertise by calling her "complete overhaul of the Gate diagnostic system," a "science project." It's in the category of small things, but there are times when the line between O'Neill acting dumb and O'Neill being insulting is extremely thin.

The problem with "Enemy Mine" is that it sets up the Unas as an underdeveloped race. Despite Daniel's efforts at mediating, the Earth contingent has a decidedly difficult decision to make in this episode. There are definitely large issues at stake — the naquadah mine opens the door for the development of technology to defeat the Goa'uld — but there are ethical issues, too, and it's wince-worthy to watch the complete disregard shown by the other SG team toward the Unas' beliefs. We don't need to be hit over the head with the idea that humans can be small-minded hypocrites; that's hardly a revelation.

What's good about this episode is the great lengths to which director Peter DeLuise goes to make the Unas language and culture seem authentic. Even though we don't understand every bark and guttural sound that's uttered, there's no doubt that we can follow the conversation without any problem. For such a foreign people, the writers and directors really do an amazing job of helping the viewer understand them. Says Alex Zahara, who played Iron Shirt in this episode: "Peter's so serious, and so dedicated, and actually so devoted. . . he loves what he's doing so much and it's so much fun for him."

The ending of "Enemy Mine" is a surprise, but it doesn't feel tacked on. This is mostly due to Michael Rooker (Colonel Edwards), whose own surprise and eventual understanding of the alien culture is, from the middle of the episode on, very authentic. The Unas do not play by the same rules that humans do. Their designating of dignity over labor is a didactic message that works because it doesn't stem from an Unan sense of moral superiority. They couldn't care less what the humans *do* with the stuff, but they do care about their stake in the process. A nice, relativistic episode floating amongst the more usual rigid, polarized fare of television viewing.

Gods & Scientists: We are not sure if the Unas have religious convictions. However, Peter DeLuise has done a lot of work on the Goa'uld language. He says, "The Unas language, it doesn't have to be English, it could be an idea. They use words like ideas. This is an idea, and then if you put a negative in front of it, it's the opposite of that idea. The word *no na* is "home," and so *ka no na* is "not home," some place other than home. And *no na* doesn't have to be your specific cave. It could be your hunting ground or your planet. It all depends on what the context is. It's up to the listener to figure out what you mean. It's all very interpretive."

Interesting Fact: The title of the episode is taken from a book of the same title, written by Barry Longyear in 1979. In it, two beings whose people are at war crash land on a barren planet and must learn each other's language, ways, and culture so that they may coexist and survive. It won the Nebula Best Novella prize in 1979; and in 1985, it was made into a movie starring Dennis Quaid and Louis Gossett Jr.

Parlez-vous Gate?:
O'NEILL: Daniel, go to your happy place.

708. Space Race

Original airdate: August 1, 2003
Written by: Damian Kindler
Directed by: Andy Mikita

Carter copilots in an interplanetary space race, but she finds out too late that the competition has been rigged. It's up to Jack and Teal'c to get to the bottom of the conspiracy.

Sam Carter shows her fun-loving, thrill-seeking side in a way we haven't been privy to before. SG-1 puts their lives on the line every episode to save

Finally after seven years, Amanda gets do a little comedy in "Space Race" (COURTESY MICHELLE)

the world — theirs or someone else's — and it's good to see that, once in a while, they'll take a risk just to have fun. That aspect of Carter's character has been seen before in small moments — repairing her motorcycle in "The Curse," for example — but this is the first time it's been showcased. Andy Mikita does a good job with the quirky shots and with capturing Tapping's facial expressions at their most mischievous.

"Space Race" takes a long time to pick up and the various threads aren't as carefully sewn together as is usual on this series. And there are plot holes a mile wide. For instance, how does Eamon so quickly deduce TechCon's guilt? The clever gimmick of the newscast is amusing, but gets tired about halfway through the episode — there are only so many times you can poke not-so-gentle fun at a media-hyped society.

"Space Race" is intimately framed with Sam/Daniel conversations — a rarity in themselves, and well acted by Tapping and Shanks — each of which provides some insight into Sam, and allows us to identify with her. While the beginning sequence shows us Carter desirous of fun, the end sequence eloquently sums up the inevitable letdown after a thrill. Who hasn't regretted life's apparent dreary routine when just coming off the high of something exciting and out of the ordinary? Amanda's body language changes completely from the beginning to the end of the episode, highlighting her character's change in attitude and mood.

One very cool touch is the teaser shot of Carter at the beginning of the episode. As previously noted, the last shot in both the teaser and in the full episode usually lingers on Richard Dean Anderson, but "Space Race" does a good job compensating for his absence (which is nonetheless starting to make itself felt — the show is lacking the unifying factor of both RDA and O'Neill). It's nice to see Carter get some extra attention.

Gods & Scientists: The race's different challenges are reminiscent of the medieval gauntlet, and the trials of Greek hero Heracles (Hercules). In medieval times, whether for entertainment, punishment, or to determine guilt or innocence, people ran a "gauntlet," in which they were forced to run between two lines of armored men wielding clubs, trying to strike the runner. In an interesting analogy with the episode, the gauntlet was sometimes run to prove guilt or innocence, the idea being that a supernatural power would intervene to reveal the truth. Heracles (or the Roman Hercules) was the son of Zeus and Alcmene, and is well known for performing twelve labors to regain his honor.

Interesting Fact: "Way back when — okay three years ago — they used to tape one episode at a time, roughly each seven working days," said *SG-1* fan Denise. "Occasionally a second unit would be used or they'd do more than one episode at once, such as when they were on location and were making the most of their time. But now, even the actors have commented how they're doing multiple episodes at once and how tough it is to concentrate. [. . .] In the 'Death Knell' commentary Amanda talks about being off on her own for days and not even seeing the guys and they were off doing whole other episodes."

Why We're Space Monkeys: Plot problems aside, this episode is fun. And when is the last time we saw Sam Carter have fun? When's the last time we saw *any* of them have fun? Every so often, the writers bring out a facet of the characters that we didn't know was there, or that we rarely get to see; this is one such episode. Damian Kindler usually writes these later, funny offerings. Sam's cheeky "What's a girl to do?" and her enthusiastic agreement to Warrick's plan before even checking with General Hammond makes us smile — and sometimes, that's what television is for.

Parlez-vous Gate?:
BORON: Does your ship have what it takes to survive that kind of super intense heat?
HADRAIG: And if it doesn't?
BORON: You'd be instantly vaporized.
HADRAIG: Interesting . . . in a horrifying sense.

709. Avenger 2.0

Original airdate: August 8, 2003
Written by: Joseph Mallozzi, Paul Mullie
Directed by: Martin Wood

Jay Felger, in imminent danger of losing his job, produces a computer virus that goes wrong. Really, really wrong. He keeps telling everyone it's not his fault. . . .

Even Carter looks bored as she follows Felger around trying to straighten out the mess he's gotten himself (and the whole Gate system) into. Then we find out it's Baal. Then we find out it may or may not be a dream.

Dream or not, it's too bad we don't see more of Baal. A cunning and versatile enemy, Baal sees an opportunity here and takes it without hesitation. Compare this Baal to the Anubis of "Lost City," where he dawdles, threatens, and generally waits around to get killed.

As we've also seen in some other episodes ("The Curse" in particular), tangential characters run the danger of being little more than foils or templates upon which the action and plot are based. While a "stock" character in any story is highly helpful and performs roles we know and easily recognize, there is a difference between stock character and stereotyped character. The stock character still manages to come across as having their own goals and needs, which they pursue (as Jay Felger does more readily in "The Other Guys"). Stereotyped characters are just that — a reflection of a common belief (or misbelief) boiled down to simplistic components (in this case, the nerdy, inept bumbler) that we neither care about nor care to see again.

To make matters worse, this is the single worst ending of any *SG-1* episode, ever. Whether it's a "dream sequence" or another fantasy or whatever, it still reeks of misogyny, and viewers were outraged. "I think 'Avenger 2.0' was a dismal failure. As much as I truly wanted to love this ep, I found that I couldn't," wrote one fan. Another fan was less polite. "I liked this episode for the sole reason that it will extend the life of my VCR tape by one week since I will have no regrets taping over 'Avenger 2.0' and putting something better over top of it." A common complaint was that the plot veered from the kind of really silly tackiness we see in "Wormhole X-Treme" and "Sight Unseen" to serious drama. An entire Gate system shutting down is not a laughing matter, within the show's own logic, but here it's the entire premise of the episode.

The lighthearted touch of "Urgo" and "The Nox" is gone. The tongue-in-cheek aspect of "Window of Opportunity" and "Deadman Switch" is missing. The jokes fly fast and furious, and if physical comedy is your thing, the scene of Felger in his apartment meeting Carter is hilarious. Otherwise, unless you put your brain on hold, repeated viewings of this episode aren't going to happen. And please let them not give us a 3.0, because we couldn't take it.

Interesting Fact: In an homage to his other well-known character, Harold Green of *The Red Green Show*, Pat McKenna (as Felger) packs duct tape into his rucksack as he gets ready to go off-world with Carter. *The Red Green Show* is famous for its obsession with duct tape, which they dub "the handyman's secret weapon."

Why We're Space Monkeys: This episode provoked a great deal of debate on online message boards and mailing lists. While most people either loved it or hated it, room was made for both sides of the discussion. Episodes that generate this kind of discussion (with courtesy) are another aspect of the series that makes us proud to be space monkeys.

Parlez-vous Gate?:
O'NEILL (speaking through the MALP to the SGC): I told you not to trust that brown-nosing little weasel!
FELGER: He doesn't know I'm standing here, does he?

710. Birthright

Original airdate: August 15, 2003
Written by: Christopher Judge
Directed by: Peter Woeste

SG-1 comes across a colony of Jaffa women who have been rescuing Jaffa girls who would otherwise be condemned to death by the Goa'uld god Moloc. When SG-1 discovers that these women have been killing Jaffa men in order to steal their symbiotes, they help them find another way of surviving. Oh, and Teal'c has sex.

The first scene of this episode shows a Jaffa. You think he's going to be important. But he gets a pained look on his face, and then he dies — much like this episode, in fact. I'll be up front: "Birthright" has serious issues. It may have been a fairly popular episode among fans (my brother, who hadn't watched an episode of *Stargate* before and hasn't since, tuned in solely to watch Jolene Blalock), but there are only so many times you can watch a war-of-the-sexes episode without it becoming tired. Chris Judge is a relatively "new" writer, and while he has many strengths — among them a good sense of pacing and timing, a good feel for the characters, and a real facility with building tension — his narrative techniques aren't as polished as they could be.

"Birthright" follows a very traditional storytelling scheme — here's a problem, now let's fix it. The veneer of gender role reversal is just thin, since the women still have to rely on what the men provide — the symbiotes, and then the tritonin — in order to survive. The sexualized language only adds to that — "succumbing" to the experiment for example — as does the very clichéd scene of women warriors with gaping cleavages, riding huge black stallions. I mean, really.

On the positive side, it is the women who are the most forward-thinking about using tritonin; while the Jaffa men that SG-1 has approached so far absolutely refused to give up their symbiotes, the women are much more open-minded. Traditional narratives usually portray women as the more emotional (and thus illogical) gender, but "Birthright" manages to turn that around. This is not to say that stories where women rely on men are bad or sexist — but if a writer is going to set up a binary opposition that has no room to move forward, in this case men and women, then the very *least*

Chris Judge wrote the part of Ishta specifically with Jolene Blalock in mind
(ALBERT L. ORTEGA)

they are compelled to do is tell a fresh story, and not trot out unacknowledged bias (women are, in the end, dependent on men) with a clichéd smattering of male-identified feminism (equating them with Amazon women, who can fight real good in short skirts and with long, unbound hair).

There are some good aspects to this episode. The gender separation is extremely thorough, and pushes the theme of the episode in some subtle ways — Sam walking in front of the men in the early scenes, and the scenes of tribal solidarity between the women Jaffa. Historically speaking, the killing of baby girls after birth was not unknown — in certain parts of the world, it is still practiced today — and so the adaptation of that to a different planet and a different culture makes a powerful point. The episode also takes the theme of the witchhunt and applies it very effectively to the Jaffa women's situation. It's a nice choice on Chris Judge's part to have the girls appear as teenagers, more fully formed, aware individuals, rather than swaddled prop dolls, as it builds up the tension and the character development.

Jolene Blalock's character makes a good point about the double standards to which women are held — "You speak of progress and shedding of the old ways and yet you still think a woman needs your protection." It has the added benefit of giving Teal'c something to think about, and we get to see some real dialogue between the two of them. And any episode that gives Teal'c a chance to express himself can't be all bad.

Gods & Scientists: Moloch was the Canaanite sun god to whom child sacrifices were made. His name is made up of the Hebrew *melech* (king) and *boshet* (shame), and he is often associated with the god Baal (see

"Summit"). An entirely malevolent being, his sacrifices were meant to renew the strength of the sun. He is mentioned in the Old Testament of the Bible, in the Book of Leviticus and 2 Kings. Some believe that the Moloch referred to there is actually a form of sacrifice rather than a deity.

Interesting Fact: The role of Ishta was specifically written with Jolene Blalock in mind. Chris says, "They asked me who I saw, and I said, 'Well, I kind of wrote it with Jolene Blalock in mind.' The only two people I really saw doing the role at all was either Jolene or Victoria Pratt. And we were fortunate enough to get Jolene."

Why We're Space Monkeys: From the depths of bad episodes can come some wonderful character moments. As a writer, Judge has a great grasp of the characters, and a couple of scenes really stand out. The conversation between Daniel and Nesa is especially genuine and heartfelt; we don't get to see Daniel getting to know kids very often, although we've seen Sam, Teal'c, and Jack do so. The lighting and framing of the scene lends itself to the intimacy of the moment. And it's also nice to see SG-1 helping people on an individual basis rather than a planetary one for once.

Parlez-vous Gate?: A thoroughly distasteful comment from O'Neill, which may or may not be ad-libbed:
O'NEILL: Wait, you don't suppose that's why they want us, do you? I mean, you know, the three of us?
DANIEL: You mean . . . to mate with? No, no I don't think so.
O'NEILL: Well, because you know me — I'm all for helping people!
CARTER (snorts): Oh God!

711. Evolution (Part 1)

Original airdate: August 22, 2003
Story by: Damian Kindler, Michael Shanks
Teleplay by: Damian Kindler
Directed by: Peter DeLuise

Bra'tac and Teal'c encounter a new "Super Soldier," and when Daniel Jackson and Dr. Lee go in search of a countermeasure, they get kidnapped. Col.

O'Neill, Teal'c, and Major Carter are incarcerated while trying to capture one alive. Everything points to Anubis.

"Evolution" is a carefully constructed episode for the midway point of season seven. Originally aired in the U.S. as the summer hiatus two-parter, this episode slams us with new information, a new black-hatted enemy (literally!), and a lot of visual clues that bring into focus the evolution of the show itself. While the Goa'uld thread is still there (the Goa'uld Telchek being the one who created the sarcophagus), and there is some myth inserted into the story (the fountain of youth, and Daniel's reference to Frankenstein's monster), we are being drawn more frequently out of the comfortable *Stargate* universe of Goa'uld domination and into the more political, technological, and far-reaching space (no pun intended) of the Asgard, the Replicators, and the Ascended/Ancients. But in terms of pacing and plot, "Evolution" is very much like older episodes: bad guy goes after other bad guys, trying to get the biggest, baddest army so that he can rule the universe. Basically.

Daniel Jackson's absence in season six was a catalyst for many changes in the overall shape of the series, as it moved away from its established arcs of Egyptian and other mythologies into the newer area of science fiction mythologies. And it seems expedient for season seven to continue that movement. *SG-1* is set in other worlds, after all, and although the caveat of the Goa'uld seeding humans across the galaxy is convenient, many of the really closely aligned mythological aspects have been loosened up or revised for a more "sciencey" feel. "Evolution" is a perfect example of this. The Goa'uld themselves are taking a lesser role as other stories of cloning ("Fragile Balance," "Resurrection"), invasion ("Lifeboat"), and technology ("Death Knell"), crop up. The suggestion is that it's not just Anubis who is evolving but also the show itself.

The Kull Warrior's (I like Sam's "Super Soldier" better) visual makeup is another clue to *SG-1*'s directional heading. The Darth Vader-like appearance of the drones clearly puts *SG-1* in the space genre — but again, it has more in common with *Star Wars* than *Star Trek*, a distinction that can be seen throughout the series. And wow, those foley effects when Sam and Jacob are taking off the helmet of the dead Kull? Yick!

SG-1 often delves into the "hell realms" described in different mythologies and they do it from different angles. "Jolinar's Memories," "Abyss," and "Beneath the Surface" all deal with hell-like places, and what happens to us in those places. In "Evolution" we are introduced to Tartarus, the home base of Anubis. Usually, hell realms are synonymous with evil, but this is the first time that something evil is being thrown back at us. More often we see the team go *to* hell, rather than have hell come to them. Still, as always, *SG-1* keeps one foot in its old-school roots with the allusion to a hell realm, allowing us to stay comfortable even as we are sitting on the edge of our seat, wondering what will happen to Daniel, Sam, and Teal'c.

Gods & Scientists: Tartarus was used in Greek mythology to refer to an abyss that was the lower of two parts of the Greek underworld. It was where the gods stuck their enemies, in particular. Tartarus was originally located far below another Greek nasty area, Hades, but eventually came to mean a part of Hades. Sometimes Tartarus was alive, and so was Hades. Tartarus and Hades were the opposite of Elysium, where happy souls lived after death.

Interesting Fact: "The guys who play the super soldiers are two of the biggest human beings on the face of the Earth," said Chris Judge in "From Stargate to Atlantis: A Sci Fi Lowdown" (a behind-the scenes special on Sci-Fi Channel). "They can't really see that well out of the helmets, so it's always kind of an adventure to see how certain scenes are going to go . . . especially when it involves a lot of movement."

Why We're Space Monkeys: While they normally work on their own, the members of SG-1 are not above taking on any and all help they can get. In this episode, we have the Tok'ra, Jaffa, and other SG teams helping, as well as another civilian scientist. All three contingents of the alliance are here — a subtle insertion of the same situation that gets quickly out of hand in "Death Knell."

Parlez-vous Gate?:
ROGELIO: Are you okay? I thought you were dead for sure. What happened, Señor?
DANIEL: We triggered some sort of trap.
DR. LEE: I think I figured out why those passageways were so narrow. It's to prevent people from escaping alive.
DANIEL: You're good.

712. Evolution (Part 2)

Original airdate: January 9, 2004
Story by: Damian Kindler, Peter DeLuise
Teleplay by: Peter DeLuise
Directed by: Peter DeLuise

O'Neill goes to Honduras in search of Daniel, teaming up with an old military acquaintance. Sam and Teal'c with the help of Jacob and Bra'tac infiltrate Anubis' stronghold and find something startling.

"Did you miss me?" In this second instalment of the two-parter, O'Neill's place is firmly reestablished. With his appearances on *SG-1* becoming fewer, it's nice to see some serious screen time for Richard Dean Anderson. The overall arc of the series does well in giving us "Jack time" just when we need it — it makes up for the other episodes where he is not on screen as much ("Grace," "Lifeboat," and "Space Race"). Another evolution of the series, the absence of Jack O'Neill, is felt keenly by the fans, and its effect on the team is more obvious through season seven. Each member of the team matures, learns to stand on his or her own, and use the means at their disposal. They rely more heavily on allies and their own creative resources to get the job done. In this way, Teal'c, Sam, and Daniel still embody the best that O'Neill characterized — they are all skilled, use creative means to achieve ends, and they play more — they even do smug now and then! All this can be seen as their direct evolution under the leadership of Colonel O'Neill, further helping fill the space where he usually stood. The physical leader may not be there, but his code of ethics is.

And, while they still work amazingly well as a team whether together, separate, or paired up, other aspects are being explored against the backdrop of the team. Sam's personal life and the inclusion of humor in her episodes ("Space Race"), Teal'c's reintegration in the politics and lives of the Jaffa ("Orpheus"), Daniel's reintegration to the team and into his life after so much strife ("Fallen"), and the reemergence of old friends ("Fallout," "Chimera") are all facets that receive narrative attention in this season. Because let's face it, after seven years on the air, there's a whole lot of backstory that propels the show along, and RDA's reduced airtime is a good opportunity to explore and use those aspects. Again, the writers do a good job of mimicking reality here: often the people whom we think are only sideline players (Agent Barrett is a good *SG-1* example) come back into our lives as they move and evolve.

While Anubis is no doubt the scariest of the villains SG-1 has encountered, the more we see him the more his cowl starts to erode this effect. He does much better when stationary; head bobbing just makes him look silly. The appearance of another Goa'uld queen, however, makes up for it. In the long arc of season seven, Anubis very definitely has his own agenda. We're not quite sure what it is yet — which is unnerving. As a villain, Anubis has frightening powers, and the newly resurrected henchman in Honduras (accompanied by Anubis-like music) ties the two together nicely. Super soldiers and self-resurrection? Bad.

Tony Amendola is an accomplished theater actor as well as working in television (ALBERT L. ORTEGA)

Very, very bad. The addition of backstory from season six (which also validates Jonas' contribution to the team) allows a new arc to develop. Anubis controls information, and, to a contemporary audience, that's as scary as any amount of firearms. If he knows what *we* know, where will he strike next? An excellent entry by *SG-1* veteran Peter DeLuise.

Gods & Scientists: I'm sorry, was that an *undead* person in this episode? I thought this was *SG-1*, not *Buffy*. The box that Daniel and Dr. Lee find leads them to believe it is the source of the myth of the fountain of youth. Many fountain of youth stories coincide with the opening up of America (North and South), while others date to the seventh century AD in Europe. The misuse of the alien device in this episode results in the Gothic sight of a living dead person roaming the jungles of Vancouver . . . I mean Honduras.

Interesting Fact: Daniel refers to Dr. Lee as "Bill," in the episode, which is the actor's first name (Bill Dow), not the character's. Dr. Lee's first name is listed as Seymour in "Zero Hour."

Why We're Space Monkeys: The supporting cast and guest cast. Enrico Colantoni (you might know him from *Just Shoot Me, Veronica Mars, or Galaxy Quest*) absolutely nails the slightly freaked but ultimately good guy. The tension between O'Neill and Burke is palpable and extremely well wrought. The military lives these men live are pressure cookers, and the two men play edgy sanity really well, injecting humor to alleviate the tension. And Zak Santiago (Rogelio) does a hilarious (though slightly over-the-top) job as well.

Parlez-vous Gate?: Siler speaks!
SILER (suiting up Jacob in a Kull Warrior suit): How's that, Sir?
JACOB: Pretty good. Reminds me of my old football days.
SILER: They had helmets back in those days, Sir?
JACOB (casting a withering look): Funny.

713. Grace

Original airdate: January 16, 2004
Written by: Damian Kindler
Directed by: Peter Woeste

Carter gets trapped in a ship. Oh, the puns available to the long-time viewer!

Sort of a sequel to "Prometheus," "Grace" highlights Sam much as "Orpheus" highlighted Teal'c and "Lifeboat" highlighted Daniel. However, unlike those two episodes, Sam Carter has interaction with each of her team members, while "Orpheus" and "Lifeboat" concentrated on the male actors much more explicitly. This may have been deliberate on the part of Kindler who may have hoped to show that Sam is not merely a scientist with no life; but many feminist scholars argue that showing female characters always in relation to others is a sign of patriarchal values at work.

   As this episode was written, produced, and directed by men, one could make an argument for that position, especially since every single person Sam encounters, besides Grace, is male. Where is Janet Fraiser? Where is Cassandra? In "Singularity" Sam chooses death rather than to abandon the girl, and yet Cassandra is totally absent at this extremely important point of Sam's life. Why is Carter always shown only in relation to men?

Did someone say "Cheese"?!? (ALBERT L. ORTEGA)

While the character of Grace is female, she is actually alien — should a cloud even have a sex? What's more, Grace is prepubescent and does not add any clarity to the plot, rather she confuses, which is another stereotype attributed to the female sex.

The best moments in "Grace" are silent, or in the small monologues that Sam has, as she debates the realness of her predicament with herself. Epiphanies regarding her character arise during action sequences rather than during dialogue. A moment of grace is an interior event — quite a challenge for a television series. Although this episode got mixed reviews — as did "Orpheus" and "Lifeboat" — trying to execute a mental state on film is daring, and the writers deserve some praise. The lighting at the beginning of the episode is a telltale sign that things are going to be presented in an unusual way — the initial, very white lighting (which glares unflatteringly off Amanda Tapping's forehead), and then the starkly contrasting blue and red lighting are visual clues. They are quite different from the softer shadings of light we are used to seeing in the SGC, offworld (unless for a particular purpose such as we see in "Revisions" or "The Broca Divide"), or in closeups. By zeroing in on Sam's face throughout the episode, unflattering, crisscrossed with emotion, and using those lighting techniques, the director brings out the idea of Grace as a healing agent or agent of change. In real life, there are no lighting directors following us around making sure we look perfect all the time, just as there is no soundtrack.

The episode has a *Solaris*-like feel, with the gas cloud and the feeling of uncertainty about what is real. Whereas most series are set in the future (*Star Trek*), or in an alternate galaxy (*Farscape*), *Prometheus* is a human alien hybrid and closer to our own technology. In "Grace," it binds us closer to Sam's predicament by reminding us that she is living at the same time we are. The realism that *SG-1* strives to manufacture is one of the reasons the series is taken so seriously; on *Farscape*, leather-clad villains and doppelgangers are easily relegated to the safe distance of science fiction, but the stories in this series are closely scrutinized by fans for their believability.

Some components of the episode jar a bit — Sam's head wound appears and disappears, which obscures the throughline of the story, unlike "The Changeling," for instance, where the plot, though harder to understand, is still, in retrospect, a smooth narrative. Occasionally, the voiceovers seemed redundant, neither providing enough information for new viewers, nor giving new information for long-time viewers. And Daniel Jackson's diction has become increasingly speedy since his return, and in this episode it's almost impossible to understand what he's saying.

Like the bubble that Sam sees, this episode has interesting properties that shouldn't be overlooked in terms of film technique, but the "showdown" concept between Sam and Jack seemed unnecessary to the plot. Even the moment most fraught with relationship angst, Sam and Jack kissing, is again set in an altered state (like every other kiss they've shared), and ultimately denies us the satisfaction of a resolution. Kiss or don't kiss, but do it and move on, already.

Gods & Scientists: Christian theology describes the concept of grace as the gift of divine favor that is unasked for (and occasionally unlooked for). Divine grace brings spiritual regeneration and a renewed sense of purpose. It derives from the Greek word *charis*, and is mentioned in the New Testament approximately 150 times, mostly in the writings of Paul, particularly in the letter of Paul to Titus: "For the grace of God has appeared for the salvation of all men" (2:11).

Interesting Fact: Amanda taped all the voiceovers for this episode prior to taping the episode, which may explain why the disembodied voice seems a little out of sync.

Why We're Space Monkeys: While the actor chooses an interpretation for their given role, good actors know that their interpretation is not the only one. They also know that what the audience sees is not necessarily what the actor may have chosen. As Amanda said in an interview, "Grace could be Sam's child within. Grace could be Sam's hopes and dreams for having a child. Grace could be the child Sam left behind when she focused all her energy on becoming Astrophysicist Woman. So she's a bunch of different things. In my mind, I chose to make her Sam's potential future."

Parlez-vous Gate?: One of the most talked about scenes in "Grace" is "The Kiss." Did we want to see the relationship of Sam and Jack taken to the next level, or did we want them to leave it professional? Director Peter Woeste admitted that, in fact actually, they shot two scenes while the producers were trolling online to see what the public wanted. In the end, what we see on screen was an amalgamation of both scenes, a fantasy within a dream. *Cough* chicken *cough*.

714. Fallout

Original airdate: January 23, 2004
Story by: Corin Nemec
Teleplay by: Joseph Mallozzi, Paul Mullie
Directed by: Martin Wood

Jonas' planet goes boom — maybe.

Usually *SG-1* handles its titles well — they tell us something about the plot, the overriding themes, and give us a reference to work with. This is one of a handful of episodes whose titles seem just a bit off. While the similarities to the World War II era are somewhat interesting — in gross, three factions with different agendas all competing for their own best interest — the story of Jonas and Kianna is what really draws us in. While the "fallout" of the relationship between the two is evident, it is more reminiscent of stories where German citizens fell in love with or harbored Jews. It has a happy ending, or least a happyish ending. But the term "fallout" resonates far more strongly with atomic or nuclear fallout, and the relationship story line doesn't fit in well there.

One well-handled aspect of the story line is the problem of politics and cooperation after a conflict — how do you unite for the greater good when you can only see your mutual differences? The naquadah/naquadria explanation is a nice twist, and the politicians come across as childish paper pushers, less interested in the people's welfare than in their own petty bickerings and one-upmanship.

A couple of the larger themes we've been dealing with in the season come through here as well — identity, belonging, and the suggestion that everyone has an agenda. Season seven is the most character-driven of all the seasons. Many fans missed the team action, since episodes like "Space Race," "Abyss," "The Changeling," and "Lifeboat" focused so tightly on particular characters. As noted in "Lost City," season four and season seven share some similarities, but season four managed a better mix of simultaneous team- and character-focused episodes. In season seven, more focus is given to individual characters and their growth as opposed to individuals within a team atmosphere. Teal'c talks more in season seven than he ever has; in "Fallout" he speaks during the briefing, which is a rare decision for him. Sam reveals her funny side, and Daniel grapples with a darkness that can't be avoided. Jack remains the most stable, but this could be partly due to Richard Dean Anderson's initial characterization being more rounded, and partly due to his absence — he just doesn't have the on-air time needed to expand his character.

Gods & Scientists: Naquadria is not a naturally occurring element. The Goa'uld Thanos is mentioned. Thanos is most well known to Marvel comic readers as Thanos the Mad Titan. Thanos bears a striking resemblance to the Greco-Roman god Thanatos, who, together with his brother Hypnos, personified Death and Sleep respectively. The principle of thanatos is used in psychology to describe the impulse toward death. It's also referred to as the "death wish," and we can see how it might be operating in "Fallout" as the peoples of Kelowna seem oblivious to their chances of survival, and in fact seem bent on destroying themselves.

Interesting Fact: The Goa'uld Baal is credited with planting the naquadria, but we never see him in person. Which is too bad, because he's the sexiest bad guy *SG-1* has. Cliff Simon (who plays Baal) won the first ever "Mr. South Africa." He said, "South Africa decided to run a competition called "Mr. South Africa" which was not a bodybuilding competition, it was more of an action-man talent competition. At that time I was modeling full-time and I was sort of pushed into entering saying, 'No, you've got to enter, you've got to enter! You've got a good chance to win.'" And he did!

Why We're Space Monkeys: "I'm fresh out [of patience]." Although the person talking is Jack, anyone's decision to refuse help is a sign that we are, after all, human. Sometimes we're just out of patience, and we get sick of people's small-minded bickering. While most sci-fi shows tend to bypass the decision processes that would make their characters choose the lesser of two evils rather than the greater of two goods, *SG-1* never hesitates to show humanity in all its aspects, even the more difficult ones.

Parlez-vous Gate?: Writer Joseph Mallozzi cited this line of RDA's (which seems ad-libbed) as his favorite of the show — even though *he* didn't write it. O'NEILL: That's what you get for dicking around.

715. Chimera

Original airdate: January 30, 2004
Story by: Robert Cooper
Teleplay by: Damian Kindler
Directed by: William Waring

Daniel has disturbing dreams that feature his lost girlfriend Sarah. Sam starts a relationship with a detective, and has troubles when he asks about her job.

Right on the heels of "Fallout" is another episode dealing primarily with relationships. Season seven is getting very touchy-feely the last few episodes, and this one is no exception.

"I felt so out of my element doing these, you know, little cutesy-flirty scenes, and of course the kissy-kissy, and it's so not a side of Carter that we've ever seen," said Amanda Tapping on her character Sam Carter breaking out of her "black widow syndrome." This is a term Tapping and her fans applied to Carter's seeming inability to have a relationship with a man who isn't

David DeLuise gives a sheepish grin –
do they like me, or not? (ALBERT L. ORTEGA)

doomed to either die or disappear. "I think that it's an offshoot of what happened in 'Grace.' The writers were trying to [. . .] dispel the black widow curse that Carter has, and also to open her up for more experiences and to flesh her out just a little bit more as a human being." "Chimera" was the episode that portrayed the love interests up front and mostly unabashedly. Sam/Jack shippers screamed for days, but some people were quite happy to see something, *anything* happen to Samantha Carter. And you could get worse people to play kissyface with than David DeLuise.

Many fans were shocked and upset about the beginning of the episode due to Carter's wardrobe. Some fans thought she looked slutty, while others were merely shocked that she suddenly showed up in a coffee shop with some décolletage when she had never worn such an outfit in seven seasons. The small moments of seeing SG-1 off base in nonmilitary garb, like "Space Race" and "Upgrades," did little to prepare fans.

Anna-Louise Plowman just sweats sophistication, doesn't she? Does she even sweat at all? More like, she *exudes* class. It's easy to see why Daniel Jackson turns all googly-eyed around her at first. A great performance by Michael Shanks, as his confidence in his character allows him to choose strong motivations for pursuing the dream state, which even Jack thinks is an insane plan. "I like to draw from personal association," Shanks noted in an interview. "It's what makes acting the most personal and gives the audience true access to true feelings that you really feel or have felt in the past." This may have been why episodes such as "Forever in a Day" were so effective. Daniel and Osiris have a strong, unspoken understanding of knowledge and its relationship to power. They are not as far apart as it seems on the surface. "Chimera" starts to show us Daniel's return in a way that points to his new development as a character. The old Daniel would have broken off negotiations point-blank and probably have made a mess. The new, recently un-Ascended Daniel has become aware that, sometimes, knowledge is only powerful because you hold more than someone else. His priorities are different now, and his relationship with knowledge is different as well.

Hidden in the content of all those relationships and myth-dispelling is a nugget of plot — the Lost City. Daniel works toward transcribing the artifact, learning a trick or two from the Goa'uld. Much as the Goa'uld have used SG-1 for their information (remember "Out of Mind"?), Daniel now uses the Goa'uld to help him out.

Another hidden nugget is Teal'c's character development. Now using tritonin to compensate for the loss of his symbiote, the Jaffa is dreaming for the first time. It is he who suggests that perhaps Daniel Jackson is not in control of his own thoughts. This new, intuitive thinking on Teal'c's part is so quickly put away that it's easy to miss, but it signals a huge change on his part. We need more Teal'c; he's been missing these last few episodes, and the concentration on Jackson and Carter is starting to get a tad cloying.

Gods & Scientists: The title alludes to two of the featured elements in this episode: the chimera is a female monster composed of lion, goat, and serpent parts from Greek mythology, and a zoological reference to having two distinct types of cells in tissue — in *SG-1* terms, the Goa'uld/human hybrid.

Interesting Fact: In a behind-the-scenes sequence, Anna-Louise Plowman reveals part of the secret of her buxom figure — rubbery implants in her costume!

Why We're Space Monkeys: Anyone who can make fun of the mechanics of their job (like Anna-Louise does about wearing falsies) gets our vote. Sure, we take it seriously as "mythic narrative structure," sure we look closely for flaws and plot holes and *yadda yadda*; but we also laugh our asses off when we see someone stick their hand down the front of their shirt and say the equivalent of, "Dude. Will you *look* at this?"

Parlez-vous Gate?:
TEAL'C: Most often dreams are the mind's way of dealing with desires that cannot be fulfilled.

DANIEL: So basically, I'm never going to get another good night's sleep ever again.

TEAL'C: With all of your past experiences, Daniel Jackson, I do not know how you have slept well before now.

DANIEL: Thank you Teal'c, this session has been disturbing on many levels.

716. Death Knell

Original airdate: February 6, 2004
Written by: Peter DeLuise
Directed by: Peter DeLuise

Earth's newest off-world base is compromised, and Sam and Jacob Carter are caught in the cross fire. Jacob is rescued but Sam is missing, and things point to a leak in the Tok'ra/Jaffa/human alliance.

The term "death knell" refers to the tolling of church bells when someone has died. It was the subject of an Ernest Hemingway novel, which was based on a meditation by the poet John Donne. "Death Knell" speaks to many of the same ideas we saw way back, in season one's "Solitudes": the reality of death, the fact that death comes without remorse or pity, and that when it does arrive, we are finally, utterly alone. In this episode, however, the writers reverse the situation. Whereas "Solitudes" had Sam helping an injured Colonel O'Neill, "Death Knell" has O'Neill searching for and rescuing Sam. As the line from Donne states, "Any man's death diminishes me, because I am involved in Mankind; And therefore never send to know for whom the bell tolls; it tolls for thee." This tolling for life — human, Jaffa, or Tok'ra — crosses xenophobic boundaries. No one in the alliance can afford to indulge in practices of "us or them"; they have to widen their horizons (and their idea of ally) to include those whom they would normally exclude.

It seems that, like "Grace" or "Lost City (Part 2)," the entire purpose of this episode was the "money shot" of Jack and Sam at the end, when, after a moment of watching Major Carter, Colonel O'Neill puts an arm around her. In the aftermath of "Grace," it looks suspiciously as though the writers were doing a rather obvious "see we're still friends!" maneuver. The progress of the story is jerky, and there is no clear plot to follow — "Death Knell" is like a collection of subplots strung together. The Tok'ra/Jaffa strife, always a precarious element, seems mashed in at the last moment. The scenes that culminate in the Jaffa and Tok'ra representatives stating their respective reasons for withdrawing are more than worth the wait, however. As free people, the Jaffa feel as though they are trading one master for another — in this case, a Goa'uld for the humans at the SGC. There is truth in the idea that a newly liberated people would want to distance themselves as quickly as possible from any form of authority, like a teenager with a curfew recently lifted.

"Death Knell" signaled a great many things for *SG-1*, and that looming feeling of death strikes us where we least expect it, in the next brilliant two-parter, "Heroes." In retrospect, the tolling of that bell resonates for the rest of the season.

Gods & Scientists: In part, *For Whom the Bell Tolls* by Ernest Hemingway was about the collective struggle against overwhelming odds. The individual *could* make a difference, in short. We can see this also working in "Death Knell," as Sam struggles against odds that seem insurmountable (physical and mental exhaustion, abandonment, ethical uncertainty) to ultimately defeat the Kull warrior with the aid of the rest of the team. An individual struggling against overwhelming odds is a staple of the hero myth. Lone hero figures like Hercules and Achilles have been handed down to us from Greek mythology, but here Peter DeLuise inverts that idea of the male hero and uses a female character. The female character as hero, and the idea of a team dynamic ultimately working together to achieve a larger end, are both contemporary views that have grown out of novels such as *For Whom the Bell Tolls*. And you thought reading classics was boring.

Interesting Fact: In 2004 Legends Memorabilia put up for auction "a fully functioning original TER." The TER (Transphase Eradication Rod) was first used in "Show and Tell." It sold for $6,600.00 U.S.

Why We're Space Monkeys: Even though it gets a little tiring from a viewer's point of view, the bickering and intrigues of the Jaffa and Tok'ra are more realistic than the fare we see in most shows, where, after a token hissy fit, the good guys see the light, band together, and exchange phone numbers and bracelets, etc. These are two (three, counting the humans) strong, independent races with three very different mandates and three different methods of accomplishing them. The Tok'ra, right from the beginning (see season two's "The Tok'ra" mini-arc), maintain that it is subterfuge and secrecy that they use (and value) most. The Jaffa people have always had a strong moral code that favors up-front confrontation, usually en masse. It's no wonder the two have problems meeting in the middle. But the continued, complex relationship between all three parties reflects more accurately (albeit with a tinge of soap opera) what a real-life alliance between parties with such unlike purposes and common goals would be like.

Parlez-vous Gate?:
CARTER: Have you not had your coffee this morning?
JACOB: Selmak doesn't like coffee.

717. Heroes (Part 1)

Original airdate: February 13, 2004
Written by: Robert Cooper
Directed by: Andy Mikita

Stonewalling a film crew that has arrived at the SGC to document what's going on, SG-1 goes about its daily business.

"Originally, this script was intended as a fun, different, episode and, along the way, [it] took a very serious turn," said executive producer Joseph Mallozzi. The beginning of the episode still has the flavor of this early version, with lots of tongue-in-cheek work by the actors (not least, we finally find out what Chevron Guy does!). Tapping, Judge, and Shanks are all getting very good at playing with the camera when they can, and the beginning segments are filled with what in the theater world would be termed "asides," extra pieces of information or emotion not overheard by the other characters. Since *SG-1* is a television series, however, many of these moments are visually cued — expressions, pauses, gestures — rather than spoken. This adds to the lightness of tone without detracting from the plot; little moments of everydayness that we have come to know and love with these characters. In the second part of the mini-arc, we again see these unspoken moments but in an intensely dramatic, emotional reversal —

Daniel's infirmary vigil and Sam's tear-stained face. Neither moment needs dialogue. This bookending of silence also helps point to the larger theme of the unsung hero.

There is, however, a sharp turn toward the dramatic near the middle of "Heroes" that sends warning signals to the pit of your stomach. All of sudden, you get the sensation that everything is very, very important. It's well seamed into the episode, and again, the pacing realistically mimics an actual day. We get up in the morning, all seems well, and then suddenly news or a catastrophe changes everything — nothing is ever the same. From a storytelling point of view, this is a hard effect to achieve. Narrative lines usually require consistency and reliability, otherwise the viewer gets irritated. Again, kudos go to director Andy Mikita. This guy seems to draw the really heavy episodes. He does a competent job not only splicing in older footage from the show but also heightening the realism of the situation with handy-cam shots so that we feel present in the action. The irony, of course, is that the "action" we see is not real action, both in the world (as it's a TV series), and in the show (as Bregman is stuck at the SGC). Bregman is, in fact, the last person we think of as a hero, and yet he is the pivot point for much of the plot. Saul Rubinek is a master of juxtaposition, making his blustering character seem too eager. We don't actually *like* Bregman, or his driven personality, but at the end of the mini-arc we are forced to admit that he is one of the reasons we are aware of what's going on.

Interesting Fact: Saul Rubinek, who plays Emmett Bregman, is a Canadian actor whose film and television credits are a mile long. He was born in a refugee camp in Germany after World War II, and his ardent spirit for unsung heroes is manifested not only in his skilled acting in this episode but also on the other side of the camera as well. Like the character Bregman, Rubinek filmed a documentary in 1988 called *So Many Miracles* for the Canadian Broadcasting Corporation and Public Broadcasting Service which chronicled his parents' reunion with those who had saved their lives during the Holocaust.

Why We're Space Monkeys: Still topical after seven years on the air, *SG-1* continues to meld historical material, mythological ideals (the hero), and contemporary themes (reality television, documentaries in hot-spot situations). While the episode "Paradise Lost" does this as well, the significance of the unknown cameraman in this episode is replaced by a very much alive character, Emmett Bregman, who has his own agenda, one other than being a passive observer of events.

Parlez-vous Gate?: Any of the interview scenes are funny, but Teal'c's, which is mostly silent, is the funniest. Confronted by two hundred pounds of silence. Wow. What do you do with that?

718. Heroes (Part 2)

Original airdate: February 20, 2004
Written by: Robert Cooper
Directed by: Andy Mikita

Bregman continues to struggle to achieve his ends, with scant help from the SGC. Agent Woolsey arrives to investigate a terrible accident.

Using a video recorder twice removed to "film" Janet's death was an interesting choice. The extra distance we acquire with that technique both flattens and heightens its dramatic effect. It definitely allows for the element of surprise, as we assume, after seven years of watching the show, that it will be one of the core characters who will be captured on film and survive — or, if someone must die, a "red shirt," playing out the didactic message of heroism in a way we recognize. Every year we set aside days to remember the women and men who have served and died for their country or their ideology. We are used to the emotions these moments evoke. By transporting us back further from that action so that we are not witnessing Janet's death as voyeurs but rather accidentally, our emotional response and our idea of what the moment-to-moment experience of a hero might be is driven home with a sledgehammer.

All our expectations in these two episodes are jarred. We do not expect the annoying Bregman to be instrumental in capturing the death of Janet Fraiser, and our distaste for and complacency toward another rah-rah-America nationalistic theme get absolutely annihilated in part because of Bregman's insistence on revealing the truth. As with most supporting characters in *SG-1*, Bregman is more than he seems. Even though he does manipulate emotions for a living (and this is really where the team's and our distaste for him comes from), and though he appears to be looking for something fantastic for his personal gain, regardless of his hyperbolic speeches to General Hammond, can we really say at the end of the episode that he is not also a hero?

Director Andy Mikita ties this narrative thread in even more strongly with the scenes of Fraiser and Bregman together. The quiet flowering of interest between the two automatically makes Bregman more sympathetic, if only because, like Janet, when he strips off his professional veneer he is a very different person. Janet Fraiser's character responds because that's what she's like. Confronted with impossible situations daily, as a doctor, Janet's persona is compassionate, caring, and most definitely in command. But as she confesses to Bregman in Part 1, "Yeah, I never know what's next. You just try and keep your head on straight." But writer Robert Cooper doesn't make her heroics too pointed, either, as Janet continues describing her day-to-day reality. "Then again, we also set a lot of broken bones and prescribe a ton of antibiotics." At the end of the episode we are not given a list of unsung heroes, another convention we have come to expect from jingoistic storylines, but rather we celebrate those who still live. The "dead" — in this case, Janet Fraiser, and also Bregman, who is out of the life of the SGC now — are not touted with fanfare the way Daniel Jackson was in "Fire and Water." Instead, they are left within us, to say what they need to say through the additional silent moments of Sam, Jack, Teal'c, and Daniel. Sometimes, the realities of life just don't need to be talked about.

Perhaps some scenes were filmed and later cut (as happened with Sam and Daniel's scenes in his return in season seven), but some questions niggle. Where, for instance, was Teal'c throughout this two-parter? His silence during his interview signaled his desire to be far, far away from Emmett Bregman and the camera, and his later idea for the eulogy was wonderful and extremely good character development for the man's man of the team, but his presence was still missed. Another question was, where's Cassie? She figures large (if off-screen) in Janet's life, and is no stranger to the SGC.

But the short version is — "Heroes" are the best two episodes of *SG-1*, ever.

Interesting Fact: In a telephone interview, Teryl Rothery confessed she has not seen "Heroes" (probably because she's so busy attending conventions and working on other projects). As far as the average television viewer went, seeing the death of Janet Fraiser was totally unexpected. *Stargate*

SG-1 zealots however, caught sly references by cast and crew members that the show would lose a cast member, and knew that it was Janet, not Jack, who would die in the episode.

Why We're Space Monkeys: This entire episode is why we're space monkeys, will always be space monkeys, and are defiantly proud of our space monkey status.

Parlez-vous Gate?:
BREGMAN: What are you doing?
JAMES: I'm just white balancing.
BREGMAN: Well, go balance the white somewhere else, okay?

719. Resurrection

Original airdate: February 27, 2004
Written by: Michael Shanks
Directed by: Amanda Tapping

SG-1 finds a Goa'uld-human hybrid engineered by the NID, but the experiment has gone wrong, and the bloodthirsty Goa'uld is about to take over the host. As if that's not enough, they also discover a naquadria bomb that is set to explode.

As a first time for both Michael Shanks and Amanda Tapping — writer and director, respectively — "Resurrection" is probably one of the most pored-over episodes of the seventh season. And while it's noticeably just that, a first attempt, much like Chris Judge's "Birthright" was, it's also a well-produced episode with an interesting story line.

Amanda definitely did her homework before starting work on "Resurrection," and she uses a lot of classic shots — the slow panning-away shot on the final scene, for example, and the slow reveals of locations — but she also draws on a lot of technical work to add to the story. Her use of lighting in the interrogation room highlights the ominous side of Keffler's character, the backlit and overhead lighting placing Keffler in both an insane (overhead) and divine (backlit) model. Some very tight shots on Carter in the laboratory and Teal'c at the bomb scene give the sense of claustrophobia, a visual representation of the countdown to explosion. About the only time we don't feel shut in is, ironically enough, in the scenes with Anna and Daniel Jackson — perhaps because there is such potential for *anything* to happen. It is an undefined space, an undefined relationship, as contrasted to the other locations, where the action is more confined, and defined. The only thing that may have been defined a bit too much were the unnecessary closeups on Carter — but we noted this in Michael Shanks' first effort as a director, "Double Jeopardy," too.

The ratcheting up of tension that's felt in the direction is also present in the script. There is an adept interweaving of previous story lines, including a resurrection (hence the title?) of the NID arc — that carries over into the next episode, "Inauguration" — and there are also some well-developed characters. Despite the red herring of his Nazi heritage, Keffler is an interesting bad guy, because he truly doesn't care what happens to Anna. Morals, professional ethics, humanity — none of it means anything to him.

We see an interesting character development in Daniel when Anna accuses the archaeologist of being just like Keffler. *We* know Daniel is fighting the good fight, but she sees only the resurrection of Keffler — a thread that's actually followed through in some nice scriptwriting by Shanks. It's left up to us to decide whether Daniel will use the information he gathers from the tapes to protect Anna, or to force a confrontation with her alter ego. This is *not* the Daniel of seasons one and two; this is a Daniel who's been through the wars, can recognize ethical grey areas, and can accept the possibility of collateral damage. Daniel, too, follows his own agenda, a personal growth that is often as painful as it is saddening. In a later scene, when Daniel switches off the tapes of Anna and is faced with his own reflection in the darkened screen, it is a moment of reckoning for him, a resurrection of his earlier confrontation with the possibilities opened up by the knowledge he gained. Will he use the device as Keffler did, or not? The earlier Daniel would not; we're not so sure about this later Daniel.

Some of the story elements in "Resurrection" are tired. The ethical argument of killing one to save billions is one of the most overused clichés in storytelling, and "Resurrection" brings nothing new to the mix. And there are only so many times we can feel sympathy for the childlike woman who does evil despite herself. "The Menace," anyone?

In spite of these problems, the episode tells an interesting, fast-paced story that doesn't skimp on character development. Carter, Jackson, and Teal'c each devote themselves to their respective areas of expertise and combine their efforts to work well as a team, and they succeed in their mission. First-time efforts should always be this good.

Gods & Scientists: The scepter found by Teal'c apparently belonged to Sekhmet. According to Egyptian mythology, she was a powerful goddess of war and the destroyer of the enemies of Ra. She was the wife of Ptah, and the mother of Nefertum (see "New Ground"). Known as the Eye of Ra (a vengeful aspect of the goddess Hathor, by some accounts), she was sent by Ra to destroy those humans who were plotting against him. She got carried away with her task, and nearly eliminated the whole human race. To stop her, Ra made beer look like blood, and got her drunk. He then punished her by exiling her to Earth. In a further illustration of the contrasts that appear with many Egyptian deities, Sekhmet was said to heal the plagues and diseases she herself had wrought upon people.

Interesting Fact: The script called for Keffler to be smoking the whole time he was interrogated. Because Brad Greenquist had quit smoking a year before filming began, he's actually smoking herbal cigarettes.

Why We're Space Monkeys: Daniel's fearful assumption that he and Teal'c had armed the bomb seems like a tongue-in-cheek reference to the sheer number of times SG-1 *has* been responsible for accidentally setting off alien technology. You've got to love a show that pokes fun at itself and recognizes when its characters have no idea what they're doing.

Parlez-vous Gate?:
BARRETT: You're kidding, right?
DR. LEE (stares at him): Do I look like a practical joker to you?

720. Inauguration

Original airdate: March 5, 2004
Written by: Joseph Mallozzi, Paul Mullie
Directed by: Peter Woeste

The new president is brought up to date on the SGC, while Vice-President Kinsey pushes for the NID to control the program.

"As crazy as it sounds, we're sitting around here talking about people who are fighting aliens, right? Could we please be specific?" This is a singularly weak setup for a clip show for *SG-1*. Whereas season six's clip episode, "Disclosure," made good use of the show's past to underscore the episode's narrative, "Inauguration," season seven's offering, does no such thing. It feels like a rehash of "Disclosure" only in a different room with different players — and less interesting.

It does a very good job of setting up "Lost City," and of introducing change. And in some ways it's an interesting choice on the part of the writers, to make sure that the changes that occur in season eight (when O'Neill becomes a recurring character rather than a lead) are established beforehand, so it's not too shocking for the fans. Paving the way by using secondary characters, with whom viewers don't identify, is a nice, easy way to achieve that. A good example is the character of Woolsey whom we've seen recently: Woolsey is the cold, clear, objective view in the emotional "Heroes."

Unfortunately, halfway in, the entire episode repeats itself. Even President Hayes looks bored.

It also fulfils its purpose of introducing the new president and giving a clear overview of the political scene. William Devane's president makes for an amusing fall-back for finding out about the Stargate program — his enthusiasm, coupled with a real respect for what the program means, the sacrifices that have been made, and the potentially disastrous future the planet faces, is both plausible and laudable. The writers make an effort to show all facets of the president's thinking, and to present him as unbiased and with the best interests of the people at heart.

The quote for season seven, "Everyone has an agenda," comes from this episode, and the suggestion that the agenda is about control is well wrought, if only in terms of Kinsey's character. Also on the upside, *SG-1* references its own clip show, bringing something new to the genre and breaking the mold once again (how often does a clip show actually offer something that can be used in later episodes?).

What's disappointing about this episode is that there are no shades of grey; it's all black and white. All the work the writers, producers, and actors have done over seven years to establish the idea that there *is* no black and white but merely shades of grey is compromised in this episode. If you stack up everyone's worst moment ("Hathor," "Emancipation," "Sight Unseen," and "Avenger 2.0") one on top of the other, of course they're going to look bad. "Inauguration" has no subtlety, and in a show that's been such a huge proponent and example of that very quality for more than half a decade, it's really a shame.

Interesting Fact: The word "inaugurate" comes from the Latin *inaugurare*, which initially meant to take omens from the flight of birds. It has since come to mean to begin with good omens, and, more commonly, to admit formally into office.

Why We're Space Monkeys: The presidential office used in this episode is actually the same set used in the *X-Men* sequel, *X2*.

Parlez-vous Gate?:
MAYNARD: We've never had any proof connecting Senator Kinsey to anything nefarious.
HAYES: I'm starting to get a bad feeling about where some of that campaign financing came from.

721. Lost City (Part 1)

Original airdate: March 12, 2004
Written by: Brad Wright, Robert Cooper
Directed by: Martin Wood

Daniel Jackson is sure he's found the location of the Lost City of the Ancients, and SG-1 races to find it before Anubis does.

Season seven is very character driven, partly due to the increasing popularity of the show, and partly due to the fact that the team aspect is missing in many episodes because of Richard Dean Anderson's absence. For some fans, season seven was the best season so far because it didn't focus nearly as much on the military aspect of the show, but for others, this season was uneven because cast and crew scrambled to adjust to the absence of the man who was still billed as the main star.

"Lost City" is a good example of this vacuum effect. While it presents a good mini-arc, with lots of all the different elements that made *SG-1* so popular — science fiction themes, explosions, the human element, all tied together by a myth — as far as arcs go, it's dropped in the middle of things with only the previous season's "Full Circle" (and "Window of Opportunity" and "Fifth Race," but who's going to remember that?) to really pull it into focus. One of the differences between the much-compared seasons four and seven is that of the mythologies — as noted in "Evolution," the series is moving out of traditional mythologies and into science fiction ones, but there is one large and extremely interesting twist — in a word, *Atlantis*.

The end of season seven prepares the viewer for season eight but it also must simultaneously prepare (and hype) viewers for the spin-off *Stargate Atlantis*. From the end of season five *SG-1* has been renewed on a year-to-year basis, which could account for some of its more uneven moments, since it's always hanging in the balance of segueing back onto the big screen. *SG-1*'s by now well-known formula of science fiction with a background of accessible mythology is used just as much in *Atlantis* as it was in early seasons of *SG-1*.

"The answer is inside." A simple declaration that encompasses many of the layers of *SG-1*, not only in the episode but in the series itself. The truth that the team is seeking is inside — inside the wall of the temple, inside O'Neill's mind, inside DNA in the form of the Ancient gene.

"Lost City" brings us some wonderful characterizations, harkening back to earlier seasons. In a quasi-revisiting of season one's "The Torment of Tantalus," Daniel is faced with the infuriating prospect of leaving behind a wealth of knowledge. At the temple, it's literally at his fingertips, and he can't access it. This is a pattern in Daniel's life that we see repeated again and again, right from season one. He's always just out of reach of something that he wants quite badly — his wife, the Harcesis child; in a moment that must bring him no end of torment, he has to watch helplessly as Jack accedes to the knowledge Daniel was willing to give his life for, knowing that his only entry to it will be translating Jack's insanity. Translating freedom rather than actively being a part of making that freedom manifest, as Teal'c does, seems to be Daniel's lot, a theme that's suggested by the statue at the temple.

The temple figure, in a very Abe Lincoln–like pose, also reflects Daniel's fate — always the political translator, never the political activist. It is the role of the translator to always be one step behind the action, and this has been Daniel's role from the feature film onward. Since his Ascension, Daniel has come a long way in being aware of the limitations of being human, and the different roles people play in the making of history. It's also a furthering of the character development we saw in season seven's "Resurrection," and "Chimera," in which Daniel accepted of the idea of collateral damage, and his understanding that knowledge gained at the expense of others is sometimes acceptable. Here, his desire to have the knowledge of the Ancients *is* the collateral damage of SG-1's mission, and he accepts it, with raging eyes and gritted teeth.

Consequently, even though *SG-1* moves more into the science fiction genre, it still holds fast to old threads of mythology. Plato's source for the myth of Atlantis describes Egyptian priests speaking of the ancient city, thereby cementing it into the *Stargate* universe as well. "Lost City" is a superb lesson in how to renew old themes.

Gods & Scientists: The Atlantis myth, conveniently for the writers, is fairly shrouded in mystery as well as history. The direct, principal sources most often used are Plato's *Timaeus* and *Critias*, but other sources may be Egyptian in origin (clever, no?). The most well-known version of the story of Atlantis is the city or island which, like the later Sodom and Gomorrah, became riddled with vice and corruption and was either swallowed by the sea (the Greek god Poseidon figures in this version) or destroyed by a cataclysmic volcanic eruption and its resulting tsunamis. Plato's philosophy was based on ideals, and it's hard to say whether he was using Atlantis as a historical reference or as a basis for an allegory.

Interesting Fact: "Lost City" lives up to its name. It was sitting in a desk drawer since the end of season five! At that time, Robert Cooper and Brad Wright were writing a finale that would segue back into feature films and into the spin-off *Stargate Atlantis*. However, *SG-1* was picked up at the last minute by the Sci-Fi Channel, and, based on fan reaction and ratings, went on for three (and now four) more seasons. Originally, it was written and shot as a two-hour finale, but Sci-Fi ultimately decided to chop it in half. As writer Robert Cooper noted, it worked fine, but you do come away with a sense that the first half is all setup for the second part.

Why We're Space Monkeys: We finally get to see SG-1 on downtime, just hanging out together. This is far better than the sly "resolution" of "Grace." Daniel gets drunk on one beer (he's so cute), and we see the team gel, not just as a military team, but as a group of people. But they look so . . . weird in civilian clothes.

HAMMOND: That was a lot of hair ago, Sir.

722. Lost City (Part 2)

Original airdate: March 19, 2004
Written by: Brad Wright, Robert Cooper
Directed by: Martin Wood

Jack goes Ancient, General Hammond proves to be tenacious, and Dr. Weir cracks a joke. Meanwhile, Anubis prepares to attack Earth, and Senator Kinsey gets his comeuppance, woohoo!

With so much buildup in the first part of the mini-arc about the danger of Anubis, the size of his fleet, and his dastardly plan of annihilation or at least total domination, it's slightly anomalous to see little evidence of his power. One shaky hologram in the White House and some threatening pacing on the deck of his ship? That doesn't really seem to be his style. When Anubis wants something, he goes after it, period. While he has been set up as a more cautious and cunning version of the Big Bad, he still seems to be wary at the most convenient times for the story line. This inauthenticity in the episode is really obvious. Even Bra'tac can't rescue this one, and he can usually impress us with his verbal reports of Anubis' movements.

In a little segue to *Atlantis*, we get to see the chair that's featured in the spin-off series here first, on a distant planet. The Ancient technology has been cropping up more often, first seen in "The Torment of Tantalus," and it spins off — literally! — into the future with open arms. Anything can happen now that the Ancient technology has been found and deciphered.

Season seven has three official two-parters, the most of any season to date. While "Evolution" showcased the show's new direction, and "Heroes" the compelling older themes, "Lost City" strives to do both. This mini-arc was allotted extra money, so the effects, while still in service to the story, are astounding. Especially worth watching twice or three times is the awesome fight sequence at the end. The textures of the *Prometheus* as enemy vessels fly across it, the shadows from ships on the

The next big thing: Joe Flanigan of *Stargate Atlantis* (ALBERT L. ORTEGA)

ground, the thousands of points of light from the various ships firing — all the gradients of cool are here.

The Han Solo jokes abounded online when the episode aired, and really, they were completely justified. Richard Dean Anderson plays part MacGyver (though pretending he knows not what he does), and part space pirate. But this silliness is almost balanced out by the best firing of the season — Senator Kinsey. "I've got enough on you to get you shot," is definitely one of my more favorite lines for the season — well, that and Sam's interrupted swearing. It is a tribute to Ronny Cox's excellent acting that we feel great vindication when he finally gets his.

And no one does belligerent innocence like Jack O'Neill. Half incredible heroism, half pain-in-the-*mik'ta*, Jack gives up his life (again, what is this, three, four times now?) for the greater good. In Part 1 he even had time to counsel wisdom just before he downloaded the repository into his brain. This episode sees him a little more chastened, a little apprehensive, but still a smart aleck. In fact, Jack imbues the first twenty minutes of the episode with almost every emotion available. Sadness and fear at the unknown future, regret about and longing for Carter, worry over his team, a tender love of Guinness. . . . Kidding aside, it's amazing that Richard has not received any nominations for his portrayal of Jack O'Neill, a man very clearly committed to being one note while reigning over a hundred subtle emotional casts. It's easy to see why fans were worried at the news that season eight would see even less of RDA.

Most of the episode is taken up with the team tracking down the Lost City, and with the coolness of the Ancients, brought to us via O'Neill (who has powers similar to those we saw in "Frozen"). But as cowriter Robert Cooper noted, it all seems squashed in there. In a little over forty minutes, we cross the galaxy *twice*, and then save the planet? The very familiar trick of making these hard-to-swallow scenes feel light through the use of quips and great team moments was too obvious. On the other hand, Teal'c's emotional farewell to a wordless O'Neill and the resulting moment was extremely well done.

One thing stood out — when they reach the planet, Bra'tac says he *thinks* there's a spot where the rings will penetrate the outer shell of the world, which is some unholy temperature and covered in lava. So the question is, what would have happened if the rings hadn't penetrated? SG-1 is chili? Regardless, the CGI effects of this episode were phenomenal, from the falling rocks of the ring transport to the final stream of

Ancient weaponry around the hull of the *Prometheus* en route to destroy Anubis' ship.

In essence, the episode brings to an end one era of *SG-1* while opening up the future. By airtime, season eight had been confirmed and was in production, but the fact that Rick would be returning for only a few episodes was well known. While RDA's new role in the SGC for season eight was handled as well as things could be, the ending of season seven is a telling portrait of how far things have come — or not, as the case may be. Sam's last angsty moment in an episode full of angsty moments was obvious and tasteless. Sure she's evolved as a person and is no longer as scared to show her feelings, but every moment onscreen between her and O'Neill is a replay of every moment they've had from season four on. Of the four team members, Teal'c and Daniel seem the most at home in their skins, not ping-ponging all over the place.

Gods & Scientists: The name of the traitorous Jaffa in service to Anubis in this two-parter, Ronan, is very auspicious. It's an excellent homonym for the Japanese word *ronin*, which was a word originally used to denote a certain class of masterless samurai warrior, but eventually came to be used to describe the many samurai who were relieved of their fiefdom through misdeeds or the death of their patron. Even later it came to describe those who voluntarily roamed Japan, seeking out unwelcome Westerners (or rebel Jaffa, as the case may be), and the Ronan we see in *SG-1* would fit in well in their ranks.

Interesting Fact: That's a real general of the Air Force in the Oval Office holding the red phone: General John P. Jumper appeared in the episode as himself, the U.S. Air Force Chief of Staff. That's the second time a general has appeared in the series (see "Prodigy").

Why We're Space Monkeys: Sam is getting more commanding; Daniel won't give up, but his strength has a leaner, meaner feel to it; and Teal'c talks more in this episode than O'Neill does. Things are shaking up again, keeping us glued to our seats for another season.

Parlez-vous Gate?:
O'NEILL: Now, see, I assume we still speak the same language . . . mostly.
DANIEL: "Sphere": planet. "Label": name.
O'NEILL: Following . . . still . . . you . . . not!

STARGATE SG-1: SEASON EIGHT
"Taking the fight to them."

801. New Order (Part 1)

Original airdate: July 9, 2004
Written by: Joseph Mallozzi, Paul Mullie
Directed by: Andy Mikita

When Sam and Teal'c ask the Asgard for help in rescuing O'Neill, they discover that the Replicators they thought were contained have escaped. Back on Earth, Elizabeth Weir and Daniel cope with a surprising turn of events that has the Goa'uld System Lords asking for a favor.

On first viewing, "New Order" felt different from other season premieres; on second viewing, it's obvious that it's *meant* to be different. The feel of the show has irredeemably changed, in ways as large as team makeup, mythological arcs, and story lines, and since it's not something that is going to go unnoticed by viewers, the writers make it a point to be honest about the upheaval. However, too much change makes fans nervous, so the whole new look is couched in old-style cosmetics — big battles, small team moments, and the familiar gold of Goa'uld ships. A great intro to a year that will have some rough (or stagnant, depending on your view) waters but in the end will come out with some heady episodes, starting with "New Order."

The end of season seven saw Jack frozen in Antarctica, with no obvious cure available. Season eight starts out by separating the team even further — Teal'c and Sam on the *Prometheus*, and Daniel and Dr. Weir at the SGC, dealing with the concept of the Goa'uld as potential allies. The writing team of "M&M" turns the show's status quo on its head in this two-parter by disturbing the enemy/alliance binary, splitting the team, upending the hierarchy of the SGC, and making SG-1 look at old enemies in new ways — from the Goa'uld to the Replicators. But you never feel out of your depth, because they cleverly base their story on some of the most enduring (and carefully cultivated) backstories of the series — the Asgard, the Replicators, Baal, and the fight against the Goa'uld. While "New Order" does take the show in a new direction, its foundations are recognizably *Stargate*; the ease with which the viewer can become immersed in the story,

Torri Higginson took over the role of Dr. Weir in *SG-1*'s eighth season, then went on to head up *SGA* (COURTESY ELIZA BENNETT)

even without the team structure of Jack, Sam, Daniel, and Teal'c fighting the good fight, is a wonderful introduction to the season.

The pairing of Daniel and Dr. Weir, whose character eventually makes the transition as one of the leads on *Stargate Atlantis* (and who's played from here on by Torri Higginson) is one that makes a lot of sense. It allows for the characters to play off each other's strengths as diplomats and humanists, without geeking out too much. Their interaction with the System Lords is both amusing and stimulating, and while those scenes could have been boring from an action-seeking perspective, the twisted tales of diplomatic hide-and-seek are intriguing and tense. Higginson manages to dismantle most fans' objections to her character (there are many General Hammond loyalists) by playing Weir with an appealing mix of self-assuredness and a sense of being lost — a feeling with which most people in a new job can identify. While Dr. Weir seems ineffectual and slightly cringey at the beginning of the episode, halfway through she picks up steam. It's as though she needed some time to realize the truly galactic proportions of the stakes — and the egos — involved.

"New Order" takes off from season six's "Unnatural Selection," which is the last time we saw the Replicators — even the progression of the titles indicates a careful plotting of course and action, a new beginning. Patrick Currie's interpretation of his character Fifth, the "Replicator with a heart," was so well done you couldn't help but ache for him at the end of "Unnatural Selection," and he outplays Tapping in their scene on the Replicator ship in this episode as well — although his tired, obsessed-creep mien is teeth-grittingly obvious. Still, you can't dispute that Fifth's interactions with SG-1 have irrevocably changed him; no longer an innocent, he has discovered the "dark side" of humanity, and remains mostly unmoved by Carter's fearful pleadings. Speaking of which, those were the worst crocodile tears, ever. The scene would not have lacked punch without them; with them, they take away from Carter's inherent strength, as though she is crying merely *to* cry. The fakery of the scene makes Fifth the more human of the two.

One of the larger arcs of the season is introduced here, as Carter faces up to the very real consequences of SG-1's betrayal of Fifth. While it's irritating to see yet *another* stalker type appear in Carter's life (see "Affinity" for more on that), the episode offers a glimpse of the ambivalence she must feel when confronted with the harsh realities of her job. She didn't want to leave Fifth behind, but she was under orders. In a way, she now has to create her own orders; with her immediate superior in cryogenic stasis, and her own future (and survival) uncertain, she must devise a means of survival, relying on her own mind to rescue her.

"New Order" very nicely posits the power of the mind — and the strength of Carter's mind in particular — as it helps her overcome fear, pain, and no doubt a fair amount of anger. There's a new order to *SG-1* and one again we're glued to our seats watching. While the galactic battles are fought in space and at the SGC, Carter and Fifth remind us that whatever else happens, it all comes down to the interpersonal relationship. Betrayal, jealousy, love, hatred — all these feelings can be made large scale, even galactic, but in the end, it's the personal attacks that can cut the deepest.

Gods & Scientists: Neutronium is the composite needed to fashion human Replicators, as opposed to the bug-like Replicators, which are fashioned out of keron blocks. Neutronium is the densest matter possible outside of a black hole, and is composed primarily of closely packed neutrons. This phase of matter occurs in the core of neutron stars, and is still not fully understood; it is, however, one of the mainstays for writers of science fiction shows.

Interesting Fact: Michael Shanks was injured by a rope on set during the production of this episode. Despite the fact that his eye was red and watering, he ignored the injury until shooting was done before going to the hospital. Talk about devotion to the job.

Why We're Space Monkeys: The CGI. *Farscape* fans had the muppets, Trekkies had the bridge, and *Dr. Who* fans had . . . the scarf? But Gaters have been privy to some pretty spectacular computer effects, and "New Order" raises the bar again, much as "Lost City (Part 2)" did with its great fight scene over the Antarctic. The Replicators, the holograms, even the disembodied voice of O'Neill make for a seamless integration into the story. Another example of CGI in service to, rather than taking over, the story.

Parlez-vous Gate?:
DANIEL: On the bright side, out of all the Goa'uld, Lord Yu has been the most co-operative with us in the past.
WEIR: I thought you said none of them could be trusted.
DANIEL: Oh, they can't, especially not a crazy one.
WEIR: Huh. That's the bright side?
DANIEL: More of a slightly less dark side.

802. New Order (Part 2)

Original airdate: July 9, 2004
Written by: Robert Cooper
Directed by: Andy Mikita

SG-1 and the Asgard make a final stand against the Replicators, trying to rescue Carter.

An aspect of this season opener, besides the new dynamics of the team, is the continuation of contemporary science fiction tropes, replacing older, traditional ones. By carefully placing new contexts in old landscapes, the writers of these two episodes have more flexibility where characters are concerned. The team's interaction in the first part of "New Order" is a great microcosm: Carter as leader; Teal'c as emotional, talking person (with hair!); and Daniel walking his own path. These are all elements we've seen swirling around in an indirect way for eight years, but now it looks like these facets are going to be addressed directly.

Season eight is going to see significant changes, and this is where we get a taste of it. With the Replicators highlighted in these first two episodes, we can surmise that there's going to be a new order to the baddies, too. And it's time — the Goa'uld have been an admirable enemy, but later episodes seem to make them more . . . irritating than a true nemesis should be. And

The first season cast of *Stargate Atlantis* (ALBERT L. ORTEGA)

while the Replicators were chilling when they first arrived on the scene, it was a good move to revamp them into a human form. While the sheer alienness of the Replicators was a good springboard for storytelling, over the long haul, a machine enemy would have become repetitive and annoying. Whether we admit it or not, we tune in to see the characters interact, not the machines. This is a theme we encounter again in "Avatar," and it's handled well in both places. So the end of the Goa'uld reign, hinted at in these beginning episodes, will make way for a more contemporary foil with a contemporary look.

And the CGI is once again flawless. When Fifth mutates from Pete Shanahan to his "real" form, the transformation is scary in its effortlessness. Gone is the posturing, blustering, "old school" Goa'uld. Replacing pride with avarice and gluttony, the latest rendition of Replicators are more and more integrated into the landscape itself. In that sense, the Replicators stand in for the heading that the show has been on the past three years — away from their traditional mythic arc of the Egyptian deities and into a more contemporary, science fiction flavor. In "New Order," the Replicators are no longer constrained to flat surfaces (where they are more easily rendered); now they move in a 3D world, around corners, up trees, and over rocks, with different perspectives and fully mobile shadows; the sheer mass of them at the end of the episode is just freaky.

Another big theme for season eight is the question of virtual worlds and the nature of reality — who decides where reality starts and ends? Fifth might perhaps live quite happily in his created world with Carter, if that's what it would take to make his world complete. To him, that would be "real." Fifth's insistence that Carter will learn to love him — even though he removes her dignity, freedom, and autonomy to better fit his own worldview — is a backhanded compliment/complaint to the fans, perhaps. But Fifth's initial creation of a perfect Carter world — and when that doesn't work, a perfect Carter replica — mimics not just rabid fans but people in general. We try and try and try again to make things "good," and in trying, we create ourselves as much as we create our world. Moral issues like right and wrong become contextual, and it's hard not to empathize a little bit with Fifth there. It's kind of heavy philosophizing for television.

Writer Robert Cooper, as well as the "M&M" team, is also putting in for some new order — orders to the fans. Like Fifth, fans often demonstrate an extremely powerful but occasionally misguided loyalty. While it's a stretch to say that Fifth is a reflection of viewers who want to manipulate the show till it reflects their own perfect reality, the writers *are* using the story to make the point that the show isn't only about small, vocal contingents who want Sam and Jack together, or Jack and Daniel together, or Pete Shanahan killed, or more action and less talking, or more mythology and less stuff blowing up. The characters *themselves* need to find their way, and from their fumbling around — even if it's in an embarrassingly sheer nightgown, what were they thinking? — the team of SG-1 must find their own place in the new order of the galaxy.

The scene of O'Neill getting promoted was . . . well, it was okay. O'Neill's signature smart-aleckyness has survived for eight years. One can't help but wonder where the O'Neill from earlier seasons went, the one from "Cold Lazarus" or "Beneath the Surface"? Heck, even in "A Hundred Days" O'Neill packs more emotional punch than in some of the later seasons, where he is occasionally reduced to Quip Guy. And even though Rick controls his penchant for humor in the promotion scene, when it comes right down to it, all around that moment are flippant lines and a casual pose that has come to be his "signature O'Neill." On the upside, he is *finally* allowed to get through a whole speech without getting beamed up halfway through it!

Season eight starts out at high speed, with great character development, both good and bad, new challenges, and some great old-style action.

Gods & Scientists: The System Lord Camulus has been disowned from the Goa'uld community, having asked for asylum on Earth. In Celtic mythology, Camulus was a war god, the tribal god of the Remi, a Gallic tribe living in Belgium. He is associated with Mars, or Ares, the Roman/Greek god of war. *Camulus* means "heaven" in Celtic.

Interesting Fact: When I asked Joseph Mallozzi (who cowrote the first part of "New Order") what wisdom he would take away with him after working on *Stargate SG-1*, he responded, "Be open to the ideas offered by your fellow writers, never miss an opportunity for humor, and don't eat more than one dessert serving a day no matter how good those chocolate tuxedo squares look."

Why We're Space Monkeys: Daniel takes his various roles almost always in stride. He's left on the planet with Dr. Weir, but pragmatically realizes that this *is* his new place, as he has a coin that's very hard to find at this galactic level — knowledge. Not to say he doesn't occasionally have hissy fits and demand some hard truths, but he's come a long way from the tentative archaeologist we saw in season one. Michael Shanks invests conscientious energy in making sure his character isn't a cardboard cutout of the faithful nerdy sidekick.

Parlez-vous Gate?:
DANIEL: On the flip side of the coin, there's the fact that nobody knows how this place should be run better than you.
O'NEILL: Why thank you, Daniel.
DANIEL: With a little guidance from your good friends and advisors, of course.
CARTER: If you don't take the job, we could end up with someone much worse. (A pause while O'Neill stares at her) Okay, that did not come out right.

803. Lockdown

Original airdate: July 23, 2004
Written by: Joseph Mallozzi, Paul Mullie
Directed by: William Warring

*Just when Teal'c finally gets his own place, O'Neill locks down the SGC when
a virus contaminates the base. But it's not a virus — it's an Anubis.*

"You'd think that getting blasted out of orbit would have slowed the guy
down!" Anubis isn't dead. Is anyone else getting Apophis flashbacks? At
least he's gotten rid of the cowl.

The theme of sacrifice is one frequently employed by the "M&M"
writing team — think of "Chain Reaction," "Fail Safe," or "Scorched Earth,"
for example — and here it's revisited again with new aims. Many fans were
disappointed with Richard Dean Anderson's reduced schedule, but closer
examination of the first few episodes can reveal that, though there is not
much O'Neill time in terms of quantity, what there is has subtle quality.
The sacrifice that the new Brigadier General O'Neill makes — trading his
job as an active member of SG-1 to become the head of the base — isn't
explained to us so much as shown. From the start, O'Neill has made it clear
that he's going to be neither very good at the job, nor very appealing to his
superiors with his methods. "Zero Hour," the next episode after this one,
approaches O'Neill's decision to become head of the base in a much more
direct way. Here O'Neill's seeming ineptitude is exposed for everyone to
see, a small window into the intricacies of a massive and mostly thankless
job. Can O'Neill's leadership abilities bear the brunt of this kind of attack,
when he can no longer just pass it up the line, when he *is* the top of the
line? His reluctance to add a fourth to SG-1 may be seen as a writerly trick,
but it's also a reflection of O'Neill: loyal, antagonistic, and protective.
Buttoned-down types like Colonel Vaselov just wouldn't fit the mold for
SG-1 — precisely because there is no mold.

This episode also continues the relationship between the SGC and Russia.
Since "Watergate," the Russian/U.S. thread has been included in almost
every season ("Watergate", "The Tomb," "Desperate Measures," "48 Hours,"
"Redemption"), including another season eight episode, "Full Alert." The
Russians have moved from Cold War enemies to potential allies to
omnipresent, with a team at the SGC. They are proving to be more than just

a convenient point of departure for espionage episodes like "Watergate" or "The Tomb." Colonel Vaselov, with his impressive, almost foreboding stance and diction, reminds us a lot of the Jaffa, and shares many of their traits as well — honor, dignity, the ability to see (and fight for) the greater cause. The episode doesn't so much set up the Russians as another "alien" in this sense as it brings together the human and Jaffa, pointing out their similarities.

Remember that photo from the "Fanchise" chapter? At least Teryl got a T-shirt . . . (COURTESY ZOE BENNETT)

Unfortunately, the problem with the Russian and the NID mini-arcs is that espionage stories are hard to tell if they concentrate on certain film noir or "telling" techniques — the so-called "talky" episodes. The Russian episodes seem to be better interwoven into the narratives than the NID episodes; the tension mounts quickly, and we are more aware of potential jeopardy, but this could be because we are familiar with the idea of Russia as a threat in a way that we are not with the NID, Jaffa, or other alien elements. Plus, most of the Russian elements have been gotten out of the way at the beginning of the episode, and the story concentrates on the threat posed by Anubis. "M&M" get most of the talky stuff out of the way there, too.

Vaselov's sacrifice alludes to Daniel's sacrifice — Daniel takes on Ascension, sacrificing his earthly life, much as Vaselov takes on Anubis. Another similarity is that both Vaselov and Daniel are infected by Anubis. The parallels are clearly drawn, with each one sacrificing in his way: Daniel, who always seems to bumble into these scenarios, but nevertheless accepts the hard tasks with grace, such as when Vaselov asks him to carry a final note to his sister; and Vaselov by making sure that Anubis does not get away in O'Neill's body. In a way, secondary characters like Dr. Fraiser or Colonel Vaselov stand in for main characters, enacting their death in a cathartic way ("Tin Man" works on the same premise, allowing the viewers to experience the deaths of the main characters without any of the consequences) which alleviates the pressure, so to speak. And, speaking of Dr. Fraiser, Alisen Down (as Dr. Brightman) has a thankless job in this episode, playing a role that has been skirted around since "Heroes." The question, "Who will take Dr. Fraiser's place?" however, can't be avoided forever. Unfortunately Dr. Brightman gets some lines from hell (trauma manifesting symptoms that range from memory loss to psychosis? Wow, way to narrow it down there), and more than a few of her lines were lost in background noise and just plain mumbling.

Like a thief, Anubis tries to break into the SGC, collecting information and other valuables as he goes. Daniel's eventual idea to make Anubis do something to be accountable to them seems good — but it's flawed. Hasn't Anubis already done enough with his knowledge of the Ancients (trying to get the Eye of Tiamat and then trying to get the Antarctic base, for starters) to warrant a reprisal? What exactly constitutes personal interference for the Ascended? Hundreds of lives lost is okay, but when Daniel stands against Anubis *one time* he gets thrown back to corporeal form? For a being as powerful and relentless as Anubis has been, it seems a shame to use him as a sort of interstellar lockpicker.

Gods & Scientists: The term "DEFCON," which is used by General O'Neill in this episode, is used by North American Air Defense (NORAD) to determine its threat alert level. It stands for Defense Readiness Condition, and goes from five (at peace) to one (at war).

Interesting Fact: Aaron Pearl, who plays Major Kearney in this episode, also played the younger version of General Hammond in season two's "1969."

Why We're Space Monkeys: You have to love it when the people involved point out where they went wrong. If you thought that Sam drawing the curtain against Colonel Vaselov's hearing about his condition was ridiculous, writer Joseph Mallozzi agrees. On GateWorld, he writes, "One particular moment that never failed to elicit giggles whenever we screened the episode comes when Carter visits Daniel in the infirmary. Daniel asks about Colonel Vaselov's condition. Carter pauses, then reaches back and draws the curtain separating Daniel's bed from that of the Russian lying right beside him, perhaps presuming it will magically render the ensuing conversation inaudible. As Carter fills Daniel in on the Vaselov's dire state, someone in the room would invariably pipe up in a bad Russian accent: 'I can heeeaaar yooooou. I am lying right heeeeere!'"

Parlez-vous Gate?: The wordless interplay between the team members after Daniel asks (for the second time) who shot him, was priceless. Teal'c's first slantwise glance!

804. Zero Hour

Original airdate: July 30, 2004
Written by: Robert Cooper
Directed by: Peter Woeste

O'Neill faces the trials and tribulations of being in command of the SGC.

The phrase "zero hour" is a contradiction, and in that way it reflects admirably the character of Jack O'Neill. While in this case it refers to the culmination of cascading events, taken out of context it can seem like a complete contradiction, an oxymoron. Fans not familiar with the show or those fans newly introduced to the character of O'Neill might come into season eight and see an inept smart-aleck and wonder why he's been put in charge of the SGC. His whole story line about the bunting, for example, sets O'Neill up as bumbling and indecisive, which is anathema to the military world; it does not seem as though he reflects the professional and military qualities the SGC has come to represent, and certainly not the ones embodied by General Hammond. When we see his acceptance of the new position, and the first few times we see him acting in that new role, we can't help but wonder why exactly he was chosen for the task. Heroism aside, he's not exactly office material.

Still, the fact remains that Jack *did* accept the new position, knowing that it would take him out of the field, and in that way, the show is challenging the way we view heroes. It can't always be about the glory of the battlefield, and this is something that Jack has obviously come to appreciate and accept in himself. The character is changing in ways the viewer can't perceive except in retrospect, looking back on the progression of season eight. It sometimes seems as though his character doesn't change or engage at all; this season makes it clear that sometimes, the stillest waters run the deepest.

And while Jack makes his decisions in a firmly comedic manner in "Zero Hour," episodes like "Sacrifices" have him making tougher decisions maturely and responsibly, as befits a man of his position. It's the small potatoes that bug O'Neill, the bureaucracy, and this becomes apparent in "Zero Hour." It may seem flippant, but Jack's character has undergone some deep changes that have him moving past his own personal misgivings. The season allows O'Neill to grow into his job, and it allows viewers to adapt to the team's new dynamics. It culminates in episodes like "Full Alert" and "Endgame," as his sense of purpose becomes steadier, and we realize that even heroes can change.

While "Zero Hour" has some problems, including a title that seems to be as ambiguous as the story, *SG-1* once again confronts philosophical issues, although more indirectly than we've seen in the past, in episodes like "Beast of Burden," "Maternal Instinct," and "1969." Like "Icon," "Avatar," and "Gemini," "Zero Hour" is a metonymical look at Jack O'Neill: he *is* a contradiction. The entire framework of the episode seems to be a contradiction, as well, since it's using a proleptic (flashforward or anticipation) technique to invoke a sense of jeopardy — we keep expecting something big to happen — when in fact we're being shown a series of small events which could accumulate to a kind of zero hour — in Jack's life. Each event on its own would not lead to such a high-stakes sense of jeopardy, but the accumulation of them does. The story sets up a contradiction between our expectations and the "payoff."

These small events are also making us aware of other contradictions. The different threats apparent in this episode — the plant, which is overtaking the SGC at an alarming rate, and the squabbling Amran delegates — combine to contradict our assumptions: science is always contained and perfectly understandable, and passion is always uncontained and imperfect. In "Zero Hour," the plant very quickly becomes uncontainable, while the delegates are literally contained in a room in order to work out their differences. In Western culture, passion is commonly seen as being messy, immature, unconstructive. In the beginning of the episode, the Amran do reflect that ideology. By placing them together in a room, however, Jack — as the agent of contradiction — forces the delegates to construct their passion differently, and (eventually) productively. Conversely, the pragmatism with which the plant is viewed at first — it is a plant and therefore under science's authority — is overturned; suddenly, the SGC is confronted with a science it cannot understand, control, or even destroy.

For all intents and purposes, "Zero Hour" is a light episode with a strange title and a strange narrative setup, but when it's all put together, it works, mostly thanks to RDA's steady performance.

Interesting Fact: Joseph Mallozzi in an interview: "A couple of weeks before this episode went to camera, we learned that *Stargate SG-1* had been mentioned on the *Conan O'Brien* show. In a segment called 'Recliner of Rage,' Pierre Bernard expressed his passionate take on the show's direction. It was a funny bit and we, of course, appreciated the fact that *Stargate* had been mentioned. Days later, we were contacted by one of the producers of the *Conan O'Brien* show. It turns out that Pierre was such a huge fan of the show that they wanted to know if they could bring him up for a visit and a possible cameo in an upcoming episode. We were more than happy to accommodate him and so, 'Zero Hour' marks the acting debut of Conan's own Pierre Bernard. He plays the erstwhile young technician at the controls at episode's end when the gate room comes under attack."

Why We're Space Monkeys: Any show that can make fun of bunting for forty minutes . . .

Parlez-vous Gate?:
CARTER: General.
O'NEILL: Colonel! We've all met.
DANIEL: Yes, actually, we know each other's life stories.
O'NEILL: Is that snippiness?
DANIEL: Is that a word?

805. Icon

Original airdate: August 6, 2004
Written by: Damian Kindler
Directed by: Peter Woeste

Daniel awakens on an alien planet to find himself in the midst of a civil war.

Metonymy is a rhetorical device used to show the entirety of something through a part of the same thing; a modern example is calling business people "suits," because their attire represents their livelihood, set of attitudes, and ideology. There are three instances in season-eight episode titles where single words are used to denote a larger idea: "Avatar" as a metonym for Teal'c; "Gemini" for Carter; and "Icon" for Daniel. An avatar is an embodiment of an ideal, as Teal'c is the embodiment of the untiring warrior; the schism between the "bad" Replicator Carter, who does what she wants, and the "cult of true womanhood" Carter, who represents humility, devotion, and servitude is the metonymy operating in "Gemini"; in "Icon," we are presented with the immediate surface icon of the Stargate and all that it has come to represent over eight years — freedom, exploration, discovery, danger, excitement, mystery — but beneath that, the episode deals with another icon of *SG-1*, Daniel Jackson. Daniel's values include humanism, higher emotions such as empathy and compassion, and being a moral compass; and there are his physical attributes: he looks good and represents good things.

The writers in season eight seem to be treading a fine line between presenting viewers with strong story lines and undermining those stories with secondary presences, and "Icon" is an example. Although the main plot denounces the use of war as an icon for freedom, the underlying message is that the icon people should be looking at is Daniel. And it highlights another recurrent use of metonymy throughout the season: thanks to the reorganization of the team, in many episodes, one of the central characters will often stand in for the whole team. While this may have been the physical reality due to Richard Dean Anderson's absence, it doesn't excuse the backhanded dissing of fans in such episodes as "New Order," "Icon," and "Citizen Joe." One of the reasons many fans love the show is because of the writers' regard for continuity; this late in the game though, it feels like the writers have eschewed tightly woven continuity and instead resorted to the use of sly in-jokes and teasing to show their awareness of the fans' presence.

Right from the beginning of the episode, Daniel Jackson (introduced as "Dr." when he is usually called Daniel), is relegated to his archaeologist days. It is he who points out that the people of the unnamed planet wear iconography of the Stargate around their necks. Just before that, Gareth speaks about the impossibility of an "artifact" coming to life. In a way, Jackson is also an artifact — a written one, then filmed — and his iconography is built with each episode that adds or detracts from his "story."

Unfortunately, when the needs of the story are weak or suggest a subtext as "Icon" does, Daniel is relegated into an older version of himself, the scientist, but this version doesn't quite gel with his later role. Gareth mentions a little later that people wear the Stargate symbol around their neck more for fashion than anything. It seems as though in this episode *Daniel* is more fashion than anything. Does this mean that Daniel is merely a fashionable but ridiculous bauble, that his ideology is outdated but still useful as a cheap plot device? Plot is the underlying network of every character's emotional and psychological characteristics: story is just what happens. To cheaply introduce a plot device in the form of Daniel for the sake of the story and not the sake of the plot makes "Icon" seem not iconic but gaudy. Throw in lame techniques like ultra-soft, overhead, beaming-upon-him lighting, *Casablanca*-esque period costumes, a rote love interest, and the requisite physical discomfort, and you have one of the least well-done episodes season eight has to offer. Take another look at "Need," a second-season entry that dealt with some of the same themes, especially Daniel as an icon, but with far more subtle and engaging techniques. For a character who has denied the plausibility of the Goa'uld as gods for eight years running, it's more than shameful to see him assigned that very role.

Gods & Scientists: Iconography is the study and interpretation of symbols and themes in visual art. The earliest such studies were published in the sixteenth century, and the science was not commonly linked to religious symbolism until the nineteenth century. Icons are in some ways visual metonyms: the cross used as a symbol for Christ in Christianity; the Star of David used as a symbol for the Jewish faith; and the Stargate used as a symbol for the worlds that lie beyond it.

Parlez-vous Gate?:
O'NEILL: You coming home or what?
DANIEL: Trying to. As soon as I find my *kal'tesh*.
O'NEILL: What?
DANIEL: Err, looks a lot like my *rin'kalnok*. You know, I lent it to the . . . uh . . . for *grel'ka greenor* day.
O'NEILL (to the others in the control room): He's changed.

806. Avatar

Original airdate: August 13, 2004
Written by: Damian Kindler
Directed by: Martin Wood

Teal'c is trapped in a combat simulation that won't let him win, or leave.

The first Teal'c-centric episode of the season, "Avatar" is fantastic. Just as "Icon" and "Gemini" show the challenges faced by Daniel and Carter respectively, as they grow into their new roles in a reordered team, so does "Avatar" provide the grounds for Teal'c to come to his own understanding of what challenges him.

While most episodes that repeat the same premise over and over while the characters figure out how to rectify the situation are dull to the point of unwatchable (*The Next Generation*'s "Cause and Effect" leaps to mind), the *Stargate* writers pull off another win here in the same vein as season four's "Window of Opportunity." Full credit for that has to go to Chris Judge for playing each of Teal'c's permutations slightly differently, just enough to allow viewers an understanding of the character's state of mind while allowing them to track the progression of his physical and mental well-being. For someone who has always prided himself on, and even defined himself through, his physical prowess, his strength as a warrior, and skills as a strategist, Teal'c's downslide into complete exhaustion over the course of "Avatar" must have been as emotionally difficult as it was physically challenging, and Judge plays the part perfectly. The resigned desperation that he emanates as he slides down the wall near the end of the episode captures that difficulty; it's impossible not to feel for him.

"Avatar" is wonderfully layered: a theme within a theme within a theme. The word itself has several meanings. The literal interpretation would be the digital representation of a user in a virtual reality space, but the episode also plays with the ideas of the corporeal representation of a familiar idea. Just as Teal'c is projected into the simulation to teach the program combat strategies, he is also the three-dimensional representation of the larger story, which involves SG-1 having to become better at what they do. While it seems as though the episode revolves around the program's all too rapid learning curve, in fact the central theme is Teal'c's own learning curve. He has always been the one character who never ceases, never backs down — in "Solitudes" he went to planet after planet searching for Jack and Sam; in "A Hundred Days" he stubbornly held on to life as he dug through the earth to reach the stranded Jack O'Neill — and in "Avatar" he's pitted against someone even *he* can't best — himself. He very painfully has to learn his own limits, the same way the scientists are learning the limitations of their simulation, and Jack is learning that there are limits to what he can do, even as commander of the SGC.

Speaking of Jack, the arc that Teal'c follows in this episode mimics Jack's arc throughout season eight, but in reverse. While Jack learns to bear with grace his role as protector and manager of the SGC, in "Avatar" Teal'c learns to let himself be lead. When Daniel first appears in the simulation, Teal'c is quick to distrust him, and the subsequent game sequences show him gradually letting down his defenses and coming to the inescapable conclusion that he cannot win the game alone. He needs Daniel. For someone who's always been so staunchly self-reliant, Teal'c's acceptance of Daniel's help must have come at no small cost to his pride. But the writers of the show have constantly tried to make sure the lessons learned by the characters never come at a too low a cost. As in real life, the harshest lessons are usually the ones we have the most need of learning, and in "Avatar," the lesson that Teal'c learns is one that will change the way he thinks and acts from here on in. An excellent redemption for "Icon."

Gods & Scientists: Virtual reality (VR) is an old standard in science fiction shows. Every series, from *Star Trek* to *The X-Files* to *Farscape* to *Red Dwarf*, has placed its characters in a virtual reality situation. VR technology was first used in the 1960s when pilots were taught to fly through simulators. It was further developed in the 1980s, with the creation of new interactive systems by the U.S. military and NASA. The use of VR as a military training tool is not new; VR was used to prepare U.S. troops for the Gulf War in 1991, for example.

Interesting Fact: Teal'c's line, "I play 'Def Jam Vendetta'" is a tongue-in-cheek reference to the fact that actor Chris Judge does the voice for the character D-Mob in the computer game.

Why We're Space Monkeys: *Stargate* isn't afraid to show its characters failing. And it's interesting to see the very authentic theme of "you are your own worst enemy" being developed on the show. Teal'c faces off against his own mind in "Avatar," much like Carter against her own doppelganger in "Gemini."

Parlez-vous Gate?:
O'NEILL: Carter, all I heard was "matrix," and I found those films quite confusing.

807. Affinity

Original airdate: August 20, 2004
Written by: Peter DeLuise
Directed by: Peter DeLuise

Teal'c is accused of some hefty crimes when his neighbor's boyfriend is found dead. Pete asks Sam for more commitment.

An episode that deals with *how* as much as *why* we like, "Affinity" only gets bogged down with some sad archetypes and a lack of any sense of jeopardy, much like what we've seen recently in "Icon" and "New Order (Part 2)." Otherwise, it is an episode that could have made a great addition to season eight.

In the long arc of season eight, as the humans "take the fight to the stars," so, in his way, does Teal'c take the fight back to Earth. It does seem a little ridiculous after eight years for him to live on base, and the questions of Teal'c's affinity to the humans is posed nicely. Instead of telling us how Teal'c feels *about* the humans — a fact that has been well established by this time — writer Peter DeLuise instead comes at it from the question, "why does Teal'c *still* like the humans?" It's a good question, and one that is not answered as much by Teal'c's own story as by Pete and Sam. Sam, undergoing the predicaments of her own personal life, takes the time to make sure she is making the right decision. Pete Shanahan, far from being the "stalker" that he calls himself (and nice tongue-in-cheek reference to the fandom), does not pressure Sam into giving him an answer. This so-called "secondary plot" is actually a reflection of the best that Teal'c has come to see in the humans, an inverse to the thieves, hoods, and NID agents we also see in "Affinity." Patience, perseverance, and a capacity to earn love instead of demanding it, these are the human traits that he admires and is willing to sacrifice a lot for. While most humans around him act like little more than spoiled children, Pete and Sam continue to hold for us the best that humans have to offer.

Unfortunately, this episode can get dismissed because of its heavy-handed use of character. The character of Krista — waiflike, big innocent eyes, *yadda yadda* — and her boyfriend straight from *Trailer Park Boys* present us with not much of a foil for Teal'c. Instead, they seem to be caricatures that don't act so much as take the well-known positions of the wailing damsel and the evil villain. Speaking of positions, check out Chris Judge's Shaft pose at the beginning, when the crane scoots up to an overhead view after Teal'c's effortless dispatching of three men. A little cheesy (and oh-so Peter DeLuise), with the thumping bass background and the flapping whites on the hero, it does however do its job, reminding us that Teal'c is not just a potted plant (did you catch that line, about talking to the plant?) but a viable warrior. Teal'c can talk, and he's finally moving out of the earlier part of the season's role of stating the obvious — "New Order" is a particularly teeth-gritting example of that.

The only things that sit poorly are the inexplicable tie-ups. Suddenly Krista is the killer, but at the end of the episode she still beams whimsically (aren't there police procedures for murder, even if in self-defence?), looking more childlike than ever beside the now Officially Branded Kid (and I could make a sly reference here to MGM branding, but I won't). How did Daniel suddenly come out with the "So you're The Trust" thing? That came from nowhere and absolutely reeked of plot convenience. And Teal'c's straight-from-Chulak martial art bears a strange resemblance to many karate forms.

Gods & Scientists: The word affinity is derived from Middle English and originally meant "relationship by marriage." These days we use it to mean more of a spontaneous liking, but it's a good clue to the many layers this episode could have offered.

Interesting Fact: Look closely at the monitor on which Daniel gets the "coded" message — it can be translated alright, and looks suspiciously like "Actual Words Are Hard to Decide So This Will Work."

Why We're Space Monkeys: In the scene in the park, it looks almost like Daniel has a little gut. And hey, isn't that cool? He is, after all, an academic — and lately not seeing so much action. It's nice to see Michael Shanks not walking around with his gut sucked in like some 1950s bodybuilder.

Parlez-vous Gate?:
TEAL'C: On Chulak, a dispute between a man and a woman that cannot be resolved necessitates a pledge break. It must be requested by one and granted by the other.
DANIEL: And if that doesn't work?
TEAL'C: A weapon is required.

808. Covenant

Original airdate: August 27, 2004
Written by: Ron Wilkerson
Teleplay by: Ron Wilkerson, Robert Cooper
Directed by: Martin Wood

An eccentric billionaire decides to go public about the Stargate project.

As a title, "Covenant" alerts us to a darker story, especially with its biblical overtones. It also makes way for some real-life answers in the universe of *SG-1*: what *does* happen to all the stuff that gets carted back from other worlds? While we've seen some glimmers in "Shades of Grey" and "Smoke and Mirrors" especially, "Covenant" puts particular faces to the shadowy idea of culpability. One of the longest arcs of the series — the consequences of previous actions — comes up, and with a sombre twist. Characters from the past (reporters Julia Donovan and Emmet Bregman) haunt the story, reminding us that they haven't disappeared. The episode interweaves covenants of declaration (between governments) as well as covenants of restriction (property laws that govern the use of articles, such as the alien DNA, and Donovan's nondisclosure contract), allowing much more weight than usual to permeate the story. Another tricky episode for the so-called "light fare" of television.

O'Neill's quip, "Some of us [know Colson] better than others," about Sam's relationship with Colson does not seem either warranted or really O'Neill-like. However, it's nice to see any relationship between Sam and a man not based on obtuse flattery (not to mention the hapless guy's death). Alec Colson's company has done much R&D (research and development) in its various guises, for the military and the SGC. He personally worked on the engine that enabled the alien-enhanced ships from Earth to get off the ground. The NID's rogue faction has officially adopted a name — The Trust — to distinguish them from the less-evil-but-still-icky regular NID.

Actor Charles Shaughnessy (remember *The Nanny*?) does a good job of showing Colson as professionally driven to the exclusion of almost everything else, and yet he's almost innocent about the world. This sort of innocence (some might say he's wearing blinders) is usually seen in creative, driven people. Colson's ability to hold on to "the truth" as his savior — since, after all, the truth is "always right," as he says — reflects the American ideal of "the truth shall set you free" in operation. Colson *believes* in the covenant between himself as a citizen and his government. He knows that he would do the right thing, and because of that belief, he continues to operate as though it will make things happen. After all, it always did in the past. In that respect, even The Trust has a rightful place in the game — after all, they believe, as Colson does, that the government has broken its covenant with them, which justifies their zealous actions.

Unfortunately, Colson's character becomes mediocre near the end of the episode. We are never really made to feel the strong bonds between Colson and his best friend, Brian. So when Sam arrives (and boy, she does a lot more personal relationship work as a commander than Jack ever did) to find Colson with a gun in his hand, it just doesn't feel real. A man who bounced back from his family's death but caves after a friend's? Too bad about the final minutes, because the rest of the episode shone.

Interesting Fact: "I asked the Air Force a long time ago what would happen if somebody did find out, and did want to go public," noted Brad Wright. "They said, 'Well, we would bring them in. We would show them everything, and then say, now that you've seen everything, you see why we can't tell the world.' Because that happens. I mean, that happens in war. Reporters see stuff they're not supposed to see, and they're asked not to reveal it, and they don't. But in this case, the twist on this story is that, they do bring him in, and he goes, 'Now I want to show the world even more.'"

Why We're Space Monkeys: The covenant between the cast and crew to maintain a show that has continuing stories and threads that are intermittently picked and given new treatment. Although *SG-1*'s format is episodic, it gives continuous viewers very long story lines and complex consequences.

Parlez-vous Gate?: A moment in which the team discuss who's nuts:
CARTER: Colson Aviation developed the multi-engine control systems for the F-302s. Colson didn't know what they were for, of course, but he *is* a brilliant engineer.
O'NEILL: He's also a little *nuts*, isn't he?
CARTER: You've test-flown experimental aircraft.
DANIEL: We all go through the Gate.
O'NEILL (pause): This isn't about us.

809. Sacrifices

Original airdate: September 10, 2004
Written by: Christopher Judge
Directed by: Andy Mikita

Teal'c and Ishta clash over Rya'c's wedding, and over the best way to fight the Goa'uld.

There can be no doubt that *SG-1* tackles issues of gender more often than other sci-fi shows. The characters of Janet Fraiser and Samantha Carter immediately stand out as more approachable representations not only of women in the military, but women in general. Episodes like "Foothold," "Heroes," and "The Warrior" portray women as being just as capable, tough, and uncompromising as men. Unfortunately, "Sacrifices," while it aims to continue in that vein, does not do as good a job. Instead, it comes across as a sort of updated "Hathor" with some "Emancipation" thrown in.

Writer Christopher Judge continues his Teal'c arc from "Birthright," and as was mentioned in that episode, little in the way of a didactic message about the equality of men and women as warriors, as mates, or as sentient beings gets through all the muck and mess of outdated sexist clichés and scenes that could have been tense but deteriorate into shouting matches. Jolene Blalock, looking a little worried at the size of her acting partner, in a key moment not only shouts to distract us (we are led to assume she's emoting), but shouts at a tent wall to boot. There is no true tension between Teal'c and Ishta's ideological differences — between talking the path of equality, and walking it — since each time we are shown the two sides, in their alternate version of Kar'yn and Rya'c, they are sexistly portrayed. The betrothed Kar'yn talks her problems out with Ishta, while Rya'c smashes his frustration out with a weapon, only to be confronted by the wise Bra'tac who drops a few pearls of wisdom on the boy's sweaty brow before departing. The wilting Ishta can barely stand up when deprived of tritonin, and is reduced to casting a glazed glare at the tyrant Moloc; whereas Teal'c, similarly bereft, hikes half a kilometer at breakneck speed and then takes out three fully trained and armed Jaffa warriors. How are we supposed to take away the full import of equal hands for equal work from that? Thankfully, Tony Amendola, as Bra'tac, holds up his character admirably, as always, even when faced with a spitting and slightly shabby-looking Rya'c.

The Goa'uld Moloc was given up for dead in "Birthright," but he reappears, in weirdly Roman regalia, in this episode — just in time to be painted by his own troops as the target for a big missile. So big a missile, in fact, that one wonders how the Stargate itself survived, being in such close proximity.

The real central premise, hidden beneath the red herrings and sidebars that were used more effectively in Judge's episode "The Changeling," is Teal'c's apprehension about Rya'c having to make the same choices he did — to choose the warrior's path over a wife and family. Again, like "The Changeling," it doesn't come up until quite far into the episode, which is a nice change from the grey, Plot A to Plot B color scheme of most television fare. But by then, all the fun of the team (the hilarious Bobsey Twins act of Sam and Daniel, or Jack and Teal'c playing table tennis) has been leeched out by insane logical leaps in the plot (an *entire* world is being evacuated because of a missed meeting?) and silly additions — like a horse in the Gate room. The remnants of the original premise for a lighter episode are not integrated into the final, dark overtones of this story, and their juxtapositioning just does not work.

The stakes have been set high enough (the immediate goal of one Goa'uld's death versus the death of many at a later date) for us to be able to choose a side. But the philosophical and strategic play is weakened by placing all of the checks in Teal'c's side, and little on Ishta's side, besides sheer bloodymindedness.

Gods & Scientists: A fairly well-known fictional covenant is the one in the *Indiana Jones* movie *Raiders of the Lost Ark*. The Ark supposedly contains the Ten Commandments, written by God for Moses. These laws were part of the original covenant between God and the people of Israel.

Interesting Fact: According to director Peter DeLuise, the original title for the episode was "My Big Fat Jaffa Wedding," but the story didn't turn out as lighthearted as anyone had originally thought it would. This isn't unusual according to show producer and writer Robert Cooper, who said, "A lot of times [episodes] start out in our minds as what's going to be kind of a lighter episode. But when there are issues that you have to deal with because of an ongoing story line, a lot of times it doesn't end up the way you envisioned it because you have to address certain issues."

Parlez-vous Gate?: After a lengthy discourse from Daniel:
O'NEILL: What was my question again?

DANIEL: How's it going?

O'NEILL: Seemed so innocuous at the time . . .

810. Endgame

Original airdate: September 17, 2004
Written by: Joseph Mallozzi, Paul Mullie
Directed by: Peter DeLuise

The Stargate is stolen, and SG-1 uncovers more of The Trust while appre-hending it.

One of the realities we face in life is that all things must end. Whether we decide to approach our existence as a game, a one-shot deal, or as one aspect of a larger journey, within each context there is a sense of finality — even the afterlife must begin with the end of this life. Enter "Endgame," an episode that relieves a lot of the early frippery of season eight, ending the slightly unbalanced feel of the first few episodes, and dumping us back into the kind of full-scale *SG-1* story line we've come to admire so much.

This endgame is all about the strategic use of an advantage to achieve a victory. The humans, in the form of The Trust, have had several years of skirmishes and confrontations with the Goa'uld. With most of the System Lords busy trying to defeat Baal, committing most of their resources to that end, The Trust decides to take advantage of a weak link in the military defense, some advanced technology, and the instability of communications between everyone else to achieve their aim of ridding the galaxy once and for all of the Goa'uld. Rebel Jaffa, Tok'ra operatives, and other nonmilitary types are deemed "acceptable losses," an eerie parallel to other, contempo-rary machinations we see on the news. But continuing in the long arc of the season, certain factions of the population are tired of waiting for dis-aster, and instead seek to take the fight to the enemy. Like the endgame, this kind is another classic chess scenario — a quick and brutal offense that could win a game in less than twenty moves. It is militarily demonstrated by Hoskins' team's wholesale wipeout of entire populations. It also returns us to much earlier in the series, "Shades of Grey," with a more annoying Harry Maybourne (who's about to make an appearance), where the question of a counterattack was first raised. Great oppositions that make for great action, all backed up by the familiar mythology and the gold-and-red background of Osiris' *al'kesh*.

However, while The Trust is being set up as the newly validated bad-guy-from-within, the reappearance of Hoskins and his team makes them seem less than lethal — or organized, for that matter. What happened to the Hoskins we saw in "Affinity," the one who tells Daniel that he is more of a "surveillance team"? We are led to assume he meant his particular team, and yet there they are, a team of four stealing the Stargate itself and masterminding a huge plan for the ultimate destruction of the Goa'uld. While The Trust is a good addition to season eight, here and in "Affinity" it's hard to see the grand scheme of things — which, admittedly, is pretty true to real-life, where things often don't come into focus until a culminating event occurs and we get some hindsight. Even though Sam mentions in "Covenant" the group of businessmen who may or may not be pulling the strings of The Trust, it still feels like there's more talk than evidence about how big they are. And it's not made better by Sam's shiny *Matrix*-like jacket…

On the other hand, "Endgame" gives us a serious dose of jeopardy, the likes of which we've seen little of thus far in the season. It also incorporates a throughline that once again demonstrates the steadiness of the *SG* universe. When Sam notes that P5R-357, the planet The Trust is going to destroy next, is barren, only a fan who's watching closely will be able to remember that that planet was also in "Affinity" — it's the planet where Teal'c's new love interest, Ishta, now resides. Within the cut and thrust of the galactic game of war, moments of intense importance like this allow viewers a more seamless integration into the universe, simultaneously cueing newer viewers to the fact that there's a whole lot more going on than it might seem. This is also a really nice interweaving of personal stakes into a galactic problem, something we see a lot of in season eight ("New Order," "Reckoning"), and Sam's quick thinking in distracting The Trust definitely saves the day in more than one way.

"Endgame" also brings the frailty of the Jaffa/Tok'ra/human alliance into focus — a thread we haven't seen much of since season seven's "Death Knell." With the Jaffa being eliminated on a genocidal scale, and the Tok'ra responsible for the existence of the drug that targets symbiotes for death, the humans in this episode find themselves in a position where they have to act as mediators between the two races. While the Jaffa and the Tok'ra have never enjoyed a fully trusting relationship, the reactions of the Jaffa (including Teal'c) in this episode remind us that for them, it's not just about creating a peaceful alliance; there's far more at stake for them — it is, literally, a matter of life and death.

Another thing "Endgame" delivers on is emotion. Mark Gibbon does a great job with M'Zel's swan song; more than anything, the big Jaffa seems not only ready for his death, but also tired. His ritual exclamation, "I die free," marks his passing at a time when he thought it was the Tok'ra who were trying to kill his people instead of the Goa'uld, and those three short words and the lifetime of struggle that they represent bring tears to the eyes. The weariness in his voice is tempered with absolute resolution that the end of his life was worth the long road he has traveled, because he tasted freedom. His freedom, and the freedom of all Jaffa, is not a game to be played by powerful players like the Tok'ra and the Goa'uld, but an individual utterance, repeated over and over again.

Gods & Scientists: Biological warfare almost never accurately hits its target. Mongol raiders purportedly dumped plague-ridden bodies over the walls of their enemies, who then transported the disease to Europe, inciting a massive epidemic of plague, or the Black Death.

Interesting Fact: Mark Gibbon also doubled as the (human) body of Thor in "Thor's Hammer" and "Thor's Chariot."

Why We're Space Monkeys: While Jack's understated, "Yeah, tough choice," at the end of the episode may have sounded flippant, it sure got across a plethora of emotions in three words: humor aimed at his teammates, acceptance that his new role as commanding officer of the SGC includes making difficult decisions, admittance that his personal bias may have come into play when he decided not to fire on the enemy ship, and rebellion against being held accountable for breaking the rules. As usual, Rick's understatement goes a long, long way.

Parlez-vous Gate?: Sam and Daniel, who share great onscreen moments this season, have a hilarious wordless exchange on board the *al'kesh*. No "What are you doing here?", not even an "Are you okay?" Just Sam's nod to Daniel, as if to say, "Well, here we are again, in trouble, imminent death, what can you do?" as Daniel goes to sit by her.

811. Gemini

Original airdate: January 21, 2005
Written by: Peter DeLuise
Directed by: William Waring

SG-1 fights the Replicators who have made it to Earth's galaxy with the help of Replicator Carter.

"Gemini" is certainly not something we'd expect to see from Peter DeLuise — the guy who gives us touching tales from oppressed peoples, either the Jaffa or the Unas or the fun episodes like "Wormhole X-Treme." He's not known for his villains, or his core character portrayals, as he usually focuses on peripheral characters. "Gemini," however, shows that he's as aware of the characters as are Robert Cooper and the "M&M" team. Just one question, though — where the hell is Daniel Jackson? He gets into an elevator, and we don't see him for the rest of the episode.

Carter's character has stayed true to form for eight seasons now; her exploits *do* make one wonder why, after so long, she *isn't* the President of the United States. The argument could be made that because of the ideologies of the Western culture, Carter isn't allowed to be bad, but instead must be split into separate entities in order to encapsulate badness. But Amanda Tapping does a good job of making Replicator Carter both eerie and approachable, in effect replacing her character with a more feminist version of what Carter could have been. This Replicator Carter *does* have emotion and *does* manifest it. The question then becomes not one of gender but of humanity, what it means to be human. We've also seen this thread in "Sacrifices" and "Affinity" but "Gemini" gives us a new take on it by asking, are Replicators machines any more than we are machines? Both O'Neill and Replicator Carter work with a single end in mind: the destruction of the other. Who's to say which one is human and which a machine? Carter's line at the end of the episode, "Because that's what I would have done," makes the safe separation of good and bad even less clear — in one line, she announces the philosophical premise behind the episode and ends it on a disturbing note.

Strangely, the only real implausibility in "Gemini" comes from the human Carter's characterization. While her personality trait of wanting to save everyone has been demonstrated throughout the series ("Singularity,"

"A Hundred Days," "Paradise Lost"), she has never willingly denied the risks involved in the actions she contemplates. She's never until now "geminied" herself by telling O'Neill that she knows her job and will complete it, and then at every turn doing the opposite. The rift between her words and actions has never been as large. In that sense, she's revisiting season eight's theme of learning to lead, as she grapples with a situation that her superiors are not fully aware of and that she doesn't have time to fully explain. Especially since the "situation" thinks just as fast as she does, and perhaps faster.

The actions and inactions of "Gemini" carry immense consequences for both Carter and the galaxy, and as such the episode again fits into the series-long arc of facing the consequences of one's actions. Here though, the stakes are doubled, as Carter and the SGC face an imminent threat not only from a galactic point of view (the arrival of the Replicators) but also from a personal one. This interweaving of personal and universal is something that's been done several times on the show, usually with great results — season one's "Cold Lazarus" is just one example.

From a personal angle, the concerns in "Gemini" mimic those found in real life. How many times do we come up against our own limitations, or get the chance to heal, change things, right wrongs, make ourselves better? Faced with ourselves, with our humanity staring us in the face, it would be hard for *anyone* to remain objective. Taken to the extreme, what would have happened if Carter had succeeded in getting Replicator Carter back to Earth, going directly against her orders? She would have, in effect, replayed the same timeline she skirted in "Unnatural Selection" when she betrayed Fifth, only this time she'd be betraying O'Neill. Another moment of doubleness and duplicity, flawlessly interwoven into the story.

Another flawless aspect of "Gemini" is the CGI. Seeing Carter behind herself, beside herself (literally) only serves to highlight the episode's theme of duplicity in all its various aspects. Starting with the episode's number (11), there are many elements of doubling in "Gemini," and as usual, this great show makes the effects work *for* the story, not as gratuitous flashiness.

Replicator Carter's interrogation room is the most obvious of visual twinned elements, with its doubled pot lights, chairs, and hanging fluorescents. The episode title comes at a moment when we see Replicator Carter on the screen and Carter in the foreground — an obvious signal, but still arresting and well done. Many of the shots throughout the episode are done with only two people in them, which also lends an effect of intensity and a sense that the situation is inescapable, and we're bound by the edges of the television screen the way Replicator Carter is bound by the flickering light around her and Fifth in their subspace communications.

It's a chilling thought to consider *Carter* as Earth's dire enemy. It's a great idea for a villain, a Replicator with Carter's extensive resources, and it introduces new high-level stakes. While Carter has invariably come up with solutions to problems over eight years, what can she do when faced with a copy of her own mind as a foe?

We've come a long way since "Emancipation." Thank goodness.

Gods & Scientists: Replicator Carter is now immune to the Ancient weapon designed to destroy the Replicators. Generally, there are two kinds of immunity — humoral innate, immunity that's found in bodily fluids, and cellular innate, immunity that's found in the cells. Because Replicator Carter is a machine, she doesn't fall into either of those categories, but it's an interesting question — how *does* she get immunity through knowledge alone?

Interesting Fact: Says Amanda Tapping, "['Gemini'] is actually for me probably the hardest episode I've ever shot in eight years, doing the two-character arc. Playing the two of them, trying to find enough differences so that you could see the difference but [also] making them alike enough that you could believe Fifth created her from the same consciousness as Carter, was a challenge."

Why We're Space Monkeys: Teal'c's insane happy grin at the thought of killing a Replicator — who cares if she looks like Carter!

Parlez-vous Gate?:
REPLICATOR CARTER: My name is Samantha Carter.
O'NEILL: Alright, we've got a little conflict with that statement — we've already got one here.

812. Prometheus Unbound

Original airdate: January 28, 2005
Written by: Damian Kindler
Directed by: Andy Mikita

Daniel accompanies General Hammond and a skeleton crew aboard the Prometheus *on a search and rescue mission for the Atlantis crew.*

An outlandish stand-alone episode. Even though it's meant to be linked to both the episode "Prometheus" and the *Atlantis* spin-off, "Prometheus Unbound" earned a massive fan response; on the GateWorld forums alone, over 350 responses were logged after its airing. The much-anticipated guest starring of *Farscape* star Claudia Black provoked a lot of back-and-forth, and her character, Vala, didn't disappoint in terms of controversy. Vala is overtly sexual, manipulative, cunning, and apparently a great liar. In some ways she is an amalgamation of many of the female characters we've seen — Hathor in her sexuality, Linea in her capacity for lying, Sha're in her instant attraction to Daniel, and Nirrti in her cold calculations. In fact, the only woman she *doesn't* resemble is Sam.

It's hard to say for sure why the episode is titled "Prometheus Unbound" since that immediately brings to mind the season-six episode "Prometheus" — which has nothing to do with this one, except for the presence of the ship. But the episode isn't even really *about* the ship, and that's made clear by the complete lack of intensity or jeopardy throughout. You would think that, with the entire crew on a crippled ship and Daniel alone with a Super Soldier (an enemy used so effectively in "Avatar"), the writers would trade in on that potential tension and danger; instead, it's an episode with lots of space shots and cutesy fight scenes.

As usual, the two female characters — Lindsey Novak and Vala — are polar opposites, emphasizing the trouble the writers have with creating an inclusive female character. It's hard to believe the writers could go backward after the more subtle Carter/Replicator Carter characterization, but Damian Kindler seems to be a hit-or-miss kind of writer.

It's nice to see Daniel after his disappearance into an elevator at the beginning of "Gemini," and he's even having the same argument — that's some continuity! His eagerness to be a part of the Atlantis expedition is warranted; after all, it *is* his life's work that is becoming a reality. His frustration with Jack's refusal to let him go is clearly intense; it must be infuriating to see something so huge loom so close and not be able to participate. In that sense, his smile when General Hammond countermands O'Neill's order suggests that he's really ready to be unbound from the SGC and his current restraints.

We've always loved that *SG-1* makes fun of itself. Sometimes they go a bit too far — this may or may not be one such episode, depending on the version of *SG-1* you prefer. "Prometheus Unbound" plays like an updated "Deadman Switch," with the wily, debonair alien rogue at odds with most of the people she comes into contact with. There are some great character moments: Hammond's easy requisitioning of his old chair, Walter's surreptitious sliding of the glass of water toward the hiccupping Novak, and Daniel's "holy crap" dive to safety when he first catches sight of the Drone. After eight years, boy has that guy learned to get the hell out of the way!

The story line of Jackson stuck on a ship with an alien entity gives us a sense of déjà-vu, until we remember season seven's "Grace" where Carter was in the exact same situation. But where "Grace" was played very much for drama, "Prometheus Unbound" relies on physical comedy. To that end, you have give kudos to the cast because it's not often that actors are called upon to give the range of emotions we see on *SG-1*. In season eight alone, Daniel has had intensely dramatic episodes ("Icon"), action sequences ("New Order"), and now physical comedy. Versatility is one of Michael Shanks' strong points.

Nevertheless, physical comedy is not an excuse for a script to perpetrate a homophobic point of view. In a show that purports to direct itself to a reasonably mature audience, the cultivation of homophobia for comic value is out of place. These are military officers, trained in CPR — for them to hesitate before performing a potentially lifesaving maneuver is not only denigrating to the character, whom we respect, but also to the military itself. While we "get" Daniel's reaction to the Drone as an ostensibly alien and male being, the scene in the ring room with General Hammond and Colonel Reynolds is unbelievably behind the times, and inexcusable.

Gods & Scientists: *Vala* was the northern Germanic term for a *shamanka*, or female shaman. She was a wise woman, capable of insight and an understanding of both the past and present. In some versions of Norse mythology, Vala was also said to be the son of Odin and Rindr, created to avenge his brother's death. In that story, his name means "Slayer," and he is the god of vengeance, rebirth, light, and love. In other Norse mythology, *vala* can mean *volva*, or priestess. And in J. R. R. Tolkien's own mythology, *vala* is the singular of the plural *valar*, representing the fourteen spirits who were to give order to the world and fight evil.

Interesting Fact: Claudia Black had this to say on her choices as Vala: "I still think sci-fi actors are underestimated by audiences who may not know what's required of them. They work even faster on *Stargate* than we did on *Farscape*, but *Stargate* often get their scripts on time. There's a reason why Patrick Stewart was hired to do the job that he did, even though he came from a Shakespearian background. You have to understand how to play the stakes for heightened drama, and you learn that or die, in theater. While it's a little bit safer on television or on a film set to call 'cut' and go again, you don't have the time; so a disciplined actor is really going to save the producer time and money if they can be a one-take wonder."

Why We're Space Monkeys: General Hammond is first and foremost an Air Force officer, and his return to the SGC, though brief, is welcome. Plus, his glee at being able to "pull a Jack" on Jack O'Neill is such fun to watch.

Parlez-vous Gate?:
DANIEL: Because I'll quit.
O'NEILL: Why don't you just hold your breath? You haven't done that in a while.

813. It's Good to Be King

Original airdate: February 4, 2005
Story by: Michael Greenburg, Peter DeLuise, Joseph Mallozzi, Paul Mullie
Teleplay by: Joseph Mallozzi, Paul Mullie
Directed by: William Gereghty

SG-1 goes after Harry Maybourne after Tok'ra intelligence reports that his planet is in imminent danger from the Goa'uld.

Back to bittersweet. It's sweet to see Harry do the right thing (which may or may not be an intrinsic part of his character) and it's certainly an outgrowth of the time he's spent with O'Neill, a man whose actions are his character. On the other hand, the episode felt almost bitter because there was a distinct lack of the back-and-forth we've come to love between Jack and Harry. While the main story of Maybourne and his little band of merry aliens is a little lacking in tension, the surrounding material and its import for the future (and past) of SG-1 make this episode worthwhile.
    Like the song of the same name by Tom Petty, "It's Good to Be King"

shows us that Maybourne's position is both privileged and ironic. It's built on knowledge that isn't his — he is a king because he knows more than the rest of the people on the planet. With that position, as in the song, Maybourne acquires friends and sexual partners. The perks are good, and Maybourne likes them.

Take a look at everyone who wrote this episode. More than a little ironic? At times, especially near the end of the episode, where Jack (sort of) chastizes Maybourne for his sexual antics, it seems self-congratulatory on the part of the writers. But Maybourne's grin — haphazard, half-hearted, a little chagrined — reminds us that he's learned a little more about the rigors of leadership. As he's stated, he's worked hard to make a life, and to make a difference — he can't leave. He's far from the Maybourne we met in season one.

"It's Good to Be King" is also a microcosmic portrait of *Stargate SG-1* in its current state, in terms of both the season and the series as a whole. As *Atlantis* continues to air, the newer, very cool show could be in danger of "taking over." The worlds that the Atlantis teams explore offer a new paradigm, one that is more contemporary than *SG-1*'s, which was conceived of in the eighties for the film and the nineties for the series. There are new technologies, baddies, and allies to explore. Just as "It's Good to Be King" melds Ancient technology with an almost Arthurian or Norse setting, the writers work hard to meld *SG-1* and *Atlantis*' technologies together, yoking the older viewers' love of *SG-1* to the exciting possibilities that the Ancients and their technology can offer.

We've seen the arc of the demise of the Goa'uld in season eight. The Goa'uld (and Egyptian mythology) is being replaced with more contemporary science fiction tropes and ideas. This episode continues that evolution. We see the First Prime of Ares as being ineffectual, almost right from the start, while the discovery of a time machine devised by the Ancients in a place with pillars reminiscent of Celtic standing stones closer to the beginning of the episode seems exciting and new — so new that even Carter can't jerry-rig the thing. New paradigms must be employed — including O'Neill entering the field with his sought-after Ancient gene — and the Goa'uld are fading away. The Jaffa in the village are so out of place we can't wait for them to be gone so that we can concentrate on the new things we've learned. How did the Ancients tell the future without impinging on the timeline construct that Carter so faithfully set up way back in "1969"? How does the time machine work? Can SG-1 begin to use the cool new stuff we've seen in *Atlantis*?

Amidst all the newness, however, there is the return of something that we've hardly ever in season eight: Teal'c, Daniel, Sam, and Jack, all together, working as a team for an objective. The casual banter between Jack and Sam, the respect and camaraderie of Teal'c and Daniel, the team working cooperatively, are all "old-school" elements, and in the context of the shifting paradigm of *SG-1*, they all provide a needed handhold for the fans. Change is fine, but the writers do a good job once again of intermingling the established with the new.

Gods & Scientists: A homophone for King Arkhan is the ancient position of the *archon*, or chief magistrate. Archons wielded their power usually in groups, as contrasts with the powers of a single head of state like a king. Perhaps an ironic twist on the illusion of Harry being a king, as he was in fact using knowledge he derived from the Ancients, who might be seen as the "kings" of our ancestors. It's also the first appearance of the time machine devised and built by the Ancients.

Interesting Fact: Fans of *Whose Line Is It Anyway?* and *The Wayne Brady Show* may or may not recognize comic crooner Wayne Brady in his role as the First Prime of Ares.

Why We're Space Monkeys: The exchange between Teal'c and First Prime Trelak reminds us that there is a great deal of honor in the Jaffa, regardless of their loyalties. Trelak's simple death sentence, "You are a man of your word," to Teal'c is strong and almost intimate. Both men are fully prepared to die in battle, and honor their mutual code.

Parlez-vous Gate?:
MAYBOURNE: I get to name all kinds of stuff. You should see the Grateful Dead Burial Grounds.

814. Full Alert

Original airdate: February 11, 2005
Written by: Joseph Mallozzi, Paul Mullie
Directed by: Andy Mikita

O'Neill must deal with a serious situation at the SGC, as the Russian military prepares for full-out war.

We've seen this plot in several guises already, namely in "New Ground" and "The Other Side," where two elements of the same planet wage war on one another. Actually, we've already seen it season eight, in "Icon," so it's a little baffling to see it trotted out again. Of the two, "Full Alert" is by far a better episode, and the inclusion of all the team members in their various spaces, working together although they may be far apart, is good to see. Daniel's diplomacy (and his Russian), gets a workout. The secondary character of Daria Varonakova is a much better foil for Daniel than the weirdly named Leda of "Icon," and Jack gets a full workout of diplomacy as well, dealing with the Russian government and the Russian faction within the SGC. Teal'c, who is getting a lot more action these days besides just standing behind the rest of the team with a zat gun or a staff weapon, seems so at home with the ins and outs of the SGC that it's easy to forget that his primary objective is still the freedom of his people.

This episode is the continuation of Jack's relinquishing of his old ways; in "Lockdown" there was the inkling that he might be fostering a Cold War mentality, but in "Full Alert" he really shows us the stuff of a commanding officer, setting aside old rivalries (for instance with Colonel Chekhov), to resolve the greater conflict. Now, here is a situation we haven't seen before — we've always looked at the infighting of nations from the outside, but "Full Alert" puts us in uncomfortable range of the immediate here and now. We can no longer complacently say that this side is bad and that side is good, because they're suddenly up close and complex. It seems a shame to have "Full Alert" after "Icon," when it was a better episode. It would have had more impact had it been the only factions-warring-against-each-other story of the season.

Sometimes the in-jokes stretch a little thin — O'Neill's quip to Kinsey about his loyalties, "I must have missed an episode," is not that amusing. And check out the beginning of "Gemini" and "Prometheus Unbound," and then again this episode and "Citizen Joe." Is anyone getting the feeling that season eight is like one big "Window of Opportunity"?

The intrigue of the Goa'uld getting Earth to do the dirty work of killing themselves off is pretty good, but a little sketchy at times. It's plausible that the Russian government would start to become worried about the SGC project. After all, the Stargate is theirs, and so far all they've gotten is one lousy team at the SGC. That plus the fact that a highly decorated officer, one of their best, arrives at the SGC to promptly die, as Colonel Vaselov does in "Lockdown." It's rather implausible that the now disgraced Senator Kinsey would be either used by The Trust or go to the SGC. His sovereignty of nations speech aside, Kinsey's lines and motions seemed jerky. And he's always got a drink in his hand, making him seem like an out-of-control alcoholic rather than a savvy political animal using the best means available to achieve his goals — which ultimately would be the reason for his reinstatement to power. Usually, Ronny Cox is stellar as Senator Kinsey, but his dialogue here is seriously lacking something. And they're getting a heck of a lot of mileage out of that one *al'kesh* of Osiris', aren't they? Eight years of *ha'tak*'s and cargo ships and Asgard ships, and this little *al'kesh* gets four consecutive episodes?

While "Full Alert" highlighted Jack's ability to confront and surmount old patterns of leadership and ways of thinking, the episode is continuing on the downward spiral that was only alleviated by "Endgame" and "Gemini." Hoping that the writers dig deeper into character, we wait another week, digging in ourselves, with the silent prayer that *SG-1* does its usual trick of taking something that looks like a train wreck in progress and turning it into a bullet train instead.

Interesting Fact: Did you see the name on the side of the surveillance truck tailing Senator Kinsey? "Mikita," in homage to veteran director Andy Mikita.

Why We're Space Monkeys: Walter Harriman, the "Chevron Guy." You know, the guy who says, "Chevron one encoded"? The man's had more lines this season alone that he has in the past eight years — and he got to do comic acting, too!

Parlez-vous Gate?:
O'NEILL: Five bucks says Carter has a theory.

815. Citizen Joe

Original airdate: February 18, 2005
Excerpts written by: Robert C. Cooper, James Crocker, Peter DeLuise, Jonathan Glassner, V. C. James, Damian Kindler, Joseph Mallozzi, Paul Mullie, Brad Wright

Story by: Robert Cooper
Teleplay by: Damian Kindler
Directed by: Andy Mikita

A barber from Indiana interrupts General O'Neill at home to tell him he and the rest of SG-1 have ruined his life.

"Citizen Joe" is a tricky episode. Like "Prometheus Unbound" it got a lot of attention from Internet fans, again over 350 responses on GateWorld alone. Some were tickled pink, and some were furious.

Why all the fuss? Many fans thought that "Citizen Joe" was the culminating slap in the face after a season full of little digs. They thought the writers were putting in snarky lines based on online fan feedback, digs like Pete Shanahan calling himself a stalker in response to his behavior (some fans had voiced anger at his behavior toward Sam), or the quip from O'Neill in "Full Alert" about missing an episode. It made some fans feel that their interest in the show was a laughing matter to the writers. In an e-mail interview, Snarkhunt said of this episode, "I get that the writers are trying to make the fans feel involved in the show, but not at the expense of my intelligence, please. After 'Citizen Joe,' I seriously started to reconsider why I watched *SG-1* since it had seemed to turn into a back-patting boys' club. The tongue-in-cheek 'slyness' just started to really get to me, like it wasn't about respecting the fans anymore but rather, poking fun at them. Constantly. However, it *does* seems slightly silly to be upset about a show that's gone out of its way to make fun of itself for years." Maybe some fan reaction came about because, for once, the mirror wasn't pointed back at the show itself, as we see so admirably done in "Wormhole X-Treme," but was instead pointed outward at the viewers. Was it an homage or a parody?

There are so many interwoven threads and lines of wordplay that it's impossible to get them all on the first watching. "Citizen Joe," with its reference to the film *Citizen Kane*, isn't just about some crazy barber who hears things. Like the story by Orson Welles, it also focuses on the rise and fall of an individual, as he becomes, piece by piece, day by day, threaded in to a world that isn't real in the sense of his personal existence but is more real to him in a psychological, emotional sense. Like *Citizen Kane*, it uses a barrage of flashbacks to tell the "story," which is in itself a retelling of the story of SG-1 and their adventures. It's an intriguing and frankly amazing way to approach a "clips" episode. It pays homage to the individual (of course, all in fun, but this seems to be Damian Kindler's stock-in-trade). As well, it involves the intertextuals and continuity that the fans love and demand (Homer Simpson has been alluded to many times on the show, and avid fans know that *The Simpsons is* one of Rick's faves), and the episode races along, not just summing up the season but the entire career of the SG-1 team. In doing so it jumps over season six's "Disclosure" for best clip show, and still maintains a sense of urgency, emotional resonance — Joe's bereft wailing at Daniel's death is *awesomely* done — and action. It even makes fun of itself for making fun of itself: who else does that?

"Citizen Joe" is not the bleak assessment of the ultimate cost of self-imposed solitude, as *Citizen Kane* is, and it's not a parody of the rabidity shown by some fans, despite the occasional, hilarious line of dialogue, such as when Joe's wife Charlene says, "The team interaction isn't what it used to be in the beginning." It's definitely satire — but parody and satire, though linked, are not the same. Parody does not delve deeply into character. A parody would not bother to have a character truly embroiled in the lives of this so-called imaginary team. "Citizen Joe" is tricky, because, as with most *SG-1* episodes, the tricks employed are so seamlessly interwoven with the necessity of the story that they can be easily skipped over or taken out of context. And that's the problem with stories. They are like Replicator blocks, and like blocks they need each other to communicate and have a sense of wholeness. In order to make "Citizen Joe" work, Joe had to be a "nobody," so that he could tell the stories and not threaten national security, he had to be a little off-the-wall, because otherwise there'd be no sense of normalcy to set him against, which was *also* being satirized. The satire extends not just to the fans, but also to the *writers*: if there were no viewers, there would be no show. In that sense, it is the writers who are the nobodies, squirreling themselves away like so many Citizen Kanes in their writing holes, coming up with stories that may or may not seem ridiculous. If anything, "Citizen Joe" is an homage to the community of *SG-1*, not a parody of it. While this episode can also be compared to season four's "Window of Opportunity," in that it took a hard line on something (fans and fan culture) that didn't necessarily sit well with all viewers, it's still a nice revision of the regular clip show, something we've come to expect from the series — even if it is a somewhat outlandish curate's egg of a satire.

Interesting Fact: In the garage sale scene, a box of comic books is one of the items for sale. Because of copyright restrictions, the producers couldn't use real comic books, so art director James Robbins used the comic book he had designed for "Avenger 2.0," *The Amazing Avenger*, and then drew covers for several other comic books.

Why We're Space Monkeys: In an interview, *SG-1* fan Julie had this to say about the show's more humorous moments: "One of the things that I love about *Stargate* is that even in mythology or arc-driven episodes, you still get lots of fabulous character moments. I'm into this show for the characters, so that's what draws me into any episode. But I do have a deep, deep love of the humor episodes, especially those that are a meta-commentary on the show itself ('Wormhole X-Treme'? Hilarious). It always boggles my mind when I hear fans complain about those episodes, claiming that they're not true *Stargate*. I end up thinking, 'What show have they been watching?' *SG-1* is *all* about the humor."

Parlez-vous Gate?: This wonderful monosyllabic dialogue between Jack and Daniel is hilarious:
DANIEL: Jack?
O'NEILL: He's a barber.
DANIEL: Broke into your house?
O'NEILL: Yeah.
DANIEL: Second week in a row.
O'NEILL: Uh-huh.
DANIEL: Alarm.
O'NEILL: I'm thinking dog.
JOE: You could just try locking your front door.

816. Reckoning (Part 1)

Original airdate: February 25, 2005
Written by: Damian Kindler
Directed by: Peter DeLuise

The Replicators, led by Replicator Carter, begin an attack on Earth's galaxy, leading to a surprising alliance between Earth and Baal. Teal'c leads the Jaffa into a battle that will turn the tide of the rebellion.

What an outstanding episode. This two-parter is the first of the upward spiral of episodes that ends season eight — not just an upward spiral, but a ninety-degree angle. "Reckoning" delivers from all perspectives: character, action, emotion, tension, mythology. This episode is what fans have been waiting for all season — a gripping adventure with some real stakes, both personal and professional. Season eight left many fans feeling ambivalent about the show, doubting it could stagger on to a ninth without doing serious damage to its integrity. Here though, writer Damian Kindler, who in the past has been responsible for such episodes as "Sight Unseen" and "Space Race," puts all the cards on table and shows us what the show has got going for it and, whatever might have been said about earlier episodes, it's a lot. "Reckoning" is like a gift to all the people who have been watching for any substantial amount of time, and a mini-reckoning for Kindler himself, who delivers the best episode he's penned to date.

While, individually, all the threads of "Reckoning" stand up and deliver, what's really happening is that they're all coalescing. The two parts of the episode bring together all the major threads of the series and raise the stakes exponentially until there's nothing left for the situation to do but explode. The thread of the Goa'uld, that of the Jaffa rebellion, that of the Replicators, that of the Ancients, and then the more personal threads of Carter's feelings of guilt over Replicator Carter, the mystery of Daniel's Ascension, Jack's command post — they all merge here, and the pacing of the episode is incredible. You can literally feel the tension mounting at every stage.

How amazing is it to see everything that Teal'c has fought for suddenly loom so near? The Jaffa rebellion, while at times clumsily handled, is one of the most serious and intriguing throughlines of the show. The painful realization of an entire people that the gods to whom they're enslaved are not in fact gods but usurpers and users, and the slow culmination of their anger into a formidable force about to gain its freedom, is something that's awe-inspiring to watch. It's fitting that Teal'c and Bra'tac should see this story through to its end together, as Bra'tac was the first to teach Teal'c of the lies the Goa'uld told. Though he's certainly aged a lot since losing his symbiote ("The Changeling"), Bra'tac has an air of calm regality and he easily controls the situation where Teal'c would have spoken more forcefully. Bra'tac's mentoring personality is coming out more and more since he spoke of his mortality to Teal'c in "Maternal Instinct," and the looks shared between the two men speak volumes regarding their devotion to each other, and to their cause.

Teal'c's speech on sacrifice, on seeing all that the Jaffa have lost finally coming to something, after years of fighting and dying and losing, is heartrending. He has given up so much, and it all leads up to this fight, this place. The culmination is intense, and there's not one lost moment in this episode. Chris Judge plays his part to perfection, drawing every ounce of restraint and passion from his character to create a controled fierceness that perfectly represents the mix that's made Teal'c so interesting over the years.

Carter, O'Neill, and Daniel face challenges of their own. One of the things that season eight hasn't done enough of until now is give us a sense of the stakes that are at hand for each character. "Reckoning" changes that. Things that we thought had been set aside, like Daniel's search for his missing memories of being one of the Ascended, suddenly reappear in a completely unexpected way. That thread takes up the interweaving of the personal and the galactic that we saw so effectively done in "Gemini," with Daniel and Replicator Carter facing off for the fate of the universe against the backdrop of Daniel's subconscious. Replicator Carter is one heck of a villain — you can sense the fear that emanates from Daniel, and it's almost impossible not to shiver when she smiles, looking so much like Sam, and yet with eyes so calculating and unlike Sam's.

Carter is put to the test again, as she teams up with Thor (those two make such a great pair) to once more defeat the Replicators. Each time they make some headway, it seems like the Replicators find something else to throw at them, but the twist here is that for once, Carter and Thor aren't fighting to save only Thor's homeworld, but the entire galaxy.

A tone of intense jeopardy engulfs these two episodes. From the moment we see Replicator Carter skewer Yu and the music swells, we *know* that "Reckoning" will be just that, a reckoning. The music echoes that of the end of "Gemini" where Replicator Carter decimates the SGC personnel, and it's used to great effect in this two-parter. Music is something that was noticeably lacking in several episodes this season ("Full Alert," for example), but in "Reckoning" it serves to ratchet up the tension and excitement. We *hear* the threat of Replicator Carter; we *hear* the imminent loss of the galaxy to the Replicators; we *hear* the passion of the Jaffa warriors. The music is not only a presence in "Reckoning," it's practically a character. This is *Stargate* at its best.

Gods & Scientists: The Temple of Dakara is a sacred site for Jaffa and Goa'uld alike, as it is where the first Prim'ta ceremony took place, and symbolizes the Jaffa's enslavement to the Goa'uld. It may be based on the

Japanese word *takara*, which means *treasure*. Certainly the temple represents a treasure of untold value to the Jaffa people. The name is also reminiscent of the Ancient Greek city, Tanagra, which took over as lead town from Thebes after the Greco-Persian wars. It was the site of a massive battle in 457 BC, a battle where Athens lost to Sparta and its allies. Tanagra today is only ruins.

Interesting Fact: Isaac Hayes, who plays the Jaffa warrior Tolok in this two-parter and "Threads," is a well-known R&B artist, as well as an accomplished musician, songwriter, composer (he wrote and performed the theme from *Shaft*), and actor (he voices "Chef" on *South Park*). Chris Judge was thrilled to play opposite him, and said, "It was such an honor to work with Isaac Hayes. He's one of the priests that has become a rebel. No one on the planet says 'Goa'uld' like Isaac Hayes!"

Why We're Space Monkeys: Very few sci-fi shows have demonstrated the respect for viewers that *Stargate* has. This includes not handling the audience with kid-gloves, with such shocking scenes as Sha're's full frontal nudity in the pilot episode, and the casual slaughter of System Lord Yu in "Reckoning."

Parlez-vous Gate?: A hilarious scene featuring Jack, Walter Harriman (also known as Chevron Guy), Sam, and Thor's transporter beam.
HARRIMAN: Sir, we're receiving a message from Thor. He said he's ready to trans—
(Sam is suddenly transported to Thor's ship.)
O'NEILL: You were saying?
HARRIMAN: Never mind.

817. Reckoning (Part 2)

Original airdate: March 4, 2005
Written by: Damian Kindler
Directed by: Peter DeLuise

Sam and Jacob try to find the Ancient weapon to destroy the Replicators, Daniel faces off against Replicator Carter, Teal'c defends the Jaffa hold on the sacred temple, and Jack defends the SGC.

An incredible follow-up to "Reckoning (Part 1)." This episode gives you goosebumps. It makes you care about the characters. It makes you grab hold of the edge of your seat. It is everything you love about *Stargate SG-1* and more. Starting, as Part 1 did, with Replicator Carter. As a villain, she rocks. It's a shame that the writers ended her reign so quickly (understandable though, considering season nine was far from a sure thing when the end of the season eight was being filmed) because her vicious manipulations are incredible to watch. She is riveting, more so than Apophis' four-year stint, more than the ever-vanishing-or-maybe-dying Anubis. She makes you *fear* for SG-1.

While Part 1 gathered the various threads of the series and the season and brought them into one giant episode, Part 2 brings them together to one location, the sacred Temple of Dakara, that the Jaffa have won and now must hold against Baal's attack — and against Anubis (did anyone really think he was dead?). Both metaphorically and physically, all threads are leading to one spot, marking a definite climax to these two episodes and to the show. The stakes are high right from the start, and they just keep getting higher as Carter and Jacob discover that the weapon they've been sent to destroy could potentially be reprogrammed to destroy only the Replicators. It's an episode marked by twists and turns, from the surprising alliance with Baal to Jacob's collapse, from Daniel's mind-bending face-off with Replicator Carter to her shocking murder of him at the end. The episode ends on a question mark: what's happened to Daniel? What's happening to Jacob? What's going to happen now that the Goa'uld have been more or less defeated by the Jaffa? What's next?

Jack's growth as a leader has never been clearer than in this episode, where he flawlessly leads the people of the SGC into battle against the Replicators without batting an eyelid. He marks his actions with the same stalwart, no-nonsense strength that we saw in General Hammond under similar circumstances ("Small Victories" and "Menace," for example). It's one of the moments where you can look back and really see the changes that O'Neill's character has so gradually undergone. He is now a fearless and astute leader, in charge of a whole program, not just four people.

Daniel Jackson's thread is the most enthralling of the episode. He has such a strong mind and incredible courage, and that comes out more than anything in his fight against Replicator Carter. The scene when he uses her ambition to probe his mind against her and manages to gain some control over the Replicators who are under her metallic thumb is thrilling; Michael Shanks plays these scenes with intensity, giving everything he has to show viewers Daniel's strength of character and mind. Their conflict is a wonderful metaphor also for the power of knowledge, one of *Stargate*'s most fertile themes ("Torment of Tantalus," "Secrets," "Out of Mind," for example). It almost seems at one point like he's going to blow Replicator Carter up by overloading her system with knowledge. "Reckoning (Part 1)" introduced the possibility of Daniel Ascending again, and although Oma is never really there, it's still interesting to watch Daniel fight himself at every turn, desperate to recall his memories, and desperate to win against his foe; even more interesting is to see him open himself to the possibility *of* remembering. Daniel's openness is one of the most enduring qualities of this character, and to watch him struggle with that so intently just makes you realize that remaining open, remaining *human* in the face of all the evil, is something he's been fighting with for a while.

Perhaps what is most striking about this episode is how everyone fights the battle on their own turf. Sam and Jacob struggle to solve a highly complex problem to make the weapon work, Jack takes up arms to defend the SGC and Earth, Teal'c fights the Goa'uld, and Daniel fights an invisible battle of the mind. Each has come so far since the pilot episode, each has developed his or her skills and range, but for this ultimate fight, it's clear that they each have to do what they do best.

The musical montage is one of the show's best scenes ever, with slow-motion close-ups of Sam machine-gunning the Replicators at the Temple, Jack shooting those at the SGC, Teal'c preparing to die at the hands of the enemy ship, and finally, Daniel dying. It's a scene that you can't watch without tearing up, as you see each character's jeopardy collide and explode, embodied by one metallic enemy, and realize that the end is coming, one way or another. This is a one-hundred-and-eighty-degree turn from "Meridian," and just as compelling.

When "Reckoning" was shot, it was not yet known if season nine would become a reality or not, and watching it with that same uncertainty is intensely emotional. As each story is born, so it must die, and this two-parter sets up the creation and destruction of new mythologies wonderfully. In a way, the Jaffa rebellion is the metaphor for the whole series: by taking Dakara, the Jaffa rebels have unveiled the false gods that are the Goa'uld, and now the mythology upon which entire civilizations are based

— including Earth's — is destroyed, so a new one must be created. In the same way, the mythology upon which the *show* was created has drawn to a close. "Reckoning" leaves you with the sense that what is old has died, and something new must arise to take its place.

Let the reckoning begin.

Gods & Scientists: Historically, when pantheons go down, it's usually a protracted death. But in the *SG-1* universe, the Goa'uld house of cards is falling fast. System Lord Yu is dead, Anubis is back, Baal is on the loose, having all but lost the fight against the Jaffa warriors. The Goa'uld, who have been Earth's archenemies for the past eight years, have finally been reduced to the status of non-deities by the end of Part 2.

Interesting Fact: Stunt coordinator Dan Shea, who plays Siler, was taken aback at the heat during his scenes fighting the Replicators in the SGC alongside Richard Dean Anderson. According to him, "There's another scene where I'm firing a gun into these Replicators and blowing them away. The SFX guys had to shoot off the propane cannon again, and I was in the foreground. Usually, I'd put fire retardant on my hands and face but I thought, 'This isn't going to be that big of deal.' All of a sudden boy, oh, boy, it got hot, we had our helmets and military gear on, but it was still pretty warm. I mean, I'm shooting my gun and there's a halo of flame around my head. So for takes two and three I made sure I put the gel on my face and hands."

Why We're Space Monkeys: The scene where all the Stargates in the galaxy are dialed at once, and we get shots of several different Gates, all on planets visited by SG-1 over the past eight years, is what being a *Stargate* fan is all about. The use of the Gate as an integral part of the plot, not just as a device but almost a participant in the action, is something we've yet to see in season eight, which is, comparatively, Gate-light. And a really nice tip of the hat to fans of the show who see the planets in question and think, "Hey, that looks familiar!"

Parlez-vous Gate?:
CARTER: You know, you blow up *one* sun, and suddenly everyone expects you to walk on water. (She succeeds at setting up the interface between the computer and the weapon.) Next up, parting the Red Sea.

818. Threads

Original airdate: March 11, 2005
Written by: Robert Cooper
Directed by: Andy Mikita

Daniel finds himself in an old fashioned diner, and his waitress is Oma Desala. As Daniel contemplates how best to do the right thing for humanity, the rest of SG-1 must battle long-time issues of their own.

By itself, a single thread or strand is easily lost, frayed, or broken. Knitting or working many threads together requires cohesiveness, strength, shelter. "Threads" brings us back to a nice place for the near-end of season eight. Originally the team of SG-1 was united by a common goal, and although individual aims may have differed, the meshing of this crazy team brought cohesiveness to the SGC, a strengthening of the hope for the future, and shelter from the storm that raged outside in the galaxy. "Threads" is a grand drama after the pulse-racing action sequences of "Reckoning," a more pensive episode that delivers the effects of threads not just from season eight but from the series as a whole.

Break ups, get-togethers, clarity, deception and lies, ceremony, mundanity, intense emotional moments, and moments of epiphany that seem devoid of histrionics —"Threads" goes a long way to showing how polar opposites can and do exist side by side.

And it's an episode that defines itself as something special, not just with a tightly woven story but also in its physical makeup. It's an unusual ninety minutes long — a hard thing to do in the rather rigidly scheduled world of television — and this suggests that it is only a portion of a story (not one or two full hours, which would be more traditional), which underscores the idea that the stories that we weave, like a piece of knitting, can always be picked up again because, in a sense, they're always still in the telling.

The Jaffa story line is still starkly authentic. Bra'tac and Teal'c's initiation ritual as blood kin to all Jaffa is touching, and as usual Bra'tac's humility saves the scene from becoming too testosterone-heavy and cheesy. His line to Teal'c, "Then I will be proud of and for you," when Teal'c demurs claiming the day as his, is also touching. Steady for eight years, the solid character of Bra'tac and his role as a father figure is always calm, compassionate, and the kind of role model sadly lacking in much of today's entertainment. And the jeopardy involved in Teal'c's appointment to the newly formed Free Jaffa Council is another thread fraught with tension. To finally achieve the ends that he's fought for for so many years is a coup for the SG-1 member, but at what cost to SG-1?

The irony and cruelty of Jim's singing "Amazing Grace" in the restaurant is not lost on us. Forced to watch Anubis' machinations helplessly, Oma's grace in the face of Jim's taunting shows how fine the line is that the she must walk. And perfect irony, to have the number one Super Bad Guy in the innocuous form of George Dzunda's character, a likeable, affable fellow whose first impression is that he's the only other guy besides Daniel who has an opinion. Which, of course, he does.

Jacob Carter (Carmen Argenziano), gone but not forgotten (COURTESY MICHELLE)

There's more continuity as well between *SG-1* and *Atlantis*. If you look closely at the papers that Daniel reads, you'll see stories from the Pegasus galaxy and see Wraith ships above it. And it's an interesting choice to place much of the scene of development within a diner, to use another polarity, the one between life and death itself. While Daniel contemplates his path, and Jim chuckles over the imminent death of all life in the galaxy (would that include Ascended beings, or would they just not be able to come back to this plane of existence, since Anubis is going to "remake" the galaxy to his own specifications?), the assembled people at the diner eat. Eating is a very ingrained ritual not just for survival but also as a reification of life. In the face of all the death that Anubis and his vision mean, eating is a method of resistance that is available to the assembled diners.

Jacob Carter's imminent death is another thread that is interwoven into the grand drama of the episode. A very different farewell from Dr. Fraiser's in "Heroes," Jacob's death picks up where he left off in "The Tok'ra." But why was such a point made to refer to Jacob nearly dying four years before, instead of seven ("The Tok'ra")? It could have been a writing error, or perhaps a setup for a future flashback episode that would clarify the time-line — and give fans a chance to see Jacob again with new material. And what happens to Oma? Does she sacrifice herself to take out Anubis, or does she just go head to head with him forever, keeping him contained?

And finally, the fishing. For Internet fans, the euphemism for Sam and Jack to "just go fishing" (meaning to get together and/or have sex) is finally laid to rest. Who says the writers don't listen? It's another tip of the hat from them, actually, continuing from "Citizen Joe." Although there are the odd back-handed snarks in season eight that seem to point to the obsessiveness of some fans, there's no doubt that the powers that be are listening to the fans. And truly, it would be absolutely ludicrous to not have *some* kind of resolution for this particular gaping question. But first, remember waaaay back in season three, the episode "Upgrades," with Anise? The other "finally" that should be pointed out here is that *one* of the three men gets a girlfriend who's "normal." Of course, she then dumps him, but hey, for those couple episodes. . . .

Gods & Scientists: There are many threads relating to death in this episode. Jacob and Selmak's death, quiet and calm amongst all the galactic strife, as they relinquish the corporeal body, has an almost Gnostic atti-tude, where the spirit is finally good, and its material existence is a burden, or even evil. Daniel's time in the diner suggests a kind of limbo, where the soul waits to be weighed — an ideology we see operating in many reli-gions, like Christianity, some sects of Buddhism, and other Near East reli-gions. Anubis' and Oma's deaths have a more myth-like flavor (Ancient Egypt in particular), where gods and demigods were not omnipotent but rather could die and be revived. The two characters' final fight is not cor-poreal however, as the two powers shift to a noncorporeal state for that final reckoning. In contrast, Ancient Egyptians believed that the corporeal body of mortals would be needed in some way to continue or accomplish the journey to the afterlife, which is what gave rise to the practice of mum-mification, or preservation, of the dead person's body.

Interesting Fact: The set where Daniel and Oma and Jim have their meeting is the set from *Dead Like Me*, the Wafflehouse.

Why We're Space Monkeys: Jacob Carter and Selmak. Two gentle souls who were nevertheless untiring warriors for good. Jacob's death is not so much anticlimactic as it is a reflection of his life: calm, understanding, unafraid.

Parlez-vous Gate?:

DANIEL: Menus?

OMA: We don't need them here — just order what you'd like.

DANIEL: Okay, I'll have the truth, with a side order of clarity, please.

OMA: The Replicator version of Sam was in your head trying to access the knowledge buried in your subconscious, but you gained control of her instead. She killed you to stop you. That's where I stepped in. How's that?

DANIEL: Pretty clear.

OMA: Well, we aim to please. The customer comes first, you know.

819. Moebius (Part 1)

Original airdate: March 18, 2005
Story by: Joseph Mallozzi, Paul Mullie, Brad Wright, Robert Cooper
Teleplay by: Joseph Mallozzi, Paul Mullie
Directed by: Peter DeLuise

Daniel convinces Jack to take the rest of SG-1 back in time to retrieve a zero-point module so that they can use it in the future.

This episode is a great exploration of science fiction themes and an acting showcase, especially for Amanda Tapping and Michael Shanks. It takes a little while to get this episode off the ground, but once it's there, it pretty much takes your idea of space-time and turns it into a pretzel.

Okay not a pretzel; this episode turns space-time, conveniently for the title, into a "Moebius" strip. The Mobius strip is named after a German mathematician August Mobius, who did a simple experiment to show how something with two sides can be connected so that it has only one side. (If you want to impress geeky math students, you can tell them the following joke: "Why did the chicken cross the Mobius strip? To get to the same side.") In mathematics, this area is known as the topology of math — how things connect to each other, even though they seem random or contradictory. A Mobius strip has a great many intriguing properties, not the least of which is that, when assembled, it has no "outside" or "inside," defying its own characteristics. Why all the fuss about it? Well, according to some scientists, a Mobius strip could be integral to another theory of physics that is currently not in favor due to its untestability — superstring theory, sometimes known as TOE or Theory of Everything. Time and space have no inside, outside, left, or right, but a continuous interchange that affects the whole.

Wow. All this in a science fiction show? You bet. The idea of the Mobius strip in the episode starts right at the beginning — and not just of the series. The locket given to Daniel by Catherine Langford's niece is right from the *Stargate* movie, and a touchstone (not the "Citizen Joe" kind) for the love that Catherine had for the project, as well as Daniel's earliest ideals, the ones that led him to going through the Stargate that first, fateful time. The premise is a little shaky, since the entire idea for the zero-point module (ZPM) is a little confusing if you're not simultaneously watching *Atlantis*. It's mentioned only peripherally in *SG-1*, but we've had episodes resting on less solid ground than this ("Sight Unseen," anyone?), and a diligent viewer would be able to follow. Plus it's nicely summed up by Daniel in his line about a ZPM being able to power both a Gate back to the Pegasus galaxy *and* power Earth's defences, a nice return to the quandary of "New Order."

Once we are into the whole timeline/alternate timeline idea, one disappointment comes out — a perfect opportunity to resurrect Dr. Fraiser gets overlooked. We've seen Dr. McKay (who loves lemon chicken), Major Davis (and his little menacing moustache), Major Samuels (wow, from season one no less!), Major Kawalsky (yay!) and General Hammond; it's a shame they didn't take the opportunity to bring back Fraiser as well.

The first part of the episode concentrates on the original team and their antics, with the ending warning by Sam as they trudge across the sand to not do anything to misuse the timeline wafting into the desert winds. This is the Mobius strip laid out flat, before it is twisted and turned. The one thing that's really lacking is the explanation of *why* timelines are so dangerous to muck with, and that's a shame. Since "1969" there has been little in the way of explanation, from a scientific viewpoint, of why timelines can be mucked up, or what the fallout is all about. There's a great deal of reiteration of "just don't do it, it's dangerous," which gets annoying. The fun starts when the strip gets twisted as something in the timeline is adjusted (although we don't know what at first) and wham!, one weirdly haired Daniel Jackson teaching English as a second language, and one Samantha Carter as an oppressed girl Friday. From this long, straight setup things move quickly into a recasting of the entire show (compressed mightily), which is close to, but exactly like, the one we know. It is as though we are skirting the Mobius strip again, but with a fractional adjustment as to *where* on the strip we are. Then Sam and Daniel figure out the import of what they're doing, then they get Jack to care, then *they* go back, repeating the same mistake.

Amanda Tapping really gets to stretch her talents, much like Michael Shanks did this season and Christopher Judge last season. Tapping makes the Sam Carter of SG-1, Sam Carter of the alternate timeline, and Replicator Sam all different enough to be autonomous but similar enough to be recognizable. Michael and Chris did good jobs of recasting themselves as well: the nerdier Daniel still finds plenty of strength when he needs it, and we get a stalwart Teal'c the likes of which we haven't seen in five years or more — impenetrable, aloof, and staunchly loyal.

A couple of times, the alternate-timeline Daniel/Sam nerdy Dynamic Duo goes a little over the top — facial expressions start to look a little pasted on instead of natural to the situation — but for the most part their moments are very good. Daniel never palms his glasses *once*, but takes them off completely (a thing our Daniel never does), and Sam's nervous cuff holding (and good lord her *wardrobe*) are just precious. The salty dog O'Neill is also hilarious, along with his perfect Canadian accent. So, while the pickup of "Moebius" is a tad sluggish, especially after the monumental "Reckoning" and the slick "Threads," it's the science and the viable humor that keeps us in our seats — even if we've never heard of a Mobius strip.

Gods & Scientists: Sam makes reference to the new ship in production, an update on *Prometheus* called *Daedalus*. Another Greek reference, Daedalus was the maker of the labyrinth that housed the Minotaur, and he fashioned wings of wax for himself and his son Icarus, to fly off an island where they were imprisoned. Daedalus means "skillfully wrought" in Greek. Lots of potential for stories for season nine right there!

Interesting Fact: Catherine niece's name is Sabrina Gosling, perhaps an allusion to Sharon Gosling, editor of the official *Stargate SG-1 Magazine*.

Why We're Space Monkeys: The little touches. Jack's boat's name is *Homer*, instead of the more traditional female name. Sam's line about sexual organs (which she said in "Children of the Gods"), the return of Ra, and the return of older, movie *Stargate* music along with him. It's the combination of payoff and the inspired renewal of old material that makes *SG-1* so watchable.

Parlez-vous Gate?:
DANIEL: We don't know where it is *now*, but we do know where it *was*. Giza, 3000 BC.
CARTER: You can't be serious.
O'NEILL: What?
DANIEL: It's the only way.
O'NEILL: What?
CARTER: No, we agreed.
O'NEILL: If I have to say "what" one more time, heads are going to roll!

820. Moebius (Part 2)

Original airdate: March 25, 2005
Story by: Joseph Mallozzi, Paul Mullie, Brad Wright, Robert Cooper
Teleplay by: Robert Cooper
Directed by: Peter DeLuise

In an alternate timeline, Daniel and Sam join Jack O'Neill to try to right the mistakes of the distant past.

Any of the last five episodes could have ended *SG-1*. "Threads" or "Reckoning" each had huge, arcing story lines that wrapped up many questions in the *Stargate* universe and delivered an ending that would have satisfied any fan. In "Reckoning," the team is confronted physically, and a significant threat is eradicated. In "Threads," the team is confronted emotionally, and a significant threat is eradicated. While the episodes were still in the conception and writing stages, the future of the show was not clear. With that in mind, it's easy to see why the end of season eight feels so heavy and uncompromising.

Thankfully, season nine was renewed by "Skiffy" (the Sci-Fi Channel), and so, at the end of "Moebius," while it is for some intents and purposes a finale, it also allows enough leeway that the writers could always follow it up with more stories.

For our purposes, it's good to end on this episode. It's light, Daniel's alive at the end (well, one of him is, little tongue-in-cheek there for the Daniel-whumping again), Jack and Sam have declared their love — like, out *loud* and stuff — Teal'c is freed from oppression and that dastardly

First Prime headgear, and there's more fishing; neatly tying in that pesky Mobius strip idea once again, as we see the ending for "Threads" relived, only better!

The big splash of course is the Sam and Jack relationship. Although it can be argued that, as always, The Kiss is not between the Sam and Jack *we* know but some version or alteration thereof, at this point in the story, with timelines affecting other timelines, the writers do a good job absolving *themselves* of some of their errors. *SG-1* has always worked closely with the U.S. Air Force, but has always taken the stand that fraternizing is not allowed. But, since the episodes are based on narrative, they also want to tell good stories — thus the alternate reality and time-loop scenarios. "Moebius" is

Fans look forward to more Amanda Tapping in the show's incredible ninth season (COURTESY MAUREEN THAYER)

one step beyond even that thinking because, as Sam (pick whichever one) says over and over, one small change in any timeline affects the others. So, when Jack and Sam finally do meet in the middle, so to speak, complete with soft lens, imminent death, a nod to *Star Wars*, sparkling lights, and swelling music, we watch . . . and some small part of us thinks, "This is going to make a difference in *our* timeline. I just know it will!"

But it's not all just about the shippers. It's great to see some resolution there, with a hint of Jack's retirement (an idea put forward by his own lover, just after she dumps him, hats off to Brad, "Coop," and "M&M"), but "Moebius" still takes us back to the older themes of season seven. While "Moebius" is sometimes seen as a variation of "Mobius," it also suggests a sense of everydayness. We see the 'Moe' character of Sam and Daniel and Jack. While Jack has always stood in for the Everyman, in this mini-arc he, Sam, and Daniel are not just everyday people but the comic version of these people — and in their incarnation of three, don't they remind you of another comic threesome, Larry, Curly, and Moe? — which also harkens us back to another "Everyman" character in season eight, Joe from "Citizen Joe." Just as Joe was a comic version of the fandom (although I argued it could also be a comic version of the writers, as well), "Moebius" presents us with the comic version of SG-1, reminding us that even *they* are not immune to some satirization, and this time not the slightly distanced "Wormhole X-Treme" satire, but one that is up close and personal.

Science, philosophy, comedy, action, and drama. If it had to end here, I couldn't have asked for a better way to go. As it is, we get to look forward to a record-breaking ninth season — and maybe beyond. Anything is possible.

Gods & Scientists: Continuity . . . continues: Ancient Egyptian gods often had animal representations. Here you'll see that Ra's Jaffa wear his traditional headpiece, the falcon, as opposed to Apophis' jackal-headed minions. The animal representations were used to signify the attributes or powers of the particular deity, which is why some deities had more than one headdress, depending on the circumstances.

Interesting Fact: Writer Joseph Mallozzi makes his own myths, even off-screen: "It's the time travel/alternate timeline story to end all time travel/alternate timeline stories — a story so full of twists and turns that one of the producer's heads actually exploded trying to understand it."

Why We're Space Monkeys: Daniel doesn't often get to make fun of things, but when he makes fun of the military, it's *so* worth it: check out alternate-timeline Daniel's mocking "What's with the. . . .?" in reference to Jack's military hand signals on Chulak.

Parlez-vous Gate?: If you haven't seen *Stargate Atlantis*, you'll miss this in-joke; but it's a great reason to start watching!
McKAY: Gateship One, you're go for launch. (At Hammond's look) What? It's a ship that goes through the Gate. Gateship. Well, I thought it was clever.

Resources

Fans of *Stargate SG-1* are lucky; there is a large and comprehensive online fandom, as well as a wide variety of print artifacts. Some are official, some are not. For the fervent fan, here's a sampling of where to look for your *SG-1* fix:

BOOKS & ARTICLES

American Science Fiction TV: Star Trek, Stargate, And Beyond – Jan Johnson-Smith
This is a critical analysis of science fiction and television, with some *Stargate SG-1* content. Unofficial.

Beyond the Gate – Keith Topping. An early season episode guide to *Stargate SG-1* from the UK. Topping has also written guides for *Buffy* and *Doctor Who*. High on nitpicks, low on analysis. Unofficial.

Reading Stargate and Beyond – Lisa Dickson, Stan Beeler, editors. A critical look at *SG-1*, covering individual episodes and characters, cultural impact, political climate. Look for an article by yours truly. Unofficial.

"Resistance Re-Examined: Gender, Fan Practices, and Science Fiction Television" – Christina Scodari. *Popular Communications*, Vol. 1 Issue 2, 111-130. 2003. Scodari has written an academic essay on the impact of fans on *SG-1* and *Farscape*.

Stargate SG-1: The Illustrated Companion – Thomasina Gibson. This is a series of four guides to the show. Full of photos and plot recaps from episodes, with some interviews. Official.

Stepping through the Stargate – P.N. Elrod, Roxanne Conrad, editors. A collection of eclectic essays from multiple sources about different aspects of the show. Unofficial.

The Essential Scripts – Brad Wright, Jonathan Glassner. As the title explains, these are scripts from various seasons (nothing past season six). Official.

MAGAZINES AND 'ZINES

Ashton Press – fanzines.ashtonpress.net/stargate.htm. 'Zines on demand. Slash, gen, and ship are available.

Pyramid Press – www.pyramidspress.com/zine.html. Limited availability of select fanzines.

The Official SG-1 Magazine – *Titan* magazine's officially sanctioned glossy. Behind the scenes looks, centerfold posters, cast interviews. Published six times a year.

ONLINE

Online content is volatile at best. Most sites listed have been around for a while, but keep in mind that Internet content is not infallible.

Abydos Gate – www.stargate-sg1.hu. Fan site that has a great many articles, past and current, as well as a wonderful photo section. And it's pretty, too.

Amanda Tapping Web page – amandatapping.com. Fan maintained, but the actor endorses it. Biography, events, and appearances; highlights include personal statements and exclusive interviews.

Arduinna's *Stargate SG-1* Handbook – www.stargatehandbook.org/sg1. A type of encyclopaedia for the Stargate series. It includes an episode guide, as well as a series timeline and information on the different races, and the planets and galaxies SG-1 has visited.

Clonejanet – savejanetfraiser.com/clone/main.php. An offshoot of a fan site devoted to getting the character of Janet Fraiser back onto *SG-1*, this site has to be my vote for weirdest *SG-1*-related site.

Five Minute Stargate – www.fiveminute.net/stargate. Entire episodes of the series compressed (hilariously), into five-minute chunks. While this site is no longer maintained (it's on an extended hiatus), it still has quite a few older episodes of *SG-1*. And it is so funny. Warning: some adult language and content.

GateWorld – gateworld.net. Darren Sumner's labor of love that spawned a singularly comprehensive site. Recently started including *Stargate Atlantis* as well as other science fiction television.

Goa'uld Translation – members.liwest.at/reno/transl_goa.htm. Wondering how to insult someone in Goa'uld? Want to follow Teal'c's conversations with other Jaffa? Well, this site offers some of the basic words and phrases of the Goa'uld language.

Heliopolis – www.sg1-heliopolis.com. The Mecca for fanfiction that is exclusively *SG-1*.

Jaffa Kree! – www.jaffakree.pwp.blueyonder.co.uk/jaffakree. Christopher Judge site, with lots of info, links, and a sense of humor.

Le Delirium – www.ledelirium.com/index.php. Comprehensive French fan site, with an episode, character, and actor guide, as well as a *Stargate* lexicon and other fun items.

MGM official site – www.mgm.com/stargate. Just what it says. It doesn't stand out compared to the fan-run sites, but it has cooler graphics due to its much larger budget.

Michael Shanks Online – www.michaelshanks-online.com/news/index.shtml. A fan-maintained Web site devoted to the actor, but so far not endorsed by him. Lots of swag for auction, including non-*SG-1* related merchandise. Photos, interviews, background on Michael. Nice to navigate.

Richard Dean Anderson Web page – rdanderson.com. Maintained by a longtime friend, this is a very comprehensive site on the actor, with a separate section devoted to *SG-1*. Interviews with RDA, lots of pictures and background content. Great site.

Sam/Jack archives – samandjack.net/directory/frames.html. The repository for fan fiction with a particularly Sam/Jack bent.

Save Daniel Jackson – www.savedanieljackson.com. Although originally started as a campaign to bring back Michael Shanks after his season five departure, this site has become loaded with interesting information and interviews.

Sci Fi – www.scifi.com/stargate. The official site for "Skiffy," the network that airs the new *SG-1* episodes in the U.S.

Selmak.org – www.selmak.org. A great site for the smaller recurring characters like Master Bra'tac and Selmak. Interviews, bios, pics.

Sevgate – cartoons.sev.com.au/index.php?catid=65. Comic strips by Australian cartoonist John Cook that parody *Stargate* (you can also access strips on just about every other science fiction television show from the main page). My personal favorite is "Sevgate technobabble." Unfortunately, due to rising costs, he is now charging a subscription rate to access the site, but it's an inexpensive one.

SG-1 Archives – www.sg1archive.com/sg1. Another comprehensive site for the series with a neat intro page. They also carry news on *Stargate Atlantis*.

SG-1 Spoilergate – www.sg-1spoilergate.jackfic.com. Spoilergate, a site devoted to upcoming news on *SG-1*, as well as cross referencing the series with many other publications.

SG-Command.Net – www.sg-command.net. Prop and costuming resource site. You can buy *everything* here, and there's a photo gallery and forum section, too. Affiliated with Stargate6.com.

SkyOne – www.skyone.co.uk/programme/pgeprogramme.aspx?pid=6. The official site for the network that airs the new *SG-1* episodes in the UK.

Stargate6.com – Another site for props and costuming, affiliated with SG-Command.net. It has a photo gallery, forums, a huge online shop – if you're at all interested in the *SG-1* franchise and fandom, this is one site you won't want to miss.

Stargate Alpha – stargate-alpha.com. A fun site that doesn't take itself too seriously, it features a reality show spoof called "Bigg Jaffa," news, articles, forums. "Think of Stargate Alpha as the Switzerland of *Stargate* Web sites."

Stargate-Project – stargate-project.de. A huge German fan site with episode guide, interviews, articles, and more. The site is in German, but a lot of the articles have been translated into English.

Stargatesolutions – stargate-sg1-solutions.com. A large site that is still being built up. Nice place to visit if you're still getting to know the *SG-1* universe and want to fill yourself in without watching twenty hours of television straight.

Stargate Wars – www.stargatewars.com. Multiplayer online game.

The Joint – www.lehopictures.com/the_joint. Visual effects supervisor James Tichenor no longer works on *SG-1*, but does work on the spin-off, *Stargate Atlantis*. His blog is chock-full of behind-the-scenes info on the series, as well as the his previous work on *SG-1*. Well worth the read.

The Official Teryl Rothery Site – www.terylrothery.com

The Official Web site of Alex Zahara – www.alexzahara.com

Toezone – www.twtid.org/toezone/intro.htm. Second place winner for weird *SG-1* sites is this one, devoted to a particular piece of Daniel Jackson's anatomy.

Bibliography

Approaching the Possible: The World of *Stargate SG-1*

Abrams, M. H. *A Glossary of Literary Terms*. Sixth edition. Fort Worth: Harcourt Brace, 1993.

Hamilton, Edith. *Mythology*. Boston: Little, Brown, 1969.

Internet Movie Database, imdb.com.

Phillips, Mark. *Science Fiction Television Series*. Jefferson, NC: McFarland, 1996.

Pinch, Geraldine. *Egyptian Myth*. New York: Oxford University Press, 2004.

Making Myth: The Story of *Stargate SG-1*

All Music Guide, www.allmusic.com.

"Amanda on Season 7." *Icon Magazine*. 2002.

Bellamy, Alan. "Executive Decision." *The Official* Stargate SG-1 *Magazine*. November/December, 2004.

Box Office Guru. www.boxofficeguru.com.

Brady, James. "In Step With Richard Dean Anderson." *Parade Magazine*. December 27, 1998: p. 20.

Brooks, Tim, & Earle F. Marsh. *The Complete Directory to Prime Time Network and Cable TV Shows, 1946–Present*, sixth ed. New York: Ballantine, 1995.

British Broadcasting Corporation. "Stargate Stars Visit Swindon." BBC Wiltshire.

Online. March 20, 2004.

CBC News. "'MacGyver' Tackles Seal Hunt." www.cbc.ca/story/Canada/
national/2005/03/07/macgyver050307.html (accessed March 8, 2005.)

Cinefantastique. cfq.com (accessed March 29, 2005.)

Counts, Kyle. "Intelligence Officer." *Starlog*. April, 1998.

Cult Times #62. November, 2000.

Daeidziak, Mark. "Winkler Refuses Un-Cool Things For *MacGyver*." *Akron Beacon
Journal*. June 26, 1985: p. B6.

Dearsley, Jayne. "SFX Profile: Richard Dean Anderson." *SFX*. June, 2002. www.rdan-
derson.com/archives/a2-06-01.htm (accessed August 8 2005).

Don S. Davis Web site. www.donsdavis.com (accessed March 29, 2005.)

Eby, Douglas. "Amanda Tapping Interview." *Talent Development Resources*. www.
talentdevelop.com/atapping.html (accessed August 31, 2004.)

Eramo, Steven. "Michael Shanks: Action Jackson." *TV Zone*. November, 2000.

———. "So Long, Daniel Jackson." *TV Zone #42*. December, 2001.

Eslinger, Amy. "OnSat Interview with Amanda Tapping." www.amanda
tapping.com/Scripts/PostNuke/index.php?module-htmlpages&func-
displays&pid-61 (accessed April 30, 2002.)

Fleming, Michael. "The Rivalry Between MGM and Sony Over the James Bond
Franchise Thickens." *Variety*. December 11, 1997.

GateWorld. gateworld.net

Gibson, Thomasina. "Father Figure." *Xposé*. February, 2001.

———. "Judge Mental!" *Xposé*. August, 2001.

———. "Shanks for the Memories." *Dreamwatch*. November, 2001.

———. "Stargazers." *Dreamwatch*. February, 2001.

———. "We Love Amanda in Uniform." *Cult Times Special #30*. May, 2000.

Gosling, Sharon. "Using the Force!" *The Official* Stargate SG-1 *Magazine #1*.
November/December, 2004.

———. "The Way of the Warrior." *The Official* Stargate SG-1 *Magazine #3*.
March/April, 2005.

Gross, Edward & Jordan, Sean. "Heaven's 'gate." *Femme Fatales*. September/October
2004.

Hirai, Miwa. "Anything Can Happen: Cybernex Chat with Michael Shanks." July
2002. www.savedanieljackson.com/history/originalspirit/originalspirit.shtml

Huddleston, Kathy. "Richard Dean Anderson Steps through the Stargate for a Fifth
Season." www.scifi.com/sfw/issue212/interview2.html (accessed March 29, 2005.)

Internet Movie Database. www.imdb.com

Miller, Karen. "Gate Crashing." *Frontier: Australian Science Fiction Media Magazine*

#13. November, 1998 – January, *1999.*

———. "Doctoring the Gate." *Frontier: Australian Science Fiction Media Magazine.* www.amandatapping.com/Scripts/PostNukes?index.php? module-htmlpages&func-display&pid-49

P., Ken. "An interview with Dean Devlin." Filmforce. filmforce.ign.com/ articles/365/365034pl.html (accessed July 16, 2002.)

Peter Williams Official Web site, www.peter-williams.info (accessed March 29, 2005.)

Prevue Magazine. February, 2002.

———. July, 2002.

Ragaine, Franck. "Ma petite Wylie, mon bonheur." ("My Little Wylie, My Happiness.") *Télé Poche Magazine.* No. 1727, March 15, 1999: 10-13

Richard Dean Anderson Web site, rdanderson.com (accessed March 29, 2005.)

Sargent, Martin. "The Screen Savers on TechTv." Transcript of television interview. June 11, 2002. rdanderson.com/archives/a2-06-11 (accessed August 8, 2005.)

Sci-Fi.com. Interview with Michael Shanks. April 16, 2003. www.scifi.com/ transcripts/2003/mshanks4.16.html

———. Interview with Christopher Judge. June 19, 2003. www.scifi.com/ transcripts/2003/cjudge6.19.html

Spelling, Ian. "Silent Sentinel." *Sci-Fi TV Magazine.* June, 1999.

"Stargate's Christopher Judge on Radio's Sci-Fi Overdrive." MGM *Sci-Fi Newsletter Vol. 23.* March, 2004. www.mgm.com/scifi/04march/judge.html (accessed August 8, 2005.)

"Stargate's Amanda Tapping." *Icon Magazine.* Spring, 2004.

Strachan, Alex. "Tapping: From a 'mostly dead' *X-Files* role to *Stargate*." *The Vancouver Sun.* Monday, June 28, 1997.

Sumner, Darren. "Honorable Mention! *The Official* Stargate SG-1 *Magazine #1.* November/December 2004.

———. "New Orders." *The Official* Stargate SG-1 *Magazine #3.* March/ April, 2005.

Tichenor, James. E-mail interview with the author, October 24, 2005.

The Corin Nemec Web site, www.corinnemec.com/homepage.htm (accessed March 29, 2005.)

The Official Amanda Tapping Web site, www.amandatapping.com (accessed March 29, 2005.)

"The Biggest Gambles of 1997." *Entertainment Weekly.* January 10, 1997.

The Screen Savers Television Interview with Richard Dean Anderson. rdanderson.com/archives/a2-06-11.htm. June 11, 2002.

Vicki Gabereau Live. Television Interview with Michael Shanks. CTV, February 2, 1999.

Wright, Jonathan. "Reopening the Stargate." *TV Zone #103.* June, 1998.

Everybody CanCon:
Stargate SG-1 in the Great White North

Bridge Studios, www.bridgestudios.com (accessed March 29, 2005.)

Canadian Audio-Visual Certification Office, Programs. www.pch.gc.ca /progs/ac-ca/progs/bcpac-cavco/pubs/2001-02/ra-ar/prog_e.cfm (accessed June 8, 2005.)

Canadian Radio-television and Telecommunications Commission. "Canadian Content." www.crtc.gc.ca/eng/cancon.htm (accessed March 29, 2005.)

Edwards, Ian. "Wright, Cooper Prosper as *Stargate* Keepers." *Playback*. March 1, 2004.

Gordon, Carole. "Anubis in London: The Man Behind the Cowl." Stargate SG-1

Solutions Interview with David Palffy. www.stargate-sg1-solutions.com/interviews/dp/0402.dpsol.shtml (accessed February 7, 2004.)

Government of British Columbia. "Ministry of Management Services — Exports — December 2001." (accessed March 29, 2005.)

Parker, Maureen. "RE: Public Notice CAVCO 2005-001 — Draft Amendments to the Income Tax Act." www.pch.gc.ca/progs/ac-ca/progs/bcpac-cavco/docs/wgc.cfm (accessed April 29, 2005.)

Robertson, Colin. "Stand up for Canada, Eh!" www.dfait-maeci.gc.ca (accessed June 5, 2002.)

SciFi.com. Interview with Richard Dean Anderson. June 18, 2003. www.scifi.com/transcripts/2003/rdanderson6.18.html

Slotek, Jim. "Did Schwarzenegger's political plans play role in T3 move?" *Toronto Sun*. February 19, 2002. jam.canoe.ca/Movies/Artists/S/Schwarzenegger_Arnold/2002/02/19/761526.html

Stargate SG-1 Official Magazine. "New Orders." March/April, 2005.

Out of the Blue: The Franchise of *Stargate SG-1*

Brown, Paul. "Legends in Time to Make Stargate Collectibles." Press release from Legends Memorabilia. www.legends-memorabilia.com November 24, 2005.

Creation Entertainment, www.creationent.com/index.htm (accessed March 29, 2005.)

Gatecon Conventions, www.gatecon.com (accessed March 29, 2005.)

JoWood Productions. Official site of the Stargate SG-1 computer game. www.stargate-thealliance.com/index.php (accessed March 29, 2005.)

Stargate Novels, www.stargatenovels.com/index.shtml (accessed March 29, 2005.)

Stargate SG-1—Avatar Press. www.avatarpress.com/stargate1 (accessed March 29, 2005.)

A.j. E-mail interview with the author, January 6, 2005.

Byrne, Tricia. E-mail interview with the author, January 6, 2005.

Denise. E-mail interview with the author, January 6, 2005.

Encyclopaedia Britannica. www.britannica.com.

Gordon, Carole. "Dead Man Talking." ourstargate.com/osdeadman.shtml (accessed February 20, 2005.)

"lab_brat." E-mail interview with the author, January 6, 2005.

Mallozzi, Joseph. E-mail interview with the author, December 15, 2004.

Science Fiction News of the Week. Issue 166. www.scifi.com/sfw/issue166 (accessed March 29, 2005.)

SciFi.com. "Sci-Fi Opens the 'Gates' to More Adventures." www.thefutoncritic.com/cgi/pr.cgi&id-20041115scifi01 November 15, 2004.

"Snarkhunt." E-mail interview with the author, January 6, 2005.

"Suz Voy." E-mail interview with the author, January 6, 2005.

Winningham, Julie. E-mail interview with the author, January 6, 2005.

Stargate SG-1: Episode Guide

Abrams, M. H. *A Glossary of Literary Terms*. sixth edition. Fort Worth, TX: Harcourt Brace College, 1993.

BioTech. "Normal Flora." BioTech, biotech.icmb.utexas.edu November 20, 2004.

Brown, Leslie, Ed. *The New Shorter Oxford English Dictionary*. New York: Oxford University Press, 1993.

Budge, Wallis. *Osiris and the Egyptian Resurrection, Vol II*. The Medici Society, 1911.

Canadian Broadcasting Corporation. "Behind the Scenes of *Da Vinci's Inquest*." www.cbc.ca/television/behindthescenes_davinci.html (accessed November 21, 2004.)

Carmody, Denise Lardner. *Mythological Woman: Contemporary Reflections on Ancient Religious Stories*. New York: Crossroad, 1992.

Colman, Andrew M. *A Dictionary of Psychology*. Oxford: Oxford University Press, 2001.

Darvill, Timothy. *The Concise Oxford Dictionary of Archaeology*. New York: Oxford University Press, 2002.

David, Greg. "Star Gazing." *TV Guide*. October 23, 2004.

Donne, John. "Meditation XVII." *Devotions Upon Emergent Occasions and Death's Duel*. New York: Random House, 1999.

Eramo, Steven. "Still Waters Run Deep." *TV Zone #115*. June, 1999.

————. "Peter DeLuise: Like Father, Like Son." *TV Zone #157*. August, 2000.

————. "Michael Shanks: Action Jackson." *TV Zone #134*. November, 2000.

————. "Propping It Up." *TV Zone Special #54*. December, 2003.

————. "Deep, Deep Trouble." *TV Zone #177*. May, 2004.

Encyclopaedia Britannica. www.britannica.com

Encyclopaedia Mythica. www.pantheon.org

Fulford, Robert. *The Triumph of Narrative*. Toronto: House of Anansi, 1999.

Gendreau, Paul. "Amanda Tapping's Vow: 'Until The Mission is Completed.'" MGM: Sci-Fi Newsletter. www.mgm.com/scifi/ozapril/ amanda.html April, 2002.

Gibson, Thomasina. "Father Figure." *Xposé #53*. February, 2001.

————. "Who'd Live in a House Like This?" *Cult Times #69*. June, 2001.

————."We Love Amanda in Uniform." *Cult Times Special #30*. May, 2000.

Gross, Edward & Jordan, Sean. "Heaven's 'gate." *Femme Fatales*. September/October, 2004.

Hamilton, Edith. *Mythology*. Boston: Little, 1969.

Hornblower, Simon. *Who's Who in the Classical World*. Ed. by Spawforth, Antony, & Tony Spawforth Oxford: Oxford University Press, 2000.

Jung, Carl Gustav. *The Essential Jung*. Ed. by Anthony Storr. London: HarperCollins, 1983.

Kingston, Maxine Hong. *The Woman Warrior: Memoirs of a Girlhood Among Ghosts*. New York: Random House, 1976.

Kramer, Samuel Noah. Ed. *Mythologies of the Ancient World*. New York: Doubleday, 1961.

Larue, Gerald. *Ancient Myth and Modern Man*. Englewood Cliffs, NJ: Prentice-Hall, 1975.

Linokelly17. "Don S. Davis — Yahoo! Chat Interview." hometown.aol. co.uk/linokelly17/page22.html September 8, 1998.

Mallozzi, Joseph. E-mail interview with the author, December 15, 2004.

Matthews, P.H. *The Concise Oxford Dictionary of Linguistics*. New York: Oxford University Press, 1997.

Mathworld, "Singularity." mathworld.wolfram.com. (accessed May 20, 2005.)

MGM Home Entertainment. *Stargate: SG-1: Season Seven*. 2003.

————. *Stargate: SG-1: Season Six*. 2002.

————. *Stargate: SG-1: Season Five*. 2001.

————. *Stargate: SG-1: Season Four*. 2000.

————. *Stargate: SG-1: Season Three*. 1999.

————. *Stargate: SG-1: Season Two*. 1998.

————. *Stargate: SG-1: Season One.* 1997.

Milton, John. *Paradise Lost.* New York: Longman, 1998.

Perenson, Melissa. "*Stargate SG-1*'s cast and crew blow out the candles on its 100th birthday." *SciFi.com.* www.scifi.com/sfw/issue228/interview.html

Ritter, Kate. "SG-1 Explorer Unit Team Briefing." rdanderson.com/archives/93-03-20.htm (accessed March 20, 2003.)

Oxford Reference Online. Oxford University Press. (accessed February 11, 2005.)

Read, David. "Amanda Speaks Out." *GateWorld.* www.gateworld.net February, 2004.

————. "Hanging With Harry." *GateWorld.* www.gateworld.net November, 2004.

Richard Dean Anderson Web site, rdanderson.com (accessed March 29, 2005.)

Rothery, Teryl. Telephone interview with the author, November 27, 2004.

"ShadowMaat." "Avenger 2.0." *GateWorld Forum.* forum.gateworld.net/showthread.php?t=278 May 12, 2004.

"Shipper Ahoy." "The Changeling." *GateWorld Forum.* forum.gateworld.net/showthread.php?t=266 November 27, 2004.

"Star Bores." *TV Guide Online.* tvguide.com/tv/showguide/showPage.asp?iProgramID-910117 August 5, 2004.

"Stargate: SG-1 Special." *TV Zone #42.* July 2001.

"Stargate: SG-1 Special." *TV Zone #38.* August 2000.

StargateSG-1.net. www.sg-1.net (accessed August 2, 2004.)

The Military Education Network, www.militaryedu.com (accessed September 9, 2004.)

Alex Zahara Web site, www.alexzahara.com (accessed August 20, 2004.)

Reuters, Associated Press. "Hawking Recants Whole Theory." *The Toronto Star*, July 22, 2004.

"Snarkhunt." E-mail interview with the author, January 6, 2005.

Stevenson, James. "Richard Dean Anderson on his Stargate Departure." *Now Playing.* June 2, 2005.

The U.S. Air Force Entertainment Liaison Office: Services. www.airforce hollywood.af.mil/services.html

Tichenor, James. E-mail interview with the author, October 24, 2005.

————. *The Joint*, www.lehopictures.com/the_joint

Thorpe, Kim. "Don S. Davis Interview." *Prevue Magazine.* July, 2002.

Winningham, Julie. E-mail interview with the author, January 6, 2005.

Wortham, Ann. "Michael Shanks Saturday Q&A." United Fan Con — Springfield, MA. photos.ashtonpress.net/ufc.htm August 17, 2004.

XVR27's Improv Interviews, www.com-www.com/whoseline/int October 1, 2004.

Zahara, Alex. Telephone interview with the author, November 20, 2004.